LAWYERS AND FUNDAMENTAL MORAL RESPONSIBILITY

Second Edition

LAWYERS AND FUNDAMENTAL MORAL RESPONSIBILITY

Second Edition

Daniel R. Coquillette
J. Donald Monan, S.J. University Professor and Former Dean
Boston College Law School
Charles Warren Visiting Professor of American Legal History
Harvard Law School

R. Michael Cassidy
Professor of Law and Associate Dean for Academic Affairs
Boston College Law School

Judith A. McMorrow
Professor of Law and Former Associate Dean for Academic Affairs
Boston College Law School

Library of Congress Cataloging-in-Publication Data

Coquillette, Daniel R.
Lawyers and fundamental moral responsibility / Daniel R. Coquillette, R. Michael Cassidy, Judith A. McMorrow. — 2nd ed.
    p. cm.
Includes index.
ISBN 978-1-4224-7025-1 (hard cover)
1. Legal ethics—United States. 2. Legal ethics. I. Cassidy, R. Michael. II. McMorrow, Judith A., 1955- III. Title.
KF306.C66 2010
174'.3—dc22

2010019628

NOTE TO USERS
To ensure that you are using the latest materials available in this area, please be sure to periodically check the LexisNexis Law School web site for downloadable updates and supplements at www.lexisnexis.com/lawschool.

Editorial Offices
121 Chanlon Rd., New Providence, NJ 07974 (908) 464-6800
201 Mission St., San Francisco, CA 94105-1831 (415) 908-3200
www.lexisnexis.com

MATTHEW◆BENDER

(2010–Pub.3556)

Dedication

This book is in honor of our parents, who set the foundation for our interest in issues both ethical and pragmatic, and our families, who have blessed us with their love and support.

Preface

It is a dangerous illusion that codes of professional responsibility "can and ought to provide clear and generally acceptable guidance to [all] attorney conduct."[1] The toughest ethical problems faced by lawyers often cannot be solved by a standardized process or set of rules, at least not by individuals who value their moral character.

The greatest flaw of many standard professional responsibility texts is their failure to acknowledge the connection between ethics and moral philosophy. These books rarely investigate the relationship between "professional ethics," narrowly construed in the context of attorney regulation and discipline, and "ethics" as seen in a broader historical, philosophical, or religious context. The most sensitive and intelligent authors of such texts have acknowledged this challenge quite frankly.[2]

This book was conceived as a way to fill that gap. It can be used as a supplement to a traditional professional responsibility course, or as the basis for a seminar in its own right. But by using the word "supplement," we do not want to characterize the book as being some kind of ancillary enrichment. Teaching professional responsibility wholly outside the context of moral philosophy condemns the field to a second-class intellectual status. Even worse, it is simply unrealistic.

The book's historical and philosophical structure is of great help to law students. The materials are organized around specific problems designed to encourage and focus class discussion. (Indeed, most class groups quickly split into differing philosophical camps, a great boon to course interest!) We have deliberately avoided assigning reported cases. Law students read too many of these already, and not enough philosophy.

There are two other inherent organizing principles for the book that are less obvious, at least initially. First, the philosophical materials are roughly ordered as the ideas themselves evolved in the history of philosophy. For example, Chapter One focuses on Pre-Socratic, Socratic, and Platonic themes, taken from early classical Greek philosophy, Chapter Two focuses on ideas introduced later by Aristotle's Nichomachean Ethics, Chapter Three focuses on notions of legal reasoning first developed by the Romans, Chapter Four explores the moral philosophy of Thomas Aquinas, etc. Later chapters

---

[1] E.H. Greenebaum, *Attorneys' Problems in Making Ethical Decisions*, 52 IND. L.J. 627, 628–629 (1977). *See generally* Bruce A. Green, *The Role of Personal Values in Professional Decisionmaking*, 11 GEO. J. LEGAL ETHICS 19, 39 (1997) (identifying circumstances where "the lawyer must make a decision within prescribed bounds or limits, but within those limits the grounds on which the lawyer exercises discretion are left to personal conscience").

[2] "What is left out, except in bits and pieces relating to specific topics, is any historical, comparative or sociological study of the profession or any study of the relationship between professional ethics and 'ethics' considered in an appropriate philosophical context." ANDREW L. KAUFMAN, PROBLEMS IN PROFESSIONAL RESPONSIBILITY xix (1976). "So far there has been little cross-fertilization, as a *practical* matter, between the philosophical and the professional enterprises." STEPHEN GILLERS, REGULATION OF LAWYERS 14 (2009). *See also* ANDREW L. KAUFMAN & DAVID B. WILKINS's excellent 4th edition, PROBLEMS IN PROFESSIONAL RESPONSIBILITY FOR A CHANGING PROFESSION (2002), which fills in many of these gaps.

Preface

introduce students to more modern theorists such as Reinhold Niebuhr, Lawrence Kohlberg, and Martha Nussbaum.

There is also a structure based on the topics of ethical philosophy itself. For example, Chapter One asks students to contemplate Plato's classical Greek question: "Is there any true test of goodness?" Chapter Two asks Aristotle's key question, "Assuming I can tell good from bad, what is the extent of my responsibility for the evil around me?" Chapter Three explores whether legal order and the threat of legal sanction set the limits of moral responsibility, and so forth. The book concludes with a discussion of pragmatism, moral realism, and the political and organizational impediments to principled individual decision making.

This book is intended to give law students a grounding in moral philosophy so that they may have a more sophisticated approach to issues of legal ethics. It not only assists them in relating this course to earlier studies in college and elsewhere, but also provides them an intellectual framework for analyzing tough ethical issues when these problems arise in the complexity of human life, and more particularly in law practice. While it could be seen as a highly theoretical form of study, many former students have reported, after using the book, that it was one of the most practical and useful subjects they studied in law school.

We are indebted to our students Caitlin Akins, Andrew Bender, John D. Holden, and Jessica Yau (Boston College Law School, Class of 2011) for their very capable assistance with researching and editing this second edition. Charles Riordan, Editorial Assistant to the Monan Chair and also a student at Boston College Law School, was invaluable, as always. We are very grateful to Pali Chheda at LexisNexis for her constant and patient assistance. We also thank our distinguished colleagues Profs. Scott Fitzgibbon and Paul Tremblay for their generous and thoughtful comments on earlier drafts.

Permissions

Permissions

Table of Contents

Table of Contents

Table of Contents

Table of Contents

Table of Contents

Table of Contents

Chapter I

THE MORAL PERSON

A. LAW SCHOOL AND ETHICS: "THE BRAMBLE BUSH"

In 1929, a young law professor named Karl Llewellyn delivered a brilliant set of introductory lectures to the in-coming first-year students at Columbia Law School. These lectures, which were to become very famous, were published under the title, *The Bramble Bush*.[1] Llewellyn's point was simple: like the man in the Mother Goose rhyme who "jumped into a *Bramble Bush* and scratched out both his eyes," legal education can be a narrowing experience that displaces the moral vision and perspective gained over a lifetime. What's the cure? To jump back "into another one and [scratch] them in again."

This course will be another "bramble bush," designed to scratch your moral eyes in again. Many of you will find this course unites your experience in law school and legal practice with something you had left behind—your liberal arts education—and, indeed, your moral training as a youth. If so, these materials will be a success, even though you will find that both the legal lessons learned in law school and the moral lessons learned long before will be challenged; before we are done, both may take a new form for you.

The legal profession—your profession—is in deep trouble today.[2] Recent developments in legal education, particularly legal realism, have emphasized the function of law as an "instrument" to achieve particular political, social, and economic ends.[3] The older ideals of a "neutral" rule of law have been debunked as, at best, a pious myth, and, at worst, a deliberate effort by the powerful to exploit the weak under an illusion of "fairness" of principle. Many students become convinced that professionalism means being willing to pursue the ends of others, irrespective of the means. It ultimately puts the client, for better or worse, in the driver's seat, and the ideal of justice becomes secondary.

This theory of education is very old. Indeed, it goes back to Greek philosophical schools known as the "Pre-Socratics."[4] One of these groups taught that all morality is relative: what's good for you is up to you, and our notion of goodness is entirely personal as well. There is no objective standard of a good person or of good conduct. This group was called the Cynics, from which we derive the pejorative word

---

[1] *See* K. N. LLEWELLYN, THE BRAMBLE BUSH: CLASSIC LECTURES ON THE LAW AND LAW SCHOOL (2008).

[2] *See* D. R. Coquillette, *Professionalism: The Deep Theory*, 72 N.C. L. REV. 1271 (1994).

[3] *See* Roger C. Cramton, *The Ordinary Religion of the Law School Classroom*, 29 J.L. & EDUC. 247, 250 (1978).

[4] For an engaging, if elementary, introduction to the Pre-Socratics, see BERTRAND RUSSELL, A HISTORY OF WESTERN PHILOSOPHY 3-81 (2007). *See also* ALASDAIR MACINTYRE, A SHORT HISTORY OF ETHICS 14–25 (1998).

"cynical." The Pre-Socratics, however, did not treat the notions of moral relativism as inherently bad, and neither do many modern American law teachers.

If one subscribes to the view of the Cynics, or moral relativism, the goal of teaching ethics is to equip each student with the ability to pursue as effectively as possible her individual view of what is good. The Greek Pre-Socratics called such teachers Sophists. The Sophists taught rhetoric, logic, and advocacy. If you used these skills to promote a military dictatorship, such as Sparta, well, fine. If you used them to support a democracy, such as Athens, fine again. If your view of the good led you to become a swindler, well, that was your business, too. Cynicism and Sophism, in the classical Greek sense, are alive and well in American law schools today. Moral relativism and its corollary—a theory of "professional" teaching that equips each future lawyer to pursue whatever ends she or her client may choose—may be found everywhere.

We will be discussing alternative theories later in this book. But let us start with the Pre-Socratics, Cynics, and Sophists. The challenges they represent may face us in legal education today, but they were first confronted by Socrates himself, two thousand and four hundred years ago.

B. IS THERE ANY REAL POINT IN TALKING ABOUT "GOOD AND BAD"?: THE CHALLENGE OF THE CYNICS AND THE SOPHISTS

The core of the moral relativism, as illustrated by the Cynics and Sophists, is the proposition that it is impossible to define moral absolutes in a way that will command universal acceptance. Most law students assume that they "know it when they see it" when it comes to distinguishing good from evil. But this test works as badly in achieving moral consensus as it did for Justice Stewart in defining pornography.[5] Try an experiment in class. Ask each person to define a characteristic of a "good person" that is immediately and objectively verifiable. Some will suggest "non-smoker," or "trained in emergency medicine to save lives," or "gives blood," or "helps others." But even these "qualifications" will be challenged. Defining the difference between "good" and "evil" conduct is no easier.

Socrates (469-399 B.C.), according to Plato's accounts of his teaching, understood these problems well.[6] He believed that despite the difficulty of understanding the nature of good and evil, these qualities are facts, like the laws of physics, and are knowable. Just because we have difficulty in defining the nature of good does not mean that there is no difference between good and evil, or that the nature of good can be changed by democratic votes, public opinion, judicial proceedings, or military victories. Further, Socrates believed that being good did not necessarily lead to being popular, successful, wealthy, or powerful. Indeed, in his own case, seeking the good led to his execution.

---

[5] *See* Jacobellis v. Ohio, 378 U.S. 184, 197 (1964).

[6] Because what we know of Socrates comes through Plato's writing, it is hard to know where the historic Socrates ends and Plato's character begins. For our purposes, this problem is pretty irrelevant. *See* BERTRAND RUSSELL, A HISTORY OF WESTERN PHILOSOPHY, *supra* note 4, at 82–93.

But Socrates also believed that being good was the only thing that ultimately made human life worthwhile. In his final address to his jury, Socrates asked one favor only:

> When my sons are grown up, I would ask you, O my friends, to punish them; and I would have you trouble them, as I have troubled you, if they seem to care about riches, or anything, more than about virtue; or if they pretend to be something when they are really nothing—then reprove them, as I have reproved you, for not caring about that for which they ought to care, and thinking that they are something when they are really nothing. And if you do this, I and my sons will have received justice at your hands.[7]

In the words of Alasdair MacIntyre, Socrates' successors "move in two main directions."

> Plato accepts the fact that moral concepts are only intelligible against the background of a certain sort of social order; he then tries to delineate it [as in *The Republic*]. . . . The Cynics and Cyrenaics by contrast seek to provide a moral code independent of society, tied only to the individual's choices and decisions, and attempting to make the individual moral life self-sufficient.[8]

MacIntyre adds that "[P]hilosophers, like Socrates, whose analysis of moral concepts suggest defects in contemporary morality" are likely "to be unwelcome" by authorities.[9] By suggesting that both individuals and legal orders can be tested by moral absolutes, Socrates was more than "unwelcome." He was executed after one of the most important "trials" in the history of Western thought.

C.   THE TRIAL OF SOCRATES (399 B.C.)

In 399 B.C., when Socrates was 70 years old, he was put on trial for his life. This event has engendered such sustained debate over the centuries that I. F. Stone's *The Trial of Socrates*, first published in 1988, became a national bestseller, and there are still scores of articles and books on this subject coming out. The trial, as we will see, has proven to be of special interest to lawyers.[10]

It is worth taking a moment to review what passed for "legal procedure" in Athens at the time. Criminal accusations were filed in writing by Athenian citizens, and the "indictment" set out the charges in advance with some specificity. In the case of this trial, the indictment survives from three classical sources: Xenophon's *Memorabilia*, Diogenes Laertius's *Life of Socrates*, and the summary by Socrates himself as recorded in Plato's *Apology*.[11] According to Laertius, the original indictment survived in the Athenian archives for nearly 600 years, at least until the reign of the Roman Emperor Hadrian in the second century A.D.

---

[7] *Materials, infra* at 1F.

[8] MacIntyre, *supra* note 4, at 25.

[9] *Id.*

[10] For a juristic approach, see R. E. Allen, Socrates and Legal Obligation (1980).

[11] *See* I. F. Stone, The Trial of Socrates 198–199 (1988).

Socrates' indictment was brought by three Athenian citizens: Anytus, a democratic politician; Meletus, "aggrieved on behalf of the poets," and Lycon, an orator.[12] (There was no "legal profession" in ancient Athens, but orators, such as Lycon, could be retained to argue on your behalf in public.) The indictment was summarized by Socrates himself. "It is about as follows: it states that Socrates is a wrongdoer because he corrupts the youth and does not believe in the gods the state believes in, but in other new spiritual beings."[13]

The cases were usually tried outdoors before 501 selected Athenian citizens, called "*dikasts.*" *Dikasts* were both judge and jury, in our sense, and were sworn to "vote according to the laws where there are laws, and where there is not, to vote justly as in us lies."[14] As we will see, because they were such a large group in a fairly small city, *dikasts* frequently were witnesses as well, and defendants could call on their direct knowledge. Socrates did this frequently in his trial. But, as we will also see, because the *dikasts* were such a large group, they could only vote on "yes" or "no" questions. Athenian procedure was designed with that in mind.

The trial began by having the accusers present their case in person to the *dikasts.* Then the defendant replied, also in person. Following that, the *dikasts* voted "yes" or "no" on the issue of guilt by dropping the right token into a jar cleverly designed so that the vote was confidential. (Each *dikast* had two bronze tokens, one with a hollow tube in the center [Guilty] and one filled [Innocent]. By covering the tube with their fingers and walking past two jars, one for the real vote and the other not, *dikasts* could drop both tokens with their actual vote secret.) If there was a majority vote of "guilty," the victorious accusers proposed a penalty, and the defendant proposed an alternative punishment. Again, there was a vote of the *dikasts,* and the majority selected the penalty. If there was a vote for acquittal, the accusers could be fined. In particular, if the accusers got fewer than 100 votes, they were fined heavily.[15]

The account of Socrates' trial was from Plato's memory, and was possibly written many years after the fact. (There was no official "transcript" or record.) It is contained in Plato's *The Apology,* set out in these *Materials.*[16] *The Apology* consists of Socrates' initial speech of defense, his answer to the proposed death sentence, and his final remarks to the *dikasts.*

Plato does not give us the speeches of the accusers, but we can determine what they must have said from Socrates' own remarks and from our own experience. After all, the selection of accusers was highly symbolic. Who do you know who would dislike the idea that there were absolute standards of good and bad discoverable only by certain elite philosophers? We can start with democratically elected politicians, such as Anytus.[17] In a democracy, the majority rules, and democratically

---

[12] *Materials, infra* at 1F.

[13] I. F. STONE, *supra* note 11, at 198 (from Plato's *Apology*). *See Materials, infra* at 1F.

[14] *Id.* at 96.

[15] PLATO, THE LAST DAYS OF SOCRATES 43–44, 192, n. 35 (Hugh Tredennick trans. with intro., London, rev. ed. 1969). *See also* DOUGLAS MACDOWELL, THE LAW IN CLASSICAL ATHENS 252 (1986).

[16] *See Materials, infra* at 1F.

[17] *See* Hugh Tredennick's notes in THE LAST DAYS OF SOCRATES 189, n.2 (Hugh Tredennick trans. with

elected representatives enact laws based on a plurality. To say that an individual could call the acts of a duly elected majority "evil," and thus oppose them, attacks the system at its core. Of course, judicial review by the United States Supreme Court can, in practice, come close to this, and there are many democratically elected politicians who resent it.

Artists are another group who dislike absolute standards of morality, whether they are playwrights, poets (such as Meletus), painters, photographers, novelists, or even musicians. But their reasoning is polar opposite from the democratic politician. Censorship, whether by a democratic legislator or a philosopher, is something to be feared. Later we will discuss Nietzsche and his theory of the *übermensch*, the "super" individual whose "energy of greatness" and artistic sensitivity achieves virtue beyond any uniform standards of good or evil.[18] Today, Nietzsche is uncomfortably associated with fascist heroes, but great individual artists could also fit the bill as "super heroes," entitled to be free from uniform tests of good and bad.

Finally, there is Lycon, an "orator" or "advocate." As lawyers, we understand the comfort of a belief that there is no "good" or "bad" side to a case, but just "differing interests" or even differing personal "realities." This provides reassurance to all but those few advocates who never represent anyone except for those with whom they totally agree. All the rest of us frequently represent the "bad" side of a case, and the notion that no one can unequivocally determine "good" or "bad" in a legal proceeding is highly reassuring. It is no surprise that the professional orator joined the democratic politician and the artist to make the accusations!

To provoke discussion of the "justice" of Socrates' conviction, we have added short excerpts from two great authors with very different perspectives. At the height of the Italian renaissance, Niccolò Machiavelli (1469–1527) published a famous "guide book" to political success, *Il Principe*, ("*The Prince*"). Machiavelli was certainly familiar with Plato's *Apology*, but does he ignore all of Socrates' teaching about goodness and return to genuine cynicism about human morals?[19]

The second excerpt is part of a work of fiction, the first of several to be included in these *Materials*. It is from Ralph Ellison's (1914-1994) famous novel *Invisible Man*, first published in 1952 and winner of the National Book Award.[20] Ellison explores the life of a young black man, who gradually became "invisible" and took to living in a cellar. He is "invisible" because those he meets "see only my surroundings, themselves, or figments of their imagination."[21] The book is written from a black perspective, but it addresses the universal law of humanity and vision under the conditions of modern life.

> Life is to be lived, not controlled; and humanity is won by continuing to play
> in face of certain defeat. Our fate is to become one, and yet many—This is

---

intro., London, Penguin Classics, rev. ed. 2003). Ironically, Anytus was accused of trying to bribe jurors in his own trial for the loss of Pylos to Sparta. *See* DOUGLAS MACDOWELL, THE LAW IN CLASSICAL ATHENS 173 (1986).

[18] *See* BERTRAND RUSSELL, A HISTORY OF WESTERN PHILOSOPHY, *supra* note 4, at 760–773.

[19] *See Materials, infra* at 1F.

[20] *See Materials, infra* at 1F.

[21] *See* JAMES D. HARD, THE OXFORD COMPANION TO AMERICAN LITERATURE 319 (1995).

not prophecy, but description. Thus one of the greatest jokes in the world is the spectacle of the whites busy escaping blackness and becoming blacker every day, and the blacks striving toward whiteness, becoming quite dull and gray. None of us seems to know who he is or where he's going.[22]

Ellison particularly addresses the problem facing those who are truly honest under the conditions of modern life. "When one is invisible he finds such problems as good and evil, honesty and dishonesty, of such shifting shapes that he confuses one with the other, depending upon who happens to be looking through him at the time."[23]

It is clear from Ellison's "Epilogue" to *Invisible Man*, set out in part below, that he regards "invisibility" as a kind of moral sickness, the result of losing one's true identity and moral compass. "[I]f you don't know where you are, you probably don't know who you are."[24] Ellison suggests a view sharply different from the Cynics about the objective truth of good and evil.

D.　FURTHER READING

For a fascinating account of Karl Llewellyn's life, see WILLIAM TWINING, KARL LLEWELLYN AND THE REALIST MOVEMENT (1985). For a concise "readable" introduction to the Pre-Socratics, Socrates, Plato, and Greek Philosophy generally, see ALASDAIR MACINTYRE, A SHORT HISTORY OF ETHICS 14–56 (1998); BERTRAND RUSSELL, A HISTORY OF WESTERN PHILOSOPHY 3–158 (2007). *See also* F. M. Cornford's excellent BEFORE AND AFTER SOCRATES 1–84 (1964).

The best source of the original texts of Plato's dialogues relating to the trial of Socrates is PLATO, THE LAST DAYS OF SOCRATES (Hugh Tredennick trans. with intro., London, rev. ed. 1969). Also in the "Penguin Classics" series are PLATO, THE REPUBLIC (Desmond Lee trans. with intro. London, 2d rev. ed. 1974) and PLATO, THE LAWS (Trevor J. Saunders trans. with intro., London, 1970). Another excellent collection of Plato's dialogues in GREAT DIALOGUES OF PLATO (E. H. Warmington, P. G. Ross eds., W. H. D. Rouse trans., Signet Classics, rev. ed. 2008).

For a good edition of THE PRINCE (first published 1532), see NICCOLO MACHIAVELLI, THE PRINCE (Ricci trans., Oxford, 1952). This edition has a helpful introduction. *See also* the amusing introductory account in BERTRAND RUSSELL, A HISTORY OF WESTERN PHILOSOPHY, *supra*, 504–511; and ALASDAIR MACINTYRE, A SHORT HISTORY OF ETHICS, *supra*, at 127–129.

On the general issue of teaching ethics in law school, see Roger Cramton, *The Ordinary Religion of the Law School Classroom*, 29 AM. J. LEGAL EDUC. 247 (1978); Katharine T. Bartlett, *Teaching Values: A Dilemma*, 37 AM. J. LEGAL EDUC. 519 (1987); and Paul G. Haskell, *Teaching Moral Analysis in Law School*, 66 NOTRE DAME L. REV. 1025 (1991).

---

[22] RALPH ELLISON, INVISIBLE MAN 577 (2d Vintage International ed., 1995).

[23] *Id.* at 572.

[24] *Id.* at 578.

E.   DISCUSSION PROBLEMS

PROBLEM I

The trial of Socrates will be set for argument in class, with roles assigned. Assume that it was true that Socrates had, through his teaching, weakened the political and ideological unity of young Athenians of good class and of military age. In fact, his former pupil, Alcibiades, committed serious treason against Athens. Assume further that Athens was, in 399 B.C., a fundamentally democratic state facing dangerous enemies.

Volunteers will be accepted for the roles of Socrates and his accusers: Meletus (a poet), Anytus (a democratic politician), and Lycon (an orator). Why do Socrates' ideas threaten artists like Meletus? Or democratic politicians like Anytus? Or those who advocate for others, like Lycon? A guest counsel, one Niccolò Machiavelli, will also be heard. What will his argument be?

Put yourself in the place of a concerned Athenian serving as a *dikast*. Your city has morale problems within and powerful military foes without. How do you cast your token?

PROBLEM II

Your law firm has recently hired a new lawyer who is widely viewed as a "disaster." While all agree that the individual is bright and hardworking, this new lawyer constantly criticizes members of the firm for accepting clients whose economic, political, or social goals are not consistent with the new lawyer's view of the public good.

Moreover, this new lawyer intrudes into everyone else's business and objects to "over-adversarial tactics" employed by other partners and associates—even when these tactics are clearly permitted by the ABA Model Rules of Professional Conduct. The lawyer's constant, nagging remarks are hurting firm morale and, even worse, several excellent applicants and one new associate have actually gone to other firms—partly because of this lawyer's influence. While so far no clients have been lost, several of the partners are concerned about that, too.

Matters have now come to a head. The new lawyer has accused a senior partner of failing to make full disclosures "to the investing public" in a major securities case, even while conceding that the senior partner probably has not "technically" violated professional and SEC guidelines.

It was tactfully suggested that this lawyer might be happier somewhere else. But this person will not resign, stating: "I love this firm and the legal profession. That is why I behave the way I do. Law is the business to which my life is devoted, and I should show less than devotion if I did not do what lies in me to improve it." [Quoting O. W. HOLMES, JR., THE PATH OF THE LAW (1897). *See Materials, infra* at 1F.] The new lawyer also said "It is literally true, even if it sounds rather comical, that [fate] has specially appointed me to this [firm], as though it were a large thoroughbred horse which because of its great size is inclined to be lazy and needs the stimulation of some stinging fly." [Quoting Socrates, Tredennick translation.

See Materials, infra at 1F.]

An emergency firm meeting has been called. You serve as a partner in the firm. What is your position? What is the "fair" way to resolve this dispute? What are this new lawyer's other career options? Would Karl Llewellyn take this lawyer "by the hand"? Will you?

Consider:

ABA Model Rules of Professional Conduct:

Rules 1.2(b), 1.16(b), 2.1, 5.1, and 5.2

F. MATERIALS

KARL N. LLEWELLYN, THE BRAMBLE BUSH
(Oxford University Press, 2008, First Published 1930)

X. Before Sunrise

The time approaches when you will put on fresh raiment, and shake the dust of these halls off your feet, and go down into the marketplace. When you have done that, you will have little time for thinking. Having ceased to be a child, you will cease to think as a child, you will, I take it, put away these childish things. Your mind will be on doing; if it should wander there will be no lack of hooks to drag it back. So that it may not be out of place before you go to stop for a moment, to look over, a little, what this profession is to which you go. What is the lawyer and his relation to the life about him? What is the part he plays in this society? Perhaps, too, you will pause with me over some of the things a lawyer does, some of the opportunities which come to him, some of the responsibilities he carries.

And I suppose that the first and the outstanding thing is that the lawyer is not popular. I think he never has been popular. I strongly suspect that there have never been laws or lawyers too heartily approved by the lay population they professed to serve. Certainly radicals have never loved them. "The first thing we will do is to hang all the lawyers"; and lawyers, and records, have been cast for burning since there have been such things as revolutions. Nor does such disapproval rest among the reds. The healthy spirited men of many ages have lifted up their clubs to bring them down upon the lawyer's skull. Cromwell, his law reforms defeated: "The sons of Zeruiah are too much for us." Rabelais, robustious, pungent in his scorn:

"Who being thus met together, after they had thereupon consulted for the space of six-and-forty weeks, finding that they could not fasten their teeth in it. . . .

"But Pantagruel said unto them, Are the lords between whom this debate and process is yet living? It was answered him, Yes. To what a devil, then, said he, serve so many paltry heaps and bundles of papers and copies which you give me? Is it not better to hear their controversy from their own mouths whilst they are face to face before us, than to read these vile fopperies, which are nothing but trumperies, deceits, diabolical cozenages of Cepola, pernicious slights and subversions of equity. . . .

"Furthermore, seeing that the laws are excerpted out of the middle of moral and natural philosophy, how should these fools have understood it, that have, by God, studied less in philosophy than my mule."

*   *   *

By this time you have discovered that I do not think the lawyer popular, and that his unpopularity appears to me as natural as whiskers on a cat.

The curious thing is the extent to which the counts against him prove on examination to be undeserved, or at worst, half-truths; and to disregard in the burst of complaint the merits of the accused.

Look the counts over. What you find is this. For part, the profession is charged with being what any profession should hope to be: expert enough to develop a sort of black art of its own. All that makes law grotesque and dubious is that any man thinks he has adequate knowledge by his common sense to judge of "rights" and "wrongs". What lawyers do must therefore be the diabolical cozenages of Cepola. The common man does not arrogate such knowledge to himself in engineering. The art of engineers is thus white magic more than black.

For part, the charge is one of trickery. Here we tread on delicate ground. So much of that accusation as concerns the mere and more obvious need of some technical order of business, I think we may waive away. Reason enough, as before, to see why the ununderstanding are intolerant; no cause for shame. Not so, I fear, some of the other phases. Not so the mazed mass of most procedure, which spells a profession either incompetent in arranging its own business, or wedded to a stubborn ritualism that makes work as three-inch brushes would make work for painters. Not so as to the charge that law procedure, and the combat aspects of the trial, tend to make lawyers forget their clients' interests in their own, and to forget in both the interests—if such there be—of justice.

Apart from procedure, and touching the charges that remain: as to the twisting of rules to win; as to there being no gain at law except at the flat expense of trampling, of putting the boots to a loser; as to the longer purse holding unfair advantage; as to the closed ranks of the law in favor of what is—surely three-fourths of the sting of the charges is drawn, and mud clapped on the wound, when one looks to the obvious truth: that in these matters law and lawyers do not show themselves, distinctively, at all. In these matters the lawyers mirror undistorted the very society that makes the charge. It is clients who wish to win, and to beat down other clients. Nor are lawyers to be held responsible for the clash of interests. Not law or lawyers, but society, gives fighting advantages to the propertied, puts the screws on in favor of the Ins. True, that the law presents a dubious method of adjusting conflict. But true again, that it serves, *somehow*, to settle those conflicts no other machinery has availed to solve at all. Three-fourths of the sting, I say, is drawn. But a part remains. Shall we deny that as we thus meddle trade-wise with the purer pitch of life, some pitch will stick? I have small patience with the man who scorns the man who does his dirty work. I have small patience, either, with the pitch worker who hides behind the skirts of him he serves. "Woe unto you, lawyers! for ye have taken away the key of knowledge: ye entered not in yourselves, and them that were entering in ye hindered."

The worst of the charges, then, seem to me in good part undeserved. The worst of them lie ill in the mouths of most of those who make them. For us in our own hearts they do give cause, they do give heavy cause for searching. Yet not for failing spirit. We have achievements to set off against our flaws.

For who is it who does the heavy work of bringing a limping, halting, clanking legal structure down to date? Who is it manages to unfold enough of that rarest of commodities, human ingenuity, social invention, to make old institutions serve new needs? Which is as much as saying, to make new institutions which are needed? I think if you turn to the work of counsel in the office you will find unlimited, unbelievable, output of that rare ore. The books are full of its traces. Most of our present law can be shown to be its product. Granted that the lawyer may not be the first actor in events, granted that he brings forth few novel needs to serve, he is none the less a precious social engineer. He observes the need that has arisen. He finds a way to meet it. It seems to have been the business man and not the lawyer who, in the first instance, brought about bills of exchange and bills of lading. It was, however, the lawyer who devised the mortgage, who made possible the giving of security in goods or land, while leaving the beneficial use of the borrower during the period for which the security was needed; made possible, therefore, the secured production loan whereby a debtor had the chance of financing a new venture out of whose own profits he might hope to meet the debt. *The land of a farmer wishes him back again*: it was the lawyer who despite the other lawyer built up the concept of the equity of redemption. It was the lawyer who turned the note-of-hand of commerce into the banker's ironclad collateral note, the lawyer who out of the same stock and the ancient covenant produced the bond that forms the base of the investment market. He did not act alone, as I have said. His was perhaps not the first drive, his was not always the full perception of the need. But his the skill, his was the engineering. It was the lawyer who devised the long-term lease for real estate improvement, and the collateral trust for real estate financing, or for financing new equipment for a mortgaged railroad. And, greatest perhaps of any single line of growth within our law, it was the lawyer who from the outset has shaped the thousand uses of the law of trusts—who made party politics a possibility when to lose an election meant the penalties of treason, who built up the possibilities of the permanent charitable gift, who turned the trust to keep family land together in the teeth of rules, who first opened to married women an independent income, who maneuvered by way of trust the first great consolidations, and turned that concept to the new fields of importing and motorcar finance. This last step, that of the trust receipt, I find peculiarly illuminating, perhaps because I know its course in more detail. You can see its growth, follow its invention, its steady step-wise spread. First in financing grain from upper New York to the sea. The early litigation that went unnoticed. The crucial case that caught the eye of metropolitan counsel. The introduction of the device, now modified, elaborated, into the importing business. The major firms that participated in its development, and the development itself, case by case, in litigation, clause by clause, in the increasing adequacy of the drafting. And in the course of the past ten years we can trace out its spread and readaptation to the financing of automobiles. Again we know the men, the means, the problems. In this one history we can see something of the energy, thought and originality that must go into creation of even such a single, simple tool as this. And this history, we may be certain, is but typical of a course of building as steady, as irresistible, as craftsmanlike, in some ways as beautiful, as that which through the medieval centuries raised cathedrals.

Nor are inventions of the lawyers limited to office counsel. Growth in law, especially growth in case law, has been attributed too lightly in most legal writing to the courts. I would neither deny nor belittle the part that the courts play in that growth. But how many judges do you know of whom it can be said, as it was once of Holmes, "the trouble with that fellow is that he is always deciding cases on points that were not raised in the briefs of either side"? How many judges do you know whose analysis of the case and of the situation is a major fresh creation, a "Let there be light!", rather than that lesser type of building which consists in merely modifying the theory of one advocate or of the other? The job of choosing wisely between the inventions of counsel is a difficult one. The job of consistent wise choice is tremendous. Yet it is not of itself the major work. That has been done, consistently, continuously, by the bar. Webster, not Marshall, made the Dartmouth College case. And when I say invention, I mean invention. To produce out of raw facts a theory of a case is prophecy. To produce it persuasively, and to get it over, is prophecy fulfilled. *Singers of songs and dreamers of plays*—though they be lawyers—*build a house no wind blows over.*

I say, then, that both in the office and in court it is the profession that keeps the law alive. It is the profession that keeps the law from sitting too closely strait-jacketed upon the social body. I have already indicated why the lawyer gets, why he will continue to get, the least of credit for his work. But the fact that he has it to do puts upon him a responsibility that reaches beyond his clients, beyond his surroundings, that reaches to the future of the people. A responsibility to his kind which there is no escaping. That laymen do not know he carries it, and do not care, makes it no more escapable. His, and his only, is the choice. He can either set himself across the path of progress, he can either check and block, by the exercise of utmost ingenuity, each new forward step. Or he can do the opposite.

Meantime, however, he must survive. It irks me to intrude such thoughts upon a high discussion—but he must pay the rent. Ours is a money economy. The man must have an income. Income and standing up under responsibility; it is a troublous team to ride.

Thus we come to that peculiar engine built up by the profession for the purpose of helping a lawyer ride the team—that system of practices and norms we know as legal ethics. There are two of those norms which look with incisive directness to our problem.

The one is the established view, respectable as few other things are respectable, accepted as such not only by the profession but the public, that a lawyer should believe in his cause. If he believes in his cause he will fight, he will fight more vigorously, he will think more skillfully, his whole self will be unchained by his conviction. That way lies, among other things, success. And as the lawyer becomes the symbol for his cause, and gains weight before the jury when he "stakes his reputation on his case"—so also the finer type of lawyer has through the centuries worked himself up into full belief in his cause before his work took on full value to himself. So much so that the lay-folk speak of an advocate's temperament as of a type, and smile (or jibe) to watch the speed with which most lawyers can achieve conviction.

Believing in one's causes involves, however, comes inevitably and almost imperceptibly to involve believing in one's client, when one's client brings a considerable succession of cases. The same loyalty which the finer ethic calls toward the cause is bound to develop in the course of time toward the client as well. But in this day of group activity, of corporate practice, the client with the succession of cases is the goal of all delight. He, or it, his or its retainer—if I may be again sordid for a moment—pays the rent. This comes inevitably to mean the substantial identification of a lawyer with a particular client or particular interest. He is a banking lawyer, or a railroad lawyer, or a sugar company lawyer. In such capacity, and with such loyalties, he should of course turn down the cases in which he does not believe. Those, you may notice, will be cases against the banking house, the sugar company, the railroad.

Thus, naturally and easily, one works out a harmonization between one's duty to the public and one's duty to one's pocket. And I wish to make here particularly the point that the ethic of believing in one's case is of peculiar value when one discovers that the case of a poor man is not worthy of such belief.

But there may be a pleasant paunch upon your client. His wallet may look fat. Suppose now that his case does not at first blush seem appealing. Then what to do? Courage, my friend, there is another ethic! There is that admirable ethic of the profession which makes it clear that the lawyer is neither judge nor jury; that the lawyer has neither duty nor right to usurp the constitutional function of the judicial tribunal. It is not for him to condemn a man who has not been found guilty by twelve jurymen. It is not for him to condemn a practice which has not been found unwarranted by the court. It is of the essence of justice that every man be given a fair hearing, be given vigorous representation at the hearing; in a word, that he be assured a fair trial of his case; that he be not condemned until that trial is had, until the court has spoken.

No ethic is more respectable among ourselves.

The public does not always understand it. But reasons of the gravest import and most far reaching effect are and should be urged in its support. To insist upon the identification of lawyer and clients is in practice to jeopardize the representation of any unpopular cause, of any unpopular litigant; it is in essence to deny a trial. Shame to those members of the profession who, knowing this, have yet so often shrunk from unpopular causes, have even joined in the pressure against counsel in such causes! If popularity were always rightness, either short range or long, there would be no grave danger in thus lumping counsel and client. But the contrary proves true. And here is also a situation continually met with, in which the lawyer himself finds it impossible to accurately judge the facts. Only either at trial, or long after it, does the true set of facts appear, which contradicts what he himself has believed to hold against his client. Here again a client is entitled to the benefit of the fair trial. He should have it. The bar exists to insure it.

Yet you will tell me these two ethics contradict each other—that one cannot at the same time believe wholly in his cause, and yet secure fair hearing for a cause he does not believe in. Do not be so naive. Already you are almost lawyers. Three years you have been studying the law. Are you still unaware that every doubtful point is regularly answered both ways by authority? Are you still blind to the fact that rules do not *control* decisions when the case is troublesome? In every field, on every point, when there is doubt, the law will offer you technique and rules, respectable, respected, to work *either* goal. There is the Janus-face of Precedent. The same with logic: you can if you will reject the rule because you do not see its end: "We cannot take this step; we do not see where to draw the line." Or, "The rule here contended for would lead to this, and this, which we cannot accept; therefore we must reject it in the present case as well." Or, on the other hand, if you prefer, you can decide the case regardless of such far, imagined difficulties: "It has been urged upon us that the rule proposed would lead to this and this. Such cases are not before us. It will be time to test them when they come. The present case, in any event, now is within the line."

Within the law, I say, therefore, rules *guide*, but they do not control decision. There is no precedent the judge may not at his need either file down to razor thinness or expand into a bludgeon. Why should you expect the ethics of the game to be different from the game itself? Of course, from one angle, the two guides are inconsistent. But each, for itself, is true, is sound, is vital—in its place. When to use which? A search for outside answer is an empty quest. Empty, delusive, footless—"Repose", says Holmes, "is not the destiny of man." Choice is your own. You answer for your choice. There are no rules to shoulder your responsibility.

Yet there are rules which can be made to seem to shoulder it. For, see, I have set before you two norms of legal ethics, both of which, as I understand it, are completely respectable, accepted, impeccable, and either of which is always available. All that is needed, to assure you of success (once you acquire any clients) is for you to choose the convenient ethic at the convenient time. You have only to insist upon the need for a fair hearing when a fat client's case looks bad; and to insist upon the need for believing in your case, either when you do by good fortune believe in a fat client's case, or when you find it difficult to believe some starved, pinched fellow. Whatever you do then, you will have done respectably. Men will look up to you. You will sleep at night. Your conscience will be clear. Your income tax will grow.

For your esteem, for your ideal, you then can take the squid, the cuttlefish. Spine he has not, but O, a beak he has. The spine is absent, but the beak is strong. There are ten counted legs, each leg alive with suckers, all waving through the water after prey. The world, the whole world, offers hope for prey. When pressed some time too hard by enemies, most lawyer-like he hides himself behind a cloud of ink.—Why does a hearse horse snicker?

I may seem to you to have been somewhat lightly ironic, somewhat idly cynical, in what I have just said. I may seem to be mocking at the precious things of life. I should be sorry to have you mistake me. I speak in bitter seriousness. I speak in behalf of all ideals I know. I speak without expectation, but I speak in hope. The unpopularity of our profession, the accusations against it, must not and cannot be permitted to hide its finer service from our eyes. We, and no others, carry the burden of making the law worth having—over the long run and from day to day. I see so clearly the responsibility. But I see also so very clearly the ease with which it can be shunted, and shunted, even, in all ignorance of the shunting. I see so clearly this two-edged ethic, I see the balm and smugness with which it baits invertebrates among us. The pressure to let the burden slide will fall so soon on you. As things stand, it is a pressure well-nigh irresistible. There will be very few whose eyes it does not close. There will be very few of you who will resist it. But twenty years from now it will give pleasure, it will give foolish pride, it will give honor, to meet those few and take them by the hand.

QUESTIONS

1. Do you agree with Rabelais that "laws are excerpted out of the middle of moral and natural philosophy"? If so, why have many lawyers "studied less in philosophy than my mule"? *See Materials, supra* at 1F.

2. Do you agree with Llewellyn that a lawyer is "a specialist in *winning*"? *See* THE BRAMBLE BUSH, *supra* at 1F.

3. Llewellyn, writing in 1936, constantly uses only the male pronoun. At that time, many law schools, including Harvard, did not admit women. Has the influx of women into the legal profession changed anything that Llewellyn said?

4. Is Llewellyn's "cuttlefish" totem fair? Or is he being too unkind to the profession?

5. What is the answer to the "two-edged ethic"? Is the answer Llewellyn's assertion that the "two-edged ethic" baits "the invertebrates among us," or is this too simplistic an approach? How helpful is this approach in practice? Does the answer depend on the nature of one's legal practice? Should it?

PLATO, THE APOLOGY OF SOCRATES
(399 B.C.)

[Note: from PLATO, THE APOLOGY (Benjamin Jowett trans., Oxford, 1871). Benjamin Jowett (1817-1893) was Professor of Greek at Oxford and Master of Balliol College. He is still famous for his great translation. For another excellent translation incorporating more recent scholarly insights, see PLATO, THE LAST DAYS OF SOCRATES (Hugh Tredennick trans. with intro., London, rev. ed., 2003), a "Penguin" paperback.]

How you have felt, O men of Athens, at hearing the speeches of my accusers, I cannot tell; but know that their persuasive words almost made me forget who I was, such was the effect of them; and yet they have hardly spoken a word of truth. But many as their falsehoods were, there was one of them which quite amazed me: I mean when they told you to be upon your guard, and not to let yourself be deceived by the force of my eloquence. They ought to have been ashamed of saying this, because they were sure to be detected as soon as I opened my lips and displayed my deficiency; they certainly did appear to be most shameless in saying this, unless by the force of eloquence they mean the force of truth: for then I do indeed admit that I am eloquent. But in how different a way from theirs! Well, as I was saying, they have hardly uttered a word, or not more than a word, of truth; but you shall hear from me the whole truth: not, however, delivered after their manner, in a set oration duly ornamented with words and phrases. No, indeed! but I shall use the words and arguments which occur to me at the moment; for I am certain that this is right, and that at my time of life I ought not to be appearing before you, O men of Athens, in the character of a juvenile orator let no one expect this of me. And I must beg of you to grant me one favor, which is this—if you hear me using the same words in my defense which I have been in the habit of using, and which most of you may have heard in the *agora*, and at the tables of the moneychangers, or anywhere else, I would ask you not to be surprised at this, and not to interrupt me. For I am more than seventy years of age, and this is the first time that I have ever appeared in a court of law, and I am quite a stranger to the ways of the place; and therefore I would have you regard me as if I were really a stranger, whom you would excuse if he spoke in his native tongue, and after the fashion of his country: that I think is not an unfair request. Never mind the manner, which may or may not be good; but think only of the justice of my cause, and give heed to that: let the judge decide justly and the speaker speak truly.

And first, I have to reply to the older charges and to my first accusers, and then I will go to the later ones. For I have had many accusers, who accused me of old, and their false charges have continued during many years; and I am more afraid of them than of Anytus and his associates, who are dangerous, too, in their own way. But far more dangerous are these, who began when you were children, and took possession of your minds with their falsehoods, telling of one Socrates, a wise man, who speculated about the heaven above, and searched into the earth beneath, and made the worse appear the better cause. These are the accusers whom I dread; for they are the circulators of this rumor, and their hearers are too apt to fancy that speculators of this sort do not believe in the gods. And they are many, and their charges against me are of ancient date, and they made them in days when you were impressible—in childhood, or perhaps in youth—and the cause when heard went by default, for there was none to answer. And, hardest of all, their names I do not know and cannot tell; unless in the chance of a comic poet. But the main body of these slanderers who from envy and malice have wrought upon you—and there are some of them who are convinced themselves, and impart their convictions to others—all these, I say, are most difficult to deal with; for I cannot have them up here, and examine them, and therefore I must simply fight with shadows in my own defense, and examine when there is no one who answers. I will ask you then to assume with me, as I was saying, that my opponents are of two kinds—one recent, the other ancient; and I hope that you will see the propriety of my answering the latter first, for these accusations you heard long before the others, and much oftener.

Well, then, I will make my defense, and I will endeavor in the short time which is allowed to do away with this evil opinion of me, which you have held for such a long time; and I hope I may succeed, if this be well for you and me, and that my words may find favor with you. But I know that to accomplish this is not easy—I quite see the nature of the task. Let the event be as God wills: in obedience to the law I make my defense.

I will begin at the beginning, and ask what the accusation is which has given rise to this slander of me, and which has encouraged Meletus to proceed against me. What do the slanderers say? They shall be my prosecutors, and I will sum up their words in an affidavit: "Socrates is an evildoer, and a curious person, who searches into things under the earth and in heaven, and he makes the worse appear the better cause; and he teaches the aforesaid doctrines to others." That is the nature of the accusation, and that is what you have seen yourselves in the comedy of Aristophanes; who has introduced a man whom he calls Socrates, going about and saying that he can walk in the air, and talking a deal of nonsense concerning matters of which I do not pretend to know either much or little—not that I mean to say anything disparaging of anyone who is a student of natural philosophy. I should be very sorry if Meletus could lay that to my charge. But the simple truth is, O Athenians, that I have nothing to do with these studies. Very many of those here present are witnesses to the truth of this, and to them I appeal. Speak then, you who have heard me, and tell your neighbors whether any of you have ever known me hold forth in few words or in many upon matters of this sort. . . . You hear their answer. And from what they say of this you will be able to judge of the truth of the rest.

As little foundation is there for the report that I am teacher, and take money; that is no more true than the other. Although, if a man is able to teach, I honor him for being paid. There is Gorgias of Leontium, and Prodicus of Ceos, and Hippias of Elis, who go the round of the cities, and are able to persuade the young men to leave their own citizens, by whom they might be taught for nothing, and come to them, whom they not only pay, but are thankful if they may be allowed to pay them. There is actually a Parian philosopher residing in Athens, of whom I have heard; and I came to hear of him in this way: I met a man who has spent a world of money on the Sophists, Callias the son of Hiponicus, and knowing that he had sons, I asked him: "Callias," I said, "if your two sons were foals or calves, there would be no difficulty in finding someone to put over them; we should hire a trainer of horses or a farmer probably who would improve and perfect them in their own proper virtue and excellence; but as they are human beings, whom are you thinking of placing over them? Is there anyone who understands human and political virtue? You must have thought about this as you have sons; is there anyone?" "There is," he said. "Who is he?" said I, "and of what country? and what does he charge?" "Evenus the Parian," he replied; "he is the man, and his charge is five minæ." Happy is Evenus, I said to myself, if he really has this wisdom, and teaches at such a modest charge. Had I the same, I should have been very proud and conceited; but the truth is that I have no knowledge of the kind, O Athenians.

I dare say that someone will ask the question, "Why is this, Socrates, and what is the origin of these accusations of you: for there must have been something strange which you have been doing? All this great fame and talk about you would never have arisen if you had been like other men: tell us, then, why this is, as we should be sorry to judge hastily of you." Now I regard this as a fair challenge, and I will endeavor to explain to you the origin of this name of "wise", and of this evil fame. Please to attend them, and although some of you may think I am joking, I declare that I will tell you the entire truth. Men of Athens, this reputation of mine has come of a certain sort of wisdom which I possess. If you ask me what kind of wisdom, I reply, such wisdom as is attainable by man, for to that extent I am inclined to believe that I am wise; whereas the persons of whom I was speaking have a superhuman wisdom, which I may fail to describe, because I have it not myself; and he who says that I have, speaks falsely, and is taking away my character. And here, O men of Athens, I must beg you not to interrupt me, even if I seem to say something extravagant. For the word which I will speak is not mine. I will refer you to a witness who is worthy of credit, and will tell you about my wisdom—whether I have any, and of what sort—and that witness shall be the god of Delphi. You must have known Chærephon; he was early a friend of mine, and also a friend of yours, for he shared in the exile of the people, and returned with you. Well, Chærephon, as you know, was very impetuous in all his doings, and he went to Delphi and boldly asked the oracle to tell him whether—as I was saying, I must beg you not to interrupt—he asked the oracle to tell him whether there was anyone wiser than I was, and the Pythian prophetess answered that there was no man wiser. Chærephon is dead himself, but his brother, who is in court will confirm the truth of this story.

Why do I mention this? Because I am going to explain to you why I have such an evil name. When I heard the answer, I said to myself, What can the god mean? and what is the interpretation of this riddle? For I know that I have no wisdom, small or great. What can he mean when he says that I am the wisest of men? And yet he is a god and cannot lie; that would be against his nature. After a long consideration, I at last thought of a method of trying the question. I reflected that if I could only find a man wiser than myself, then I might go to the god with a refutation in my hand. I should say to him, "Here is a man who is wiser than I am; but you said that I was the wisest." Accordingly I went to one who had the reputation of wisdom, and observed to him—his name I need not mention; he was a politician whom I selected for examination—and the result was as follows: When I began to talk with him, I could not help thinking that he was not really wise, although he was thought wise by many, and wiser still by himself; and I went and tried to explain to him that he thought himself wise, but was not really wise; and the consequence was that he hated me, and his enmity was shared by several who were present and heard me. So I left him, saying to myself, as I went away: Well, although I do not suppose that either of us knows anything really beautiful and good, I am better off than he is—for he knows nothing, and thinks that he knows. I neither know nor think that I know. In this latter particular, then, I seem to have slightly the advantage of him. Then I went to another, who had still higher philosophical pretensions, and my conclusion was exactly the same. I made another enemy of him, and of many others besides him.

After this I went to one man after another, being not unconscious of the enmity which I provoked, and I lamented and feared this: but necessity was laid upon me—the word of God, I thought, ought to be considered first. And I said to myself, Go I must to all who appear to know, and find out the meaning of the oracle. And I swear to you, Athenians, by the dog I swear!—for I must tell you the truth—the result of my mission was just this: I found that the men most in repute were all but the most foolish; and that some inferior men were really wiser and better. I will tell you the tale of my wanderings and of the "Herculean" labors, as I may call them, which I endured only to find at last the oracle irrefutable. When I left the politicians, I went to the poets; tragic, dithyrambic [passionate], and all sorts. And there, I said to myself, you will be detected; now you will find out that you are more ignorant than they are. Accordingly, I took them some of the most elaborate passages in their own writings, and asked what was the meaning of them—thinking that they would teach me something. Will you believe me? I am almost ashamed to speak of this, but still I must say that there is hardly a person present who would not have talked better about their poetry than they did themselves. That showed me in an instant that not by wisdom do poets write poetry, but by a sort of genius and inspiration; they are like diviners or soothsayers who also say many fine things, but do not understand the meaning of them. And the poets appeared to me to be much in the same case; and I further observed that upon the strength of their poetry they believed themselves to be the wisest of men in other things in which they were not wise. So I departed, conceiving myself to be superior to them for the same reason that I was superior to the politicians.

At last I went to the artisans, for I was conscious that I knew nothing at all, as I may say, and I was sure that they knew many fine things; and in this I was not mistaken, for they did know many things which I was ignorant, and in this they certainly were wiser than I was. But I observed that even the good artisans fell into the same error as the poets; because they were good workmen they thought that they also knew all sorts of high matters, and this defect in them overshadowed their wisdom—therefore I asked myself on behalf of the oracle, whether I would like to be as I was, neither having their knowledge nor their ignorance, or like them in both; and I made answer to myself and the oracle that I was better off as I was.

This investigation has led to my having many enemies of the worst and most dangerous kind, and has given occasion also to many calumnies, and I am called wise, for my hearers always imagine that I myself possess the wisdom which I find wanting in others: but the truth is, O men of Athens, that God only is wise; and in this oracle he means to say that the wisdom of men is little or nothing; he is not speaking of Socrates, he is only using my name as an illustration, as if he said, He, O men, is the wisest, who, like Socrates, knows that his wisdom is in truth worth nothing. And so I go my way, obedient to the god, and make inquisition into the wisdom of anyone, whether citizen or stranger, who appears to be wise; and if he is not wise, then in vindication of the oracle I show him that he is not wise; and this occupation quite absorbs me, and I have no time to give either to any public matter of interest or to any concern of my own, but I am in utter poverty by reason of my devotion to the god.

There is another thing:—young men of the richer classes, who have not much to do, come about me of their own accord; they like to hear the pretenders examined, and they often imitate me, and examine others themselves; there are plenty of persons, as they soon enough discover, who think that they know something, but really know little or nothing: and then those who are examined by them instead of being angry with themselves are angry with me: This confounded Socrates, they say; this villainous misleader of youth!—and then if somebody asks them, Why, what evil does he practice or teach? They do not know, and cannot tell; but in order that they may not appear to be at a loss, they repeat the ready-made charges which are used against all philosophers about teaching things up in the clouds and under the earth, and having no gods, and making the worse appear the better cause; for they do not like to confess that their pretense of knowledge has been detected—which is the truth: and as they are numerous and ambitious and energetic, and are all in battle array and have persuasive tongues, they have filled your ears with their loud and inveterate calumnies. And this is the reason why my three accusers, Meletus and Anytus and Lycon, have set upon me; Meletus, who has a quarrel with me on behalf of the poets; Anytus, on behalf of the craftsmen; Lycon, on behalf of the rhetoricians: and as I said at the beginning, I cannot expect to get rid of this mass of calumny all in a moment. And this, O men of Athens, is the truth and the whole truth; I have concealed nothing, I have dissembled nothing. And yet I know that this plainness of speech makes them hate me, and what is their hatred but a proof that I am speaking the truth?—this is the occasion and reason of their slander of me as you will find out either in this or in any future inquiry.

I have said enough in my defense against the first class of my accusers; I turn to the second class, who are headed by Meletus, that good and patriotic man, as he calls himself. And now I will try to defend myself against them: these new accusers must also have their affidavit read. What do they say? Something of this sort: That Socrates is a doer of evil, and corrupter of the youth, and he does not believe in the gods of the State, and has other new divinities of his own. That is the sort of charge; and now let us examine the particular counts. He says that I am a doer of evil, who corrupt the youth; but I say, O men of Athens, that Meletus is a doer of evil, and the evil is that he makes a joke of a serious matter, and is too ready at bringing other men to trial from a pretended zeal and interest about matters in which he really never had the smallest interest. And the truth of this I will endeavor to prove.

Come hither, Meletus, and let me ask a question of you. You think a great deal about the improvement of youth?

Yes, I do.

Tell the judges, then, who is their improver; for you must know, as you have taken the pains to discover their corrupter, and are citing and accusing me before them. Speak, then, and tell the judges who their improver is. Observe, Meletus, that you are silent, and have nothing to say. But is not this rather disgraceful, and a very considerable proof of what I was saying, that you have no interest in the matter? Speak up, friend, and tell us who their improver is.

The laws.

But that, my good sir, is not my meaning. I want to know who the person is, who, in the first place, knows the laws.

The judges, Socrates, who are present in court.

What do you mean to say, Meletus, that they are able to instruct and improve youth?

Certainly they are.

What, all of them, or some only and not others?

All of them.

By the goddess Hera, that is good news! There are plenty of improvers, then. And what do you say of the audience—do they improve them?

Yes, they do.

And the Senators?

Yes, the Senators improve them.

But perhaps the ecclesiasts corrupt them?—or do they too improve them? They improve them.

Then every Athenian improves and elevates them; all with the exception of myself; and I alone am their corrupter? Is that what you affirm?

That is what I stoutly affirm.

I am very unfortunate if that is true. But suppose I ask you a question: Would you say that this also holds true in the case of horses? Does one man do them harm and all the world good? Is not the exact opposite of this true? One man is able to do them good, or at least not many; the trainer of horses, that is to say, does them good, and others who have to do with them rather injure them? Is not that true, Meletus, of horses, or any other animals? Yes, certainly. Whether you and Anytus say yes or no, that is no matter. Happy indeed would be the condition of youth if they had one corrupter only, and all the rest of the world were their improvers. And you, Meletus, have sufficiently shown that you never had a thought about the young: your carelessness is seen in your not caring about matters spoken of in this very indictment.

And now, Meletus, I must ask you another question: Which is better, to live among bad citizens, or among good ones? Answer friend, I say; for that is a question which may be easily answered. Do not the good do their neighbors good, and the bad do them evil?

Certainly.

And is there anyone who would rather be injured than benefited by those who live with him? Answer, my good friend; the law requires you to answer—does anyone like to be injured?

Certainly not.

And when you accuse me of corrupting and deteriorating the youth, do you allege that I corrupt them intentionally or unintentionally?

Intentionally, I say.

But you have just admitted that the good do their neighbors good, and the evil do them evil. Now is that a truth which your superior wisdom has recognized thus early in life, and am I, at my age, in such darkness and ignorance as not to know that if a man with whom I have to live is corrupted by me, I am very likely to be harmed by him, and yet I corrupt him, and intentionally, too? that is what you are saying, and of that you will never persuade me or any other human being. But either I do not corrupt them, or I corrupt them unintentionally, so that on either view of the case you lie. If my offense is unintentional, the law has no cognizance of unintentional offenses: you ought to have taken me privately, and warned and admonished me; for if I had been better advised, I should have left off doing what I only did unintentionally—no doubt I should; whereas you hated to converse with me or teach me, but you indicted me in this court, which is a place not of instruction, but of punishment.

I have shown, Athenians, as I was saying, that Meletus has no care at all, great or small, about the matter. But still I should like to know, Meletus, in what I am affirmed to corrupt the young. I suppose you mean, as I infer from your indictment, that I teach them not to acknowledge the gods which the State acknowledges, but some other new divinities or spiritual agencies in their stead. These are the lessons which corrupt the youth, as you say.

Yes, that I say emphatically.

Then, by the gods, Meletus, of whom we are speaking, tell me and the court, in somewhat plainer terms, what you mean! for I do not as yet understand whether you affirm that I teach others to acknowledge some gods, and therefore do believe in gods and am not an entire atheist—this you do not lay to my charge; but only that they are not the same gods which the city recognizes—the charge is that they are different gods. Or, do you mean to say that I am an atheist simply, and a teacher of atheism?

I mean the latter—that you are a complete atheist.

That is an extraordinary statement, Meletus. Why do you say that? Do you mean that I do not believe in the god-head of the sun or moon, which is the common creed of all men?

I assure you, judges, that he does not believe in them; for he says that the sun is stone, and the moon earth.

Friend Meletus, you think that you are accusing Anaxagoras; and you have but a bad opinion of the judges, if you fancy them ignorant to such a degree as not to know that those doctrines are found in the books of Anaxagoras the Clazomenian, who is full of them. And these are the doctrines which the youth are said to learn of Socrates, when there are not infrequently exhibitions of them at the theatre (price of admission one drachma at the most); and they might cheaply purchase them, and laugh at Socrates if he pretends to father such eccentricities. And so, Meletus, you really think that I do not believe in any god?

I swear by Zeus that you believe absolutely in none at all.

You are a liar, Meletus, not believed even by yourself. For I cannot help thinking, O men of Athens, that Meletus is reckless and impudent, and that he has written this indictment in a spirit of mere wantonness and youthful bravado. Has he not compounded a riddle, thinking to try me? He said to himself: I shall see whether this wise Socrates will discover my ingenious contradiction, or whether I shall be able to deceive him and the rest of them. For he certainly does appear to me to contradict himself in the indictment as much as if he said that Socrates is guilty of not believing in the gods, and yet of believing in them—but this surely is a piece of fun.

I should like you, O men of Athens, to join me in examining what I conceive to be his inconsistency; and do you, Meletus, answer. And I must remind you that you are not to interrupt me if I speak in my accustomed manner.

Did ever man, Meletus, believe in the existence of human things, and not of human beings? . . . I wish, men of Athens, that he would answer, and not be always trying to get up an interruption. Did ever any man believe in horsemanship, and not in horses? or in flute-playing and not in flute-players? No, my friend; I will answer to you and to the court, as you refuse to answer for yourself. There is no man who ever did. But now please to answer the next question: Can a man believe in spiritual and divine agencies, and not in spirit or demigods?

He cannot.

I am glad that I have extracted that answer, by the assistance of the court; nevertheless you swear in the indictment that I teach and believe in divine or spiritual agencies (new or old, no matter for that); at any rate, I believe in spiritual agencies, as you say and swear in the affidavit; but if I believe in divine beings, I must believe in spirits or demigods; is not that true? Yes, that is true, for I may assume that your silence gives assent to that. Now what are spirits or demigods? are they not either gods or the sons of gods? Is that true?

Yes, that is true.

But this is just the ingenious riddle of which I was speaking: the demigods or spirits are gods, and you say first that I don't believe in gods, and then again that I do believe in gods; that is, if I believe in demigods. For if the demigods are the illegitimate sons of gods, whether by Nymphs or by any other mothers, as is thought, that, as all men will allow, necessarily implies the existence of their parents. You might as well affirm the existence of mules, and deny that of horses and asses. Such nonsense, Meletus, could only have been intended by you as a trial of me. You have put this into the indictment because you had nothing real of which to accuse me. But no one who has a particle of understanding will ever be convinced by you that the same man can believe in divine and superhuman things, and yet not believe that there are gods and demigods and heroes.

I have said enough in answer to the charge of Meletus: any elaborate defense is unnecessary; but as I was saying before, I certainly have many enemies, and this is what will be my destruction if I am destroyed; of that I am certain; not Meletus, nor yet Anytus, but the envy and detraction of the world, which has been the death of many good men, and will probably be the death of many more; there is no danger of my being the last of them.

Someone will say: And are you not ashamed, Socrates, of a course of life which is likely to bring you to an untimely end? To him I may fairly answer: There you are mistaken: a man who is good for anything ought not to calculate the chance of living or dying; he ought only to consider whether in doing anything he is doing right or wrong—acting the part of a good man or of a bad. Whereas, according to your view, the heroes who fell at Troy were not good for much, and the son of Thetis above all, who altogether despised danger in comparison with disgrace; and when his goddess mother said to him, in his eagerness to slay Hector, that if he avenged his companion Patroclus, and slew Hector, he would die himself—"Fate," as she said, "waits upon you next after Hector"; he, hearing this, utterly despised danger and death, and instead of fearing them, feared rather to live in dishonor, and not to avenge his friend. "Let me die next," he replies, "and be avenged of my enemy, rather than abide here by the beaked ships, a scorn and a burden of the earth." Had Achilles any thought of death and danger? For wherever a man's place is, whether the place which he has chosen or that in which he has been placed by a commander, there he ought to remain in the hour of danger; he should not think of death or of anything, but of disgrace. And this, O men of Athens, is a true saying.

Strange, indeed, would be my conduct, O men of Athens, if I who, when I was ordered by the generals whom you chose to command me at Potidæa and Amphipolis and Delium, remained where they placed me, like any other man, facing death—if, I say, now, when, as I conceive and imagine, God orders me to fulfill the philosopher's mission of searching into myself and other men, I were to desert my post through fear of death, or any other fear, that would indeed be strange, and I might justly be arraigned in court for denying the existence of the gods, if I disobeyed the oracle because I was afraid of death: then I should be fancying that I was wise when I was not wise. For this fear of death is indeed the pretense of wisdom, and not real wisdom, being the appearance of knowing the unknown; since no one knows whether death, which they in their fear apprehend to be the greatest evil, may not be the greatest good. Is there not here conceit of knowledge, which is a disgraceful sort of ignorance? And this is the point in which, as I think, I am superior to men in general, and in which I might perhaps fancy myself wiser than other men—that whereas I know but little of the world below, I do not suppose that I know: but I do know that injustice and disobedience to a better, whether God or man, is evil and dishonorable, and I will never fear or avoid a possible good rather than a certain evil. And therefore if you let me go now, and reject the counsels of Anytus, who said that if I were not put to death I ought not to have been prosecuted, and that if I escape now, your sons will all be utterly ruined by listening to my words—if you say to me, Socrates, this time we will not mind Anytus, and will let you off, but upon one condition, that you are not to inquire and speculate in this way any more, and that if you are caught doing this again you shall die—if this was the condition on which you let me go, I should reply: Men of Athens, I honor and love you; but I shall obey God rather than you, and while I have life and strength I shall never cease from the practice and teaching of philosophy, exhorting anyone whom I meet after my manner, and convincing him, saying: O my friend, why do you who are a citizen of the great and mighty and wise city of Athens, care so much about laying up the greatest among of money and honor and reputation, and so little about wisdom and truth and the greatest improvement of the soul, which you never regard or heed at all? Are you not ashamed of this? And if the person with whom I am arguing says: Yes, but I do care; I do not depart or let him go at once: I interrogate and examine and cross-examine him, and if I think that he has no virtue, but only says that he has, I reproach him with undervaluing the greater, and overvaluing the less. And this I should say to everyone whom I meet, young and old, citizen and alien, but especially to the citizens, inasmuch as they are my brethren. For this is the command of God, as I would have you know; and I believe that to this day no greater good has ever happened in the State than my service to the God. For I do nothing but go about persuading you all, old and young alike, not to take thought for your persons and your properties, but first and chiefly to care about the greatest improvement of the soul. I tell you that virtue is not given by money, but that from virtue come money and every other good of man, public as well as private. This is my teaching, and if this is the doctrine which corrupts the youth, my influence is ruinous indeed. But if anyone says that this is not my teaching, he is speaking an untruth. Wherefore, O men of Athens, I say to you, do as Anytus bids or not as Anytus bids, and either acquit me or not; but whatever you do, know that I shall never alter my ways, not even if I have to die many times.

Men of Athens, do not interrupt, but hear me; there was an agreement between us that you should hear me out. And I think that what I am going to say will do you good: for I have something more to say, at which you may be inclined to cry out; but I beg that you will not do this. I would have you know that, if you kill such a one as I am, you will injure yourselves more than you will injure me. Meletus and Anytus will not injure me: they cannot; for it is not in the nature of things that a bad man should injure a better than himself. I do not deny that he may, perhaps, kill him, or drive him into exile, or deprive him of civil rights; and he may imagine, and others may imagine, that he is doing him a great injury: but in that I do not agree with him; for the evil of doing as Anytus is doing—of unjustly taking away another man's life—is greater far. And now, Athenians, I am not going to argue for my own sake, as you may think, but for yours, that you may not sin against the God, or lightly reject his boon by condemning me. For if you kill me you will not easily find another like me, who, if I may use such a ludicrous figure of speech, am a sort of gadfly, given to the State by the God; and the State is like a great and noble steed who is tardy in his motions owing to his very size, and requires to be stirred into life. I am that gadfly which God has given the State and all day long and in all places am always fastening upon you, arousing and persuading and reproaching you. And as you will not easily find another like me, I would advise you to spare me. I dare say that you may feel irritated at being suddenly awakened when you are caught napping; and you may think that if you were to strike me dead, as Anytus advises, which you easily might, then you would sleep on for the remainder of your lives, unless God in his care of you gives you another gadfly. And that I am given to you by God is proved by this: that if I had been like other men, I should not have neglected all my own concerns, or patiently seen the neglect of them during all these years, and have been doing yours, coming to you individually, like a father or elder brother, exhorting you to regard virtue; this, I say, would not be like human nature. And had I gained anything, or if my exhortations had been paid, there would have been some sense in that: but now, as you will perceive, not even the impudence of my accusers dares to say that I have ever exacted or sought pay of anyone; they have no witness of that. And I have a witness of the truth of what I say; my poverty is a sufficient witness.

Someone may wonder why I go about in private, giving advice and busying myself with the concerns of others, but do not venture to come forward in public and advise the State. I will tell you the reason of this. You have often heard me speak of an oracle or sign which comes to me, and is the divinity which Meletus ridicules in the indictment. This sign I have had ever since I was a child. The sign is a voice which comes to me and always forbids me to do something which I am going to do, but never commands me to do anything, and this is what stands in the way of my being a politician. And rightly, as I think. For I am certain, O men of Athens, that if I had engaged in politics, I should have perished long ago and done no good either to you or to myself. And don't be offended at my telling you the truth: for the truth is that no man who goes to war with you or any other multitude, honestly struggling against the commission of unrighteousness and wrong in the State, will save his life; he who will really fight for the right, if he would live even for a little while, must have a private station and not a public one.

I can give you as proofs of this, not words only, but deeds, which you value more than words. Let me tell you a passage of my own life, which will prove to you that I should never have yielded to injustice from any fear of death, and that if I had not yielded I should have died at once. I will tell you a story—tasteless, perhaps, and commonplace, but nevertheless true. The only office of State which I ever held, O men of Athens, was that of Senator; the tribe Antiochis, which is my tribe, had the presidency at the trial of the generals who had not taken up the bodies of the slain after the battle of Arginusæ; and you proposed to try them all together, which was illegal, as you all thought afterwards; but at the time I was the only one of the Prytanes who was opposed to the illegality, and I gave my vote against you; and when the orators threatened to impeach and arrest me, and have me taken away, and you called and shouted, I made up my mind that I would run the risk, having law and justice with me, rather than take part in your injustice because I feared imprisonment and death. This happened in the days of the democracy. But when the oligarchy of the Thirty was in power, they sent for me and four others into the rotunda, and bade us bring Leon the Salaminian from Salamis, as they wanted to execute him. This was a specimen of the sort of commands which they were always giving with the view of implicating as many as possible in their crimes; and then I showed, not in words only, but in deed, that, if I may be allowed to use such an expression, I cared not a straw for death, and that my only fear was the fear of doing an unrighteous or unholy thing. For the strong arm of that oppressive power did not frighten me into doing wrong; and when we came out of the rotunda the other four went to Salamis and fetched Leon, but I went quietly home. For which I might have lost my life, had not the power of the Thirty shortly afterwards come to an end. And to this many will witness.

Now do you really imagine that I could have survived all these years, if I had led a public life, supposing that like a good man I had always supported the right and had made justice, as I ought, the first thing? No, indeed, men of Athens, neither I nor any other. But I have been always the same in all my actions, public as well as private, and never have I yielded any base compliance to those who are slanderously termed my disciples or to any other. For the truth is that I have no regular disciples: but if anyone likes to come and hear me while I am pursuing my mission, whether he be young or old, he may freely come. Nor do I converse with those who pay only, and not with those who do not pay; but any one, whether he be rich or poor, may ask and answer me and listen to my words; and whether he turns out to be a bad man or a good one; that cannot be justly laid to my charge, as I never taught him anything. And if anyone says that he has ever learned or heard anything from me in private which all the world has not heard, I should like you to know that he is speaking an untruth.

But I shall be asked, Why do people delight in continually conversing with you?

I have told you already, Athenians, the whole truth about this: they like to hear the cross examination of the pretenders to wisdom; there is amusement in this. And this is a duty which the God has imposed upon me, as I am assured by oracles, visions, and in every sort of way in which the will of divine power was ever signified to anyone. This is true, O Athenians; or, if not true, would be soon refuted. For if I am really corrupting the youth, and have corrupted some of them already, those of them who have grown up and have become sensible that I gave them bad advice in the days of their youth should come forward as accusers and take their revenge; and if they do not like to come themselves, some of their relatives, fathers, brothers, or other kinsmen, should say what evil their families suffered at my hands. Now is their time. Many of them I see in the court. There is Crito, who is of the same age and of the same *deme* with myself; and there is Critobulus his son, whom I also see. Then again there is Lysanias of Sphettus, who is the father of Æscines—he is present; and also there is Antiphon of Cephisus, who is the father of Epignes; and there are the brothers of several who have associated with me. There is Nicostratus the son of Theosdotides, and the brother of Theodotus (now Theodotus himself is dead, and therefore he, at any rate, will not seek to stop him); and there is Paralus the son of Demodocus, who had a brother Theages; and Adeimantus the son of Ariston, whose brother Plato is present; and Æantodorus, who is the brother of Apollodorus, whom I also see. I might mention a great many others, any of whom Meletus should have produced as witnesses in the course of his speech; and let him still produce them, if he has forgotten; I will make way for him. And let him say, if he has any testimony of the sort which he can produce. Nay, Athenians, the very opposite is the truth. For all these are ready to witness on behalf of the corrupter, of the destroyer of their kindred, as Meletus and Anytus call me; not the corrupted youth only—there might have been a motive for that—but their uncorrupted elder relatives. Why should they too support me with their testimony? Why, indeed, except for the sake of truth and justice, and because they know that I am speaking the truth, and that Meletus is lying.

Well, Athenians, this and the like of this is nearly all the defense which I have to offer. Yet a word more. Perhaps there may be someone who is offended at me, when he calls to mind how he himself, on a similar or even a less serious occasion, had recourse to prayers and supplications with many tears, and how he produced his children in court, which was a moving spectacle, together with a posse of his relations and friends; whereas I, who am probably in danger of my life, will do none of these things. Perhaps this may come into his mind, and he may be set against me, and vote in anger because he is displeased at this. Now if there be such a person among you, which I am far from affirming, I may fairly reply to him: My friend, I am a man, and like other men, a creature of flesh and blood, and not of wood or stone, as Homer says; and I have a family, yes, and sons, O Athenians, three in number, one of whom is growing up, and the two others are still young; and yet I will not bring any of them hither in order to petition you for an acquittal. And why not? Not from any self-will or disregard of you. Whether I am or am not afraid of death is another question, of which I will not now speak. But my reason simply is that I feel such conduct to be discreditable to myself, and you, and the whole State. One who has reached my years, and who has a name for wisdom, whether deserved or not, ought not to debase himself. At any rate, the world has decided that Socrates is in some way superior to other men. And if those among you who are said to be superior in wisdom and courage, and any other virtue, demean themselves in this way, how shameful is their conduct! I have seen men of reputation, when they have been condemned, behaving in the strangest manner: they seemed to fancy that they were going to suffer something dreadful if they died, and that they could be immortal if you only allowed them to live; and I think that they were a dishonor to the State, and that any stranger coming in would say of them that the most eminent men of Athens, to whom the Athenians themselves give honor and command, are no better than women. And I say that these things ought not to be done by those of us who are of reputation; and if they are done, you ought not to permit them; you ought rather to show that you are more inclined to condemn, not the man who is quiet, but the man who gets up a doleful scene, and makes the city ridiculous.

But, setting aside the question of dishonor, there seems to be something wrong in petitioning a judge, and thus procuring an acquittal instead of informing and convincing him. For his duty is, not to make a present of justice, but to give judgment; and he has sworn that he will judge according to the laws, and not according to his own good pleasure; and neither he nor we should get into the habit of perjuring ourselves—there can be no piety in that. Do not then require me to do what I consider dishonorable and impious and wrong, especially now, when I am being tried for impiety on the indictment of Meletus. For if, O men of Athens, by force of persuasion and entreaty, I could overpower your oaths, then I should be teaching you to believe that there are no gods, and convict myself, in my own defense, of not believing in them. But that is not the case; for I do believe that there are gods, and in a far higher sense than that in which any of my accusers believe in them. And to you and to God I commit my cause, to be determined by you as is best for you and me.

SOCRATES LOSES THE VOTE. ABOUT 280 *DIKASTS* VOTED FOR CONVICTION, 221 AGAINST. MELETUS ASKS FOR THE DEATH SENTENCE. SOCRATES MUST SUGGEST AN ALTERNATIVE PENALITY.

There are many reasons why I am not grieved, O men of Athens, at the vote of condemnation. I expect this, and am only surprised that the votes are so nearly equal; for I had thought that the majority against me would have been far larger; but now, had thirty votes gone over to the other side, I should have been acquitted. And I may say that I have escaped Meletus. And I may say more; for without the assistance of Anytus and Lycon, he would not have a fifth part of the votes, as the law requires, in which case he would have incurred a fine of a thousand drachmæ, as is evident.

And so he proposes death as the penalty. And what shall I propose on my part, O men of Athens? Clearly that which is my due. And what is that which I ought to pay or to receive? What shall be done to the man who has never had the wit to be idle during his whole life; but has been careless of what the many care about—wealth and family interests and military offices, and speaking in the assembly, and magistracies, and plots [secret societies], and [political] parties. Reflecting that I was really too honest a man to follow in this way and live, I did not go where I could do no good to you or to myself; but where I could do the greatest good privately to everyone of you, thither I went, and sought to persuade every man among you that he must look to himself, and seek virtue and wisdom before he looks to his private interests, and look to the [welfare of the] State before he looks to the interests of the State [i.e., his interests and advantages]; and that this should be the order which he observes in all his actions. What shall be done to such a one? Doubtless some good thing, O men of Athens, if he has his reward; and the good should be a kind suitable to him. What would be a reward suitable to a poor man who is your benefactor, who desires leisure that he may instruct you? There can be no more fitting reward than maintenance in the Prytaneum, O men of Athens, a reward which he deserves far more than the citizen who has won the prize at Olympia in the horse or chariot race, whether the chariots were drawn by two horses or by many. For I am in want, and he has enough; and he only gives you the appearance of happiness, and I give you the reality. And if I am to estimate the penalty justly, I say that maintenance in the Prytaneum is the just return.

Perhaps you may think that I am braving you in saying this, as in what I said before about the tears and prayers. But that is not the case. I speak rather because I am convinced that I never intentionally wronged anyone, although I cannot convince you of that—for we have had a short conversation only; but if there were a law at Athens, such as there is in other cities, that a capital cause should not be decided in one day, then I believe that I should have convinced you; but now the time is too short. I cannot in a moment refute great slanders; and, as I am convinced that I never wronged another, I will assuredly not wrong myself. I will not say of myself that I deserve any evil, or propose any penalty. Why should I? Because I am afraid of the penalty of death which Meletus proposes? When I do not know whether death is a good or an evil, why should I propose a penalty which would certainly be an evil? Shall I say imprisonment? And why should I live in prison, and be the slave of the magistrates of the year—of the Eleven? Or shall the penalty be a fine, and imprisonment until the fine is paid? There is the same objection. I should have to lie in prison, for money I have none, and I cannot pay. And if I say exile (and this may possibly be the penalty which you will affix), I must indeed be blinded by the love of life if I were to consider that when you, who are my own citizens, cannot endure my discourses and words, and have found them so grievous and odious that you would fain have done with them, others are likely to endure me. No, indeed, men of Athens, that is not very likely. And what a life should I lead, at my age, wandering from city to city, living in ever changing exile, and always being driven out! For I am quite sure that into whatever place I go, as here so also there, the young men will come to me; and if I drive them away, their elders will drive me out at their desire: and if I let them come, their fathers and friends will drive me out for their sakes.

Someone will say: Yes, Socrates, but cannot you hold your tongue, and then you may go into a foreign city, and no one will interfere with you? Now I have great difficulty in making you understand my answer to this. For if I tell you that this would be a disobedience to a divine command, and therefore that I cannot hold my tongue, you will not believe that I am serious; and if I say again that the greatest good of man is daily to converse about virtue, and all that concerning which you hear me examining myself and others, and that the life which is unexamined is not worth living—that you are still less likely to believe. And yet what I say is true, although a thing of which it is hard for me to persuade you. Moreover, I am not accustomed to think that I deserve any punishment. Had I money I might have proposed to give you what I had, and have been none the worse. But you see that I have none, and can only ask you to proportion the fine to my means. However, I think that I could afford a mina [100 drachmæ], and therefore, I propose that penalty: Plato, Crito, Critobulus, and Apollodorus, my friends here, bid me say thirty minæ [3,000 drachmæ], and they will be the sureties. Well then, say thirty minæ, let that be the penalty; for that they will be ample security to you.

THE *DIKASTS* VOTE FOR DEATH

Not much time will be gained, O Athenians, in return for the evil name which you will get from the detractors of the city, who will say that you killed Socrates, a wise man; for they will call me wise even although I am not wise when they want to reproach you. If you had waited a little while, your desire would have been fulfilled in the course of nature. For I am far advanced in years, as you may perceive and not far from death. I am speaking now only to those of you who have condemned me to death. And I have another thing to say to them: You think that I was convicted through deficiency of words—I mean, that if I had thought fit to leave nothing undone, nothing unsaid, I might have gained an acquittal. Not so; the deficiency which led to my conviction was not of words—certainly not. But I had not the boldness or impudence or inclination to address you as you would have liked me to address you, weeping and wailing and lamenting, and saying and doing many things which you have been accustomed to hear from others, and which, as I say, are unworthy of me. But I thought that I ought not to do anything common or mean in the hour of danger: nor do I now repent of the manner of my defense, and I would rather die having spoken after my manner, than speak in your manner and live. For neither in war nor yet at law ought any man to use every way of escaping death. For often in battle there is no doubt that if a man will throw away his arms, and fall on his knees before his pursuers, he may escape death; and in other dangers there are other ways of escaping death, if a man is willing to say and do anything. The difficulty, my friends, is not in avoiding death, but in avoiding unrighteousness; for that runs faster than death. I am old and move slowly, and the slower runner has overtaken me, and my accusers are keen and quick, and the faster runner, who is unrighteousness, has overtaken them. And now I depart hence condemned by you to suffer the penalty of death, and they, too, go their ways condemned by the truth to suffer the penalty of villainy and wrong; and I must abide by my award—let them abide by theirs. I suppose that these things may be regarded as fated—and I think that they are well.

And now, O men who have condemned me, I would fain prophesy to you; for I am about to die, and that is the hour in which men are gifted with prophetic power. And I prophesy to you who are my murderers, that immediately after my death punishment far heavier than you have inflicted on me will surely await you. Me you have killed because you wanted to escape the accuser, and not to give an account of your lives. But that will not be as you suppose: far otherwise. For I say that there will be more accusers of you than there are now; accusers whom hitherto I have restrained: and as they are younger they will be more severe with you, and you will be more offended at them. For if you think that by killing men you can avoid the accuser censuring your lives, you are mistaken; that is not a way of escape which is either possible or honorable; the easiest and noblest way is not to be cursing others, but to be improving yourselves. This is the prophecy which I utter before my departure, to the judge who have condemned me.

Friends, who would have acquitted me, I would like also to talk with you about this thing which has happened, while the magistrates are busy, and before I go to the place at which I must die. Stay then awhile, for we may as well talk with one another while there is time. You are my friends, and I should like to show you the meaning of this event which has happened to me. O my judges—for you I may truly call judges—I should like to tell you of a wonderful circumstance. Hitherto the familiar oracle within me has constantly been in the habit of opposing me even about trifles, if I was going to make a slip or error about anything; and now as you see there has come upon me that which may be thought, and is generally believed to be, the last and worst evil. But the oracle made no sign of opposition, either as I was leaving my house and going out in the morning, or when I was going up into this court, or while I was speaking, at anything which I was going to say; and yet I have often been stopped in the middle of a speech; but now in nothing I either said or did touching this matter has the oracle opposed me. What do I take to be the explanation of this? I will tell you. I regard this as a proof that what has happened to me is a good, and that those of us who think that death is an evil are in error. This is a great proof to me of what I am saying, for the customary sign would surely have opposed me had I been going to evil and not to good.

Let us reflect in another way, and we shall see that there is great reason to hope that death is a good, for one of two things: either death is a state of nothingness and utter unconsciousness, or, as men say, there is a change and migration of the soul from this world to another. Now if you suppose that there is no consciousness, but a sleep like the sleep of him who is undisturbed even by the sight of dreams, death will be an unspeakable gain. For if a person were to select the night in which his sleep was undisturbed even by dreams, and were to compare with this the other days and nights of his life, and then were to tell us how many days and nights he had passed in the course of his life better and more pleasantly than this one, I think that any man, I will not say a private man; but even the great king, will not find many such days or nights, when compared with the others. Now if death is like this, I say that to die, is gain; for eternity is then only a single night. But if death is the journey to another place, and there, as men say, all the dead are, what good, O my friends and judges, can be greater than this? If indeed when the pilgrim arrives in the world below, he is delivered from the professors of justice in this world, and finds the true judges who are said to give judgment there, Minos and Rhadamanthus and Æacus and Triptolemus, and other sons of God who were righteous in their own life, that pilgrimage will be worth making. What would not a man give if he might converse with Orpheus and Musæus and Hesiod and Homer? Nay, if this be true, let me die again and again. I, too, shall have a wonderful interest in a place where I can converse with Palamedes, and Ajax the son of Telamon, and other heroes of old, who have suffered death through an unjust judgment; and there will be no small pleasure, as I think, in comparing my own sufferings with theirs. Above all, I shall be able to continue my search into true and false knowledge; as in this world, so also in that; I shall find out who is wise, and who pretends to be wise, and is not. What would not a man give, O judges, to be able to examine the leader of the great Trojan expedition; or Odysseus or Sisyphus, or numberless others, men and women too! What infinite delight would there be in conversing with them and asking them questions! For in that world they do not put a man to death for this; certainly not. For besides being happier in that world than in this, they will be immortal, if what is said is true.

Wherefore, O judges, be of good cheer about death, and know this of a truth—that no evil can happen to a good man, either in life or after death. He and his are not neglected by the gods; nor has my own approaching end happened by mere chance. But I see clearly that to die and be released was better for me; and therefore the oracle gave no sign. For which reason also, I am not angry with my accusers, or my condemners; they have done me no harm, although neither of them meant to do me any good; and for this I may gently blame them.

Still I have a favor to ask of them. When my sons are grown up, I would ask you, o my friends, to punish them; and I would have you trouble them, as I have troubled you, if they seem to care about riches, or anything, more than about virtue; or if they pretend to be something when they are really nothing—then reprove them, as I have reproved you, for not caring about that for which they ought to care, and thinking that they are something when they are really nothing. And if you do this, I and my sons will have received justice at your hands.

The hour of departure has arrived, and we go our ways—I to die, and you to live. Which is better, God only knows.

QUESTIONS

1.   In Athenian society, the closest thing to a lawyer would be an "orator," like Lycon, who would speak on behalf of others. Socrates says that he is a poor orator "unless by the force of eloquence they mean the force of truth." If so, Socrates would admit to being an orator or advocate, "But in how different a way from theirs!" What would Socrates think of legal education today, including the "Socratic method"?

2.   Socrates, when challenged as to why he did not enter public life as a politician, replied, "Now do you really imagine that I could have survived all these years, if I had led a public life, supposing that like a good man I had always supported the right and had made justice, as I ought, the first thing? No indeed, men of Athens, neither I nor any other." Earlier, Socrates states "[H]e who will really fight for the right, if he would live even for a little while, must have a private station, and not a public one." The Tredennick translation puts it more strongly.

No man on earth who conscientiously opposes either you or any other organized democracy, and flatly prevents a great many wrongs and illegalities from taking place in the state to which he belongs, can possibly escape with his life. The true champion of justice, if he intends to survive even for a short time, must . . . leave politics alone.

THE LAST DAYS OF SOCRATES, *supra*, at 64. What do you think of Socrates' reply? How do you feel about public life and politics?

3.   One of the great lines of classic literature is Socrates' conclusion "No evil can happen to a good man, either in life or after death. He and his are not neglected by the gods." (Tredennick trans. *See Materials*, *supra* at 1F.) Ignoring the gender pronouns, what do you think of this remark? If it is true, why does personal virtue seem to be so casually regarded today? Does it make a difference if you are a politician, a financier, a movie star, or an athlete? Should it matter if you are a lawyer?

NICCOLO MACHIAVELLI, THE PRINCE (1532)
(Luigi Ricci trans., London, 1903)

15

OF THE THINGS FOR WHICH MEN, AND ESPECIALLY PRINCES, ARE PRAISED OR BLAMED

It remains now to be seen what are the methods and rules for a prince as regards his subjects and friends. And as I know that many have written of this, I fear that my writing about it may be deemed presumptuous, differing as I do, especially in this matter, from the opinions of others. But my intention being to write something of use to those who understand it, it appears to me more proper to go to the real truth of the matter than to its imaginations; and many have imagined republics and principalities which have never been seen or known to exist in reality; for how we live is so far removed from how we ought to live, that he who abandons what is done for what ought to be done, will rather learn to bring about his own ruin than his preservation. A man who wishes to make a profession of goodness in everything must necessarily come to grief among so many who are not good. Therefore it is necessary for a prince, who wishes to maintain himself, to learn how not to be good, and to use it and not use it, according to the necessity of the case. Leaving on one side, then, those things which concern only an imaginary prince, and speaking of those that are real, I state that all men, when spoken of, and especially princes, who are placed at a greater height, are noted for some of those qualities which bring them either praise or blame. Thus one is considered liberal, another miserly; one a free giver, another rapacious; one cruel, another merciful; one a breaker of his word, another faithful; one effeminate and pusillanimous, another fierce and high-spirited; one humane, another proud; one lascivious, another chaste; one frank, another astute; one hard, another easy; one serious, another frivolous; one religious, another an incredulous, and so on. I know that every one will admit that it would be highly praiseworthy in a prince to possess all the above-named qualities that are reputed good, but as they cannot all be possessed or observed, human conditions not permitting of it, it is necessary that he should be prudent enough to avoid the disgrace of those vices which would lose him the state, and guard himself against those which will not lose it him, if possible, but if not able to, he can indulge them with less scruple. And yet he must not mind incurring the scandal of those vices, without which it would be difficult to save the state, for if one considers well, it will be found that some things which seem virtues would, if followed, lead to one's ruin, and some others which appear vices result, if followed, in one's greater security and wellbeing.

*   *   *

17

OF CRUELTY AND CLEMENCY, AND WHETHER IT IS BETTER TO BE LOVED OR FEARED

Proceeding to the other qualities before named, I say that every prince must desire to be considered merciful and not cruel. He must, however, take care not to misuse this mercifulness. Cesare Borgia was considered cruel, but his cruelty had settled the Romagna, united it, and reduced it to peace and confidence. If this is considered a benefit, it will be seen that he was really much more merciful than the Florentine people, who, to avoid the name of cruelty, allowed Pistoia to be destroyed. A prince, therefore, must not mind incurring the charge of cruelty for the purpose of keeping his subjects united and confident; for, with a very few examples, he will be more merciful than those who, from excess of tenderness, allow disorders to arise, from whence spring murders and rapine; for these as a rule injure the whole community, while the executions carried out by the prince injure only one individual. And of all princes, it is impossible for a new prince to escape the name of cruel, new states being always full of dangers. Wherefore Virgil maked Dido excuse the inhumanity of her rule by its being new, where she says:

Res dura, et regni novitas me talia cogunt
Moliri, et lale fines custode tueri.
[Trans. *"My hard lot and the newness of my reign*
Force me to guard my domain carefully"]

Nevertheless, he must be cautious in believing and acting, and must not inspire fear of his own accord, and must proceed in a temperate manner with prudence and humanity, so that too much confidence does not render him incautious, and too much diffidence does not render him intolerant. From this arises the question whether it is better to be loved more than feared, or feared more than loved. The reply is, that one ought to be both feared and loved, but as it is difficult for the two to go together, it is much safer to be feared than loved, if one of the two has to be wanting. For it may be said of men in general that they are ungrateful, voluble, dissemblers, anxious to avoid danger, and covetous of gain; as long as you benefit them, they are entirely yours; they offer you their blood, their goods, their life, and their children, as I have before said, when the necessity is remote; but when it approaches, they revolt. And the prince who has relied solely on their words, without making other preparations, is ruined, for the friendship which is gained by purchase and not through grandeur and nobility of spirit is merited but is not secured, and at a time is not to be had. And men have less scruple in offending one who makes himself loved than one who makes himself feared; for love is held by a chain of obligations which, men being selfish, is broken whenever it serves their purpose; but fear is maintained by a dread of punishment which never fails. Still, a prince should make himself feared in such a way that if he does not gain love, he at any rate avoids hatred; for fear and the absence of hatred may well go together, and will be always attained by one who abstains from interfering with the property of his citizens and subjects or with their women. And when he is obliged to take the life of any one, to him do so when there is a proper justification and manifest reason for it; but above all he must abstain from taking the property of others, for men forget more easily the death of their father than the loss of their patrimony. Then also pretexts for seizing property are never wanting, and one who begins to live by rapine will always find some reason for taking the goods of others, whereas causes for taking life are rarer and more quickly destroyed. But when the prince is with his army and has a large number of soldiers under his control, then it is extremely necessary that he should not mind being thought cruel; for without this reputation he could not keep an army united or disposed to any duty.

Among the noteworthy actions of Hannibal is numbered this, that although he had an enormous army, composed of men of all nations and fighting in foreign countries, there never arose any dissension either among them or against the prince, either in good fortune or in bad. This could not be due to anything but his inhuman cruelty, which together with his infinite other virtues, made him always venerated and terrible in the sight of his soldiers, and without it his other virtues would not have sufficed to produce that effect. Thoughtless writers admire on the one hand his actions, and on the other blame the principal cause of them.

And that it is true that his other virtues would not have sufficed may be seen from the case of Scipio (very rare not only in his own times, but in all times of which memory remains), whose armies rebelled against him in Spain, which arose from nothing but his excessive kindness, which allowed more license to the soldiers than was consonant with military discipline. He was reproached with this in the senate by Fabius Maximus, who called him a corrupter of the Roman militia.

The Locri having been destroyed by one of Scipio's officers were not revenged by him, nor was the insolence of that officer punished, simply by reason of his easy nature; so much so, that some one wishing to excuse him in the senate, said that there were many men who knew rather how not to err, than how to correct the errors of others. This disposition would in time have tarnished the fame and glory of Scipio had he persevered in it under the empire, but living under the rule of the senate this harmful quality was not only concealed but became a glory to him.

I conclude, therefore, with regard to being feared and loved, that men love at their own free will, but fear at the will of the prince, and that a wise prince must rely on what is in his power and not on what is in the power of others, and he must only trouble himself to avoid incurring hatred, as has been explained.

18

IN WHAT WAY PRINCES MUST KEEP FAITH

How laudable it is for a prince to keep good faith and live with integrity, and not with astuteness, every one knows. Still the experience of our times shows those princes to have done great things who have had little regard for good faith, and have been able by astuteness to confuse men's brains, and who have ultimately overcome those who have made loyalty their foundation. You must know, then, that there are two methods of fighting, the one by law, the other by force: the first method is that of men, the second of beasts; but as the first method is often insufficient, one must have recourse to the second. It is therefore necessary to know well how to use both the beast and the man. This was covertly taught to princes by ancient writers, who relate how Achilles and many others of those princes were given to Chiron the centaur to be brought up, who kept them under his discipline; this system of having for teacher who was half beast and half man is meant to indicate that a prince must know how to use both natures, and that the one without the other is not durable. A prince being thus obliged to know well how to act as a beast must imitate the fox and the lion, for the lion cannot protect himself from snares, and the fox cannot defend himself from wolves. One must therefore be a fox to recognize snares, and a lion to frighten wolves. Those that wish to be only lions do not understand this. Therefore, a prudent ruler ought not to keep faith when by so doing it would be against his interest, and when the reasons which made him bind himself no longer exist. If men were all good, this precept would not be a good one; but as they are bad, and would not observe their faith with you, so you are not bound to keep faith with them. Nor are legitimate grounds ever wanting to a prince to give colour to the non-fulfillment of his promise. Of this one could furnish an infinite number of modern examples, and show how many times peace has been broken, and how many promises rendered worthless, by the faithlessness of princes, and those that have been best able to imitate the fox have succeeded best. But it is necessary to be able to disguise this character well, and to be a great feigner and dissembler; and men are so simple and so ready to obey present necessities, that one who deceives will always find those who allow themselves to be deceived. I will only mention one modern instance. Alexander VI did nothing else but deceive men, he thought of nothing else, and found the way to do it; no man was ever more able to give assurances, or affirmed things with stronger oaths, and no man observed them less; however, he always succeeded in his deceptions, as he knew well this side of the world. It is not, therefore, necessary for a prince to have all the above-named qualities, but it is very necessary to seem to have them. I would even be bold to say that to possess them and to always observe them is dangerous, but to appear to possess them is useful. Thus it is well to seem pious, faithful, humane, religious, sincere and also to be so; but you must have the mind so watchful that when it is needful to be otherwise you may be able to change to the opposite qualities. And it must be understood that a prince, and especially a new prince, cannot observe all those things which are considered good in men, being often obliged, in order to maintain the state, to act against faith, against charity, against humanity, and against religion. And, therefore, he must have a mind disposed to adapt itself according to the wind, and as the variations of fortune dictate, and, as I said before, not deviate from what is good, if possible, but be able to do evil if necessitated. A prince must take great care that nothing goes out of his mouth which is not full of the above-named five qualities, and, to see and hear him, he should seem to be all faith, all integrity, all humanity, and all religion. And nothing is more necessary than to seem to have this last quality, for men in general judge more by the eyes than by the hands, for every one can see, but very few have to feel. Everybody sees what you appear to be, few feel what you are, and those few will not dare to oppose themselves to the many, who have the majesty of the state to defend them; and in the actions of men, and especially of princes, from which there is no appeal, the end is everything.

Let a prince therefore aim at living [conquering] and maintaining the state, and the means will always be judged honorable and praised by every one, for the vulgar is always taken by appearances and the result of things; and the world consists only of the vulgar, and the few find a place when the many have nothing to rest upon [i.e., the few who are not vulgar are isolated]. A certain prince of the present time, whom it is well not to name, never does anything but preach peace and good faith, but he is really a great enemy to both, and either of them, had he observed them, would have lost him both state and reputation on many occasions.

QUESTIONS

1.   Much is said in law schools about "legal ethics." Has anyone ever said to you that the "real truth of the matter" is that a person "who wishes to make a profession of goodness must necessarily come to grief among so many who are not good"? MACHIAVELLI, THE PRINCE, *Materials*, *supra* at 1F. Would Machiavelli make a good law professor? Commencement speaker? What do students actually think about the "real truth" in practice? What would Socrates say? Is Machiavelli right that some vices "result in one's greater security and wellbeing"?

2.   Machiavelli states "There are two methods of fighting the one by the law, the other by force; the first method is that of men, the other of beasts; but as the first method is often insufficient, one must have recourse to the second." Does this mean that one must behave in an "illegal" way to succeed? If not, what does Machiavelli mean?

3.   According to Machiavelli, "[the Prince] must have a mind disposed to adapt itself according to the wind, and as the variations of fortune dictate, and, as I said before, not deviate from what is good, if possible, but be able to do evil if necessitated." What would Socrates say about this? If one adopts Machiavelli's view of life, what kind of legal philosophy would be required? Is Machiavelli's view "realistic"?

4.   Assume Machiavelli is a partner at your law firm. What is his "solution" to Problem II? What is your response? Does Machiavelli acknowledge a difference between being "good" and "bad"? If so, what does it mean in "practice"?

5.   Alasdair MacIntyre, a great ethicist, observed that "Machiavelli was not a bad man." A SHORT HISTORY OF ETHICS, *supra*, at 127. What could that possibly mean?

RALPH ELLISON, INVISIBLE MAN
(1952)

EPILOGUE

So there you have all of it that's important. Or at least you *almost* have it. I'm an invisible man and it placed me in a hole—or showed me the hole I was in, if you will—and I reluctantly accepted the fact. What else could I have done? Once you get used to it, reality is as irresistible as a club, and I was clubbed into the cellar before I caught the hint. Perhaps that's the way it had to be; I don't know. Nor do I know whether accepting the lesson has placed me in the rear or in the *avant-garde*. *That*, perhaps, is a lesson for history, and I'll leave such decisions to Jack and his ilk while I try belatedly to study the lesson of my own life.

Let me be honest with you—a feat which, by the way, I find of the utmost difficulty. When one is invisible he finds such problems as good and evil, honesty and dishonesty, of such shifting shapes that he confuses one with the other, depending upon who happens to be looking through him at the time. Well, now I've been trying to look through myself, and there's a risk in it. I was never more hated than when I tried to be honest. Or when, even as just now I've tried to articulate exactly what I felt to be the truth. No one was satisfied—not even I. On the other hand, I've never been more loved and appreciated than when I tried to "justify" and affirm someone's mistaken beliefs; or when I've tried to give my friends the incorrect, absurd answers they wished to hear. In my presence/ they could talk and agree with themselves, the world was nailed down, and they loved it. They received a feeling of security. But here was the rub: Too often, in order to justify *them*, I had to take myself by the throat and choke myself until my eyes bulged and my tongue hung out and wagged like the door of an empty house in a high wind. Oh, yes, it made them happy and it made me sick. So I became ill of affirmation, of saying "yes" against the nay-saying of my stomach—not to mention my brain.

There is, by the way, an area in which a man's feelings are more rational than his mind, and it is precisely in that area that his will is pulled in several directions at the same time. You might sneer at this, but I know now. I was pulled this way and that for longer than I can remember. And my problem was that I always tried to go in everyone's way but my own. I have also been called one thing and then another while no one really wished to hear what I called myself. So after years of trying to adopt the opinions of others I finally rebelled. I am an *invisible* man. Thus I have come a long way and returned and boomeranged a long way from the point in society toward which I originally aspired.

So I took to the cellar; I hibernated. I got away from it all. But that wasn't enough. I couldn't be still even in hibernation. Because, damn it, there's the mind, the *mind*. It wouldn't let me rest. Gin, jazz and dreams were not enough. Books were not enough. My belated appreciation of the crude joke that had kept me running, was not enough. And my mind revolved again and again back to my grandfather. And, despite the farce that ended my attempt to say "yes" to the Brotherhood, I'm still plagued by his deathbed advice. . . . Perhaps he did his meaning deeper than I thought, perhaps his anger threw me off—I can't decide.

Could he have meant—hell, he *must* have meant the principle, that we were to affirm the principle on which the country was built and not the men, or at least not the men who did the violence. Did he mean say "yes" because he knew that the principle was greater than the men, greater than the numbers and the vicious power and all the methods used to corrupt its name? Did he mean to affirm the principle, which they themselves had dreamed into being out of the chaos and darkness of the feudal past, and which they had violated and compromised to the point of absurdity even in their own corrupt minds? Or did he mean that we had to take the responsibility for all of it, for the men as well as the principle, because we were the heirs who must use the principle because no other fitted our needs?

* * *

"Agree 'em to death and destruction," grandfather had advised. Hell, weren't they their own death and their own destruction except as the principle lived in them and in us? And here's the cream of the joke: Weren't we *part of them* as well apart from them and subject to die when they died? I can't figure it out; it escapes me. But what do *I* really want, I've asked myself. Certainly not the freedom of a Rinehart or the power of a Jack, nor simply the freedom not to run. No, but the next step I couldn't make, so I've remained in the hole.

I'm not blaming anyone for this state of affairs, mind you; nor merely crying *mea culpa.* The fact is that you carry part of your sickness with you, at least I do as an invisible man. I carried my sickness and though for a long time I tried to place it in the outside world, the attempt to write it down shows me that at least half of it lay within me. It came upon me slowly, like that strange disease that affects those black men whom you see turning slowly from black to albino, their pigment disappearing as under the radiation of some cruel, invisible ray. You go along for years knowing something is wrong, then suddenly you discover that you're as transparent as air. At first, you tell yourself that it's all a dirty joke, or that it's due to the "political situation." But deep down you come to suspect that you're yourself to blame, and you stand naked and shivering before the millions of eyes who look through you unseeingly. *That* is the real soulsickness, the spear in the side, the drag by the neck through the mob-angry town, the Grand Inquisition, the embrace of the Maiden, the rip in the belly with the guts spilling out, the trip to the chamber with the deadly gas that ends in the oven so hygienically clean—only it's worse because you continue stupidly to live. But live you must, and you can either make passive love to your sickness or burn it out and go on to the next conflicting phase.

Yes, but what *is* the next phase? How often have I tried to find it! Over and over again I've gone up above to seek it out. For, like almost everyone else in our country, I started out with my share of optimism. I believed in hard work and progress and action, but now, after first being "for" society and then "against" it, I assign myself no rank or any limit, and such an attitude is very much against the trend of the times. But my world has become one of infinite possibilities. What a phrase—still it's a good phrase and a good view of life, and a man shouldn't accept any other, that much I've learned underground. Until some gang succeeds in putting the world in a strait jacket, its definition is possibility. Step outside the narrow borders of what men call reality and you step into chaos—ask Rinehart, he's a master of it—or imagination. That too I've learned in the cellar, and not by deadening my sense of perception; I'm invisible, not blind.

No indeed, the world is just as concrete, ornery, vile and sublimely wonderful as before, only now I better understand my relation to it and it to me. I've come a long way from those days when, full of illusion, I lived a public life and attempted to function under the assumption that the world was solid and all the relationships therein. Now I know men are different and that all life is divided and that only in division is there true health. Hence again I have stayed in my hole, because up above there's an increasing passion to make men conform to a pattern. Just as in my nightmare, Jack and the boys are waiting with their knives, looking for the slightest excuse to . . . well, to "ball the jack," and I do not refer to the old dance step, although what they're doing is making the old eagle rock dangerously.

Whence all this passion toward conformity anyway?—diversity is the word. Let man keep his many parts and you'll have no tyrant states. Why, if they follow this conformity business they'll end up by forcing me, an invisible man, to become white, which is not a color but the lack of one. Must I strive toward colorlessness? But seriously, and without snobbery, think of what the world would lose if that should happen. America is woven of many strands; I would recognize them and let it so remain. It's "winner take nothing" that is the great truth of our country or of any country. Life is to be lived, not controlled; and humanity is won by continuing to play in face of certain defeat. Our fate is to become one, and yet many—This is not prophecy, but description. Thus one of the greatest jokes in the world is the spectacle of the whites busy escaping blackness and becoming blacker every day, and the blacks striving toward whiteness, becoming quite dull and gray. None of us seems to know who he is or where he's going.

Which reminds me of something that occurred the other day in the subway. At first I saw only an old gentleman who for the moment was lost. I knew he was lost, for as I looked down the platform I saw him approach several people and turn away without speaking. He's lost, I thought, and he'll keep coming until he sees me, then he'll ask his direction. Maybe there's an embarrassment in it if he admits he's lost to a strange white man. Perhaps to lose a sense of *where* you are implies the danger of losing a sense of *who* you are. That must be it, I thought—to lose your direction is to lose your face. So here he comes to ask his direction from the lost, the invisible. Very well, I've learned to live without direction. Let him ask.

QUESTIONS

1. What does Ellison's narrator mean by being "invisible"?

2. What would Socrates think of Ellison's narrator?

3. Ellison's narrator remarks that "I was never more hated than when I tried to be honest." *Materials*, *supra* at 1F. What would Socrates say? Machiavelli? What kind of a moral solution is "invisibility"?

4. Before his death in 1994, Ralph Ellison said of the narrator, "The protagonist's story is his social bequest. And I'll tell you something else: The bequest is

hopeful." N.Y. Times Mag., Jan. 1, 1995, at 23. What is "hopeful" about the "invisible man"?

Chapter II

MORAL RESPONSIBILITY

A. MORAL RESPONSIBILITY: ARISTOTLE'S CHALLENGE

The last section focused on the question of how you define a "good" person. If you decide, like the Pre-Socratics, that being "good" is a purely subjective, personal matter, then this section will not concern you. The next section that will interest you is Chapter III: *The Legal Mentality*. You would not be alone. Many distinguished jurists, including Oliver Wendell Holmes, Jr., have argued for the utility of viewing the positive law from a "bad" person's point of view.[1] According to Holmes,

> If you want to know the law and nothing else, you must look at it as a bad man, who cares only for the material consequences which such knowledge enables him to predict, not as a good one, who finds his reason for conduct, whether inside the law or outside of it, in the vaguer sanctions of conscience.[2]

Let us assume, however, that you are like Plato and Socrates. Let us assume that you believe there is a universally recognizable and verifiable difference between a "good" person and "bad" person. In short, let us assume you believe that the difference between good and evil is *real*. This leads to a second and equally difficult question. If I recognize the difference between good and evil, and I am trying myself to be a "good" person, how much responsibility do I have for the evil that is around me?

This was one of the fundamental questions addressed by another preeminent Greek philosopher, Aristotle. Aristotle lived from 384-322 B.C. From the time he was 18, he was a student of Plato in Athens and remained in Plato's school there for nearly 20 years. (Plato died in 347 B.C.) After Plato's death, Aristotle developed his own approach to major philosophical problems and addressed almost every area of human knowledge of his day in dozens of works. These included the *Organon* (logical treatises); works on natural sciences, such as *De Coelo* and *Physics*; biological works, such as *De Partibus Animalium* and *De Motu*; works on psychology (e.g., *De Anima*); works on metaphysics; and works on the arts (the *Rhetoric* and the *Poetics*).[3] Far more than Plato, Aristotle favored direct observation of nature and the life of empirical experience, as opposed to purely abstract thought. As such, he would have a profound effect on modern philosophers from

---

[1] O. W. Holmes, Jr., *The Path of the Law, in* COLLECTED LEGAL PAPERS 167–171 (1920).

[2] *Id.* at 171.

[3] *See* THE DICTIONARY OF PHILOSOPHY 20–21 (D.D. Runes ed., 4th ed. 1942).

Thomas Aquinas to Francis Bacon.[4] Aristotle actually invented the notion of "common sense" as a supplement to the five physical senses. He saw it as a kind of rational capacity to unite physical data into a unified, basic idea of what an object really "is."[5]

For our purposes, however, Aristotle's great work was on ethics, the *Nicomachean Ethics*. This book was said to have been written for Aristotle's son, Nicomachus. While it is impossible to summarize here all of Aristotle's theory of ethics, his most important ideas were predicated on the idea that human beings are fundamentally different from all other animals. This difference takes two forms. Humans are different because:

1. they can subordinate sensuality and appetite to rational rule and principle; and

2. they can use reason to seek for and contemplate truth.

In this section are included Aristotle's chapters on our responsibility for our conduct and the conduct we see around us. It was Aristotle's view that the special qualities of human nature that make humans "a breed apart" also demand a very high sense of responsibility. If what makes humans "special" is our capacity to subordinate our sensual and material desires to principle, and to seek and appreciate truth, then we must always pursue these ends, or be less than fully "human."

Aristotle, as you will see, is very strict about "excuses." Let us take the most common "excuses" for tolerating or permitting bad conduct. The first is coercion. "I *had* to do it." The second is ignorance. "How was I to know?" or "I wasn't sure what was going on!" The third is that it was outside our control or area of authority. "It wasn't my job!" or "It wasn't my business to ask" or "I was told to mind my own affairs."

Basically, Aristotle holds all human beings responsible for any evil they have, in fact, the power to prevent. If you see a bus full of school children hurtling along a road and you know the bridge is out, it is not an excuse for failing to warn that you are under no legal duty to the children, or that you are not a police officer, or that you are only visiting from another town. The only excuse would be that the bus was going so fast that no one could see or hear you, and you had nothing else you could do. Let us assume, for example, that you learn from a client that a poisonous batch of food has been released negligently by the client, and that you have a professional duty to keep that confidence. This does not relieve you of Aristotelian moral responsibility if you could act in time to warn the potential consumers of the poison.

Aristotle also takes a very tough view on "coercion." For him, coercion excuses an act only if the actor physically cannot resist, for example, my finger is squeezed by force of another on a trigger that then shoots a gun. "Losing a job," or "facing bar discipline," or "potential legal liability" are not irresistible physical forces. Social or professional pressures influence all of life's choices; if the presence of such factors constituted legal coercion, none of life's actions would be truly voluntary.

[4] *Id.* at 16–17. *See* DANIEL R. COQUILLETTE, FRANCIS BACON 93–97 (1992).

[5] DICTIONARY OF PHILOSOPHY, *supra* note 3, at 22.

Aristotle would agree that most "coercion" is no excuse. Human dignity requires recognition of human free will. What make humans remarkable is how they can resist "coercion," including the coercion of sensuality and greed. It follows that humans can, and should, resist all coercion to do evil if they still have a choice. Only when there is physically no choice, as when you actually lose control of your muscles and the power to control your actions, are you exonerated from an evil act.

We can discuss endlessly the "gray" areas of Aristotelian "coercion." What if I have to kill another—even an innocent person—to save my own life? What if I could save the lives of hundreds if I killed only one? But the bottom line is that most "coercion" familiar to law students and lawyers—e.g., the need for grades, jobs, income, professional security, etc.—is not recognized by Aristotle as "coercion" which excuses bad conduct.

The same is true of "ignorance." Aristotle makes it very clear that only genuine, excusable ignorance counts. Suppose you shoot an arrow at what you think is a target, but behind the target is your mother, and she is killed. That is ignorance excusing the act of matricide, assuming you were not negligent in failing to examine the target. On the other hand, drunkenness is not usually an excuse for irresponsible behavior because you know, or ought to know, what the consequences could be. Deliberately turning "a blind eye" to evil acts, or maintaining what in political circles is called "deniability," is not excusable ignorance for Aristotle. As a good person, you have an obligation to stay informed and educated about any situation where your acts, or lack of action, could promote or prevent evil.

Some commentators, such as Bertrand Russell, have made fun of Aristotle.

> There is something unduly smug and comfortable about Aristotle's speculations on human affairs. . . . What he has to say is what will be useful to comfortable men of weak passions; but he has nothing to say to those who are possessed by a god or a devil. . . ."[6]

Indeed, Aristotle's views have been criticized as elitist and exclusionary (e.g., he did not think that slaves or women, as nonmembers of the *polis*, could even aspire to lead flourishing lives). From the comfort of wealth and political power, isn't it rather easy to preach the virtue of resisting societal pressure? On the other hand, there is nothing particularly *comfortable* about Aristotle's views on moral responsibility because they excuse very little. If we weaken these standards, what does it say about human nature and dignity, including our own and that of others perhaps less fortunate?

B. MORAL RESPONSIBILITY AND THE LAW: NUREMBERG AND CATHERINE GENOVESE

Following the excerpts from Aristotle are accounts of three modern events, one of historic proportions and the other two more individual tragedies. Each story presents forcefully the question of a person's "excuses" for not preventing evil conduct, and how this relates to "legal" responsibility.

---

[6] BERTRAND RUSSELL, A HISTORY OF WESTERN PHILOSOPHY 184 (2007) (1st published 1945).

Everyone is familiar with the Nuremberg trials that followed the conclusion of World War II. The chief prosecutor for the United States (following Robert Jackson) was Brigadier General Telford Taylor. An excerpt of Taylor's account of the Nuremberg trials has been included in this book. The primary defenses of the accused were *not* to deny that evil conduct had occurred or to argue that "all was fair in war." Horrendous crimes against Germany's own citizens and other civilians had been discovered, including the Holocaust of Jews. The primary defenses were, instead, our old Aristotelian friends, ignorance and coercion. The defense counsel also argued that, even if the accused were morally wrong in failing to act or in "following orders," there was no legal basis for punishment. Their acts were permitted, even required, by the legal system in force at the time. Was Nuremberg simply an application of "winner's law," rather than an objective, principled, *legal trial*?

Telford Taylor, as you will see, remained deeply concerned about these arguments, and about how the principles of Nuremberg were applied to American soldiers in later wars, such as Vietnam. Is it really fair to expect punishment of enlisted men for "reacting" to a "dehumanized" environment when they were drafted and "forced" to fight? What about the responsibility of their superiors? Finally, why have people placed such an emphasis on establishing a "legal" basis for punishment and responsibility?

The story of Catherine (Kitty) Genovese is set out next, in excerpts from the *New York Times*. This is a single, tragic slaying, in a city where many occur. A man was quickly arrested and punished for Kitty's death. True, Kitty Genovese's death could have been prevented by any of 38 neighbors who saw her being stalked by the killer. But the law of New York specifically provides no such duty to act, even where there is no personal risk. What is the problem here? Is it a "legal" problem, or a problem of educating and socializing our citizens?

The third set of stories in the materials involves prosecutors in high profile murder cases who doubted the guilt of the defendants they were assigned to prosecute. Each prosecutor assumed that it was his or her moral responsibility to try to overturn an unjust conviction, or at least *not* to fight to uphold it. Yet each took a radically different approach to his or her role. The questions that follow this particular set of materials urge you to think about the role of conscience for a government attorney.

One can never tell when the more dramatic and universal situations represented by Catherine Genovese's death, or by an international human rights violation, may touch our lives. The defenses of "superior orders" and "exigent circumstances" were recently heard during the Iraq War, and will doubtlessly be heard again. But clashes between professional expectations and moral responsibility occur for attorneys on a daily basis in a variety of contexts. The problems that follow are designed to urge you to think about a lawyer's individual moral responsibility for the goals and objectives of his or her clients.

C. FURTHER READING

For a particularly good, concise treatment of Aristotle's Ethics, see ALASDAIR MACINTYRE, A SHORT HISTORY OF ETHICS 57–83 (1998). *See also* F. M. CORNFORD, BEFORE AND AFTER SOCRATES 84–109 (1964); JOHN HERMAN RANDALL, JR., ARISTOTLE (1960); and BERTRAND RUSSELL, A HISTORY OF WESTERN PHILOSOPHY 172–184 (2007) (1st ed. 1945).

For a good paperback edition of the original text, with a very helpful introduction, see ARISTOTLE, NICOMACHEAN ETHICS (J. A. K. Thomson trans. with intro., rev. ed. H. Tredennick, Penguin 2004). Those wishing to go on in studying Aristotle's writing might consider as well the "Penguin" edition of THE POLITICS (T. A. Sinclair trans. with intro., Harmondsworth 1992). For a particularly fine selected anthology, with an excellent general introduction, see RICHARD MCKEON, INTRODUCTION TO ARISTOTLE (2d ed. 1973).

For those wishing more background in the setting of classical Greek thought, see ALFRED ZIMMERN, THE GREEK COMMONWEALTH (1956). For an approach to Aristotle from a "legal" or "jurisprudential" point of view, see HUNTINGTON CAIRNS, LEGAL PHILOSOPHY FROM PLATO TO HEGEL 77–126 (1949). For a leading scholarly treatment of Aristotle's methodology, see J. DONALD MONAN, S. J., MORAL KNOWLEDGE AND ITS METHODOLOGY IN ARISTOTLE (1968).

It is hard to find a better introduction to the Nuremberg trials than Telford Taylor's own NUREMBERG AND VIETNAM: AN AMERICAN TRAGEDY (1970). For a full "recap" of the Genovese murder, 20 years later, see Maureen Dowd, *Twenty Years After Kitty Genovese's Murder, Experts Study Bad Samaritanism*, N.Y. TIMES, Mar. 12, 1984, at B1, B4. *See also* Diane Kiesel, *Who Saw This Happen?*, 69 A.B.A. J. 1208–1209 (1983).

D. DISCUSSION PROBLEMS

PROBLEM III

Llewellyn: [to the students of Columbia Law School] "The pressure to let the burden slide will fall so soon on you. As things stand it is a pressure well-nigh irresistible. There will be *very few whose eyes* it does not close." *See Materials, supra* at 1F.

Aristotle:

> The man, then, must be a perfect fool who is unaware that people's characters take their bias from the steady direction of their activities. If a man, well aware of what he is doing, behaves in such a way that he is bound to become unjust, we can only say that he is voluntarily unjust.

ARISTOTLE, ETHICS, *infra* Book III, Chapter 5, page 91 (A. K. Thomson trans.). *See Materials, infra* at 2E for W. D. Ross's translation.

You are a young lawyer with three children. You are your family's sole source of financial support. Times are tight. You accept the only "law" job you can get, "office counsel," for a small loan collection agency. You discover that you are expected to draft "fool-proof" small loan "agreements" that go to the absolute limits of the state "small loan" laws. You are also to be zealous in filing suits and attachments against those in default, who are usually struggling, poor, and from disadvantaged racial or ethnic backgrounds. To aid the company's lobbying efforts, you also draft legislation to minimize state control of small loan interest rates and to permit garnishment of wages. As soon as you can get another job, you'll be leaving, but there's nothing on the horizon.

One night you stop at a bar on the way home. You discover that you're sitting between Karl Llewellyn and Aristotle. Do you have any questions for them? Telford Taylor and William Calley[7] walk in to have a drink following a joint speaking engagement. For some reason, the conversation shifts to the problem of an individual's responsibility to do good when the surrounding "system" is evil. What position do you take? The others?

PROBLEM IV

One of your most important clients is a contractor. You are often asked to review this client's legal problems and to be sure that various city requirements for work to be performed, including safety certificates, zoning variances, etc., are in order. It is not actually your responsibility to get these certificates or to deal with city building inspectors. That is done by your client's employees. You simply "check off" these requirements to be sure that all necessary permissions have been obtained. As you have increasing contact with this client, you become aware that even "difficult" certificates and variances are obtained with considerable ease, particularly compared with your other clients. You become suspicious of bribery. Should you raise this matter with your client? What problems, including problems with the ABA Model Rules, could result if you did?

Later, one of your client's buildings collapses, killing several people. Apparently the structural steel, although fully inspected, was clearly in violation of the Building Code. Two building inspectors and your client are indicted but, of course, not you. Have you any "responsibility" for what happened? What would be the view of your fellow lawyers on this question? The bereaved family of one of the deceased? A "disinterested" member of the general public? Incidentally, will you represent your client against the criminal prosecution?

PROBLEM V

As Telford Taylor notes in *Materials infra* at 2E, soldiers often attempt to avoid responsibility for alleged offenses committed during warfare by claiming that either (1) a military officer in superior position of authority ratified or ordered their conduct, or (2) although what they did may have been illegal, it was not in a moral sense "wrong" due to the exigencies of war. The latter argument is not a true defense at all—it is an attempt at jury nullification. The former argument is strictly bounded by the laws of war: to succeed, the soldier would have to prove that he or she actually received an explicit order from a superior officer to engage in the

---

[7] The lieutenant in command at My Lai, Vietnam. My Lai is a hamlet of Son My district. *See Materials, infra* at 2E.

charged conduct, *and* that they acted reasonably in following what they thought was a lawful order.[8] Following clearly *unlawful* orders is not a defense, even during time of war.

During the Iraq War, the "following orders" defense was once again raised in the Abu Ghraib prison scandal. Iraqi prisoners at Abu Ghraib were allegedly subjected to indignities, torture, and abuse at the hands of U.S. soldiers. The allegations included intimidating prisoners with snarling dogs, stripping them naked and photographing them in humiliating poses, and requiring them to masturbate in front of others. Images of such treatment were captured on film and broadcast across the Internet.

Twelve United States soldiers ultimately were court-martialed with respect to conditions at the prison. But only one officer working inside the prison was charged. Lieutenant Colonel Stephen Jordan, who ran the interrogation center at Abu Ghraib prison, was court-martialed for alleged dereliction of duty and lying to investigators, even though he was not alleged to have tortured or humiliated prisoners himself. He was subsequently acquitted of all charges except the charge of disobeying the orders of a superior officer.

While an independent commission established by the Department of Defense suggested that other military intelligence officers had encouraged or condoned certain interrogation techniques, no senior officials who worked outside the Abu Ghraib prison were ever criminally charged by court-martial.[9]

What might Aristotle say about whether the prison guards at Abu Ghraib acted "voluntarily"? *See Materials infra* at 2E. Were their actions products of "vices of the soul" over with they had control? Or were their acts purely the product of the environment and culture in which these soldiers found themselves? What should Private Lynddie England have done when fellow military police suggested she parade a prisoner around the prison the complex naked on a dog leash? To whom should she have complained?

Where senior officials create a culture of condoning or tacitly encouraging criminal misconduct—but never directly "order" it—who should bear ultimate moral responsibility for the abuse? The Abu Ghraib scandal, like Nuremberg and My Lai, teaches us that the soldiers themselves are certainly legally accountable for their own conduct in most contexts because the following orders defense is so strictly construed. But is it morally just for a society to prosecute subordinate soldiers where superior officers are beyond the reach of the law?

---

[8] *See* Calley v. Callaway, 519 F.2d 184, 193 (5th Cir. 1975).

[9] INDEPENDENT PANEL TO REVIEW DEPARTMENT OF DEFENSE DETENTION OPERATIONS (2004), *available at* http:// ww.defenselink.mil/news/Aug2004/d20040824finalreport.pdf.

Lt. William Calley during his court-martial at Fort Benning, Georgia, April 1971. Courtesy, Associated Press and *New York Times*. Photographer Joe Holloway, Jr. On August 24, 2009, Mr. Calley, now 66, was quoted as having said in a speech to the Kiwanis Club of Cleveland, "There is not a day that goes by that I do not feel remorse for what happened that day in My Lai. I feel remorse for the Vietnamese who were killed, for their families, for the American soldiers involved, and their families. I am very sorry." *See* Robert Mackey, *William Calley: An Apology for My Lai Four Decades Later*, THE LEDE BLOG, *available at* nytimes.com, August 24, 2009.

Consider:

ABA Model Rules of Professional Conduct:

Rules 1.2(b), 1.2(d), 1.4, 1.6(a), 1.6(b), 1.8(b), 2.1, 3.1, 3.3(a), 3.8(a), 4.1(b), 5.1(a), 5.1(c), 5.2, 8.4(a), and 8.4(c).

E. MATERIALS

ARISTOTLE, THE NICOMACHEAN ETHICS (*circa* 330 B.C.)
THE WORKS OF ARISTOTLE
(W. D. Ross, Trans., 1915)

Note: For a later, paperback translation, see THE ETHICS OF ARISTOTLE *(J. A. K. Thomson trans., Harmondsworth 1953, rev. ed. by H. Tredennick, 2004), a "Penguin" paperback.*

BOOK III

Since virtue is concerned with passions and actions, and on voluntary passions and actions praise and blame are bestowed, on those that are involuntary pardon, and sometimes also pity, to distinguish the voluntary and the involuntary is presumably necessary for those who are studying the nature of virtue, and useful also for legislators with a view to the assigning both of honours and of punishments.

Those things, then, are thought involuntary, which take place under compulsion or owing to ignorance; and that is compulsory of which the moving principle is outside, being a principle in which nothing is contributed by the person who is acting or is feeling the passion, e.g., if he were to be carried somewhere by a wind, or by men who had him in their power.

But with regard to the things that are done from fear of greater evils or for some noble object (e.g., if a tyrant were to order one to do something base, having one's parents and children in his power, and if one did the action they were to be saved, but otherwise would be put to death), it may be debated whether such actions are involuntary or voluntary. Something of the sort happens also with regard to the throwing of goods overboard in a storm; for in the abstract no one throws goods away voluntarily, but on condition of its securing the safety of himself and his crew any sensible man does so. Such actions, then, are mixed, but are more like voluntary actions; for they are worthy of choice at the time when they are done, and the end or an action is relative to the occasion. Both the terms, then, 'voluntary' and 'involuntary,' must be used with reference to the moment of action. Now the man acts voluntarily; for the principle that moves the instrumental parts of the body in such actions is in him, and the things of which the moving principle is in a man himself are in his power to do or not to do. Such actions, therefore, are voluntary, but in the abstract perhaps involuntary; for no one would choose any such act in itself.

For such actions men are sometimes even praised, when they endure something base or painful in return for great and noble objects gained; in the opposite case they are blamed, since to endure the greatest indignities for no noble end or for a trifling end is the mark of an inferior person. On some actions praise indeed is not bestowed, but pardon is, when one does what he ought not under pressure which overstrains human nature and which no one could withstand. But some acts, perhaps, we cannot be forced to do, but ought rather to face death after the most fearful sufferings; for the things that 'forced' Euripides's Alcmaeon to slay his mother seem absurd. It is difficult sometimes to determine what should be chosen at what cost, and what should be endured in return for what gain, and yet more difficult to abide by our decisions; for as a rule what is expected is painful, and what we are forced to do is base, whence praise and blame are bestowed on those who have been compelled or have not.

What sort of acts, then, should be called compulsory? We answer that without qualification actions are so when the cause is in the external circumstances and the agent contributes nothing. But the things that in themselves are involuntary, but now and in return for these gains are worthy of choice, and whose moving principle is in the agent, are in themselves involuntary, but now and in return for these gains voluntary. They are more like voluntary acts; for actions are in the class of particulars, and the particular acts here are voluntary. What sort of things are to be chosen, and in return for what, it is not easy to state; for there are many differences in the particular cases.[10]

But if someone were to say that pleasant and noble objects have a compelling power, forcing us from without, all acts would be for him compulsory; for it is for these objects that all men do everything they do. And those who act under compulsion and unwillingly act with pain, but those who do acts for their pleasantness and nobility do them with pleasure; it is absurd to make external circumstances responsible, and not oneself, as being easily caught by such attractions, and to make oneself responsible for noble acts but the pleasant objects responsible for base acts. The compulsory, then, seems to be that whose moving principle is outside, the person compelled contributing nothing.

Everything that is done by reason of ignorance is *not* voluntary; it is only what produces pain and repentance that is *in* voluntary. For the man who has done something owing to ignorance, and feels not the least vexation at his action, has not acted voluntarily, since he did not know what he was doing, nor yet involuntarily, since he is not pained. Of people, then, who act by reason of ignorance he who repents is thought an involuntary agent, and the man who does not repent *may*, since he is different, be called a not voluntary agent; for, since he differs from the other, it is better that he should have a name of his own.

Acting by reason of ignorance seems also to be different from acting in ignorance; for the man who is drunk or in a rage is thought to act as a result not of ignorance but of one of the causes mentioned, yet not knowingly but in ignorance.

---

[10] Editors' Note: For this paragraph, we prefer J. A. K. Thomson's translation from his ARISTOTLE, ETHICS, *supra* at 79:

> What class of actions, then, ought we to distinguish as "compulsory"? It is arguable that the bare description will apply to any case where the cause of the action is found in things external to the agent when he contributes nothing to the result. But it may happen that actions, though, abstractly considered, involuntary, are deliberately chosen at a given time and in given circumstances in preference to a given alternative. In that case, their origin being in the agent, these actions must be pronounced voluntary in the particular circumstances and because they are preferred to their alternatives. In themselves they are involuntary, yet they have more of the voluntary about them, since conduct is a sequence of particular acts, and the particular things done in the circumstances we have supposed are voluntary. But when it comes to saying which of two alternative lines of action should be preferred—then difficulties arise. For the differences in particular cases are many.

Now every wicked man is ignorant of what he ought to do and what he ought to abstain from, and it is by reason of error of this kind that men become unjust and in general bad; but the term "involuntary" tends to be used not if a man is ignorant of what is to his advantage—for it is not mistaken purpose that causes involuntary action (it leads rather to wickedness), nor ignorance of the universal (for *that men* are *blamed*), but ignorance of particulars, i.e., of the circumstances of the action and the objects with which it is concerned. For it is on these that both pity and pardon depend, since the person who is ignorant of any of these acts involuntarily.

Perhaps it is just as well, therefore, to determine their nature and number. A man may be ignorant, then, of who he is, what he is doing, what or whom he is acting on, and sometimes also what (e.g., what instrument) he is doing it with, and to what end (e.g., he may think his act will conduce to someone's safety), and how he is doing it (e.g., whether gently or violently). Now of all of these no one could be ignorant unless he were mad, and evidently also he could not be ignorant of the agent; for how could he not know himself? But of what he is doing a man might be ignorant, as for instance people say "it slipped out of their mouths as they were speaking," or "they did not know it was a secret," as Aeschylus said of the mysteries, or a man might say he "let it go off when he merely wanted to show its working," as the man did with the catapult. Again, one might think one's son was an enemy, as Merope did, or that a pointed spear had a button on it, or that a stone was pumice-stone; or one might give a man a draught to save him, and really kill him; or one might want to touch a man, as people do in sparring, and really wound him. The ignorance may relate, then, to any of these things, i.e., of the circumstances of the action, and the man who was ignorant of any of these is thought to have acted involuntarily, and especially if he was ignorant on the most important points; and these are thought to be the circumstances of the action and its end. Further, the doing of an act that is called involuntary in virtue of ignorance of this sort must be painful and involve repentance.

Since that which is done under compulsion or by reason of ignorance is involuntary, the voluntary would seem to be that of which the moving principle is in the agent himself, he being aware of the particular circumstances of the action. Presumably acts done by reason of anger or appetite are not rightly called involuntary. For in the first place, on that showing none of the other animals will act voluntarily, nor will children; and secondly, is it meant that we do not do voluntarily *any* of the acts that are due to appetite or anger, or that we do the noble acts voluntarily and the base acts involuntarily? Is not this absurd, when one and the same thing is the cause? But it would surely be odd to describe as involuntary the things one ought to desire; and we ought both to be angry at certain things and to have an appetite for certain things, e.g. for health and for learning. Also what is involuntary is thought to be painful, but what is in accordance with appetite is thought to be pleasant. Again, what is the difference in respect of involuntariness between errors committed upon calculation and those committed in anger? Both are to be avoided, but the irrational passions are thought not less human than reason is, and therefore also the actions which proceed from anger or appetite are the man's actions. It would be odd, then, to treat them as involuntary.

2

Both the voluntary and the involuntary having been delimited, we must next discuss choice; for it is thought to be most closely bound up with virtue and to discriminate characters better than actions do.

Choice, then, seems to be voluntary, but not the same thing as the voluntary; the latter extends more widely. For both children and the lower animals share in voluntary action, but not in choice, and acts done on the spur of the moment we describe as voluntary, but not as chosen.

Those who say it is appetite or anger or wish or a kind of opinion do not seem to be right. For choice is not common to irrational creatures as well, but appetite and anger are. Again, the incontinent man acts with appetite, but not with choice; while the continent man on the contrary acts with choice, but not with appetite. Again, appetite is contrary to choice, but not appetite to appetite. Again, appetite relates to the pleasant and the painful, choice neither to the painful nor to the pleasant.

Still less is it anger; for acts due to anger are thought to be less than any others objects of choice.

But neither is it wish, though it seems near to it; for choice cannot relate to impossibles, and if anyone said he chose them he would be thought silly; but there may be a wish even for impossibles, e.g., for immortality. And wish may relate to things that could in no way be brought about by one's own efforts, e.g., that a particular actor or athlete should win in a competition; but no one chooses such things, but only the things that he thinks could be brought about by his own efforts. Again, wish relates rather to the end, choice to the means; for instance, we wish to be healthy, but we choose the acts which will make us healthy, and we wish to be happy and say we do, but we cannot well say we choose to be so; for, in general, choice seems to relate to the things that are in our own power.

For this reason, too, it cannot be opinion; for opinion is thought to relate to all kinds of things, no less to eternal things and impossible things than to things in our own power; and it is distinguished by its falsity or truth, not by its badness or goodness, while choice is distinguished rather by these.

Now with opinion in general perhaps no one even says it is identical. But it is not identical even with any kind of opinion; for by choosing what is good or bad we are men of a certain character, which we are not by holding certain opinions. And we choose to get or avoid something good or bad, but we have opinions about what a thing is or whom it is good for or how it is good for him; we can hardly be said to opine to get or avoid anything. And choice is praised for being related to the right object rather than for being rightly related to it, opinion for being truly related to its object. And we choose what we best know to be good, but we opine what we do not quite know; and it is not the same people that are thought to make the best choices and to have the best opinions, but some are thought to have fairly good opinions, but by reason of vice to choose what they should not. If opinion precedes choice or accompanies it, that makes no difference; for it is not this that we are considering, but whether it is *identical* with some kind of opinion.

What, then, or what kind of thing is it, since it is none of the things we have mentioned? It seems to be voluntary, but not all that is voluntary to be an object of choice. Is it, then, what has been decided on by previous deliberation? At any rate choice involves a rational principle and thought. Even the name seems to suggest that it is what is chosen before other things.

3

Do we deliberate about everything, and is everything a possible subject of deliberation, or is deliberation impossible about some things? We ought presumably to call not what a fool or a madman would deliberate about, but what a sensible man would deliberate about, a subject of deliberation. Now about eternal things no one deliberates, e.g., about the material universe or the incommensurability of the diagonal and the side of a square. But no more do we deliberate about the things that involve movement but always happen in the same way, whether of necessity or by nature or from any other cause, e.g., the solstices and the risings of the stars; nor about things that happen now in one way, now in another, e.g., droughts and rains; nor about chance events, like the finding of treasure. But we do not deliberate even about all human affairs; for instance, no Spartan deliberates about the best constitution for the Scythians. For none of these things can be brought about by our own efforts.

We deliberate about things that are in our power and can be done; and these are in fact what is left. For nature, necessity, and chance are thought to be causes, and also reason and everything that depends on man. Now every class of men deliberates about the things that can be done by their own efforts. And in the case of exact and self contained sciences there is no deliberation, e.g., about the letters of the alphabet (for we have no doubt how they should be written); but the things that are brought about by our own efforts, but not always in the same way, are the things about which we deliberate, e.g., questions of medical treatment or of money making. And we do so more in the case of the art of navigation than in that of gymnastics, inasmuch as it has been less exactly worked out, and again about other things in the same ratio, and more also in the case of the arts than in that of the sciences; for we have more doubt about the former. Deliberation is concerned with things that happen in a certain way for the most part, but in which the event is obscure, and with things in which it is indeterminate. We call in others to aid us in deliberation on important questions, distrusting ourselves as not being equal to deciding.

We deliberate not about ends but about means. For a doctor does not deliberate whether he shall heal, nor an orator whether he shall persuade, nor a statesman whether he shall produce law and order, nor does anyone else deliberate about his end. They assume the end and consider how and by what means it is to be attained; and if it seems to be produced by several means they consider by which it is most easily and best produced, while if it is achieved by one only they consider how it will be achieved by this and by what means *this* will be achieved, till they come to the first cause, which in the order of discovery is last. For the person who deliberates seems to investigate and analyze in the way described as though he were analyzing a geometrical construction(^{11} (not all investigation appears to be deliberation—for instance mathematical investigations—but all deliberation is investigation), and what is last in the order of analysis seems to be first in the order of becoming. And if we come on an impossibility, we give up the search, e.g., if we need money and this cannot be got; but if a thing appears possible we try to do it. By 'possible' things I mean things that might be brought about by our own efforts; and these in a sense include things that can be brought about by the efforts of our friends, since the moving principle is in ourselves. The subject of investigation is sometimes the instruments, sometimes the use of them; and similarly in the other cases—sometimes the means, sometimes the mode of using it or the means of bringing it about. It seems, then, as has been said, that man is a moving principle of actions; now deliberation is about the things to be done by the agent himself, and actions are for the sake of things other than themselves. For the end cannot be a subject of deliberation, but only the means; nor indeed can the particular facts be a subject of it, as whether this is bread or has been baked as it should; for these are matters of perception. If we are to be always deliberating, we shall have to go on to infinity.

The same thing is deliberated upon and is chosen, except that the object of choice is already determinate, since it is that which has been decided upon as a result or de-liberation that is the object of choice. For every one ceases to inquire how he is to act when he has brought the moving principle back to himself and to the ruling part of himself; for this is what chooses. This is plain also from the ancient constitutions, which Homer represented; for the kings announced their choices to the people. The object of choice being one of the things in our own power which is desired after deliberation, choice will be deliberate desire of things in our own power; for when we have decided as a result of deliberation, we desire in accordance with our deliberation.

We may take it, then, that we have described choice in outline, and stated the nature of its objects and the fact that it is concerned with means.

4

That *wish* is for the end has already been stated; some think it is for the good, others for the apparent good. Now those who say that the good is the object of wish must admit in consequence that that which the man who does not choose aright wishes for is not an object of wish (for if it is to be so, it must also be good; but it was, if it so happened, bad); while those who say the apparent good is the object of wish must admit that there is no natural object of wish, but only what seems good to each man. Now different things appear good to different people, and, if it so happens, even contrary things.

If these consequences are unpleasing, are we to say that absolutely and in truth the good is the object of wish, but for each person the apparent good; that that

---

[11] Aristotle had in mind a method of discovering the solution of a geometrical problem. The problem being to construct a figure of a certain kind, we suppose it constructed and then analyse it to see if there is some figure by constructing which we can construct the required figure, and so on till we come to a figure which our existing knowledge enables us to construct. [Translator's note]

which is in truth an object of wish is an object of wish to the good man, while any chance thing may be so to the bad man, as in the case of bodies also the things that are in truth wholesome are wholesome for bodies which are in good condition, while for those that are diseased other things are wholesome—or bitter or sweet or hot or heavy, and so on; since the good man judges each class of things rightly, and in each the truth appears to him? For each state of character has its own ideas of the noble and the pleasant, and perhaps the good man differs from others most by seeing the truth in each class of things, being as it were the norm and measure of them. In most things the error seems to be due to pleasure; for it appears a good when it is not. We therefore choose the pleasant as a good, and avoid pain as an evil.

5

The end, then, being what we wish for, the means what we deliberate about and choose, actions concerning means must be according to choice and voluntary. Now the exercise of the virtues is concerned with means. Therefore virtue also is in our own power, and so too vice. For where it is in our power to act it is also in our power not to act, and *vice versa*; so that, if to act, where this is noble, is in our power, not to act, which will be base, will also be in our power, and if not to act, where this is noble, is in our power, to act, which will be base, will also be in our power. Now if it is in our power to do noble or base acts, and likewise in our power not to do them, and this was what being good or bad meant, then it is in our power to be virtuous or vicious.

The saying that "no one is voluntarily wicked nor involuntarily happy" seems to be partly false and partly true; for no one is involuntarily happy, but wickedness is voluntary. Or else we shall have to dispute what has just been said, at any rate, and deny that man is a moving principle or begetter of his actions as of children. But if these facts are evident and we cannot refer actions to moving principles other than those in ourselves, the acts whose moving principles are in us must themselves also be in our power and voluntary.

Witness seems to be borne to this both by individuals in their private capacity and by legislators themselves; for these punish and take vengeance on those who do wicked acts (unless they have acted under compulsion or as a result of ignorance for which they are not themselves responsible), while they honour those who do noble acts, as though they meant to encourage the latter and deter the former. But no one is encouraged to do the things that are neither in our power nor voluntary; it is assumed that there is no gain in being persuaded not to be hot or in pain or hungry or the like, since we shall experience these feelings nonetheless. Indeed, we punish a man for his very ignorance, if he is thought responsible for the ignorance, as when penalties are doubled in the case of drunkenness; for the moving principle is in the man himself, since he had the power of not getting drunk and his getting drunk was the cause of his ignorance. And we punish those who are ignorant of anything in the laws that they ought to know and that is not difficult, and so too in the case of anything else that they are thought to be ignorant of through carelessness; we assume that it is in their power not to be ignorant, since they have the power of taking care.

But perhaps a man is the kind of man not to take care. Still they are themselves by their slack lives responsible for becoming men of that kind, and men make themselves responsible for being unjust or self-indulgent, in the one case by cheating and in the other by spending their time in drinking bouts and the like; for it is activities exercised on particular objects that make the corresponding character. This is plain from the case of people training for any contest or action; they practice the activity the whole time. Now not to know that it is from the exercise of activities on particular objects that states of character are produced is the mark of a thoroughly senseless person. Again, it is irrational to suppose that a man who acts unjustly does not wish to be unjust or a man who acts self-indulgently to be self-indulgent. But if *without* being ignorant a man does the things which will make him unjust, he will be unjust voluntarily. Yet it does not follow that if he wishes he will cease to be unjust and will be just. For neither does the man who is ill become well on those terms. We may suppose a case in which he is ill voluntarily, through living incontinently and disobeying his doctors. In that case it was *then* open to him not to be ill, but not now, when he has thrown away his chance, just as when you have let a stone go it is too late to recover it; but yet it was in your power to throw it, since the moving principle was in you. So, too, to the unjust and to the self-indulgent man it was open at the beginning not to become men of this kind, and so they are unjust and self-indulgent voluntarily; but now that they have become so it is not possible for them not to be so.

But not only are the vices of the soul voluntary, but those of the body also for some men, whom we accordingly blame; while no one blames those who are ugly by nature, we blame those who are so owing to want of exercise and care. So it is, too, with respect to weakness and infirmity; no one would reproach a man blind from birth or by disease or from a blow, but rather pity him, while everyone would blame a man who was blind from drunkenness or some other form of self-indulgence. Of vices of the body, then, those in our own power are blamed, those not in our power are not. And if this be so, in the other cases also the vices that are blamed must be in our own power.

Now someone may say that all men desire the apparent good, but have no control over the appearance, but the end appears to each man in a form answering to his character. We reply that if each man is somehow responsible for his state of mind, he will also be himself somehow responsible for the appearance; but if not, no one is responsible for his own evildoing, but everyone does evil acts through ignorance of the end, thinking that by these he will get what is best and the aiming at the end is not self-chosen but one must be born with an eye, as it were, by which to judge rightly and choose what is truly good, and he is well endowed by nature who is well endowed with this. For it is what is greatest and most noble, and what we cannot get or learn from another, but must have just such as it was when given us at birth, and to be well and nobly endowed with this will be perfect and true excellence of natural endowment. If this is true, then, how will virtue be more voluntary than vice? To both men alike, the good and the bad, the end appears and is fixed by nature or however it may be, and it is by referring everything else to this that men do whatever they do.

Whether, then, it is not by nature that the end appears to each man such as it does appear, but something also depends on him, or the end is natural but because the good man adopts the means voluntarily virtue is voluntary, vice also will be none the less voluntary; for in the case of the bad man there is equally present that which depends on himself in his actions even if not in his end. If, then, as is asserted, the virtues are voluntary (for we are ourselves somehow partly responsible for our states of character, and it is by being persons of a certain kind that we assume the end to be so and so), the vices also will be voluntary; for the same is true of them.

With regard to the virtues in *general* we have stated their genus in outline, viz. that they are means and that they are states of character, and that they tend, and by their own nature, to the doing of the acts by which they are produced, and that they are in our power and voluntary, and act as the right rule prescribes. But actions and states of character are not voluntary in the same way; for we are masters of our actions from the beginning right to the end, if we know the particular facts, but though we control the beginning of our states of character the gradual progress is not obvious, any more than it is in illnesses; because it was in our power, however, to act in this way or not in this way, therefore the states are voluntary.

QUESTIONS

1.   Aristotle has been described as a "bourgeois" philosopher because of his emphasis on the "staid" and "middle class" values of responsibility and deliberate, restrained choice. But, as he asks, are not these values essential if we have a view of human nature that emphasizes dignity and self-determination? What are the alternatives to regarding human beings as responsible for their acts, outside of Aristotle's very narrow definition of excusable ignorance and coercion? In Bernstein's musical "West Side Story," the gang leader announces that he is either "deprived because he's depraved" or "depraved because he's deprived." What would Aristotle think of this?

2.   Aristotle is particularly strict about "excuses." Putting yourself in a state of careless, inexcusable ignorance, or "under the influence" of alcohol and drugs—or even fatigue—makes you responsible for what follows, even though in a less impaired state, you would be horrified by your own conduct. Does our law really work this way? Should it?

3.   Would Aristotle regard a legal mandate as the kind of "coercion" which would excuse an otherwise immoral act? How about disbarment by the Board of Bar Overseers for violation of a disciplinary rule? How about the threat of losing your job?

TELFORD TAYLOR, NUREMBERG AND VIETNAM: AN AMERICAN TRAGEDY
(1970)

4. Nuremberg

*   *   *

To summarize, the Nuremberg, Tokyo, and other post-World War II war crimes trials brought to the development of the international penal law of war an international jurisdiction, a strong affirmation of the individual's obligation to comply with internationally recognized standards of conduct, a first enforcement within narrow limits of the concept of "crimes against peace," and a considerable expansion of the area of criminal liability for violations of the laws of war.

Outside the legal dimension, however, the Nuremberg trials had perhaps an even more significant impact on the governments and peoples of the world, in spreading a sense of the moral and political importance of the issues with which the trials were concerned. Before Nuremberg, the laws of war were embodied in professional military tradition, field manuals, international law treatises, and occasionally, in little-noticed court-martial proceedings. Nuremberg made them the preoccupation of great statesmen and generals, and the stuff of newspaper headlines.

The setting at Nuremberg was prestigious and highly dramatic. The defendants were colorful and infamous or notorious, and the spectacle of their confrontation with the documents, films, and other records of their doings was now disgusting, now poignant, and always gripping. Lawyers of great renown appeared at the bar of the courts, and Robert Jackson's extraordinary gift for the written word projected the terrible events and searching issues in unforgettable language.

Military courts and commissions have customarily rendered their judgments stark and unsupported by opinions giving the reasons for their decisions. The Nuremberg and Tokyo judgments, in contrast, were all based on extensive opinions detailing the evidence and analyzing the factual and legal issues, in the fashion of appellate tribunals generally.

Needless to say, they were not of uniform quality, and often reflected the logical shortcomings of compromise, the marks of which commonly mar the opinions of multi-member tribunals. But the process was *professional* in *a* way seldom achieved in military courts, and the records and judgments in these trials provided a much-needed foundation for a corpus of judge-made international penal law. The results of the trials commended themselves to the newly formed United Nations, and on Dec. 11, 1946, the General Assembly adopted a resolution affirming "the principles of international law recognized by the Charter of the Nuremberg Tribunal and the judgment of the Tribunal."

However, history may ultimately assess the wisdom or unwisdom of the war crimes trials, one thing is indisputable: At their conclusion, the United States Government stood legally, politically, and morally committed to the principles enunciated in the charters and judgments of the tribunals. The President of the United States, on the recommendation of the Departments of State, War and

Justice, approved the war crimes programs. Thirty or more American judges, drawn from the appellate benches of the states from Massachusetts to Oregon, and Minnesota to Georgia, conducted the later Nuremberg trials and wrote the opinions. General Douglas MacArthur, under authority of the Far Eastern Commission, established the Tokyo tribunal and confirmed the sentences it imposed and it was under his authority as the highest American military officer in the Far East that the Yamashita and other such proceedings were held. The United States delegation to the United Nations presented the resolution by which the General Assembly endorsed the Nuremberg principles.

Thus, the integrity of the nation is staked on those principles, and today the question is how they apply to our conduct of the war in Vietnam, and whether the United States Government is prepared to face the consequences of their application.

*   *   *

7. Crime and Punishment

Opinion or "reaction" samplings taken shortly after the first news of the Son My incidents revealed that nearly two-thirds of those interviewed denied feeling any shock. [Son My is a Vietnamese district containing the hamlet of My Lai.] Some observers found this lack of public indignation or shame, as well as some of the comments recorded by the samplers, more upsetting than the killings themselves.

It is neither surprising nor particularly disturbing, however, that many of those interviewed refused to believe that anything untoward had occurred. "I can't believe an American servicemen would purposely shoot any civilian," declared Alabama's George Wallace, "any atrocities in this war were caused by the Communists." Others described the reports as "a prefabricated story by a bunch of losers," or labeled them incredible because "it's contrary to everything I've learned about America." These outright rejections of undisputed information are a familiar defense mechanism, activated in order to ward off the shock which would accompany acceptance.

There was also a widespread disposition to discount the Son My stories on the ground that "incidents such as this are bound to happen in a war." So, too, are murders and robberies "bound to happen" in our streets, and they are likely to happen much more often if we cease to regard them as reprehensible. In fact Son My was unusual, both in its scale and the candor with which the operation was carried on, with Army photographers on the scene and commanders in helicopters circling overhead. Those who resorted to this "sloughing-off" justification are, nonetheless, correct in assuming that unjustifiable killings of prisoners and civilians on a smaller scale are bound to and indeed do happen in a war, and what they overlook is that in the United States Army, when detected they have generally not gone unpunished. During the Second World War many American soldiers were court-martialed and severely punished for killing or assaulting civilians in violation of local law or the laws of war. The fact that we are now fighting in Asia instead of Europe is hardly a worthy basis for suspending their application.

Now the Son My court-martial proceedings carry the prospect of inquiry into those ominous problems—into body counts, and zippo raids, and free-fire zones, and "mere gook rules." The motive force will be the defendants' effort to shake off culpability either by showing that what they did was not "wrong," however unlawful, or that if wrong, others more highly placed were primarily responsible. Such an inquiry is unlikely to be either complete or dispassionate.

"Regardless of the outcome of . . . the My Lai courts-martial and other legal actions," Col. William Corson has written, "the point remains that American judgment as to the effective prosecution of the war was faulty from beginning to end and that the atrocities, alleged or otherwise, are a result of a failure of judgment, not criminal behavior." Colonel Corson overlooks, I fear, that negligent homicide is generally a crime of bad judgment rather than evil intent. Perhaps he is right in the strictly causal sense that if there had been no failure of judgment, the occasion for criminal conduct would not have arisen. The Germans in occupied Europe made gross errors of judgment which no doubt created the conditions in which the slaughter of the inhabitants of Klissura occurred, but that did not make the killings any less criminal.

Still, there is a real question how far the criminal process is appropriate as a scale in which to weigh the responsibility of those in high authority for the crimes committed in Vietnam. The pages of The Washington Monthly and the New York Village Voice have recently been the vehicle for a running debate on the subject between Townsend Hoopes, former Under Secretary of the Air Force and author of an interesting account of top-level policy formulation from 1965-1969, and two newspaper reporters, Geoffrey Cowan and Judith Coburn. The reporters thought that if Justice Jackson's promise at Nuremberg were to be kept, President Johnson and his associates ought to be brought before a like bar of justice; Mr. Hoopes's reaction to this, not unnaturally, was one of dismay. The antagonists never squarely locked horns, so that not even the most dispassionate judge could award the laurels of victory to either side. Mr. Hoopes's defense, nonetheless, was something less than satisfying, for the burden of it was that American leaders are intrinsically "good" men. "Lyndon Johnson, though disturbingly volatile, was not in his worst moments an evil man in the Hitlerian sense," Mr. Hoopes declared, while "his principal advisers were, almost uniformly, those considered to be among the ablest, the best, the most humane and liberal men that could be found for public trust."

That is what trial lawyers call "character testimony." Whatever its value in a fraud or perjury case, it is not very relevant to a determination whether certain proven conduct is criminal, and whether the defendant was implicated. How much the President and his close advisers in the White House, Pentagon and Foggy Bottom knew about the volume and cause of civilian casualties in Vietnam, and the physical devastation of the country-side, is speculative. Something was known, for the late John McNaughton (then Assistant Secretary of Defense) returned from the White House one day in 1967 with the message that "We seem to be proceeding on the assumption that the way to eradicate the Vietcong is to destroy all the village structures, defoliate all the jungles, and then cover the entire surface of South Vietnam with asphalt."

Whatever the limits and standards of culpability for civilians in Washington, the proximity and immediate authority of the military commanders ties the burden of responsibility much more tightly to their shoulders. The divisional and other commands in Quang Ngai Province, within which Son My is situated and where civilian casualties and physical destruction have been especially heavy, were subordinated to the Third Marine Amphibious Force, commanded by Lieut. Gen. Robert E. Cushman, who in turn was directly responsible to the top Army headquarters in Vietnam, the Military Assistance Command Vietnam (MACV). At the time of Son My, Gen. William Westmoreland headed MACV, with Gen. Creighton Abrams as his deputy, and Lieut. Gen. William B. Rossen in charge of a headquarters of MACV in northern South Vietnam. From MACV, the chain of command runs through the Commander-in-Chief Pacific (Adm. Ulysses Grant Sharp Jr.) to the Chiefs of Staff in Washington.

It is on these officers that command responsibility for the conduct of operations has lain. From General Westmoreland down they were more or less constantly in Vietnam, and splendidly equipped with helicopters and other aircraft, which gave them a degree of mobility unprecedented in earlier wars, and consequently endowed them with every opportunity to keep the course of the fighting and its consequences under close and constant observation. Communications were generally rapid and efficient, so that the flow of information and orders was unimpeded.

These circumstances are in sharp contrast to those that confronted General Yamashita in 1944 and 1945, with his forces reeling back in disarray before the oncoming American military powerhouse. For failure to control his troops so as to prevent the atrocities they committed, Brig. Gens. Egbert F. Bullene and Morris Handwerk and Maj. Gens. James A. Lester, Leo Donovan and Russel B. Reynolds found him guilty of violating the laws of war and sentenced him to death by hanging. The sentence was first confirmed by the area commander, Lieut. Gen. William D. Styer, and then by Gen. Douglas MacArthur, as Commander-in-Chief, United States Army Forces in the Pacific. In his statement on the confirmation, General MacArthur said of Yamashita:

> It is not easy for me to pass penal judgment upon a defeated adversary in a major military campaign. I have reviewed the proceedings in vain search for some mitigating circumstance on his behalf. I can find none. Rarely has so cruel and wanton a record been spread to public gaze. Revolting as this may be in itself, it pales before the sinister and far-reaching implication thereby attached to the profession of arms. . . . This officer, of proven field merit, entrusted with high command involving authority adequate to responsibility, has failed this irrevocable standard; has failed his duty to his troops, to his country, to his enemy, to mankind; has failed utterly his soldier faith. The transgressions resulting there from as revealed by the trial are a blot upon the military profession, a stain upon civilization and constitute a memory of shame and dishonor that can never be forgotten. . . . I approve the findings and sentence of the Commission and direct the Commanding General, Army Forces in the Western Pacific, to execute the judgment upon the defendant, stripped of uniform, decorations and other appurtenances signifying membership in the military profession.

Whether or not individuals are held to criminal account is perhaps not the most important question posed by the Vietnam war today. But the Son My courts-martial are shaping the question for us, and they can not be fairly determined without full inquiry into the higher responsibilities. Little as the leaders of the Army seem to realize it, this is the only road to the Army's salvation, for its moral health will not be recovered until its leaders are willing to scrutinize their behavior by the same standards that their revered predecessors applied to Tomayuki Yamashita 25 years ago.

QUESTIONS

1.   General MacArthur said of General Yamashita, before Yamashita's execution by hanging, that his conduct was "a blot upon the military profession." Yet "[t]here was no charge that General Yamashita had approved, much less ordered these barbarities, and no evidence that he knew of them other than the inference that he must have because of their extent." TELFORD TAYLOR, NUREMBERG AND VIETNAM: AN AMERICAN TRAGEDY. What are the canons that define the "military profession"? If Yamashita was "a blot" upon that profession, what about Gen. William Westmoreland or Gen. Creighton Abrams, commander at the time of the Vietnamese massacres? Or should they all be excused because of ignorance, lack of direct control, and no evidence that they approved such conduct?

2.   Most law firms are controlled by hierarchical systems, with managing partners setting general policy and, often, regulating client selection. They are like generals, concerned with strategy. The partners and senior associates conducting the practice are similar to field officers, and the junior associates and paralegals are the soldiers. Who should bear primary responsibility for ethical judgments? The ABA Model Rules divides responsibility into three different "layers" reflecting these hierarchies: Rule 5.1 ("Partner or Supervisory Lawyer"); Rule 5.2 ("Subordinate Lawyer"); and Rule 5.3 ("Nonlawyer Assistants"). Rule 5.2(b) states that "[a] subordinate lawyer does not violate the Rules of Professional Conduct if that lawyer acts in accordance with a supervisory lawyer's reasonable resolution of an arguable question of professional duty." What would Telford Taylor think of Rule 5.2(b)? Aristotle? You? Who decides what is a "reasonable resolution" or an "arguable question"?

MARTIN GANSBERG, 37 WHO SAW MURDER DIDN'T CALL THE POLICE
N.Y. TIMES, March 27, 1964, at 1, 38, col. 4

Twenty-eight-year-old Catherine Genovese, who was called Kitty by almost everyone in the neighborhood, was returning home from her job as manager of a bar in Hollis. She parked her red Fiat in a lot adjacent to the Kew Gardens' Long Island Railroad Station, facing Mowbray Place. Like many residents of the neighborhood, she had parked there day after day since her arrival from Connecticut a year ago, although the railroad frowns on the practice.

She turned off the lights of her car, locked the door and started to walk the 100 feet to the entrance of her apartment at 82-70 Austin Street, which is in a Tudor building, with stores on the first floor and apartments on the second.

The entrance to the apartment is in the rear of the building because the front is rented to retail stores. At night the quiet neighborhood is shrouded in the slumbering darkness that marks most residential areas.

Miss Genovese noticed a man at the far end of the lot, near a seven-story apartment house at 82-10 Austin Street. She halted. Then, nervously, she headed up Austin Street towards Lefferts Boulevard, where there is a call box to the 102d Police Precinct in nearby Richmond Hill.

"He Stabbed Me!"

She got as far as a street light in front of a bookstore before the man grabbed her. She screamed. Lights went on in the 10-story apartment house at 82-67 Austin Street, which faces the bookstore. Windows slid open and voices punctured the early-morning stillness.

Miss Genovese screamed: "Oh, my God, he stabbed me! Please help me! Please help me!"

From one of the upper windows in the apartment house, a man called down: "Let that girl alone!"

The assailant looked up at him, shrugged and walked down Austin Street toward a white sedan parked a short distance away. Miss Genovese struggled to her feet.

Lights went out. The killer returned to Miss Genovese, now trying to make her way around the side of the building by the parking lot to get to her apartment. The assailant stabbed her again.

"I'm dying!" she shrieked. "I'm dying!"

A City Bus Passed

Windows were opened again and lights went on in many apartments. The assailant got into his car and drove away. Miss Genovese staggered to her feet. A city bus, Q-10, the Lefferts Boulevard line to Kennedy International Airport, passed. It was 3:35 a.m.

The assailant returned. By then, Miss Genovese had crawled to the back of the building, where the freshly painted brown doors to the apartment house held out hope of safety. The killer tried the first door; she wasn't there. At the second door, 82-62 Austin Street, he saw her slumped on the floor at the foot of the stairs. He stabbed her a third time—fatally.

It was 3:50 by the time the police received their first call, from a man who was a neighbor of Miss Genovese. In two minutes they were at the scene.

WHAT KIND OF PEOPLE ARE WE?
New York Times, March 28, 1964, Editorial

Seldom has *The Times* published a more horrifying story than its account of how 38 respectable, law-abiding, middle-class Queens citizens watched a killer stalk his young woman victim in a parking lot in Kew Gardens over a half-hour period, without one of them making a call to the Police Department that might have saved her life. They would not have been exposed to any danger themselves; a simple telephone call in the privacy of their own homes was all that was needed. How incredible it is that such motivations as "I didn't want to get involved" deterred them from this act of simple humanity. Does residence in a great city destroy all sense of personal responsibility for one's neighbors? Who can explain such shocking indifference on the part of a cross section of our fellow New Yorkers? We regretfully admit that we do not know the answers.

QUESTIONS

1. Within three months, a man was arrested and convicted of Catherine Genovese's murder. *See* N.Y. TIMES, June 16, 1964, at 1, col. 6. He was sentenced to death. Does that make you feel better? Eventually, his sentence was changed to life imprisonment, due to an error in the sentencing process. People v. Moseley, 20 N.Y.2d. 64, 281 N.Y.S.2d. 782, 228 N.E.2d 765 (1967). Does this make you feel better?

2. Would it make you feel any better if the bystanders who could have saved Catherine Genovese's life were also punished? A very few American states make it a criminal offense to refuse to render aid to a person in peril (so-called "Good Samaritan" statutes). *See, e.g.,* R.I. Gen. Laws § 11-56-1 (1998); Vt. Stat. Ann. tit. 12, § 519 (2006). Most, like New York, do not. The European experience is very different. "European countries have long used the criminal law to enforce a duty to aid a person in distress." KADISH, SCHULHOFER, & STEIKER, CRIMINAL LAW AND ITS PROCESSES 200 (8th ed. 2007). *See, e.g.,* French Penal Code art. 63(2) (1945). Who has it right, France or New York?

3. What would Aristotle have said about this situation? Would legal responsibility for such failures promote or discourage adequate moral responsibility?

BENJAMIN WEISER, DOUBTING CASE, CITY PROSECUTOR AIDED DEFENSE
NEW YORK TIMES, June 23, 2008

The Manhattan District Attorney, Robert M. Morgenthau, had a problem. The murder convictions of two men in one of his office's big cases—the 1990 shooting of a bouncer outside the Palladium nightclub—had been called into question by a stream of new evidence.

So the office decided on a re-examination, led by a 21-year veteran assistant, Daniel L. Bibb.

Mr. Bibb spent nearly two years reinvestigating the killing and reported back: He believed that the two imprisoned men were not guilty, and that their convictions should be dropped. Yet top officials told him, he said, to go into a court hearing and defend the case anyway. He did, and in 2005 he lost.

But in a recent interview, Mr. Bibb made a startling admission: He threw the case. Unwilling to do what his bosses ordered, he said, he deliberately helped the other side win.

He tracked down hard-to-find or reluctant witnesses who pointed to other suspects and prepared them to testify for the defense. He talked strategy with defense lawyers. And when they veered from his coaching, he cornered them in the hallway and corrected them.

"I did the best I could," he said. "To lose."

Today, the two men are free. At the end of the hearing, which stretched over six weeks, his superiors agreed to ask a judge to drop the conviction of one, Olmedo Hidalgo. The judge granted a new trial to the other, David Lemus, who was acquitted in December.

Mr. Bibb, 53, who said it was painful to remain in the office, resigned in 2006 and is trying to build a new career as a defense lawyer in Manhattan—with some difficulty, friends say, in a profession where success can hang on the ability to cut deals with prosecutors.

Mr. Morgenthau's office would not comment on Mr. Bibb's claims. Daniel J. Castleman, chief assistant district attorney, would say only: "Nobody in this office is ever required to prosecute someone they believe is innocent. That was true then, as it is now. That being the case, no useful purpose would be served in engaging in a debate with a former staff member." The office has said it had good reason to believe that the two men were guilty.

Yet whatever the facts of the murder, the dispute offers an unusual glimpse of a prosecutor weighing the demands of conscience against his obligation to his office, and the extraordinary measures he took to settle that conflict in his own mind.

"I was angry," Mr. Bibb said, "that I was being put in a position to defend convictions that I didn't believe in."

The case also reveals a rare public challenge to one of the nation's most powerful district attorneys from within his office. As the hearing unfolded in 2005, Mr. Morgenthau, running for re-election, was sharply criticized by an opponent who said he had prosecuted the wrong men.

By then, the Palladium case had become one of the most troubled in the city's recent history, stirred up every few years by fresh evidence, heralded in newspaper and television reports, that pointed to other suspects.

It is not as if Mr. Morgenthau has refused to admit mistakes. In 2002, in spectacular fashion, his office recommended dismissing the convictions of five men in the attack on a jogger in Central Park, after its reinvestigation showed that another man had acted alone. "It's my decision," Mr. Morgenthau said then. "The buck stops here."

In fact, the prosecutor who led that inquiry, Nancy E. Ryan, was Mr. Bibb's supervisor in the Palladium case—though Mr. Bibb would not detail his conversations with her or other superiors, saying they were privileged.

Defense lawyers confirmed that Mr. Bibb helped them, though he never explicitly stated his intentions. Some praised his efforts to see that justice was done. Others involved in the case suggested he did a disservice to both sides—shirking his duty as an assistant district attorney, and prolonging an injustice by not quitting the case, or the office.

And some blame Mr. Bibb's superiors. Steven M. Cohen, a former federal prosecutor who pushed Mr. Morgenthau's office to reinvestigate, said that while Mr. Bibb should have refused to present the case, his bosses should not have pressed him.

"If Bibb is to be believed, he was essentially asked to choose between his conscience and his job," Mr. Cohen said. "Whether he made the right choice is irrelevant; that he was asked to make that choice is chilling."

At 6-foot-6, Mr. Bibb looks every inch the lawman, with a square jaw, a gravelly voice and a negotiating style that lawyers describe as brutally honest. He joined the district attorney's office right out of Seton Hall Law School in 1982 and went on to handle some of its major murder cases and cold-case investigations.

The Palladium case certainly looked open and shut in 1992, when Mr. Lemus and Mr. Hidalgo were sentenced to 25 years to life. Several bouncers identified them as the men they scuffled with outside the East Village nightclub. Mr. Lemus's ex-girlfriend said he claimed to have shot a bouncer there.

But the next decade brought a string of nagging contradictions. A former member of a Bronx drug gang confessed that he and a friend had done the shooting. That spurred new examinations by the district attorney's office, federal prosecutors, defense lawyers, the police and the press.

When Mr. Morgenthau's office was asked to take another look, Mr. Bibb said, his supervisors gave him carte blanche. "It really was, leave no stone unturned," he said.

Over 21 months, starting in 2003, he and two detectives conducted more than 50 interviews in more than a dozen states, ferreting out witnesses the police had somehow missed or ignored.

Mr. Bibb said he shared his growing doubts with his superiors. And at a meeting in early 2005, he recalled, after defense lawyers won court approval for a hearing into the new evidence, he urged that the convictions be set aside. "I made what I considered to be my strongest pitch," he said.

Instead, he said, he was ordered to go to the hearing, present the government's case and let a judge decide—a strategy that violated his sense of a prosecutor's duty.

"I had always been taught that we made the decisions, that we made the tough calls, that we didn't take things and throw them up against the wall" for a judge or jury to sort out, he said. "If the evidence doesn't convince me, then I'm never going to be able to convince a jury."

Still, Mr. Bibb said, he worried that if he did not take the case, another prosecutor would—and possibly win.

Defense lawyers said he plunged in. In long phone conversations, he helped them sort through the new evidence he had gathered.

"If I make a mistake in my interpretation of what he said, he'll correct me," said

Gordon Mehler, who represented Mr. Lemus. "If there's a piece of evidence that bears on another piece of evidence I'm talking about, he'll remind me of it. That's not something that a prosecutor typically does."

As the defense decided which witnesses to call, he again hunted them down—sometimes in prison or witness protection—and, when necessary, persuaded them to testify in State Supreme Court in Manhattan.

"I made sure all of their witnesses were going to testify in a manner that would have the greatest impact, certainly consistent with the truth," Mr. Bibb said. "I wasn't telling anybody to make anything up."

He told them what questions to expect, both from the defense and his own cross-examination—which he admitted felt "a little bit weird." Defense lawyers say they first met some of their witnesses on the day of testimony, outside the courtroom.

During breaks, Mr. Bibb confronted the lawyers when he felt they were not asking the right questions. "Don't you understand?" one lawyer recalled him saying. "I'm your best friend in that courtroom."

Cross-examining the witnesses, Mr. Bibb took pains not to damage their credibility. Facing a former gang member who had pleaded guilty to six murders, he asked only a few perfunctory questions about the man's record.

Daniel J. Horwitz, the other defense lawyer, said the help was invaluable. "Did Dan play a useful role in making sure that justice prevailed in that courtroom? The answer is unequivocally yes."

When the testimony was over, Mr. Bibb said he made one last appeal to his superiors to drop the convictions. They agreed to do so for Mr. Hidalgo, but not for Mr. Lemus—who was still implicated by "strong evidence," the office said at the time.

"I said, 'I'm done,' " Mr. Bibb recalled. "I wanted nothing to do with it."

Another prosecutor made final written arguments, and in October 2005, Justice Roger S. Hayes ordered the new trial for Mr. Lemus. Demoralized by the case, Mr. Bibb resigned a few months later.

A close friend, Robert Mooney, a New York City police detective, said that if not for the Palladium case, Mr. Bibb "would have spent his entire professional life at the prosecutor's office."

"He's brokenhearted that he's not doing this anymore."

In a brief interview after he quit, Mr. Bibb defended Mr. Morgenthau against criticism that the case had been mishandled. "There was never any evil intent on the part of the D.A.'s office," Mr. Bibb said then.

But around the same time, he distanced himself from the office's decisions in remarks to "Dateline NBC." He said that during the hearing, he already believed the two men were not guilty, but proceeded because he had a client to represent: Mr. Morgenthau.

"He was aware of what was going on," Mr. Bibb told the interviewer. "The decision to go to a hearing was not made in my presence."

As for Mr. Bibb's new revelation that he helped the defense, lawyers and others are divided.

Stephen Gillers, a legal ethics professor at the New York University School of Law, said he believed that Mr. Bibb had violated his obligation to his client, and could conceivably face action by a disciplinary panel. "He's entitled to his conscience, but his conscience does not entitle him to subvert his client's case," Mr. Gillers said. "It entitles him to withdraw from the case, or quit if he can't."

On the other hand, he added, Mr. Morgenthau could have defused any conflict by assigning another prosecutor.

John Schwartz, a former detective who worked to exonerate the convicted men, said Mr. Bibb did them no favor by continuing in the case. "He effectively took part in keeping two innocent men in prison an additional year at least, for not going with what he felt was the truth," Mr. Schwartz said.

But Mr. Mehler, the defense lawyer, said Mr. Bibb acted honorably. While lawyers on both sides must advocate for their clients, he said, "a prosecutor has an additional duty to search out the truth.

"I say that he lived up to that."

Today, Mr. Bibb says he does not believe he crossed any line.

"I didn't work for the other side," he said. "I worked for what I thought was the right thing."

DEBRA CASSENS MOSS, A PROSECUTOR'S DUTY—ASSISTANT A.G. RESIGNS RATHER THAN DEFEND CONVICTION SHE FEELS IS WRONG
ABA JOURNAL (June 1992)

A lot of people who have investigated the 1983 rape and murder of a 10-year-old Chicago-area girl have come to believe that the wrong men were convicted of the crime.

But the most telling conversion to date may have come from former Illinois Assistant Attorney General Mary Brigid Kenney, who was supposed to defend a death sentence for one of the two men before the state supreme court.

Kenney resigned in March on ethical grounds, saying she now believes that death row inmate Rolando Cruz and a co-defendant are innocent, and publicly called on Illinois Attorney General Roland Burris to drop his prosecution of the case.

Like many people before her, Kenney said she started out believing that Cruz and Alejandro Hernandez, both 28, were guilty. After reviewing the trial record, she became convinced that convicted child-killer Brian Dugan, who has confessed to the crime, is the real murderer.

"I cannot sit idly as this office continues to pursue the unjust prosecution and execution of Rolando Cruz," Kenney said in her March 5 resignation letter. "I have no doubt that had the juries that convicted [the two men] heard the evidence about [Dugan's] crimes and confessions, they could not have possibly come to the conclusion that anyone but Brian Dugan was responsible."

Cruz and Hernandez were convicted of the brutal murder of Jeanine Nicarico, who was abducted from her suburban Naperville home and driven to a remote area, where she was raped and beaten to death. Both men are appealing.

Cruz was sentenced to death and Hernandez to 80 years in prison in trials held after their original convictions and death sentences were overturned. The state high court had ordered new trials because the men were not tried separately.

Kenney joins a growing list of current and former officials involved in the investigation and prosecution of the case who have come to the conclusion that Dugan, who is serving a life sentence for two other rapes and murders, including that of a 7-year-old girl, also killed Nicarico.

The list includes former State Police Director Jeremy Margolis; former Naperville Police Chief James Teal; Kane County, Ill., State's Attorney Gary Johnson, who once defended a third co-defendant in the case; and three of the jurors who helped convict Cruz and Hernandez.

Dugan, 35, not only has confessed to the Nicarico killing, but has described the girl's murder in details that Kenney and other converts say are strongly corroborated by the evidence. Dugan, however, has refused to tell his story in court without a grant of immunity from the death penalty, which DuPage County, Ill., State's Attorney James Ryan has so far refused to consider.

Not My Job

Kenney's public appeal to her boss, though, appears to have fallen on deaf ears. At a press conference following her resignation, Burris said he had no choice but to defend the two convictions in court. To do otherwise, he said, would probably constitute grounds for impeachment.

Burris said it was not his job to review a conviction and substitute his judgment for a jury's. "Unfortunately, we do not have the luxury to be able to pick and choose" the cases in which his office will represent the state on appeal, he said.

But defense lawyers, legal experts and Kenney all say that Burris is mistaken. According to them, the attorney general has an ethical obligation to seek justice, not merely to uphold a conviction.

In support of their position, they cite a 1935 U.S. Supreme Court ruling, the ABA's Standards Relating to the Administration of Criminal Justice and the Illinois Rules of Professional Conduct.

In *Berger v. United States*, 295 U.S. 78, the Court said that the prosecution's interest in a criminal case "is not that it shall win a case, but that justice shall be done."

The ABA's standards also describe a dual role for prosecutors as advocates and administrators of justice.

And the Illinois rules spell out the special responsibilities of a prosecutor, including a duty to reveal evidence that may negate the guilt of an accused or mitigate the offense.

"I think that prosecutors should vigorously prosecute the guilty," said Ronald Rotunda, a law school professor who teaches ethics at the University of Illinois at Champaign-Urbana. "But deterrence will not work if it is the innocent who go to jail because the prosecutor is concerned about his batting average," he said.

"For [Burris] to say he's not worried about whether somebody is guilty or innocent-he's just doing his job-is a very ugly position to take," said Northwestern University Law School Professor Lawrence Marshall, Cruz's appellate lawyer. "Anybody who looks at this case objectively, without a political agenda, can see that Brian Dugan is guilty and Rolando Cruz is innocent."

Despite mounting pressure, Burris has shown no intention of backing down. In its 150-page brief, filed April 10, the state contends that Dugan is lying. It says the physical evidence and expert testimony at Cruz's trial contradict Dugan's claims that he alone killed the girl.

Through a spokesman, Burris repeated his assertion that it is up to the courts to determine whether the convictions should stand. The attorney general feels critics "should direct their concerns to the court, not him," the spokesman said.

QUESTIONS

1.   Compare the stories of prosecutors Daniel Bibb (New York) and Mary Brigid Kenney (Illinois) in the newspaper stories above. Both prosecutors were assigned the task of defending, in post-conviction proceedings, the validity of murder convictions they believed to be unjust. Kenney resigned from her office rather than argue on appeal that the conviction should be affirmed. Bibb took on the assignment, but secretly aided the defense in marshaling and fashioning its evidence in support of a motion for new trial. Which approach is more consistent with a lawyer's moral responsibility? Note that Professor Stephen Gillers of NYU School of Law believed that Assistant District Attorney Bibb may have violated professional responsibilities to his own client—the State of New York. *See Materials, supra* at 2E and ABA Model Rules 1.2 and 1.4. Who is a prosecutor's "client" for purposes of the disciplinary rules? How is the resolution of this question effected by comment (1) to ABA Model Rule 3.8, which provides that "[a] prosecutor has the responsibility of a minister of justice and not simply that of an advocate"?

2.   If you are uncomfortable with the path taken by either Bibb or Kenney in these cases, what do you think of yet a third approach? Might a prosecutor attempt to convince his or her superiors of another course of action, and if that advocacy is unsuccessful, ask that the prosecution be reassigned to another attorney in the office? What are the consequences, both legal and pragmatic, likely to flow from that approach?

3.   What if the prosecutor simply accedes to their supervisors' request and defends the conviction? Would the narrowly circumscribed "following orders"

defense in ABA Model Rule 5.2 protect the prosecutor from professional discipline? Should it?

4. Which of these approaches, if any, would Aristotle favor?

Chapter III

THE LEGAL MENTALITY

A. THE CONTRIBUTION OF ROMAN LEGALISM

The United States Capitol Building, the Supreme Court Building, the Department of Justice, and hundreds of other federal and state law buildings, even in the smallest country town, are likely to have one thing in common: they are modeled after Roman buildings. In the case of the Supreme Court Building, this extends to the details of the bronze doors, the busts of former Chief Justices (some complete with togas!), and even the fountains and lighting fixtures. Subconsciously, we have learned to equate Roman style with government and, most particularly, with law.

How appropriate. Most of our fundamental "legal" mentality also derives, directly or indirectly, from Roman models. Even the words "justice," "judge," "jurisprudence," "legislation," "regulation," "equity," "equitable," "constitution," and "code" are derived from the Romans, as is the word "legal" itself. The direct history of Roman law extends from at least the *Lex Valeria* of 508 B.C. through the great codification of Justinian between 529 and 534 A.D. This period of over 1000 years makes our own legal history, with a constitutional government of slightly over 200 years, seem like a flash in time. Even so, it is only half the story. Roman legal ideas continued to influence the development of modern legal systems long after the death of the Empire. Whether it was the Code Napoleon or the early law of our own republic, Roman models are widely known and used.[1]

The Romans had conquered Greece, and they were familiar with the great heritage of Greek philosophy that we have touched upon in our accounts of Plato and Aristotle.[2] But Roman society was very different from that of Athens. To begin with, it was far larger, more complex, more secular, and more materialistic. By 50 A.D., the height of the Roman Empire, Rome ruled the known world. It even occupied England from 43 to 410 A.D., a period far longer than the existing government of the United States.

Reflective scholars have long perceived similarities between our own culture and the Roman Empire. We, too, are a highly secular, materialistic, and complex society with a vast web of international influence. We put a high premium on military power, and we are both socially diverse and very hierarchical. While we have abandoned slavery, its invidious mark is still felt in our society, as it was in Rome. And, like the Romans, we ultimately look not to philosophy or to religion but to *law* to order our

---

[1] *See, e.g.,* D. R. Coquillette, *Justinian in Braintree: John Adams, Civilian Learning, and Legal Elitism, 1758–1775, in* Law in Colonial Massachusetts 359–418 (Coquillette, Brink, & Menand eds., 1984).

[2] *See* Bertrand Russell, A History of Western Philosophy 270–297 (2007).

affairs, protect our security, and bind us together.

What are the characteristics of a "legal" mentality? The first is the supremacy of a system of formal rules as the basis for social order. Suppose we injure someone, say by running into them with a car. Or suppose we wish to have a solemn agreement with someone. In other societies, even quite sophisticated ones, people would turn first to tribal custom or to religious practices to define their rights and duties and "what to do next." Here, our first thought would be of the law.

The second characteristic follows from the first. "Legal" societies not only have widely encompassing systems of formal rules, but they also promulgate and enforce these rules through a legal process. Romans did not confuse their civil law with social mores or religious beliefs, and neither do we. Roman legal literature, which consisted both of legislation and juristic writing, was eventually consolidated by the great Byzantine Emperor Justinian (482–565 A.D.). Emperor Justinian wanted existing Roman law to be collected into a simple and clear system of rules, or "code." His legal minister, Tribonian, lead a group of scholars in a two-year effort to codify existing Roman law. The result was the great Justinian Code, or *Corpus Juris*, completed in 534 A.D.

The *Corpus Juris* was composed of a *Digest* (533 A.D.) containing abridgments of the best work of prior jurists, the *Code* (534 A.D.) containing a codification of statutes, and the famous *Institutes* (533 A.D.), a text book for law students. This formal law was originally enforced by the Praetors through an ingenious system of lay judges, backed by legal sanctions.[3]

It is impossible here to give you any real sense of the sophistication and elegance of the *Corpus Juris*. The Justinian Code was a lucid and concise codification of Roman law. Indeed, Roman commercial law is still unequaled for its clarity and structure. (Even the Uniform Commercial Code borrowed Roman ideas—and the Roman numbering systems!) In addition, the Roman distinctions between "natural law" (*ius naturale*),"law of nations" (*ius gentium*), and the "civil law" of an individual state (*ius civile*) inspired many later jurists, from Thomas Aquinas to those of the present day. Most importantly, the Romans placed a system of general, uniform, and public laws—capable of coercive enforcement—at the heart of their society. As we shall see, most modern systems of jurisprudence owe at least something to the Romans.

Enforcement by official sanctions of the formal commands of a sovereign power, duly promulgated and adopted by a "legitimizing" process whereby norms are identified as "law," has become seen as the touchstone of modern "positive" law. But, more importantly, the recognition by a complex society that such a system prevails over other social ordering devices, including philosophy and religion, is the touchstone of the "legal mentality." For both, we are deeply indebted to the Romans.

The *Corpus Juris*—Justinian's uniform and comprehensive rewriting of Roman law—has formed the basis of civil law in many modern states. The first item in this chapter's "Materials" is the beginning of Justinian's great textbook for law students,

---

[3] *See* JOHN P. DAWSON, THE ORACLES OF THE LAW 100–147 (1986).

the *Institutes* (533 A.D.). Its structure is a model of logic, and it defines its terms carefully. Justinian observed the following in defining the source of legal obligation:

> That which seems good to the emperor has also the force of law; for the people, by the *lex regia* which is passed to confer on him his power, make over to him their whole power and authority.[4]

We see in the Justinian Code an early recognition that individual citizens delegate to others (senators, magistrates, the emperor) the power to make laws for the benefit of the whole, in exchange for the peace, stability, and security that come from living in an ordered society.

B. POSITIVISM

One system of jurisprudence that owes its ancestry to the Romans is "positivism." Articulated by the renowned John Austin (1790-1859) in his great *The Province of Jurisprudence Determined* (1832), "positivism" limits the term "law" to the system of formal, promulgated rules backed by sanctions that actually exist in a society, not any "ideal" system or concept of what a law "ought" to be. Its leading modern proponents have been H. L. A. Hart, whose work will be found in the next chapter, and Hans Kelsen, whose "pure theory" of law purports to describe law in an entirely formal manner "free from all taint of history, ethics, politics, sociology, idealism and other external influences."[5] Thus, a positivist would examine the "law" as it was enacted on statute books and coercively enforced by the police and the courts. Issues such as whether the law was "good" or "bad" would be irrelevant.[6] To use Roman terms, only the law of the state, the *ius civile*, and perhaps the law of nations if duly enacted by international treaty (*ius gentium*) are the "real law."

Roberto Unger's book *Knowledge and Politics* (1975) explores the nature of "positivism" by comparing it to its chief juristic rival, "natural rights" theory. "Natural rights" theory was also indirectly inspired by a Roman idea, that of "natural law" or the "*ius naturale.*" While Romans used that term in reference only to those "laws" of nature that no human will can change, that is, the laws of physics or the laws of biology, later theorists extended the concept to define a "natural" law as that which governs or limits the *ius civile* or state law. For example, consider a

---

[4] *Materials, infra* at 3G.

[5] David H. Walker, The Oxford Companion to Law 969–970 (1980). *See* Hans Kelson, The Pure Theory of Law (1934, rev. 1960). "Positivism" as a system of jurisprudence is distantly related to the "positive philosophy" of writers such as Auguste Comte (1798-1857). The latter argues that in nature there are scientific laws that can be known empirically, but the ultimate causes of things, in a theological or metaphysical sense, cannot be known. *See* The Dictionary of Philosophy 60–61, 243 (2006).

[6] Lon L. Fuller has argued that there are tests of "good" and "bad" law making that are fairly independent of spiritual or ideological bias. For example, he argues that laws which are properly promulgated, prospective, consistent, possible of compliance, clear, and uniformly and consistently enforced are inherently better than having no laws, secret laws, retroactive laws, inconsistent laws, impossible laws, unintelligible laws, or laws that are enforced in an arbitrary way or in a way in which there is no consequence between the law as announced and actual administration. *See* Lon L. Fuller, The Morality of Law 39 (1964). Even these "rules for making rules" have been challenged as containing moral bias. *See id.* 187–244. For a fine study of Fuller's jurisprudence, see Robert S. Summers, Lon L. Fuller (1984).

state law mandating genocide. Some would argue that this "law" violates "natural law" and thus is actually not a valid "law" even though formally promulgated and coercively enforced. Unger observes:

> To the positivist, society has no inherent order of its own. He sees rules as the impositions of a will, even though of an enlightened one, on the chaos of social life. The universal laws are simply conventions which set the boundaries among particular interests so that these interests will not destroy each other.

The natural rights theorist, on the contrary, claims to discover an intrinsic order in social relations, an order it is his purpose to make explicit and to develop. For him, the universals that describe this order—rights, rules, and institutional categories—have an existence and a worth quite independent of the particular interests that may take advantage of them. Thus, the natural rights thinker treats the system of private law concepts and property or the doctrine of separation of powers in public law as if they had an autonomous logic that survived in all their transmutation.[7]

To the extent that positive law is based solely on coercion, and that "positivism" separates legality from moral, political, or religious underpinnings, there will be obvious problems of legitimacy. People might not be convinced to obey rules against their self-interest solely by threat of punishment. Police cannot be everywhere. At some point, people must "believe" in the law. Unger effectively describes the dilemma:

> The assumption of the belief that the laws must be capable of coercive enforcement is the artificial view of society. According to this view, even though society may have an implicit order, as the natural rights theorist claims, it is not a self-regulating or self-enforcing one. Because individuals and individual interests are the primary elements of social life, and because they are locked in a perpetual struggle with one another, social order must be established by acts of will and protected against the ravages of self-interest.
>
> The ideas that there is no natural community of common ends and that group life is a creature of will help explain the importance of rules and of their coercive enforcement. But the same factors may also account for the fascination of terror, the systematic use of violence unlimited by law, as a device of social organization. The less one's ability to rely on participation in common ends, the greater the importance of force as a bond among individuals. Punishment and fear take the place of community.
>
> Moreover, when they view everything in the social world as a creation of the will, men come to believe there is nothing in society a will sufficiently violent cannot preserve or destroy. Thus, legalism and terrorism, the commitment to rules and the seduction of violence, are rival brothers, but brothers nonetheless.[8]

---

[7] *Materials, infra* at 3G.

[8] *Materials, infra* at 3G.

C. ALTERNATIVES TO LAW

The "might makes right" aspects of positivism have led some philosophers to consider whether law is necessary at all. In the late 1960s, the Oxford University Anarchist Society embarked on an interesting experiment. ("Anarchism" derives from the Greek term for a "society without an *arkhos*, that is to say without a ruler."[9]) The Oxford Anarchists bought hundreds of old bicycles and painted them white. They were then left at convenient corners throughout the city. Anyone who needed a bike could simply use a white one, and then leave it on the side of the road for the next person. The idea was that bicycle theft, a real problem for the "law," was caused by private property. If there were many communal "white" bicycles, there would be no need for a coercive law against bicycle theft. (The scheme worked beautifully until one night most of the bikes were expropriated by a capitalist with a truck!)

As Dennis Lloyd, later Lord Lloyd of Hampstead, observed in his *The Idea of Law* (1964):

> Fantastic though this viewpoint may seem to the members of a well-ordered democratic society—whatever its particular shortcomings or imperfections may be—it is useful to remember that in many less well-regulated societies the operation of law may appear in a more unfavourable guise. Moreover, the feeling that law inherently is or should be necessary for man in a properly ordered society receives little encouragement from the long succession of leading Western philosophers from Plato to Karl Marx who, in one way or another, have lent their support to the rejection of law. Hostility towards law has also played an important part in many of the great religious systems of East and West, and was a crucial element in the ideology of the Christian Church in its formative period. And, apart from Marxists, there are still to be found other serious supporters of a doctrine of anarchism as an answer to man's besetting personal and social problems.[10]

The best known modern anarchist was Karl Marx. According to Lloyd:

> Marx envisaged the overthrow of the capitalist society by a violent revolution of the oppressed proletariat. Law was nothing but a coercive system devised to maintain the privileges of the property-owning class; by the revolution a classless society would be brought into being, and law and the state would 'wither away' as being no longer needed to support an oppressive regime.[11]

Even today, devoted Marxists will argue that the repression of Stalinism was contrary to the true spirit of Marxism, which was, and is, ultimately to make coercive law unnecessary by removing the root causes of injustice in society. While such "pure" Marxists are now an endangered species, many still believe that laws

---

[9] *Materials, infra* at 3G.

[10] *Materials, infra* at 3G.

[11] *Materials, infra* at 3G.

are inherently suspect, and must always justify themselves by their political, economic, and social usefulness.

Another common modern phenomenon is having law "on the books," but with no real enforcement mechanism in practice. This can be true both on city streets and in the corporate jungle, and it often leads to other forms of social ordering. The tribal Anglo-Saxons had no police and often no effective coercive sanctions. Nevertheless, they had written *dooms* or "laws" to act as guidelines in negotiating private disputes. Many geographic areas, even in closely ordered societies, have no effective police. Although the common stereotype of such a "lawless" community is a big city neighborhood run by gangs or the mafia, a more common situation is represented by remote rural areas. Consider some of the towns in northern Maine where the fishing is excellent and the nearest police station is over two hours away. If official "coercion" is a required prerequisite for "positive" law, these places often function largely in the absence of law. Whether in a tribal society, an urban ghetto, or a remote fishing village, social customs, "mores," and religious beliefs can substitute for the rule of law, at least in an informal sense. Is that better or worse than conventional operation of positive law?[12]

As Lloyd points out, the answer to this last question depends very much on one's belief in the inherent goodness of human beings. To Saint Augustine (354–430 A.D.), watching the collapse of the Roman legal order from his vantage in North Africa, the answer was clear. "[L]aw was a natural necessity to curb man's sinful nature," at least until God's kingdom comes.[13] As we will see, more hopeful times led to more positive views, and by the time of Saint Thomas Aquinas (1225–1274) law was seen not "as a necessary evil but was a natural foundation in the development of human welfare," that is, even good people benefit from good laws.[14] Where the laws were bad and the people good, however, Aquinas would pioneer the idea of a legitimate kind of freedom from law, that is, where positive law violates God's law, the obligation to obey the civil law ends. The nature of this "freedom" will be our focus in Chapter IV.

D. POSITIVISM, LEGAL ETHICS, AND MORAL REASONING

What does all this mean for legal ethics? As we will see, an individual lawyer's attitude to legal rules, including the disciplinary rules governing the legal profession itself, is central to that lawyer's approach to moral responsibility. Some lawyers see the positive rules as defining the four corners of moral responsibility; they will comply strictly to these rules even when personal, spiritual, or cultural values are jeopardized. These lawyers are true believers in the "positive" legal mentality as representing the democratic and objective legal norms of our society, and they will

---

[12] For a description of such "lawless" social orders, see Margaret Hasluck, *The Albanian Blood Feud, in* LAW AND WARFARE 381–382 (Paul Bohannan ed., 1967); and Robert Nedfield, *Primitive Law, in* LAW AND WARFARE, *supra* at 3–24. *See also* P. H. BLAIR, AN INTRODUCTION TO ANGLO-SAXON ENGLAND 194–244 (1962).

[13] *Materials, infra* at 3G.

[14] *Materials, infra* at 3G.

see spiritual or cultural values as far too "subjective" and "individualistic" to provide reliable guidelines for conduct. Lawyers with a skeptical view of human nature will also put a high premium on enforcement of these positive rules through coercive punishments by boards of bar overseers. Other lawyers see the positive rules as secondary, and even subordinate, to other sources of ethical guidance, such as religious, cultural, or communitarian values. In the following chapters, we will explore more closely the challenges and problems of taking the latter approach, both to the individual lawyer and to society at large.

As you think through the relationship between positive rules and your own responsibility, consider the work of psychologist Lawrence Kohlberg, who developed an influential theory of moral development that provides an interesting link between positivism and individual moral reasoning. Building on the work of Jean Piaget, Kohlberg envisioned three levels and six stages of moral development. For purposes of our discussion, we will rely on a simple description of Kohlberg's theory. Does Kohlberg's theory resonate with you?

Level I: Pre-Conventional/Pre-Moral (egocentric perspective)

Stage 1: The first stage of moral analysis involves deference to those of greater power or prestige, such as a parent or other authority figure. Fixed rules should be obeyed unquestioningly. At this first stage, actors are motivated by a concern for obedience and a desire to avoid punishment.

Stage 2: At the second stage, the actor realizes that different decision makers may have different viewpoints. The actor looks heavily to instrumental justifications that satisfy oneself or sometimes others. The analytical process often looks like a relative comparison of values, with a "naïve egalitarianism" that focuses on exchange and reciprocity. Punishment is seen as a risk to be avoided. Both stages of Level I are categorized as "preconventional" because the actor is analyzing the situation as an individual rather than focusing on family or societal values.

Level II: Conventional/Role Conformity (moral reciprocity)

Stage 3: By stage three, which often emerges as children reach their teens, Kohlberg envisioned that moral values focus on maintaining conventional expectations and order. In stage three, the actor seeks approval of others and has the desire to please, often conforming behavior to expected roles. The actor looks to the intention of the action to determine its moral value.

Stage 4: At stage four, the actor looks more to duty and showing respect for authority or a desire to maintain social order. As a member of society, the actor identifies the social consequences of doing a bad act for good reasons. The actor is looking beyond an egocentric perspective.

Level III: Post-Conventional (reasoning from moral principles)

Stage 5: At stage five, actors consider the theoretical needs of a good society. Actors have a contractual or legalistic orientation, examining right or wrong in terms of rational laws or rules. The social value of law or the value of contract often prevails over the needs of individuals, but concern about morality or rights may justify violating a particular law.

Stage 6: At stage six, the actor focuses not only on existing social rules but also on individual principles of conscience. Moral choice is seen as involving universalities and consistency. Individuals have internalized ideals that exert a pressure to act without regard to the reactions of others.

Kohlberg's approach was criticized by Prof. Carol Gilligan for drawing on studies of boys, which yielded too much focus on a justice and rights analysis.[15] Instead she urged an "ethic of care" as another way to assess moral development. Others argue that we cannot talk about moral reasoning without more fully discussing content (right and wrong).[16] Yet others have critiqued Kohlberg for failing to account more fully for the role of culture in moral reasoning.[17]

Accept for purposes of discussion that Kohlberg's theory offers some insights (albeit raising many questions) into moral reasoning. What stage of moral development do the following individuals exhibit under Kohlberg's scheme? Why do you categorize them in this way?

- A lawyer avoids conflicts because the lawyer does not want to receive professional sanction for violating the Rules of Professional Conduct or be sued by her client.

- A young associate, deeply in debt, finds a damaging document during discovery. When the associate goes to a senior partner to show the document prior to disclosure, the partner tells the associate to "lose it." When the associate expresses concern about that course of action, the partner heaves a big sigh, mutters under her breath about "naïve puppies," and tells the associate that she will take over managing the discovery of documents. Fearful of what might happen, the young associate acquiesces to the partner's request.

At a bare minimum, to even discuss moral reasoning suggests there is something more than positive law that shapes our analysis. Whatever approach you choose will have a profound effect on how you see your moral responsibilities as a lawyer.

E.   FURTHER READING

There are two excellent introductions to Roman legal culture: BARRY NICHOLAS, INTRODUCTION TO ROMAN LAW (1962) and HANS JULIUS WOLFF, ROMAN LAW: AN HISTORICAL INTRODUCTION (1951). *See also* the excellent summary in JOHN P. DAWSON, THE ORACLES OF THE LAW 100–147 (1968). For a view of what it was really like to live in ancient Rome, see JANE F. GARDNER, BEING A ROMAN CITIZEN (1993). Finally there

---

[15] CAROL GILLIGAN, IN A DIFFERENT VOICE: PSYCHOLOGICAL THEORY AND WOMEN'S DEVELOPMENT (1982).

[16] Laurence Thomas, *Morality and Psychological Development, in* A COMPANION TO ETHICS 472 (Peter Singer ed., 1993) ("It seems absolutely ludicrous and thoroughly contrary to common sense to say that a Stage 4 Canadian who embraces the ideals of equality and a Stage 4 member of the Third Reich who embraces the ideals of Nazi ideology are both making equally good progress along the road of moral development.") Kohlberg gave attention to this issue as well. LARRY P. NUCCI, EDUCATION IN THE MORAL DOMAIN xii (foreword by Elliot Turiel).

[17] ELLIOT TURIEL, THE DEVELOPMENT OF SOCIAL KNOWLEDGE: MORALITY & CONVENTION (1983).

is the classic source, H. F. JOLOWICZ, HISTORICAL INTRODUCTION TO THE STUDY OF ROMAN LAW (3d ed. 1972).

There is no substitute for actually reading Roman legal texts and legal arguments, particularly in Latin. There are also many good translations of the *Institutes*, but our favorite is still the INSTITUTES OF JUSTINIAN (Thomas C. Sanders trans., 7th ed. 1883, reprinted 1962). *See also* CICERO, SELECTED WORKS 35–57 (Michael Grant trans., Harmondsworth 1960), for one of Cicero's great legal arguments.

The best introduction to positivism remains H. L. A. HART'S, GREAT THE CONCEPT OF LAW (1994). Far more difficult are JOHN AUSTIN'S ORIGINAL THE PROVINCE OF JURISPRUDENCE DETERMINED (1832), which is still in print, and HANS KELSEN, THE PURE THEORY OF LAW (1934, rev. 1960, 1967). For a most helpful guide, see NEIL MACCORMICK, H. L. A. HART (2d. ed. 2008).

Highly recommended for a view of the entire controversy surrounding positivism are LON C. FULLER, THE MORALITY OF LAW (1969 rev. ed.), particularly pages 95–151, 187–242, ROBERT SUMMERS, LON L. FULLER (1984), and ESSAYS IN LEGAL PHILOSOPHY (Robert S. Summers ed., 1968).

For further reading on Kohlberg's theory of moral development, see LAWRENCE KOHLBERG, FROM IS TO OUGHT: HOW TO COMMIT THE NATURALISTIC FALLACY AND GET AWAY WITH IT IN THE STUDY OF MORAL DEVELOPMENT (1971); Lawrence Kohlberg, *Moral Stages and Moralization: The Cognitive-Developmental Approach, in* MORAL DEVELOPMENT AND BEHAVIOR: THEORY, RESEARCH AND SOCIAL ISSUES (T. Lickona ed., 1976), *available at* http://en.wikipedia.org/wiki/Kohlberg%27s_stages_of_moral_development—cite_ref-moralization_7-9; LAWRENCE KOHLBERG, CHARLES LEVINE, ALEXANDRA HEWER, MORAL STAGES: A CURRENT FORMULATION AND A RESPONSE TO CRITICS (1983).

F. DISCUSSION PROBLEMS

PROBLEM VI

You are sent to negotiate the release of hostages held by rioting prisoners at an Ohio State Prison. The leader of the prisoners, well-read and highly intelligent, begins a serious discussion with you about anarchy and terrorism. Quoting Unger [*Materials, infra* at 3G], the leader states: "Legalism and terrorism, the commitment to rules and the seduction of violence, are rival brothers, but brothers nonetheless." How do you make the case for legal order in the prisons to rioters who reject the system's legal authority? Why should an anarchist go through "proper channels" in registering their grievances about prison conditions with an authority they reject?

If you think this problem is at all far-fetched, see *Talks Go On Over Hostages at Ohio Prison Where 6 Inmates Die*, N.Y. TIMES INT'L, Apr. 13, 1993. In April 1993, roughly 450 prisoners barricaded themselves in the "L Block" of the Southern Ohio Correctional Facility at Lucasville for 11 days during one of the longest and bloodiest prison riots in U.S. History. Before the end of the stalemate, seven prisoners were viciously beaten and killed by fellow inmates, and one guard was strangled to death. Another ten officers and nine inmates were severely injured. The rioters presented public officials with 21 demands related to prison rules and prison conditions, which were considered deplorable by modern standards. After officials agreed to consider these demands, the prisoners surrendered.

Paramedics remove the body of a prison guard held hostage at the Southern Ohio Correctional Facility, 15 April 1993. Eugene Garcia/AFP/Getty Images.

PROBLEM VII

Does a lawyer who complies with the literal mandates of the disciplinary rules act with "moral responsibility"? Consider the disciplinary rule pertaining to client confidences. ABA Model Rule 1.6(a) requires a lawyer to keep her client's secrets, even beyond the client's death. Model Rule 1.6(b) sets forth a number of narrow and limited circumstances in which a lawyer may disclose client confidences.

Imagine a case where several alleged gang members are involved in drug dealing. The police break up a group of men on a street corner one evening, and attempt to arrest them for drug distribution. All of the suspects flee. The police take chase, and suddenly shots are fired. One police officer is critically wounded, and subsequently dies. Your client, among several other suspects, is apprehended with drugs in his possession. He is charged with distribution of narcotics.

Hired to represent your client on drug charges, you interview him about what happened that evening. Your client tells you in confidence that he fired the shot that killed the police officer, and that he subsequently abandoned his pistol in the nearby woods.

The police subsequently find the abandoned firearm, and test it for fingerprints. The only fingerprints on the gun belong to one of your client's associates in the drug ring. Unbeknownst to the police, your client was wearing gloves on the evening in question. The co-defendant is indicted for murder of the police officer. Your client refuses to give you permission to reveal his admission to the authorities or to the lawyer representing the co-defendant. As a result, an innocent person is convicted of first degree murder and sentenced to life in prison.

One year after these tragic events, your client dies in prison while serving a relatively short sentence for drug dealing. Your conscience has been racked with guilt during the intervening period. You see your former client's death as an opportunity to "come clean" and do the right thing. You approach counsel for the murder defendant and reveal to him the nature of your client's confidence. You offer to testify in support of the co-defendant's motion for a new trial.

Model Rule 1.6(b)(1) allows a lawyer to reveal a client confidence if believed necessary "to prevent reasonably certain death or substantial bodily harm." Is life imprisonment for a crime that one did not commit "substantial bodily harm" within the meaning of that rule?[18]

If there is no controlling authority in your state on this precise question, what should you do? If there *is* authority in the state that false imprisonment does *not* constitute "substantial bodily harm," would a morally responsible lawyer nonetheless disclose the deceased client's confidence and risk disbarment? Might a legal positivist argue that a lawyer acts responsibly when he obeys the *letter* of an ethical rule, notwithstanding that an injustice may result in particular circumstances?

For a modern example of this anguish-ridden dilemma, see Maurice Possley, *Inmate's Freedom May Hinge on Secret Kept for 26 Years*, CHI. TRIB., Jan. 19, 2008, at 1.

Consider:

ABA Model Rules of Professional Conduct:

    Preamble and Scope

ABA Model Rule of Professional Conduct 1.6

---

[18] Some state disciplinary rules allow for the disclosure of client confidences to prevent the wrongful incarceration of another person. *See, e.g.*, Massachusetts Rules of Professional Conduct, Rule 1.6(b)(1). Others do not. *See, e.g.*, Illinois Rule of Professional Conduct Rule 1.6(c). *See generally* Colin Miller, *Why There Should Be a Wrongful Incarceration/Execution Exception to Attorney-Client Confidentiality*, 102 NW. U. L. REV. COLLOQUY 391 (2008).

G. MATERIALS

THE INSTITUTES OF JUSTINIAN (533 A.D.), TITLE I, TITLE II, PR.-11 LIBER PRIMUS
(Lib. I) (Thomas Collett Sanelars trans., 1883)

TIT I. DE JUSTITIA ET JURE

Justice is the constant and perpetual wish to render every one his due.

1. Jurisprudence is the knowledge of things divine and human; the science of the just and the unjust.

2. Having explained these general terms, we think we shall commence our exposition of the law of the Roman people most advantageously, if our explanation is at first plain and easy, and is then carried on into details with the utmost care and exactness. For, if at the outset we overload the mind of the student, while yet new to the subject and unable to bear much, with a multitude and variety of topics, one of two things will happen—we shall either cause him wholly to abandon his studies, or, after great toil, and often after great distrust of himself (the most frequent stumbling-block in the way of youth), we shall at least conduct him to the point, to which, if he had been led by a smoother road, he might, without great labour, and without any distrust of his own powers, have been sooner conducted.

3. The maxims of law are these: to live honestly, to hurt no one, to give every one his due.

4. The study of law is divided into two branches: that of public and that of private law. Public law is that which regards the government of the Roman Empire; private law, that which concerns the interests of individuals. We are now to treat of the latter, which is composed of three elements, and consists of precepts belonging to natural law, to the law of nations, and to the civil law.

TIT II. DE JURE NATURALI GENTIUM ET CIVILI

The law of nature is that law which nature teaches to all animals. For this law does not belong exclusively to the human race, but belongs to all animals, whether of the air, the earth, or the sea. Hence comes that yoking together of male and female, which we term matrimony; hence the procreation and bringing up of children. We see, indeed, that all the other animals besides man are considered as having knowledge of this law.

1. Civil law is thus distinguished from the law of nations. Every community governed by laws and customs uses partly its own law, partly laws common to all mankind. The law which a people makes for its own government belongs exclusively to that state, and is called the civil law, as being the law of the particular state. But the law which natural reason appoints for all mankind obtains equally among all nations, and it is called the law of nations, because all nations make use of it. The people of Rome, then, are governed partly by their own laws, and partly by the laws which are common to all mankind. What is the nature of these two

component parts of our law we will set forth in the proper place.

2. Civil law takes its name from the state which it governs, as, for instance, from Athens; for it would be very proper to speak of the laws of Solon or Draco as the civil law of Athens. And thus the law which the Roman people make use of is called the civil law of the Romans, or that of the Quirites, as being used by the Quirites; for the Romans are called Quirites from Quirthus. But whenever we speak of civil law, without adding of what state we are speaking, we mean our own law: just as when 'the poet' is spoken of without any name being expressed, the Greeks mean the great Homer, and we Romans mean Virgil. The law of nations is common to all mankind, for nations have established certain laws, as occasion and the necessities of human life required. Wars arose, and in their train followed captivity and then slavery, which is contrary to the law of nature; for by that law all men are originally born free. Further, from this law of nations almost all contracts were at first introduced, as, for instance, buying and selling, letting and hiring, partnership, deposits, loans returnable in kind, and very many others.

3. Our law is written and unwritten, just as among the Greeks some of their laws were written and others not written. The written part consists of laws, *plebiscite*, *senatus-consulta*, enactments of emperors, edicts of magistrates and answers of jurisprudences.

4. A law is that which was enacted by the Roman people on its being proposed by a senatorian magistrate, as a consul. A *plebiscitum* is that which was enacted by the *plebs* on its being proposed by a plebeian magistrate, as a tribune. The *plebs* differs from the people as a species from its genus; for all the citizens, including patricians and senators, are comprehended in the people; but the plebs only includes citizens, not being patricians or senators. But *plebiscita*, after the Hortensian law had been passed, began to have the same force as laws.

5. A *senatus-consultum* is that which the senate commands and appoints: for, when the Roman people was so increased that it was difficult to assemble it together to pass laws, it seemed right that the senate should be consulted in the place of the people.

6. That which seems good to the emperor has also the force of law; for the people, by the *lex regia* which is passed to confer on him his power, make over to him their whole power and authority. Therefore whatever the emperor ordains by rescript, or decides in adjudging a cause, or lays down by edict, is unquestionably law; and it is these enactments of the emperor that are called constitutions. Of these, some are personal, and are not to be drawn into precedent, such not being the intention of the emperor. Supposing the emperor has granted a favour to any man on account of his merits, or inflicted some punishment, or granted some extraordinary relief, the application of these acts does not extend beyond the particular individual. But the other constitutions, being general, are undoubtedly binding on all.

7. The edicts of the praetors are also of great authority. These edicts are called the *jus honorarium*, because those who bear honours in the state, that is, the magistrates, have given it their sanction. The curule aediles also used to publish an

edict relative to certain subjects, which edict also became part of the *jus honorarium*.

8. The answers of the jurisprudents are the decisions and opinions of persons who were authorized to determine the law. For anciently it was provided that there should be persons to interpret publicly the law, who were permitted by the emperor to give answers on questions of law. They were called jurisconsults; and the authority of their decisions and opinions, when they were all unanimous, was such, that the judge could not, according to the constitutions, refuse to be guided by their answers.

9. The unwritten law is that which usage has established; for ancient customs, being sanctioned by the consent of those who adopt them, are like laws.

10. The civil law is not improperly divided into two kinds, for the division seems to have had its origin in the customs of the two states Athens and Lacedaemon. For in these states it used to be the case, that the Lacedaemonians rather committed to memory what they were to observe as law, while the Athenians rather kept safely what they had found written in their laws.

11. The laws of nature, which all nations observe alike, being established by a divine providence, remain ever fixed and immutable. But the laws which every state has enacted, undergo frequent changes, either by the tacit consent of the people, or by a new law being subsequently passed.

* * *

QUESTIONS

1. What do you think of a text book for law students that begins with a definition of "justice"? Is that a good place to begin? If so, is it accurate to describe justice as "a perpetual wish to render every one his due"?

2. The *Institutes* divides "law" (*ius*) into three divisions: (1) "natural law" (*ius naturale*: "that law which nature teaches to all animals"); (2) the "law of nations" (*ius gentium*: "the law which natural reason appoints for all mankind" and which "obtains equally among all nations"); and (3) the "civil law" (*ius civile*: the law which a people "makes for its own government" and "belongs exclusively to the state"). Do you agree that "law" is the right term for all three forms of "*ius*"? What if a government enacted a "law" which violates a "natural law" or a "law of nations"? Is the "civil law" void? What do you believe the Romans thought?

ROBERTO UNGER, KNOWLEDGE AND POLITICS
64–75 (1975)

* * *

THE UNREFLECTIVE VIEW OF SOCIETY

Recall my description in Chapter One of the mind as a machine. The individual is made up of reason and will. Will directs reason, but does not control the content of knowledge. Society is the plurality of individuals with understanding and desire.

As desiring beings, men are blind creatures of appetite. Nevertheless, with the important qualifications suggested by the antinomy of theory and fact, they are capable of an objective understanding of the world. Different men, each by the use of his own mind, can come ever closer to the same truth about reality. On the other hand, the things men want, and therefore the purposes they make their minds serve, are infinitely diverse.

Amidst this abundance of ends, there are some goals almost everyone pursues. Men want comfort and honor, and avoid the opposite of these. Above all, they try to keep life, for desire wants to be satisfied, not annihilated. Comfort is the satisfaction of material wants by material things. Honor is the satisfaction of the wish to be the object of other men's obedience or admiration. Accordingly, there are two kinds of honor: power and glory.

Power is the capacity to command, to subordinate the wills of others to one's own will. Glory is the winning of admiration, the applause with which one is favored. The tranquil exercise of power, which men call authority, depends either on the acknowledgment of the glory of the powerholder or on the limitation of power by impersonal laws. The laws make possible power without glory. Glory may be a source of power, and power of glory, but not all powerful men are glorious, nor all glorious men powerful. Freedom is the condition in which a person is not under the control of an alien will, or is only under the control of a will limited by impersonal laws in whose making, according to those who are democrats as well as liberals, he must participate. The love of freedom is part of the avoidance of enslavement to another, which is the opposite of power. The weakening of the want of comfort and honor is called holiness when its cause is the love for God and madness when it has a different cause.

A society of individuals who seek to achieve their particular objectives and to satisfy their needs for comfort and honor must be characterized by mutual hostility and mutual dependence. Both hostility and dependence are based on the nature of human ends and on the scarcity of means to satisfy them.

The first source of hostility, given the scarcity of material resources, is the desire for comfort. There are not enough of the goods people want in order to be comfortable. They must therefore scramble. Scrambling is all the more inevitable because men want not just to have, but to have more than their fellows. Only by fighting to get more can they be assured of keeping what they already possess. The reason for this is that the control of things is a tool of power.

Power is the second cause of antagonism in society. The power of some is the powerlessness of others. The more one man's desire for power is satisfied, the more will his fellows' wish for it remain frustrated. The fight for power must be as unceasing as the struggle for things.

Glory too stimulates hostility, for it shines by contrast to insignificance of person. There is not enough time to admire everyone, and then, if everyone were equally famous, fame would lose its meaning. The race for glory is as exacting and brutal as the battle for comfort and power, though it is usually more ceremonious.

The same goals that make men enemies also make them indispensable allies. To satisfy their hunger for comfort, they depend on each other's labor. In a sense, the necessary reliance on other people's work is a consequence of the scarcity of time. No man has enough time to satisfy his desire for material things through his own efforts, for death comes soon. Hence, individuals must find ways to buy and sell one another's time. There must be a labor market and the institution of contract for services.

The control of labor is the most direct form of power, and the wish for power is the second source of cooperation, just as it is the second cause of personal rivalry. By definition, power requires obedience, and obedience, if it is to last, must be given as well as taken. Men cannot foresee what would happen to them in a free-for-all fight for power. But if they collaborate to establish a policy under law, they can be assured that each will have a chance to exercise some modest form of power or, at least, that no one will be completely deprived of freedom.

Finally, human interdependence is a consequence of the general love for glory. Aside from the recognition he gains from his fellows, a person has no coherent self, for his ends do not form a stable system, and the different parts of his being are at war with one another. He is defined by others. Thus, individuals must join together to give one another a self, and, by their mutual admiration, to console as much as possible their fear of death.

Though everyone cannot be admired in the same measure, we can, by establishing a well organized society, make sure that no one need be completely defeated in his wish for glory. By performing social roles according to expectation, men can secure the modicum of approval necessary to lend a semblance of coherence to their persons.

We may insist that in our policy all be entitled to a measure of recognition simply because they are humans. Kant called this kind of recognition respect. Respect and approval for the performance of one's role moderate the hostility the struggle for glory produces in the same way that law tempers the battle for power through its guarantees of freedom. While there are freedom and respect, the loss of power and glory will never be an unmitigated disaster.

The wants of comfort and honor, together with the circumstance of scarcity, which is implied in them, make reciprocal antagonism and reciprocal need the everlasting conditions of society. To promote their interests in hostility and collaboration, men are constantly making alliances by forming groups. But these groups are always precarious. Left to themselves, they would last only as long as the common convenience that brought them into being. The two fundamental problems of politics, order and freedom, are the consequences of the conditions of mutual antagonism and need, and of the drives that underlie those conditions.

The first task of society is to place the restraints on mutual antagonism necessary to satisfy mutual need. The struggle for comfort, power, and glory can be moderated so that everyone may be assured that he will not be threatened by the worst of discomfort, enslavement, and disrespect, or by violent death. But how is the control of hostility to be achieved? This is the problem of order.

As soon as men seek to place limits on their antagonism, they confront a second difficulty. For each person, the good is the satisfaction of his own desires; no other good exists. Freedom, to rephrase the earlier definition, is the power to choose arbitrarily the ends and means of one's striving. In principle, nothing makes one man's goals worthier of success than another's. Yet it seems that whatever restraints are established to ensure order will benefit the purposes of some individuals more than those of their fellows. Any such preference would be arbitrary, in the sense that it could not be justified. How then can order be instituted in such a way that no one's liberty is unjustifiably preferred or downgraded and that everyone has the largest amount of liberty compatible with the absence of such arbitrariness? This is the problem of freedom.

The common solution to the problems of order and freedom is the making and applying of impersonal rules or laws.

The Principle of Rules and Values

The distinction between rules and values, as the two basic elements of social order, is the first principle of liberal political thought. It may be called simply the principle of rules and values. It articulates the conception, embraced by the unreflective view of society, that the eternal hostility of men to one another requires that order and freedom by maintained by government under law.

To explain what is meant by the principle of rules and values and to work out its implications, I begin by defining the concepts of value and of rule. Then I discuss how the relationship between rules and values is conceived. Lastly, I suggest ways in which the idea of a society governed by law ties together several seemingly unrelated aspects of liberal thought.

Value and Rule

Value is the social face of desire. It refers to an end of action or to a want when the emphasis is on relations among persons. In contrast, the term desire is used when the discussion concerns the relation within an individual between the setting of goals and the understanding of facts. End, objective, goal, and will are generic concepts that cover both usages.

The satisfaction of an individual's wants is his good. Assuredly, through lack of understanding, men may fail to appreciate that a single-minded insistence on the pursuit of a particular objective may prejudice the attainment of other goals. Moreover, they may also distinguish between what they think is right or proper and what they want. In this sense, the concept of value is ambiguous as between want or interest and standard or ideal. Nevertheless, as the discussion of liberal psychology has already suggested and the study of liberal political thought will confirm, the second sense of value ultimately collapses into the first. The sole measure of good that remains is the wants of an individual or some combination of the wants of different individuals revealed by the choices they make. The good has no existence outside the will.

The need for rules arises from the undying enmity and the demands of collaboration that mark social life. Because there are no conceptions of the good that stand above the conflict and impose limits on it, artificial limits must be created. Otherwise, the natural hostility men have for one another will run its course relentlessly to the prejudice of their interdependence.

Self-interest, the generalized search for comfort and glory, and any sharing of common values will all be insufficient to keep the peace. It is in the individual's self-interest to benefit from a system of laws established by others but not to obey or establish that system himself. As long as most persons are not robbers, robbery can be a profitable business. Furthermore, though everyone has similar interests in comfort and glory, they are interests that, because of the scarcity of their objects, throw men against one another as much as they bring men together. Finally, every other sharing of values is bound to be both precarious and morally indifferent. It is precarious because the individual will is the true and only seat of value, forever changing direction as the dangers and opportunities of the struggle for comfort and glory shift. The sharing of values is also without ethical significance. We are not entitled to pass from the fact that we happen to agree upon our ends to the claim that someone else ought to agree to them, or at least should do nothing to stop us from attaining them.

Peace must therefore be established by rules. By its significance to society, by its origin, and by its form, a rule differs from a value. A good way to develop the point is to make the concept of rule used in liberal political thought more precise. One can do this by distinguishing different kinds of rule with respect to their uses in social life and then by focusing on the type of rule with which liberal political doctrine is most directly concerned.

Rules are general and they bear on conduct. Beyond this, however, little can be said before we have distinguished three sorts of rules: constitutive, technical or instrumental, and prescriptive.

Constitutive rules define a form of conduct in such a way that the distinction between the rule and the ruled activity disappears. It has been said that the rules of games and the rules of logic are of this sort. The moves of a game and thus the game as a whole are defined by its rules. The laws of identity and contradiction determine a particular mode of discourse.

Technical or instrumental rules are guides for the choice of the most effective means to an end. They take the form, do x if you want y. They simply state a generalization about what means are most likely on the whole to produce the desired result. In any given situation, one may find a more efficient means than the one indicated by the rule.

Prescriptive rules are imperatives that state what some category of persons may do, ought to do, or ought not to do. Accordingly, they are permissions, general commands, and prohibitions. Prescriptive rules differ from constitutive rules because they are clearly distinguishable from the conduct they govern and from instrumental rules because they are not hypothetical.

The rules to which the first principle of liberal political doctrine refers must be prescriptive. The war of men against one another lacks the voluntary or unthinking stability of conduct presupposed by constitutive rules. Moreover, the same antagonism precludes the constant and general agreement about ends that would be necessary for instrumental rules to serve effectively as a basis for the ordering of social relations.

The prescriptive rules established by government are usually called laws. Many laws, to be sure, lend themselves easily to being viewed as instrumental or constitutive rules. Indeed, it is possible to see the whole legal order as either instrumental or constitutive; the implications of these alternative possibilities will be mentioned later. Nevertheless, for the moment it is enough to remember that for a powerful if not dominant strain in liberal political thought laws are above all prescriptive rules.

They place limits on the pursuit of private ends, thereby ensuring and that natural egoism will not turn into a free-for-all in which everyone and everything is endangered. They also facilitate mutual collaboration. The two tasks are connected because a peaceful social order in which we know what to expect from others is a condition for the accomplishment of any of our goals. More specifically, it is the job of the laws to guarantee the supreme goods of social life, order, and freedom.

Positivism and Natural Right

The two basic manners in which the political doctrine of liberalism defines the opposition of rules and values correspond to two ideas about the source of the laws and to two conceptions of how freedom and order may be established. To establish order and freedom the laws must be impersonal. They must embody more than the values of an individual or of a group. Rules whose source is the interest of a single person or class of persons destroy the good of freedom because, by definition, they constitute a dominion of some wills over the wills of others. Furthermore, they leave order without any support except the terror by which it is imposed, for the oppressed will not love the laws.

There are other ways to avoid the dictatorship of private interest. One way is to imagine that public rules are made by a will that stands above the contending private wills and somehow represents them. Hobbes's sovereign monarch and Hegel's bureaucratic class and king exemplify this notion of a political deity. The political deity's circumstances supposedly allow it to understand and to promote the common interest men have in the control of hostility and in the furtherance of collaboration.

According to this view, which one might call in an ample sense positivism or absolutism, the problem of determining *in general* the best way to guarantee coordination and to limit antagonism is insoluble. This may be either because there are no solid standards for choosing the best solution or because the complexity of the task exceeds the powers of the mind. The right laws will therefore be whatever rules are chosen by the sovereign, whose condition allegedly places him beyond the contention of individual wants.

The absolutist view leads to a kind of legislative agnosticism that makes it impossible to define when the laws are impersonal other than by the standard of their origin. Moreover, the sovereign, the government, or the class in whose impartiality the positivist conception trusts are always in danger of sinking into the very battle of private interests from which they claim to escape. Indeed, given the impossibility of rising above individual choice as a measure of the good, this disaster seems unavoidable.

For these reasons, there arises within liberal thought a second family of attempts to define the relationship between rules and values. It consists in trying to formulate standards or procedures that will establish in a general fashion which laws are impersonal and therefore capable of securing order and freedom in society. The more familiar liberal theories of legislation fall into this category.

Among such views, there is one that calls for separate and immediate treatment because of its direct bearing on the relationship between rules and values. It starts from the premise that the circumstances of reciprocal hostility and need, and the universal interest in comfort and glory, carry implications of their own for how society ought to be arranged. Intelligence can spell out the implications and then take them as a basis for impersonal legislation. Thus, the solution to problems of order and freedom preexists the making of the laws and can be used as a standard with which to judge them. It is this preexisting solution that settles the entitlements of individuals; rights precede rules. Here you have the core of the modern theory of natural right, under whose star the liberal state was born.

There is in most statements of the natural rights conception an ambiguity that obscures a fatal dilemma. If we treat the rights as somehow derived from the circumstances of social life, we are forced to explain how evaluative standards can be inferred from facts. If, on the contrary, we present the rights as simply prudent means to achieve agreed-upon ends, like peace and prosperity, we have to explain how we go about judging divergence from these ends and what happens when, in a particular case, the purpose seems to be better served by disrespecting the right. These and other consequences of such an attempt to view the law as a system of instrumental rules are discussed at greater length later on.

Despite their divergence, the positivist and natural right interpretations of the principle of rules and values have in common the insistence that it is on the whole better for men to live under the laws than to be without them. The two doctrines agree that the absence of coercively enforced public rules would deny us the blessings of collaboration and security in the search for comfort and glory. The point can be put in an altogether more inclusive form. Whenever we want something, we must also want not to have it kept away from us or taken away once it is already ours. When we want to carry out a course of action, we must also want not to be stopped by others from executing it.

To will intelligently and consequentially is to will that others respect our objectives. We wish to be entitled to the objects of our choices. Entitlements, however, are possible only when there is a system of general rules that limits the wants of each man in comparison to those of his fellows so that each may be safe in the enjoyment of what is his. In short, will implies the will to be entitled, which in turn implies the acceptance of a system of rules either to distribute or to confirm and enforce the entitlements. With similar arguments, some have even suggested that a legal order is entailed by the concept of a society of men with conflicting values.

At a still more basic level, positivism and natural rights theory may be viewed as expressions in political thought of opposing yet complementary views of the dualism of the universal and the particular. In Chapter One, I pointed out that this dualism is the common ground of the antinomies of theory and fact and of reason and desire. In this chapter, it will reappear as the basis of an antinomy of rules and values.

To the positivist, society has no inherent order of its own. He sees rules as the impositions of a will, even though of an enlightened one, on the chaos of social life. The universal laws are simply conventions which set the boundaries among particular interests so that these interests will not destroy each other.

The natural rights theorists, on the contrary, claims to discover an intrinsic order in social relations, an order it is his purpose to make explicit and to develop. For him the universals that describe this order—rights, rules, and institutional categories—have an existence and a worth quite independent of the particular interests that may take advantage of them. Thus, the natural rights thinker treats the system of private law concepts of contract and property or the doctrine of separation of powers in public law as if they had an autonomous logic that survived in all their transmutations.

Though they differ in the priorities they assign to the universal and the particular, positivism and natural rights doctrine are at one in accepting a radical distinction between universals and particulars and in identifying the former with the abstract and the latter with the concrete. The significance of this assumption for the entire system of liberal thought will gradually become clear.

The Legal Mentality

To explain the principle of rules and values [*sic*] I have defined its constituent terms and suggested how the liberal doctrine conceives their relationship to each other. Now I shall complete my study of the principle by describing some of its links to a more general view of social life.

The society evoked and described by the first postulate of liberal political thought is a society governed by law. Only a system of prescriptive rules with the characteristics of law can resolve the problems of order and freedom. These characteristics are already implicit in the preceding discussion of what prescriptive rules have to be like to satisfy the requirement of impersonality. For liberal political thought, the laws must be general, uniform, public, and capable of coercive enforcement.

Because the laws are general, it is possible to state what sorts of acts are commanded, prohibited, or permitted to categories of persons before specific problems of choice under the laws arise. The generality of the laws makes it possible for them to be impersonal either because they may represent some ideal outcome of conflicting private interests or because they somehow abstract altogether from considerations of private interest.

To be meaningful, generality requires uniformity of application. Some decisions under the rules may be attacked as mistaken, and others defended as correct. Entitlements or rights are interests of individuals protected by uniformly applied laws.

If they are impersonal, the laws must also be public. They are the rules established by a particular institution, the government or the state. The state is viewed either as above the antagonism of private values or as the framework within which those interests are represented and reconciled. Only such an institution can hope to frame laws that do more than embody a factional interest.

Hence, a clear line is drawn between the state and other social groups, and between the laws of the former and the rules of the latter. But the distinction is always breaking down. The government takes on the characteristics of a private body because private interests are the only interests that exist in the situation of which it is a part. Thus, the state is like the gods on Olympus, who were banished from the earth and endowed with superhuman powers, but condemned to undergo the passions of mortals.

Lastly, the laws must on the whole be capable of coercive enforcement. Failure to achieve one's goals has an automatic sanction. In psychology, the sanction is described as discontentment; in political thought, as the loss of comfort and glory. If, however, the laws, by virtue of their very impersonality, fail to live up completely to the interests of any person, obedience to the public rules cannot be spontaneously protected by self-interest. A sufficiently stiff punishment, however, will make it in the interest of all to obey them by outweighing the advantages that might be gained from disobedience.

Generality, uniformity, publicity, and coercion are therefore the distinguishing attributes of impersonal laws. Each of them is connected with a deeper set of presuppositions about thought or society. The relationship of the attributes of law to their assumptions, and of the assumptions to one another, is neither logical nor causal, but is of a kind described later as a relationship of common meaning. These foundations of the idea of law are aspects of the peculiar legal mentality that animates liberal political thought.

Generality is associated with the political ideal of formal equality and with the moral ideal of universalism. Formal equality means that as citizens of the state and legal persons men are viewed and treated by the law as fundamentally equal. Social circumstances must therefore be clearly distinguished from legal-political status. By disregarding or accepting the inequality of the former in order to emphasize all the more intensely the equality of the latter, we commit ourselves to general laws. To equalize men's social circumstances with respect to even a few of the divergences among those circumstances, we would have to treat each man or each group differently and thus to move away from the attribute of generality. The language of formal equality is a language of rights as abstract opportunities to enjoy certain advantages rather than a language of the concrete and actual experience of social life.

The ethical analogue to formal equality is universalism. It is the belief that moral judgment, like political order, is primarily a matter or rights and duties. The rights and duties are established by principles whose formulation becomes more general and therefore more perfect the less their applicability turns on who and where one is. The morality of reason is a classic form of the universalist ethic.

Formal equality and moral universalism both include the conception of universals and particulars encountered before. The legal person or the moral agent are constructed, as abstract and formal universals, out of individual lives, and then treated as if they were real and independent beings. Particular interests, experiences, or circumstances are viewed as a contingent substance of the forms, or as concrete examples of the abstract propositions. Thus, one can define a right independently of the interests an individual may use it to promote.

The basis of uniformity is the formal conception of reason. Reason cannot establish the ends of action, nor does it suffice to determine the concrete implications of general values on which we may happen to agree. That is why rules are so important in the first place. Nevertheless, if the laws are to be uniformly applied, we need a technique of rule application. This technique must rely on the powers that reason possesses because it is a machine for analysis and combination: the capacity to deduce conclusions from premises and the ability to choose efficient means to accept ends. Consequently, the major liberal theories of adjudication view the task of applying law either as one of making deductions from the rules or as one of choosing the best means to advance the ends the rules themselves are designed to foster.

The public character of law has its immediate ground in the distinction between state and society and in the more inclusive dichotomy of public and private life. The state appears in a double light, as the providential alternative to the blindness of private cupidity and as the supreme weapon of some men in their self-interested struggle against others. The separation of the public and the private alternates with the destruction of the latter by the former. In either event, the conflict between the two is never resolved.

The assumption of the belief that the laws must be capable of coercive enforcement is the artificial view of society. According to this view, even though society may have an implicit order, as the natural rights theorist claims, it is not a self-regulating or self-enforcing one. Because individuals and individual interests are the primary elements of social life, and because they are locked in a perpetual struggle with one another, social order must be established by acts of will and protected against the ravages of self-interest.

The ideas that there is no natural community of common ends and that group life is a creature of will help explain the importance of rules and of their coercive enforcements. But the same factors may also account for the fascination of terror, the systematic use of violence unlimited by law, as a device of social organization. The less one's ability to rely on participation in common ends, the greater the importance of force as a bond among individuals. Punishment and fear take the place of community.

Moreover, when they view everything in the social world as a creation of the will, men come to believe there is nothing in society a will sufficiently violent cannot preserve or destroy. Thus, legalism and terrorism, the commitment to rules and the seduction of violence, are rival brothers, but brothers nonetheless.

QUESTIONS

1. Unger states that "the first principle of liberal thought" is "the distinction between rules and values." Why must a "liberal" make such a distinction? He further argues that this first principle "articulates the conception, embraced by the unreflective view of society, that the eternal hostility of men to one another requires that order and freedom be maintained by government under law." Why does he call this an "unreflective view of society"? Is it your view?

2. Unger concludes that "[t]he less one's ability to rely on participation in common ends, the greater the importance of force as a bond between individuals." Is this an argument for or against the legal mentality?

3. Unger notes that the view that "the laws must be capable of coercive enforcement" assumes that "even though society may have an implicit order, as the natural rights theorists claim, it is not a self-regulating or self-enforcing one." He continues, "Because individuals and individual interests are the primary elements of social life, and because they are locked in a perpetual struggle with one another, social order must be established by acts of will and protected against the ravages of self-interest." What do you think of this assumption?

DENNIS LLOYD (DENNIS LLOYD OF HAMPSTEAD, BARON),THE IDEA OF LAW
(1964)

IS LAW NECESSARY?

*   *   *

It may seem strange that at the very outset of our inquiry into the Idea of Law the question should be raised whether law is really necessary at all. In fact, however, this is a question of primary significance which we ought not and indeed cannot take for granted. For it arises out of an uneasy and perplexing doubt not only whether law may be 'expendable' as being unnecessary to the creation of a just society, but also whether law may not perhaps be something positively evil in itself, and therefore a dangerous impediment to the fulfillment of man's social nature. Fantastic though this viewpoint may seem to the members of a well-ordered democratic society—whatever its particular shortcomings or imperfections may be—it is useful to remember that in many less well-regulated societies the operation of law may appear in a more unfavorable guise. Moreover, the feeling that law inherently is or should be necessary for man in a properly ordered society receives little encouragement from the long succession of leading Western philosophers from Plato to Karl Marx who, in one way or another, have lent their support to the rejection of law. Hostility towards law has also played an important part in many of the great religious systems of East and West, and was a crucial element in the ideology of the Christian Church in its formative period. And, apart from Marxists, there are still to be found other serious supporters of a doctrine of anarchism as an answer to man's besetting personal and social problems. Every age—and certainly our own is no exception—produces individuals or groups who feel a general restlessness against all authority and who respond to this feeling by giving vent to various acts or demonstrations against the forces of law and order. No doubt such people are often sincerely motivated by the vague notion that in some mysterious way their demonstrations will lead to a better and happier life for mankind, but such sporadic outbursts have generally had little influence on the main currents of human thought and feeling. We must therefore look deeper than the external manifestations of social restiveness in trying to explore the ideological foundations of dissatisfaction with the very idea of law in order to find out what it is that has urged so many, in civilizations geographically and culturally so far apart, and throughout human history, either to reject law altogether or to regard it at best as a necessary evil suited only to an utterly imperfect state of human society.

Later in this book the role of law as a social phenomenon will engage our attention as well as its function as part of the cement of social control and its relation to a conception of a just society. We shall not here anticipate the discussion of these matters but will concentrate on the lines of thought which have led, on the one hand, to the total rejection of the need for law at all, or, on the other, to the notion that law is an evil thing only to be tolerated as a temporary expedient while man remains unwilling or unable to achieve a just society.

The Nature of Man

When we talk of some idea or concept as being 'ideological' in character, we mean that it forms part of our outlook upon the world, upon the relation of man to the world and to society in all its manifestations. The idea of law certainly partakes of this ideological character so that our view of it will inevitably be coloured by our general thinking about man's place in the world, the view we may adopt of the nature of man, or the 'human condition', as some modern writers prefer to call it, and the aims or purposes which man may be called upon or required to fulfill. When we assert that law either is, or is not necessary to man, we are clearly not just trying to state a simple physical fact, such as that man cannot live without food and drink—we are engaged in a process of evaluation. What we are really saying is that man's nature is such that he can only attain a truly human condition given the existence or non-existence of law. Such a statement contains implicit within it an assumption as to man's goal or purposes, as to what is good for man, and what he needs for the attainment of those objectives.

It is no doubt because of man's perennial and intense preoccupation with such issues that thinkers of all ages and societies have been drawn into the interminable dispute as to the ethical quality or potentiality of man's nature. This dispute may indeed be thought by many today to be not only interminable but also senseless, but whether this is so or not, the position taken up has formed the major premise in leading to the deduction whether, or to what extent, law is necessary for man, and so its importance for this purpose remains undeniable. For those who see in man either the incarnation of evil or at best an amalgam of good and bad impulses constantly in conflict, the bad tending repeatedly to prevail over the good, it seems evident that there are dark and dangerous forces implanted in man's very nature which need to be sternly curbed and which, if not curbed, will lead to the total destruction of that social order in whose absence man's state would be no higher than that of the animals. Law then, in this view, is the indispensable restraint upon the forces of evil, and anarchy of the absence of law the supreme horror to be warded off. On the other hand, those who view man's nature as inherently good seek to find the sources of the ills of man's present condition in situations external to man himself and hence look for some fundamental defect in man's social environment as the true cause of the evils which afflict him. And as the most conspicuous features of this environment are of course the government of the reigning powers and the legal system through which they exert their political authority, it is hardly surprising that criticisms center upon these as the true source of human tribulations.

In an age of social reforms, such as the last hundred years in the West, it might seem that such critics would have better directed their shafts to the reform of the existing law rather than to its total elimination, but on the other hand it must be borne in mind that in many societies the evils of the legal regime must have seemed to the religious or philosophically minded to be inescapable, and that to replace one regime based on legal repression by another could only result in a comparable series of afflictions and oppressions. The only course, therefore, was to condemn legal restraint root and branch.

THE LAW AND THE FORCES OF EVIL

Two very different starting-points were taken by those who looked upon law as a means of attaining social harmony by the curbing of the evil passions of man. On the one hand, some postulated that man's nature was intrinsically evil and that no social progress could be attained without the restraints of penal laws. On the other hand were those who held that man was originally created good by nature but that due to sin, corruption, or some other internal weakness, such as avarice, man's original and true nature had become distorted and thus required for its control the rigors of a punitive system of law. Those who favoured this more optimistic assessment of human failings tended to look backwards to an earlier Golden Age of primeval innocence when men lived simple, happy, and well-ordered lives without the need for any external system of legal rules or coercion to restrain their impulses, which were wholly unselfish and directed to the common good of mankind. Such was the idyllic primitive scene as depicted by many writers from Seneca to Rousseau and even in our own day, and this roseate view of man's remote past has often served as a pattern for a movement towards a return to nature, in the sense of man's primitive, unspoiled nature, and therefore opened up a future prospect of a happier society in which uncorrupted natural impulse will replace a coercive regime of law.

Examples of both these ideological views of man's nature and destiny can be drawn from very widely scattered sources. Only a few need to be mentioned here. In ancient China of the third century B.C. we find, for instance, the important school of so-called 'Legists', who argued that man's nature was initially evil and that the good ways in which men often acted were due to the influence of the social environment, particularly the teaching of rituals and the restraints of penal laws. 'A single law, enforced by severe penalties, is worth more for the maintenance of order than all the words of all the sages,' was one of their governing maxims. About the same period the *shastra* writers in India were asserting that men are by nature passionate and covetous and that if left to themselves the world would resemble a 'devil's workshop', where the 'logic of the fish' would reign, that is, the big ones would eat up all the little ones. Comparable views are not difficult to locate among some of the seminal writers of modern Western Europe. Thus for Bodin the original state of man was one of disorder, force, and violence, and Hobbes's description of the life of primitive man as a state of perpetual warfare, where individual existence was 'brutish, nasty, and short,' has become classical. For Hume, too, without law, government, and coercion, human society could not exist and so in this sense law was a natural necessity for man. Machiavelli based his celebrated advice to princes to disregard their pledges when these conflicted with their own interests on the argument that men 'are naturally bad and will not observe their faith towards you, so you must, in the same way, not observe yours to them.'

The hypothesis of a primitive Golden Age has in one form or another also played an important role in the history of Western ideology. Two of the best-known statements of this hypothesis in classical antiquity are to be found in the pages of Ovid and of Seneca. Ovid, in the first book of his *Metamorphoses* refers to it in these terms:

The Golden Age was first; when Man yet new,
No rule but uncorrupted reason knew;
And with a native bent, did Good pursue.
Unforc'd by punishment, unaw'd by fear.
His words were simple, and his soul sincere:
Needless was written Law, where none opprest;
The Law of Man was written in his breast;
No suppliant crowds before the Judge appeared:
No Court erected yet, nor cause was hear'd;
But all was safe, for Conscience was their guard.

Seneca's celebrated account, as befitted a philosopher, was more circumstantial:

> In this primitive state men lived together in peace and happiness, having all things in common; there was no private property. We may infer that there could have been no slavery, and there was no coercive government. Order there was of the best kind for men followed nature without fail and the best and wisest men were their rulers. They guided and directed men for their good, and were gladly obeyed as they commanded wisely and justly. . . . As time passed, the primitive innocence disappeared; men became avaricious and dissatisfied with the common enjoyment of the good things of the world, and desired to hold them in their private possession. Avarice rent the first happy society asunder . . . and the kingship of the wise gave place to tyranny, so that men had to create laws which should control their rulers.

Although Seneca asserts that this primitive innocence was rather the result of ignorance than of virtue, he attributes the later social evils and the necessity for the introduction of a regime of law to the corruption of human nature from its initial state of innocence, and this corruption he explains as due specifically to the development of the vice of avarice. This idea of vice and corruption as the reason for the establishment of coercive institutions became a key feature of Western thought for many centuries, adapted as it was by the early Church Fathers to the Judeo-Christian version of the Fall of Man. The Biblical account of paradise was equated with Seneca's primitive state of innocence, and the necessity for human law and all its familiar institutions, such as the coercive state, private property, and slavery, was derived from man's sinful nature, which resulted from the Fall. Law was a natural necessity after the Fall to mitigate the evil effects of sin. Even the family treated as a consequence of the Fall, for it represented the coercive domination of the male as against the freedom and equality of the primitive paradise. Slavery, too, was regarded as one of the inevitable consequences of the Fall, for man, though in his uncorrupt state free and equal, as a result of sin was made a fit subject for enslavement, and thus in a corrupt age slavery was a legitimate institution.

This theory of law and government attained its classic restatement in the writings of Augustine. State-law and coercion were not in themselves sinful but were part of the divine order as a means of restraining human vices due to sin. Hence all the established legal institutions and the state powers were legitimate and coercion could properly be used to enforce them. Augustine saw the future hope for mankind, not in the sphere of social reform by promoting a juster social regime on earth, but rather by the attainment of a commonwealth of God's elect, a mystical society, which would ultimately, in God's good time, replace the existing regime dominated by man's sinful nature.

Augustine's assertion that law was a natural necessity to curb man's sinful nature held the field for many centuries. Augustine wrote at a time when the great system of the Roman Empire was on the point of disintegration and there seemed but little prospect of a rise of an orderly, let alone a just, society by mere human dispensation. But gradually life became more settled and provided scope for social and economic advancement. Moreover, by the thirteenth century, some of the more scientific and philosophic reflections of classical antiquity upon man's social condition, especially those of Aristotle, had filtered through to Western Europe. The time was ripe for a change of emphasis. Man's nature might be corrupt and sinful but he still possessed a natural virtue which was capable of development. Leaning heavily upon Aristotle's conception of the natural development of the state from man's social impulses, Aquinas held that the state was not a necessary evil but was a natural foundation in the development of human welfare. Aquinas, as a pillar of orthodoxy of the medieval Catholic Church, strove to reconcile this position with the established theology of his day. Nevertheless, he also provided an important basis for the later secular view of law as at least potentially a beneficent force, not merely for restraining the evil impulses of man but also for setting him upon the path of social harmony and welfare. In this way law came to be envisaged not as a purely negative force, for the restraint of evil, but as a positive instrument for realizing those goals towards which man's good or social impulses tend to direct him.

Is Man Naturally Good? The Anarchist's Viewpoint

We have seen how the attempt to regard law as a natural necessity directed to restraining, in the only way possible, the evil instincts of man gave way to a new view of law as a means of rationalizing and directing the social side of man's nature. Yet in all ages there have been thinkers who have utterly rejected this approach to the coercive forces of law and order. For such thinkers man's nature is and remains basically good, but it is the social environment which is responsible for the evils of man's condition, and above all the existence of a regime of law imposed by force from above.

A mood of wistful primitivism, a nostalgia for a primeval Golden Age, has coloured a good deal of what may be termed anarchist thought from ancient to modern times. Plato, for instance, showed strong leanings towards primitivism as is illustrated by his assertion that "the men of early times were better than we are and nearer to the Gods." Yet this approach tends to be an altogether more sophisticated one, concentrating far less on a mythical past than on man's potentiality in the future for an ideally just society. Moreover, such a society is not to be one with an ideally conceived legal regime but, on the contrary, one free from all legal rules in which rational harmony will prevail as a result of the good sense and social impulses of its members.

An idealist picture of a state without law, whose inner harmony derives from human reason carried to its highest potential of development by a succession of philosopher-kings chosen for their wisdom and knowledge, is presented by Plato in his *Republic*. Plato pins his faith upon a system of education which will not only produce adequate rulers but will also serve to condition the rest of the population to the appropriate state of obedience. Modern experience certainly supports Plato in his belief that education or 'brain-washing' may condition people to subservience but remains divided on the notion that any system of education can provide a royal road to wisdom, or that there is any foolproof manner of selecting or training persons who are naturally preordained for rulership.

It may be said that Plato's leanings were not so much towards anarchism as towards what we should today term 'totalitarianism', as his proposals for an inflexible and rigorously enforced legal system in his late dialogue, *The Laws*, sufficiently demonstrate. Again, though there was unquestionably an anarchic flavour about certain aspects of primitive Christianity this was manifested in a contempt for, rather than a rejection of, human law, and indeed the injunction to render unto Caesar what was Caesar's became accepted as conferring a divine legitimacy on the established powers. At the same time the cult of non-violence appeared to many opponents of the early Christians as a threat to state authority and has afforded a base for the anarchistic doctrines of some influential modern writers, such as Bakunin and Tolstoy.

The modern period from the seventeenth century has been marked by the rise of science and technology and with this has developed the ideology of human progress, a world-view which rejects the belief in a primitive paradise and looks forward to an ever brighter future for mankind. For long this doctrine was wedded to the notion that the social evolution of man could be left to the free play of economic forces which, if not interfered with, could be assumed to work towards ultimate social harmony. This was the theory of *laissez faire*, which, though applied by Adam Smith especially to economic affairs, carried with it the broader doctrine that all government and law were in principle evil in so far as they constricted or distorted the natural development of the economy and of society. Far from being anarchist, however, this theory strongly favoured the use of coercive law for the protection of private property, which it regarded as an indispensable feature of free market.

The nineteenth century represented perhaps the heyday of the more sophisticated anarchist writers, though Godwin's celebrated contribution, *Political Justice*, first appeared in 1793. Godwin argued that the evils of society arose not from man's corrupt or sinful nature but from the detrimental effects of oppressive human institutions. Man is inherently capable of unlimited progress and only coercive institutions and ignorance stand in the way. With touching faith in human reason and perfectibility Godwin held that voluntary cooperation and education would enable all law to be abolished. Such moral and social norms as were required for maintaining social order and progress would be made effective in that their violation would incur the moral censure of the free individuals of which society would consist. This type of philosophic anarchism was further expounded by the leaders of the Russian school of anarchists, Bakunin and Kropotkin, for whom the state, law, coercion, and private property were the enemies of human happiness and welfare. These writers stressed the beneficent role of cooperation in human history and believed that in the inevitable course of evolution the principle of mutual aid would replace the miseries of the coercive community. Tolstoy, on the other hand, propounded a form of anarchy based on his conception of the simple Christian God-inspired life led by the early Christian communities. Many of his enthusiastic supporters attempted to set up 'Tolstoy colonies' on these lines in various parts of the world, but the results were hardly inspiring. In his very sympathetic *Life of Tolstoy*, Aylmer Maude relates some of the strange and comic ways in which these societies speedily collapsed. In one such colony, for instance, a boy stole a waistcoat from a fellow-colonist. This youth had previously been indoctrinated by his companions in the view that private property is wrongful and that the police and the law-courts are part of an immoral regime of coercion. When the return of the waistcoat was demanded, the youth proved to have learned his lessons only too well. If property is wrong, he inquired, why was it more wrong for a boy to have it than a man? He wanted the waistcoat as much as the man did. He was quite willing to discuss the subject but he would not alter his opinion that he was going to keep the waistcoat and that it would be very wrong to take it from him.

Another such colony came to a rather drastic end. The property of the colony was bought in the name of a member who held it for the use of his fellow-members. One day an eccentric individual appeared on the scene and after some discussion with the colonists suddenly rose and made the following announcement. "Gentlemen! I have to inform you that from today your colony will have neither house nor land. You are astonished? Then I will speak more plainly. Your farmhouse, with its outbuildings, gardens, and fields, now belongs to me. I allow you three days to go!" The colonists were thunderstruck but none of them resisted and they all cleared out of the place. Two days later the legal owner presented the property to the local Commune.

A cynic might well chuckle at this vindication of his disbelief in the natural goodness of man, but the outcome of these naive anarchist exercises undoubtedly points to the fundamental dilemma which must face those who believe that human society can function without the external cement of coercive law. As Maude remarks: "Remove the law, and induce men to believe that no fixed code or seat of judgment should exist, and the only people who will be able to get on at all decently will be those who, like the Russian pre-revolutionary peasantry, follow a traditional way of life. . . . The root evil of Tolstoyism is that it disdains and condemns the result of the experience gained by our forefathers, who devised a system which, in spite of the many defects that still hamper it, made it possible for men to cooperate practically and to carry on their diverse occupations with a minimum of friction."

Perhaps the most remarkable of the theses of the modern anarchists, and certainly the most influential, is that of Karl Marx. Marx envisaged the overthrow of the capitalist society by a violent revolution of the oppressed proletariat. Law was nothing but a coercive system devised to maintain the privileges of the property-owning class; by the revolution a classless society would be brought into being, and law and the state would 'wither away' as being no longer needed to support an oppressive regime. The Marxist looks forward rather than backward to a Golden Age when social harmony will be attuned to the natural goodness of man unimpeded by such environmental snares as the institution of private property. Such a social paradise cannot, however, arise overnight and therefore we have the paradox that during an interim period—likely to be of indefinite duration—there is need for a vast increase of state activity supported by all the apparatus of legal coercion so abhorrent to the anarchist. More will be said of the Marxist theory of law later on in this work, but it seems incontestable that the introduction of Marxist socialism has so far entailed more and more law and legal repression rather than its abolition.

Innate Goodness and the Price of Civilization

Despite these discouraging experiences there still remain distinguished exponents of the view that man at the primitive level is innately good and that it is the social and political organization of civilized life which has introduced the seeds of violence and disorder and which in their turn have led to systems of legal coercion. One of the main theses of Elliot Smith's book on *Human History*, first published in 1930, is the innate goodness and peacefulness of mankind. 'The evidence is so definite and abundant that it becomes a problem of psychological interest to discuss why men persist in denying the fact of Man's innate peacefulness. Each of us knows from his own experience that his fellows are, on the whole, kindly and well-intentioned. Most of the friction and discord of our lives are obviously the result of such exasperations and conflicts as civilization itself creates. Envy, malice, and all uncharitableness usually have for the object of their expression some artificial aim, from the pursuit of which Primitive Man is exempt.'

Few will deny that numerous ills from which we suffer are the direct result of the stresses, tensions, and conflicts characteristic of a civilized and therefore complex mode of existence. All the same Elliot Smith's contrast between natural and civilized man seems one-sided and oversimplified. Readers of Mary Shelley's *Frankenstein* will recall how Frankenstein creates a monster in human form, which, though possessed of human feelings, eventually turns upon and slays its creator. The romance seems symbolic of the duality of human nature. Man may well possess innate tendencies towards what we call 'goodness', namely, those relationships which arise out of sympathy and cooperation, for without these all social life—the distinctive character of man—would be impossible. But there is also a dynamic side to human nature, which may be directed to either creative or destructive ends.

The well-meaning philosophic anarchist, even when he is most concerned to give scope to man's creative impulses, is apt to gloss over or ignore the darker side of the nature of man. Sir Herbert Read, for instance, argues that human groups have always spontaneously associated themselves into groups for mutual aid and to satisfy their needs, and so can be relied upon voluntarily to organize a social economy which will ensure the satisfaction of their needs. The anarchist, he tells us conceives, society as a balance or harmony of groups. The only difficulty is their harmonious interrelation. But is not the promotion of such harmony a function which must be conferred on some state organization? Sir Herbert Read's answer is two-fold. In the first place, he believes that this function would largely disappear with the elimination of economic motivation from society. Crime, for example, is largely a reaction to the institution of private property. And secondly, matters such as infant education and public morality are matters of common sense, to be solved by reference to the innate good will of the community. With the universal decentralization of authority and the simplification of life, including the disappear-ance of 'inhuman entities' like the modern city, any disputes can be resolved on a local basis. "Local associations may form their courts and these courts are sufficient to administer a common law based on common sense." It will be noted that Read differs from some anarchists in recognizing the need for some kind of general law and insists only on rejecting all the coercive apparatus of centralized control. "Anarchism," he explains, "means literally a society without an *arkhos*, that is to say without a ruler. It does not mean a society without law and therefore it does not mean a society without order. The anarchist accepts the social contract, but he interprets that contract in a particular way, which he believes to be the way most justified by reason."

The recognition that even in the simplest form of society some system of rules is necessary seems almost inevitable. In any society, whether primitive or complex, it will be necessary to have rules which lay down the conditions under which men and women may mate and live together; rules governing family relationships; conditions under which economic and food-gathering or hunting activities are to be organized; and the exclusion of acts which are regarded as inimical to the welfare of the family, or of larger groups such as the tribe or the whole community. Moreover, in a complex civilized community, even if simplified to the degree dear to the heart of an anarchist like Read, there will have still to be a large apparatus of rules governing family, social, and economic life. The idea that human society, on whatever level, could ever conceivably exist on the basis that each man should simply do whatever he thinks right in the particular circumstances is too fanciful to deserve serious consideration. Such a society would not be merely, as Read puts it, "a society without order," but the very negation of society itself.

At this point then, the discussion can move over from the necessity of law in human society to the closely related question: whether the idea of law can be divorced from a regime of coercion.

QUESTIONS

1. Lloyd observes that a "long succession of leading Western philosophers from Plato to Karl Marx . . . in one way or another have lent their support to the rejection of law." Why is that?

2. St. Augustine, observing the decline of the Roman Empire, concluded that, in Lloyd's words, "law was a natural necessity to curb man's sinful nature." But suppose you believe that human beings are inherently good? And what about Sir Herbert Read's point that *arkhos* means "to live without a ruler," not to live "without law"? Can an anarchist legitimately argue that a society that has a non-coercive system of rules is superior to one which must use force? Or is this just "wistful primitivism, a nostalgia for a primeval Golden Age"? *Materials, supra* at 3G.

Chapter IV

THE MORAL CONSTRAINTS ON RULE MAKING

In the last three chapters, we have been concerned with whether it is possible to distinguish good from evil. In this chapter and the two that follow, we turn our attention to the connection between law and morality. Is there a higher source of moral authority than the civil law? If so, how can it be discerned? Is a law that contravenes such authority a "valid" law? How should a person striving to do what is morally right behave when confronted with a law that may have been properly enacted and promulgated, but that will result in an injustice in its particular application to specific circumstances?

A. THE JUDEO-CHRISTIAN TRADITION AND ST. THOMAS AQUINAS (1225-1274 A.D.)

The collapse of Roman civilization left intact two great religious traditions, Judaism and Christianity. The two were closely interrelated. Many primary elements of Christian ethics, including the sacred history of the creation, the notion of the salvation of a chosen people and the idea of "righteousness" itself, were directly derived from Judaism. The close relationship of Jewish settlements after the Dispersion with both Greek and Arabic communities led to important intellectual exchanges, particularly in Moorish Spain, long after vicious anti-Semitism in Europe excluded Jews from a directly active role in Christian education and culture.[1] The work of Maimonides of Cordoba (1135-1204 A.D.) and other Jewish scholars helped to preserve knowledge of Greek and Arabic texts, including the texts of Aristotle.[2]

The powerful monastic orders of Europe also preserved Roman, Greek, and Hebrew texts, and the greatest symbol of their learning was doubtless the Dominican, St. Thomas Aquinas (1225-1274 A.D.). St. Thomas was thoroughly familiar with the texts of Aristotle, and studied extensively at the University of Paris, one of the oldest of the great medieval universities. For most of his life, however, he worked in Dominican communities in Italy, where he had access to many Greek texts.

St. Thomas's principal work, at least for jurisprudence, was the *Summa Theologica*, written between 1265 and 1273 A.D. In this great work, St. Thomas developed his own extensions of Aristotle's ethical philosophy, and created a decidedly new synthesis of Greek philosophy, Roman legalism, and Judeo-Christian

---

[1] *See* ALASDAIR MacINTYRE, A SHORT HISTORY OF ETHICS 110–120 (1998).

[2] BERTRAND RUSSELL, A HISTORY OF WESTERN PHILOSOPHY 323 (2007). *See* translation of MAIMONIDES'S *Logic* and other texts in MEDIEVAL POLITICAL PHILOSOPHY 188–270 (Ralph Lerner & Muhsin Mahdi eds., 1963).

spiritualism. The durability of St. Thomas's work was so extraordinary that it became the underpinning of the official philosophy of the Roman Catholic Church; even today, Thomism and Neo-Thomism are the leading schools of natural law jurisprudence.[3]

St. Thomas's ethical philosophy is predicated on the existence of God and, indeed, his other great work *Summa contra Gentiles* (1259-1265 A.D.) contains a careful proof of God's existence and goodness. God has a will, and "divine law" directs us to obey that will, even though humans, and even priests, have the capacity to be wicked and refuse to obey. Failure to recognize and obey divine law is sin. By contrast, a sincere effort to ascertain, appreciate, and comply with God's will leads to human flourishing and happiness.

According to St. Thomas, the task of "considering and determining the ultimate end of life and human affairs" is the principal *"practical science,"* called by Aristotle "ethics" and by himself "moral philosophy."[4] It is "practical" because it leads to "realizing or getting intrinsically desirable human good(s)."[5] Put roughly, leading a life of moral virtue, in accordance with God's will, leads to human good in very immediate, concrete ways, "not simply as a vision of truth, nor even simply as a participation in holiness and grace, but as a participation by a plurality of persons in a plurality of goods . . . 'a kingdom of truth and life, holiness and grace, justice, love and peace.' "[6]

It is the very practicality and optimism of St. Thomas that has made his work so durable. This also certainly extends to his views on law. Reproduced in this book are his famous *Question 96* and *Of the Power of Human Law*. St. Thomas actually asks six questions:

Should human law be laid down as a general command?
Should it restrain all the vices?
Is it competent to order the acts of all the virtues?
Does it bind a man in conscience?
Are all men subject to human law?
May its subjects lawfully act against the letter of the law?[7]

Note how each question is argued on both sides. This is the style of the medieval disputation. The last question is particularly crucial. May a citizen legitimately disobey a positive law? St. Thomas already had said "yes," if "they [the laws] are contrary to Divine good; such are the laws of tyrants which promote idolatry."[8] But the actor needs to be cautious, as an orderly, law abiding government is inherently

---

[3] *See* JOHN FINNIS, NATURAL LAW AND NATURAL RIGHTS (1980) and John Finnis, *Practical Reasoning, Human Goods and the End of Man, in* PROCEEDINGS OF THE AMERICAN CATHOLIC PHILOSOPHIC ASSOCIATION 23–36 (1984).

[4] THOMAS AQUINAS, COMMENTARY ON ARISTOTLE'S NICOMACHEAN ETHICS, Lecture I § 2 (C. I. Litzinger ed., 1983).

[5] Finnis, *Practical Reasoning, Human Goods and the End of Man, supra*, at 24.

[6] *Id.* at 33.

[7] Citing here the Blackfriars translation, THOMAS AQUINAS, SUMMA THEOLOGICA, I—II q. 96, art. 4 (1966). Compare with *Materials, infra* at 4E.

[8] AQUINAS, SUMMA THEOLOGICA, *supra*, art. 4. Compare with *Materials, infra* at 4E.

good. If burdens are "inequitably dispensed" or against the common good, then, "these are outrages rather than laws. . . . Such commands do not oblige in the court of conscience."[9] Likewise, "every law is ordained for the common well-being, and to that extent gets the force and quality of law; in so far as it falls short here it has no binding force."[10] But, again, St. Thomas is cautious not to encourage disrespect for the legal order in most cases.

> Now it happens often that the observance of some point of law conduces to the common weal in the majority of instances, and yet, in some cases, is very hurtful. Since then the lawgiver cannot have in view every single case, he shapes the law according to what happens most frequently, by directing his attention to the common good. Wherefore if a case arise wherein the observance of that law would be hurtful to the general welfare, it should not be observed. For instance, suppose that in a besieged city it be an established law that the gates of the city are to be kept closed, this is good for public welfare as a general rule: but, if it were to happen that the enemy are in pursuit of certain citizens, who are defenders of the city, it would be a great loss to the city, if the gates were not opened to them: and so in that case the gates ought to be opened, contrary to the letter of the law, in order to maintain the common weal, which the lawgiver had in view.
>
> Nevertheless it must be noted, that if the observance of the law according to the letter does not involve any sudden risk needing instant remedy, it is not competent for everyone to expound what is useful and what is not useful to the state: those alone can do this who are in authority, and who, on account of suchlike cases, have the power to dispense from the laws. If, however, the peril be so sudden as not to allow of the delay involved by referring the matter to authority, the mere necessity brings with it a dispensation, since necessity knows no law.[11]

St. Thomas's careful definition of when disobedience of the letter of the law is permitted, or required, is always set against the presumptive good of being law-abiding. In general, God's will is to obey the positive law, except where to do so is to violate God's own laws, or to reduce the law to something the law giver did not actually intend. The former idea, of course, ultimately supports religious civil disobedience—but only in clear cases. The latter idea is the basis of what we today call "equity," but, again, it should only occur when there is no doubt as to intention.[12] The "benefit of the doubt" in St. Thomas's work is with the positive law. On this basis, the Church and secular authority can in general peacefully coexist, as is still very much the case today.

---

[9] Aquinas, Summa Theologica, *supra*, art. 4.

[10] Aquinas, Summa Theologica, *supra*, at 139.

[11] Aquinas, Summa Theologica, *supra*, at 139. *Materials, infra* at 4E.

[12] *See* D. R. Coquillette, *Equity Before 1530, in* Dictionary of the Middle Ages (1989).

B. PERSONAL VALUES AND THE LAW

St. Thomas's *Question 96* and its six articles were one of the earliest and most lucid guides in the Judeo-Christian tradition on "civil disobedience"; that is, when it is permissible, or required, to disobey a law. It remains one of the most influential today. But is it consistent with your own values and religious beliefs?

To begin, St. Thomas's "jurisprudence" is God-centered. Once one accepts the proofs of God contained in the *Summa contra Gentiles*, it is easy to see God's will as a limitation on secular law. But for the most part, we in the United States do not live in a God-centered legal order, and the First Amendment prohibits establishment of a state religion. Further, God's will appears differently to different religious groups, and even to different individuals. The Davidians of Waco, Texas believed they were doing God's will, but secular power was ruthlessly inflicted on them. To persuade such a diverse and secular society as our own to accept belief-based religious limitations on secular law is easier said than done. Thus, those whose personal values conflict with positive law have turned to more "rationalist" arguments, even when their motivations are religious. We will discuss the non-religious arguments for inherent limitations on positive law in the next chapter.

Certain jurists have argued strongly that confusing personal values and law is bad philosophy and bad jurisprudence. Perhaps the most famous of these is H. L. A. Hart (1907-1992). In his famous *The Concept of Law* (2d ed. 1994), Hart argued the essential "positivist" thesis "that it is in no sense a necessary truth that laws reproduce or satisfy certain demands of morality, though in fact they have often done so."[13] Hart continued:

> There are many types of relation between law and morals and there is nothing which can be profitably singled out for study as *the* relation between them. Instead it is important to distinguish some of the many different things which may be meant by the assertion or denial that law and morals are related. Sometimes what is asserted is a kind of connexion which few if any have ever denied; but its indisputable existence may be wrongly accepted as a sign of some more doubtful connexion, or even mistaken for it. Thus, it cannot seriously be disputed that the development of law, at all times and places, has in fact been profoundly influenced both by the conventional morality and ideals of particular social groups, and also by forms of enlightened moral criticism urged by individuals, whose moral horizon has transcended the morality currently accepted. But it is possible to take this truth illicitly, as a warrant for a different proposition: namely that a legal system *must* exhibit some specific conformity with morality or justice, or *must* rest on a widely diffused conviction that there is a moral obligation to obey it. Again, though this proposition may, in some sense, be true, it does not follow from it that the criteria of legal validity of particular laws used in a legal system must include, tacitly if not explicitly, a reference to morality or justice.

---

[13] *Materials, infra* at 4E.

During his lifetime, Hart was a stalwart defender of personal liberty. He opposed all efforts to regulate, in the name of "morality," acts between consenting adults that had no adverse effects on non-consenting third parties. This led him to be a pioneer against laws punishing homosexuality and inhibiting freedom of the press.

But "positivism" is easier in theory than in practice. Lon Fuller (1902-1978), a cordial but long-time critic of Hart, delighted in setting up intellectual puzzles that illustrated the weaknesses of "pure" positivism and also attempted to limit positivism through belief in natural law. One of the most famous of these puzzles, "The Problem of the Grudge Informer" is set out in this chapter. At first reading, the puzzle may seem diabolically clever, but far-fetched. On reflection, however, it becomes clear that this situation has regularly occurred, in different forms, throughout history. For example, in the late 20th century, a newly united Germany was forced to grapple with what to do with the past members of the infamous East German *Stasi* and their web of informers.[14]

In the next chapter, we will work through a second famous puzzle by Lon Fuller, "The Case of the Speluncean Explorers." In analyzing both Fuller puzzles, try to identify and define the legal philosophy of each of the participants. In "The Problem of the Grudge Informer," Fuller challenges us to select among the conflicting recommendations of five Deputy Ministers of Justice. Define the jurisprudence of each of the Deputies and test their assumptions before you choose. Do you think that Fuller is being totally fair in the way he sets up his puzzle, or does he have his own secret ax to grind? Your answers may predict a great deal about your own legal philosophy, and what kind of a lawyer you are or are likely to become.

Fuller's famous "puzzles," of course, are an effort to teach by getting students to define more closely their own values, without the instructor/author disclosing his or her own. Does Fuller succeed in this endeavor? This book is trying to do somewhat the same thing. The closer you scrutinize and challenge your own values, the more resilient they may become. This truth has been recognized by people as diverse as St. Thomas More, a famous doubter in his time, and Admiral Stockdale, who found philosophical self-examination to be among the best defenses to brainwashing techniques during his eight years as a prisoner in Vietnam. *See* Robert F. Drinan, S.J., *Renaissance Lawyer, Renaissance Man*, 99 HARV. L. REV. 499, 499–507 (1985) (reviewing RICHARD MARIUS, THOMAS MORE: A BIOGRAPHY (1985)); James Bond Stockdale, *The World of Epictetus: Reflections on Survival and Leadership*, THE ATLANTIC MONTHLY, Apr. 1978, at 98–106; JAMES BOND STOCKDALE, COURAGE UNDER FIRE: TESTING EPICTETUS'S DOCTRINES IN A LABORATORY OF HUMAN BEHAVIOR (1993).

C.   FURTHER READING

For a good general summary of the influence of the Judeo-Christian tradition on ethical philosophy, see ALASDAIR MACINTYRE, A SHORT HISTORY OF ETHICS 110–120 (1998) and J. M. KELLY, A SHORT HISTORY OF WESTERN LEGAL THEORY 79–158 (1992). There is also a good summary of St. Thomas Aquinas's legal philosophy in HUNTINGTON CAIRNS, LEGAL PHILOSOPHY FROM PLATO TO HEGEL 163–204 (1949). For an

---

[14] *See, e.g.*, Stephen Kinzes, *Germany's New Custodian of Stasi Secrets Insists on Justice*, N.Y. TIMES INT'L, Jan. 20, 1991, at 12.

in-depth analysis of the legal and ethical philosophy of St. Thomas Aquinas, see the classic work by ETIENNE GILSON, THE PHILOSOPHY OF ST. THOMAS AQUINAS (*LE THOMISME*) (1st ed. 1924, 2d ed. English trans. Edward Bullough, 1929).

The leading modern proponent of a Natural Law philosophy that is God-centered is John Finnis. His book NATURAL LAW AND NATURAL RIGHTS (1980), is a great classic and demonstrates a sophisticated continuation of the spirit of St. Thomas. *See also* JOHN FINNIS, FUNDAMENTALS OF ETHICS (1983).

For invaluable insights on H. L. A. Hart and Lon L. Fuller, see NEIL MACCORMICK, H. L. A. HART (2d ed. 2008) and ROBERT S. SUMMERS, LON L. FULLER (1984).

For those interested in reading more about the challenges of teaching values in law school, the starting point is Roger C. Cramton's provocative *The Ordinary Religion of the Law School Classroom*, 29 J. LEGAL EDUC. 247, 250 (1978). The subject of the impact of an instructor's ideology on students was also explored at the 1993 Dan K. Moore Program on Ethics at the University of North Carolina, and papers by Katharine Bartlett, Paul Haskell, John Conley, and Daniel Coquillette are published in 72 N.C. L. REV. 1249–1277 (1994).

D. DISCUSSION PROBLEMS

PROBLEM VIII

Prepare Fuller's "The Problem of the Grudge Informer." *Materials, infra* at 4E. Be ready to argue the position of any of the five Deputies. As Minister of Justice, what would your final decision be? Defend your views.

PROBLEM IX

The "Netherlands Government in London" (NGL) purported to be the legitimate Dutch government during the Nazi occupation of Holland during World War II. The government-in-exile also purported to pass statutes binding on all Dutch subjects—statutes often contradictory to those of the Nazi occupation government. Were these statutes "law"? Should Dutch subjects who broke these "laws" be punished after the war? Would it make any difference if copies of these NGL statutes were sprinkled from NGL planes over the occupied country? What if one NGL statute forbade compliance with the Nazi laws designed to exterminate Jews?

Consider:

ABA Model Rule of Professional Conduct 1.2(b)

E.   MATERIALS

THE SUMMA THEOLOGICA OF ST. THOMAS AQUINAS
Part II (First Part) [Prima Secundae (Circa 1265-1272 A.D.)

Translated by Fathers of the English Dominican Province
(2d ed., London, 1927) Third Number (qq. XC.—CXIV.)

QUESTION XCVI.
OF THE POWER OF HUMAN LAW.
(IN SIX ARTICLES.)

We must now consider the power of human law. Under this head there are six points of inquiry: (1) Whether human law should be framed for the community? (2) Whether human law should repress all vices? (3) Whether human law is competent to direct all acts of virtue? (4) Whether it binds man in conscience? (5) Whether all men are subject to human law? (6) Whether those who are under the law may act beside the letter of the law?

FIRST ARTICLE.

WHETHER HUMAN LAW SHOULD BE
FRAMED FOR THE COMMUNITY
RATHER THAN FOR THE
INDIVIDUAL?

We proceed thus to the First Article:—

Objection 1. It would seem that human law should be framed not for the community, but rather for the individual. For the Philosopher says (*Ethic.* v. 7) that *the legal just . . . includes all particular acts of legislation . . . and all those matters which are the subject of decrees*, which are also individual matters, since decrees are framed about individual actions. Therefore law is framed not only for the community, but also for the individual.

Obj. 2. Further, law is the director of human acts, as stated above (Q. XC., AA. 1, 2). But human acts are about individual matters. Therefore human laws should be framed, not for the community, but rather for the individual.

Obj. 3. Further, law is a rule and measure of human acts, as stated above (Q. XC., AA. 1, 2). But a measure should be most certain, as stated in *Metaph.* X. Since therefore in human acts no general proposition can be so certain as not to fail in some individual cases, it seems that laws should be framed not in general but for individual cases.

On the contrary, The jurist says (*Pandect. Justin,* lib.1., tit. iii., art. ii., *De legibus,* etc.) that *laws should be made to suit the majority of instances; and they are not framed according to what may possibly happen in an individual case.*

I answer that, Whatever is for an end should be proportionate to that end. Now the end of law is the common good; because, as Isidore says (*Etym.* v. 21) that *law should be framed, not for any private benefit, but for the common good of all citizens.* Hence human laws should be proportionate to the common good. Now the common good comprises many things. Wherefore law should take account of many things, as to persons, as to matters, and as to times. Because the community of the state is composed of many persons; and its good is procured by many actions; nor is it established to endure for only a short time, but to last for all time by the citizens succeeding one another, as Augustine says (*De Civ. Dei* 21; xxii., 6).

Reply Obj. 1. The Philosopher (*Ethic.* v. 7) divides the legal just, i.e., positive law, into three parts. For some things are laid down simply in a general way: and these are the general laws. Of these he says that *the legal is that which originally was a matter of indifference, but which, when enacted, is so no longer:* as the fixing of the ransom of a captive.—Some things affect the community in one respect, and individuals in another. These are called *privileges, i.e., private laws,* as it were, because they regard private persons, although their power extends to many matters; and in regard to these, he adds, *and further, all particular acts of legislation.*—Other matters are legal, not through being laws, but through being applications of general laws to particular cases: such are decrees which have the force of law, and in regard to these, he adds *all matters subject to decrees.*

Reply Obj. 2. A principle of direction should be applicable to many; wherefore (*Metaph.* x., text 4) the Philosopher says that all things belonging to one genus, are measured by one, which is the principle in that genus. For if there were as many rules or measures as there are things measured or ruled, they would cease to be of use, since their use consists in being applicable to many things. Hence law would be of no use, if it did not extend further than to one single act. Because the decrees of prudent men are made for the purpose of directing individual actions; whereas law is a general precept, as stated above (Q. XCII., A.2, Obj. 2).

Reply Obj. 3. *We must not seek the same degree of certainty in all things* (*Ethic.* i. 3). Consequently in contingent matters, such as natural and human things, it is enough for a thing to be certain, as being true in the greater number of instances, though at times and less frequently it fail.

SECOND ARTICLE.

WHETHER IT BELONGS TO HUMAN LAW TO REPRESS ALL VICES?

We proceed thus to the Second Article:—

Objection 1. It would seem that it belongs to human law to repress all vices. For Isidore says (*Etym.* v. 20) that *laws were made in order that, in fear thereof, man's audacity might be held in check.* But it would not be held in check sufficiently, unless all evils were repressed by law. Therefore human law should repress all evils.

Obj. 2. Further, the intention of the lawgiver is to make the citizens virtuous. But a man cannot be virtuous unless he forbear from all kinds of vice. Therefore it belongs to human law to repress all vices.

Obj. 3. Further, human law is derived from the natural law, as stated above (Q. XCV., A. 2). But all vices are contrary to the law of nature. Therefore human law should repress all vices.

On the contrary, We read in *De Lib. Arb.* i 5: *It seems to me that the law which is written for the governing of the people rightly permits these things, and that Divine providence punishes them.* But Divine providence punishes nothing but vices. Therefore human law rightly allows some vices, by not repressing them.

I answer that, As stated above (Q.XC., AA. 1, 2), law is framed as a rule or measure of human acts. Now a measure should be homogenous with that which it measures, as stated in *Metaph.* x., text. 3, 4, since different things are measured by different measures. Wherefore laws imposed on men should also be in keeping with their condition, for, as Isidore says (*Etym.* v. 21), law should be *possible both according to nature, and according to the customs of the country.* Now possibility or faculty of action is due to an interior habit or disposition: since the same thing is not possible to one who has not a virtuous habit, as is possible to one who has. Thus the same is not possible to a child as to a full-grown man: for which reason the law for children is not the same as for adults, since many things are permitted to children, which in an adult are punished by law or at any rate are open to blame. In like manner many things are permissible to men not perfect in virtue, which would be intolerable in a virtuous man.

Now human law is framed for a number of human beings, the majority of whom are not perfect in virtue. Wherefore human laws do not forbid all vices, from which the virtuous abstain, but only the more grievous vices, from which it is possible for the majority to abstain; and chiefly those that are to the hurt of others, without the prohibition of which human society could not be maintained: thus human law prohibits murder, theft and suchlike.

Reply Obj. 1. Audacity seems to refer to the assailing of others. Consequently it belongs to those sins chiefly whereby one's neighbor is injured: and these sins are forbidden by human law, as stated.

Reply Obj. 2. The purpose of human law is to lead men to virtue, not suddenly, but gradually. Wherefore it does not lay upon the multitude of imperfect men the burdens of those who are already virtuous, viz., that they should abstain from all evil. Otherwise these imperfect ones, being unable to bear such precepts, would break out into yet greater evils: thus it is written (Prov. xxx. 33): *He that violently bloweth his nose, bringeth out blood*; and (Matth. ix. 17) that if *new wine,* i.e., precepts of a perfect life, is *put into old bottles,* i.e., into imperfect men, *the bottles break, and the wine runneth out,* i.e., the precepts are despised, and those men, from contempt, break out into evils worse still.

Reply Obj. 3. The natural law is a participation in us of the eternal law: while human law falls short of the eternal law. Now Augustine says (De Lib. Arb. i. 5): *The law which is framed for the government of states, allows and leaves unpunished many things that are punished by Divine providence. Nor, if this law does not attempt to do everything, is this a reason why it should be blamed for what it does.* Wherefore, too, human law does not prohibit everything that is forbidden by the natural law.

THIRD ARTICLE.

WHETHER HUMAN LAW PRESCRIBES ACTS OF ALL THE VIRTUES?

We proceed thus to the Third Article:—

Objection 1: It would seem that human law does not prescribe acts of all the virtues. For vicious acts are contrary to acts of virtue. But human law does not prohibit all vices, as stated above (A.2). Therefore neither does it prescribe all acts of virtue.

Obj. 2. Further, a virtuous act proceeds from a virtue. But virtue is the end of law; so that whatever is from a virtue, cannot come under a precept of law. Therefore human law does not prescribe all acts of virtue.

Obj. 3. Further, law is ordained to the common good, as stated above (Q. XC., A. 2). But some acts of virtue are ordained, not to the common good, but to private good. Therefore the law does not prescribe all acts of virtue.

On the contrary, The Philosopher says (*Ethic.* v. 1) that the law *prescribes the performance of the acts of a brave man, . . . and the acts of the temperate man, . . . and the acts of the meek man: and in like manner as regards the other virtues and vices, prescribing the former, forbidding the latter.*

I answer that, The species of virtues are distinguished by their objects, as explained above (Q. LIV., A. 2; Q. LX., A. 1; Q. LXII., A. 2). Now all the objects of virtues can be referred either to the private good of an individual, or to the common good of the multitude: thus matters of fortitude may be achieved either for the safety of the state, or for upholding the rights of a friend, and in like manner with the other virtues. But law, as stated above (Q. XC., A. 2) is ordained to the common good. Wherefore there is no virtue whose acts cannot be prescribed by the law. Nevertheless human law does not prescribe concerning all the acts of every virtue: but only in regard to those that are ordainable to the common good,—either immediately, as when certain things are done directly for the common good,—or mediately, as when a lawgiver prescribes certain things pertaining to good order, whereby the citizens are directed in the upholding of the common good of justice and peace.

Reply Obj. 1. Human law does not forbid all vicious acts, by the obligation of a precept, as neither does it prescribe all acts of virtue. But it forbids certain acts of each vice, just as it prescribes some acts of each virtue.

Reply Obj. 2. An act is said to be an act of virtue in two ways. First, from the fact that a man does something virtuous; thus the act of justice is to do what is right, and an act of fortitude is to do brave things: and in this way law prescribes certain acts of virtue.—Secondly an act of virtue is when a man does a virtuous thing in a way in which a virtuous man does it. Such an act always proceeds from virtue: and it does not come under a precept of law, but is the end at which every lawgiver aims.

Reply Obj. 3. There is no virtue whose act is not ordainable to the common good, as stated above, either mediately or immediately.

FOURTH ARTICLE.

WHETHER HUMAN LAW BINDS A MAN IN CONSCIENCE?

We proceed thus to the Fourth Article:—

Objection 1. It would seem that human law does not bind a man in conscience. For an inferior power has no jurisdiction in a court of higher power. But the power of man, which frames human law, is beneath the Divine power. Therefore human law cannot impose its precept in a Divine court, such as is the court of conscience.

Obj. 2. Further, the judgment of conscience depends chiefly on the commandments of God. But sometimes God's commandments are made void by human laws, according to Matth. xv. 6: *You have made void the commandment of God for your tradition.* Therefore human law does not bind a man in conscience.

Obj. 3. Further, human laws often bring loss of character and injury on man, according to Isa. x. 1 *et seq.*: *Woe to them that make wicked laws, and when they write injustice; to oppress the poor in judgment, and do violence to the cause of the humble of My people.* But it is lawful for anyone to avoid oppression and violence. Therefore human laws do not bind man in conscience.

On the contrary, It is written (1 Pet. ii. 19): *This is thanks-worthy, if for conscience . . . a man endure sorrows, suffering wrongfully.*

I answer that, Laws framed by man are either just or unjust. If they be just, they have the power of binding in conscience, from the eternal law whence they are derived, according to Prov. viii. 15: *By Me kings reign, and lawgivers decree just things.* Now laws are said to be just, both from the end, when, to wit, they are ordained to the common good,—and from their author, that is to say, when the law that is made does not exceed the power of the lawgiver,—and from their form, when, to wit, burdens are laid on the subjects, according to an equity of proportion and with a view to the common good. For, since one man is a part of the community, each man, in all that he is and has, belongs to the community; just as a part, in all that it is, belongs to the whole; wherefore nature inflicts a loss on the part, in order to save the whole: so that on this account, such laws as these, which impose proportionate burdens, are just and binding in conscience, and are legal laws.

On the other hand laws may be unjust in two ways: first, by being contrary to human good, through being opposed to the things mentioned above:—either in respect of the end, as when an authority imposes on his subjects burdensome laws, conducive, not to the common good, but rather to his own cupidity or vainglory;—or in respect of the author, as when a man makes a law that goes beyond the power committed to him;—or in respect of the form, as when burdens are imposed unequally on the community, although with a view to the common good. The like are acts of violence rather than laws; because, as Augustine says (*De Lib. Arb.* i. 5), *a law that is not just, seems to be no law at all.* Wherefore such laws do not bind in conscience, except perhaps in order to avoid scandal or disturbance, for which cause a man should even yield his right, according to Matth. v. 40, 41: *If a man . . . take away thy coat, let go thy cloak also unto him; and whosoever will force thee one mile, go with him other two.*

Secondly, laws may be unjust through being opposed to the Divine good: such are the laws of tyrants inducing to idolatry, or to anything else contrary to the Divine law: and laws of this kind must nowise be observed, because, as stated in Acts v. 29, *we ought to obey God rather than men.*

Reply Obj. 1. As the Apostle says (Rom. xiii. 1, 2), all human power is from God . . . *therefore he that resisteth the power*, in matters that are within its scope, *resisteth the ordinance of God*; so that he becomes guilty according to his conscience.

Reply Obj. 2. This argument is true of laws that are contrary to the commandments of God, which is beyond the scope of (human) power. Wherefore in such matters human law should not be obeyed.

Reply Obj. 3. This argument is true of a law that inflicts unjust hurt on its subjects. The power that man holds from God does not extend to this: wherefore neither in such matters is man bound to obey the law, provided he avoid giving scandal or inflicting a more grievous hurt.

FIFTH ARTICLE.

WHETHER ALL ARE SUBJECT TO THE LAW?

We proceed thus to the Fifth Article:—

Objection 1. It would seem that not all are subject to the law. For those alone are subject to a law for whom a law is made. But the Apostle says (1 Tim. i. 9): *The law is not made for the just man.* Therefore the just are not subject to the law.

Obj. 2. Further, Pope Urban says[15] *he that is guided by a private law need not for any reason be bound by the public law.* Now all spiritual men are led by the private law of the Holy Ghost, for they are the sons of God, of whom it is said (Rom. viii. 14): *Whosoever are led by the Spirit of God, they are the sons of God.* Therefore not all men are subject to human law.

Obj. 3. Further, the jurist says[16] that *the sovereign is exempt from the laws.* But he that is exempt from the law is not bound thereby. Therefore not all are subject to the law.

---

[15] *Decret.* Caus. Xix., qu. 2.

[16] Pandect. Justin. i. ff., tit. 3, *De Leg. Et Senat.*

On the contrary, The Apostle says (Rom. xiii. 1): *Let every soul be subject to the higher powers*. But subjection to a power seems to imply subjection to the laws framed by that power. Therefore all men should be subject to human law.

I answer that, As stated above (Q. XC., AA. 1, 2; A. 3 *ad2*), the notion of law contains two things; first, that it is a rule of human acts; secondly, that it has coercive power. Wherefore a man may be subject to law in two ways. First, as the regulated is subject to the regulator: and, in this way, whoever is subject to a power, is subject to the law framed by that power. But it may happen in two ways that one is not subject to a power. In one way, by being altogether free from its authority: hence the subjects of one city or kingdom are not bound by the laws of the sovereign of another city or kingdom, since they are not subject to his authority. In another way, by being under a yet higher law; thus the subject of a proconsul should be ruled by his command, but not in those matters in which the subject receives his orders from the emperor: for in these matters, he is not bound by the mandate of the lower authority, since he is directed by that of a higher. In this way, one who is simply subject to a law, may not be subject thereto in certain matters, in respect of which he is ruled by a higher law.

Secondly, a man is said to be subject to a law as the coerced is subject to the coercer. In this way the virtuous and righteous are not subject to the law, but only the wicked. Because coercion and violence are contrary to the will: but the will of the good is in harmony with the law, whereas the will of the wicked is discordant from it. Wherefore in this sense the good are not subject to the law, but only the wicked.

Reply Obj. 1. This argument is true of subjection by way of coercion: for, in this way, *the law is not made for the just men*: because *they are a law to themselves*, since they *shew the work of the law written in their hearts*, as the Apostle says (Rom. ii. 14, 15). Consequently the law does not enforce itself upon them as it does on the wicked.

Reply Obj. 2. The law of the Holy Ghost is above all law framed by man: and therefore spiritual men, insofar as they are led by the law of the Holy Ghost, are not subject to the law in those matters that are inconsistent with the guidance of the Holy Ghost. Nevertheless the very fact that spiritual men are subject to law, is due to the leading of the Holy Ghost, according to 1 Pet. ii. 13: *Be ye subject . . . to every human creature for God's sake.*

Reply Obj. 3. The sovereign is said to be *exempt from the law*, as to its coercive power; since, properly speaking, no man is coerced by himself, and law has no coercive power save from the authority of the sovereign. Thus then is the sovereign said to be exempt from the law, because none is competent to pass sentence on him, if he acts against the law. Wherefore on Ps. L. 6: *To Thee only have I sinned*, a gloss says that *there is no man who can judge the deeds of a king*—But as to the directive force of law, the sovereign is subject to the law by his own will, according to the statement (*Extra, De Constit.* cap. *Cum omnes*) that *whatever law a man makes for another, he should keep himself* And a wise authority[17] says: 'Obey the law that thow makest thyself.' Moreover the Lord reproaches those who *say and do*

---

[17] Dionysius Cato, *Dist. de Moribus.*

not; and who *bind heavy burdens and lay them on men's shoulders, but with a finger of their own they tat not move them* (Matth. alit. 3, 4). Hence, in the judgment of God, the sovereign is not exempt from the law, as to its directive force; but he should fulfil it of his own free-will and not of constraint.—Again the sovereign is above the law, insofar as, when it is expedient, he can change the law, and dispense in it according to time and place.

SIXTH ARTICLE.

WHETHER HE WHO IS UNDER A LAW MAY ACT BESIDE THE LETTER OF THE LAW?

We proceed thus to the Sixth Article:—

Objection 1. It seems that he who is subject to a law may not act beside the letter of the law. For Augustine says (*De Vera Relig.* xxxi.): *Although man judge about temporal laws when they make them, yet when once they are made they must pass judgment not on them, but according to them.* But if anyone disregard the letter of the law, saying that he observes the intention of the lawgiver, he seems to pass judgment on the law. Therefore it is not right for one who is under a law to disregard the letter of the law, in order to observe the intention of the lawgiver.

Obj. 2. Further, he alone is competent to interpret the law who can make the law. But those who are subject to the law cannot make the law. Therefore they have no right to interpret the intention of the lawgiver, but should always act according to the letter of the law.

Obj. 3. Further, every wise man knows how to explain his intention by words. But those who framed the laws should be reckoned wise: for Wisdom says (Prov. viii. 15): *By Me kings reign, and lawgivers decree just things.* Therefore we should not judge of the intention of the lawgiver otherwise than by the words of the law.

On the contrary, Hilary says (*De Trin.* iv.): *The meaning of what is said is according to the motive for saying it: because things are not subject to speech, but speech to things.* Therefore we should take account of the motive of the lawgiver, rather than to his very words.

I answer that, As stated above (A.4), every law is directed to the common weal of men, and derives the force and nature of law accordingly. Hence the jurist says: *By no reason of law, or favour of equity, is it allowable for us to interpret harshly, and render burdensome, those useful measures which have been enacted for the welfare of man.*[18] Now it happens often that the observance of some point of law conduces to the common weal in the majority of instances, and yet, in some cases, is very hurtful. Since then the lawgiver cannot have in view every single case, he shapes the law according to what happens most frequently, by directing his attention to the common good. Wherefore if a case arise wherein the observance of that law would be hurtful to the general welfare, it should not be observed. For

---

[18] *Pandect* Justin. lib. i. ff. tit. 3. *De Leg. et Senat.*

instance, suppose that in a besieged city it be an established law that the gates of the city are to be kept closed, this is good for public welfare as a general rule: but, if it were to happen that the enemy are in pursuit of certain citizens, who are defenders of the city, it would be a great loss to the city, if the gates were not opened to them: and so in that case the gates ought to be opened, contrary to the letter of the law, in order to maintain the common weal, which the lawgiver had in view.

Nevertheless it must be noted, that if the observance of the law according to the letter does not involve any sudden risk needing instant remedy, it is not competent for everyone to expound what is useful and what is not useful to the state: those alone can do this who are in authority, and who, on account of suchlike cases, have the power to dispense from the laws. If, however, the peril be so sudden as not to allow of the delay involved by referring the matter to authority, the mere necessity brings with it a dispensation, since necessity knows no law.

Reply Obj. 1. He who in a case of necessity acts beside the letter of the law, does not judge of the law; but of a particular case in which he sees that the letter of the law is not to be observed.

Reply Obj. 2. He who follows the intention of the lawgiver, does not interpret the law simply; but in a case in which it is evident, by reason of the manifest harm, that the lawgiver intended otherwise. For if it be a matter of doubt, he must either act according to the letter of the law, or consult those in power.

Reply Obj. 3. No man is so wise as to be able to take account of every single case; wherefore he is not able sufficiently to express in words all those things that are suitable for the end he has in view. And even if a lawgiver were able to take all the cases into consideration, he ought not to mention them all, in order to avoid confusion: but should frame the law according to that which is of most common occurrence.

QUESTIONS

1.   St. Thomas observed that "Laws framed by man are either just or unjust. If they be just, they have the power of binding in conscience, from the eternal law whence they are derived, according to Proverbs viii. 15: *By Me kings reign, and lawgivers decree just things.*" (Fourth Article). Does this mean we should all feel morally obliged to obey just law, quite apart from any chance of coercion or punishment? If so, would it not be of great importance to law compliance that the positive law in general reflect religious and moral truth? And, if this is so, should not lawmakers seriously consider the religious and moral culture of the governed in promulgating positive law? Lord Devlin, for example, argued that without the support of religious and moral beliefs, positive law would be unenforceable in practice, and that Christianity, therefore, is central to English law. Patrick Devlin, The Enforcement of Morals 10 (1965). What do you think of this argument?

2.   St. Thomas, by arguing that the just, positive law maker has divine sanction, places the Church firmly behind a good, positive legal order. Further, he suggests that, when in doubt, the governed should defer to the wisdom of authority of the lawgiver. Does this view "co-opt" religion and conscience to the benefit of secular

power? Or, does it make St. Thomas's arguments as to when one should *not* obey positive law all the more potent? (Incidentally, St. Thomas would probably ask you to obey parking laws as a matter of conscience, even when there was no chance of a ticket.)

H. L. A. HART, THE CONCEPT OF LAW
(2d ed. 1994)

LAWS AND MORALS

1. Natural Law and Legal Positivism

There are many different types of relation between law and morals and there is nothing which can be profitably singled out for study as *the* relation between them. Instead it is important to distinguish some of the many different things which may be meant by the assertion or denial that law and morals are related. Sometimes what is asserted is a kind of connection which few if any have ever denied; but its indisputable existence maybe wrongly accepted as a sign of some more doubtful connection, or even mistaken for it. Thus, it cannot seriously be disputed that the development of law, at all times and places, has in fact been profoundly influenced both by the conventional morality and ideals of particular social groups, and also by forms of enlightened moral criticism urged by individuals, whose moral horizon has transcended the morality currently accepted. But it is possible to take this truth illicitly, as a warrant for a different proposition: namely that a legal system *must* exhibit some specific conformity with morality or justice, or *must* rest on a widely diffused conviction that there is a moral obligation to obey it. Again, though this proposition may, in some sense, be true, it does not follow from it that the criteria of legal validity of particular laws used in a legal system include, tacitly if not explicitly, a reference to morality or justice.

Many other questions besides these may be said to concern the relations between law and morals. In this chapter we shall discuss only two of them, though both will involve some consideration of many others. The first is a question which may still be illuminatingly described as the issue between Natural Law and Legal Positivism, though each of these titles has come to be used for a range of different theses about law and morals. Here we shall take Legal Positivism to mean the simple contention that it is in no sense a necessary truth that laws reproduce or satisfy certain demands of morality, though in fact they have often done so. But just because those who have taken this view have either been silent or differed very much concerning the nature of morality, it is necessary to consider two very different forms in which Legal Positivism has been rejected. One of these is expressed most clearly in the classical theories of Natural Law: that there are certain principles of human conduct, awaiting discovery by human reason, with which man-made law must conform if it is to be valid. The other takes a different, less rationalist view of morality, and offers a different account of the ways in which legal validity is connected with moral value. We shall consider the first of these in this section and the next.

In the vast literature from Plato to the present day which is dedicated to the assertion, and also to the denial, of the proposition that the ways in which men ought to behave may be discovered by human reason, the disputants on one side seem to say to those on the other, 'You are blind if you cannot see this' only to receive in reply, 'You have been dreaming.' This is so, because the claim that there are true principles of right conduct, rationally discoverable, has not usually been advanced as a separate doctrine but was originally presented, and for long defended, as part of a general conception of nature, inanimate and living. This outlook is, in many ways, antithetic to the general conception of nature which constitutes the framework of modern secular thought. Hence it is that, to its critics, Natural Law theory has seemed to spring from deep and old confusions from which modern thought has triumphantly freed itself; while to its advocates, the critics appear merely to insist on surface trivialities, ignoring profounder truths.

Thus many modern critics have thought that the claim that laws of proper conduct may be discovered by human reason rested on a simple ambiguity of the word 'law,' and that when this ambiguity was exposed Natural Law received its death-blow. It is in this way that John Stuart Mill dealt with Montesquieu, who in the first chapter of the *Esprit des Lois* naively inquires why it is that, while inanimate things such as the stars and also animals obey 'the law of their nature,' man does not do so but falls into sin. This, Mill thought, revealed the perennial confusion between laws which formulate the course or regularities of nature, and laws which require men to behave in certain ways. The former, which can be discovered by observation and reasoning, may be called 'descriptive' and it is for the scientist thus to discover them; the latter cannot be so established, for they are not statements or descriptions of facts, but are 'prescriptions' or demands that men shall behave in certain ways. The answer therefore to Montesquieu's question is simple: prescriptive laws may be broken and yet remain laws, because that merely means that human beings do not do what they are told to do; but it is meaningless to say of the laws of nature, discovered by science, either that they can or cannot be broken. If the stars behave in ways contrary to the scientific laws which purport to describe their regular movements, these are not broken but they lose their title to be called 'laws' and must be reformulated. To these differences in the sense of 'law,' there correspond systematic differences in the associated vocabulary of words like 'must,' 'bound to,' 'ought,' and 'should.' So, on this view, belief in Natural Law is reducible to a very simple fallacy: a failure to perceive the very different senses which those law-impregnated words can bear. It is as if the believer had failed to perceive the very different meaning of such words in 'You are bound to report for military service' and 'It is bound to freeze if the wind goes round to the north.'

Critics like Bentham and Mill, who most fiercely attacked Natural Law, often attributed their opponents' confusion between these distinct senses of law, to the survival of the belief that the observed regularities of nature were prescribed or decreed by a Divine Governor of the Universe. On such a theocratic view, the only difference between the law of gravity and the Ten Commandments—God's law for Man—was, as Blackstone asserted, the relatively minor one that men, alone of created things, were endowed with reason and free will; and so unlike things, could discover and disobey the divine prescriptions. Natural Law has, however, not always been associated with belief in a Divine Governor or Lawgiver of the universe, and even where it has been, its characteristic tenets have not been logically dependent on that belief. Both the relevant sense of the word 'natural', which enters into Natural Law, and its general outlook minimizing the difference, so obvious and so important to modern minds, between prescriptive and descriptive laws, have their roots in Greek thought which was, for this purpose, quite secular. Indeed, the continued reassertion of some form of Natural Law doctrine is due in part to the fact that its appeal is independent of both divine and human authority, and to the fact that despite a terminology, and much metaphysics, which few could now accept, it contains certain elementary truths of importance for the understanding of both morality and law. These we shall endeavor to disentangle from their metaphysical setting and restate here in simpler terms.

*   *   *

2. The Minimum Content of Natural Law

In considering the simple truisms which we set forth here, and their connexion with law and morals, it is important to observe that in each case the facts mentioned afford a *reason* why, given survival as an aim, law and morals should include a specific content. The general form of the argument is simply that without such a content laws and morals could not forward the minimum purpose of survival which men have in associating with each other. In the absence of this content men, as they are, would have no reason for obeying voluntarily any rules; and without a minimum of co-operation given voluntarily by those who find that it is in their interest to submit to and maintain the rules, coercion of others who would not voluntarily conform would be impossible. It is important to stress the distinctively rational connexion between natural facts and the content of legal and moral rules in this approach, because it is both possible and important to inquire into quite different forms of connexion between natural facts and legal or moral rules. Thus, the still young sciences of psychology and sociology may discover or may even have discovered that, unless certain physical, psychological, or economic conditions are satisfied, e.g. unless young children are fed and nurtured in certain ways within the family, no system of laws or code of morals can be established, or that only those laws can function successfully which conform to a certain type. Connexions of this sort between natural conditions and systems of rules are not mediated by reasons; for they do not relate the existence of certain rules to the conscious aims or purpose of those whose rules they are. Being fed in infancy in a certain way may well be shown to be a necessary condition or even a *cause* of a population developing or maintaining a moral or legal code, but it is not a *reason* for their doing so. Such causal connexions do not of course conflict with the connexions which rest on purposes or conscious aims; they may indeed be considered more important or fundamental than the latter, since they may actually explain why human beings have those conscious aims or purposes which Natural Law takes as its starting-points. Causal explanations of this type do not rest on truisms nor are they mediated by conscious aims or purposes: they are for sociology or psychology like other sciences to establish by the methods of generalization and theory, resting on observation and, where possible, on experiment. Such connexions therefore are of a different kind from those which relate the content of certain legal and moral rules to the facts stated in the following truisms.

(i) Human vulnerability. The common requirements of law and morality consist for the most part not of active services to be rendered but of forbearances, which are usually formulated in negative form as prohibitions. Of these the most important for social life are those that restrict the use of violence in killing or inflicting bodily harm. The basic character of such rules may be brought out in a question: If there were not these rules what point could there be for beings such as ourselves in having rules of *any* other kind? The force of this rhetorical question rests on the fact that men are both occasionally prone to, and normally vulnerable to, bodily attack. Yet though this is a truism it is not a necessary truth; for things might have been, and might one day be, otherwise. There are species of animals whose physical structure (including exoskeletons or a carapace) renders them virtually immune from attack by other members of their species and animals who have no organs enabling them to attack. If men were to lose their vulnerability to each other there would vanish one obvious reason for the most characteristic provision of law and morals: *Thou shalt not kill.*

(ii) Approximate equality. Men differ from each other in physical strength, agility, and even more in intellectual capacity. Nonetheless it is a fact of quite major importance for the understanding of different forms of law and morality, that no individual is so much more powerful than others, that he is able, without co-operation, to dominate or subdue them for more than a short period. Even the strongest must sleep at times and, when asleep, loses temporarily his superiority. This fact of approximate equality, more than any other, makes obvious the necessity for a system of mutual forbearance and compromise which is the base of both legal and moral obligation. Social life with its rules requiring such forbearances is irksome at times; but it is at any rate less nasty, less brutish, and less short than unrestrained aggression for beings thus approximately equal. It is, of course, entirely consistent with this and an equal truism that when such a system of forbearance is established there will always be some who will wish to exploit it, by simultaneously living within its shelter and breaking its restrictions. This, indeed is, as we later show, one of the natural facts which makes the step from merely moral to organized, legal forms of control a necessary one. Again, things might have been otherwise. Instead of being approximately equal there might have been some men immensely stronger than others and better able to dispense with rest, either because some were in these ways far above the present average, or because most were far below it. Such exceptional men might have much to gain by aggression and little to gain from mutual forbearance or compromise with others. But we need not have recourse to the fantasy of giants among pygmies to see the cardinal importance of the fact of approximate equality: for it is illustrated better by the facts of international life, where there are (or were) vast disparities in strength and vulnerability between the states. This inequality, as we shall later see, between the units of international law is one of the things that has imparted to it a character so different from municipal law and limited the extent to which it is capable of operating as an organized coercive system.

(iii) Limited altruism. Men are not devils dominated by a wish to exterminate each other, and the demonstration that, given only the modest aim of survival, the basic rules of law and morals are necessities, must not be identified with the false view that men are predominantly selfish and have no disinterested interest in the

survival and welfare of their fellows. But if men are not devils, neither are they angels; and the fact that they are a mean between these two extremes is something which makes a system of mutual forbearances both necessary and possible. With angels, never tempted to harm others, rules requiring forbearances would not be necessary. With devils prepared to destroy, reckless of the cost to themselves, they would be impossible. As things are, human altruism is limited in range and intermittent, and the tendencies to aggression are frequent enough to be fatal to social life if not controlled.

(iv) Limited resources. It is a merely contingent fact that human beings need food, clothes, and shelter; that these do not exist at hand in limitless abundance; but are scarce, have to be grown or won from nature, or have to be constructed by human toil. These facts alone make indispensable some minimal form of the institution of property (though not necessarily individual property), and the distinctive kind of rule which requires respect for it. The simplest forms of property are to be seen in rules excluding persons generally other than the 'owner' from entry on, or the use of land, or from taking or using material things. If crops are to grow, land must be secure from indiscriminate entry, and food must, in the intervals between its growth or capture and consumption, be secure from being taken by others. At all times and places life itself depends on these minimal forbearances. Again, in this respect, things might have been otherwise than they are. The human organism might have been constructed like plants, capable of extracting food from air, or what it needs might have grown without cultivation in limitless abundance.

The rules which we have so far discussed are static rules, in the sense that the obligations they impose and the incidence of these obligations are not variable by individuals. But the division of labour, which all but the smallest groups must develop to obtain adequate supplies, brings with it the need for rules which are dynamic in the sense that they enable individuals to create obligations and to vary their incidence. Among these are rules enabling men to transfer, exchange, or sell their products; for those transactions involve the capacity to alter the incidence of those initial rights and obligations which define the simplest form of property. The same inescapable division of labour, and perennial need for co-operation, are also factors which make other forms of dynamic or obligation-creating rule necessary in social life. These secure the recognition of promises as a source of obligation. By this device individuals are enabled by words, spoken or written, to make themselves liable to blame or punishment for failure to act in certain stipulated ways. Where altruism is not unlimited, a standing procedure providing for such self-binding operations is required in order to create a minimum form of confidence in the future behavior of others, and to ensure the predictability necessary for co-operation. This is most obviously needed where what is to be exchanged or jointly planned are mutual services, or wherever goods which are to be exchanged or sold are not simultaneously or immediately *available*.

(v) Limited understanding and strength of will. The facts that make rules respecting persons, property, and promises necessary in social life are simple and their mutual benefits are obvious. Most men are capable of seeing them and of sacrificing the immediate short-term interests which conformity to such rules demands. They may indeed obey, from a variety of motives: some from prudential calculation that the sacrifices are worth the gains, some from a disinterested

interest in the welfare of others, and some because they look upon the rules as worthy of respect in themselves and find their ideals in devotion to them. On the other hand, neither understanding of long-term interest, nor the strength or goodness of will, upon which the efficacy of these different motives towards obedience depends, are shared by all men alike. All are tempted at times to prefer their own immediate interests and, in the absence of a special organization for their detection and punishment, many would succumb to the temptation. No doubt the advantages of mutual forbearance are so palpable that the number and strength of those who would co-operate voluntarily in a coercive system will normally be greater than any likely combination of malefactors. Yet, except in very small closely-knit societies, submission to the system of restraints would be folly if there were no organization for the coercion of those who would then try to obtain the advantages of the system without submitting to its obligations. 'Sanctions' are therefore required not as the normal motive for obedience, but as a guarantee that those who would voluntarily obey shall not be sacrificed to those who would not. To obey, without this, would be to risk going to the wall. Given this standing danger, what reason demands is *voluntary* co-operation in a *coercive* system.

It is to be observed that the same natural fact of approximate equality between men is of crucial importance in the efficacy of organized sanctions. If some men were vastly more powerful than others, and so not dependent on their forbearance, the strength of the malefactors might exceed that of the supporters of law and order. Given such inequalities, the use of sanctions could not be successful and would involve dangers at least as great as those which they were designed to suppress. In these circumstances instead of social life being based on a system of mutual forebearances, with force used only intermittently against a minority of malefactors, the only viable system would be one in which the weak submitted to the strong on the best terms they could make and lived under their 'protection.' This, because of the scarcity of resources, would lead to a number of conflicting power centres, each grouped round its 'strong man': these might intermittently war with each other, though the natural sanction, never negligible, of the risk of defeat might ensure an uneasy peace. Rules of a sort might then be accepted for the regulation of issues over which the 'powers' were unwilling to fight. Again we need not think in fanciful terms of pygmies and giants in order to understand the simple logistics of approximate equality and its importance for law. The international scene, where the units concerned have differed vastly in strength, affords illustration enough. For centuries the disparities between states have resulted in a system where organized sanctions have been impossible, and law has been confined to matters which did not affect 'vital' issues. How far atomic weapons, when available to all, will redress the balance of unequal power, and bring forms of control more closely resembling municipal criminal law, remains to be seen.

The simple truism we have discussed not only disclose the core of good sense in the doctrine of Natural Law. They are of vital importance for the understanding of law and morals, and they explain why the definition of the basic forms of these in purely formal terms, without reference to any specific content or social needs, has proved so inadequate. Perhaps the major benefit to jurisprudence from this outlook is the escape it affords from certain misleading dichotomies which often obscure the discussion of the characteristics of law. Thus, for example, the traditional question whether every legal system must provide for sanctions can be presented in a fresh and clearer light, when we command the view of things presented by this simple version of Natural Law. We shall no longer have to choose between two unsuitable alternatives which are often taken as exhaustive: on the one hand that of saying that this is required by 'the' meaning of the words 'law' or 'legal system,' and on the other that of saying that it is 'just a fact' that most legal systems do provide for sanctions. Neither of these alternatives is satisfactory. There are no settled principles forbidding the use of the word 'law' of systems where there are no centrally organized sanctions, and there is good reason (though no compulsion) for using the expression 'international law' of a system, which has none. On the other hand we do need to distinguish the place that sanctions must have within a municipal system, if it is to serve the minimum purposes of being constituted as men are. We can say, given the setting of natural facts and aims, which make sanctions both possible and necessary in a municipal system, that this is a *natural necessity*; and some such phrase is needed also to convey the status of the minimum forms of protection for persons, property, and promises which are similarly indispensable features of municipal law. It is in this form that we should reply to the positivist thesis that 'law may have any content'. For it is a truth of some importance that for the adequate description not only of law but of many other social institutions, a place must be reserved, besides definitions and ordinary statements of fact, for a third category of statements: those the truth of which is contingent on human beings and the world they live in retaining the salient characteristics which they have.

3. Legal Validity and Moral Value

The protections and benefits provided by the system of mutual forbearances which underlies both law and morals may, in different societies, be extended to very different ranges of persons. It is true that the denial of these elementary protections to any class of human beings, willing to accept the corresponding restrictions, would offend the principles of morality and justice to which all modern states pay, at any rate, lip service. Their professed moral outlook is, in general, permeated by the conception that in these fundamentals at least, human beings are entitled to be treated alike and that differences of treatment require more to justify them than just an appeal to the interests of others.

Yet it is plain that neither the law nor the accepted morality of societies need extend their minimal protections and benefits to all within their scope, and often they have not done so. In slave-owning societies the sense that the slaves are human beings, not mere objects to be used, may be lost by the dominant group, who may yet remain morally most sensitive to each other's claims and interests. Huckleberry Finn, when asked if the exposition of a steamboat boiler had hurt anyone, replied, 'No'm: killed a nigger.' Aunt Sally's comment 'Well it's lucky because sometimes people do get hurt' sums up a whole morality which has often prevailed among men. Where it does prevail, as Huck found to his cost, to extend to slaves the concern for others which is natural between members of the dominant group may well be looked on as a grave moral offense, bringing with it all the sequelae of moral guilt. Nazi Germany and South Africa offer parallels unpleasantly near to us in time.

Though the law of some societies has occasionally been in advance of the accepted morality, normally law follows morality and even the homicide of a slave may be regarded only as a waste of public resources or as an offence against the master whose property he is. Even where slavery is not officially recognized, discriminations on grounds of race, colour, or creed may produce a legal system and a social morality which does not recognize that all men are entitled to a minimum of protection from others.

These painful facts of human history are enough to show that, though a society to be viable must offer *some* of its members a system of mutual forbearances, it need not, unfortunately, offer them to all. It is true, as we have already emphasized in discussing the need for and the possibility of sanctions, that if a system of rules is to be imposed by force on any, there must be a sufficient number who accept it voluntarily. Without their voluntary co-operation, thus creating *authority*, the coercive power of law and government cannot be established. But coercive power, thus established on its basis of authority, may be used in two principal ways. It may be exerted only against malefactors who, though they are afforded the protection of the rules, yet selfishly break them. On the other hand, it may be used to subdue and maintain, in a position of permanent inferiority, a subject group whose size, relatively to the master group, may be large or small, depending on the means of coercion, solidarity, and discipline available to the latter, and the helplessness or inability to organize of the former. For those thus oppressed there may be nothing in the system to command their loyalty but only things to fear. They are its victims, not its beneficiaries.

In the earlier chapters of this book we stressed the fact that the existence of a legal system is a social phenomenon which always presents two aspects, to both of which we must attend if our view of it is to be realistic. It involved the attitudes and behaviour involved in the voluntary acceptance of rules and also the simpler attitudes and behaviour involved in mere obedience or acquiescence.

Hence a society with law contains those who look upon its rules from the internal point of view as accepted standards of behaviour, and not merely as reliable predictions of what will befall them, at the hand of officials, if they disobey. But it also comprises those upon whom, either because they are malefactors or mere helpless victims of the system, these legal standards have to be imposed by force or threat of force; they are concerned with the rules merely as a source of possible punishment. The balance between these two components will be determined by many different factors. If the system is fair and caters genuinely for the vital interests of all those from whom it demands obedience, it may gain and retain the allegiance of most for most of the time, and will accordingly be stable. On the other hand it may be a narrow and exclusive system run in the interests of the dominant group, and it may be made continually more repressive and unstable with the latent threat of upheaval. Between these two extremes various combinations of these attitudes to law are to be found, often in the same individual.

Reflection on this aspect of things reveals a sobering truth: the step from the simple form of society, where primary rules of obligation are the only means of social control, into the legal world with its centrally organized legislature, courts, officials, and sanctions brings its solid gains at a certain cost. The gains are those of adaptability to change, certainty, and efficiency, and these are immense; the cost is the risk that the centrally organized power may well be used for the oppression of numbers with whose support it can dispense, in a way that the simpler regime of primary rules could not. Because this risk has materialized and may do so again, the claim that there is some further way in which law *must* conform to morals beyond that which we have exhibited as the minimum content of Natural Law, needs very careful scrutiny. Many such assertions either fail to make clear the sense in which the connexion between law and morals is alleged to be necessary; or upon examination they turn out to mean something which is both true and important, but which it is most confusing to present as a necessary connexion between law and morals. We shall end this chapter by examining six forms of this claim.

(i) Power and authority. It is often said that a legal system must rest on a sense of moral obligation or on the conviction of the moral value of the system, since it does not and cannot rest on mere power of man over man. We have ourselves stressed, in the earlier chapters of this book, the inadequacy of orders backed by threats and habits of obedience for the understanding of the foundations of a legal system and the idea of legal validity. Not only do these require for their elucidation the notion of an accepted rule of recognition, as we have argued at length in Chapter VI, but, as we have seen in this chapter, a necessary condition of the existence of coercive power is that some at least must voluntarily co-operate in the system and accept its rules. In this sense it is true that the coercive power of law presupposes its accepted authority. But the dichotomy of 'law based merely on power' and 'law which is accepted as morally binding' is not exhaustive. Not only may vast numbers be coerced by laws which they do not regard as morally binding, but it is not even true that those who do accept the system voluntarily, must conceive of themselves as morally bound to do so, though the system will be most stable when they do so. In fact, their allegiance to the system may be based on many different considerations: calculations of long-term interest; disinterested interest in others; an unreflecting inherited or traditional attitude; or the mere wish to do as others do. There is indeed no reason why those who accept the authority of the system should not examine their conscience and decide that, morally, they ought not to accept it, yet for a variety of reasons continue to do so.

These commonplaces may have become obscured by the general use of the same vocabulary to express both the legal and the moral obligations which men acknowledge. Those who accept the authority of a legal system look upon it from the internal point of view, and express their sense of its requirements in internal statements couched in the normative language which is common to both law and morals: 'I (You) ought,' 'I (he) must,' 'I (they) have an obligation.' Yet they are not thereby committed to a *moral* judgment that it is morally right to do what the law requires. No doubt if nothing else is said, there is a presumption that any one who speaks in these ways of his or others' legal obligations, does not think that there is any moral or other reason against fulfilling them. This, however, does not show that nothing can be acknowledged as legally obligatory unless it is accepted as morally obligatory. The presumption which we have mentioned rests on the fact that it will often be pointless to acknowledge or point out a legal obligation, if the speaker has conclusive reasons, moral or otherwise, to urge against fulfilling it.

(ii) The influence of morality on law. The law of every modern state shows at a thousand points the influence of both the accepted social morality and wider moral

ideals. These influences enter into law either abruptly and avowedly through legislation, or silently and piecemeal through the judicial process. In some systems, as in the United States, the ultimate criteria of legal validity explicitly incorporate principles of justice or substantive moral values; in other systems, as in England, where there are no formal restrictions on the competence of the supreme legislature, its legislation may yet no less scrupulously conform to justice or morality. The further ways in which law mirrors morality are myriad, and still insufficiently studied: statutes may be a mere legal shell and demand by their express terms to be filled out with the aid of moral principles; the range of enforceable contracts may be limited by reference to conceptions of morality and fairness; liability for both civil and criminal wrongs may be adjusted to prevailing views of moral responsibility. No 'positivist' could deny that these are facts, or that the stability of legal systems depends in part upon such types of correspondence with morals. If this is what is meant by the necessary connexion of law and morals, its existence should be conceded.

(iii) Interpretation. Laws require interpretation if they are to be applied to concrete cases, and once the myths which obscure the nature of the judicial processes are dispelled by realistic study, it is patent, as we have shown in Chapter VI, that the open texture of law leaves a vast field for a creative activity which some call legislative. Neither in interpreting statutes nor precedents are judges confined to the alternatives of blind, arbitrary choice, or 'mechanical' deduction from rules with predetermined meaning. Very often their choice is guided by an assumption that the purpose of the rules which they are interpreting is a reasonable one, so that the rules are not intended to work injustice or offend settled moral principles. Judicial decision, especially on matters of high constitutional import, often involves a choice between moral values, and not merely the application of some single outstanding moral principle; for it is folly to believe that where the meaning of the law is in doubt, morality always has a clear answer to offer. At this point judges may again make a choice which is neither arbitrary nor mechanical; and here often display characteristic judicial virtues, the special appropriateness of which to legal decision explains why some feel reluctant to call such judicial activity 'legislative'. These virtues are: impartiality and neutrality in surveying the alternatives; consideration for the interest of all who will be affected; and a concern to deploy some acceptable general principle as a reasoned basis for decision. No doubt because a plurality of such principles is always possible it cannot be *demonstrated* that a decision is uniquely correct: but it may be made acceptable as the reasoned product of informed impartial choice. In all this we have the 'weighing' and 'balancing' characteristic of the effort to do justice between competing interests.

Few would deny the importance of these elements, which may well be called 'moral' in rendering decisions acceptable; and the loose and changing tradition or canons of interpretation, which in most systems govern interpretation, often vaguely incorporate them. Yet if these facts are tendered as evidence of the *necessary* connexion of law and morals, we need to remember that the same principles have been honored nearly as much in the breach as in the observance. For, from Austin to the present day, reminders that such elements *should* guide decision have come, in the main, from critics who have found that judicial lawmaking has often been blind to social values, 'automatic,' or inadequately reasoned.

(iv) The criticism of law. Sometimes the claim that there is a necessary connexion between law and morality comes to no more than the assertion that a *good* legal system must conform at certain points, such as those already mentioned in the last paragraph, to the requirements of justice and morality. Some may regard this as an obvious truism; but it is not a tautology, and in fact, in the criticism of law, there may be disagreement both as to the appropriate moral standards and as to the required points of conformity. Does the morality, with which law must conform if it is to be good, mean the accepted morality of the group whose law it is, even though this may rest on superstition or may withhold its benefits and protection from slaves or subject classes? Or does morality mean standards which are enlightened in the sense that they rest on rational beliefs as to matters of fact, and accept all human beings as entitled to equal consideration and respect?

No doubt the contention that a legal system must treat all human beings within its scope as entitled to certain basic protections and freedoms, is now generally accepted as a statement of an ideal of obvious relevance in the criticism of law. Even where practice departs from it, lip service to this ideal is usually forthcoming. It may even be the case that a morality which does not take this view of the right of all men to equal consideration, can be shown by philosophy to be involved in some inner contradiction, dogmatism, or irrationality. If so, the enlightened morality which recognizes these rights has special credentials as the true morality, and is not just one among many possible moralities. These are claims which cannot be investigated here, but even if they are conceded, they cannot alter, and should not obscure, the fact that municipal legal systems, with their characteristic structure of primary and secondary rules, have long endured though they have flouted these principles of justice. What, if anything, is to be gained from denying that iniquitous rules are law, we consider below.

(v) Principles of legality and justice. It may be said that the distinction between a good legal system which conforms at certain points to morality and justice, and a legal system which does not, is a fallacious one, because a minimum of justice is necessarily realized whenever human behaviour is controlled by general rules publicly announced and judicially applied. Indeed we have already pointed out, in analyzing the idea of justice, that its simplest form (justice in the application of the law) consists in no more than taking seriously the notion that what is to be applied to a multiplicity of different persons is the same general rule, undeflected by prejudice, interest, or caprice. This impartiality is what the procedural standards known to English and American lawyers as principles of 'Natural Justice' are designed to secure. Hence, though the most odious laws may be justly applied, we have, in the bare notion of applying a general rule of law, the germ at least of justice.

Further aspects of this minimum form of justice which might well be called 'natural' emerge if we study what is in fact involved in any method of social control—rules of games as well as law—which consists primarily of general standards of conduct communicated to classes of persons, who are then expected to understand and conform to the rules without further official direction. If social control of this sort is to function, the rules must satisfy certain conditions: they must be intelligible and within the capacity of most to obey, and in general they must not be retrospective, though exceptionally they may be. This means that, for the most part, those who are eventually punished for breach of the rules will have had the ability and opportunity to obey. Plainly these features of control by rule are closely related to the requirements of justice which lawyers term principles of legality. Indeed one critic of positivism has seen in these aspects of control by rules, something amounting to a necessary connexion between law and morality, and suggested that they be called 'the inner morality of law'. Again, if this is what the necessary connexion of law and morality means, we may accept it. It is unfortunately compatible with very great iniquity.

(vi) Legal validity and resistance to law. However incautiously they may have formulated their general outlook, few legal theorists classed as positivists would have been concerned to deny the forms of connexion between law and morals discussed under the last five headings. What then was the concern of the great battle-cries of legal positivism: 'The existence of law is one thing; its merit or demerit another';[19] 'The law of a State is not an ideal but something which actually exists . . . it is not that which ought to be, but that which is';[20] 'Legal norms may have any kind of content'?[21]

What these thinkers were, in the main, concerned to promote was clarity and honesty in the formulation of the theoretical and moral issues raised by the existence of particular laws which were morally iniquitous but were enacted in proper form, clear in meaning, and satisfied all the acknowledged criteria of validity of a system. Their view was that, in thinking about such laws, both the theorist and the unfortunate official or private citizen who was called on to apply or obey them, could only be confused by an invitation to refuse the title of 'law' or 'valid' to them. They thought that, to confront these problems, simpler, more candid resources were available, which would bring into focus far better, every relevant intellectual and moral consideration: we should say, 'This is law; but it is too iniquitous to be applied or obeyed.'

The opposed point of view is one which appears attractive when, after revolution or major upheavals, the Courts of a system have to consider their attitude to the moral iniquities committed in legal form by private citizens or officials under an earlier regime. Their punishment may be felt socially desirable, and yet, to procure it by frankly retrospective legislation, making criminal what was permitted or even required by the law of the earlier regime, may be difficult, itself morally odious, or perhaps not possible. In these circumstances it may seem natural to exploit the moral implications latent in the vocabulary of the law and especially in words like *ius, recht, diritto, droit* which are laden with the theory of Natural Law. It may then appear tempting to say that enactments which enjoined or permitted iniquity should not be recognized as valid, or have the quality of law, even if the system in which they were enacted acknowledged no restriction upon the legislative competence of its legislature. It is in this form that Natural Law arguments were revived in Germany after the last war in response to the acute social problems left by the iniquities of Nazi rule and its defeat. Should informers who, for selfish ends, procured the imprisonment of others for offences against monstrous statutes

---

[19] Austin, The Province of Jurisprudence Defined, Lecture V, at 184–85.

[20] Gray, The Nature and Sources of the Law, § 213.

[21] Kelsen, General Theory of Law and State 113.

passed during the Nazi regime, be punished? Was it possible to convict them in the courts of postwar Germany on the footing that such statutes violated the Natural Law and were therefore void so that the victims' imprisonment for breach of such statutes was in fact unlawful, and procuring it was itself an offence?[22] Simple as the issue looks between those who would accept and those who would repudiate the view that morally iniquitous rules cannot be law, the disputants seem often very unclear as to its general character. It is true that we are here concerned with alternative ways of formulating a moral decision not to apply, obey, or allow others to plead in their defense morally iniquitous rules: yet the issue is ill presented as a verbal one. Neither side to the dispute would be content if they were told, 'Yes: you are right, the correct way in English (or in German) of putting that sort of point is to say what you have said.' So, though the positivist might point to a weight of English usage, showing that there is no contradiction in asserting that a rule of law is too iniquitous to be obeyed, and that it does not follow from the proposition that a rule is too iniquitous to obey that it is not a valid rule of law, their opponents would hardly regard this as disposing of the case.

Plainly we cannot grapple adequately with this issue if we see it as one concerning the proprieties of linguistic usage. For what really is at stake is the comparative merit of a wider and a narrower concept or way of classifying rules, which belong to a system of rules generally effective in social life. If we are to make a reasoned choice between these concepts, it must be because one is superior to the other in the way in which it will assist our theoretical inquiries, or advance and clarify our moral deliberations, or both.

The wider of these two rival concepts of law includes the narrower. If we adopt the wider concept, this will lead us in theoretical inquiries to group and consider together as 'law' all rules which are valid by the formal tests of a system of primary and secondary rules, even though some of them offend against a society's own morality or against what we may hold to be an enlightened or true morality. If we adopt the narrower concept we shall exclude from 'law' such morally offensive rules. It seems clear that nothing is to be gained in the theoretical or scientific study of law as a social phenomenon by adopting the narrower concept: it would lead us to exclude certain rules even though they exhibit all the other complex characteristics of law. Nothing, surely, but confusion could follow from a proposal to leave the study of such rules to another discipline, and certainly no history or other form of legal study has found it profitable to do this. If we adopt the wider concept of law, we can accommodate within it the study of whatever special features morally iniquitous laws have, and the reaction of society to them. Hence the use of the narrower concept here must inevitably split, in a confusing way, our effort to understand both the development and potentialities of the specific method of social control to be seen in a system of primary and secondary rules. Study of its use involves study of its abuse.

What then of the practical merits of the narrower concept of law in moral

---

[22] *See* the judgment of 27 July 1940, Oberlandsgericht Bamberg, 5 *Süddeutsche Juristen-Zeitung*, 207, discussed at length in H. L. A. Hart, *Legal Positivism and the Separation of Law and Morals* Harvard L. Rev. lxxi (1958), 598, and in L. Fuller, Positivism and Fidelity to Law, *ibid.*, at 630. But note corrected account of this judgment *infra* pp. 254–55.

deliberation? In what way is it better, when faced with morally iniquitous demands, to think 'This is in no sense law' rather than 'This is law but too iniquitous to obey or apply'? Would this make men more clear-headed or readier to disobey when morality demands it? Would it lead to better ways of disposing of the problems such as the Nazi regime left behind? No doubt ideas have their influence; but it scarcely seems that an effort to train and educate men in the use of a narrower concept of legal validity, in which there is no place for valid but morally iniquitous laws, is likely to lead to a stiffening of resistance to evil, in the face of threats of organized power, or a clearer realization of what is morally at stake when obedience is demanded. So long as human beings can gain sufficient co-operation from some to enable them to dominate others, they will use the forms of law as one of their instruments. Wicked men will enact wicked rules which others will enforce. What surely is most needed in order to make men clear sighted in confronting the official abuse of power, is that they should preserve the sense that the certification of something as legally valid is not conclusive of the question of obedience, and that, however great the aura of majesty or authority which the official system may have, its demands must in the end be submitted to a moral scrutiny. This sense, that there is something outside the official system, by reference to which in the last resort the individual must solve his problems of obedience, is surely more likely to be kept alive among those who are accustomed to think that rules of law may be iniquitous, than among those who think that nothing iniquitous can anywhere have the status of law.

But perhaps a stronger reason for preferring the wider concept of law, which will enable us to think and say, 'This is law but iniquitous,' is that to withhold legal recognition from iniquitous rules may grossly oversimplify the variety of moral issues to which they give rise. Older writers who, like Bentham and Austin, insisted on the distinction between what law is and what it ought to be, did so partly because they thought that unless men kept these separate they might, without counting the cost to society, make hasty judgments that laws were invalid and ought not to be obeyed. But besides this danger of anarchy, which they may well have overrated, there is another form of oversimplification. If we narrow our point of view and think only of the person who is called upon to *obey* evil rules, we may regard it as a matter of indifference whether or not he thinks that he is faced with a valid rule of 'law' so long as he sees its moral iniquity and does what morality requires. But besides the moral question of obedience (Am I to do this evil thing?) there is Socrates' question of submission: Am I to submit to punishment for disobedience or make my escape? There is also the question which confronted the post-war German courts, 'Are we to punish those who did evil things when they were permitted by evil rules then in force?' These questions raise very different problems of morality and justice, which we need to consider independently of each other: they cannot be solved by a refusal, made once and for all, to recognize evil laws as valid for any purpose. This is too crude a way with delicate and complex moral issues.

A concept of law which allows the invalidity of law to be distinguished from its immorality, enables us to see the complexity and variety of these separate issues; whereas a narrow concept of law which denies legal validity to iniquitous rules may blind us to them. It may be conceded that the German informers, who for selfish ends procured the punishment of others under monstrous laws, did what morality forbad; yet morality may also demand that the state should punish only those who, in doing evil, did what the state at the time forbad. This is the principle of *nulla poena sine lege*. If inroads have to be made on this principle in order to avert something held to be a greater evil than its sacrifice, it is vital that the issues at stake be clearly identified. A case of retroactive punishment should not be made to look like an ordinary case of punishment for an act illegal at the time. At least it can be claimed for the simple positivist doctrine that morally iniquitous rules may still be law, that this offers no disguise for the choice between evils which, in extreme circumstances, may have to be made.

QUESTIONS

1.   Hart observes that "to its critics, Natural Law theory has seemed to spring from deep and old confusions from which modern thought has triumphantly freed itself; while to its advocates, the critics appear merely to insist on surface trivialities, ignoring profounder truths." Where do you stand?

2.   Do you believe that "laws of proper conduct may be discovered by human reason"? If not, how are they discovered? Are the ABA Model Rules of Professional Conduct dictated by reason? Or are they shaped by accidents of politics and economics? Or a bit of both? What is the source of their legitimacy for you?

3.   Hart concludes his description of natural law theory with this statement: "At least it can be claimed for the simple positivist doctrine that morally iniquitous rules may still be law, that this offers no disguise for the choice between evils which, in extreme circumstances, may have to be made." Several professional rules of "ethics" make clear choices between evils. Take for example the confidentiality rules, which in the latest ABA form arguably prohibit revealing confidences from clients even if the result is the criminal conviction of an innocent person. *See* Model Rule 1.6, discussed *supra* at 3F. St. Thomas Aquinas would certainly argue that such a rule could, in some circumstances, be against God's will, or should be disobeyed for reasons of equity. Does calling such a rule "the law" make sense? Does that give it added legitimacy, or simply accurately state the empirical fact that a lawyer violating such a rule may be punished?

LON L. FULLER, THE MORALITY OF LAW
245–253 (rev. ed. 1969)

APPENDIX: THE PROBLEM OF THE GRUDGE INFORMER

By a narrow margin you have been elected Minister of Justice of your country, a nation of some twenty million inhabitants. At the outset of your term of office you are confronted by a serious problem that will be described below. But first the background of this problem must be presented.

For many decades your country enjoyed a peaceful, constitutional and democratic government. However, some time ago it came upon bad times. Normal relations were disrupted by a deepening economic depression and by an increasing antagonism among various factional groups, formed along economic, political, and religious lines. The proverbial man on horseback appeared in the form of the

Headman of a political party or society that called itself the Purple Shirts.

In a national election attended by much disorder the Headman was elected President of the Republic and his party obtained a majority of the seats in the General Assembly. The success of the party at the polls was partly brought about by a campaign of reckless promises and ingenious falsifications, and partly by the physical intimidation of night-riding Purple Shirts who frightened many people away from the polls who would have voted against the party.

When the Purple Shirts arrived in power they took no steps to repeal the ancient Constitution or any of its provisions. They also left intact the Civil and Criminal Codes and the Code of Procedure. No official action was taken to dismiss any government official or to remove any judge from the bench. Elections continued to be held at intervals and ballots were counted with apparent honesty. Nevertheless, the country lived under a reign of terror.

Judges who rendered decisions contrary to the wishes of the party were beaten and murdered. The accepted meaning of the Criminal Code was perverted to place political opponents in jail. Secret statutes were passed, the contents of which were known only to the upper levels of the party hierarchy. Retroactive statutes were enacted which made acts criminal that were legally innocent when committed. No attention was paid by the government to the restraints of the Constitution, of antecedent laws, or even of its own laws. All opposing political parties were disbanded. Thousands of political opponents were put to death, either methodically in prisons or in sporadic night forays of terror. A general amnesty was declared in favor of persons under sentence for acts "committed in defending the fatherland against subversion." Under this amnesty a general liberation of all prisoners who were members of the Purple Shirt party was effected. No one not a member of the party was released under the amnesty.

The Purple Shirts as a matter of deliberate policy preserved an element of flexibility in their operations by acting at times through the party "in the streets," and by acting at other times through the apparatus of the state which they controlled. Choice between the two methods of proceeding was purely a matter of expediency. For example, when the inner circle of the party decided to ruin all the former Socialist-Republicans (whose party put up a last-ditch resistance to the new regime), a dispute arose as to the best way of confiscating their property. One faction, perhaps still influenced by prerevolutionary conceptions, wanted to accomplish this by a statute declaring their goods forfeited for criminal acts. Another wanted to do it by compelling the owners to deed their property over at the point of a bayonet. This group argued against the proposed statute on the ground that it would attract unfavorable comment abroad. The Headman decided in favor of direct action through the party to be followed by a secret statute ratifying the party's action and confirming the titles obtained by threats of physical violence.

The Purple Shirts have now been overthrown and a democratic and constitutional government restored. Some difficult problems have, however, been left behind by the deposed regime. These you and your associates in the new government must find some way of solving. One of these problems is that of the "grudge informer."

During the Purple Shirt regime a great many people worked off grudges by reporting their enemies to the party or to the government authorities. The activities reported were such things as the private expression of views critical of the government, listening to foreign radio broadcasts, associating with known wreckers and hooligans, hoarding more than the permitted amount of dried eggs, failing to report a loss of identification papers within five days, etc. As things then stood with the administration of justice, any of these acts, if proved, could lead to a sentence of death. In some cases this sentence was authorized by "emergency" statutes; in others it was imposed without statutory warrant, though by judges duly appointed to their offices.

After the overthrow of the Purple Shirts, a strong public demand grew up that these grudge informers be punished. The interim government, which preceded that with which you are associated, temporized on this matter. Meanwhile it has become a burning issue and a decision concerning it can no longer be postponed. Accordingly, your first act as Minister of Justice has been to address yourself to it. You have asked your five Deputies to give thought to the matter and to bring their recommendations to conference. At the conference the five Deputies speak in turn as follows:

FIRST DEPUTY: "It is perfectly clear to me that we can do nothing about these so-called grudge informers. The acts they reported were unlawful according to the rules of the government then in actual control of the nation's affairs. The sentences imposed on their victims were rendered in accordance with principles of law then obtaining. These principles differed from those familiar to us in ways that we consider detestable. Nevertheless they were then the law of the land. One of the principal differences between that law and our own lies in the much wider discretion it accorded to the judge in criminal matters. This rule and its consequences are as much entitled to respect by us as the reform which the Purple Shirts introduced into the law of wills, whereby only two witnesses were required instead of three. It is immaterial that the rule granting the judge a more or less uncontrolled discretion in criminal cases was never formally enacted but was a matter of tacit acceptance. Exactly the same thing can be said of the opposite rule which we accept that restricts the judge's discretion narrowly. The difference between ourselves and the Purple Shirts is not that theirs was an unlawful government—a contradiction in terms—but lies rather in the field of ideology. No one has a greater abhorrence than I for Purple Shirtism. Yet the fundamental difference between our philosophy and theirs is that we permit and tolerate differences in viewpoint, while they attempted to impose their monolithic code on everyone. Our whole system of government assumes that law is a flexible thing, capable of expressing and effectuating many different aims. The cardinal point of our creed is that when an objective has been duly incorporated into a law or judicial decree it must be provisionally accepted even by those that hate it, who must await their chance at the polls, or in another litigation, to secure a legal recognition for their own aims. The Purple Shirts, on the other hand, simply disregarded laws that incorporated objectives of which they did not approve, not even considering it worth the effort involved to repeal them. If we now seek to unscramble the acts of the Purple Shirt regime, declaring this judgment invalid, that statute void, this sentence excessive, we shall be doing exactly the thing we most condemn in them.

I recognize that it will take courage to carry through with the program I recommend and we shall have to resist strong pressures of public opinion. We shall also have to be prepared to prevent the people from taking the law into their own hands. In the long run, however, I believe the course I recommend is the only one that will insure the triumph of the conceptions of law and government in which we believe."

SECOND DEPUTY: "Curiously, I arrive at the same conclusion as my colleague, by an exactly opposite route. To me it seems absurd to call the Purple Shirt regime a lawful government. A legal system does not exist simply because policemen continue to patrol the streets and wear uniforms or because a constitution and code are left on the shelf unrepealed. A legal system presupposes laws that are known, or can be known, by those subject to them. It presupposes some uniformity of action and that like cases will be given like treatment. It presupposes the absence of some lawless power, like the Purple Shirt Party, standing above the government and able at any time to interfere with the administration of justice whenever it does not function according to the whims of that power. All of these presuppositions enter into the very conception of an order of law and have nothing to do with political and economic ideologies. In my opinion law in any ordinary sense of the word ceased to exist-when the Purple Shirts came to power. During their regime we had, in effect, an interregnum in the rule of law. Instead of a government of laws we had a war of all against all conducted behind barred doors, in dark alleyways, in palace intrigues, and prison-yard conspiracies. The acts of these so-called grudge informers were just one phase of that war. For us to condemn these acts as criminal would involve as much incongruity as if we were to attempt to apply juristic conceptions to the struggle for existence that goes on in the jungle or beneath the surface of the sea. We must put this whole dark, lawless chapter of our history behind us like a bad dream. If we stir among its hatreds, we shall bring upon ourselves something of its evil spirit and risk infection from its miasmas. I therefore say with my colleague, let bygones be bygones. Let us do nothing about the so-called grudge informers. What they did do was neither lawful nor contrary to law, for they lived, not under a regime of law, but under one of anarchy and terror."

THIRD DEPUTY: "I have a profound suspicion of any kind of reasoning that proceeds by an 'either-or' alternative. I do not think we need to assume either, on the one hand, that in some manner the whole of the Purple Shirt regime was outside the realm of law, or, on the other, that all of its doings are entitled to full credence as the acts of a lawful government. My two colleagues have unwittingly delivered powerful arguments against these extreme assumptions by demonstrating that both of them lead to the same absurd conclusion, a conclusion that is ethically and politically impossible. If one reflects about the matter without emotion it becomes clear that we did not have during the Purple Shirt regime a 'war of all against all.' Under the surface much of what we call normal human life went on—marriages were contracted, goods were sold, wills were drafted and executed. This life was attended by the usual dislocations—automobile accidents, bankruptcies, unwitnessed wills, defamatory misprints in the newspapers. Much of this normal life and most of these equally normal dislocations of it were unaffected by the Purple Shirt ideology. The legal questions that arose in this area were handled by the courts much as they had been formerly and much as they are being handled today. It would invite an intolerable chaos if we were to declare everything that happened under the Purple Shirts to be without legal basis. On the other hand, we certainly cannot say that the murders committed in the streets by members of the party acting under orders from the Headman were lawful simply because the party had achieved control of the government and its chief had become President of the Republic. If we must condemn the criminal acts of the party and its members, it would seem absurd to uphold every act which happened to be canalized through the apparatus of a government that had become, in effect, the alter ego of the Purple Shirt Party. We must therefore, in this situation, as in most human affairs, discriminate. Where the Purple Shirt philosophy intruded itself and perverted the administration of justice from its normal aims and uses, there we must interfere. Among these perversions of justice I would count, for example, the case of a man who was in love with another man's wife and brought about the death of the husband by informing against him for a wholly trivial offense, that is, for not reporting a loss of his identification papers within five days. This informer was a murderer under the Criminal Code which was in effect at the time of his act and which the Purple Shirts had not repealed. He encompassed the death of one who stood in the way of his illicit passions and utilized the courts for the realization of his murderous intent. He knew that the courts were themselves the pliant instruments of whatever policy the Purple Shirts might for the moment consider expedient. There are other cases that are equally clear. I admit that there are also some that are less clear. We shall be embarrassed, for example, by the cases of mere busybodies who reported to the authorities everything that looked suspect. Some of these persons acted not from desire to get rid of those they accused, but with a desire to curry favor with the party, to divert suspicions (perhaps ill-founded) raised against themselves, or through sheer officiousness. I don't know how these cases should be handled, and make no recommendation with regard to them. But the fact that these troublesome cases exist should not deter us from acting at once in the cases that are clear, of which there are far too many to permit us to disregard them."

FOURTH DEPUTY: "Like my colleague I too distrust 'either-or' reasoning, but I think we need to reflect more than he has about where we are headed. This proposal to pick and choose among the acts of the deposed regime is thoroughly objectionable. It is, in fact, Purple Shirtism itself, pure and simple. We like this law, so let us enforce it. We like this judgment, let it stand. This law we don't like, therefore it never was a law at all. This governmental act we disapprove, let it be deemed a nullity. If we proceed this way, we take toward the laws and acts of the Purple Shirt government precisely the unprincipled attitude they took toward the laws and acts of the government they supplanted. We shall have chaos, with every judge and every prosecuting attorney a law unto himself. Instead of ending the abuses of the Purple Shirt regime, my colleague's proposal would perpetuate them. There is only one way of dealing with this problem that is compatible with our philosophy of law and government and that is to deal with it by duly enacted law, I mean, by a special statute directed toward it. Let us study this whole problem of the grudge informer, get all the relevant facts, and draft a comprehensive law dealing with it. We shall not then be twisting old laws to purposes for which they were never intended. We shall furthermore provide penalties appropriate to the offense and not treat every informer as a murderer simply because the one he informed against was ultimately executed. I admit that we shall encounter some difficult problems of draftmanship. Among other things, we shall have to assign a definite legal meaning to 'grudge' and that will not be easy. We should not be deterred by these difficulties, however, from adopting the only course that will lead us out of a condition of lawless, personal rule."

FIFTH DEPUTY: "I find a considerable irony in the last proposal. It speaks of putting a definite end to the abuses of the Purple Shirtism, yet it proposes to do this by resorting to one of most hated devices of the Purple Shirt regime, the ex post facto criminal statute. My colleague dreads the confusion that will result if we attempt without a statute to undo and redress 'wrong' acts of the departed order, while we uphold and enforce its 'right' acts. Yet, he seems not to realize that his proposed statute is a wholly specious cure for this uncertainty. It is easy to make a plausible argument for an undrafted statute; we all agree it would be nice to have things down in black and white on paper. But just what would this statute provide? One of my colleagues speaks of someone who had failed for five days to report a loss of his identification papers. My colleague implies that the judicial sentence imposed for that offense, namely death, was so utterly disproportionate as to be clearly wrong. But we must remember that at that time the underground movement against the Purple Shirts was mounting in intensity and that the Purple Shirts were being harassed constantly by people with false identification papers. From their point of view they had a real problem, and the only objection we can make to their solution of it (other than the fact that didn't want them to solve it) was that they acted with somewhat more rigor than the occasion seemed to demand. How will my colleague deal with this case in his statute, and with all of its cousins and second cousins? Will he deny the existence of any need for law and order under the Purple Shirt regime? I will not go further into the difficulties involved in drafting this proposed statute, since they are evident enough to anyone who reflects. I shall instead turn to my own solution. It has been said on very respectable authority that the main purpose of the criminal law is to give an outlet to the human instinct for revenge. There are times, and I believe this is one of them, when we should allow that instinct to express itself directly without the intervention of forms of law. This matter of the grudge informers is already in process of straightening itself out. One reads almost every day that a former lackey of the Purple Shirt regime has met his just reward in some unguarded spot. The people are quietly handling things in their own way and if we leave them alone, and instruct our public prosecutors to do the same, there will soon be no problem left for us to solve. There will be some disorders, of course, and a few innocent heads will be broken. But our government and our legal system will not be involved in the affair and we shall not find ourselves hopelessly bogged down in an attempt to unscramble all the deeds and misdeeds of the Purple Shirts."

As Minister of Justice which of these recommendations would you adopt?

QUESTION

1. Answer Fuller's question, above. Do the five deputies present all possible options? Should there be a transcendent opinion from a "Sixth Deputy"? If so, what is it? By the way, in *The Morality of Law, supra,* Fuller articulates eight pitfalls of rulemaking: "The first and most obvious lies in a failure to achieve rules at all, so that every issue must be decided on an ad hoc basis. The other routes are: (2) a failure to publicize, or at least to make available to the affected party, the rules he is expected to observe; (3) the abuse of retroactive legislation, which not only cannot itself guide action, but undercuts the integrity of rules prospective in effect, since it puts them under the threat of retrospective change; (4) a failure to make rules understandable; (5) the enactment of contradictory rules or (6) rules that require conduct beyond the powers of the affected party; (7) introducing such frequent changes in the rules that the subject cannot orient his action by them; and, finally, (8) a failure of congruence between the rules as announced and their actual administration." THE MORALITY OF LAW, *supra.* Are rules that bear any of these deficiencies "moral" rules?

Chapter V

NATURAL LAW: THE LAW IN THE SKY AND IN THE CAVE

A. THE RENAISSANCE: THE "LAW OF REASON" AND SECULAR NATURAL LAW

For St. Thomas Aquinas, and many devout people today, "Natural Law" centers on religion. If God exists, then God's will is certainly where the responsibility to make and obey positive law begins.

Starting with the Western Renaissance, a number of jurists and political theorists began to strive toward defining a "Law of Reason," a kind of Natural Law without God based on empirical reasoning, science, and a rationalist philosophy. Of course, many of these jurists, including great rationalists such as Francis Bacon (1561–1626) and Hugo Grotius (1583–1645), professed belief in God. They argued that laws of science and reason, created by God, would not contradict God's will; thus it was not blasphemous to prove or support theories by empirical data alone.[1] God was simply not necessary for the proof. Of course, no one can be sure how devout these rationalists really were. Disbelief was still dangerous. As Bertrand Russell observed of Francis Bacon, "[h]ow far Bacon's orthodoxy was sincere it is impossible to know."[2]

The rationalist argument for Natural Law is particularly important today, as we live in a secular and doubting world. H. L. A. Hart observed:

> Natural Law has, however, not always been associated with belief in a Divine Governor or Lawgiver of the universe, and even where it has been, its characteristic tenets have not been logically dependent on that belief. Both the relevant sense of the word 'natural', which enters into Natural Law, and its general outlook minimizing the difference, so obvious and so important to modern minds, between prescriptive and descriptive laws, have their roots in Greek thought which was, for this purpose, quite secular. Indeed, the continued reassertion of some form of Natural Law doctrine is due in part to the fact that its appeal is independent of both divine and

---

[1] *See* discussion in DANIEL R. COQUILLETTE, FRANCIS BACON 16–17 (1992); A. P. D'ENTREVES, NATURAL LAW 48–63.

[2] *See* BERTRAND RUSSELL, A HISTORY OF WESTERN PHILOSOPHY 542 (2007). Bacon may have been quite sincere, but the point is that this makes little difference in evaluating his work. *See* D. R. COQUILLETTE, FRANCIS BACON 17 (1992). Grotius was a devout Christian, although imprisoned for heretical beliefs by Dutch Calvinists. Grotius had a "burning desire" for the reunification of Christendom, a desire which could be perceived as heretical by many, now and then. *See* EDWARD DUMBAULD, THE LIFE AND LEGAL WRITINGS OF HUGO GROTIUS 14 (1969). On rationalist arguments generally, see RICHARD TUCK, NATURAL RIGHTS THEORIES (1981).

human authority, and to the fact that despite a terminology, and much metaphysics, which few could now accept, it contains certain elementary truths of importance for the understanding of both morality and law.[3]

Hart's description of Natural Law's popularity as "due in part to the fact that its appeal is independent of both divine and human authority" assumes a Natural Law very different from that postulated by St. Thomas Aquinas. To that "Natural Law," a law based on reason rather than God's will, we now turn.

Hugo Grotius (1583–1645), also known as Huigh de Groot, was a famous Dutch jurist. The explosion of commerce and nationalism during the 17th century led to major international confrontations about free trade, diplomatic immunity, and "just" wars. As a skilled diplomat, Grotius was deeply involved in these disputes, and wrote two books that are widely regarded as the beginning of modern public international law, *Mare Liberum* (1609), defending the freedom of the seas, and *De Jure Belli ac Pacis* (1625), describing the laws of war and peace.

International "law" has always been a problem for positivist legal theory. Here there is no "sovereign," and often no promulgated rules—at least no rules backed by any effective sanction. There may be a "law" of nuclear nonproliferation, and even a treaty signed by North Korea, but North Korea recognizes no sovereign that can enforce such a law, and it is unclear whether anything short of a total war will change that matter. So, is international law really "law"?

The short answer is that only a theory of natural law independent of the positivist tests of "sovereignty" and "coercion" will suffice in making international law "law." And this was the task Grotius set out to perform. In addition, Grotius sought to prove a natural law "based on man's own nature and independent of God, and that on the basis of the law of nature it was possible to formulate a coherent code suitable for all times and places."[4] This law not only would bind all nations, but would provide a test as to the "rightness" of all positive legal systems.[5]

In making his argument, Grotius returns to the Roman ideas of *ius naturale* and *ius gentium*, which we discussed in Chapter III. But this time, there is a substantial difference. As Grotius notes, the Romans defined the "law of nature" (*ius naturale*) as "that law which nature teaches to all animals." *Institutes* I., 2. pr.[6] For them, it was like the laws of physics or biology, principles that positive law can do nothing to influence. (The legislature of a sovereign state can repeal the "law" of gravity if it wishes, but there will be no effect on that "law," although people may be punished for pointing that out!) Closer to a "law of reason" was the Roman idea of "the law of nations" (*ius gentium*). This was defined by the Romans as "the law which natural reason appoints for all mankind." This law "obtains equally among all nations, and is called the law of nations, because all nations make use of it."[7]

---

[3] *Materials, supra* at 4E.

[4] DAVID M. WALKER, THE OXFORD COMPANION TO LAW 541 (1980). *See also* EDWARD DUMBAULD, THE LIFE AND LEGAL WRITINGS OF HUGO GROTIUS (1969) and RICHARD TUCK, NATURAL RIGHTS THEORIES 58–81 (1981).

[5] WALKER, *supra*, at 541.

[6] *Materials, supra* at 3G.

[7] *Materials, supra* at 3G.

Presumably this law can be ascertained empirically by observing the actual conduct of nations, but both the original jurists and Justinian's compilers could get quite confused when it came to specifics. "Slavery," for example, was against the law of nature "for by that law all men are originally born free," but historically it was part of the law of nations as "[w]ars arose, and in their train followed captivity and slavery."[8] Another example given of the "law of nations" was "almost all contracts . . . as, for instance, buying and selling, letting and hiring, partnership, deposits, loans returnable in kind, and very many others."[9]

By the Renaissance, these definitions have shifted. To Grotius, the "law of nature" becomes "not only . . . such things as depend not upon Human Will, but also many things which have been allowed by the general Consent of Mankind."[10] This includes a prohibition against all things "intrinsically evil," such as deprivation of private property. The content of "the Law of Nature is so unalterable, that God himself cannot change it. . . . For instance then, as twice two should not be four, God himself cannot effect; so neither can he, that what is intrinsically evil, should not be evil."[11]

Thus Grotius's law of nature could prohibit slavery, even though practiced historically by many nations, because it is "intrinsically evil" as a matter of right reason, just like "twice two" is four. Human laws that purport to "legalize" slavery are as invalid as laws that attempt to repeal gravity or the principles of mathematics; they are of no legitimate effect, even though capable of coercive enforcement. This is, of course, a combination of the unalterable Roman "*ius natural*," the laws of physics and such, with the Roman "*ius gentium*," based on universal "natural reason" among "all mankind," to create something completely different, an unalterable "law of nature," based on reason alone, binding on all peoples, despite their national and historical practices.

So, how is this "law of nature" to be discovered? Certainly not by seeking the lowest common denominator among all cultures, if that even exists. Grotius instead turns to that "which is generally believed to be so by all, or at least, the most civilized, Nations."[12] The power of the collective human mind and of its consequence, civilization, can establish the difference between slavery and genocide and the law. This great leap of faith in human intelligence and wisdom, surpassing anything in Roman legal culture, was the foundation of modern public international law, and much of modern constitutionalism as well.

---

[8] *Materials, supra* at 3G.

[9] *Materials, supra* at 3G. Ulpian originally made the point relating to slavery and Hermogenian made the point as to the commercial transactions. *See* JUSTINIAN'S DIGEST 1.1 4–5. Gaius, on the other hand, gives no such examples, and simply defined the *ius gentium* as "the law that natural reason establishes among all mankind . . . followed by all people alike." THE INSTITUTES OF GAIUS 1.1. This is significant as THE INSTITUTES OF GAIUS was the only Roman text that survived from classical times without digesting and changes by Justinian's Byzantine compilers. (It had accidentally survived Justinian's order to destroy all texts that preceded his CORPUS JURIS!)

[10] *Materials, infra* at 5E.

[11] *Id.*

[12] *Id.*

B. NATURAL LAW AND THE LEGAL PROFESSION

Lawyers have long reacted with passion to the arguments of secular natural law. Some, such as Telford Taylor and A. P. d'Entrèves, have seen the terrible historical lessons of the Holocaust and World War II as vindicating the need for a "law" that tests laws.[13] A vivid example was the Jewish Historical Museum in its former location at the "Waag" in Amsterdam. After many rooms of treasure, the last, and largest, seemed bare. All along the walls were books of legal records bound by chains to reading stands. Visitors turned the pages of the books, slowly realizing in horror that these were the legal papers, carefully promulgated under German occupational law, ordering the extermination of individual Jews. For any lawyer, those "legal" records were unforgettable, and there were thousands.

Yet some very great lawyers have seen "natural law" as a kind of fraud. No jurist is likely to see more war and suffering than did Oliver Wendell Holmes, Jr., who was seriously wounded three times in the Civil War, and barely survived.[14] He went on to live 94 years. In the middle of another ghastly war, World War I, he wrote his eloquent essay, "Natural Law," set out in full in this chapter.

Holmes's portrait stands at the entrance to Harvard Law School's "Holmes Field" (now Hauser) Building, and copies grace thousands of courtrooms and lawyers' offices. His views have greatly shaped modern legal culture. Central to Holmes's thought was a rejection of natural law theory, either God-centered or secular. In Holmes's view "[t]he jurists who believe in natural law seem to me to be in that naïve state of mind that accepts what has been familiar and accepted by them and their neighbors as something that must be accepted by all men everywhere."[15] Law to Holmes was a prediction of what courts were likely to do, a prediction grounded in a "new jurisprudence" which, in turn, was based on a realistic study of court behavior against a political and economic backdrop. This "realism," shared with his friend Louis Brandeis and with others such as Roscoe Pound, Harlan Stone, Benjamin Cardozo, and Felix Frankfurter, became the underpinnings of a "sociological jurisprudence" that still has a profound influence in law schools today.[16] As Roscoe Pound argued in 1923, "[m]ore than anything else, the theory of natural rights . . . served to cover up what the legal order really was and what court and lawmaker and judge really were doing."[17]

Even in the heat of World War I, Holmes observed that "I used to say when I was young, that truth was the majority vote of that nation that could lick all others."[18] He continued, "certainly we may expect that the received opinion about the present war will depend a good deal upon which side wins (I hope with all my soul it will be mine), and I think that the statement was correct in so far as it implied that our test

---

[13] *See Materials, supra* at 2E, and *infra* at 5E.

[14] CATHERINE DRINKER BOWEN, YANKEE FROM OLYMPUS (1944), remains the most "readable" and gripping account of Holmes's life. *See* pages 149–197 for Holmes's war experiences.

[15] *Materials, infra* at 5E.

[16] *See* Henry Steele Commages, *The Masters of the New Jurisprudence: Pound and Holmes, in* THE AMERICAN MIND 374–381 (1950).

[17] *Id.* 375.

[18] *Materials, infra* at 5E.

of truth is a reference to either a present or an imagined future majority in favor of our view."[19] The nature of legal rights was much the same. "No doubt behind these legal rights is the fighting will of the subject to maintain them, and the spread of his emotions to the general rules by which they are maintained; but that does not seem to me the same thing as the supposed a priori discernment of a duty or the assertion of a pre-existing right. A dog will fight for his bone."[20]

Holmes, like his fellow Yankee Herman Melville (1819-1891), wondered at the unknowable universe, but without spiritual certainty. He noted "[t]hat the universe has in it more than we understand, that the private soldiers have not been told the plan of campaign, or even that there is one . . . has no bearing upon our conduct."[21] Melville, the son-in-law of Lemuel Shaw, Holmes's predecessor as Chief Justice of Massachusetts, had symbolized God in *Moby Dick* (1851) as an awesome natural force, indifferent like the Great White Whale to man's fate. The American theology of *Moby Dick* had none of the comfort or certainty of the *Summa Theologica*, and there was a clear consequence for legal thought. Holmes, perhaps, had more optimism, but no more certainty. "As I listen," he said in a Memorial Day address in 1884, "the great chorus of life and joy begins again, and amid the awful orchestra of seen and unseen powers and destinies of good and evil our trumpets sound once more a note of daring, hope, and will."[22] We will return to Melville and Shaw in Chapters VI and VII.

A. P. d'Entrèves's chapter "The Ideal Law" from his *Natural Law* (1951) and Oliver Wendell Holmes's essay "Natural Law" are among the most powerful and concise arguments for their contrasting views to be found anywhere. Their only common ground is that neither argument assumes the existence of a benevolent God. Both are reproduced here for your consideration.

In addition, there is included a second great puzzle by Lon Fuller, "The Case of the Speluncean Explorers."[23] Like the "The Problem of the Grudge Informer," this case is another test of your analytical abilities and your juristic beliefs. Ask yourself how Holmes and d'Entrèves would solve Fuller's test.

Lon Fuller's methods of analysis are very relevant to the underpinnings of professional rules. He had an influence on the *ABA Code of Professional Responsibility* (1969) and may have first suggested the division of that Code into "Ethical Considerations" ("ECs"), which were aspirational, and "Disciplinary Rules" ("DRs") which were mandatory. Fuller believed that while we may not all agree as to the "best" ends of professional responsibility, we can at least agree as to the minimum content of that responsibility.[24] Thus, we may not all agree how much time

---

[19] *Materials, infra* at 5E.

[20] *Materials, infra* at 5E.

[21] *Materials, infra* at 5E.

[22] Oliver Wendell Holmes, Jr., Speeches 12 (1891).

[23] 62 Harv. L. Rev. 616 (1949).

[24] *See* Lon L. Fuller, The Morality of Law (rev. ed. 1969), for his notion of the "Moral Scale" which "begins at the bottom with the most obvious demands of social living and extends upward to the highest reaches of human aspiration." *Id.* 9–10. Fuller continued: "Somewhere along this scale there is an invisible pointer that marks the dividing line where the pressure of duty leaves off [i.e., mandatory

a lawyer should contribute to pro bono work, or even what pro bono means, so this is an aspirational goal. But we are able to agree that a lawyer must not steal money from a client. Fuller argues that just because we cannot all agree on the full content of moral duty does not mean we cannot reach consensus on much of the minimum content of such a moral duty.[25] The legal profession continues to struggle with the balance of aspirational statements and rules of minimum conduct. Over the last century the legal profession has moved away from reliance on aspirational statements in our systems of self-regulation, going from Canons of Ethics, to Code of Professional Responsibility to the very positivist Rules of Professional Conduct.

This chapter concludes with a real case, *Repouille v. United States*, 165 F.2d 152 (2d Cir. 1947). As you will see, it has close similarities to Lon Fuller's "Case of the Speluncean Explorers." Even more important, the three judges were three of the most brilliant ever to sit in American courts: Learned Hand, Augustus N. Hand, and Jerome Frank. All three were strongly influenced by Holmes's judicial philosophy, and Jerome Frank was a great advocate of "legal realism."[26] But they could not agree in the *Repouille* case about how to define the words "good moral character" as used in the immigration law, 8 U.S.C. § 707(a)(3). Note, the old *ABA Model Code* also prohibited lawyers from engaging in "illegal conduct involving moral turpitude" and "conduct that is prejudicial to the administration of justice." *See* DR-1-102 (A)(3), (5). This rule was not an "aspirational" "EC," but a mandatory "DR."[27] The *Model Rules of Professional Conduct* abandoned the aspirational "ECs," and have only mandatory rules, but there is still a rule which prohibits lawyers from committing criminal acts that reflect "adversely on the lawyer's honesty, trustworthiness or fitness as a lawyer in other respects" and engaging "in conduct that is prejudicial to the administration of justice," Model Rule 8.4.[28] What do these terms mean? Fuller would argue that we may not be able to agree on some aspects of "good moral character," or "moral turpitude" or "conduct . . . prejudicial to the administration of justice," but we should nevertheless seek a consensus as to what we can agree on. What would that be? Do the three great judicial minds at work in the *Repouille* case help? Can Oliver Wendell Holmes, Jr. help?

C. FURTHER READING

For excellent, concise accounts of the impact of the Renaissance and the Reformation on ethical philosophy, see A. P. D'ENTREVES, NATURAL LAW 33–94 (1951); ALASDAIR MACLNTYRE, A SHORT HISTORY OF ETHICS 121–156 (1998); and

---

obligation] and the challenge of excellence begins [i.e., aspirational goals]. The whole field of moral argument is dominated by a great undeclared war over the location of this pointer." *Id.* 10.

[25] *Id.* 32. "In the social practices I have just described there is a standing refutation for the notion, so common in moral argument, that we must know the perfectly good before we can recognize the bad or barely adequate. . . . [O]ur common sense tells us that we can apply more objective standards to departures from satisfactory performance than we can to performances reaching toward perfection. And it is on this common sense view that we build our institutions and practices." *Id.* 32.

[26] *See* JEROME FRANK, LAW AND THE MODERN MIND (1930, reprint 2008).

[27] "EC 1-5" states that a lawyer should "refrain from . . . morally reprehensible conduct," but that is just "aspirational." *See* ABA CODE OF PROFESSIONAL RESPONSIBILITY 1983.

[28] *See* ABA MODEL RULES OF PROFESSIONAL CONDUCT (2009).

BERTRAND RUSSELL, A HISTORY OF WESTERN PHILOSOPHY 491–596 (2007). Excellent translations of Grotius were created by the Carnegie Endowment for International Peace. Particularly recommended is Francis Kelsey's translation of DE JURE BELLI AC PACIS (1927, I, II, 1928, III) and Ralph van Daman Magoffin's translation of MARE LIBERUM (1916, reprint 2001). EDWARD DUMBAULD'S, THE LIFE AND LEGAL WRITINGS OF HUGO GROTIUS (1969) is a captivating introduction to Grotius as a jurist and as an individual. For the empirical philosophy of another great Renaissance jurist, Grotius's contemporary Francis Bacon, see DANIEL R. COQUILLETTE, FRANCIS BACON (1992).

For an introduction to the jurisprudence of Oliver Wendell Holmes, Jr., see the magnificent Holmes Lectures of 1981 by Benjamin Kaplan, Patrick Atiyah, and Jan Vetter, celebrating the centennial of the publication of THE COMMON LAW (1981), published as HOLMES AND THE COMMON LAW: A CENTURY LATER (1983). *See also* the excellent anthology edited by ROBERT W. GORDON, THE LEGACY OF OLIVER WENDELL HOLMES, JR. (1992), and the provocative chapter on *The Place of Justice Holmes in American Legal Thought, in* MORTON J. HORWITZ'S, THE TRANSFORMATION OF AMERICAN LAW 1870–1960, 109–143 (1992). Holmes's greatest essays, *The Path of the Law* (1897) and *Natural Law* (1918) are reproduced in OLIVER WENDELL HOLMES, COLLECTED LEGAL PAPERS 167–202, 310–316 (1920). Again, as an introduction to Holmes as an extraordinary individual, it is still hard to surpass Catherine Drinker Bowen's imaginative YANKEE FROM OLYMPUS (1944).

For the legal "realism" of Holmes and his successors, including Jerome Frank, see HENRY STEELE COMMAGER, THE AMERICAN MIND 375, 381 (1950) and the innovative new study by MORTON J. HORWITZ, in THE TRANSFORMATION OF AMERICAN LAW 1870-1960, at 169–246. Best of all is Jerome Frank's own account in LAW AND THE MODERN MIND (1930).

Particularly valuable for its lucid and thorough analysis of the secular "natural law" controversy is LLOYD L. WEINREB'S, NATURAL LAW AND JUSTICE (1987). *See also* the excellent ESSAYS IN LEGAL PHILOSOPHY (1968), selected and edited by Robert S. Summers, and RICHARD TUCK, NATURAL RIGHTS THEORIES (1979). Defining the two sides of a dispute over enforcement of morality are PATRICK DEVLIN'S THE ENFORCEMENT OF MORALS (1965) ("For") and H. L. A. HART'S LAW, LIBERTY AND MORALITY (1963) ("Against"). BASIL MITCHELL'S LAW, MORALITY AND RELIGION IN A SECULAR SOCIETY (1967) provides a "score card," particularly in his introductory chapter, *The Debate Between Lord Devlin and Professor Hart*. Mitchell also explores the issue raised by Fuller, *In What Sense is a Shared Morality Essential for Society, in* LAW, MORALITY AND RELIGION IN A SECULAR SOCIETY 18–35. Finally, for the "latest word," see John Finnis, *The "Natural Law Tradition,"* Donald H. Regan, *What a Sensible Natural Law and a Sensible Utilitarian Agree About and Disagree About: Response to Finnis,* and Lloyd L. Weinreb, *The Natural Law Tradition: Comments on Finnis,* all in 36 J. LEGAL EDUC. (1986) (pages 492–495, 496–500, and 501–504, respectively).

D. DISCUSSION PROBLEMS

PROBLEM X

Prepare *The Case of the Speluncean Explorers*, Fuller, 62 Harv. L. Rev. 616, 616–645 (1949). *Materials, infra* at 5E. As a judge, how would you have decided this case? Support your decision. If you think this case is at all far-fetched, read *United States v. Holmes*, 26 F. Cas. 360 (C.C.E.D. Pa. 1842), and *Regina v. Dudley & Stephens*, 14 Q.B. 273 (1881–1885), All E.R. Rep. 61 (1884).

PROBLEM XI

Prepare *Repouille v. United States*, 165 F.2d 152 (2d Cir. 1947). *Materials, infra* at 5E. The judges sitting on this case were, of course, three of the greatest of their time, Learned Hand, Augustus Hand, and Jerome Frank. Do you agree with the opinion of Judge Learned Hand or with Judge Jerome Frank? Does Judge Frank's view present problems in a democracy?

PROBLEM XII

After the World Trade Center attacks in New York on September 11, 2001, the U.S. government embarked on a massive anti-terrorism campaign. Central to that goal was improved intelligence gathering, including the use of aggressive interrogation techniques. Questions quickly arose about the use of torture by U.S. personnel. The Office of Legal Counsel (OLC) is a division of the Department of Justice that provides authoritative legal advice to the President and executive branch agencies, and also serves as general counsel to the Department of Justice. From 2001 to the present, the lawyers in the OLC were intimately involved in determining the legality of government actions in the war on terror, including what interrogation techniques may legally be employed. Memos written by the OLC lawyers would eventually give legal sanction to waterboarding (a process of pouring water over a person's head to give the sensation of drowning), placing a person in a small box, sleep deprivation, forced nudity, slapping, and throwing a person against a flexible wall, and other interrogation techniques.

You are a lawyer in the Office of Legal Counsel. You are deeply committed to protecting your country from harm. Assume for purposes of discussion that (1) you and your fellow lawyers are extremely bright and able to come up with very aggressive interpretations of the Constitution, statutes, and treaties that would justify these interrogation techniques, including a claim that as Commander-in-Chief the president is not subject to any legislative constraints on what he may do in that role, and (2) there are very strong contrary legal arguments that would strongly support prohibiting these same interrogation techniques. What will you advise? Does natural law have any relevance in the arguments you make as a lawyer? If so, how do you justify your concerns? Does natural law give you any insights on whether you should include contrary arguments in whatever advice you give?

A wide range of additional information and analysis is available on the "torture memos." For a justification of the lawyers' conduct, see JOHN YOO, WAR BY OTHER

MEANS: AN INSIDER'S ACCOUNT OF THE WAR ON TERROR (2006). For a different view, see JACK GOLDSMITH, THE TERROR PRESIDENCY: LAW AND JUDGMENT INSIDE THE BUSH ADMINISTRATION (2007). Those roundly criticizing the lawyers include Daniel Kanstroom, *Law, Torture, and the "Task of the Good Laywer:—Mukasey Agnostites,"* 32 B.C. INT'L & COMP. L. REV. 187 (2009). *See also* W. Bradley Wendel, *Legal Ethics and the Separation of Law and Morals,* 91 CORNELL L. REV. 67 (2005), W. Bradley Wendel, *Deference to Clients and Obedience to Law: The Ethics of the Torture Lawyers (A Response to Professor Hatfield),* 104 NW. U. L. REV. COLLOQUY 58 (2009). The published OLC memos are available online at http://www.usdoj.gov/olc.

E. MATERIALS

HUGO GROTIUS, OF THE RIGHTS OF WAR AND PEACE
Vol. 1 pages 45–49, 50–51, 53–54 (John Morrice trans., 1715)
(Orig. Pub. 1625)

BOOK I

CHAPTER I

WHAT WAR IS, AND WHAT RIGHT IS

X. 1.[29] Natural Right is the Rule and Dictate of Right Reason, Shewing the Moral Deformity, or Moral Necessity there is in any Act, by either its complying, or disagreeing with Human Nature it self, and consequently that such an Act is either forbid, or commanded by God, the Author of Nature.

2. The Actions upon which such a Dictate is given, are Morally and in themselves either Obligatory or Unlawful, and therefore must consequently be understood to be either commanded, or forbid by God himself; and this makes the Law of Nature differ not only from Human Right, but from a Voluntary Divine Right; for that does not command or forbid such things as are in themselves, or in their own Nature Obligatory and Unlawful, but by forbidding it renders the one Unlawful, and by commanding the other Obligatory.

3. But that we may the better understand this Law of Nature, we must observe, that some things are said to belong to it, not properly, but (as the Schoolmen love to speak) by way of Reduction, and indirectly, that is, to which the Law of Nature

---

[29] "Natural Right is the Rule and Dictate of Right Reason." Philo in his Book, entitled, *Every Good Man Free:* "Right Reason is a Law that cannot deceive or be Erroneous, a Law not to be corrupted by this or that mortal Man, not a dead lifeless Thing on lifeless Paper or Pillars, but from its own Immortal Nature unperishable, deeply ingraved on the Immortal Mind." And Tertullian, *of the Soldier's Crown:* "Will you then inquire for the Law of God, a written Law to prove it, when you have in common with all the World the Natural Law impressed on your Minds?" And M. Autominus: "The End and Purpose of Rational Animals is to observe and follow that Reason and Law which has prevailed in the City and Government of greatest Antiquity."

is not repugnant; as some things, we just now said, are called just, because they have no Injustice in them; and sometimes by the wrong use of the Word, those things which our Reason declares to be honest, or comparatively good, tho' they are not enjoyed us, are said to belong to this Natural Law.

4. We must further observe, that this Natural Law does not only respect such things as depend not upon Human Will, but also many things which have been allowed by the general Consent of Mankind. Thus Dominion, as now in use, was introduced by Man's Consent, and being once admitted, this Law of Nature informs us, that it is a wicked thing to take away from any Man against his Will what is properly his own. Wherefore *Paulus* the Lawyer infers, that[30] Theft is forbid by the Law of Nature; *Ulpian*, that it is dishonest by Nature, and *Euripides* calls it hateful to God, as you may see in these Verses of *Helena*.

> *For God hates Violence; and ne'er approves*
> *What's not by fair Means, but Oppression, gain'd.*
> *Wealth got by Fraud deserves our utmost Scorn.*
> *The Air and Earth are Human Property,*
> *And afford the World sufficient room:*
> *No need at all t' invade another's Right.*

5. But the Law of Nature is so unalterable, that God himself cannot change it. For tho' the Power of God be Immense, yet may we say, that there are some things unto which this infinite Power does not extend. Indeed when we speak so, 'tis only a manner of speaking, that is so far from signifying any thing, that it implies in it a manifest Contradiction. For instance then, as twice two should not be four, God himself cannot effect; so neither can he, that what is intrinsically evil, should not be evil. And this is Aristotle's Meaning when he says, *some things are no sooner mention'd, than we discover Depravity in 'em.* For as the Being of things after they exist, and in the manner they exist, depends not upon any other, so neither do the Properties which necessarily follow that Being. Now such is the Evil of some Actions, compared with Nature guided by right Reason. Therefore God suffers himself to be judged of according to this Rule, as we may find, *Gen. xviii. 25. Efai v. 3. Ezek. Xviii. 25. Ferem, ii. 9. Mich. vi 2. Rom ii. 6. iii. 6.*

6. Yet it sometimes happens, that in these Acts, concerning which the Law of Nature has determined something, some shew of Change may deceive the Unthinking, whereas indeed the Law of Nature is not changed; but the Things, concerning which the Law of Nature determines, may undergo a Change. As for Example: If my Creditor forgive me my Debt, I am not then obliged to pay it; not that the Law of Nature ceases to command me to pay what I owe, but because what I did owe ceases to be a Debt. For as *Arrian* rightly argues in *Epictetus, to make a just Debt, it is not enough that the Mony was lent, but it is also requisite, that the Obligation continue undischarg'd.* So when God commands any Man to be put to Death, or his

---

[30] "Theft is forbid by the Law of Nature." Julian. "There's a Second law" (after that of acknowledging and worshipping God) "a Law in its own Nature Sacred and Divine, which Commands us at all Times, and in all Places to abstain from what belongs to others; and which permits us neither in Word nor Deed, nor even in our most private thoughts to confound each other's Properties." And *Cicero* in his 3d Book of Offices, from *Chrylippus:* "In Life tis allowable that every one should get what is useful and convenient for his comfortable Substance, but it is not to take it away from other People."

Goods to be taken away, Murder and Theft do not thereby become lawful, which very words always include a Crime; but that cannot be Murder, or Theft, which is done by the express Command of him who is the Sovereign Lord of our Lives and Estates.

7. There are also some things allowed by the Law of Nature, not absolutely, but according to the present posture of Affairs; so' till a Property was admitted, the common Use of things was natural, and before the erecting of Courts of Judicature, it was lawful to recover our own by Force.

XI. 1. But that Distinction which we find in the Books of the *Roman* Laws, that this immutable Right is of two sorts, either such as is common to Men with Beasts, which they call in a stricter Sense the Law of Nature; or that which is peculiar to Men, which they often style the Law of Nations, is of very little or no use; for nothing is properly capable of a Law, but that Nature which can practice general Precepts; which *Hesiod* has well observ'd:

> *(n) To us great Jove has kindly given Laws:*
> *But Fish, and Beasts, and Birds, for want of these*
> *Devour each other; they no 'Justice have.*
> *Blest Man's possest of This, the best of Goods.*

*   *   *

2. If at any time Justice be attributed to Brute Beasts, it is improperly, and only on the Account of some Shadow or Resemblance of Reason. But it is not Material to the very Essence of Right, whether the Act itself, on which the Law of Nature has decreed, be common to us, with other Creatures, as the *bringing up of* our Offspring, or peculiar to us only, as the Worship of God.

XII. Now that any thing is or is not by the Laws of Nature, is generally proved by Arguments drawn either from what goes before or from what follows. The former way of Reasoning is the finer and more abstracted; the later more popular. The Proof by the former is by shewing the necessary Agreement or Disagreement of any thing, with a Nature that's reasonable and designed for Society. But the Proof by the latter is, when we cannot by perfect Demonstration, yet with very great Probability, conclude that to be the Effect of the Law of Nature, which is generally believed to be so by all, or at least, the most civilized, Nations. For an universal Effect, requires an universal Cause. And there cannot well be any other cause assigned for this General Opinion than that General Sense, which is said to be common to all Mankind.

*   *   *

XIII. The other kind of Right, we told you, is the Voluntary Right, as being derived from the Will, and is either Human or Divine.

XIV. We will begin with the Human, as more generally known; and this is either a Civil, a Particular, or a Common Right. The *Civil* Right is that which results from the Civil Power. The *Civil* Power is that which governs the *State*. The State is a compleat Company of Free Persons, associated together to enjoy the Protection of Laws for their common Benefit. The Particular Right, and which is not derived from the Civil Power, though subject to it, is various, including in it that of a Father over his Child, of a Master over his Servant, and the like. But the common Right, is the Right of Nations, which derives its Authority from the unanimous Approbation of all, or at least of many, Nations. I said *of many*, because there is scarce any Right found, except that of Nature, which is also called the Right of Nations, common to all Nations. Nay, that which is reputed the Right or Law of Nations in one part of the World, is not so in another, as we shall shew hereafter, when we come to treat of *Prisoners of War*, and *Postliminy* or the *Right of Returning*. Now the Proofs on which the Law of Nations is founded, are the same with those of the Unwritten Civil law, *viz.* continued Use, and the Testimony of Men skilled in the Laws. For this Law is, as *Dio Chrysostom* well observes, the Invention of Time and Experience. And to this purpose the eminent Authors of the World's Annals are of excellent use to us.

QUESTIONS

1. Grotius said that "the Law of Nature is so unalterable, that God himself cannot change it." What does he mean by this?

2. Grotius uses as one test of the "Law of Nature" that "which is generally believed to be so by all, or at least, the most civilized, Nations." Which are the "most civilized Nations" today? Do they agree on some fundamental things?

3. Grotius gives protection of private property and human life as two of the cornerstones of the "Law of Nature." Do you agree?

A. P. D'ENTREVES, NATURAL LAW
95–98, 102–103, 108–111 (1951)

CH. VI. THE IDEAL LAW

It has been the purpose of this enquiry to show that the theory of natural law provided answers to many problems which still face the modern legal philosopher. No assessment of that theory would, however, be complete without taking into account what may well be said to constitute its most constant feature all through the ages: the assertion of the possibility of testing the validity of all laws by referring them to an ultimate measure, to an ideal law which can be known and appraised with an even greater measure of certainty than all existing legislation. Natural law is the outcome of man's quest for an absolute standard of justice. It is based upon a particular conception of the relationship between the ideal and the real. It is a dualist theory which presupposes a rift, though not necessarily a contrast, between what is and what ought to be.

This must not be taken to mean that the doctrine of natural law is at heart a revolutionary doctrine. Nothing indeed would be more remote from the truth. If natural law played a revolutionary part at certain epochs of Western history, it is equally true that, during most of its age-long development, the doctrine was limited to a mildly progressive, and at times to a frankly conservative function. The recognition of the existence of an ideal law did not necessarily imply that positive law should be overruled by it in cases of conflict. Natural law could serve as well to support revolutionary claims as to justify an existing legal order. It could even lead to the glorification of a particular system of law, as when Roman law, after its reception on the Continent as the "common" law of Europe, came to be considered as the *ratio scripta*, or as when Sir Edward Coke described the English Common law as "nothing else but reason". Justice Holmes humorously described this particular outcome of natural law by remarking:

> It is not enough for the knight of romance that you agree that his lady is a very nice girl—if you do not admit that she is the best that God ever made or will make, you must fight. There is in all men a demand for the superlative, so much so that the poor devil who has no other way of reaching it obtains it by getting drunk. It seems to me that this demand is at the bottom of the philosopher's effort to prove that truth is absolute and of the jurist's search for criteria of universal validity which he collects under the head of natural law (Holmes, *Natural Law*, in "Harvard Law Review," 1918).

This is not a very charitable judgment: but there is no doubt that natural law was the *belle dame sans merci* who inspired the crusading spirit of old-time jurisprudence. That spirit has gone. It has given way to a realistic approach which is in keeping with an age of prosaic undertakings. The study of the ideal law is no longer conceived as being of any relevance to the lawyer. "The juridical science of the nineteenth and twentieth century expressly declares itself incapable of drawing the problem of justice into the scope of its enquiries" (Kelsen). It actually prides itself on being able to master and to construct into a system any given legal material without resorting to the delusion of natural law. The abandonment of natural law marks the rise of modern jurisprudence. This is the fundamental fact which we must keep in mind in order to understand, if only from a negative angle, what natural law ultimately stood for. It may well be that after we have examined the achievements and limitations of modern jurisprudence, the case for natural law may once again be assessed in a positive manner.

The rise of modern jurisprudence is marked by the abandonment of natural law and by a new or "positive" approach to legal experience. But the notion of natural law as the embodiment of justice and as the ultimate ground of the validity of all laws had been criticized long before the advent of positive jurisprudence. Nor can the new approach be described as the outcome of any particular doctrinal standpoint. The word "positivism," if one cares to use it in this connection, can indicate only an attitude rather than a definite philosophical creed. Indeed, the oldest argument against natural justice is the sceptical argument. It goes back to the very beginnings of speculative thought. It has a long history which stretches down from the Sophists to the present day. I need only refer the reader, for a classical treatment of the subject, to Hume's *Treatise of Human Nature*, Book II, part ii, or to the section in Cicero's *Republic* (III, vi—xx), where Carneades' argument is set forth with sufficient vigor and clearness to remind us how little there is that can be called entirely new in legal and political philosophy.

Modern or positive jurisprudence is not necessarily based upon scepticism, nor does it imply a denial that the problem of justice exists. Modern jurists may be willing to leave the discussion of the ultimate reason why law should be regarded as binding to the legal philosopher, without taking a definite stand about the existence of natural law. Nor do they accept as a matter of course the "monist" view of the coincidence of the ideal and the real which, as we have seen in a preceding chapter, consecrated the law of the State as the embodiment of ethical values. All they do is to put the problem of the ideal of natural law, as it were, within brackets. However influenced they may have been or still are by one or other philosophical current, their implicit or explicit philosophy is not the determining factor. They are indeed anxious to convince us that theirs is not a philosophical, but a "scientific" concern.

This, I understand, is apparent among English jurists. To the foreign observer English jurisprudence—with some notable exceptions—may still seem to have a flavour of utilitarianism as a distinctive national characteristic. And indeed, if we think of Austin, we may well believe that the cradle of modem English jurisprudence was utilitarian philosophy. But Austin himself, if I am not mistaken, was careful not to tie his notion of jurisprudence to any particular philosophical assumption. He actually avoided any final pronouncement on the possibility of evaluating legal experience from a standpoint other than that of the "analytical" jurist. Of general jurisprudence he wrote:

> It is concerned directly with principles and distinctions which are common to various systems of particular or positive law; and which each of these various systems inevitably involves, let it be worthy of praise or blame, or let it accord or not with an assumed measure or test. (AUSTIN, *Lectures*, Campbell's ed., I, 33).

He seems clearly to admit that "the goodness or badness of laws" might be tried "by the test of utility (or by any of the various tests which divide the opinions of mankind)." He contented himself with declaring that with this kind of undertaking general jurisprudence "has no immediate concern." The problem of the ideal law is neither denied nor declared insoluble. It is simply put within brackets as irrelevant to the task of the jurist.

*   *   *

The real question was to determine which laws are sufficiently "definite," or "binding," or "positive" to deserve the name of laws. It is on this point that the difficulties began, and that the peculiarities of legal empiricism soon became apparent. It gradually dawned upon lawyers and jurists that the validity or "positiveness" of law cannot consist, or at least cannot consist solely, in the mere fact of its enforcement. The use of force, or the possibility of its use, is only the outward or material aspect of positive law. From a strictly juridical or "formal" point of view the validity of a particular law cannot depend upon its varying degree of effectiveness. It consists in the fact that that particular law belongs to a system which is singled out and recognized as the only positive and valid system.

That this system, to nineteenth century jurists, was the system or legal order of the State, has only a relative importance. The formal or logical side of their argument is the side which calls for attention. To say that the positiveness of law derives from its belonging to a positive system is in fact only a different way of saying that the recognition of its validity as a law depends on the possibility of referring it back, directly or indirectly, to a common source from which all legal precepts ultimately proceed. This is what the jurists, borrowing an old term with which we are already acquainted, indicated under the name of sovereignty. Sovereignty became the sacred dogma of positive jurisprudence, because it was the condition of the positiveness of law. Sovereignty may be, and indeed is, a fact. But from the juridical angle it was also, and essentially, a formal criterion: the criterion which made it possible to recognize a rule or a body of rules as part of a positive order, and, therefore to pronounce on their validity as laws.

Thus the restriction of all law to positive law and the quest for a systematic construction of the legal order went hand in hand. They are indeed the two fundamental aspects of modern jurisprudence. Its tendency to become more and more "formal" was only a consequence of its purpose to be a "positive" science, that is, to steer clear of any criterion of validity of law—such as natural law—extraneous to the system.

*   *   *

I would like to conclude this long argument with the mention of some recent examples of the inadequacy of legal positivism to solve the problem of the ultimate validity of law. Examples of this kind are, in our troubled days, only too frequent. I remember a time, not very remote, when there was in my country not one but four different legal orders, all of which could have claimed some degree of "positiveness." I prefer to use a simpler example which was given by Professor Goodhart in a recent article.

A statute is promulgated during the war by the Netherlands Government in London, purporting to bind Dutch subjects in Holland. Professor Goodhart asks "is this law?"—by which he means, I presume, "is it positive law?", law the validity of which can be ascertained by the criteria of positive jurisprudence. Now, as Professor Goodhart points out, the statute was certainly a law from the point of view of the Netherlands Government, who regarded themselves as having the right to issue it, independently of the fact whether it could ever be made efficacious. Yet, on the other hand, the German authorities would never have regarded it as a law, not even if every citizen in Holland had obeyed it. From the standpoint of a third party, such as the British courts, the question might have been dubious. "The real difficult question arises, however, when we consider the position of the inhabitant of Holland."

Professor Goodhart suggests that, at the end of the war, the Netherlands courts would have considered his particular views as immaterial. They would have confined themselves to assessing the actual observance or violation of the statute. And, indeed, so they should according to "positive" jurisprudence. But, as Professor Goodhart frankly admits, "this does not mean that the view of the individual is unimportant. On the contrary, a large part of political history has been concerned with disputes between individuals and governments regarding the authority of the latter to declare law."

I submit that what Professor Goodhart seems to consider a political issue is what our benighted ancestors would have called a clear issue of natural law. I submit that this issue can be solved only on the traditional lines of calling the validity of positive law into question, and that it is impossible for the individual to do so unless he decides on the justice of the law which he is asked to obey. But I further submit that it is possible to find in quite recent developments of legal theory and practice a clear indication of a return to the obsolete notions which positivism had criticized and declared to be unacceptable.

That the whole question of the trial of war criminals at the end of the war would raise a "natural law" issue was an authoritative opinion which events have fully confirmed. No doubt the provisions for the Nürnberg Tribunal were based, or purported to be based, on existing or "positive" international law. Apart from the preliminary and controversial question of individual responsibility under international law, the violation of international treaties, of the laws and customs of war, and above all of Article I of the Preamble to the Fourth Hague Convention of 1907 (the "Martens clause" which formally included the "laws of humanity" and the "dictates of the public conscience" within the boundaries of international law) certainly provided a "positive" basis for the prosecution.

But I strongly suspect that the boundaries of legal positivism were overstepped, and had to be overstepped, the moment it was stated that the trials were a "question of justice." The principle *nullum crimen sine poena*, [no crime goes unpunished], on which the sentences were grounded, was a flat contradiction of one of the most generally accepted principles of positive jurisprudence, the principle *nulla poena sine lege* [no punishment without law]. Whether or not the assertion of that principle constitutes a dangerous precedent is not for me to judge. All I suggest is that the words used by the Court ("So far from it being unjust to punish him, it would be unjust if his wrong were allowed to go unpunished") are clearly reminiscent of old natural law argumentations. The rejection of the defence of superior orders makes that reminiscence even more poignant: for it is nothing less than the old doctrine that the validity of laws does not depend on their "positiveness," and that it is the duty of the individual to pass judgment on laws before he obeys them.

Thus, after a century of effort to eliminate the dualism between what is and what ought to be from the field of legal and political experience, natural law seems to have taken its revenge upon the very champions of the pernicious doctrine that there is no law but positive law, or that might equals right, since for all practical purposes the two propositions are perfectly equivalent.

QUESTIONS

1.   D'Entrèves states that "[t]he rise of modern jurisprudence is marked by the abandonment of natural law and by a new or 'positive' approach to legal experience." *Id.* Assuming this is true, why should this be? Does it help explain the relative paucity of discussion about justice in U.S. law school classrooms?

2.   D'Entrèves makes a pointed reference to the Nuremburg Tribunal. Was there a basis for that Tribunal other than natural law? What difference does it make?

3.   D'Entrèves concludes by identifying positivism with "might equals right, since for all practical purposes the two propositions are perfectly equivalent." Do you agree?

OLIVER WENDELL HOLMES, JR., NATURAL LAW
Collected Legal Papers
310–316 (1920)
from 32 HARVARD LAW REVIEW 40 (1918)

NATURAL LAW

It is not enough for the knight of romance that you agree that his lady is a very nice girl—if you do not admit that she is the best that God ever made or will make, you must fight. There is in all men a demand for the superlative, so much so that the poor devil who has no other way of reaching it attains it by getting drunk. It seems to me that this demand is at the bottom of the philosopher's effort to prove that truth is absolute and of the jurist's search for criteria of universal validity which he collects under the head of natural law.

I used to say, when I was young, that truth was the majority vote of that nation that could lick all others. Certainly we may expect that the received opinion about the present war will depend a good deal upon which side wins (I hope with all my soul it will be mine), and I think that the statement was correct in so far as it implied that our test of truth is a reference to either a present or an imagined future majority in favor of our view. If, as I have suggested elsewhere, the truth may be defined as the system of my (intellectual) limitations, what gives it objectivity is the fact that I find my fellow man to a greater or less extent (never wholly) subject to the same *Can't Helps*. If I think that I am sitting at a table I find that the other persons present agree with me; so if I say that the sum of the angles of a triangle is equal to two right angles. If I am in a minority of one they send for a doctor or lock me up; and I am so far able to transcend the to me convincing testimony of my senses or my reason as to recognize that if I am alone probably something is wrong with my works.

Certitude is not the test of certainty. We have been cock-sure of many things that were not so. If I may quote myself again, property, friendship, and truth have a common root in time. One can not be wrenched from the rocky crevices into which one has grown for many years without feeling that one is attacked in one's life. What we most love and revere generally is determined by early associations. I love granite rocks and barberry bushes, no doubt because with them were my earliest joys that reach back through the past eternity of my life. But while one's experience thus makes certain preferences dogmatic for oneself, recognition of how they came to be so leaves one able to see that others, poor souls, may be equally dogmatic about something else. And this again means scepticism. Not that one's belief or love does not remain. Not that we would not fight and die for it if important—we all, whether we know it or not, are fighting to make the kind of a world that we should like—but that we have learned to recognize that others will fight and die to make a different world, with equal sincerity or belief. Deep-seated preferences can not be argued about—you can not argue a man into liking a glass of beer—and therefore, when differences are sufficiently far reaching, we try to kill the other man rather than let him have his way. But that is perfectly consistent with admitting that, so far as appears, his grounds are just as good as ours.

The jurists who believe in natural law seem to me to be in that naive state of mind that accepts what has been familiar and accepted by them and their neighbors as something that must be accepted by all men everywhere. No doubt it is true that, so far as we can see ahead, some arrangements and the rudiments of familiar institutions seem to be necessary elements in any society that may spring from our own and that would seem to us to be civilized—some form of permanent association between the sexes—some residue of property individually owned—some mode of binding oneself to specified future conduct—at the bottom of all, some protection for the person. But without speculating whether a group is imaginable in which all but the last of these might disappear and the last be subject to qualifications that most of us would abhor, the question remains as to the *Ought* of natural law.

It is true that beliefs and wishes have a transcendental basis in the sense that their foundation is arbitrary. You can not help entertaining and feeling them, and there is an end of it. As an arbitrary fact people wish to live, and we say with various degrees of certainty that they can do so only on certain conditions. To do it they must eat and drink. That necessity is absolute. It is a necessity of less degree but practically general that they should live in society. If they live in society, so far as we can see, there are further conditions. Reason working on experience does tell us, no doubt, that if our wish to live continues, we can do it only on those terms. But that seems to me the whole of the matter. I see no *a priori* duty to live with others and in that way, but simply a statement of what I must do if I wish to remain alive. If I do live with others they tell me that I must do and abstain from doing various things or they will put the screws on to me. I believe that they will, and being of the same mind as to their conduct I not only accept the rules but come in time to accept them with sympathy and emotional affirmation and begin to talk about duties and rights. But for legal purposes a right is only the hypostasis of a prophecy—the imagination of a substance supporting the fact that the public force will be brought to bear upon those who do things said to contravene it—just as we talk of the force of gravitation accounting for the conduct of bodies in space. One phrase adds no more than the other to what we know without it. No doubt behind these legal rights is the fighting will of the subject to maintain them, and the spread of his emotions to the general rules by which they are maintained; but that does not seem to me the same thing as the supposed *a priori* discernment of a duty or the assertion of a preexisting right. A dog will fight for his bone.

The most fundamental of the supposed preëxisting rights—the right to life—is sacrificed without a scruple not only in war, but whenever the interest of society, that is, of the predominant power in the community, is thought to demand it. Whether that interest is the interest of mankind in the long run no one can tell, and as, in any event, to those who do not think with Kant and Hegel it is only an interest, the sanctity disappears. I remember a very tenderhearted judge being of opinion that closing a hatch to stop a fire and the destruction of a cargo was justified even if it was known that doing so would stifle a man below. It is idle to illustrate further, because to those who agree with me I am uttering commonplaces and to those who disagree I am ignoring the necessary foundations of thought. The *a priori* men generally call the dissentients superficial. But I do agree with them in believing that one's attitude on these matters is closely connected with one's general attitude toward the universe. Proximately, as has been suggested, it is determined largely by early associations and temperament, coupled with the desire to have an absolute guide. Men to a great extent believe what they want to—although I see in that no basis for a philosophy that tells us what we should want to want.

Now when we come to our attitude toward the universe I do not see any rational ground for demanding the superlative—for being dissatisfied unless we are assured that our truth is cosmic truth, if there is such a thing—that the ultimates of a little creature on this little earth are the last word of the unimaginable whole. If a man sees no reason for believing that significance, consciousness and ideals are more than marks of the finite, that does not justify what has been familiar in French sceptics; getting upon a pedestal and professing to look with haughty scorn upon a world in ruins. The real conclusion is that the part can not swallow the whole—that our categories are not, or may not be, adequate to formulate what we cannot know. If we believe that we come out of the universe, not it out of us, we must admit that we do not know what we are talking about when we speak of brute matter. We do know that a certain complex of energies can wag its tail and another can make syllogisms. These are among the powers of the unknown, and if, as may be, it has still greater powers that we can not understand, as Fabre in his studies of instinct would have us believe, studies that gave Bergson one of the strongest strands for his philosophy and enabled Maeterlinck to make us fancy for a moment that we heard a clang from behind phenomena—if this be true, why should we not be content? Why should we employ the energy that is furnished to us by the cosmos to defy it and shake our fist at the sky? It seems to me silly.

That the universe has in it more than we understand, that the private soldiers have not been told the plan of campaign, or even that there is one, rather than some vaster unthinkable to which every predicate is an impertinence, has no bearing upon our conduct. We still shall fight—all of us because we want to live, some, at least, because we want to realize our spontaneity and prove our powers, for the joy of it, and we may leave to the unknown the supposed final valuation of that which in any event has value to us. It is enough for us that the universe has produced us and has within it, as less than it, all that we believe and love. If we think of our existence not as that of a little god outside, but as that of a ganglion within, we have the infinite behind us. It gives us our only but our adequate significance. A grain of sand has the same, but what competent person supposes that he understands a grain of sand? That is as much beyond our grasp as man. If our imagination is strong enough to accept the vision of ourselves as parts inseverable from the rest, and to extend our final interest beyond the boundary of our skins, it justifies the sacrifice even of our lives for ends outside of ourselves. The motive, to be sure, is the common wants and ideals that we find in man. Philosophy does not furnish motives, but it shows men that they are not fools for doing what they already want to do. It opens to the forlorn hopes on which we throw ourselves away, the vista of the farthest stretch of human thought, the chords of a harmony that breathes from the unknown.

QUESTIONS

1.   Holmes wrote "Natural Law" while the world was convulsed in World War I. He, himself, saw terrible slaughter in the Civil War and was badly wounded. Yet he writes, "I used to say, when I was young, that truth was the majority vote of that nation that could lick all others," and goes on, "Certainly we may expect that the received opinion about the present war will depend a good deal upon which side wins (I hope with all my soul it will be mine) . . . our test of truth is a reference to either a present or an imagined future majority in favor of our view." Holmes, Jr., *Natural Law.* What would Holmes have thought of the Nuremberg Tribunal? Of Telford Tayor and d'Entrèves? Of arguments based on "justice"?

2.   Holmes argues that "jurists who believe in natural law seem to me to be in that naïve state of mind that accepts what has been familiar and accepted by them and their neighbors as something that must be accepted by all men everywhere." Later, in the definition of legal rights, he observes simply that, "A dog will fight for his bone." Holmes, Jr., *Natural Law.* What would Holmes see as the basis for legal rights? For professional responsibility? For the ABA Model Rules?

3.   Holmes rightly points out that we may have deeply felt differences about what is correct in particular circumstances. Is this a fatal blow to the idea of natural law? Why not?

4.   In concluding, Holmes returns to the analogy of war. He notes "[t]hat the universe has in it more than we understand, that the private soldiers have not been told the plan of campaign, or even that there is one." Holmes, Jr., *Natural Law.* What would St. Thomas Aquinas think of this? Plato? For lawyers of Holmes's belief, is there any alternative to positivism?

LON L. FULLER, THE CASE OF THE SPELUNCEAN EXPLORERS
62 HARVARD LAW REVIEW 616 (1949)

IN THE SUPREME COURT OF NEWGARTH, 4300

The defendants, having been indicted for the crime of murder, were convicted and sentenced to be hanged by the Court of General Instances of the County of Stowfield. They bring a petition of error before this Court. The facts sufficiently appear in the opinion of the Chief Justice.

TRUEPENNY, C. J. The four defendants are members of the Speluncean Society, an organization of amateurs interested in the exploration of caves. Early in May of 4299 they, in the company of Roger Whetmore, then also a member of the Society, penetrated into the interior of a limestone cavern of the type found in the Central Plateau of this Commonwealth. While they were in a position remote from the entrance to the cave, a landslide occurred. Heavy boulders fell in such a manner as to block completely the only known opening to the cave. When the men discovered their predicament they settled themselves near the obstructed entrance to wait until a rescue party should remove the detritus that prevented them from leaving their underground prison. On the failure of Whetmore and the defendants to return to their homes, the Secretary of the Society was notified by their families. It appears that the explorers had left indications at the headquarters of the Society concerning the location of the cave they proposed to visit. A rescue party was promptly dispatched to the spot.

The task of rescue proved one of overwhelming difficulty. It was necessary to supplement the forces of the original party by repeated increments of men and machines, which had to be conveyed at great expense to the remote and isolated region in which the cave was located. A huge temporary camp of workmen, engineers, geologists, and other experts was established. The work of removing the obstruction was several times frustrated by fresh landslides. In one of these, ten of the workmen engaged in clearing the entrance were killed. The treasury of the Speluncean Society was soon exhausted in their rescue effort, and the sum of eight hundred thousand frelars, raised partly by popular subscription and partly by legislative grant, was expended before the imprisoned men were rescued. Success was finally achieved on the thirty-second day after the men entered the cave.

Since it was known that the explorers had carried with them only scant provisions, and since it was also known that there was no animal or vegetable matter within the cave on which they might subsist, anxiety was early felt that they might meet death by starvation before access to them could be obtained. On the twentieth day of their imprisonment it was learned for the first time that they had taken with them into the cave a portable wireless machine of both sending and receiving messages. A similar machine was promptly installed in the rescue camp and oral communication established with the unfortunate men within the mountain. They asked to be informed how long a time would be required to release them. The engineers in charge of the project answered that at least ten days would be required even if no new landslides occurred. The explorers then asked if any physicians were present, and were placed in communication with a committee of medical experts. The imprisoned men described their condition and the rations they had taken with them, and asked for a medical opinion whether they would be likely to live without food for ten days longer. The chairman of the committee of physicians told them that there was little possibility of this. The wireless machine within the cave then remained silent for eight hours. When communication was re-established the men asked to speak with the physicians. The chairman of the physicians' committee was placed before the apparatus, and Whetmore, speaking on behalf of himself and the defendants, asked whether they would be able to survive for ten days longer if they consumed the flesh of one of their number. The physicians' chairman reluctantly answered this question in the affirmative. Whetmore asked whether it would be advisable for them to cast lots to determine which of them should be eaten. None of the physicians present was willing to answer the question. Whetmore then asked if there were among the party a judge or other official of the government who would answer this question. None of those attached to the rescue camp was willing to assume the role of advisor in this matter. He then asked if any minister or priest would answer their question, and none was found who would do so. Thereafter no further messages were received from within the cave, and it was assumed (erroneously, it later appeared) that the electric batteries of the explorers' wireless machine had become exhausted. When the imprisoned men were finally released it was learned that on the twenty-third day after their entrance into the cave Whetmore had been killed and eaten by his companions.

From the testimony of the defendants, which was accepted by the jury, it appears that it was Whetmore who first proposed that they might find the nutriment without which survival was impossible in the flesh of one of their own number. It was also Whetmore who first proposed the use of some method of casting lots, calling the attention of the defendants to a pair of dice he happened to have with him. The defendants were at first reluctant to adopt so desperate a procedure, but after the conversations by wireless related above, they finally agreed on the plan proposed by Whetmore. After much discussion of the mathematical problems involved, agreement was finally reached on a method of determining the issue by the use of the dice.

Before the dice were cast, however, Whetmore declared that he withdrew from the arrangement, as he had decided on reflection to wait for another week before embracing an expedient so frightful and odious. The others charged him with a breach of faith and proceeded to cast the dice. When it came Whetmore's turn, the dice were cast for him by one of the defendants, and he was asked to declare any objections he might have to the fairness of the throw. He stated that he had no such objections. The throw went against him, and he was then put to death and eaten by his companions.

After the rescue of the defendants, and after they had completed a stay in a hospital where they underwent a course of treatment for malnutrition and shock, they were indicted for the murder of Roger Whetmore. At the trial, after the testimony had been concluded, the foreman of the jury (a lawyer by profession) inquired of the court whether the jury might not find a special verdict, leaving it to the court to say whether on the facts as found the defendants were guilty. After some discussion, both the Prosecutor and counsel for the defendants indicated their acceptance of this procedure, and it was adopted by the court. In a lengthy special verdict the jury found the facts as I have related them above, and found further that if on these facts the defendants were guilty of the crime against them, then they found the defendants guilty. On the basis of this verdict, the trial judge ruled that the defendants were guilty of murdering Roger Whetmore. The judge then sentenced them to be hanged, the law of our Commonwealth permitting him no discretion with respect to the penalty to be imposed. After the release of the jury, its members joined in a communication to the Chief Executive asking that the sentence be commuted to an imprisonment of six months. The trial judge addressed a similar communication to the Chief Executive. As yet no action with respect to these pleas has been taken, as the Chief Executive is apparently awaiting our disposition of this petition of error.

It seems to me that in dealing with this extraordinary case the jury and the trial judge followed a course that was not only fair and wise, but the only course that was open to them under the law. The language of our statute is well known: "Whoever shall willfully take the life of another shall be punished by death." N.C.S.A. (N.S.) § 12-A. This statute permits of no exception applicable to this case, however our sympathies may incline us to make allowance for the tragic situation in which these men found themselves.

In a case like this the principle of executive clemency seems admirably suited to mitigate the rigors of the law, and I propose to my colleagues that we follow the example of the jury and the trial judge by joining in the communications they have addressed to the Chief Executive. There is every reason to believe that these requests for clemency will be heeded, coming as they do from those who have studied the case and had an opportunity to become thoroughly acquainted with all its circumstances. It is highly improbable that the Chief Executive would deny these requests unless he were himself to hold hearings at least as extensive as those involved in the trial below, which lasted for three months. The holding of such hearings (which would virtually amount to a retrial of the case) would scarcely be compatible with the function of the Executive as it is usually conceived. I think we may therefore assume that some form of clemency will be extended to these defendants. If this is done, then justice will be accomplished without impairing either the letter or spirit of our statutes and without offering any encouragement for the disregard of law.

FOSTER, J. I am shocked that the Chief Justice, in an effort to escape the embarrassments of this tragic case, should have adopted, and should have proposed to his colleagues, an expedient at once so sordid and so obvious. I believe something more is on trial in this case than the fate of these unfortunate explorers; that is the law of our Commonwealth. If this Court declares that under our law these men have committed a crime, then our law is itself convicted in the tribunal of common sense, no matter what happens to the individuals involved in this petition of error. For us to assert that the law we uphold and expound compels us to a conclusion we are ashamed of, and from which we can only escape by appealing to a dispensation resting within the personal whim of the Executive, seems to me to amount to an admission that the law of this Commonwealth no longer pretends to incorporate justice.

For myself, I do not believe that our law compels the monstrous conclusion that these men are murderers. I believe, on the contrary, that it declares them to be innocent of any crime. I rest this conclusion on two independent grounds, either of which is of itself sufficient to justify the acquittal of these defendants.

The first of these grounds rests on a premise that may arouse opposition until it has been examined candidly. I take the view that the enacted or positive law of this Commonwealth, including all of its statutes and precedents, is inapplicable to this case, and that the case is governed instead by what ancient writers in Europe and America called "the law of nature."

This conclusion rests on the proposition that our positive law is predicated on the possibility of men's coexistence in society. When a situation arises in which the coexistence of men becomes impossible, then a condition that underlies all of our precedents and statutes has ceased to exist. When that condition disappears, then it is my opinion that the force of our positive law disappears with it. We are not accustomed to applying the maxim *cessante ratione legis, cessat et ipsa lex* (the reason of the law ceasing, the law itself also ceases) to the whole of our enacted law, but I believe that this is a case where the maxim should be so applied.

The proposition that all positive law is based on the possibility of men's coexistence has a strange sound, not because the truth it contains is strange, but simply it is a truth so obvious and pervasive that we seldom have occasion to give words to it. Like the air we breathe, it so pervades our environment that we forget that it exists until we are suddenly deprived of it. Whatever particular objects may be sought by the various branches of our law, it is apparent on reflection that all of them are directed toward facilitating and improving men's coexistence and regulating with fairness and equity the relations of their life in common. When the assumption that men may live together loses its truth, as it obviously did in this extraordinary situation where life only became possible by the taking of life, then the basic premises underlying our whole legal order have lost their meaning and force.

Had the tragic events of this case taken place a mile beyond the territorial limits of our Commonwealth, no one would pretend that our law was applicable to them. We recognize that jurisdiction rests on a territorial basis. The grounds of this principle are by no means obvious and are seldom examined. I take it that this principle is supported by an assumption that it is feasible to impose a single legal order upon a group of men only if they live together within the confines of a given area of the earth's surface. The premise that men shall coexist in a group underlies, then, the territorial principle, as it does all of law. Now I contend that a case may be removed morally from the force of a legal order, as well as geographically. If we look to the purposes of law and government, and to the premises underlying our positive law, these men when they made their fateful decision were as remote from our legal order as if they had been a thousand miles beyond our boundaries. Even in a physical sense, their underground prison was separated from our courts and writ-servers by a solid curtain of rock that could be removed only after the most extraordinary expenditures of time and effort.

I conclude, therefore, that at the time Roger Whetmore's life was ended by these defendants, they were, to use the quaint language of nineteenth-century writers, not in a "state of civil society" but in a "state of nature." This has the consequence that the law applicable to them is not the enacted and established law of this Commonwealth, but the law derived from those principles that were appropriate to their condition. I have no hesitancy in saying that under those principles they were guiltless of any crime.

What these men did was done in pursuance of an agreement accepted by all of them and first proposed by Whetmore himself. Since it was apparent that their extraordinary predicament made inapplicable the usual principles that regulate men's relations with one another, it was necessary for them to draw, as it were, a new charter of government appropriate to the situation in which they found themselves.

It has from antiquity been recognized that the most basic principle of law or government is to be found in the notion of contract or agreement. Ancient thinkers, especially during the period from 1600 to 1900, used to base government itself on a supposed original social compact. Skeptics pointed out that this theory contradicted the known facts of history, and that there was no scientific evidence to support the notion that any government was ever founded in the manner supposed by the theory. Moralists replied that, if the compact was a fiction from a historical point of view, the notion of compact or agreement furnished the only ethical justification on which the powers of government, which include that of taking life, could be rested. The powers of government can only be justified morally on the ground that these are powers that reasonable men would agree upon and accept if they were faced with the necessity of constructing anew some order to make their life in common possible.

Fortunately, our Commonwealth is not bothered by the perplexities that beset the ancients. We know as a matter of historical truth that our government was founded upon a contract of free accord of men. The archeological proof is conclusive that in the first period following the Great Spiral the survivors of that holocaust voluntarily came together and drew up a charter of government. Sophistical writers have raised questions as to the power of those remote contractors to bind future generations, but the fact remains that our government traces itself back in an unbroken line to that original charter.

If, therefore, our hangmen have the power to end men's lives, if our sheriffs have the power to put delinquent tenants in the street, if our police have the power to incarcerate the inebriated reveler, these powers find their moral justification in that original compact of our forefathers. If we can find no higher source for our legal order, what higher source should we expect these starving unfortunates to find for the order they adopted for themselves?

I believe that the line of argument I have just expounded permits of no rational answer. I realize that it will probably be received with a certain discomfort by many who read this opinion, who will be inclined to suspect that some hidden sophistry must underlie a demonstration that leads to so many unfamiliar conclusions. The source of this discomfort is, however, easy to identify. The usual conditions of human existence incline us to think of human life as an absolute value, not to be sacrificed under any circumstances. There is much that is fictitious about this conception even when it is applied to the ordinary relations of society. We have an illustration of this truth in the very case before us. Ten workmen were killed in the process of removing the rocks from the opening to the cave. Did not the engineers and government officials who directed the rescue effort know that the operations they were undertaking were dangerous and involved a serious risk to the lives of the workmen executing them? If it was proper that these ten lives should be sacrificed to save the lives of five imprisoned explorers, why then are we told it was wrong for these explorers to carry out an arrangement which would save four lives at the cost of one?

Every highway, every tunnel, every building we project involves a risk to human life. Taking these projects in the aggregate, we can calculate with some precision how many deaths the construction of them will require; statisticians can tell you the average cost in human lives of a thousand miles of a four-lane concrete highway. Yet we deliberately and knowingly incur and pay this cost on the assumption that the values obtained for those who survive outweigh the loss. If these things can be said of a society functioning above ground in a normal and ordinary manner, what shall we say of the supposed absolute value of a human life in the desperate situation in which these defendants and their companion Whetmore found themselves?

This concludes the exposition of the first ground of my decision. My second ground proceeds by rejecting hypothetically all the premises on which I have so far proceeded. I concede for purposes of argument that I am wrong in saying that the situation of these men removed them from the effect of our positive law, and I assume that the Consolidated Statutes have the power to penetrate five hundred feet of rock and to impose themselves upon these starving men huddled in their underground prison.

Now it is, of course, perfectly clear that these men did an act that violates the literal wording of the statute which declares that he who "shall willfully take the life of another" is a murderer. But one of the most ancient bits of legal wisdom is the saying that a man may break the letter of the law without breaking the law itself. Every proposition of positive law, whether contained in a statute or a judicial precedent, is to be interpreted reasonably, in the light of its evident purpose. This is a truth so elementary that it is hardly necessary to expatiate on it. Illustrations of its application are numberless and are to be found in every branch of the law. In *Commonwealth v. Staymore* the defendant was convicted under a statute making it a crime to leave one's car parked in certain areas for a period longer than two hours. The defendant had attempted to remove his car, but was prevented from doing so because the streets were obstructed by a political demonstration in which he took no part and which he had no reason to anticipate. His conviction was set aside by this Court, although his case fell squarely within the wording of the statute. Again, in *Fehler v. Neegas* there was before this Court for construction a statute in which the word "not" had plainly been transposed from its intended position in the final and most crucial section of the act. This transposition was contained in all the successive drafts of the act, where it was apparently overlooked by the draftsmen and sponsors of the legislation. No one was able to prove how the error came about, yet it was apparent that, taking account of the contents of the statute as a whole, an error had been made, since a literal reading of the final clause rendered it inconsistent with everything that had gone before and with the object of the enactment as stated in its preamble. This Court refused to accept a literal interpretation of the statute, and in effect rectified its language by reading the word "not" into the place where it was evidently intended to go.

The statute before us for interpretation has never been applied literally. Centuries ago it was established that a killing in self-defense is excused. There is nothing in the wording of the statute that suggests this exception. Various attempts have been made to reconcile the legal treatment of self-defense with the words of the statute, but in my opinion these are all merely ingenious sophistries. The truth is that the exception in favor of self-defense cannot be reconciled with the *words* of the statute, but only with its *purpose*.

The true reconciliation of the excuse of self-defense with the statute making it a crime to kill another is to be found in the following line of reasoning. One of the principal objects underlying any criminal legislation is that of deterring men from crime. Now it is apparent that if it were declared to be the law that a killing in self-defense is murder such a rule could not operate in a deterrent manner. A man whose life is threatened will repel his aggressor, whatever the law may say. Looking therefore to the broad purposes of criminal legislation, we may safely declare that this statute was not intended to apply to cases of self-defense.

When the rationale of the excuse of self-defense is thus explained, it becomes apparent that precisely the same reasoning is applicable to the case at bar. If in the future any group of men ever find themselves in the tragic predicament of these defendants, we may be sure that their decision whether to live or die will not be controlled by the contents of our criminal code. Accordingly, if we read this statute intelligently it is apparent that it does not apply to this case. The withdrawal of this situation from the effect of the statute is justified by precisely the same considerations that were applied by our predecessors in office centuries ago to the case of self-defense.

There are those who raise the cry of judicial usurpation whenever a court, after analyzing the purpose of a statute, gives to its words a meaning that is not at once apparent to the casual reader who has not studied the statute closely or examined the objectives it seeks to attain. Let me say emphatically that I accept without reservation the proposition that this Court is bound by the statutes of our Commonwealth and that it exercises its powers in subservience to the duly expressed will of the Chamber of Representatives. The line of reasoning I have applied above raises no question of fidelity to enacted law, though it may possibly raise a question of the distinction between intelligent and unintelligent fidelity. No superior wants a servant who lacks the capacity to read between the lines. The stupidest housemaid knows that when she is told "to peel the soup and skin the potatoes" her mistress does not mean what she says. She also knows that when her master tells her to "drop everything and come running" he has overlooked the possibility that she is at the moment in the act of rescuing the baby from the rain barrel. Surely we have a right to expect the same modicum of intelligence from the judiciary. The correction of obvious legislative errors or oversights is not to supplant the legislative will, but to make that will effective.

I therefore conclude that on any aspect under which this case may be viewed these defendants are innocent of the crime of murdering Roger Whetmore, and that the conviction should be set aside.

TATTING, J. In the discharge of my duties as a justice of this Court, I am usually able to dissociate the emotional and intellectual sides of my reactions, and to decide the case before me entirely on the basis of the latter. In passing on this tragic case I find that my usual resources fail me. On the emotional side I find myself torn between sympathy for these men and a feeling of abhorrence and disgust at the monstrous act they committed. I had hoped that I would be able to put these contradictory emotions to one side as irrelevant, and to decide the case on the basis of a convincing and logical demonstration of the result demanded by our law. Unfortunately, this deliverance has not been vouchsafed me.

As I analyze the opinion just rendered by my brother Foster, I find that it is shot through with contradictions and fallacies. Let us begin with his first proposition: these men were not subject to our law because they were not in a "state of civil society" but in a "state of nature." I am not clear why this is so, whether it is because of the thickness of the rock that imprisoned them, or because they were hungry, or because they had set up a "new charter of government" by which the usual rules of law were to be supplanted by a throw of the dice. Other difficulties intrude themselves. If these men passed from the jurisdiction of our law to that of "the law of nature," at what moment did this occur? Was it when the entrance to the cave was blocked, or when the threat of starvation reached a certain undefined degree of intensity, or when the agreement for the throwing of the dice was made? These uncertainties in the doctrine proposed by my brother are capable of producing real difficulties. Suppose, for example, one of these men had had his twenty-first birthday while he was imprisoned within the mountain. On what date would we have to consider that he had attained his majority—when he reached the age of twenty-one, at which time he was, by hypothesis, removed from the effects of our law, or only when he was released from the cave and became again subject to what my brother calls our "positive law"? These difficulties may seem fanciful, yet they only serve to reveal the fanciful nature of the doctrine that is capable of giving rise to them.

But it is not necessary to explore these niceties further to demonstrate the absurdity of my brother's position. Mr. Justice Foster and I are the appointed judges of a court of the Commonwealth of Newgarth, sworn and empowered to administer the laws of that Commonwealth. By what authority do we resolve ourselves into a Court of Nature? If these men were indeed under the law of nature, whence comes our authority to expound and apply that law? Certainly we are not in a state of nature.

Let us look at the contents of this code of nature that my brother proposes we adopt as our own and apply to this case. What a topsy-turvy and odious code it is! It is a code in which the law of contracts is more fundamental than the law of murder. It is a code under which a man may make a valid agreement empowering his fellows to eat his own body. Under the provisions of this code, furthermore, such an agreement once made is irrevocable, and if one of the parties attempts to withdraw, the others may take the law into their own hands and enforce the contract by violence—for though my brother passes over in convenient silence the effect of Whetmore's withdrawal, this is the necessary implication of his argument.

The principles my brother expounds contain other implications that cannot be tolerated. He argues that when the defendants set upon Whetmore and killed him (we know not how, perhaps by pounding him with stones) they were only exercising the rights conferred upon them by their bargain. Suppose, however, that Whetmore had had concealed upon his person a revolver, and that when he saw the defendants about to slaughter him he had shot them to death in order to save his own life. My brother's reasoning applied to these facts would make Whetmore out to be a murderer since the excuse of self-defense would have to be denied to him. If his assailants were acting rightfully in seeking to bring about his death, then of course he could no more plead the excuse that he was defending his own life than could a condemned prisoner who struck down the executioner lawfully attempting to place the noose about his neck.

All of these considerations make it impossible for me to accept the first part of my brother's argument. I can neither accept his notion that these men were under a code of nature which this Court was bound to apply to them, nor can I accept the odious and perverted rules that he would read into that code. I come now to the second part of my brother's opinion, in which he seeks to show that the defendants did not violate the provisions of N.C.S.A. (N.S.) § 12-A. Here the way, instead of being clear, becomes for me misty and ambiguous, though my brother seems unaware of the difficulties that inhere in his demonstrations.

The gist of my brother's argument may be stated in the following terms: No statute, whatever its language, should be applied in a way that contradicts its purpose. One of the purposes of any criminal statute is to deter. The application of the statute making it a crime to kill another to the peculiar facts of this case would contradict this purpose, for it is impossible to believe that the contents of the criminal code could operate in a deterrent manner on men faced with the alternative of life or death. The reasoning by which this exception is read into the statute is, my brother observes, the same as that which is applied in order to provide the excuse of self-defense.

On the face of things this demonstration seems very convincing indeed. My brother's interpretation of the rationale of the excuse of self-defense is in fact supported by a decision of this court, *Commonwealth v. Parry*, a precedent I happened to encounter in my research on this case. Though *Commonwealth v. Parry* seems generally to have been overlooked in the texts and subsequent decisions, it supports unambiguously the interpretation my brother has put upon the excuse of self-defense.

Now let me outline briefly, however, the perplexities that assail me when I examine my brother's demonstration more closely. It is true that a statute should be applied in the light of its purpose, and that one of the purposes of criminal legislation is recognized to be deterrence. The difficulty is that other purposes are also ascribed to the law of crimes. It has been said that one of its objects is to provide an orderly outlet for the instinctive human demand for retribution. *Commonwealth v. Scape*. It has also been said that its object is the rehabilitation of the wrongdoer. *Commonwealth v. Makeover*. Other theories have been propounded. Assuming that we must interpret a statute in the light of its purpose, what are we to do when it has many purposes or when its purposes are disputed?

A similar difficulty is presented by the fact that although there is authority for my brother's interpretation of the excuse of self-defense, there is other authority which assigns to that excuse a different rationale. Indeed, until I happened on *Commonwealth v. Parry* I had never heard of the explanation given by my brother. The taught doctrine of our law schools, memorized by generations of law students, runs in the following terms: The statute concerning murder requires a "willful" act. The man who acts to repel an aggressive threat to his own life does not act "willfully," but in response to an impulse deeply ingrained in human nature. I suspect that there is hardly a lawyer in this Commonwealth who is not familiar with this line of reasoning, especially since the point is a great favorite of the bar examiners.

Now the familiar explanation for the excuse of self-defense just expounded obviously cannot be applied by analogy to the facts of this case. These men acted not only "willfully" but with great deliberation and after hours of discussing what they should do. Again we encounter a forked path, with one line of reasoning leading us in one direction and another in a direction that is exactly the opposite. This perplexity is in this case compounded, as it were, for we have to set off one explanation, incorporated in a virtually unknown precedent of this Court, against another explanation, which forms a part of the taught legal tradition of our law schools, but which, so far as I know, has never been adopted in any judicial decision.

I recognize the relevance of the precedents cited by my brother concerning the displaced "not" and the defendant who parked overtime. But what are we to do with one of the landmarks of our jurisprudence, which again my brother passes over in silence? This is *Commonwealth v. Valjean*. Though the case is somewhat obscurely reported, it appears that the defendant was indicted for the larceny of a loaf of bread, and offered as a defense that he was in a condition approaching starvation. The court refused to accept this defense. If hunger cannot justify the theft of wholesome and natural food, how can it justify the killing and eating of a man? Again, if we look at the thing in terms of deterrence, is it likely that a man will starve to death to avoid a jail sentence for the theft of a loaf of bread? My brother's demonstrations would compel us to overrule *Commonwealth v. Valjean*, and many other precedents that have been built on that case.

Again, I have difficulty in saying that no deterrent effect whatever could be attributed to a decision that these men were guilty of murder. The stigma of the word "murderer" is such that it is quite likely, I believe, that if these men had known that their act was deemed by the law to be murder they would have waited for a few days at least before carrying out their plan. During that time some unexpected relief might have come. I realize that this observation only reduces the distinction to a matter of degree, and does not destroy it altogether. It is certainly true that the element of deterrence would be less in this case than is normally involved in the application of the criminal law.

There is still a further difficulty in my brother Foster's proposal to read an exception into the statute to favor this case, though again a difficulty not even intimated in his opinion. What shall be the scope of this exception? Here the men cast lots and the victim was himself originally a party to the agreement. What would we have to decide if Whetmore had refused from the beginning to participate in the plan? Would a majority be permitted to overrule him? Or, suppose that no plan were adopted at all and the others simply conspired to bring about Whetmore's death, justifying their act by saying that he was in the weakest condition. Or again, that a plan of selection was followed but one based on a different justification than the one adopted here, as if the others were atheists and insisted that Whetmore should die because he was the only one who believed in an afterlife. These illustrations could be multiplied, but enough have been suggested to reveal what a quagmire of hidden difficulties my brother's reasoning contains.

Of course I realize on reflection that I may be concerning myself with a problem that will never arise, since it is unlikely that any group of men will ever again be brought to commit the dread act that was involved here. Yet, on still further reflection, even if we are certain that no similar case will arise again, do not the illustrations I have given show the lack of any coherent and rational principle in the rule my brother proposes? Should not the soundness of a principle be tested by the conclusions it entails, without reference to the accidents of later litigational history? Still, if this is so, why is it that we of this Court so often discuss the question whether we are likely to have later occasion to apply a principle urged for the solution of the case before us? Is this a situation where a line of reasoning not originally proper has become sanctioned by precedent, so that we are permitted to apply it and may even be under an obligation to do so?

The more I examine this case and think about it, the more deeply I become involved. My mind becomes entangled in the meshes of the very nets I throw out for my own rescue. I find that almost every consideration that bears on the decision of the case is counterbalanced by an opposing consideration leading in the opposite direction. My brother Foster has not furnished to me, nor can I discover for myself, any formula capable of resolving the equivocations that beset me on all sides.

I have given this case the best thought of which I am capable. I have scarcely slept since it was argued before us. When I feel myself inclined to accept the view of my brother Foster, I am repelled by a feeling that his arguments are intellectually unsound and approach mere rationalization. On the other hand, when I incline toward upholding the conviction, I am struck by the absurdity of directing that these men be put to death when their lives have been saved at the cost of the lives of ten heroic workmen. It is to me a matter of regret that the Prosecutor saw fit to ask for an indictment for murder. If we had a provision in our statutes making it a crime to eat human flesh, that would have been a more appropriate charge. If no other charge suited to the facts of this case could be brought against the defendants, it would have been wiser, I think, not to have indicted them at all. Unfortunately, however, the men have been indicted and tried, and we have therefore been drawn into this unfortunate affair.

Since I have been wholly unable to resolve the doubts that beset me about the law of this case, I am with regret announcing a step that is, I believe, unprecedented in the history of this tribunal. I declare my withdrawal from the decision of this case.

KEEN, J. I should like to begin by setting to one side two questions which are not before this Court.

The first of these is whether executive clemency should be extended to these defendants if the conviction is affirmed. Under our system of government, that is a question for the Chief Executive, not for us. I therefore disapprove of that passage in the opinion of the Chief Justice in which he in effect gives instructions to the Chief Executive as to what he should do in this case and suggests that some impropriety will attach if these instructions are not heeded. This is a confusion of governmental functions—a confusion of which the judiciary should be the last to be guilty. I wish to state that if I were the Chief Executive I would go farther in the direction of clemency than the pleas addressed to him propose. I would pardon these men altogether, since I believe that they have already suffered enough to pay for any offense they may have committed. I want it to be understood that this remark is made in my capacity as a private citizen who by the accident of his office happens to have acquired an intimate acquaintance with the facts of this case. In the discharge of my duties as judge, it is neither my function to address directions to the Chief Executive, nor to take into account what he may or may not do, in reaching my own decision, which must be controlled entirely by the law of this Commonwealth.

The second question that I wish to put to one side is that of deciding whether what these men did was "right" or "wrong," "wicked" or "good." That is also a question that is irrelevant to the discharge of my office as a judge sworn to apply, not my conceptions of morality, but the law of the land. In putting this question to one side I think I can also safely dismiss without comment the first and more poetic portion of my brother Foster's opinion. The element of fantasy contained in the arguments developed there has been sufficiently revealed in my brother Tatting's somewhat solemn attempt to take those arguments seriously.

The sole question before us for decision is whether these defendants did, within the meaning of N.C.S.A. (N.S.) § 12-A, willfully take the life of Roger Whetmore. The exact language of the statute is as follows: "Whoever shall willfully take the life of another shall be punished by death." Now I should suppose that any candid observer, content to extract from these words their natural meaning, would concede at once that these defendants did "willfully take the life" of Roger Whetmore.

Whence arise all the difficulties of the case, then, and the necessity for so many pages of discussion about what ought to be so obvious? The difficulties, in whatever tortured form they may present themselves, all trace back to a single source, and that is a failure to distinguish the legal from the moral aspects of this case. To put it bluntly, my brothers do not like the fact that the written law requires the conviction of these defendants. Neither do I, but unlike my brothers I respect the obligations of an office that requires me to put my personal predilections out of my mind when I come to interpret and apply the law of this Commonwealth.

Now, of course, my brother Foster does not admit that he is actuated by a personal dislike of the written law. Instead he develops a familiar line of argument according to which the court may disregard the express language of a statute when something not contained in the statute itself, called its "purpose," can be employed to justify the result the court considers proper. Because this is an old issue between myself and my colleague, I should like, before discussing his particular application of the argument to the facts of this case, to say something about the historical background of this issue and its implications for law and government generally.

There was a time in this Commonwealth when judges did in fact legislate very freely, and all of us know that during that period some of our statutes were rather thoroughly made over by the judiciary. That was a time when the accepted principles of political science did not designate with any certainty the rank and function of the various arms of the state. We all know the tragic issue of that uncertainty in the brief civil war that arose out of the conflict between the judiciary, on the one hand, and the executive and the legislature, on the other. There is no need to recount here the factors that contributed to that unseemly struggle for power, though they included the unrepresentative character of the Chamber, resulting from a division of the country into election districts that no longer accorded with the actual distribution of the population, and the forceful personality and wide popular following of the then Chief Justice. It is enough to observe that those days are behind us, and that in place of the uncertainty that then reigned we now have a clear-cut principle, which is the supremacy of the legislative branch of our government. From that principle flows the obligation of the judiciary to enforce faithfully the written law, and to interpret that law in accordance with its plain meaning without reference to our personal desires or our individual conceptions of justice. I am not concerned with the question whether the principle that forbids the judicial revision of statutes is right or wrong, desirable or undesirable; I observe merely that this principle has become a tacit premise underlying the whole of the legal and governmental order I am sworn to administer.

Yet though the principle of the supremacy of the legislature has been accepted in theory for centuries, such is the tenacity of professional tradition and the force of fixed habits of thought that many of the judiciary have still not accommodated themselves to the restricted role which the new order imposes on them. My brother Foster is one of that group; his way of dealing with statutes is exactly that of a judge living in the 3900's.

We are all familiar with the process by which the judicial reform of disfavored legislative enactments is accomplished. Anyone who has followed the written opinions of Mr. Justice Foster will have had an opportunity to see it at work in every branch of the law. I am personally so familiar with the process that in the event of my brother's incapacity I am sure I could write a satisfactory opinion for him without any prompting whatever, beyond being informed whether he liked the effect of the terms of the statute as applied to the case before him.

The process of judicial reform requires three steps. The first of these is to divine some single "purpose" which the statute serves. This is done although not one statute in a hundred has any such single purpose, and although the objectives of nearly every statute are differently interpreted by the different classes of its sponsors. The second step is to discover that a mythical being called "the legislator," in the pursuit of this imagined "purpose," overlooked something or left some gap or imperfection in his work. Then comes the final and most refreshing part of the task, which is, of course, to fill in the blank thus created. *Quod erat faciendum* [Roughly, "Thereby we build by erasing."]

My brother Foster's penchant for finding holes in statutes reminds one of the story told by an ancient author about the man who ate a pair of shoes. Asked how he liked them, he replied that the part he liked the best was the holes. That is the way my brother feels about statutes; the more holes they have in them the better he likes them. In short, he doesn't like statutes.

One could not wish for a better case to illustrate the specious nature of this gap-filling process than the one before us. My brother thinks he knows exactly what was sought when men made murder a crime, and that was something he calls "deterrence." My brother Tatting has already shown how much is passed over in that interpretation. But I think the trouble goes deeper. I doubt very much whether our statute making murder a crime really has a "purpose" in any ordinary sense of the term. Primarily, such a statute reflects a deeply-felt human conviction that murder is wrong and that something should be done to the man who commits it. If we were forced to be more articulate about the matter, we would probably take refuge in the more sophisticated theories of the criminologists, which, of course, were certainly not in the minds of those who drafted our statute. We might also observe that men will do their own work more effectively and live happier lives if they are protected against the threat of violent assault. Bearing in mind that the victims of murders are often unpleasant people, we might add some suggestion that the matter of disposing of undesirables is not a function suited to private enterprise, but should be a state monopoly. All of which reminds me of the attorney who once argued before us that a statute licensing physicians was a good thing because it would lead to lower life insurance rates by lifting the level of general health. There is such a thing as over-explaining the obvious.

If we do not know the purpose of § 12-A, how can we possibly say there is a "gap" in it? How can we know what its draftsmen thought about the question of killing men in order to eat them? My brother Tatting has revealed an understandable, though perhaps slightly exaggerated revulsion to cannibalism. How do we know that his remote ancestors did not feel the same revulsion to an even higher degree? Anthropologists say that the dread felt for a forbidden act may be increased by the fact that the conditions of a tribe's life create special temptations toward it, as incest is most severely condemned among those whose village relations make it most likely to occur. Certainly the period following the Great Spiral was one that had implicit in it temptations to anthropophagy. Perhaps it was for that very reason that our ancestors expressed their prohibition in so broad and unqualified a form. MI of this is conjecture, of course, but it remains abundantly clear that neither I nor my brother Foster knows what the "purpose" of § 12-A is.

Considerations similar to those I have just outlined are also applicable to the exception in favor of self-defense, which plays so large a role in the reasoning of my brothers Foster and Tatting. It is of course true that in *Commonwealth v. Parry* an obiter dictum justified this exception on the assumption that the purpose of criminal legislation is to deter. It may well also be true that generations of law students have been taught that the true explanation of the exception lies in the fact that a man who acts in self-defense does not act "willfully," and that the same students have passed their bar examinations by repeating what their professors told them. These last observations I could dismiss, of course, as irrelevant for the simple reason that professors and bar examiners have not as yet any commission to make our laws for us. But again the real trouble lies deeper. As in dealing with the statute, so in dealing with the exception, the question is not the conjectural *purpose* of the rule, but its *scope*. Now the scope of the exception in favor of self-defense as it has been applied by this Court is plain: it applies to cases of resisting an aggressive threat to the party's own life. It is therefore too clear for argument that this case does not fall within the scope of the exception, since it is plain that Whetmore made no threat against the lives of these defendants.

The essential shabbiness of my brother Foster's attempt to cloak his remaking of the written law with an air of legitimacy comes tragically to the surface in my brother Tatting's opinion. In that opinion Justice Tatting struggles manfully to combine his colleague's loose moralisms with his own sense of fidelity to the written law. The issue of this struggle could only be that which occurred, a complete default in the discharge of the judicial function. You simply cannot apply a statute as it is written and remake it to meet your own wishes at the same time.

Now I know that the line of reasoning I have developed in this opinion will not be acceptable to those who look only to the immediate effects of a decision and ignore the long-run implications of an assumption by the judiciary of a power of dispensation. A hard decision is never a popular decision. Judges have been celebrated in literature for their sly prowess in devising some quibble by which a litigant could be deprived of his rights where the public thought it was wrong for him to assert those rights. But I believe that judicial dispensation does more harm in the long run than hard decisions. Hard cases may even have a certain moral value by bringing home to the people their own responsibilities toward the law that is ultimately their creation, and by reminding them that there is no principle of personal grace that can relieve the mistakes of their representatives.

Indeed, I will go farther and say that not only are the principles I have been expounding those which are soundest for our present conditions, but that we would have inherited a better legal system from our forefathers if those principles had been observed from the beginning. For example, with respect to the excuse of self-defense, if our courts had stood steadfast on the language of the statute the result would undoubtedly have been a legislative revision of it. Such a revision would have drawn on the assistance of natural philosophers and psychologists, and the resulting regulation of the matter would have had an understandable and rational basis, instead of the hodgepodge of verbalisms and metaphysical distinctions that have emerged from the judicial and professorial treatment.

These concluding remarks are, of course, beyond any duties that I have to discharge with relation to this case, but I include them here because I feel deeply that my colleagues are insufficiently aware of the dangers implicit in the conceptions of the judicial office advocated by my brother Foster.

I conclude that the conviction should be affirmed.

HANDY, J. I have listened with amazement to the tortured ratiocinations to which this simple case has given rise. I never cease to wonder at my colleagues' ability to throw an obscuring curtain of legalisms about every issue presented to them for decision. We have heard this afternoon learned disquisitions on the distinction between positive law and the law of nature, the language of the statute and the purpose of the statute, judicial functions and executive functions, judicial legislation and legislative legislation. My only disappointment was that someone did not raise the question of the legal nature of the bargain struck in the cave—whether it was unilateral or bilateral, and whether Whetmore could not be considered as having revoked an offer prior to action taken thereunder.

What have all these things to do with the case? The problem before us is what we, as officers of the government, ought to do with these defendants. That is a question of practical wisdom, to be exercised in a context, not of abstract theory, but of human realities. When the case is approached in this light, it becomes, I think, one of the easiest to decide that has ever been argued before this Court.

Before stating my own conclusions about the merits of the case, I should like to discuss briefly some of the more fundamental issues involved—issues on which my colleagues and I have been divided ever since I have been on the bench.

I have never been able to make my brothers see that government is a human affair, and that men are ruled, not by words on paper or by abstract theories, but by other men. They are ruled well when their rulers understand the feelings and conceptions of the masses. They are ruled badly when that understanding is lacking.

Of all branches of the government, the judiciary is the most likely to lose its contact with the common man. The reasons for this are, of course, fairly obvious. Where the masses react to a situation in terms of a few salient features, we pick into little pieces every situation presented to us. Lawyers are hired by both sides to analyze and dissect. Judges and attorneys vie with one another to see who can discover the greatest number of difficulties and distinctions in a single set of facts. Each side tries to find cases, real or imagined, that will embarrass the demonstrations of the other side. To escape this embarrassment, still further distinctions are invented and imported into the situation. When a set of facts has been subjected to this kind of treatment for a sufficient time, all the life and juice have gone out of it and we have left a handful of dust.

Now I realize that wherever you have rules and abstract principles lawyers are going to be able to make distinctions. To some extent the sort of thing I have been describing is a necessary evil attaching to any formal regulation of human affairs. But I think that the area which really stands in need of such regulation is greatly overestimated. There are, of course, a few fundamental rules of the game that must be accepted if the game is to go on at all. I would include among these the rules relating to the conduct of elections, the appointment of public officials, and the term during which an office is held. Here some restraint on discretion and dispensation, some adherence to form, some scruple for what does and what does not fall within the rule, is, I concede, essential. Perhaps the area of basic principle should be expanded to include certain other rules, such as those designed to preserve the free civilmoign system.

But outside of these fields I believe that all government officials, including judges, will do their jobs best if they treat forms and abstract concepts as instruments. We should take as our model, I think, the good administrator, who accommodates procedures and principles to the case at hand, selecting from among the available forms those most suited to reach the proper result.

The most obvious advantage of this method of government is that it permits us to go about our daily tasks with efficiency and common sense. My adherence to this philosophy has, however, deeper roots. I believe that it is only with the insight this philosophy gives that we can preserve the flexibility essential if we are to keep our actions in reasonable accord with the sentiments of those subject to our rule. More governments have been wrecked, and more human misery caused by the lack of this accord between ruler and ruled than by any other factor that can be discerned in history. Once drive a sufficient wedge between the mass of people and those who direct their legal, political, and economic life, and our society is ruined. Then neither Foster's law of nature nor Keen's fidelity to written law will avail us anything.

Now when these conceptions are applied to the case before us, its decision becomes, as I have said, perfectly easy. In order to demonstrate this I shall have to introduce certain realities that my brothers in their coy decorum have seen fit to pass over in silence, although they are just as acutely aware of them as I am.

The first of these is that this case has aroused an enormous public interest, both here and abroad. Almost every newspaper and magazine has carried articles about it; columnists have shared with their readers confidential information as to the next governmental move; hundreds of letters-to-the-editor have been printed. One of the great newspaper chains made a poll of public opinion on the question, "What do you think the Supreme Court should do with the Speluncean explorers?" About ninety per cent expressed a belief that the defendants should be pardoned or let off with a kind of token punishment. It is perfectly clear, then, how the public feels about the case. We could have known this without the poll, of course, on the basis of common sense, or even by observing that on this Court there are apparently four-and-a-half men, or ninety per cent, who share the common opinion.

This makes it obvious, not only what we should do, but what we must do if we are to preserve between ourselves and public opinion a reasonable and decent accord. Declaring these men innocent need not involve us in any undignified quibble or trick. No principle of statutory construction is required that is not consistent with the past practices of this Court. Certainly no layman would think that in letting these men off we had stretched the statute any more than our ancestors did when they created the excuse of self-defense. If a more detailed demonstration of the method of reconciling our decision with the statute is required, I should be content to rest on the arguments developed in the second and less visionary part of my brother Foster's opinion.

Now I know that my brothers will be horrified by my suggestion that this Court should take account of public opinion. They will tell you that public opinion is emotional and capricious, that it is based on half-truths and listens to witnesses who are not subject to cross-examination. They will tell you that the law surrounds the trial of a case like this with elaborate safeguards, designed to insure that the truth will be known and that every rational consideration bearing on the issues of the case has been taken into account. They will warn you that all of these safeguards go for naught if a mass opinion formed outside this framework is allowed to have any influence on our decision.

But let us look candidly at some of the realities of the administration of our criminal law. When a man is accused of crime, there are, speaking generally, four ways in which he may escape punishment. One of these is a determination by a judge that under the applicable law he has committed no crime. This is, of course, a determination that takes place in a rather formal and abstract atmosphere. But look at the other three ways in which he may escape punishment. These are: (1) a decision by the Prosecutor not to ask for an indictment; (2) an acquittal by the jury; (3) a pardon or commutation of sentence by the executive. Can anyone pretend that these decisions are held within a rigid and formal framework of rules that prevents factual error, excludes emotional and personal factors, and guarantees that all the forms of the law will be observed?

In the case of the jury we do, to be sure, attempt to cabin their deliberations within the area of the legally relevant, but there is no need to deceive ourselves into believing that this attempt is really successful. In the normal course of events the case now before us would have gone on all of its issues directly to the jury. Had this occurred we can be confident that there would have been an acquittal or at least a division that would have prevented a conviction. If the jury had been instructed that the men's hunger and their agreement were no defense to the charge of murder, their verdict would in all likelihood have ignored this instruction and would have involved a good deal more twisting of the letter of the law than any that is likely to tempt us. Of course the only reason that didn't occur in this case was the fortuitous circumstance that the foreman of the jury happened to be a lawyer. His learning enabled him to devise a form of words that would allow the jury to dodge its usual responsibilities.

My brother Tatting expresses annoyance that the Prosecutor did not, in effect, decide the case for him by not asking for an indictment. Strict as he is himself in complying with the demands of legal theory, he is quite content to have the fate of these men decided out of court by the Prosecutor on the basis of common sense. The Chief Justice, on the other hand, wants the application of common sense postponed to the very end, though like Tatting, he wants no personal part in it.

This brings me to the concluding portion of my remarks, which has to do with executive clemency. Before discussing that topic directly, I want to make a related observation about the poll of public opinion. As I have said, ninety per cent of the people wanted the Supreme Court to let the men off entirely or with a more or less nominal punishment. The ten per cent constituted a very oddly assorted group, with the most curious and divergent opinions. One of our university experts has made a study of this group and has found that its members fall into certain patterns. A substantial portion of them are subscribers to "crank" newspapers of limited circulation that gave their readers a distorted version of the facts of the case. Some thought that "Speluncean" means "cannibal" and that anthropophagy is a tenet of the Society. But the point I want to make, however, is this: although almost every conceivable variety and shade of opinion was represented in this group, there was, so far as I know, not one of them, nor a single member of the majority of ninety per cent, who said, "I think it would be a fine thing to have the courts sentence these men to be hanged, and then to have another branch of the government come along and pardon them." Yet this is a solution that has more or less dominated our discussions and which our Chief Justice proposes as a way by which we can avoid doing an injustice and at the same time preserve respect for law. He can be assured that if he is preserving anybody's morale, it is his own, and not the public's which knows nothing of his distinctions. I mention this matter because I wish to emphasize once more the danger that we may get lost in the patterns of our own thought and forget that these patterns often cast not the slightest shadow on the outside world.

I come now to the most crucial fact in this case, a fact known to all of us on this Court, though one that my brothers have seen fit to keep under the cover of their judicial robes. This is the frightening likelihood that if the issue is left to him, the Chief Executive will refuse to pardon these men or commute their sentence. As we all know, our Chief Executive is a man now well advanced in years, of very stiff notions. Public clamor usually operates on him with the reverse of the effect intended. As I have told my brothers, it happens that my wife's niece is an intimate friend of his secretary. I have learned in this indirect, but, I think, wholly reliable way, that he is firmly determined not to commute the sentence if these men are found to have violated the law.

No one regrets more than I the necessity for relying in so important a matter on information that could be characterized as gossip. If I had my way this would not happen, for I would adopt the sensible course of sitting down with the Executive, going over the case with him, finding out what his views are, and perhaps working out with him a common program for handling the situation. But of course my brothers would never hear of such a thing.

Their scruple about acquiring accurate information directly does not prevent them from being very perturbed about what they have learned indirectly. Their acquaintance with the facts I have just related explains why the Chief Justice, ordinarily a model of decorum, saw fit in his opinion to flap his judicial robes in the face of the Executive and threaten him with excommunication if he failed to commute the sentence. It explains, I suspect, my brother Foster's feat of levitation by which a whole library of law books was lifted from the shoulders of these defendants. It explains also why even my legalistic brother Keen emulated Pooh-Bah in the ancient comedy by stepping to the other side of the stage to address a few remarks to the Executive "in my capacity as a private citizen." (I may remark, incidentally, that the advice of Private Citizen Keen will appear in the reports of this court printed at taxpayers' expense.)

I must confess that as I grow older I become more and more perplexed at men's refusal to apply their common sense to problems of law and government, and this truly tragic case has deepened my sense of discouragement and dismay. I only wish that I could convince my brothers of the wisdom of the principles I have applied to the judicial office since I first assumed it. As a matter of fact, by a kind of sad rounding of the circle, I encountered issues like those involved here in the very first case I tried as Judge of the Court of General Instances in Fanleigh County.

A religious sect had unfrocked a minister who, they said, had gone over to the views and practices of a rival sect. The minister circulated a handbill making charges against the authorities who had expelled him. Certain lay members of the church announced a public meeting at which they proposed to explain the position of the church. The minister attended this meeting. Some said he slipped in unobserved in a disguise; his own testimony was that he had walked in openly as a member of the public. At any rate, when the speeches began he interrupted with certain questions about the affairs of the church and made some statements in defense of his own views. He was set upon by members of the audience and given a pretty thorough pommeling, receiving among other injuries a broken jaw. He brought a suit for damages against the association that sponsored the meeting and against ten named individuals who he alleged were his assailants.

When we came to the trial, the case at first seemed very complicated to me. The attorneys raised a host of legal issues. There were nice questions on the admissibility of evidence, and, in connection with the suit against the association, some difficult problems turning on the question whether the minister was a trespasser or a licensee. As a novice on the bench I was eager to apply my law school learning and I began studying these questions closely, reading all the authorities and preparing well-documented rulings. As I studied the case I became more and more involved in its legal intricacies and I began to get into a state approaching that of my brother Tatting in this case. Suddenly, however, it dawned on me that all these perplexing issues really had nothing to do with the case, and I began examining it in the light of common sense. The case at once gained a new perspective, and I saw that the only thing for me to do was to direct a verdict for the defendants for lack of evidence.

I was led to this conclusion by the following considerations. The melee in which the plaintiff was injured had been a very confused affair, with some people trying to get to the center of the disturbance, while others were trying to get away from it; some striking at the plaintiff, while others were apparently trying to protect him. It would have taken weeks to find out the truth of the matter. I decided that nobody's broken jaw was worth that much to the Commonwealth. (The minister's injuries, incidentally, had meanwhile healed without disfigurement and without any impairment of normal faculties.) Furthermore, I felt very strongly that the plaintiff had to a large extent brought the thing on himself. He knew how inflamed passions were about the affair, and could easily have found another forum for the expression of his views. My decision was widely approved by the press and public opinion, neither of which could tolerate the views and practices that the expelled minister was attempting to defend.

Now, thirty years later, thanks to an ambitious Prosecutor and a legalistic jury foreman, I am faced with a case that raises issues which are at bottom much like those involved in that case. The world does not seem to change much, except that this time it is not a question of a judgment for five or six hundred frelars, but of the life or death of four men who have already suffered more torment and humiliation than most of us would endure in a thousand years. I conclude that the defendants are innocent of the crime charged, and that the conviction and sentence should be set aside.

TATTING, J. I have been asked by the Chief Justice whether, after listening to the two opinions just rendered, I desire to reexamine the position previously taken by me. I wish to state that after hearing these opinions I am greatly strengthened in my conviction that I ought not to participate in the decision of this case.

The Supreme Court being evenly divided, the conviction and sentence of the Court of General Instances is affirmed. It is ordered that the execution of the sentence shall occur at 6 a.m., Friday, April 2, 4300, at which time the Public Executioner is directed to proceed with all convenient dispatch to hang each of the defendants by the neck until he is dead.

POSTSCRIPT

Now that the court has spoken its judgment, the reader puzzled by the choice of date may wish to be reminded that the centuries which separate us from the year 4300 are roughly equal to those that have passed since the Age of Pericles. There is probably no need to observe that the Speluncean Case itself is intended neither as a work of satire nor as a prediction in any ordinary sense of the term. As for the judges who make up Chief Justice Truepenny's court, they are, of course, as mythical as the facts and precedents with which they deal. The reader who refuses to accept this view, and who seeks to trace out contemporary resemblances where none is intended or contemplated, should be warned that he is engaged in a frolic of his own, which may possibly lead him to miss whatever modest truths are contained in the opinions delivered by the Supreme Court of Newgarth. The case was constructed for the sole purpose of bringing into a common focus certain divergent philosophies of law and government. These philosophies presented men with live questions of choice in the days of Plato and Aristotle. Perhaps they will continue to do so when our era has had its say about them. If there is any element of prediction in the case, it does not go beyond a suggestion that the questions involved are among the permanent problems of the human race.

QUESTIONS

1.   Do you think Fuller fairly set out the options in this great puzzle? What is his "hidden agenda," if any?

2.   Assume you were a Justice of the Supreme Court of Newgarth. How would you decide this case, and on what principles? Can you identify the schools of jurisprudence represented by the other judges?

3.   What role should prosecutorial "discretion," the jury's "power" to acquit the guilty, or executive "clemency" play in this kind of case? How can they be justified by positivism?

4.   How would Oliver Wendell Holmes, Jr. decide this case?

5.   Just for fun, see how many of Fuller's little "jokes" you can find, like the choice of 4300 A.D. for the "date" of this case. There are many hidden in the problem, including some bad puns.

Calvin and Hobbes © 1993 Watterson. Reprinted with permission of Universal Press Syndicate. All rights reserved.

Our thanks to BC Law School alumnus, Joshua M. Thayer, who bravely defended the views of Justice Foster, and then brought this cartoon to our attention.

REPOUILLE v. UNITED STATES
165 F.2d 152 (2d Cir. 1947)

Before L. HAND, AUGUSTUS N. HAND and FRANK, CIRCUIT JUDGES.

L. HAND, CIRCUIT JUDGE.

The District Attorney, on behalf of the Immigration and Naturalization Service, has appealed from an order, naturalizing the appellee, Repouille. The ground of the objection in the district court and here is that he did not show himself to have been a person of "good moral character" for the five years which preceded the filing of his petition.[31] The facts were as follows. The petition was filed on September 22, 1944, and on October 12, 1939, he had deliberately put to death his son, a boy of thirteen, by means of chloroform. His reason for this tragic deed was that the child had "suffered from birth from a brain injury which destined him to be an idiot and a physical monstrosity malformed in all four limbs. The child was blind, mute, and deformed. He had to be fed; the movements of his bladder and bowels were involuntary, and his entire life was spent in a small crib." Repouille had four other children at the time towards whom he has always been a dutiful and responsible parent; it may be assumed that his act was to help him in their nurture, which was being compromised by the burden imposed upon him in the care of the fifth. The family was altogether dependent upon his industry for its support. He was indicted for manslaughter in the second degree with a recommendation of the "utmost clemency"; and the judge sentenced him to not less than five years not more than ten, execution to be stayed, and the defendant to be placed on probation, from which he was discharged in December, 1945. Concededly, except for this act he conducted himself as a person of "good moral character" during the five years before he filed his petition. Indeed, if he had waited before filing his petition from September 22, to October 14, 1944, he would have had a clear record for the necessary period, and would have been admitted without question.

Very recently we had to pass upon the phrase "good moral character" in the Nationality Act;[32] and we said that it set as a test, not those standards which we might ourselves approve, but whether "the moral feelings, now prevalent generally in this country" would "be outraged" by the conduct in question: that is, whether it conformed to "the generally accepted moral conventions current at the time."[33] In the absence of some national inquisition, like a Gallup poll, that is indeed a difficult test to apply; often questions will arise to which the answer is not ascertainable, and where the petitioner must fail only because he has the affirmative. Indeed, in the case at bar itself the answer is not wholly certain; for we all know that there are great numbers of people of the most unimpeachable virtue, who think it morally justifiable to put an end to a life so inexorably destined to be a burden to others, and—so far as any possible interest of its own is concerned—condemned to a brutish existence, lower indeed than all but the lowest forms of sentient life. Nor

---

[31] § 707(a)(3), Title 8 U.S.C.A.

[32] § 707(a)(3), Title 8 U.S.C.A.

[33] United States v. Francioso, 2d Cir., 164 F.2d 163.

is it inevitably an answer to say that it must be immoral to do this, until the law provides security against the abuses which would inevitably follow, unless the practice were regulated. Many people—probably most people—do not make it a final ethical test of conduct that it shall not violate law; few of us exact of ourselves or of others the unflinching obedience of a Socrates. There being no unlawful means of accomplishing an end, which they believe to be righteous in itself, there have always been conscientious persons who feel no scruple in acting in defiance of a law which is repugnant to their personal convictions, and who even regard as martyrs those who suffer by doing so. In our own history it is only necessary to recall the Abolitionists. It is reasonably clear that the jury which tried Repouille did not feel any moral repulsion at his crime. Although it was inescapably murder in the first degree, not only did they bring in a verdict that was flatly in the face of the facts and utterly absurd—for manslaughter in the second degree presupposes that the killing has not been deliberate—but they coupled even that with a recommendation which showed that in substance they wished to exculpate the offender. Moreover, it is also plain, from the sentence which he imposed, that the judge could not have seriously disagreed with their recommendation.

One might be tempted to seize upon all this as a reliable measure of current morals; and no doubt it should have its place in the scale; but we should hesitate to accept it as decisive, when, for example, we compare it with the fate of a similar offender in Massachusetts, who, although he was not executed, was imprisoned for life. Left at large as we are, without means of verifying our conclusion, and without authority to substitute our individual beliefs, the outcome must needs be tentative; and not much is gained by discussion. We can say no more than that, quite independently of what may be the current moral feeling as to legally administered euthanasia, we feel reasonably secure in holding that only a minority of virtuous persons would deem the practice morally justifiable, while it remains in private hands, even when the provocation is as overwhelming as it was in this instance.

However, we wish to make it plain that a new petition would not be open to this objection; and that the pitiable event, now long passed, will not prevent Repouille from taking his place among us as a citizen. The assertion in his brief that he did not "intend" the petition to be filed until 1945, unhappily is irrelevant; the statute makes crucial the actual date of filing.

Order reversed; petition dismissed without prejudice to the filing of a second petition.

FRANK, CIRCUIT JUDGE (dissenting).

This decision may be of small practical import to this petitioner for citizenship, since perhaps, on filing a new petition, he will promptly become a citizen. But the method used by my colleagues in disposing of this case may, as a precedent, have a very serious significance for many another future petitioner whose "good moral character" may be questioned (for any one of a variety of reasons which may be unrelated to a "mercy killing") in circumstances where the necessity of filing a new petition may cause a long and injurious delay.[34] Accordingly, I think it desirable to dissent.

The district judge found that Repouille was a person of "good moral character." Presumably, in so finding, the judge attempted to employ that statutory standard in accordance with our decisions, i.e., as measured by conduct in conformity with "the generally accepted moral conventions at the time." My colleagues, although their sources of information concerning the pertinent mores are not shown to be superior to those of the district judge, reject his finding. And they do so, too, while conceding that their own conclusion is uncertain, and (as they put it) "tentative." I incline to think that the correct statutory test (the test Congress intended) is the attitude of our ethical leaders. That attitude would not be too difficult to learn; indeed, my colleagues indicate that they think such leaders would agree with the district judge. But the precedents in this circuit constrain us to be guided by contemporary public opinion about which, cloistered as judges are, we have but vague notions. (One recalls Gibbon's remark that usually a person who talks of "the opinion of the world at large" is really referring to "the few people with whom I happened to converse.")

Seeking to apply a standard of this type, courts usually do not rely on evidence but utilize what is often called the doctrine of "judicial notice," which, in matters of this sort, properly permits informal inquiries by the judges.[35] However, for such a purpose (as in the discharge of many other judicial duties), the courts are inadequately staffed,[36] so that sometimes "judicial notice" actually means judicial ignorance.

But the courts are not utterly helpless; such judicial impotence has its limits. Especially when an issue importantly affecting a man's life is involved, it seems to me that we need not, and ought not, resort to our mere unchecked surprises, remaining wholly (to quote my colleagues' words) "without means of verifying our conclusions." Because court judgments are the most solemn kind of governmental acts—backed up as they are, if necessary, by the armed force of the government—they should, I think, have a more solid foundation. I see no good reason why a man's rights should be jeopardized by judges' needless lack of knowledge.

I think, therefore, that, in any case such as this, where we lack the means of

---

[34] Consider, e.g., the case of a professional man, unable during his long delay, incident to his becoming a citizen, to practice his profession in certain states of this country.

[35] Cf. WIGMORE, EVIDENCE, 3d ed., §§ 41, 2569, 2571, 2580, 2583; Thayer, A Preliminary Treatise on Evidence (1898) 308–309; Davis, *An Approach to Problems of Evidence* in The Administrative Process, 55 HARV. LAW REV. (1942) 364, 404–405, 410; Morris, *Law and Fact*, 55 HARV. LAW REV. (1942) 1301, 1318–1325.

In this very case, my colleagues have relied on informally procured information with reference to "the fate of a similar offender in Massachusetts."

[36] Think how any competent administrative agency would act if faced with a problem like that before us here.

Cf. FRANK, IF MEN WERE ANGELS (1942) 122–127; L. Hand, J., in Parke-Davis & Co. v. H. K. Mulford Co., C.C., 189 F. 95, 115; Cohen, *Benjamin Nathan Cardozo*, 1 NAT. LAWYERS GUILD (1938) 283, 285; Morris, *Law and Fact*, 55 HARV. LAW REV. (1942) 1303, 1318–1319.

determining present-day public reactions, we should remand to the district judge with these directions: The judge should give the petitioner and the government the opportunity to bring to the judge's attention reliable information on the subject, which he may supplement in any appropriate way. All the data so obtained should be put of record. On the basis thereof, the judge should reconsider his decision and arrive at a conclusion. Then, if there is another appeal, we can avoid sheer guessing, which alone is now available to us, and can reach something like an informed judgment.

QUESTIONS

1.   Learned Hand, Augustus Hand, and Jerome Frank are among the greatest American judges of all time. But did they get this case right, either in the majority opinion or the dissent? How would you decide this case? Oliver Wendell Holmes, Jr.? A. P. d'Entrèves?

2.   Certain leading jurists, as diverse as Erwin Griswold and Francis Bacon, have argued that it is important to punish individuals who believe they are justified in disobeying the law. (Griswold was discussing Vietnam protestors and Bacon, duelists.) *See generally* Chapter VI. It could be argued that the attitude of "criminals" motivated by conscience is more threatening to the political and legal order than, say, conventional bank robbers who usually do not protest the illegality of bank robbery, or even bother to defend it as socially desirable conduct. (Indeed, bank robbery would be quite unprofitable if it were legal!) What do you think of this argument in the context of, say, abortion protests or euthanasia? We will discuss this problem at length in the next chapter.

3.   Here is an issue that frequently occurs in the context of professional discipline. Should a lawyer who violates a duty of confidentiality or loyalty to a client in pursuit of a "moral" end, say to prevent a fraud or harm to another, be punished as much or more severely than one who acts for purely selfish reasons? In *People v. Belge*, 50 A.D. 2d 1088, 376 N.Y.S.2d 771, 772 (4th Dept. 1975), *aff'd*, 41 N.Y.2d 60, 359 N.E.2d 377 (1976), two lawyers, who learned the location of the bodies of two murdered women from their incarcerated client, kept the secret despite great suffering to the families involved. Later, the New York courts and New York State Bar Association (Opinion No. 479) upheld their conduct as required by the disciplinary rules in effect in New York. *See* ANDREW L. KAUFMAN & DAVID B. WILKINS, PROBLEMS IN PROFESSIONAL RESPONSIBILITY 199–203 (4th ed. 2002). Suppose these two lawyers made the opposite choice. Should they have been punished? Should they have been punished severely?

Chapter VI

JUSTIFIED DISOBEDIENCE

In the last two chapters we have examined natural law and rationalist arguments supporting moral constraints on rulemaking. In this chapter, we consider yet another argument supporting limits on the positive law—the "natural rights" theory of John Locke. We then turn our attention to the closely related question of civil disobedience; that is, when and in what fashion is it morally justified for individuals to disobey positive law?

The subject of civil disobedience has important implications for attorneys. First, when attorneys act as private citizens and disobey the law, they may face professional discipline. Is it appropriate to suspend or revoke the license of an attorney who engages in unlawful conduct for reasons of conscientious objection? Second, lawyers may act as agents for clients who are themselves engaged in acts of civil disobedience. Is it professional misconduct for an attorney to advise a *client* to disobey a law that the client considers unjust? We turn our attention to these questions in the second part of the chapter.

A. THE HISTORICAL BACKGROUND OF AMERICAN CIVIL DISOBEDIENCE: FROM THE ENLIGHTENMENT TO THE VINEYARDS OF WRATH

The United States is a government founded by a revolution. There was a theory behind that revolution—and theory was definitely important to the likes of Washington, Jefferson, Madison, and Adams. Of special importance to them was the "natural rights" movement of the European Enlightenment, particularly as articulated by John Locke (1632–1704). This was somewhat ironic, as Locke's works were written to defend another revolution, the "Glorious Revolution" of 1688 which saw King William and Queen Mary replace King James II on the throne of England. This "Glorious Revolution" established the Whig system of limited monarchy which, in turn, was the core of the English parliamentarian government against which the Americans rebelled in 1775.

Locke's most influential political work was *Two Treatises of Government* (1690). One of the purposes of this book was to show why the "Glorious Revolution" was legitimate and could be distinguished from the Jacobite rebellion seeking to restore the Stuart monarchy in 1689. The essence of Locke's argument was contract theory. There was a "tacit consent" by the governed to the government. As Alasdair MacIntyre summarized it: "Men hand over to a legislative and executive power the authority to pass and to enforce laws which will protect their natural rights."[1] But this is a very different "social contract" from, say, that of Hobbes, whose "social covenant" establishing sovereign authority is inherently irrevocable and without limit.[2] Locke's "contract" is inherently conditional, "for insofar as the civil authority does not protect natural rights, it ceases to be a legitimate authority."[3] The "Glorious Revolution" was founded on great constitutional agreements between William and Mary and their subjects, as articulated by the group of statutes called the "Revolution Settlement," including the Bill of Rights of 1689.[4] The Jacobite rebels had no such basis of legitimacy.

Locke's idea of the content of the "natural rights," which inherently limit any sovereignty, was quite conservative. His immediate political experience was the English Civil War, which was triggered by events such as the *Five Knights* case of 1627.[5] In that case, Charles I tried to force "loans" from his subjects, having dissolved Parliament without securing approval for adequate taxes. Those who refused, such as the five knights, were thrown in jail on the King's command, without other legal justification. When Charles I was forced to recall Parliament, he had to release the five knights. Parliament then passed the "Petition of Right of 1628," which focused on two "rights": (1) the right not to be imprisoned except by the rule of law and (2) "the ancient and indubitable Right of every Free man, that he hath a full and absolute property in his goods and estate."[6]

To Locke, the *Five Knights* case would be more about the right to property than equal protection or due process of law. Illegal taxation "without representation" was a violation of the natural right of property. Yet, as MacIntyre points out, "Locke seems to have been aware of the fact that more than half the population of England was effectively propertyless. How then, is he able to reconcile his view of the right of the majority to rule with his view of the natural right to property?"[7] The answer is that Locke's "natural rights" limits on sovereignty applied to majority rule and democratic governments, as well as to all others. From this idea, of course, we get our present American constitutional doctrine of judicial review, which provides a check on unconstitutional legislative action. But in Locke's view, even a constitutional amendment could not take away a "natural" right such as private property.

There was also Locke's theory of "tacit consent." Locke stated that "every Man, that hath any Possession, or Enjoyment, of any part of the Dominions of any Government, doth thereby give his tacit Consent, and is as far forth obliged to Obedience to the Laws of that Government, during such Enjoyment, as any one under it; whether this be his Possession of Land . . . or a Lodging only for a Week;

---

[1] ALASDAIR MACINTYRE, A SHORT HISTORY OF ETHICS 158 (1998). *See* JOHN W. YOLTON, LOCKE: AN INTRODUCTION (1985).

[2] "The powers of the sovereign, in Hobbes's system, are unlimited." BERTRAND RUSSELL, A HISTORY OF WESTERN PHILOSOPHY 551 (1945).

[3] ALASDAIR MACINTYRE, A SHORT HISTORY OF ETHICS, *supra* note 1, at 158.

[4] *See* SIR GEORGE CLARK, THE LATER STUARTS 1660–1714, at 144–153 (2d ed. 1956); Paul Langford, *The Eighteenth Century (1688-1789), in* OXFORD HISTORY OF BRITAIN 399–409 (K. O. Morgan ed., 1988).

[5] 3 STATE TRIALS 1 (1627).

[6] *Id.*

[7] ALASDAIR MACINTYRE, A SHORT HISTORY OF ETHICS, *supra* note 1, at 158.

or whether it be barely traveling freely on the Highway."[8] As MacIntyre observed: "Thus it follows that the wandering gypsy on the road has consented to the authority of the government, which may therefore legitimately conscript him into its armed forces."[9]

Locke's theories dominate our current, popular view of government, and underlie both the most common argument for civil disobedience, that is, that the power of government ends when it no longer protects natural rights, and also the leading argument for compliance, that is, that one cannot "tacitly consent" to a democratic government, enjoy all its benefits, and then pick and choose among the burdens. At the height of the Vietnam protests, for example, both sides were shouting over-simplified versions of Locke at each other. The anti-war protesters advocated a "natural right" not to fight and die for a cause they rejected, while the other side said "America, love it or leave it!"

The rhetoric of the American Revolution itself strongly emphasized "natural rights" theory, and, of course, the *Declaration of Independence* tracked Locke's idea of a social contract almost exactly, reciting the "self-evident" truths that all men "are endowed by their Creator with certain unalienable Rights" and "[t]hat whenever any Form of Government becomes destructive to these ends, it is the Right of the People to alter or to abolish it."[10] But the issues of the American Revolution also focused on Locke's more narrow view of "natural rights." This was a war provoked by invasion of property rights by "taxation without representation," reminiscent of the *Five Knights* case. The assertion that "all men are created equal" was to be the subject of another, far more bloody war.

In America, the theoretical underpinnings of the new country were threatened by a fundamental flaw. The right to property had been extended to "owning" human beings. How could slaves, brought to this country in chains, be said to have "tacitly consented" to the new government? Of course they used the roads and those other, strictly limited, state amenities which were open to them, but only because they had no choice. And how could a system advocating, at least in theory, the natural rights of all persons and a rule of law founded on due process tolerate slavery?

Slavery was only the most conspicuous example of social disenfranchisement. Among American settlers, "free" blacks and Asians had harshly restricted civil rights."[11] Native Americans were systematically exploited. Women neither had the vote nor, in many cases, control over their own property. Through both legal and political maneuvers, the poor were routinely deprived of political power, and immigrants, brought to build the railways and work the fields of the great land, struggled to achieve equality.[12] These were, and are, the bitter vineyards whose

---

[8] *See* JOHN LOCKE, SECOND TREATISE OF CIVIL GOVERNMENT § 119, *quoted in* ALASDAIR MACINTYRE, A SHORT HISTORY OF ETHICS, *supra* note 1, at 159.

[9] ALASDAIR MACINTYRE, A SHORT HISTORY OF ETHICS, *supra* note 1, at 159.

[10] THE DECLARATION OF INDEPENDENCE para. 2 (U.S. 1776).

[11] *See generally* A. LEON HIGGINBOTHAM, JR., IN THE MATTER OF COLOR: RACE AND THE AMERICAN LEGAL PROCESS (1978); Robert J. Cottrol & Raymond T. Diamond, *The Second Amendment: Toward an Afro-Americanist Reconsideration*, 80 GEO. L.J. 309 (1991).

[12] *See* LAWRENCE M. FRIEDMAN, A HISTORY OF AMERICAN LAW 179–201, 428–445 (3d ed. 2005).

"Grapes of Wrath" have led to more than just a terrible Civil War. They remain today at the core of our greatest political, legal, and cultural challenges.

While we often romanticize the "Currier & Ives" pastoral world of America in the Antebellum Period, the cruel social realities were close to the surface. Concord, Massachusetts, in the 1840s, was an idyllic town. It was set on the bend of a quiet river, and woods, ponds, and farms surrounded the old houses and white steeples. Yet, to Henry David Thoreau (1817–1862), the political and social underpinnings of the town could not bear scrutiny. From a modest middle class family of French, Scottish, and Quaker descent, he struggled through Harvard College and became a school teacher in his native town, supplementing his income by working as a handyman of Ralph Waldo Emerson and Nathaniel Hawthorne, who both had houses in Concord. Thoreau was most famous for his retreat into the woods in 1845 to 1847 and his subsequent journal, *Walden* (1854), but he was also fiercely outspoken on current affairs. His *Civil Disobedience*, first published in 1849 by that most remarkable literary critic and social leader, Elizabeth Peabody, was but one example.[13]

Thoreau rejected Locke's theory of "tacit consent," which as we have seen supports a very narrow and limited window for civil disobedience. Thoreau thought that if an individual had delegated "power" to a society or a government, it was either based on a real consent or it was a bogus fiction. If it were a genuine consent, then the individual would be morally responsible for the acts of the government, because it is each person's support—or even silent submission—which makes that government possible. If the consent were bogus or fictional, it could neither be used by government as a moral justification for coercion nor by the individual as an "excuse" for cowardice or complicity. For the staunch abolitionist Thoreau, the government's complicity in slavery deprived the government of any legitimacy whatsoever. "How does it become a man to behave toward this American government to-day? I answer, that he cannot without disgrace be associated with it. I cannot for an instant recognize that political organization as *my* government which is the *slave's* government also."[14]

Unlike Locke, who thought that citizens tacitly ceded most collective decision-making to government, Thoreau believed that the conscience of the individual was paramount to the will of government. "The only obligation which I have the right to assume, is to do at any time what I think right."[15] Thoreau thought that sometimes (as in the case of slavery) the constitution is the problem, not the answer. Legal channels like judicial review and constitutional amendment are not sufficient to address injustice, because they can take too long. Citizens are born to live, not to lobby. A strong individualist, Thoreau thought that at times it was the moral duty of a citizen to follow his conscience and stand completely apart from the domain of law.

Thoreau's strong convictions made it nearly impossible for him to succeed his father as a socially prominent businessman and pencil manufacturer. They also led

---

[13] *See* Van Wyck Brooks, The Flowering of New England 295–312 (1952).

[14] *Materials, infra* at 6F.

[15] *Materials, infra* at 6F.

him to refuse to pay taxes to a government which he believed to be unjust. In fact, tax violations repeatedly landed Thoreau in jail, until benevolent neighbors paid the fines (against Thoreau's will) and bailed him out. In 1857, Thoreau met John Brown at Emerson's home, and Thoreau became increasingly active as an abolitionist. He also undertook an extensive ethnological study of Native-Americans, whose culture he greatly admired. Thoreau worked with a passion on both these social causes, a passion which led to the fatigue and tuberculosis which caused his death in 1862.

Thoreau's influence lived after him in ways he would have found both gratifying and hard to believe. His writings had a profound influence on Mahatma Gandhi, Martin Luther King, Jr., and many other moral and political leaders. Here was a solitary man who scarcely left his quiet hometown, although he claimed to have "traveled widely in Concord." Yet, the example of his life and the power of his words would move subcontinents and influence the affairs of another century.[16]

Thoreau doubtless knew of Chief Justice Lemuel Shaw (1781–1861), who was Chief Justice of Massachusetts from 1830 to 1860, most of Thoreau's adult life.[17] Shaw is today acknowledged to be one of the great jurists of 19th century America. His cases in the area of real property, commercial law, and labor law are still cited and admired.[18] But Shaw also found himself directly confronted with the horror of the Fugitive Slave Act and slavery. His reaction was quite different from Thoreau's. Despite his deep personal aversion to slavery, Shaw enforced the Fugitive Slave Act when the positive law seemed to present him with no real choice. He did this for two reasons. First, he correctly predicted that failure to reach a political compromise on slavery—a compromise represented by the Fugitive Slave Act—would lead to "national calamity" which would "threaten a great people with ruin."[19] Indeed, the Civil War, which Shaw never lived to see end, surpassed all predictions for terrible slaughter. The casualty rate for Americans has never been exceeded by any other war, including the World Wars.

Shaw had a second reason. He was to serve as Chief Justice of Massachusetts for 30 years. He did not intend to resign. But the law was what made him a judge. He doubtless knew the famous words of the medieval jurist Bracton, "the king must not be under man but under God and under the law, because law makes the king."[20] What justification did Shaw have to subvert, as a Chief Justice, the duly enacted federal law, supported by the explicit wording of the then Constitution, Article IV,

---

[16] For Thoreau's influence on Gandhi, see HARPINDER KAUR, GANDHI'S CONCEPT OF CIVIL DISOBEDIENCE: A STUDY WITH SPECIAL REFERENCE TO THOREAU'S INFLUENCE ON GANDHI (New Delhi, 1986). For Gandhi's philosophy generally, see JUDITH M. BROWN, GANDHI AND CIVIL DISOBEDIENCE: THE MAHATMA IN INDIAN POLITICS 1928-1934 (Cambridge, 1977). For Thoreau's influence on King, see "Letter from Birmingham Jail," *Materials, infra* at 6F.

[17] Shaw was a "friend of a friend" of Thoreau. The Chief Justice took long walks with Nathaniel Hawthorne (1804-1864), Thoreau's employer in Concord and close acquaintance. In turn, Herman Melville (1819-1891) married Shaw's daughter, and dedicated *Moby Dick* (1851) to Hawthorne. It was a small world in cultural Massachusetts at the time!

[18] *See* ELIJAH ADLOW, THE GENIUS OF LEMUEL SHAW (Boston, 1962).

[19] *See Materials, infra* at 6F.

[20] 2 BRACTON, DE LEGIBUS ET CONSUETUDINIBUS ANGLIAE 33 (S. E. Thorne trans., 1968).

Section 2?[21]

Many of Shaw's contemporaries disagreed. Judge Harrington of Vermont said that he would return a fugitive slave only "[i]f the master could show a bill of sale . . . from the Almighty."[22] Richard Henry Dana, author of *Two Years Before the Mast*, worked tirelessly as a young Boston attorney to defend the fugitives. More questionable, to some, were the rumored activities of certain lawyers at night. "Respectable" and "law abiding" professionals were, in the darkness, tending the Underground Railroad, which spirited thousands of escaped slaves to freedom in Canada. This was, of course, in total violation of the law. In the homes of the "best" families were secret doors, fake walls, hidden rooms. The small harbors and back roads of Massachusetts, long used to smuggle rum, were now used to smuggle people.

The great dilemmas of American civil disobedience, both open and covert, took on a special form for those under professional oath to "support the laws and Constitution [of] the United States." Both Shaw and Thoreau asked, from their different perspectives, how people could lead a "double" life—attorney at law during the day, arguing legal rules and procedures, while at night secretly subverting the entire system? Forged in the terrible vineyards of wrath and social injustice, these dilemmas were to continue to our own time.

B. THE 20TH CENTURY: A MESSAGE FROM A BIRMINGHAM JAIL

The Civil War ended legal slavery, but not the curse of racism and social inequality. Race segregated schools and universities, miscegenation laws, legal apartheid in eating, and other public places, are all within immediate living memory of many United States citizens. These barriers were not just against African-Americans. The admission of women to higher education and to the professions was both slow and segregated, and the civil rights of Latino, Asian-American, and other immigrants were violated under color of law until very recently.[23]

Much of the "progress" against social injustice was achieved by legal challenges to existing laws and institutions. Lawyers were frequently at the center of these challenges, both as political activists in their own right and as professional counsel (indeed, other lawyers were at the center of the resistance to change). In some cases, challenges to discriminatory laws and institutions could be brought without actually breaking the positive law in place, but frequently reform began with "illegal" action, whether it be "sit ins" at lunch counters or walking into a class at

---

[21] *See Materials, infra* at 6F.

[22] *Materials, infra* at 6F.

[23] *See* A. LEON HIGGINBOTHAM, JR., IN THE MATTER OF COLOR: RACE AND THE AMERICAN LEGAL PROCESS, *supra* note 11. For example, women only achieved full enfranchisement with the adoption of the XIXth Amendment, ratified August 18, 1920, and were only admitted to Harvard Law School in 1950. *See* ELEANOR FLEXNER, CENTURY OF STRUGGLE: THE WOMEN'S RIGHTS MOVEMENT IN THE UNITED STATES (1996). Japanese-American citizens were excluded from the west coast of the United States and relocated and interred at assembly camps for security reasons during World War II. This exclusion was upheld on War Powers grounds by the Supreme Court in the case of *Korematsu v. United States*, 323 U.S. 214 (1944).

a segregated state university. Thus, the "Civil Rights" movement of the 1960s became another "testing ground" for theories of civil disobedience, and for the proper role of lawyers in relation to civil disobedience.

The ultimate manifesto of the "Civil Rights" movement was the Rev. Martin Luther King's "Letter from Birmingham Jail," published on June 12, 1963, in *The Christian Century*, and reproduced in this chapter. King, of course, was a theologian, but his "Letter" shows a sophisticated understanding of both philosophical and legal issues. To begin, it is clear that he had read Plato's *Apology* closely. "Just as Socrates felt that it was necessary to create a tension in the mind so that individuals could shake off the bondage of myths and half-truths . . . so must we see the need for nonviolent gadflies to create the kind of tension in society that will help men rise from the dark depths of prejudice."[24] King also referred to both St. Augustine and St. Thomas Aquinas for the proposition that "an unjust law is no law at all."[25] He reflected that it was "illegal" to "aid and comfort a Jew in Hitler's Germany."[26] "Even so, I am sure that had I lived in Germany at the time I would have aided and comforted my Jewish brothers."[27]

But King's disobedience to the law of America was different from what he might have done in Germany. In closing his "Letter," he affirms the Lockean social contract of American constitutionalism.

> One day the south will know that when these disinherited children of God sat down at lunch counters they were in reality standing up for what is best in the American dream and for the most sacred values in our Judeo-Christian heritage, thereby bringing our nation back to those great wells of democracy which were dug deep by the founding fathers in their formulation of the Constitution and the Declaration of Independence.[28]

And, of course, he disavowed both violence and covert sabotage. His purpose was not to subvert the legal system. "That would lead to anarchy. One who breaks an unjust law must do so *openly*, *lovingly*, and with a willingness to accept the penalty."[29] King continued:

> I submit that an individual who breaks a law that conscience tells him is unjust and who willingly accepts the penalty of imprisonment in order to arouse the conscience of the community over its injustice is in reality expressing the highest respect for law.[30]

But it is doubtful that King would express "the highest respect" for a fundamental legal order in which he ultimately had no faith, say that of Nazi Germany. The influence of Locke's theory is strong in King's analysis. If the "law" still ultimately vindicates and protects natural rights, and has the potential to do so, it deserves our

---

[24] *Materials, infra* at 6F.

[25] *Id.*

[26] *Id.*

[27] *Id.*

[28] *Id.*

[29] *Id.*

[30] *Id.*

allegiance, even in disobedience. As we will see, the Platonic Socrates goes even further in defense of allegiance in the *Crito*, and King refers to that argument, as well.[31]

C.   CIVIL DISOBEDIENCE AND ATTORNEY CONDUCT

Deliberate and conscientious objection presents particular problems for the *lawyer*. Lawyers take formal oaths to uphold the laws of the state and federal government and their respective constitutions.[32] For lawyers, there is no need for Locke's "tacit consent." There is an explicit, formal contract to respect the law. In return for their allegiance and obedience to law, lawyers obtain special monopolies, immunities, and privileges, including the attorney-client privilege, a major limitation on the state's power to gather evidence. To accept these specific benefits, and then to violate the formal agreement on which they are based, seems patently disingenuous. Thoreau would certainly point out that taking such benefits and oaths involves direct complicity in the government. Chief Justice Shaw would put it differently, but would doubtless agree.

In addition to the moral and contractual obligation of the oath and received monopolies and benefits, there is also the coercive force of the professional rules. A lawyer who engages in illegal conduct—even for reasons of conscientious objection—may be subject to professional reprimand, suspension, or disbarment. But not *all* illegal conduct by a lawyer will expose the attorney to discipline. ABA Model Rule 8.4 provides for professional discipline for "a criminal act that reflects adversely on the lawyer's honesty, trustworthiness or fitness as a lawyer in other respects" and also continues the prohibition against any conduct "involving dishonesty, fraud, deceit or misrepresentation" or conduct "prejudicial to the administration of justice."[33] Again, there is no intention that a lawyer be permitted or encouraged to do other illegal acts,[34] only that professional discipline be limited to the above categories. As Comment 2 to Rule 8.4 makes clear: "Although a lawyer is *personally* answerable to the entire criminal law, a lawyer should be *profession-*

---

[31] *Materials, infra* at 6F. *See Materials*, Chapter VII, *infra*. It is an interesting issue if King would have this allegiance to a constitutional order that included the original article IV, section 2. *See Materials, infra* at 6F.

[32] Attorney oaths differ from jurisdiction to jurisdiction. Most contain a solemn promise to uphold the Constitution, but some also require sworn allegiance to state and federal laws. For example, Washington State Admission to Practice Rule 5 sets forth the oath of office in that state, which includes the sentence "I am fully subject to the laws of the state of Washington and the laws of the Untied States *and will abide by the same*." (emphasis added). The oath of admission to the federal bar requires that the attorney "solemnly swear (or affirm) that as an attorney and as a counselor of this court [he] will conduct [himself] uprightly and *according to law*, and that [he] will support the Constitution of the United States." Mary Elizabeth Basile, *Loyalty Testing for Attorneys: When Is It Necessary and Who Should Decide?* 30 CARDOZO L. REV. 1843, 1847 (2008) (emphasis added).

[33] *See* JOHN S. DZIENKOWSKI, PROFESSIONAL RESPONSIBILITY, STANDARDS, RULES & STATUTES 99 (2009-2010 ed.).

[34] EC 1-5, the "aspirational" ethical consideration contained in the Model Code of Professional Responsibility formerly in effect in many jurisdictions, made it clear that a lawyer "should refrain from *all illegal* or morally reprehensible conduct" because "obedience to law exemplifies respect for law." DZIENKOWSKI, PROFESSIONAL RESPONSIBILITY, STANDARDS, RULES & STATUTES, *supra* note 33, at 407 (emphasis added).

ally answerable only for offenses that indicate lack of those characteristics relevant to law practice" (emphasis added).[35]

Now let us suppose that Martin Luther King were a lawyer. He was arrested and charged in Birmingham with the crime of parading without a permit. Should he be subject to professional discipline for participating in the demonstration that led to this arrest? King would likely argue that he should only be disbarred or subject to discipline for "illegal conduct involving moral turpitude" (if he were practicing in a *Model Code* state) or for criminal acts that reflected "adversely on [his] honesty, trustworthiness or fitness as a lawyer in other respects" (if he were practicing in a *Model Rules* state) and that civil disobedience in the form of non-violent demonstration does not evidence either moral turpitude or disrespect for the law. But Chief Justice Shaw would likely argue that King's oath and professional identity should constrain him from *any* illegal acts, and that almost all civil disobedience could be characterized as conduct "prejudicial to the administration of justice" or "adversely reflecting on fitness to practice law," especially since the professional oath which King would have taken when sworn in as an attorney would likely have bound him to obey both state and federal law. What do you think?

This issue came to a head during the Vietnam War. Draft resistance was a felony. But was it "illegal conduct involving moral turpitude," as prohibited by Model Code of Professional Responsibility DR 1-102(A)(3), then followed in some variation by most states? Should recent law school graduates who evaded the draft be disbarred? That question would in all likelihood turn on whether the form of draft resistance involved deceit or evasion (such as assuming a new identity or entering another country illegally). Remember King's admonition: "One who breaks an unjust law must do so *openly*, *lovingly*, and with a willingness to accept the penalty."[36] Some states apparently decided that draft resisters who reported themselves to the authorities and submitted to their punishment could retain their status in the practicing bar. Other states appear to have taken a different view, holding that any felony was "illegal conduct involving moral turpitude."[37] Whether the result would be different under the *Model Rules* depends on whether the draft evasion reflected on "honesty, trustworthiness or fitness of a lawyer in other respects," ABA Model Rule 8.4(b), or involved "dishonesty, fraud, deceit or misrepresentation." ABA Model Rule 8.4(c). Whether open failure to register for the draft constitutes "deceit" is an interesting issue on which there can be serious disagreement.[38]

In addition to bar discipline, there are several other ways that the legal profession imposes its standards. Suppose Martin Luther King were a law student, not yet admitted to the bar. He would be required, in almost every state, to report his criminal record on his bar application. He would then be called before the "Character Committee" of the relevant Board of Bar Examiners, and asked to

---

[35] DZIENKOWSKI, PROFESSIONAL RESPONSIBILITY, STANDARDS, RULES & STATUTES, *supra* note 33, at 99.

[36] *Materials, infra* at 6F.

[37] DZIENKOWSKI, PROFESSIONAL RESPONSIBILITY, STANDARDS, RULES & STATUTES, *supra* note 33, at 408.

[38] *See* Donald T. Weckstein, *Maintaining the Integrity and Competence of the Legal Profession*, 48 TEX. L. REV. 267 (1970). *See also In re* Pontarelli, 66 N.E.2d 83 (Ill. 1946), for a World War II case.

explain his conduct in Birmingham. This Committee would be focusing generally on "fitness to practice law," but would have broad discretion in deciding whether a prior criminal arrest or conviction was of the sort to disqualify King to practice law.[39] Or suppose King were a lawyer nominated to be a state Chief Justice, like Shaw, or a federal judge, or the Attorney General. The confirmation process would doubtless focus on his criminal record, and, again, there would be broad discretion as to whether such conduct were appropriate for a future judge or government law officer.

But this is not all. Today, all states but Kentucky and California have "mandatory reporting" rules (so-called "snitch rules") that require lawyers to report ethical misconduct by fellow attorneys to bar disciplinary authorities. Under ABA Model Rule 8.3(a) "a lawyer having knowledge [not otherwise protected by the confidentiality rules of 1.6] that another lawyer has committed a violation of the rules of professional conduct that raises a substantial question as to that lawyer's honesty, trustworthiness or fitness as a lawyer in other respects" must inform the appropriate professional disciplinary authority of such conduct.[40] Unlike practically all other citizens, lawyers are thus required to *self-police* their profession, or face discipline themselves. Since violation of a criminal law by an attorney which falls into one of the categories listed above is considered professional misconduct, lawyers must report their knowledge of such transgressions to the bar. So, for example, if you were a lawyer in Concord Massachusetts in 1842 and had knowledge that your neighbor, Richard Henry Dana, was secreting fugitive slaves as part of the Underground Railroad, under today's rules you would be obliged to report Dana to the Board of Bar Overseers, or face discipline yourself. Not surprisingly, the so-called "snitch rules" have proven to be very hard to enforce and extremely controversial.[41]

This brings us to one final special challenge presented for lawyers by civil disobedience. What if it is not you, but your *client* that wishes to engage in illegal conduct due to reasons of conscience? ABA Model Rule 1.2(d) provides that a lawyer shall not "counsel a client to engage, or assist a client, in conduct that the lawyer knows is criminal or fraudulent, but a lawyer may discuss the legal consequences of any proposed course of conduct with a client and may counsel or assist a client to make a good faith effort to determine the validity, scope, meaning or application of the law."[42] There is also the symbolic role of the lawyer as an "officer of the court"[43]

---

[39] In 1976, one of the author's students was called before a "Character Committee" of a state Board of Bar Examiners because a search of the state draft records indicated that the student had not registered. Apparently, all males passing that bar examination were checked against the draft records as a routine matter.

[40] DZIENKOWSKI, PROFESSIONAL RESPONSIBILITY, STANDARDS, RULES & STATUTES, *supra* note 33, at 205. The Model Code of Professional Responsibility predecessor to Rule 8.3 required lawyers having "unprivileged knowledge" of "a violation of DR 1-102" to report such knowledge to a tribunal or other authority empowered to investigate or act upon such violation." *Id.* at 409.

[41] Nikki A. Ott & Heather F. Newton, *A Current Look at Model Rule 8.3: How Is It Used and What Are Courts Doing About It?*, 16 Geo. J. Legal Ethics 747, 755 (2003).

[42] Here again, there has been a major shift between the *ABA Model Rules* and the former *ABA Model Code*. The *Code* flatly stated that "a lawyer shall not . . . [c]ounsel or assist his client in conduct that the lawyer knows to be illegal or fraudulent." DR 7-102(A)(7). The more modern Rule 1.2(d)

and corresponding duties of fidelity to the law and legal system. Does a lawyer have an obligation to persuade a client to *desist* from unlawful conduct, even if he is sympathetic to the client's purpose?

To assist you with this difficult question, the chapter ends with two modern accounts of civil disobedience theory. The first, from Ronald Dworkin's famous *Taking Rights Seriously* (1977), focuses on disobedience of the draft laws "out of conscience." The domestic turmoil following the entry into the war in Vietnam soon equaled the "Civil Rights Movement" as a source of difficult moral challenges, particularly to middle class university students. The draft laws were also clearly constitutionally valid, at least as a basic idea, and violation of these laws was a serious crime, a felony punishable by years in jail.

Dworkin's argument was that civil disobedience is actually good for a well-functioning, democratic legal system, and, in certain ways, is actually necessary. To begin at the most obvious point, there is a need to create judicial test cases. This means that individuals must disobey some rules, executive orders, official decisions, and even statutes, to create an opportunity for judicial review. Further, in a complex federal system, even judicial decisions may be inconsistent with other court decisions, or reversed on appeal. Finally, the Supreme Court of the United States has reversed itself on key legal issues, as the fate of the infamous *Dred Scott* (1857) and *Plessy v. Ferguson* (1896) cases attest.[44] To the extent a client wishes to pursue such a course of conscience, the lawyer faces no true dilemma between loyalty to the client and to the legal system, because the one actually benefits the other. Indeed, as we have seen, ABA Model Rule 1.2(d) explicitly permits such a role.

On the other hand, what if it is crystal clear that the client's conduct will be found to be criminal? Erwin Griswold, former Dean of Harvard Law School and Solicitor General, had no trouble with that question. "[I]t is of the essence of the law that it is equally applied to all, that it finds all alike, irrespective of personal motive."[45]

---

explicitly resolves the easier "civil disobedience" issues discussed later in the materials by Dworkin and McMorrow; i.e., when the lawyer has a genuine "good faith" doubt as to the validity or application of a law. It does not, however, resolve the issue where the civil disobedience is a criminal act in clear violation of a law found to be valid by the courts, except that it is permissible for the lawyer to "discuss the consequences of any proposed course of conduct." Apparently, however, a lawyer may not "counsel" such action under Rule 1.2(d).

[43] Since the 13th century, there has been a close supervision of the legal profession by the official court system, and in most American jurisdictions the bar is officially licensed and regulated by court-appointed officials. *See* J. H. BAKER, AN INTRODUCTION TO ENGLISH LEGAL HISTORY 177–199 (3d ed. 1990); THEODORE F. T. PLUCKNETT, A CONCISE HISTORY OF THE COMMON LAW 215–230 (1956). Whether lawyers, thus regulated, are "officers of the court" with independent duties not only to their clients but also to the justice system has been hotly debated. Certainly the ABA Model Rules have provided for special obligations of candor, good behavior, and good faith for lawyers appearing before a tribunal. *See* ABA Model Rules 3.2, 3.3, 3.4, 3.5. There have also been controls on publicity likely to affect the fairness of trials and on lawyers appearing in cases where they could be called as witnesses. *See* ABA Model Rules 3.6, 3.7. *But see* Eugene R. Gaetke, *Lawyers as Officers of the Court*, 42 VAND. L. REV. 39, 90–91 (1989), arguing that "the characterizations of lawyers as officers of the court under contemporary law is largely disingenuous."

[44] *See* Dred Scott v. Sandford, 19 How. 393 (1857); Plessy v. Ferguson, 163 U.S. 537 (1896).

[45] *Materials, infra* at 6F. On April 16, 1968, in the middle of the Vietnam controversy and after Martin Luther King's assassination, Erwin Griswold stated in New Orleans, at Tulane Law School, that there

Dworkin disagrees. It is legitimate, he argues, that prosecutors "go easy" on genuine conscientious objection, that judges adjust sentences, or that juries nullify the law through acquittal. He concludes:

> Some lawyers will be shocked by my general conclusion that we have a responsibility toward those who disobey the draft laws out of conscience, and that we may be required not to prosecute them, but rather to change our laws or adjust our sentencing procedures to accommodate them. The simple Draconian propositions, that crime must be punished, and that he who misjudges the law must take the consequences, have an extraordinary hold on the professional as well as the popular imagination. But the rule of law is more complex and more intelligent than that and it is important that it survive.[46]

But is it obvious that criminal conduct undertaken for reasons of "conscience" is less dangerous to society than "ordinary" criminal conduct? To begin, the "ordinary" criminal is usually not seeking to challenge the government's moral base or its legitimacy. A bank robber will probably support laws protecting private property, or should, as without them bank robbery is not very profitable. Bank robbers do not threaten the social fabric in most societies. Political terrorists, on the other hand, are often acting from deep conviction and conscience, and often in a selfless way. This is one reason they can be so dangerous.

So how does a lawyer distinguish between a client with Dworkin's "benign," but illegal, objectives and a client whose illegal objectives threaten the legal order? Is this a subjective judgment for every lawyer? Professor Judith McMorrow tackles these issues in her excellent article, "Civil Disobedience and the Lawyer's Obligation to the Law," which is also excerpted in this chapter. McMorrow begins with some of the difficulties identified by Dworkin. Counseling "illegal" conduct certainly could be justified where there is genuine doubt about the applicability or validity of the law in question. Even if there is direct precedent against a client on an issue, how can a lawyer assume that the courts might not reverse themselves? And what about the factors discussed by Dworkin at the end of his chapter? Should a lawyer point out to a client considering clearly criminal conduct that a sympathetic jury might, nevertheless, acquit? Or that a prosecutor might, for policy reasons, decide not to proceed? Or that a judge could select a lenient sentence? McMorrow concludes that "[a]ffirmatively telling the client about the option of civil disobedi-

---

was a "moral right of dissenters to disobey laws they believe in conscience to be unjust," but that there was no "legal right to disobey any laws, no matter how unjust they might seem." Griswold added, "those who adopted the civil disobedience tactic of disobeying the law should be prepared to go to jail." N.Y. TIMES, April 17, 1968, at 1. Griswold observed that: "One of the monuments to the memory of the late Rev. Dr. Martin Luther King, Jr. is that he practiced civil disobedience only under such circumstances and by nonviolent means." *Id.* at 16. The next day, the *New York Times* ran an editorial praising Griswold and stating that his remarks could be "read with profit" by the 9,300 university faculty members who had signed a statement calling on the federal government to quash its indictments of Dr. Benjamin Spock and four others on charges of conspiring to encourage violations of the draft law. According to the editorial, "the faculty protesters confused moral rights with legal responsibilities." The editorial concluded that "if after due process, the defendants are found guilty, they must in good conscience accept any penalty imposed by law. . . . To deny this obligation is to challenge not a law but the whole democratic framework of laws." N.Y. TIMES, April 18, 1968, at 46. Do you agree?

[46] *Materials, infra* at 6F.

ence. . . . reaches to the heart of the lawyer's relationship to the law."[47] Lawyers should neither be required to raise the possibility nor always be prohibited from discussing it. But, she warns, "lawyers have a special obligation to exercise . . . caution before engaging in civil disobedience. Because of the limitation of the concept of self-regulation, this standard appropriately is not incorporated into narrow 'rules' of conduct, but should be part of the individual lawyer's consideration when evaluating an unjust law."[48]

But where does this leave us? Back to the core problems of this course. If, as McMorrow argues, guidance should not be provided by disciplinary rule, then the issue must be resolved by the individual lawyer. But how? Hopefully by application of some principled form of moral reasoning. This, in turn, leads us back to the question of whether one can ever distinguish between a "just" and "unjust" law, or whether, as positivists would argue, that simply is an exercise in personal prejudice. And there is a final issue. Suppose we can agree that a specific law or legal outcome is "unjust." Does that justify *criminal* disobedience, particularly for a lawyer? In the next chapter we will reflect on one of the most powerful arguments ever made for an unbending allegiance to the rule of law, even in the face of patent injustice. This was Plato's *Crito*.

D. FURTHER READING

There are good introductory accounts of the philosophical liberalism of the European "Enlightenment" and the works of John Locke in our standard "companion" paperbacks, ALASDAIR MACINTYRE, A SHORT HISTORY OF ETHICS 157–177 (1998); BERTRAND RUSSELL, A HISTORY OF WESTERN PHILOSOPHY 596–647 (2007); and HUNTINGTON CAIRNS, LEGAL PHILOSOPHY FROM PLATO TO HEGEL 335–361 (1949). For further accounts, see Richard Ithamar Aaron's classic JOHN LOCKE (1971) and John W. Yolton's more modern approach, LOCKE: AN INTRODUCTION (1985). *See also* STERLING P. LAMPRECHT, MORAL AND POLITICAL PHILOSOPHY OF JOHN LOCKE (1902). There are some very good "in print" paperback editions of the *Second Treatise of Government*, such as JOHN LOCKE, THE SECOND TREATISE OF GOVERNMENT (Thomas P. Peardon ed., with intro. 1952). Finally, for an overview of the "Enlightenment," see CARL L. BECKER'S GREAT, THE HEAVENLY CITY OF THE EIGHTEENTH-CENTURY PHILOSOPHERS (1932) and FRANK E. MANUEL, THE AGE OF REASON (1951).

For an account of Thoreau's important influence on Mahatma Gandhi, see HARPINDER KAUR, GANDHI'S CONCEPT OF CIVIL DISOBEDIENCE: A STUDY WITH SPECIAL REFERENCE TO THOREAU'S INFLUENCE ON GANDHI (New Delhi, 1986). For a general study of Gandhi's philosophy, see JUDITH M. BROWN, GANDHI AND CIVIL DISOBEDIENCE: THE MAHATMA IN INDIAN POLITICS 1928-1934 (Cambridge, 1977).

LEONARD LEVY'S, THE LAW OF THE COMMONWEALTH AND CHIEF JUSTICE SHAW (1957) remains a definitive scholarly source on Shaw's life and the turmoil surrounding the fugitive slave issue while Shaw was Chief Justice. For a legal introduction to the horror of American slavery, see LAWRENCE M. FRIEDMAN, A HISTORY OF AMERICAN

---

[47] *Materials, infra* at 6F.

[48] *Id.*

Law 192–201 (1973) and MARK V. TUSHNET, THE AMERICAN LAW OF SLAVERY, 1810–1860: CONSIDERATIONS OF HUMANITY AND INTEREST (1981).

One of the best accounts of the life, philosophy, and struggle of Martin Luther King, Jr. is JAMES A. COLAIACO, MARTIN LUTHER KING, JR.: APOSTLE OF MILITANT NONVIOLENCE (1992), which contains a full chapter on the "Letter from Birmingham Jail." Focusing more on King's philosophy is, HANES WALTON, JR., THE POLITICAL PHILOSOPHY OF MARTIN LUTHER KING, JR. (1971).

On the subject of civil disobedience and the lawyer, Justice Abe Fortas (1910-1982) in CONCERNING DISSENT AND CIVIL DISOBEDIENCE (1968) gives a former Supreme Court Justice's (1965-1969) view on disobedience which, predictably, is fairly deferential to the legal order. For the view that "[t]he law generally does not require lawyers to act in a manner that subordinates their own and the clients' interests in favor of the interests of the judicial system and the general public" and that lawyers should either adopt new duties or abandon any claim to be "officers of the court," see Eugene R. Gaetke, *Lawyers as Officers of the Court*, 42 VAND. L. REV. 39, 90–91 (1989).

E. DISCUSSION PROBLEMS

PROBLEM XIII

Judge Lemuel Shaw answers his door late one night in 1854. Before him stands a person wanted as a "fugitive slave." Shaw explains that, despite his personal aversion to slavery, he is going to send for the sheriff or, even worse, a federal marshal. What are Shaw's reasons for this act? What is your view? [*Optional reading*: ROBERT M. COVER, JUSTICE ACCUSED: ANTISLAVERY AND THE JUDICIAL PROCESS (1975)].

PROBLEM XIV

Italian immigrants and anarchists Fernando Sacco and Bartolomeo Vanzetti were charged and convicted of armed robbery and murder in 1921 in Dedham, Massachusetts. While their convictions were pending on appeal in the Massachusetts Supreme Judicial Court, a certain law professor named Felix Frankfurter risked his professional reputation by publishing an article in *The Atlantic* (March 1927) attempting to demonstrate their innocence. Nevertheless, their conviction was sustained, and their execution ordered.

Late one night there is a knock on Frankfurter's door. Before him stands Vanzetti, who has escaped from the County Jail while awaiting execution. Frankfurter explains that, despite his absolute belief in Vanzetti's innocence, he is going to call the police. What are Frankfurter's reasons for this act? What is your view? Is this situation identical to the Shaw question?

[For additional reading on the Sacco and Vanzetti case, see the opinion of the Massachusetts Supreme Judicial Court in *Commonwealth v. Sacco*, 255 Mass. 369 (1926). *See also* Felix Frankfurter, *The Case of Sacco and Vanzetti*, LAW & POLITICS 140–188 (1962); ROBERTA STRAUSS FEUERLICHT, JUSTICE CRUCIFIED: THE STORY OF

SACCO AND VANZETTI (1977)].

PROBLEM XV

You are a German citizen. You answer your door late one night in 1943. Before you stands a Jew, escaped from a concentration camp. Do you call the police? Is this situation identical to, or different from, Problems XIII and XIV? Suppose you turned in the Jew, out of obedience to the law and fear of punishment. Should you be punished at Nuremberg? What would be the relevant law? What would Lemuel Shaw do if he served as a judge on the Nuremberg Tribunal? Felix Frankfurter? Telford Taylor? St. Thomas Aquinas?

PROBLEM XVI

How should ABA Model Rules 1.2(d) and 8.4 be construed in regards to acts of civil disobedience committed or counseled by attorneys?

Imagine that you are an attorney who represents the right-to-life group "Operation Rescue." The local chapter of Operation Rescue is planning a demonstration and rally on National Right to Life Day. Some members of the organization want to picket and hold prayer sessions at a local Planned Parenthood clinic. Members of Operation Rescue want to get close enough to the clinic to engage patients in conversations about their healthcare options. They believe that a state statute requiring them to keep 35 feet away from the driveway or entrances to any reproductive health care facility constitutionally infringes on their First Amendment freedoms. *See, e.g., Mass. Gen. L. c. 255 § 120E 1/2.* The statute provides for misdemeanor penalties of up to three months in jail and up to a $500 fine.

Your clients want to challenge the constitutionality of this statute by violating it, getting themselves arrested, and then moving to dismiss any later-filed criminal charges. They hope that their arrest and subsequent prosecution will bring important media attention to their anti-abortion cause, and that it will be a potential vehicle for having an overbroad statute struck down.

Assume that you identify with your clients' cause, and believe that the state statute may indeed violate controlling Supreme Court precedent. *See, e.g., Hill v. Colorado,* 530 U.S. 703 (2000). Can you advise your clients to picket within 35 feet of the clinic entrance? Must you advise your clients *not* to do so? If instead you simply counsel your clients on the exact scope of the buffer zone statute, advise them of the consequences of violating it, and advise them of the likelihood under controlling precedent of having the statute later determined to be unconstitutional, have you "assisted your client . . . in conduct that the lawyer knows is criminal or fraudulent" in violation of ABA Rule 1.2(d)?

What if you join your clients in the protest and are arrested and convicted of misdemeanor trespass yourself. Are you likely to be disbarred? Does criminal trespass "reflect adversely . . . on [your] fitness as a lawyer" for purposes of ABA Model Rule 8.4(b)? Have you engaged in conduct "prejudicial to the administration of justice" under ABA Model Rule 8.4(d)?

See generally McCullen v. Coakley, 571 F.3d 167 (1st Cir. 2009).

Consider:

ABA Model Rules of Professional Conduct:

Rules 1.2(d); 1.6(b); 2.1; 8.3(a); 8.4

F. MATERIALS

THE WORKS OF JOHN LOCKE
The Twelfth Edition, Volume Fourth (1824), Chapter XIX

OF THE DISSOLUTION OF GOVERNMENT

He that will with any clearness speak of the dissolution of government ought in the first place to distinguish between the dissolution of the society and the dissolution of the government. That which makes the community and brings men out of the loose state of nature into one politic society is the agreement which everybody has with the rest to incorporate and act as one body, and so be one distinct commonwealth. The usual and almost only way whereby this union is dissolved is the inroad of foreign force making a conquest upon them; for in that case, not being able to maintain and support themselves as one entire and independent body, the union belonging to that body which consisted therein must necessarily cease, and so every one return to the state he was in before, with a liberty to shift for himself and provide for his own safety, as he thinks fit, in some other society. Whenever the society is dissolved, it is certain the government of that society cannot remain. Thus conquerors' swords often cut up governments by the roots and mangle societies to pieces, separating the subdued or scattered multitude from the protection of and dependence on that society which ought to have preserved them from violence. The world is too well instructed in, and too forward to allow of, this way of dissolving of governments to need any more to be said of it; and there wants not much argument to prove that where the society is dissolved, the government cannot remain—that being as impossible as for the frame of a house to subsist when the materials of it are scattered and dissipated by a whirlwind, or jumbled into a confused heap by an earthquake.

Besides this overturning from without, governments are dissolved from within.

First, when the legislative is altered. Civil society being a state of peace amongst those who are of it, from whom the state of war is excluded by the umpirage which they have provided in their legislative for the ending all differences that may arise amongst any of them, it is in their legislative that the members of a commonwealth are united and combined together into one coherent living body. This is the soul that gives form, life, and unity to the commonwealth; from hence the several members have their mutual influence, sympathy, and connection; and, therefore, when the legislative is broken or dissolved, dissolution and death follows; for the essence and union of the society consisting in having one will, the legislative, when once established by the majority, has the declaring and, as it were, keeping of that will. The constitution of the legislative is the first and fundamental act of society, whereby provision is made for the continuation of their union under the direction of persons and bonds of laws made by persons authorized thereunto by the consent and appointment of the people, without which no one man or number of men amongst them can have authority of making laws that shall be binding to the rest. When any one or more shall take upon them to make laws, whom the people have not appointed so to do, they make laws without authority, which the people are not therefore bound to obey; by which means they come again to be out of subjection and may constitute to themselves a new legislative as they think best, being in full liberty to resist the force of those who without authority would impose anything upon them. Everyone is at the disposure of his own will when those who had by the delegation of the society the declaring of the public will are excluded from it, and others usurp the place who have no such authority or delegation.

This being usually brought about by such in the commonwealth who misuse the power they have, it is hard to consider it aright, and know at whose door to lay it, without knowing the form of government in which it happens. Let us suppose then the legislative placed in the concurrence of three distinct persons:

(1) A single hereditary person having the constant supreme executive power, and with it the power of convoking and dissolving the other two within certain periods of time.

(2) An assembly of hereditary nobility.

(3) An assembly of representatives chosen pro tempore by the people. Such a form of government supposed, it is evident,

First, that when such a single person or prince sets up his own arbitrary will in place of the laws which are the will of the society declared by the legislative, then the legislative is changed; for that being in effect the legislative whose rules and laws are put in execution and required to be obeyed. When other laws are set up, and other rules pretended and enforced than what the legislative constituted by the society have enacted, it is plain that the legislative is changed. Whoever introduces new laws, not being thereunto authorized by the fundamental appointment of the society, or subverts the old, disowns and overturns the power by which they were made, and so sets up a new legislative.

Secondly, when the prince hinders the legislative from assembling in its due time, or from acting freely pursuant to those ends for which it was constituted, the legislative is altered; for it is not a certain number of men, no, nor their meeting, unless they have also freedom of debating and leisure of perfecting what is for the good of the society, wherein the legislative consists. When these are taken away or altered so as to deprive the society of the due exercise of their power, the legislative is truly altered; for it is not names that constitute governments but the use and exercise of those powers that were intended to accompany them, so that he who takes away the freedom or hinders the acting of the legislative in its due seasons in effect takes away the legislative and puts an end to the government.

Thirdly, when, by the arbitrary power of the prince, the electors or ways of election are altered without the consent and contrary to the common interest of the people, there also the legislative is altered; for if others than those whom the society has authorized thereunto do choose, or in another way than what the society has prescribed, those chosen are not the legislative appointed by the people.

Fourthly, the delivery also of the people into the subjection of a foreign power, either by the prince or by the legislative, is certainly a change of the legislative, and so a dissolution of the government; for the end why people entered into society being to be preserved one entire, free, independent society, to be governed by its own laws, this is lost whenever they are given up into the power of another.

Why in such a constitution as this the dissolution of the government in these cases is to be imputed to the prince is evident. Because he, having the force, treasure, and offices of the state to employ, and often persuading himself, or being flattered by others, that as supreme magistrate he is incapable of control—he alone is in a condition to make great advances toward such changes, under pretense of lawful authority, and has it in his hands to terrify or suppress opposers as factious, seditious, and enemies to the government. Whereas no other part of the legislative or people is capable by themselves to attempt any alteration of the legislative, without open and visible rebellion apt enough to be taken notice of, which, when it prevails, produces effects very little different from foreign conquest. Besides, the prince in such a form of government having the power of dissolving the other parts of the legislative, and thereby rendering them private persons, they can never in opposition to him or without his concurrence alter the legislative by a law, his consent being necessary to give any of their decrees that sanction. But yet, so far as the other parts of the legislative in any way contribute to any attempt upon the government, and do either promote or not, what lies in them, hinder such designs, they are guilty and partake in this, which is certainly the greatest crime men can be guilty of one toward another.

There is one way more whereby such a government may be dissolved, and that is when he who has the supreme executive power neglects and abandons that charge, so that the laws already made can no longer be put in execution. This is demonstratively to reduce all to anarchy, and so effectually to dissolve the government; for laws not being made for themselves, but to be by their execution the bonds of the society, to keep every part of the body politic in its due place and function, when that totally ceases, the government visibly ceases, and the people become a confused multitude, without order or connection. Where there is no longer the administration of justice for the securing of men's rights, nor any remaining power within the community to direct the force to provide for the necessities of the public, there certainly is no government left. Where the laws cannot be executed, it is all one as if there were no laws; and a government without laws is, I suppose, a mystery in politics, inconceivable to human capacity and inconsistent with human society.

In these and the like cases, when the government is dissolved, the people are at liberty to provide for themselves by erecting a new legislative, differing from the other by the change of persons or form, or both, as they shall find it most for their safety and good; for the society can never by the fault of another lose the native and original right it has to preserve itself, which can only be done by a settled legislative, and a fair and impartial execution of the laws made by it. But the state of mankind is not so miserable that they are not capable of using this remedy till it be too late to look for any. To tell people they may provide for themselves by erecting a new legislative, when by oppression, artifice, or being delivered over to a foreign power, their old one is gone, is only to tell them they may expect relief when it is too late and the evil is past cure. This is in effect no more than to bid them first be slaves, and then to take care of their liberty; and when their chains are on, tell them they may act. like freemen. This, if barely so, is rather mockery than relief; and men can never be secure from tyranny if there be no means to escape it till they are perfectly under it; and therefore it is that they have not only a right to get out of it, but to prevent it.

There is, therefore, secondly, another way whereby governments are dissolved, and that is when the legislative or the prince, either of them, act contrary to their trust.

First, the legislative acts against the trust reposed in them when they endeavor to invade the property of the subject, and to make themselves or any part of the community masters or arbitrary disposers of the lives, liberties, or fortunes of the people.

The reason why men enter into society is the preservation of their property; and the end why they choose and authorize a legislative is that there may be laws made and rules set as guards and fences to the properties of all the members of the society to limit the power and moderate the dominion of every part and member of the society; for since it can never be supposed to be the will of the society that the legislative should have a power to destroy that which every one designs to secure by entering into society, and for which the people submitted themselves to legislators of their own making. Whenever the legislators endeavor to take away and destroy the property of the people, or to reduce them to slavery under arbitrary power, they put themselves into a state of war with the people who are thereupon absolved from any further obedience, and are left to the common refuge which God has provided for all men against force and violence. Whensoever, therefore, the legislative shall transgress this fundamental rule of society, and either by ambition, fear, folly, or corruption, endeavor to grasp themselves, or put into the hands of any other, an absolute power over the lives, liberties, and estates of the people, by this breach of trust they forfeit the power the people had put into their hands for quite contrary ends, and it devolves to the people, who have a right to resume their original liberty and, by the establishment of a new legislative, such as they shall think fit, provide for their own safety and security, which is the end for which they are in society. What I have said here concerning the legislative in general holds true also concerning the supreme executor, who having a double trust put in him—both to have a part in the legislative and the supreme execution of the law—acts against both when he goes about to set up his own arbitrary will as the law of the society. He acts also contrary to his trust when he either employs the force, treasure, and offices of the society to corrupt the representatives and gain them to his purposes, or openly pre-engages the electors and prescribes to their choice such whom he has by solicitations, threats, promises, or otherwise won to his designs, and employs them to bring in such who have promised beforehand what to vote and what to enact. Thus to regulate candidates and electors, and new-model the ways of election, what is it but to cut up the government by the roots, and poison the very fountain of public security? For the people, having reserved to themselves the choice of their representatives, as the fence to their properties, could do it for no other end but that they might always be freely chosen, and, so chosen, freely act and advise as the necessity of the commonwealth and the public good should upon examination and mature debate be judged to require. This those who give their votes before they hear the debate and have weighed the reasons on all sides are not capable of doing. To prepare such an assembly as this, and endeavor to set up the declared abettors of his own will for the true representatives of the people and the lawmakers of the society, is certainly as great a breach of trust and as perfect a declaration of a design to subvert the government as is possible to be met with. To which if one shall add rewards and punishments visibly employed to the same end, and all the arts of perverted law made use of to take off and destroy all that stand in the way of such a design, and will not comply and consent to betray the liberties of their country, it will be past doubt what is doing. What power they ought to have in the society who thus employ it contrary to the trust that went along with it in its first institution is easy to determine; and one cannot but see that he who has once attempted any such thing as this cannot any longer be trusted.

To this perhaps it will be said that, the people being ignorant and always discontented, to lay the foundation of government in the unsteady opinion and uncertain humor of the people is to expose it to certain ruin; and no government will be able long to subsist if the people may set up a new legislative whenever they take offense at the old one. To this I answer: Quite the contrary. People are not so easily got out of their old forms as some are apt to suggest. They are hardly to be prevailed with to amend the acknowledged faults in the frame they have been accustomed to. And if there be any original defects, or adventitious ones introduced by time or corruption, it is not an easy thing to get them changed, even when all the world sees there is an opportunity for it. This slowness and aversion in the people to quit their old constitutions has in the many revolutions which have been seen in this kingdom, in this and former ages, still kept us to, or after some interval of fruitless attempts still brought us back again to, our old legislative of king, lords, and commons; and whatever provocations have made the crown be taken from some of our princes' heads, they never carried the people so far as to place it in another line.

But it will be said this hypotheses lays a ferment for frequent rebellion. To which I answer:

First, no more than any other hypothesis; for when the people are made miserable, and find themselves exposed to the ill-usage of arbitrary power, cry up their governors as much as you will for sons of Jupiter, let them be sacred or divine, descended or authorized from heaven, give them out for whom or what you please, the same will happen. The people generally ill-treated, and contrary to right, will be ready upon any occasion to ease themselves of a burden that sits heavy upon them. They will wish and seek for the opportunity, which in the change, weakness, and accidents of human affairs seldom delays long to offer itself. He must have lived but a little while in the world who has not seen examples of this in his time, and he must have read very little who cannot produce examples of it in all sorts of governments in the world.

Secondly, I answer, such revolutions happen not upon every little mismanage-ment in public affairs. Great mistakes in the ruling part, many wrong and inconvenient laws, and all the slips of human frailty will be born by the people without mutiny or murmur. But if a long train of abuses, prevarications, and artifices, all tending the same way, make the design visible to the people, and they cannot but feel what they lie under and see whither they are going, it is not to be wondered that they should then rouse themselves and endeavor to put the rule into such hands which may secure to them the ends for which government was at first erected, and without which ancient names and specious forms are so far from being better that they are much worse than the state of nature or pure anarchy—the inconveniences being all as great and as near, but the remedy farther off and more difficult.

Thirdly, I answer that this doctrine of a power in the people of providing for their safety anew by a new legislative, when their legislators have acted contrary to their trust by invading their property, is the best fence against rebellion, and the probablest means to hinder it; for rebellion being an opposition, not to persons, but authority which is founded only in the constitutions and laws of the government, those, whoever they be, who by force break through, and by force justify their violation of them, are truly and properly rebels; for when men, by entering into society and civil government, have excluded force and introduced laws for the preservation of property, peace, and unity amongst themselves, those who set up force again in opposition to the laws do *rebellare*—that is, bring back again the state of war—and are properly rebels; which they who are in power, by the pretense they have to authority, the temptation of force they have in their hands, and the flattery of those about them, being likeliest to do, the properest way to prevent the evil is to show them the danger and injustice of it who are under the greatest temptation to run into it.

In both the aforementioned cases, when either the legislative is changed or the legislators act contrary to the end for which they were constituted, those who are guilty are guilty of rebellion; for if any one by force takes away the established legislative of any society, and the laws of them made pursuant to their trust, he thereby takes away the umpirage which every one had consented to for a peaceable decision of all their controversies, and a bar to the state of war amongst them. They who remove or change the legislative take away this decisive power which nobody can have but by the appointment and consent of the people, and so destroying the authority which the people did, and nobody else can, set up, and introducing a power which the people has not authorized, they actually introduce a state of war which is that of force without authority; and thus by removing the legislative established by the society—in whose decisions the people acquiesced and united as to that of their own will—they untie the knot and expose the people anew to the state of war.

*   *   *

Here, it is like, the common question will be made: Who shall be judge whether the prince or legislative act contrary to their trust? This, perhaps, ill-affected and factious men may spread amongst the people, when the prince only makes use of his due prerogative. To this I reply: The people shall be judge; for who shall be judge whether his trustee or deputy acts well and according to the trust reposed in him but he who deputes him and must, by having deputed him, have still a power to discard him when he fails in his trust? If this be reasonable in particular cases of private men, why should it be otherwise in that of the greatest moment where the welfare of millions is concerned, and also where the evil, if not prevented, is greater and the redress very difficult, dear, and dangerous?

But further, this question, Who shall be judge? cannot mean that there is no judge at all; for where there is no judicature on earth to decide controversies amongst men, God in heaven is Judge. He alone, it is true, is Judge of the right. But every man is judge for himself, as in all other cases, so in this, whether another has put himself into a state of war with him, and whether he should appeal to the Supreme Judge, as Jephthah did.

If a controversy arise betwixt a prince and some of the people in a matter where the law is silent or doubtful, and the thing be of great consequence, I should think the proper umpire in such a case should be the body of the people; for in cases where the prince has a trust reposed in him and is dispensed from the common ordinary rules of the law, there, if any men find themselves aggrieved and think the prince acts contrary to or beyond that trust, who so proper to judge as the body of the people (who, at first, lodged that trust in him) how far they meant it should extend? But if the prince, or whoever they be in the administration, decline that way of determination, the appeal then lies nowhere but to heaven; force between either persons who have no known superior on earth, or which permits no appeal to a judge on earth, being properly a state of war wherein the appeal lies only to heaven; and in that state the injured party must judge for himself when he will think fit to make use of that appeal and put himself upon it.

To conclude, the power that every individual gave the society when he entered into it can never revert to the individuals again as long as the society lasts, but will always remain in the community, because without this there can be no community, no commonwealth, which is contrary to the original agreement; so also when the society has placed the legislative in any assembly of men, to continue in them and their successors with direction and authority for providing such successors, the legislative can never revert to the people while that government lasts, because having provided a legislative with power to continue for ever, they have given up their political power to the legislative and cannot resume it. But if they have set limits to the duration of their legislative and made this supreme power in any person or assembly only temporary, or else when by the miscarriages of those in authority it is forfeited, upon the forfeiture, or at the determination of the time set, it reverts to the society, and the people have a right to act as supreme and continue the legislative in themselves, or erect a new form, or under the old form place it in new hands, as they think good.

QUESTIONS

1. Speaking of Locke's theory of the "tacit consent" of the governed, Alasdair MacIntyre observed: "Locke's doctrine is important because it is the doctrine of every modern state which claims to be democratic, but which like every state wishes to coerce its citizens. Even if the citizens are not consulted and have no means of expressing their views on a given topic, they are held to have tacitly consented to the actions of governments."[49] Is this a fair depiction of Locke's theory? If so, what do

---

[49] ALASDAIR MACINTYRE, A SHORT HISTORY OF ETHICS, *supra* note 1, at 159.

you think of it? How would American slavery fit this theory?

2.　Locke argues that "the power that every individual gave the society when he entered into it can never revert to the individuals again so long as the society lasts" and that the same is true of the power a society places in its governing body, unless society has "set limits to the duration" of this power or the power is "forfeited." *Materials, supra* at 6F. Do you agree that individuals have lost their right to act independently of society? What, in practical terms, would terminate our society's delegation of power to the sovereign states and the federal constitutional government? Is Locke a philosopher of rebellion and revolution, or status quo?

3.　Locke observed that "[t]he reason why men enter into society is the preservation of their property." *Materials, supra* at 6F. Bertrand Russell later observed that "[t]he greatest political defect of Locke and his disciples, from a modern point of view, was their worship of property. But those who criticized them on this account often did so in the interests of classes that were more harmful than the capitalists, such as monarchists, aristocrats, and militarists."[50] What do you think of this? Do you agree?

HENRY DAVID THOREAU, CIVIL DISOBEDIENCE
A Yankee in Canada, with Anti-slavery and Reform Papers
(1866)

[This essay first appeared, in a slightly different form, under the title "Resistance to Civil Government" in Elizabeth Peabody's *Aesthetic Papers* (Boston, 1849).]

"CIVIL DISOBEDIENCE"

I heartily accept the motto,—"That government is best which governs least", and I should like to see it acted up to more rapidly and systematically. Carried out, it finally amounts to this, which I also believe,—"That government is best which governs not at all"; and when men are prepared for it, that will be the kind of government which they will have. Government is at best but an expedient; but most governments are usually, and all governments are sometimes, inexpedient. The objections which have been brought against a standing army, and they are many and weighty, and deserve to prevail, may also at last be brought against a standing government. The standing army is only an arm of the standing government. The government itself, which is only the mode which the people have chosen to execute their will, is equally liable to be abused and perverted before the people can act through it. Witness the present Mexican war, the work of comparatively a few individuals using the standing government as their tool; for, in the outset, the people would not have consented to this measure.

This American government,—what is it but a tradition, though a recent one, endeavoring to transmit itself unimpaired to posterity, but each instant losing some of its integrity? It has not the vitality and force of a single living man; for a single man can bend it to his will. It is a sort of wooden gun to the people themselves. But

---

[50] Bertrand Russell, A History of Western Philosophy, *supra* note 2, at 646.

it is not the less necessary for this; for the people must have some complicated machinery or other, and hear its din, to satisfy that idea of government which they have. Governments show thus how successfully men can be imposed on, even impose on themselves, for their own advantage. It is excellent, we must all allow. Yet this government never of itself furthered any enterprise, but by the alacrity with which it got out of its way. *It* does not keep the country free. *It* does not settle the West. *It* does not educate. The character inherent in the American people has done all that has been accomplished; and it would have done somewhat more, if the government had not sometimes got in its way. For government is an expedient by which men would fain succeed in letting one another alone; and, as has been said, when it is most expedient, the governed are most let alone by it. Trade and commerce, if they were not made of India-rubber, would never manage to bounce over the obstacles which legislators are continually putting in their way; and, if one were to judge these men wholly by the effects of their actions and not partly by their intentions, they would deserve to be classed and punished with those mischievous persons who put obstructions on railroads.

But, to speak practically and as a citizen, unlike those who call themselves no-government men, I ask for, not at once no government, but *at once* a better government. Let every man make known what kind of government would command his respect, and that will be one step toward obtaining it.

After all, the practical reason why, when the power is once in the hands of the people, a majority are permitted, and for a long period continue, to rule, is not because they are most likely to be in the right, nor because this seems fairest to the minority, but because they are physically the strongest. But a government in which the majority rule in all cases cannot be based on justice, even as far as men understand it. Can there not be a government in which majorities do not virtually decide right and wrong, but conscience?—in which majorities decide only those questions to which the rule of expediency is applicable? Must the citizen ever for a moment, or in the least degree, resign his conscience to the legislator? Why has every man a conscience, then? I think that we should be men first, and subjects afterward. It is not desirable to cultivate a respect for the law, so much as for the right. The only obligation which I have the right to assume, is to do at any time what I think right. It is truly enough said, that a corporation has no conscience; but a corporation of conscientious men is a corporation *with* a conscience. Law never made men a whit more just; and, by means of their respect for it, even the well-disposed are daily made the agents of injustice. A common and natural result of an undue respect for law is, that you may see a file of soldiers, colonel, captain, corporal, privates, powder-monkeys, and all, marching in admirable order over hill and dale to the wars, against their wills, ay, against their common sense and consciences, which makes it very steep marching indeed, and produces a palpitation of the heart. They have no doubt that it is a damnable business in which they are concerned; they are all peaceably inclined. Now, what are they? Men at all? or small movable forts and magazines, at the service of some unscrupulous man in power? Visit the Navy-Yard, and behold a marine, such a man as an American government can make, or such as it can make a man with its black arts,—a mere shadow and reminiscence of humanity, a man laid out alive and standing, and already, as one may say, buried under arms with funeral accompaniments, though it may be,—

Not a drum was heard, not a funeral note,

As his corse to the rampart we hurried;

Not a soldier discharged his fare-well shot

O'er the grave where our hero we buried.

The mass of men serve the state thus, not as men mainly, but as machines, with their bodies. They are the standing army, and the militia, jailers, constables, posse comitatus, &c. In most cases there is no free exercise whatever of the judgment or of the moral sense; but they put themselves on a level with wood and earth and stones; and wooden men can perhaps be manufactured that will serve the purpose as well. Such command no more respect than men of straw or a lump of dirt. They have the same sort of worth only as horses and dogs. Yet such as these even are commonly esteemed good citizens. Others,—as most legislators, politicians, law-yers, ministers, and office-holders, serve the state chiefly with their heads; and, as they rarely make any moral distinctions, they are as likely to serve the Devil, without *intending* it, as God. A very few, as heroes, patriots, martyrs, reformers in the great sense, and men, serve the state with their consciences also, and so necessarily resist it for the most part; and they are commonly treated as enemies by it. A wise man will only be useful as a man, and will not submit to be "clay," and "stop a hole to keep the wind away," but leave that office to his dust at least:—

I am too high-born to be propertied,

To be a secondary at control,

Or useful serving-man and instrument

To any sovereign state throughout the world.

He who gives himself entirely to his fellowmen appears to them useless and selfish; but he who gives himself partially to them is pronounced a benefactor and philanthropist.

How does it become a man to behave toward this American government to-day? I answer, that he cannot without disgrace be associated with it. I cannot for an instant recognize that political organization as *my* government which is the *slave's* government also.

All men recognize the right of revolution; that is, the right to refuse allegiance to, and to resist, the government, when its tyranny or its inefficiency are great and unendurable. But almost all say that such is not the case now. But such was the case, they think, in the Revolution of '75. If one were to tell me that this was a bad government because it taxed certain foreign commodities brought to its ports, it is most probable that I should not make an ado about it, for I can do without them. All machines have their friction; and possibly this does enough good to counterbalance the evil. At any rate, it is a great evil to make a stir about it. But when the friction comes to have its machine, and oppression and robbery are organized, I say, let us not have such a machine any longer. In other words, when a sixth of the population of a nation which has undertaken to be the refuge of liberty are slaves, and a whole country is unjustly overrun and conquered by a foreign army, and subjected to military law, I think that it is not too soon for honest men to rebel and revolutionize. What makes this duty the more urgent is the fact, that the country so overrun is not our own, but ours is the invading army.

Paley, a common authority with many on moral questions, in his chapter on the "Duty of Submission to Civil Government," resolves all civil obligation into expediency; and he proceeds to say, "that so long as the interest of the whole society requires it, that is, so long as the established government cannot be resisted or changed without public inconveniency, it is the will of God that the established government be obeyed, and no longer. . . . . This principle being admitted, the justice of every particular case of resistance is reduced to a computation of the quantity of the danger and grievance on the one side, and of the probability and expense of redressing it on the other." Of this, he says, every man shall judge for himself. But Paley appears never to have contemplated those cases to which the rule of expediency does not apply, in which a people, as well as an individual, must do justice, cost what it may. If I have unjustly wrested a plank from a drowning man, I must restore it to him though I drown myself. This, according to Paley, would be inconvenient. But he that would save his life, in such a case, shall lose it. This people must cease to hold slaves, and to make war on Mexico, though it cost them their existence as a people.

In their practice, nations agree with Paley; but does any one think that Massachusetts does exactly what is right at the present crisis?

> A drab, of state, a cloth-o'-silver
> slut,
> To have her train borne up, and
> her soul train in the dirt.

Practically speaking, the opponents to a reform in Massachusetts are not a hundred thousand politicians at the South, but a hundred thousand merchants and farmers here, who are more interested in commerce and agriculture than they are in humanity, and are not prepared to do justice to the slave and to Mexico, *cost what it may*. I quarrel not with far-off foes, but with those who, near at home, co-operate with, and do the bidding of, those far away, and without whom the latter would be harmless. We are accustomed to say, that the mass of men are unprepared; but improvement is slow, because the few are not materially wiser or better than the many. It is not so important that many should be as good as you, as that there be some absolute goodness somewhere; for that will leaven the whole lump. There are thousands who are *in opinion* opposed to slavery and to the war, who yet in effect do nothing to put an end to them; who, esteeming themselves children of Washington and Franklin, sit down with their hands in their pockets, and say that they know not what to do, and do nothing; who even postpone the question of freedom to the question of free-trade, and quietly read the prices-current along with the latest advices from Mexico, after dinner, and, it may be, fall asleep over them both. What is the price-current of an honest man and a patriot to-day? They hesitate, and they regret, and sometimes they petition; but they do nothing in earnest and with effect. They will wait, well disposed, for others to remedy the evil, that they may no longer have it to regret. At most, they give only a cheap vote, and a feeble countenance and God-speed, to the right, as it goes by them. There are nine hundred and ninety-nine patrons of virtue to one virtuous man. But it is easier to deal with the real possessor of a thing than with the temporary guardian of it.

All voting is a sort of gaming, like checkers or backgammon, with a slight moral tinge to it, a playing with right and wrong, with moral questions; and betting naturally accompanies it. The character of the voters is not staked. I cast my vote, perchance, as I think right; but I am not vitally concerned that that right should prevail. I am willing to leave it to the majority. Its obligation, therefore, never exceeds that of expediency. Even voting *for the right* is *doing* nothing for it. It is only expressing to men feebly your desire that it should prevail. A wise man will not leave the right to the mercy of chance, nor wish it to prevail through the power of the majority. There is but little virtue in the action of masses of men. When the majority shall at length vote for the abolition of slavery, it will be because they are indifferent to slavery, or because there is but little slavery left to be abolished by their vote. *They* will then be the only slaves. Only *his* vote can hasten the abolition of slavery who asserts his own freedom by his vote.

I hear of a convention to be held at Baltimore, or elsewhere, for the selection of a candidate for the Presidency, made up chiefly of editors, and men who are politicians by profession; but I think, what is it to any independent, intelligent, and respectable man what decision they may came to? Shall we not have the advantage of his wisdom and honesty, nevertheless? Can we not count upon some independent votes? Are there not many individuals in the country who do not attend conventions? But no: I find that the respectable man, so called, has immediately drifted from his position, and despairs of his country, when his country has more reason to despair of him. He forthwith adopts one of the candidates thus selected as the only *available* one, thus proving that he is himself *available* for any purposes of the demagogue. His vote is of no more worth than that of any unprincipled foreignor or hireling native, who may have been bought. O for a man who is a *man*, and, as my neighbor says, has a bone in his back which you cannot pass your hand through! Our statistics are at fault: the population has been returned too large. How many *men* are there to a square thousand miles in this country? Hardly one. Does not America offer any inducement for men to settle here? The American has dwindled into an Odd Fellow,—one who may be known by the development of his organ of gregariousness, and a manifest lack of intellect and cheerful self-reliance; whose first and chief concern, on coming into the world, is to see that the Almshouses are in good repair; and, before yet he has lawfully donned the virile garb, to collect a fund for the support of the widows and orphans that may be; who, in short, ventures to live only by the aid of the Mutual Insurance company, which has promised to bury him decently.

It is not a man's duty, as a matter of course, to devote himself to the eradication of any, even the most enormous wrong; he may still properly have other concerns to engage him; but it is his duty, at least, to wash his hands of it, and, if he gives it no thought longer, not to give it practically his support. If I devote myself to other pursuits and contemplations, I must first see, at least, that I do not pursue them sitting upon another man's shoulders. I must get off him first, that he may pursue his contemplations too. See what gross inconsistency is tolerated. I have heard some of my townsmen say, "I should like to have them order me out to help put down an insurrection of the slaves, or to march to Mexico;—see if I would go"; and yet these very men have each, directly by their allegiance, and so indirectly, at least, by their money, furnished a substitute. The soldier is applauded who refuses to serve in an unjust war by those who do not refuse to sustain the unjust government which makes the war; is applauded by those whose own act and authority he disregards and sets at naught; as if the State were penitent to that degree that it hired one to scourge it while it sinned, but not to that degree that it left off sinning for a moment. Thus, under the name of Order and Civil Government, we are all made at last to pay homage to and support our own meanness. After the first blush of sin comes its indifference; and from immoral it becomes, as it were, *un* moral, and not quite unnecessary to that life which we have made.

The broadest and most prevalent error requires the most disinterested virtue to sustain it. The slight reproach to which the virtue of patriotism is commonly liable, the noble are most likely to incur. Those who, while they disapprove of the character and measures of a government, yield to it their allegiance and support, are undoubtedly its most conscientious supporters, and so frequently the most serious obstacles to reform. Some are petitioning the State to dissolve the Union, to disregard the requisitions of the President. Why do they not dissolve it themselves,—the union between themselves and the State,—and refuse to pay their quota into its treasury? Do not they stand in the same relation to the State, that the State does to the Union? And have not the same reasons prevented the State from resisting the Union, which have prevented them from resisting the State?

How can a man be satisfied to entertain an opinion merely, and enjoy *it*? Is there any enjoyment in it, if his opinion is that he is aggrieved? If you are cheated out of a single dollar by your neighbor, you do not rest satisfied with knowing that you are cheated, or with saying that you are cheated, or even with petitioning him to pay you your due; but you take effectual steps at once to obtain the full amount, and see that you are never cheated again. Action from principle, the perception and the performance of right, changes things and relations; it is essentially revolutionary, and does not consist wholly with anything which was. It not only divides states and churches, it divides families; ay, it divides the *individual*, separating the diabolical in him from the divine.

Unjust laws exist: shall we be content to obey them, or shall we endeavor to amend them, and obey them until we have succeeded, or shall we transgress them at once? Men generally, under such a government as this, think that they ought to wait until they have persuaded the majority to alter them. They think that, if they should resist, the remedy would be worse than the evil. But it is the fault of the government itself that the remedy is worse than the evil. *It* makes it worse. Why is it not more apt to anticipate and provide for reform? Why does it not cherish its wise minority? Why does it cry and resist before it is hurt? Why does it not encourage its citizens to be on the alert to point out its faults, and *do* better than it would have them? Why does It always crucify Christ, and excommunicate Copernicus and Luther, and pronounce Washington and Franklin rebels?

One would think, that a deliberate and practical denial of its authority was the only offence never contemplated by government; else, why has it not assigned its definite, its suitable and proportionate penalty? If a man who has no property refuses but once to earn nine shillings for the State, he is put in prison for a period unlimited by any law that I know, and determined only by the discretion of those who placed him there; but if he should steal ninety times nine shillings from the State, he is soon permitted to go at large again.

If the injustice is part of the necessary friction of the machine of government, let it go, let it go: perchance it will wear smooth,—certainly the machine will wear out. If the injustice has a spring, or a pulley, or a rope, or a crank, exclusively for itself, then perhaps you may consider whether the remedy will not be worse than the evil; but if it is of such a nature that it requires you to be the agent of injustice to another, then, I say, break the law. Let your life be a counter friction to stop the machine. What I have to do is to see, at any rate, that I do not lend myself to the wrong which I condemn.

As for adopting the ways which the State has provided for remedying the evil, I know not of such ways. They take too much time, and a man's life will be gone. I have other affairs to attend to. I came into this world, not chiefly to make this a good place to live in, but to live in it, be it good or bad. A man has not everything to do, but something; and because he cannot do *everything*, it is not necessary that he should do *something* wrong. It is not my business to be petitioning the Governor or the Legislature any more than it is theirs to petition to me; and, if they should not hear my petition, what should I do then? But in this case the State has provided no way: its very Constitution is the evil. This may seem to be harsh and stubborn and unconciliatory; but it is to treat with the utmost kindness and consideration the only spirit that can appreciate or deserves it. So is all change for the better, like birth and death, which convulse the body.

I do not hesitate to say, that those who call themselves Abolitionists should at once effectually withdraw their support, both in person and property, from the government of Massachusetts, and not wait till they constitute a majority of one, before they suffer the right to prevail through them. I think that it is enough if they have God on their side, without waiting for that other one. Moreover, any man more right than his neighbors constitutes a majority of one already.

I meet this American government, or its representative, the State government, directly, and face to face, once a year—no more—in the person of its tax-gatherer; this is the only mode in which a man situated as I am necessarily meets it; and it then says distinctly, Recognize me; and the simplest, the most effectual, and, in the present posture of affairs, the indispensablest mode of treating with it on this head, of expressing your little satisfaction with and love for it, is to deny it then. My civil neighbor, the tax-gatherer, is the very man I have to deal with,—for it is, after all, with men and not with parchment that I quarrel,—and he has voluntarily chosen to be an agent of the government. How shall he ever know well what he is and does as an officer of the government, or as a man, until he is obliged to consider whether he shall treat me, his neighbor, for whom he has respect, as a neighbor and well-disposed man, or as a maniac and disturber of the peace, and see if he can get over this obstruction to his neighborliness without a ruder and more impetuous thought or speech corresponding with his action. I know this well, that if one thousand, if one hundred, if ten men whom I could name,—if ten *honest* men only,—ay, if *one* HONEST man, in this State of Massachusetts, *ceasing to hold slaves*, were actually to withdraw from this copartnership, and be locked up in the county jail therefor, it would be the abolition of slavery in America. For it matters not how small the beginning may seem to be: what is once well done is done forever. But we love better to talk about it: that we say is our mission. Reform keeps many scores of newspapers in its service, but not one man. If my esteemed neighbor, the State's ambassador, who will devote his days to the settlement of the question of human rights in the Council Chamber, instead of being threatened with the prisons of Carolina, were to sit down the prisoner of Massachusetts, that State which is so anxious to foist the sin of slavery upon her sister,—though at present she can discover only an act of inhospitality to be the ground of a quarrel with her,—the Legislature would not wholly waive the subject the following winter.

Under a government which imprisons any unjustly, the true place for a just man is also a prison. The proper place to-day, the only place which Massachusetts has provided for her freer and less desponding spirits, is in her prisons, to be put out and locked out of the State by her own act, as they have already put themselves out by their principles. It is there that the fugitive slave, and the Mexican prisoner on parole, and the Indian come to plead the wrongs of his race, should find them; on that separate, but more free and honorable ground, where the State places those who are not *with* her, but *against* her,—the only house in a slave State in which a free man can abide with honor. If any think that their influence would be lost there, and their voices no longer afflict the ear of the State, that they would not be as an enemy within its walls, they do not know by how much truth is stronger than error, nor how much more eloquently and effectively he can combat injustice who has experienced a little in his own person. Cast your whole vote, not a strip of paper merely, but your whole influence. A minority is powerless while it conforms to the majority; it is not even a minority then; but it is irresistible when it clogs by its whole weight. If the alternative is to keep all just men in prison, or give up war and slavery, the State will not hesitate which to choose. If a thousand men were not to pay their tax-bills this year, that would not be a violent and bloody measure, as it would be to pay them, and enable the State to commit violence and shed innocent blood. This is, in fact, the definition of a peaceable revolution, if any such is possible. If the tax-gatherer, or any other public officer, asks me, as one has done, "But what shall I do?" my answer is, "If you really wish to do anything, resign your office." When the subject has refused allegiance, and the officer has resigned his office, then the revolution is accomplished. But even suppose blood should flow. Is there not a sort of blood shed when the conscience is wounded? Through this wound a man's real manhood and immortality flow out, and he bleeds to an everlasting death. I see this blood flowing now.

I have contemplated the imprisonment of the offender, rather than the seizure of his goods,—though both will serve the same purpose,—because they who assert the purest right, and consequently are most dangerous to a corrupt State, commonly have not spent much time in accumulating property. To such the State renders comparatively small service, and a slight tax is wont to appear exorbitant, particularly if they are obliged to earn it by special labor with their hands. If there were one who lived wholly without the use of money, the State itself would hesitate to demand it of him. But the rich man,—not to make any invidious comparison,—is always sold to the institution which makes him rich. Absolutely speaking, the more money, the less virtue; for money comes between a man and his objects, and obtains them for him; and it was certainly no great virtue to obtain it. It puts to rest many questions which he would otherwise be taxed to answer; while the only new question which it puts is the hard but superfluous one, how to spend it. Thus his moral ground is taken from under his feet. The opportunities of living are diminished in proportion as what are called the "means" are increased. The best thing a man can do for his culture when he is rich is to endeavor to carry out those schemes which he entertained when he was poor. Christ answered the Herodians according to their condition. "Show me the tribute-money," said he;—and one took a penny out of his pocket;—if you use money which has the image of Caesar on it, and which he has made current and valuable, that is, *if you are men of the State*, and gladly enjoy the advantages of Caesar's government, then pay him back some of his own when he demands it; "Render therefore to Caesar that which is Caesar's, and to God those things which are God's,"—leaving them no wiser than before as to which was which; for they did not wish to know.

When I converse with the freest of my neighbors, I perceive that, whatever they may say about the magnitude and seriousness of the question, and their regard for the public tranquility, the long and the short of the matter is, that they cannot spare the protection of the existing government, and they dread the consequences to their property and families of disobedience to it. For my own part, I should not like to think that I ever rely on the protection of the State. But, if I deny the authority of the State when it presents its tax-bill, it will soon take and waste all my property, and so harass me and my children without end. This is hard. This makes it impossible for a man to live honestly, and at the same time comfortably, in outward respects. It will not be worth the while to accumulate property; that would be sure to go again. You must hire or squat somewhere, and raise but a small crop, and eat that soon. You must live within yourself, and depend upon yourself always tucked up and ready for a start, and not have many affairs. A man may grow rich in Turkey even, if he will be in all respects a good subject of the Turkish government. Confucius said: "If a state is governed by the principles of reason, poverty and misery are subjects of shame; if a state is not governed by the principles of reason, riches and honors are the subjects of shame." No: until I want the protection of Massachusetts to be extended to me in some distant Southern port, where my liberty is endangered, or until I am bent solely on building up an estate at home by peaceful enterprise, I can afford to refuse allegiance to Massachusetts, and her right to my property and life. It costs me less in every sense to incur the penalty of disobedience to the State, than it would to obey. I should feel as if I were worth less in that case.

Some years ago, the State met me in behalf of the Church, and commanded me to pay a certain sum toward the support of a clergyman whose preaching my father attended, but never I myself. "Pay," it said, "or be locked up in the jail." I declined to pay. But, unfortunately, another man saw fit to pay it. I did not see why the schoolmaster should be taxed to support the priest, and not the priest the schoolmaster; for I was not the State's schoolmaster, but I supported myself by voluntary subscription. I did not see why the lyceum should not present its tax-bill, and have the State to back its demand, as well as the Church. However, at the request of the selectmen, I condescended to make some such statement as this writing:—"Know all men by these presents, that I, Henry Thoreau, do not wish to be regarded as a member of any incorporated society which I have not joined." This I gave to the town clerk; and he has it. The State, having thus learned that I did not wish to be regarded as a member of that church, has never made a like demand on me since; though it said that it must adhere to its original presumption that time. If I had known how to name them, I should then have singed off in detail from all the societies which I never signed on to; but I did not know where to find a complete list.

I have paid no poll-tax for six years. I was put into a jail once on this account, for one night; and, as I stood considering the walls of solid stone, two or three feet thick, the door of wood and iron, a foot thick, and the iron grating which strained the light, I could not help being struck with the foolishness of that institution which treated me as if I were mere flesh and blood and bones, to be locked up. I wondered that it should have concluded at length that this was the best use it could put me to, and had never thought to avail itself of my services in some way. I saw that, if there was a wall of stone between me and my townsmen, there was a still more difficult one to climb or break through, before they could get to be as free as I was. I did not for a moment feel confined, and the walls seemed a great waste of stone and mortar. I felt as if I alone of all my townsmen had paid my tax. They plainly did not know how to treat me, but behaved like persons who are underbred. In every threat and in every compliment there was a blunder; for they thought that my chief desire was to stand the other side of that stone wall. I could not but smile to see how industriously they locked the door on my meditations, which followed them out again without let or hindrance, and *they* were really all that was dangerous. As they could not reach me, they had resolved to punish my body; just as boys, if they cannot come at some person against whom they have a spite, will abuse his dog. I saw that the State was half-witted, that it was timid as a lone woman with her silver spoons, and that it did not know its friends from its foes, and I lost all my remaining respect for it, and pitied it.

*   *   *

I think sometimes, Why, this people mean well; they are only ignorant; they would do better if they knew how: why give your neighbors this pain to treat you as they are not inclined to? But I think again, this is no reason why I should do as they do, or permit others to suffer much greater pain of a different kind. Again, I sometimes say to myself, When many millions of men, without heat, without ill wit, without personal feeling of any kind, demand of you a few shillings only, without the possibility, such is their constitution, of retracting or altering their present demand, and without the possibility, on your side, of appeal to any other millions, why expose yourself to this overwhelming brute force? You do not resist cold and hunger, the winds and the waves, thus obstinately; you quietly submit to a thousand similar necessities. You do not put your head into the fire. But just in proportion as I regard this as not wholly a brute force, partly a human force, and consider that I have relations to those millions as to so many millions of men, and not of mere brute or inanimate things, I see that appeal is possible, first and instantaneously, from them to the Maker of them, and, secondly, from them to themselves. But, if I put my head deliberately into the fire, there is no appeal to fire or to the Maker of fire, and I have only myself to blame. If I could convince myself that I have any right to be satisfied with men as they are, and to treat them accordingly, and not according, in some respects, to my requisitions and expectations of what they and I ought to be, then, like a good Mussulman and fatalist, I should endeavor to be satisfied with things as they are, and say it is the will of God. And, above all, there is this difference between resisting this and a purely brute or natural force, that I can resist this with some effect; but I cannot expect, like Orpheus, to change the nature of the rocks and trees and beasts.

I do not wish to quarrel with any man or nation. I do not wish to split hairs, to make fine distinctions, or set myself up as better than my neighbors. I seek rather, I may say, even an excuse for conforming to the laws of the land. I am but too ready to conform to them. Indeed, I have reason to suspect myself on this head; and each year, as the tax-gatherer comes round, I find myself disposed to review the acts and position of the general and State governments, and the spirit of the people, to discover a pretext for conformity.

> We must affect our country as our
> parents;
> And if at any time we alienate
> Our love or industry from doing it
> honor,
> We must respect effects and teach
> the soul
> Matter of conscience and religion,
> And not desire of rule or benefit.

I believe that the State will soon be able to take all my work of this sort out of my hands, and then I shall be no better a patriot than my fellow-countrymen. Seen from a lower point of view, the Constitution, with all its faults, is very good; the law and the courts are very respectable; even this State and this American government are, in many respects, very admirable and rare things, to be thankful for, such as a great many have described them; but seen from a point of view a little higher, they are what I have described them; seen from a higher still, and the highest, who shall say what they are, or that they are worth looking at or thinking of at all?

However, the government does not concern me much, and I shall bestow the fewest possible thoughts on it. It is not many moments that I live under a government, even in this world. If a man is thought-free, fancy-free, imagination-free, that which is *not* never for a longtime appearing *to be* to him, unwise rulers or reformers cannot fatally interrupt him.

I know that most men think differently from myself; but those whose lives are by profession devoted to the study of these or kindred subjects, content me as little as any. Statesmen and legislators, standing so completely within the institution, never distinctly and nakedly behold it. They speak of moving society, but have no resting-place without it. They may be men of a certain experience and discrimination, and have no doubt invented ingenious and even useful systems, for which we sincerely thank them; but all their wit and usefulness lie within certain not very wide limits. They are wont to forget that the world is not governed by policy and expediency. Webster never goes behind government, and so cannot speak with authority about it. His words are wisdom to those legislators who contemplate no essential reform in the existing government; but for thinkers, and those who legislate for all time, he never once glances at the subject. I know of those whose serene and wise speculations on this theme would soon reveal the limits of his mind's range and hospitality. Yet, compared with the cheap professions of most reformers, and the still cheaper wisdom and eloquence of politicians in general, his are almost the only sensible and valuable words, and we thank Heaven for him. Comparatively, he is always strong, original, and, above all, practical. Still his quality is not wisdom, but prudence. The lawyer's truth is not Truth, but consistency, or a consistent expediency. Truth is always in harmony with herself, and is not concerned chiefly to reveal the justice that may consist with wrong-doing. He well deserves to be called, as he has been called, the Defender of the Constitution. There are really no blows to be given by him but defensive ones. He is not a leader, but a follower. His leaders are the men of '87. "I have never made an effort," he says, "and never propose to make an effort; I have never countenanced an effort, and never mean to countenance an effort, to disturb the arrangement as originally made, by which the various States came into the Union." Still thinking of the sanction which the Constitution gives to slavery, he says, "Because it was a part of the original compact—let it stand." Notwithstanding his special acuteness and ability, he is unable to take a fact out of its merely political relations, and behold it as it lies absolutely to be disposed of by the intellect—what, for instance, it behooves a man to do here in America to-day with regard to slavery, but ventures, or is driven, to make some such desperate answer as the following, while professing to speak absolutely, and as a private man—from which what new and singular code of social duties might be inferred? "The manner," says he, "in which the governments of those States where slavery exists are to regulate it, is for their own consideration, under their responsibility to their constituents, to the general laws of propriety, humanity, and justice, and to God. Associations formed elsewhere, springing from a feeling of humanity, or any other cause, have nothing whatever to do with it. They have never received any encouragement from me, and they never will."

They who know of no purer sources of truth, who have traced up its stream no higher, stand, and wisely stand, by the Bible and the Constitution, and drink at it there with reverence and humility; but they who behold where it comes trickling into this lake or that pool, gird up their loins once more, and continue their pilgrimage toward its fountain-head.

No man with a genius for legislation has appeared in America. They are rare in the history of the world. There are orators, politicians, and eloquent men, by the thousand; but the speaker has not yet opened his mouth to speak, who is capable of settling the much-vexed questions of the day. We love eloquence for its own sake, and not for any truth which it may utter, or any heroism it may inspire. Our legislators have not yet learned the comparative value of free-trade and of freedom, of union, and of rectitude, to a nation. They have no genius or talent for comparatively humble questions of taxation and finance, commerce and manufactures and agriculture. If we were left solely to the wordy wit of legislators in Congress for our guidance, uncorrected by the seasonable experience and the effectual complaints of the people, America would not long retain her rank among the nations. For eighteen hundred years, though perchance I have no right to say it, the New Testament has been written; yet where is the legislator who has wisdom and practical talent enough to avail himself of the light which it sheds on the science of legislation?

The authority of government, even such as I am willing to submit to,—for I will cheerfully obey those who know and can do better than I, and in many things even those who neither know nor can do so well,—is still an impure one: to be strictly just, it must have the sanction and consent of the governed. It can have no pure right over my person and property but what I concede to it. The progress from an absolute to a limited monarchy, from a limited monarchy to a democracy, is a progress toward a true respect for the individual. Even the Chinese philosopher was wise enough to regard the individual as the basis of the empire. Is a democracy, such as we know it, the last improvement possible in government? Is it not possible to take a step further towards recognizing and organizing the rights of man? There will never be a really free and enlightened State, until the State comes to recognize the individual as a higher and independent power, from which all its own power and authority are derived, and treats him accordingly. I please myself with imagining a State at last which can afford to be just to all men, and to treat the individual with respect as a neighbor; which even would not think it inconsistent with its own repose, if a few were to live aloof from it, not meddling with it, nor embraced by it, who fulfilled all the duties of neighbors and fellowmen. A State which bore this kind of fruit, and suffered it to drop as fast as it ripened, would prepare the way for a still more perfect and glorious State, which also I have imagined, but not yet anywhere seen.

QUESTIONS

1. Thoreau observed that "the lawyer's truth is not Truth, but consistency, or a consistent expediency." *Materials, supra* at 6F. What does he mean by that? Do you agree? Socrates said almost the same thing. *See Materials, supra* at 1F.

2. Thoreau observed further: "If we were left solely to the wordy wit of legislators in Congress for our guidance, uncorrected by the seasonable experience and the effectual complaints of the people, America would not long retain her rank among the nations." *Materials, supra* at 6F. What does he have in mind when he refers to "effectual complaints"? What are the practical methods of "correcting" our legislature? Is Thoreau thinking of legal actions such as *Brown v. Board of Education*, 347 U.S. 483 (1954)? If not, what does he have in mind? Were his personal methods "effectual"? Did he really care?

3. Would Thoreau, a great enemy of racism and injustice, see any point in going to law school today? If so, would he get past the "Character and Fitness" committee of his Board of Bar Examiners after graduation?

THE UNITED STATES CONSTITUTION
(As of 1797)

ARTICLE IV

SECTION 1. Full Faith and Credit shall be given in each State to the public Acts, Records, and judicial Proceedings of every other State. And the Congress may by general Laws prescribe the Manner in which such Acts, Records and Proceedings shall be proved, and the Effect thereof.

SECTION 2. The Citizens of each State shall be entitled to all Privileges and Immunities of Citizens in the several States.

A Person charged in any State with Treason, Felony, or other Crime, who shall flee from Justice, and be found in another State, shall on Demand of the executive Authority of the State from which he fled, be delivered up, to be removed to the State having Jurisdictions of the Crime.

No Person held to Service or Labour in one State, under the Laws thereof, escaping into another, shall, in Consequence of any Law or Regulation therein, be discharged from such Service or Labour, but shall be delivered up on Claim of the party to whom such Service or Labour may be due.

SECTION 3. New States may be admitted by the Congress into this Union; but no new State shall be formed or erected with the Jurisdiction or any other State; nor any State be formed by the Junction of two or more States, or Parts of States, without the Consent of the Legislatures of the States concerned as well as of the Congress.

The Congress shall have Power to dispose of and make all needful Rules and Regulations respecting the Territory or other Property belonging to the United States: and nothing in this Constitution shall be so construed as to Prejudice any Claims of the United States, or of any particular State.

SECTION 4. The United States shall guarantee to every State in this Union a Republican Form of Government, and shall protect each of them against Invasion; and on Application of the Legislature, or of the Executive (when the Legislature cannot be convened) against domestic Violence.

(Italics added in SECTION 2.)

THE FUGITIVE SLAVE ACT
Second Congress. Seas. II. Ch 7 (Feb. 12, 1793)

CHAP. VII.—An Act respecting fugitives from justice, and persons escaping from the service of their masters.

SECTION 1. *Be it enacted by the Senate and House of Representatives of the United States of America in Congress assembled,* That whenever the executive authority of any state in the Union, or of either of the territories northwest or south of the river Ohio, shall demand any person as a fugitive from justice, of the executive authority of any such state or territory to which such person shall have fled, and shall moreover produce the copy of an indictment found, or an affidavit made before a magistrate of any state or territory as aforesaid, charging the person so demanded, with having committed treason, felony or other crime, certified as authentic by the governor or chief magistrate of the state or territory from whence the person so charged fled, it shall be the duty of the executive authority of the state or territory to which such person shall have fled, to cause him or her to be arrested and secured, and notice of the arrest to be given to the executive authority making such demand, or to the agent of such authority appointed to receive the fugitive, and to cause the fugitive to be delivered to such agent when he shall appear: But if no such agent shall appear within six months from the time of the arrest, the prisoner may be discharged. And all costs or expenses incurred in the apprehending, securing, and transmitting such fugitive to the state or territory making such demand, shall be paid by such state or territory.

Sec. 2. *And be it further enacted*, That any agent, appointed as aforesaid, who shall receive the fugitive into his custody, shall be empowered to transport him or her to the state or territory from which he or she shall have fled. And if any person or persons shall by force set at liberty, or rescue the fugitive from such agent while transporting, as aforesaid, the person or persons so offending shall, on conviction, be fined not exceeding five hundred dollars, and be imprisoned not exceeding one year.

Sec. 3. *And be it also enacted*, That when a person held to labour in any of the United States, or in either of the territories on the north-west or south of the river Ohio, under the laws thereof, shall escape into any other of the said states or territory, the person to whom such labour or service may be due, his agent or attorney, is hereby empowered to seize or arrest such fugitive from labour, and to take him or her before any judge of the circuit or district courts of the United States, residing or being within the state, or before any magistrate of a county, city or town corporate, wherein such seizure or arrest shall be made, and upon proof to the satisfaction of such judge or magistrate, either by oral testimony or affidavit taken before and certified by a magistrate of any such state or territory, that the person so seized or arrested, doth, under the laws of the state or territory from which he or she fled, owe service or labour to the person claiming him or her, it shall be the duty of such judge or magistrate to give a certificate thereof to such claimant, his agent or attorney, which shall be sufficient warrant for removing the said fugitive from labour, to the state or territory from which he or she fled.

Sec. 4. *And be it further enacted*, That any person who shall knowingly and willingly obstruct or hinder such claimant, his agent or attorney in so seizing or arresting such fugitive from labour, or shall rescue such fugitive from such claimant, his agent or attorney when so arrested pursuant to the authority herein given or declared; or shall harbor or conceal such person after notice that he or she was a fugitive from labour, as aforesaid, shall, for either of the said offences, forfeit and pay the sum of five hundred dollars. Which penalty may be recovered by and for the benefit of such claimant, by action of debt, in any court proper to try the same; saving moreover to the person claiming such labour or service, his right of action for or on account of the said injuries or either of them.

APPROVED, February 12, 1793.

QUESTIONS

1. Viewed strictly as positive law making, do you see any flaws in the "Fugitive Slave Act" of 1793? (2d Congress, Seas. II, Ch. 7, Feb. 12, 1793)? Does it meet Fuller's tests? *See Materials, supra* at 6F. Is there any problem with its constitutionality, given the contemporary form of Article IV of the Constitution (set out above in the text)?

2. Could you have served as a "judge of the circuit or district courts of the United States" given your responsibility under this statute? Could you have served on the Supreme Court of the United States?

3. Assuming you did serve as a Justice of the Supreme Court and the constitutionality of this statute were challenged, what would you do? Joseph Story (1779-1845) was the effective Founder of Harvard Law School, having rescued it from oblivion in 1829. He was also the youngest person, at 32, ever to be named to the Supreme Court (at least until you are appointed). He faced this exact issue in *Prigg v. Pennsylvania*, 41 U.S. 539 (1842). Despite his aversion to slavery, Story returned Margaret Morgan, an escaped slave, to slavery, together with her two children, "who by the laws of Pennsylvania were born free!" *See* R. KENT NEWMYER, SUPREME COURT JUSTICE JOSEPH STORY: STATESMAN OF THE OLD REPUBLIC 370 (1985). Newmyer adds: "The South had come for its pound of flesh and blood. As an advocate of the Constitutional Compromise of 1787, as the self-designated master of objective adjudication, Story felt obliged to give it to them—or not 'it' but Margaret Morgan and her children." *Id.* at 370. A large statue of Story is at the main door of Harvard Law School. What do you think?

LEONARD LEVY, THE LAW OF THE COMMONWEALTH AND CHIEF JUSTICE SHAW
72–91, 106–108 (notes deleted) (1957)

"THE FUGITIVE SLAVE LAW"
REMANDING RUNAWAYS

I.

The fugitive-slavery issue was freighted with perils to the nation. Shaw's thought on the subject was filled with apprehension for the security and harmony of the Union. He was earnestly a man of peace who would not consciously aggravate a situation offering the menace of a "great national calamity." To persons of like sensibilities, the histrionics of extremists, who rasped unceasingly on the sinful nature of slavery, were exasperating. In October 1835, two months after conservatives in a mass meeting at Faneuil Hall had apologized to the South for the abolitionism in Boston, a mob of several thousands, including many "gentlemen" from State and Milk Streets, stormed a meeting of the Boston Female Anti-Slavery Society, cowed the defenseless praying women, and nearly lynched William Lloyd

Garrison. A quietus on agitation was devoutly wished by persons of standing. Frenzied provocateurs, vowing obedience not to law and order and the Constitution, but to an unwritten "higher law" of conscience, endangered the political stability that came from allegiance to the sound nationalist doctrines of Marshall and Webster. Article IV, section 2, of the United States Constitution had provided for the return of fugitive slaves, and Congress had passed the Act of 1793 to that end. As a judge, Shaw felt duty-bound to enforce the Constitution as law regardless of whatever moral twinges he may have experienced. When the abolitionists hurled their barbs at him, they aimed at a man who reluctantly regarded the return of runaways as a legal necessity.

II.

It was not until 1842 that the first bona fide case of a fugitive slave came before Shaw; but in 1836 there occurred a case that clearly indicated his desire to avoid giving effect to the Fugitive Slave Act unless the facts at issue presented no other recourse. In August 1836, Philadelphians reading about the new slave case in Boston learned that two fugitives had been rescued in the very presence of the Supreme Judicial Court of Massachusetts—an insult "without parallel in the history of that state."

> Even the insurgents in Shays' rebellion were polite and courtly in comparison with the mob in the present case.—One might expect the very bodies of Parsons, Dana, and Parker to rise out of their graves and reprove the lawless spirit of the times for such an outrage against the majesty of the laws. Truly we are fallen upon evil days when such things can be perpetrated,—and with impunity. The most strenuous assertions . . . can offer no apology for barefaced insult to the laws of Massachusetts and the Constitution of the United States.

The monstrous event that caused a thrill of outrage to run down editors' spines occurred on a Monday, the first day of the month, before Chief Justice Shaw himself. On the preceding Saturday, the brig *Chickasaw*, Henry Eldridge, Captain, had sailed into Boston harbor carrying two Negro passengers, Eliza Small and Polly Ann Bates. Both women had with them legal documents as proof of their free status. While the *Chickasaw* lay in the stream, she was boarded by one Matthew Turner who represented himself to the captain as the agent of John B. Morris, a wealthy slave-holder of Baltimore. The women were asserted by Turner to be fugitives from Morris' service. At this point in the story, contemporary versions differ. Two newspapers, both of which voiced the politics of the State Street merchants, agreed that the women "freely admitted that they were the property of Mr. Morris, and gave him (Turner) reasons for making their escape." That they carried evidence of their freedom was not mentioned by either paper. Another journal carried the information that Turner, on being shown such evidence by one of them, "pocketed it and refused to return it." The inimitable *Liberator* reported on August 13: "We learn that Turner, the woman catcher, when he first met his intended victims on board the vessel pretended to be very friendly, and under the assumed name of James Wilson, by his professions of friendship obtained the free papers of one of the women." Failing to get the papers of the other woman by this ruse, continued *The Liberator*, Turner disclosed his real identity and design. Eliza and Polly Ann, hearing that they were to be forcibly returned, broke down; whereupon "the *kindhearted* and *pious* kidnapper read to them from the Bible for their consolation. . . ." Thus, from the evidence, it is not clear whether the women were fugitives or whether they were the victims of a mean plot by their former master to repossess them.

In any case, Captain Eldridge detained his passengers on the brig at the request of Turner until the latter obtained a warrant for their arrest as escaped slaves. News of the events on the *Chickasaw* quickly circulated. A large and excited group of Negroes collected on the wharf. During Turner's absence, a Negro citizen appeared before Chief Justice Shaw and secured a writ of habeas corpus directed against Eldridge, forcing him to release the unfortunate women pending a hearing on the question of his authority to hold them in restraint. Deputy Sheriff Huggerford, who served the writ, found the women in a state of agitation, locked in their cabin. One of them, a mulatto of about thirty, upon learning that friendly proceedings had been instituted, burst into tears, crying that "She knew God would not forsake her and send her back to the South."

Shaw was no longer available in Court that same afternoon, and on the technical objection that the writ had been signed by him, Justice Wilde postponed the hearing till nine o'clock the following Monday morning. As the Court opened that August first, the Chief Justice took the bench, sitting alone. Spectators, mostly Negroes, packed the room. The few whites present were, in the main, abolitionists concerned with the freedom of two of God's children. If there were any in the audience friendly to the cause of Eldridge or the slaveowner's agent, they were lost in a sea of sympathizers for the alleged slaves.

On the basis of the writ and the return to it by Eldridge, the question before the Court was restricted to the captain's right to detain the women. The arguments of counsel, however, ranged further afield, into the constitutional issue over fugitive slavery. A.H. Fiske, on behalf of the captain, read an affidavit by Turner, who was present in court, to the effect that the women were the property of the Baltimore citizen whom he represented. Then Fiske launched into a defense of the Fugitive Slave Law of 1793, under which the claim to the women was made. He moved for a postponement of the hearing so that evidence might be brought from Baltimore to prove that they were slaves. Samuel Eliot Sewall, the abolitionist lawyer so frequently a volunteer on behalf of any Negro's liberty, addressed the Court in opposition to the motion. He argued that Eldridge had no claim to the women, that all human beings were free-born and had a natural right to the enjoyment of their liberties. When he had finished, the larger part of the audience, much excited, burst into applause.

The Chief Justice, rising to give his opinion, stated the issue simply: "Has the captain of the brig *Chickasaw a* right to convert his vessel into a prison?" He decided that the defendant had not the least right to hold the women. They had been detained in his custody in a most unlawful manner, since he in no way brought himself within the provisions of the federal statute of 1793. Shaw concluded his opinion by saying "the prisoners must therefore be discharged from all further detention."

Turner, the agent, then arose and implied that he would make a fresh arrest under the provisions of the Fugitive Slave Law, and he inquired of the Court whether a warrant would be necessary for that purpose. At the same moment a constable was sent to lock the door leading downstairs. These actions created a wave of excitement among the spectators. The general impression was that the slave-hunter was about to make a fresh seizure right on the spot, even though the prisoners appeared to have been discharged by the Chief Justice.

Tension charged the air for a moment. Before Shaw could answer Turner, word was passed to the women informing them that they were discharged and advising that they clear out before the agent got them again. "The Court room now exhibited one of the grossest outrages of public justice that we have ever before witnessed." Could the respectable property owners in State Street have had foreknowledge of the violence that broke loose the next moment, "five-hundred men could have been rallied to the Court . . . prepared to sustain the supremacy of the laws." Someone called to the people in the room, "Take them." A chant of "Go—go!" rang out. Instantly, the tumult broke: the spectators, both white and colored, turned into a disorderly mob, rushed over the benches, and stormed down the aisle toward Eliza and Polly Ann. Shaw protested, "Stop, stop," but the mob tore on, yelling "Don't stop." Shaw climbed down out of his bench and endeavored vainly to hold the door against them. Huggerford, the only officer in the room, was grabbed, throttled, and "maltreated to the peril of his life." The crowd, bearing away the prisoners, disappeared through the private passageway of the judiciary and dashed down the stairs of the Court House. In Court Square, the fugitives were shoved into a carriage and driven out of the city, followed for a short distance by the screaming mob. Huggerford and a posse took up the pursuit. The carriage crossed over Mill Dam—where toll money was thrown out while the horses were driven at a gallop—and was gone.

The story of the shocking rescue was a sensation in Boston's newspapers. The *Columbian Centinel* excoriated the seditious "Abolition Riot," and estimated that ninety percent of the public shared its views. "A Friend of the Union," in a letter to the editor, wrote heatedly that if a few fanatics and Negroes were suffered to browbeat and put down the highest tribunals of the nation, "then adieu to its peace and union." Only exemplary punishment of the leaders and abettors of the mob, stated the writer, would "satisfy our Southern brethren, and convince them that their *rights* and *property* will be protected, at least here in New England . . . ." But the fugitives were never recaptured; nor were their rescuers ever brought to trial, because, most curiously, no one came forward to identify any of them. The editor of the merchants' paper sputtered furiously:

> The prisoners have been forcibly rescued, at noonday, from our highest court, sitting in the heart of a populous city. The outrage was committed by a mob of several hundreds, and after three days search, neither the prisoners nor one of the rioters have been arrested. Is there no person who was present who can identify one of the offenders? Could such a scene be enacted, and the Chief Justice be assailed *vi et armis* (with force of arms!) in the face of day, and in open court, and no person be able to detect one of a hundred? The case has not its parallels in the annals of crime. . . . All the money in the Treasury is but as dross compared to the importance of

sustaining the dignity and supremacy of the public tribunals in whom depend not only the rights and peace of the citizens, but the very existence of the state.

It was generally agreed that a monstrous event had happened for which Garrisonism was somehow responsible.

But only *The Liberator* carried the story that only two days after the "Abolition Riot," occurred, the Massachusetts Anti-Slavery Society had held a special meeting, during which resolves were voted expressing on the part of the members their "deep regret and decided disapprobation." *The Liberator* (August 6) also made clear its disapproval of the tumultuous conduct of the persons involved. The "incident" was an "unjustifiable" one, but the abolitionist society and the organ of the cause agreed that it was "not unpardonable," because it developed out of ignorance and misapprehension. It is true that the mob and Sewall, who was censured for "instigating" it, deserve exculpation from accusation of having planned a "rescue," that is, of having conspired to seize the prisoners from the custody of the law. The event was unforeseeable, and the friendly audience acted under the impulse of fear to get the women out of the clutches of the slave hunter *after*, it was thought, they had been released by Shaw.

The Chief Justice himself seems to have recovered his judicial composure almost at once. In spite of his active part in trying to quell the outbreak, there was, fortunately, no report of his having been physically abused. On August first, the *Daily Evening Transcript* said: 'The Judge stated that they (the women) must be brought back to be regularly discharged in open court"; but two days later informed its readers that "the Chief Justice considers the prisoners as *virtually discharged—*" and regarded the disturbance as one that could not reasonably have been anticipated. Judge Wilde, his associate, was of the same opinion.

Shaw, it should be noted, had not only refused, under the facts of the case, to allow the alleged fugitives to be held at the agent's pleasure; he had not granted a postponement of the hearing as requested, so that evidence could be brought from Baltimore to prove that they were the property of Morris. Obviously Shaw was disinclined to enforce the Fugitive Slave Law except in a case of unavoidable necessity. His opinion was based on the facts as legally brought: not on a claim to the women by Turner, but on their unlawful detention by Eldridge. Shaw never had an opportunity to reply to Turner's request for a warrant to make a new arrest, for it was at that moment that the wild rush began. The *Mercantile Journal* was confident, however, that he would have remanded the women to Turner's custody.

There was a shocking postscript to this first "rescue" of alleged fugitive slaves in Boston. Four weeks later, a United States naval officer from Baltimore entered Samuel Eliot Sewall's office and after announcing that he was a relative of Morris the slave-owner, proceeded to insult the abolitionist lawyer "with opprobrious epithets," and then struck him "a number blows with the butt end of a horsewhip." The assailant, who immediately thereafter left town, had informed his victim that he had no right to interfere with Southern property rights. It was the very week of Med's case, when the Chief Justice himself had indulged in similar interference which reduced Sewall's to insignificance.

III.

Six years later the famous Latimer case occurred. On October 19, 1842, a Constable Stratton, furnished with a warrant issued by the Boston Police Court, arrested George Latimer, "a fine looking colored man." A complaint of theft in Virginia had been brought against him by James B. Gray, a Norfolk slave master, who simultaneously claimed the fugitive from justice as his slave. Soon a crowd of "nearly three-hundred, mostly male blacks," assembled before the Court House where the prisoner was held. To defeat a rescue, he was slipped out by the back door and locked up in the Leverett Street jail. Coolidge the jailer, like Stratton, was by Gray's written authority his legal agent. Fearing that Gray and his men might smuggle Latimer out of the city late at night, parties interested in freedom's cause successfully petitioned Chief Justice Shaw for a writ of habeas corpus.

The following evening, Stratton, in compliance with the writ, produced Latimer before Shaw in the Supreme Court room. The Court was not officially in session, but since the judges were present for other purposes, they also heard this case. At the time, "immense crowds" were milling about the Court House "in a very feverish state of anxiety. . . ." Gray's attorney, E. G. Austin, defended the seizure of Latimer under the terms of the Fugitive Slave Law. Stratton justified himself by showing the police court warrant, Gray's claim to Latimer as a slave, and his own appointment as Gray's agent. Samuel Eliot Sewall and Amos Merrill, for the prisoner, argued from *Prigg v. Pennsylvania* on the illegality of all proceedings against Latimer done under color of state or local authority.

After consultation with the other judges, Shaw discharged the writ and ordered Latimer returned to the custody of his captors. In his opinion he confined himself strictly to the fugitive-slavery question, ignoring the contention that the police court warrant was void because of federal legislation on fugitives from justice. He ruled that Gray and Stratton showed sufficient authority to detain the prisoner under the Act of 1793, which the United States Supreme Court had recently upheld in Prigg's case. State courts could not interfere with the operation of a constitutional statute under whose terms Gray as claimant was entitled to arrest Latimer wherever he fled, prove his ownership before a federal court, and obtain therefrom a certificate to carry his slave away with him. Shaw also thought that Gray should be allowed reasonable time to take the necessary measures to get a certificate of rendition. Since the prisoner had been arrested only the day before, and his master made oath to apply before a federal court, Shaw found no legal ground to remove Latimer from custody. When Stratton and his assistants escorted the slave back to jail, they were riotously attacked by the mob outside the Court House. The rescue attempt failed, but one officer was given "a touch of the nose bleed" and another was "struck by a brickbat, and severely hurt. . . ." Eight of the mob were arrested, all of them Negroes.

On the next day, the twenty-first, the opposing counsel agreed to postpone examination on the larceny charge in order to settle the fugitive slave question. Bail was fixed at $200 for Latimer's appearance in police court ten days later. Austin then decided that if Latimer were released on bail, a new question would arise: who was to hold him in custody in the interval? To save trouble, Austin quashed the complaint against him as a fugitive from justice, because he could then be held by

Stratton as a fugitive slave in accordance with Shaw's order. As events showed, this move not only confirmed abolitionist suspicions that the larceny charge was originally a fictitious device to apprehend Latimer, it also created a circumstance which led eventually to the slave's freedom, for he was now being held in jail, at Gray's convenience and jailer Coolidge's profit, without the police court warrant. Gray's next move, an application before Justice Story, on circuit duty, for a certificate of rendition, did not strengthen his action in jailing Latimer. Story, holding the case over for two weeks to give Gray time to obtain evidence of his title from Norfolk, did order that he legally detain Latimer in the interim. The United States, however, had rights to use a Boston jail by permission of Massachusetts only to hold persons committed by authority of a federal court. Story did not order Latimer's commitment; he simply remanded him to Gray's personal custody. The abolitionists now began to rake the city with angry protests against the illegal and abusive use of its jail. A mass meeting was called for October 30 in Faneuil Hall.

On October 24, a final legal effort was made by Latimer's friends to free him. They sued out a writ of personal replevin, under a state personal liberty law of 1837, passed to guarantee trial by jury "on questions of personal freedom." This law did not exclude fugitive slaves from its protection. It read in part: "If any person is imprisoned. . . . unless it be in the custody of some public officer of the law, by force of a lawful warrant. . . . he shall be entitled, as of right, to a writ of personal replevin. . . ." The writ was served on Coolidge, commanding him to produce Latimer before the Court of Common Pleas, there to submit the cause of his detention before a jury. Coolidge, however, refused to acknowledge the writ. Latimer's attorneys again applied to the Chief Justice for relief, and again he issued a writ of habeas corpus, this one commanding the jailer to show why he had rejected the writ of personal replevin. The hearing was held immediately, in Coolidge's parlor adjoining the jail.

After Sewall and Merrill had argued Latimer's rights under the personal liberty law, Shaw remarked to Austin, Coolidge's counsel, that no reply would be necessary because his own judgment was fixed and required no confirmation. In the account of Shaw's opinion as reported by Garrison, who was one of the few outsiders present, an important paragraph reveals much of Shaw's thought on the fugitive-slavery question. He said, "in substance," reported *The Liberator* (November 4), that

> he probably felt as much sympathy for the person in custody as others; but this was a case in which an appeal to natural rights and the paramount law of liberty was not pertinent! It was decided by the Constitution of the United States, and by the law of Congress under that instrument, relating to fugitive slaves. These were to be obeyed, however disagreeable to our own natural sympathies and views of duty! . . . By the Constitution, the duty of returning runaway slaves was made imperative on the free states, and the act of Congress . . . was in accordance with the spirit of that instrument. He repeatedly said, that on no other terms could a union have been formed between the North and the South . . .

To the contentions that Latimer could not be held without warrant or evidence of his status as a slave, and that presumption was in favor of his freedom, Shaw replied by holding to his sworn obligation to support the Constitution. This obligation could be met only by protecting Gray's right under law to have sufficient time for producing evidence to his claim.

As to Latimer's rights under the Massachusetts Personal Liberty Law of 1837, they were non-existent, ruled Shaw. That law had been passed by state officers sworn to support the Constitution and laws of the nation; they could not pass any law in conflict with these superior obligations. Therefore, the statute relied upon by the prisoner could not be construed to embrace runaways. Such persons must be regarded as exceptions to its provisions. The statute, Shaw concluded, citing Prigg's case, was unconstitutional and void insofar as it concerned fugitive slaves. Accordingly, the writ of personal replevin was inapplicable in Latimer's case. Shaw then ordered that the slave once more be remanded to the custody of the agents of Gray, whose claim was properly pending before a federal court.

The abolitionists countered this opinion with abuse most galling. At their Faneuil Hall meeting on October 30, Sewall imputed to Shaw the "basest motives of personal feeling." Wendell Phillips pronounced his famous curse upon the Constitution, and Francis Jackson, Frederick Douglass, and Edmund Quincy did their best to incite a crowd to rescue. The intemperate Garrison wrote that Shaw's opinion proved his readiness to aid "in kidnapping a guiltless and defenseless human, and to act the part of Pilate in the Crucifixion of the Son of God. . . ." Where, asked Garrison, did Shaw's guilt differ "from that of the slave pirate on the African coast . . .?" When "A Subscriber" protested that it was "unchristian" to classify with slavers "one of the best men in the community," Garrison replied that Chief Justice Shaw had betrayed the honor of Massachusetts "when Liberty lay bleeding." The Chief Justice was also subjected to derision because he held "court" in the jailor's parlor while police stood guard. Shaw, of course, was free to hold a hearing on a writ of habeas corpus wherever he judged expedient. Moreover, according to Peleg Chandler, editor of the conservative *Law Reporter*, the suggestion to hold the hearing at the jail came from Latimer's counsel.

Chandler undertook "to deal a blow" against the "false morality, born from the sophistry of fanaticism" which sought to undermine public confidence in the judiciary and the laws of the nation. He referred indignantly to critics who insisted that Shaw should have freed Latimer in accordance with the "law" of conscience, in spite of the Constitution and Congress. Did not the abolitionist know, asked Chandler,

> that a judge has nothing to do with the moral character of the laws which society chooses to make, and which, when made, it places him upon the bench to apply the facts before him? Does he not know that the judiciary is the mere organ of society, to declare what the law is, and having ascertained, to pronounce what the law requires?

In his defense of Shaw, and of Story too, Chandler sketched an image of the neutral judge who, exercising no personal discretion, allowed none of his own considerations of morality or conscience to intrude upon the performance of his duties. The zealots who made civil disobedience sound doctrine, however, had their own image of the ideal judge. He was a Judge Harrington of Vermont who, rejecting documentary proof that a Negro claimed was in fact a fugitive slave, had allegedly remarked: "If the master could show a bill of sale, or grant, from the Almighty, then his title to him would be complete: otherwise it would not."

With such a judge in mind, Garrisonians were not given to pause in a scrupulous regard for fact or moderation when discussing Lemuel Shaw. They meant to whip public opinion into a froth of hysteria, and fortune favored them. Justice Story was too ill to hear the case as scheduled on the fifth of November, and the date when Gray might apply before a federal court for a certificate was advanced to the twenty-first. The abolitionists made the most of the opportunity which time gave to them. They bellowed animadversions at mass meetings up and down the state. A propaganda sheet, the *Latimer Journal and North Star*, rife with a sense of bitter injustice, was published tri-weekly, beginning with November 11. The editors, Dr. Henry I. Bowditch and William F. Channing, sons of famous fathers, circulated twenty thousand copies of each issue. "The slave shall never leave Boston even if to gain that end our streets pour with blood," they wrote. The judiciary was their special target. "The whole of the Latimer Journal," stated the *Law Reporter*, "was largely devoted to the most positive assertions, that the chief justice's decision upon the *habeas corpus* was grossly illegal, and he and Mr. Justice Story are accused of using their offices to oppress their fellow men."

Bowditch, Channing, Charles Sumner, and others of similar persuasion got up a petition threatening the Sheriff of Suffolk County with removal from office if he did not order his subordinate, jailor Coolidge, to release Latimer. Sheriff Eveleth did not himself consider Latimer to be properly jailed without a warrant. Spurred by the threat of removal and by public demonstrations against the use of the jail by Gray and his agents for their personal advantage, Eveleth ordered Latimer's release by noon of the eighteenth. This new development, just a few days before the slave-owner could get a certificate, put Gray in a quandary. He still had legal custody of Latimer, but if he held him privately, his slave would be rescued from him. As his counsel, Austin explained in his letter "To the Public," "to attempt to keep Latimer in any other place than the jail, was to raise at once a signal for a riot, if not bloodshed." Consequently Gray consented to sell his claim for $400. Immediately after the sale, Latimer was set free.

The Fugitive Slave Law was yet to be enforced in Massachusetts. Whittier stated its defiance in "Massachusetts to Virginia": "No fetters in the Bay State,—no slave upon our land!" An immense petition for repeal of the law, bearing 51,862 Massachusetts signatures, rolled up into the size of a barrel, was presented to Congress by "Old Man Eloquent," John Quincy Adams. Under "gag law" the petition was not received. The state legislature, however, favorably responded to anti-slavery protests. Outraged citizens had held meetings in every county and in almost every town "to demand that their ancient Commonwealth should never again be insulted by the conversion of her jails into barracoons, and her sworn servants and judicial officers into the minions of the slave catcher." On February 17, 1843, following a great demonstration in Faneuil Hall, a petition with 65,000 names, borne on the shoulders of six men, was delivered to the State House where it was presented by Charles Francis Adams. The "Latimer Law," an act "further to protect Personal Liberty," was passed. It prohibited state judges from recognizing the Act of 1793 or issuing certificates of rendition: it prohibited officers of the Commonwealth from assisting in the arrest of alleged fugitive slaves; and it prohibited the use of state jails for the confinement of fugitives. Such a law had been made legally possible by the opinion in Prigg's case by Justice Story who had, ironically, been subjected like Shaw to obloquy in the abolitionist press. Other northern states also passed personal liberty laws, converting the Act of 1793 into a nullity by the withdrawal of state aid in its enforcement.

<h1 style="text-align:center">IV.</h1>

Southern anxiety for the loss of runaways was allayed by a new Fugitive Slave Law passed by Congress, with Webster's endorsement, as part of the Compromise of 1850. The peculiar ingenuity of the new legislation was that it brought the law of bondage home to a free state. It was a law of flint, providing federal officials for its effective enforcement. When hateful scenes of slavery were transferred from the South and enacted in the streets of Boston, the old city was confronted with a choice among cherished alternatives: liberty or union? freedom or property? The new law produced a curious moral spectacle, for the question which distracted the minds of free men was whether to catch slaves or not to catch slaves.

To the anti-slavery hotspurs, fanatically devoted to a "higher law" than the Constitution, the measure was diabolical; it violated the purest promptings of conscience and Christianity. Wendell Phillips resolved for "the Abolitionists of Massachusetts" that "CONSTITUTION OR NO CONSTITUTION, LAW OR NO LAW" they would fight the sins which Black Daniel symbolized. Those who praised Webster's patriotism and defended the Act of 1850 denied that the Theodore Parkers and Charles Sumners had a monopoly on moral justification. If the conservatives like the Chief Justice had retreated from the cause of individual freedom, it was in an anxious regard for even greater moral values: peace and Union. Or so they reasoned.

Charles Francis Adams wrote that while a shallow veneer of anti-slavery sentiment had been fashionable among them, it was "mere sentiment," without roots either in conviction or in material interests. "On the contrary," contended Adams, "so far as material interests were concerned, a great change had recently taken place. The manufacturing development of Massachusetts had been rapid, and a close affiliation had sprung up between the cotton spinners of the North and the cotton producers of the South,—or as Charles Sumner put it, between 'the lords of the loom and the lords of the lash.' "

By mid-century a great majority of Boston's "best people" no longer concealed their warmness toward Southern interests. Their eagerness to keep on the best of terms with the South was later recalled by Edward L. Pierce, a student at Harvard Law School (1850–52). "A southern slave holder, or his son at Harvard," he wrote, "was more welcome in society than any guest except a foreigner. . . . The deference to rich southern planters was marked." Almost all the wealth of the city was controlled by the "Cotton Whigs," and as social and business Boston gradually became "almost avowedly a pro-slavery community," its self-justification of loyalty to the Constitution and to national security approached hysteria. When the news came from Washington that the Fugitive Slave Act had been safely passed, one hundred guns roared a joyous salute across the Common.

A few weeks later, opponents of the law swelled Faneuil Hall to fire their invective against its supporters, to pledge their aid to Negro fellow-citizens, and to demand "INSTANT REPEAL." A group of fifty—it soon grew to two hundred and ten—was appointed to act as a Committee of Vigilance and Safety which determined to render the abominable act a nullity. Then in the same hall, in November, defenders of the law swore their allegiance to it at a "Constitutional Meeting."

In the furious climate of irreconcilable loyalties and thunderous rallies engendered by the Act of 1850, men waited apprehensively to see whether a solemn act of Congress would be honored, or be superseded by the resolves of a Gideon's army of lawless agitators. A month after the law was passed, slave-hunters arrived in Boston searching for William and Ellen Craft, fugitives from a Georgia planter. Here was the first test—and the vigilance committee, led by the indomitable Parker, tracked down the slave-hunters and chased them out of town. Then on February 15, 1851, the Shadrach affair began.

From Norfolk there came to Boston a "hired kidnapper," with documents prepared in Virginia, claiming a waiter at Taft's Cornhill Coffee House as a slave. George Ticknor Curtis, "Cotton Whig" and Commissioner of the United States Circuit Court, issued a warrant for the arrest of the alleged runaway, one Frederick Wilkins, alias Shadrach. Seized as he unsuspectingly served breakfast to United States Deputy Marshal Patrick Riley, Shadrach was hustled through a back street to the Court House. Riley notified City Marshal Francis Tukey and Mayor Bigelow that he "got a nigger," sent for Commissioner Curtis and the claimant's counsel, and directed the doors of the United States Court Room to be locked and guarded. Shadrach, finally informed of the charges against him, requested counsel. In the meantime, word had spread that the marshal had captured a fugitive slave. Vigilance men Samuel Eliot Sewall, Charles Davis, Ellis Gray Loring, Charles List, Robert Morris, and Richard Henry Dana—he who had sailed before the mast—all volunteered for the defendant.

As a turbulent crowd, increasing by the moment, assembled in Court Square, Dana prepared a petition for habeas corpus addressed to Chief Justice Shaw. Morris, in Loring's presence, had obtained verbal authority from Shadrach to apply for the writ and swore before Dana that the petition was accurate. It stated that the prisoner was held by Deputy Marshal Riley on pretence of his being a fugitive slave, and that he did not know whether there was a warrant for his arrest. With this petition Dana sought out Shaw, whom he found in the lobby of the Supreme Judicial Court Room with Associate Justice Metcalf, and explained that with the writ he hoped to bring a test case on the constitutional power of a commissioner to issue a warrant under the Act of 1850. Shaw flatly refused to grant habeas corpus in Shadrach's behalf, revealing a positive disapproval of the antislavery efforts. In his diary, under the entry for that Saturday, February 15, the ardently partisan Dana recorded in detail his conversation with the Chief Justice. In what Dana considered "a most ungracious manner," Shaw had replied after reading the petition, "This won't do. I can't do anything on this." And laying it on a table, he turned away to busy himself with something else; but he was not rid of Dana so easily. To an inquiry into the defects of the petition, Shaw gave the impression of trying to "bluff" off his questioner. Finally he yielded to Dana's persistence with the objection that Shadrach had not signed the petition. The lawyer then reminded the judge that state law permitted the petition to be made on behalf of the petitioner. Dana thought to himself that the Chief Justice certainly knew that in extreme cases, when the writ was most needed to protect personal liberty, circumstances might make it impossible for the prisoner to sign personally. Shaw was obstinate:

"There is no evidence that it is in his behalf. There is no evidence of his authority."

"Do you require proof of his authority? What proof do you require, sir?"

"It is enough for me to say that the petition is not sufficient. The petition shows on its face that the writ cannot issue. It shows that the man is in legal custody of a United States marshal."

Again the lawyer instructed the judge: the fact of legal custody must appear on Riley's return to the writ *after* it was granted. Shaw tried another tack, this time complaining that Shadrach could not properly swear ignorance of the charge against him. Dana called attention to the fact that the petition stated fully the pretense of arrest. Finding this to be true, Shaw fell back on his original objection that there was want of evidence from the prisoner. He then added his final objection—"and not made," wrote Dana, "until after he had positively refused to issue the writ"—that the petition required an appended copy of the warrant of arrest or a statement that a copy had been applied for and could not be obtained. Yet the petition clearly stated that Shadrach did not know whether his imprisonment was under a warrant or not. Moreover, the Act of 1850 permitted arrests without a warrant. Dana was disconsolate: "I felt that all these objections were frivolous and invalid, but seeing the temper the Chief Justice was in, and his evident determination to get rid of the petition, I left him for the purpose of either procuring the evidence he required or of going before another judge."

Dana returned to the United States Court Room. Extending from its door into the street was a crowd of about two hundred Negroes. Inside the court room, Shadrach's counsel requested time to consult with him and to prepare the defense. Commissioner Curtis held the proceedings over until the following Tuesday. Officiously, Riley ordered the room cleared of spectators, reporters, and attorneys so that Shadrach might be left alone with his guards. At about two o'clock the door was unlocked to let out the last few persons, Charles G. Davis, Robert Morris, Elizur Wright, editor of *The Commonwealth*, all members of the abolitionist Committee of Vigilance and Safety.

As the door was opened a yell went up from the Negroes milling in the passageways. Instantly a tug of war began over the door, the officers inside straining to keep it shut, the crowd pressing to force it open. Shadrach headed for the unguarded opposite exit, and as about fifteen men streamed into the room jamming Riley into a corner behind the door, the marshal screamed from his place of safety, "Shoot him! Shoot him!" But the rescuers had already escorted Shadrach out of the room, down the stairs, and into the streets. Dana, working in his office opposite the Court House, rushed to his window at the sound of shouting in time to see two huge Negroes, bearing Shadrach between them, dash off toward Cambridge "like a black squall," the mob cheering as they departed.

The amazing rescue threatened the success of "peace measures," and the nation protested. The Washington Correspondent of the New York *Journal of Commerce* telegraphed from the capital: "Some sensation was produced here by the intelligence of the negro insurrection in Boston." Secretary of State Webster thought the rescue was "a case of treason." On February 17, President Fillmore called a special cabinet meeting to discuss measures to be taken, and on the next day, issued a proclamation commanding all civil and military officers to assist in recapturing Shadrach and to prosecute all persons who took part in the "scandalous outrage" committed against the laws of the United States. On the Senate floor, Henry Clay demanded to know whether a "government of white men was to be yielded to a government by blacks." Boston's reputation had been "badly damaged," especially in the South. The *Savannah Republican* scourged the city as a "black speck on the map—disgraced by the lowest, the meanest, the BLACKEST kind of NULLIFICATION."

In Boston, the press fulminated against the "mischief which mad Abolitionism will wantonly perpetrate." On February 18, the Board of Mayor and Aldermen expressed regret that the Commonwealth's dignity had been criminally insulted, and ordered the City Marshal to make "the whole police force" available to quell a similar breach of law should one be anticipated. Two days later, the Common Council approved unanimously the Board's action and "cordially" endorsed the President's proclamation.

The abolitionists, in their turn, ridiculed the furor which the rescue had occasioned. "Warrington" attacked as Tories the leading citizens who pretended outrage: "State-street brokers and Milk-street jobbers who . . . hold mortgages on slave property . . . dared not to disturb the good understanding between the planters and the manufacturers. . . ." And was not the rescue for the greater glory of God and His children? Dr. Bowditch marked down the day in his calendar as "a holy day," and Parker thought the rescue was "the noblest deed done in Boston since the destruction of the tea in 1773." Impishly, vigilance men recalled that Mrs. Glasse, the celebrated cook, had prudently premised in her recipe for cooking a hare, "First, *catch* your hare!"

Richard Henry Dana shared the rejoicing of his fellows, but in the aftermath of the rescue, he set down in his diary the one event that marred the day and disturbed not only him, but Judge Metcalf too. "The conduct of the Chief Justice, his evident disinclination to act, the frivolous nature of his objections, and his insulting manner to me, have troubled me. . . ." wrote Dana. Shaw's conduct, he concluded perspicaciously, "shows how deeply seated, so as to affect, unconsciously I doubt not, good men like him, is this selfish hunker-ism of the property interest on the slave question."

Shaw's Whiggery was indeed robust, and he never lost his admiration for Webster's politics or principles. There exists no statement from Shaw that he, like Webster, Choate, and Curtis, approved of the Fugitive Slave Law as an expedient to cement the sectional differences that menaced the Union; yet there is nothing in the cast of the man's mind, temperament, or associations suggesting that his judicial obligation to enforce Congressional law necessarily conflicted with his personal opinions. Four months before the death of Webster, his lifelong friend, Shaw wrote that it would have been "a glorious thing to have so distinguished a man as Mr.

Webster elected Prest [*sic*] of the U.S." With the passing years, the intensification of the slavery controversy made the security and peace of the Union Shaw's passion; long ago these values had been elevated in his mind to a case of political and even "moral" necessity. He remained an old-line Whig when less conservative men drifted to the new Republican banner; by 1860 he was advocating appeasement of the South and supported the Constitutional Unionist, heirs to the traditional compromise party. While Dana and his friends—"overzealous philanthropists" Shaw had called them—predicated their position on the natural rights of man, the Chief Justice responded to motives also worthy of respect: love for the Union and national harmony. Translated into the political values of the 1850's, this meant a love for law and order, for "peace measures," for maintaining inviolate the North's pledge to remand fugitive slaves.

*   *   *

VIII

On August 21, 1860, Shaw resigned from the bench. He was free at last to express himself on public matters as a private citizen. A divided nation was facing a Presidential election. The "Bell-Everetts," arch-conservators of compromise and national unity, pledged to "no political principle other than the Constitution of the Country, the Union of the States, and the Enforcement of the Laws," appealed to the most respected man in Massachusetts for permission to use his name as candidate for Elector-at-Large. Alluding to the dangers of secession, the Union State Committee wrote to him:

> In this state of things your appearance at the head of our electoral ticket as a revered mediator between the Northern and Southern extremes of party, would, in our humble opinion, be in entire conformity with your honored career, of vast importance to the country, and a crowning title to its grateful veneration."

On the back of this letter, eighty-year-old Lemuel Shaw scrawled, "nomination declined/Sept. 4." Great age may have made him reluctant to engage in politics, though the reason for his declination is unrecorded. Undoubtedly he was in sympathy with the cause of the party. In a real sense, he was all his life a Constitutional Unionist. Nomination would not likely have been officially tendered were his party views not known.

A few months later, in his final public act, Shaw headed a group of prominent conciliationists who hoped to appease the South by recommending unconditional repeal of Massachusetts' Personal Liberty Laws. In an "Address" published on December 18, the signatories, "impelled by no motive save the love of our country," warned:

> The foundations of our government are shaken, and unless the work of destruction shall be stayed, we may soon see that great union . . . broken into weak, discordant, and shattered fragments; and that people, who have dwelt under its protection in unexampled peace and prosperity, shedding fraternal blood in civil war.

Urging their fellow citizens first to examine their own conduct for "causes which threaten a great people with ruin," before demanding loyalty to the Constitution from the South, the signers documented their conviction that Massachusetts itself "has violated our great national compact" by its personal liberty laws. Such laws, commanding interference by the state with the laws of the national government, were "laws commanding civil war." There followed a fervent plea for sanity in the conduct of state affairs. Were Massachusetts "honestly and generously" to discharge its obligations under the Fugitive Slave Act and to repeal the provoking statutes, then secession might be given pause and the Union preserved. Five days later, South Carolina seceded.

The "Address" bore the signatures of some of the most distinguished and influential men in Massachusetts. Among the forty-two were Benjamin R. Curtis, Joel Parker, George Ticknor, Jared Sparks, Levi Lincoln, Emory Washburn, and Theophilus Parsons. The first name on the list was Lemuel Shaw's.

He who had given liberty to every slave, not a runaway, brought before him while he sat on the bench of justice, ended his public career in opposition to "An Act to protect the Rights and Liberties of the People of the Commonwealth of Massachusetts." As the "national calamity" he had always dreaded became ever and ever an increasing reality, a man of his conservative temperament and Unionist views could only retreat from the cause of individual freedom in anxious regard for an even greater value, the nation itself. Were one charitably disposed to a man who with integrity compromised under fire, it might be said of Lemuel Shaw, as Tennyson said of statesmen, that he

> knew the seasons when to take Occasion by the hand, and make the bounds
> of freedom wider yet.

QUESTIONS

1.   Leonard Levy, Shaw's brilliant biographer, is clearly "charitably disposed to a man who with integrity compromised under fire." *(Materials, supra* at 6F). How do you regard Shaw's record on the fugitive-slavery issue?

2.   Assume you were in Shaw's shoes as Chief Justice of Massachusetts. Would you resign? Would you use your position, like Judge Harrington of Vermont, to free black fugitives despite the federal law? Would you demand, as Harrington did, "a bill of sale . . . from the Almighty" before remanding a human being into slavery? How would you defend your choice?

3.   Assume you were a lawyer in Boston, such as Richard Henry Dana. Would you represent the fugitives? Would you stop there? What if Dana also secretly supported the illegal "underground railway?" If so should he be allowed to appear in court as a lawyer? Should he be disbarred? If he was working against the legal system at night, shouldn't he have at least honestly said so during the day? Why or why not? What would the ABA Model Rules say?

MARTIN LUTHER KING, JR., LETTER FROM BIRMINGHAM JAIL
The Christian Century (June 12, 1963)

A vigorous, eloquent reply to criticism expressed
by a group of eight clergymen

My Dear Fellow Clergymen:

While confined here in the Birmingham city jail I came across your recent statement calling my present activities "unwise and untimely." Seldom do I pause to answer criticism of my work and ideas. If I sought to answer all the criticisms that cross my desk, my secretaries would have little time for anything other than such correspondence in the course of the day, and I would have no time for constructive work. But since I feel that you are men of genuine good will and that your criticisms are sincerely set forth, I want to try to answer your statement in what I hope will be patient and reasonable terms.

I think I should indicate why I am here in Birmingham, since you have been influenced by the view which argues against "outsiders coming in." I have the honor of serving as president of the Southern Christian Leadership Conference, an organization operating in every southern state, with headquarters in Atlanta, Georgia. We have some 85 affiliate organizations across the south, and one of them is the Alabama Christian Movement for Human Rights. Frequently we share staff, educational and financial resources with our affiliates. Several months ago the affiliate here in Birmingham asked us to be on call to engage in a nonviolent direct action program if such were deemed necessary. We readily consented, and when the hour came we lived up to our promise. So I, along with several members of my staff, am here because I was invited here. I am here because I have organizational ties here.

I.

But more basically, I am in Birmingham because injustice exists here. Just as the prophets of the eighth century B.C. left their villages and carried their "thus saith the Lord" far afield and just as the Apostle Paul left his village of Tarsus and carried the gospel of Jesus Christ to the far corners of the Greco-Roman world, so am I compelled to carry the gospel of freedom beyond my own home town. Like Paul, I must constantly respond to the Macedonian call for aid.

Moreover, I am cognizant of the interrelatedness of all communities and states. I cannot sit idly by in Atlanta and not be concerned about what happens in Birmingham. Injustice anywhere is a threat to justice everywhere. We are caught in an inescapable network of mutuality, tied in a single garment of destiny. Whatever affects one directly affects all indirectly. Never again can we afford to live with the narrow, provincial "outside agitator" idea. Anyone who lives inside the United States can never be considered an outsider anywhere within its bounds.

You deplore the demonstrations taking place in Birmingham. But your statement, I am sorry to say, fails to express a similar concern for the conditions that brought about the demonstrations. I am sure that none of you would want to rest contentment with the superficial kind of social analysis that deals merely with effects and does not grapple with underlying causes. It is unfortunate that demonstrations are taking place in Birmingham, but it is even more unfortunate that the city's white power structure left the Negro community with no alternative.

II.

In any nonviolent campaign there are four basic steps: collection of the facts to determine whether injustices exist, negotiation, self-purification and direct action. We have gone through all these steps in Birmingham. There can be no gainsaying the fact that racial injustice engulfs this community. Birmingham is probably the most thoroughly segregated city in the United States. Its ugly record of police brutality is widely known. Its unjust treatment of Negroes in the courts is a notorious reality. There have been more unsolved bombings of Negro homes and churches in Birmingham than in any other city in the nation. These are the hard, brutal facts of the case. On the basis of these conditions Negro leaders sought to negotiate with the city fathers. But the latter consistently refused to engage in good-faith negotiation.

Then last September came the opportunity to talk with leaders of Birmingham's economic community. In the course of the negotiations certain promises were made by the merchants—for example, the promise to remove the stores' humiliating racial signs. On the basis of these promises the Rev. Fred Shuttles-worth and the leaders of the Alabama Christian Movement for Human Rights agreed to a moratorium on all demonstrations. As the weeks and months went by we realized that we were the victims of a broken promise. The signs remained.

As in so many past experiences, our hopes had been blasted, and our disappointment was keenly felt. We had no alternative except to prepare for direct action, whereby we would present our very bodies as a means of laying our case before the conscience of the local and the national community. Mindful of the difficulties involved, we decided to undertake a process of self-purification. We began a series of workshops on nonviolence, and we repeatedly asked ourselves: "Are you able to accept blows without retaliating?" "Are you able to endure the ordeal of jail?" We decided to schedule our direct action program for the Easter season, realizing that except for Christmas this is the main shopping period of the year. Knowing that a strong economic withdrawal program would be the by-product of direct action, we felt that this would be the best time to bring pressure to bear on the merchants.

But Birmingham's mayoral election was coming up in March, and when we discovered that Commissioner of Public Safety Eugene "Bull" Connor was to be in the run-off, we decided to postpone our demonstrations until the day after the run-off so that they could not be used to cloud the issues. It is evident, then, that we did not move irresponsibly into direct action. Like many others, we wanted to see Mr. Connor defeated, and to this end we endured postponement after postponement. Having aided in this community need, we felt that our direct action program could be delayed no longer.

III.

You may well ask, "Why direct action? Why sit-ins, marches, etc.? Isn't negotiation a better path?" You are quite right in calling for negotiation. Indeed, this is the very purpose of direct action. Nonviolent direct action seeks to foster such a tension that a community which has constantly refused to negotiate is forced to confront the issue. It seeks so to dramatize the issue that it can no longer be ignored. My citing the creation of tension as part of the work of the nonviolent resister may sound rather shocking. But I readily acknowledge that I am not afraid of the word "tension." I have earnestly opposed violent tension, but there is a type of constructive, nonviolent tension which is necessary for growth. Just as Socrates felt that it was necessary to create a tension in the mind so that individuals could shake off the bondage of myths and half-truths and rise to the realm of creative analysis and objective appraisal, so must we see the need for nonviolent gadflies to create the kind of tension in society that will help men rise from the dark depths of prejudice and racism to the majestic heights of understanding and brotherhood.

The purpose of our direct action program is to create a situation so crisis-packed that it will inevitably open the door to negotiation. I therefore concur with you in your call for negotiation. Too long has our beloved south-land been bogged down in a tragic effort to live in monologue rather than dialogue.

One of the basic points in your statement is that the action that I and my associates have taken in Birmingham is untimely. Some have asked, "Why didn't you give the new city administration time to act?" The only answer that I can give to this query is that the new Birmingham administration must be prodded about as much as the outgoing one before it will act. We are sadly mistaken if we feel that the election of Albert Boutwell as mayor will bring the millennium to Birmingham. While Mr. Boutwell is a much more gentle person than Mr. Connor, they are both segregationists, dedicated to maintenance of the status quo. I have hope that Mr. Boutwell will be reasonable enough to see the futility of massive resistance to desegregation. But he will not see this without pressure from devotees of civil rights. My friends, I must say to you that we have not made a single gain in civil rights without determining legal and nonviolent pressure. Lamentably, it is a historical fact that privileged groups seldom give up their privileges voluntarily. Individuals may see the moral light and voluntarily give up their unjust posture; but, as Reinhold Niebuhr has reminded us, groups tend to be more immoral than individuals.

We know through painful experience that freedom is never voluntarily given by the oppressor; it must be demanded by the oppressed. Frankly, I have yet to engage in a direct action campaign that was "well timed" in the view of those who have not suffered unduly from the disease of segregation. For years now I have heard the word "Wait!" It rings in the ear of every Negro with piercing familiarity. This "Wait" has almost always meant "Never." As one of our distinguished jurists once said, "Justice too long delayed is justice denied."

IV.

We have waited for more than 340 years for our constitutional and God-given rights. The nations of Asia and Africa are moving with jet-like speed toward gaining political independence, but we still creep at horse-and-buggy pace toward gaining a cup of coffee at a lunch counter. Perhaps it is easy for those who have never felt the stinging darts of segregation to say "Wait." But when you have seen vicious mobs lynch your mothers and fathers at will and drown you sisters and brothers at whim; when you have seen hate-filled policemen curse, kick and even kill your black brothers and sisters with impunity; when you see the vast majority of your 20 million Negro brothers smothering in an air-tight cage of poverty in the midst of an affluent society; when you suddenly find your tongue twisted as you seek to explain to your six-year-old daughter why she can't go to the public amusement park that has just been advertised on television, and see tears welling up when she is told that Funtown is closed to colored children, and see ominous clouds of inferiority beginning to form in her little mental sky, and see her beginning to distort her personality by unconsciously developing a bitterness toward white people; when you have to concoct an answer for a five-year-old son asking, "Daddy, why do white people treat colored people so mean?"; when you take a cross-country drive and find it necessary to sleep night after night in the uncomfortable corners of your automobile because no motel will accept you; when you are humiliated day in and day out by nagging signs reading "white" and "colored"; when your first name becomes "nigger," your middle name becomes "boy" (however old you are) and your last name becomes "John," and your wife and mother are never given the respected title "Mrs."; when you are harried by day and haunted by night by the fact that you are a Negro, never quite knowing what to expect next, and are plagued with inner fears and outer resentment; when you are forever fighting a degenerating sense of "nobodiness"—then you will understand why we find it difficult to wait. There comes a time when the cup of endurance runs over, and men are no longer willing to be plunged into an abyss of injustice where they experience the bleakness of corroding despair. I hope, sirs, you can understand our legitimate and unavoidable impatience.

V.

You express a great deal of anxiety over our willingness to break laws. This is certainly a legitimate concern. Since we so diligently urge people to obey the Supreme Court's decision of 1964 outlawing segregation in the public schools, at first glance it may seem rather paradoxical for us consciously to break laws. One may well ask, "How can you advocate breaking some laws and obeying others?" The answer lies in the fact that there are two types of laws: just and unjust. I agree with St. Augustine that "an unjust law is no law at all."

Now what is the difference between the two? How does one determine whether a law is just or unjust? A just law is man-made code that squares with the moral law or the law of God. An unjust law is a code that is out of harmony with the moral law. To put it in the terms of St. Thomas Aquinas, an unjust law is a human law that is not rooted in eternal law and natural law. Any law that uplifts human personality is just. Any law that degrades human personality is unjust. All segregation statutes are unjust because segregation distorts the soul and damages the personality. It gives the segregator a false sense of superiority and the segregated a false sense of inferiority. Segregation, to use the terminology of the Jewish philosopher Martin Buber, substitutes an "I-it" relationship for an "I-thou" relationship and ends up relegating persons to the status of things. Hence segregation is not only politically, economically and sociologically unsound, it is sinful. Paul Tillich has said that sin is separation. Is not segregation an existential expression of man's tragic separation, his awful estrangement, his terrible sinfulness? Thus it is that I can urge men to disobey segregation ordinances, for such ordinances are morally wrong.

Let us consider some of the ways in which a law can be unjust. A law is unjust, for example, if the majority group compels a minority group to obey the statute but does not make it binding on itself. By the same token a law in all probability is just if the majority is itself willing to obey it. Also, a law is unjust if it is inflicted on a minority that, as a result of being denied the right to vote, had no part in enacting or devising the law. Who can say that the legislature of Alabama which set up that state's segregation laws was democratically elected? Throughout Alabama all sorts of devious methods are used to prevent Negroes from becoming registered voters, and there are some counties in which, even though Negroes constitute a majority of the population, not a single Negro is registered. Can any law enacted under such circumstances be considered democratically structured?

Sometimes a law is just on its face and unjust in its application. For instance, I have been arrested on a charge of parading without a permit. Now there is nothing wrong in having an ordinance which requires a permit for a parade. But such an ordinance becomes unjust when it is used to maintain segregation and to deny citizens the First-amendment privilege of peaceful assembly and protest.

I hope you are able to see the distinction I am trying to point out. In no sense do I advocate evading the law, as would the rabid segregationist. That would lead to anarchy. One who breaks an unjust law must do so *openly, lovingly*, and with a willingness to accept the penalty. I submit that an individual who breaks a law that conscience tells him is unjust and who willingly accepts the penalty of imprisonment in order to arouse the conscience of the community over its injustice is in reality expressing the highest respect for law.

Of course, there is nothing new about this kind of civil disobedience. It was evidenced sublimely in the refusal of Shadrach, Meshach and Abednego to obey the laws of Nebuchadnezzar, on the ground that a higher moral law was at stake. It was practiced superbly by the early Christians who were willing to face hungry lions rather than submit to certain unjust laws of the Roman empire. To a degree, academic freedom is a reality today because Socrates practiced civil disobedience. We should never forget that everything Adolf Hitler did in Germany was "legal" and everything the Hungarian freedom fighters did in Hungary was "illegal." It was "illegal" to aid and comfort a Jew in Hitler's Germany. Even so, I am sure that had I lived in Germany at the time I would have aided and comforted my Jewish brothers. If today I lived in a communist country where certain principles dear to the Christian faith are suppressed, I would openly advocate disobeying that country's antireligious laws.

VI.

I must make two honest confessions to you, my Christian and Jewish brothers. First, I must confess that over the past few years I have been gravely disappointed with the white moderate. I have almost reached the regrettable conclusion that the Negro's great stumbling block in his stride toward freedom is not the White Citizen's Councilor or the Ku Klux Klanner but the white moderate who is more devoted to "order" than to justice; who prefers a negative peace which is the absence of tension to a positive peace which is the presence of justice; who constantly says "I agree with you in the goal you seek, but I cannot agree with your methods"; who paternalistically believes he can set the timetable for another man's freedom; who lives by a mythical concept of time and who constantly advises the Negro to wait for a "more convenient season." Shallow understanding from people of good will is more frustrating than absolute misunderstanding from people of ill will. Lukewarm acceptance is much more bewildering than outright rejection.

I had hoped that the white moderate would understand that law and order exist for the purpose of establishing justice and that when they fail in this purpose they block social progress. I had hoped that the white moderate would understand that the present tension in the south is a necessary phase of the transition from an obnoxious-negative peace, in which the Negro passively accepted his unjust plight, to a substantive and positive peace, in which all men will respect the dignity and worth of the human personality. Actually, we who engage in nonviolent direct action are not the creators of tension. We merely bring to the surface the hidden tension that is already alive. We bring it out in the open where it can be seen and dealt with. Like a boil that can never be cured so long as it is covered up but must be opened with all its pus-flowing ugliness to the natural medicines of air and light, injustice must be exposed, with all the tension its exposure creates, to the light of human conscience and the air of national opinion before it can be cured.

In your statement you assert that our actions, even though peaceful, must be condemned because they precipitate violence. But is this a logical assertion? Isn't this like condemning a robbed man because his possession of money precipitated an act of robbery? Isn't this like condemning Socrates because his unswerving commitment to truth and his philosophical inquiries precipitated the act by the misguided populace in which they made him drink hemlock? Isn't this like condemning Jesus because his unique God-consciousness and never-ceasing devotion to God's will precipitated the evil act of crucifixion? We must come to see that, as the federal courts have consistently affirmed, it is wrong to urge an individual to cease his efforts to gain his basic constitutional rights because the quest may precipitate violence. Society must protect the robbed and punish the robber.

I had also hoped that the white moderate would reject the myth concerning time in relation to the struggle for freedom. I have just received a letter from a white brother in Texas. He writes: "All Christians know that the colored people will receive equal rights eventually, but it is possible that you are in too great a religious hurry. It has taken Christianity almost 2,000 years to accomplish what it has. The teachings of Christ take time to come to earth." Such an attitude stems from a tragic misconception of time, from the strangely irrational notion that there is something in the very flow of time that will inevitably cure all ills. Actually, time itself is neutral; it can be used either destructively or constructively. More and more I feel that the people of ill will have used time much more effectively than have the people of good will. We will have to repent in this generation not merely for the hateful words and actions of the bad people but for the appalling silence of the good people. Human progress never rolls in on wheels of inevitability; it comes through the tireless efforts of men willing to be co-workers with God, and without this hard work time itself becomes an ally of the forces of social stagnation. We must use time creatively, in the knowledge that the time is always ripe to do right. Now is the time to make real the promise of democracy and transform our pending national elegy into a creative psalm of brotherhood. Now is the time to lift our national policy from the quicksand of racial injustice to the solid rock of human dignity.

VII.

You speak of our activity in Birmingham as extreme. At first I was rather disappointed that fellow clergymen would see my nonviolent efforts as those of an extremist. I began thinking about the fact that I stand in the middle of two opposing forces in the Negro community. One is a force of complacency made up of Negroes who, as a result of long years of oppression, are so completely drained of self-respect and a sense of "somebodiness" that they have adjusted to segregation, and of a few middle class Negroes who, because of a degree of academic and economic security and because in some ways they profit by segregation, have unconsciously become insensitive to the problems of the masses. The other force is one of bitterness and hatred, and it comes perilously close to advocating violence. It is expressed in the various black nationalist groups that are springing up across the nation, the largest and best-known being Elijah Muhammad's Muslim movement. Nourished by the Negro's frustration over the continued existence of racial discrimination, this movement is made up of people who have lost faith in America, who have absolutely repudiated Christianity, and who have concluded that the white man is an incorrigible "devil."

I have tried to stand between those two forces, saying that we need emulate neither the "do-nothingism" of the complacent nor the hatred of the black nationalist. For there is the more excellent way of love and nonviolent protest. I am grateful to God that, through the influence of the Negro church, the way of nonviolence became an integral part of our struggle.

If this philosophy had not emerged, by now many streets of the south would, I am convinced, be flowing with blood. And I am further convinced that if our white brothers dismiss as "rabble-rousers" and "outside agitators" those of us who employ nonviolent direct action and if they refuse to support our nonviolent efforts, millions of Negroes will, out of frustration and despair, seek solace and security in black nationalist ideologies—a development that would inevitably lead to a frightening racial nightmare.

VIII.

Oppressed people cannot remain oppressed forever. The yearning for freedom eventually manifests itself, and that is what has happened to the American Negro. Something within has reminded him of his birthright of freedom, and something without has reminded him that it can be gained. Consciously or unconsciously, he has been caught up by the *Zeitgeist*, and with his black brothers of Africa and his brown and yellow brothers of Asia, South America and the Caribbean, the U.S. Negro is moving with a sense of great urgency toward the promised land of racial justice. If one recognizes this vital urge that has engulfed the Negro community, he should readily understand why public demonstrations are taking place. The Negro has many pent-up resentments and latent frustrations, and he must release them. So let him march; let him make prayer pilgrimages to the city hall; let him go on freedom rides—and try to understand why he must do so. If his repressed emotions are not released in nonviolent ways, they will seek expression through violence; this is not a threat but a fact of history. I have not said to my people, "Get rid of your discontent." Rather, I have tried to say that this normal and healthy discontent can be channeled into the creative outlet of nonviolent direct action. And now this approach is being termed extremist.

But though I was initially disappointed at being categorized as an extremist, as I continued to think about the matter I gradually gained a measure of satisfaction from the label. Was not Jesus an extremist for love: "Love your enemies, bless them that curse you, do good to them that hate you, and pray for them which despitefully use you, and persecute you." Was not Amos an extremist for justice: "Let justice roll down like waters and righteousness like an everflowing stream." Was not Paul an extremist for the Christian gospel: "I bear in my body the marks of Lord Jesus." Was not Martin Luther an extremist: 'Here I stand; I can do no other so help me God." And John Bunyan: "I will stay in jail to the end of my days before I make a butchery of my conscience." And Abraham Lincoln: "This nation cannot survive half slave and half free." And Thomas Jefferson: "We hold these truths to be self-evident, that all men are created equal . . ." So the question is not whether we will be extremists but what kind of extremists we will be. Will we be extremists for hate or for love? Will we be extremist for the preservation of injustice of for the extension of justice? Perhaps the south, the nation and the world are in dire need of creative extremists.

I had hoped that the white moderate would see this need. Perhaps I was too optimistic; perhaps I expected too much. I suppose I should have realized that few members of the oppressor race can understand the deep groans and passionate yearnings of the oppressed race, and still fewer have the vision to see that injustice must be rooted out by strong, persistent and determined action. I am thankful, however, that some of our white brothers have grasped the meaning of this social revolution and committed themselves to it. They are still all too few in quantity, but they are big in quality. Some—such as Ralph McGill, Lillian Smith, Harry Golden and James McBride Dabbs—have written about our struggle in eloquent and prophetic terms. Others have marched with us down nameless streets of the south. They have languished in filthy, roach-infested jails, suffering the abuse and brutality of policemen who view them as "dirty nigger lovers." Unlike so many of their moderate brothers and sisters, they have recognized the urgency of the moment and sensed the need for powerful "action" antidotes to combat the disease of segregation.

IX.

Let me take note of my other major disappointment. Though there are some notable exceptions, I have also been disappointed with the white church and its leadership. I do not say this as one of those negative critics who can always find something wrong with the church. I say this as a minister of the gospel, who loves the church; who was nurtured in its bosom; who has been sustained by its spiritual blessings and who will remain true to it as long as the cord of life shall lengthen.

When I was suddenly catapulted into the leadership of the bus protest in Montgomery, Alabama, a few years ago I felt we would be supported by the white church. I felt that the white ministers, priests and rabbis of the south would be among our strongest allies. Instead, some have been outright opponents, refusing to understand the freedom movement and misrepresenting its leaders; all too many others have been more cautious than courageous and have remained silent and secure behind stained-glass windows.

In spite of my shattered dreams I came to Birmingham with the hope that the white religious leadership of this community would see the justice of our cause and with deep moral concern would serve as the channel through which our just grievances could reach the power structure. But again I have been disappointed.

I have heard numerous southern religious leaders admonish their worshipers to comply with a desegregation decision because it is the *law*, but I have longed to hear white ministers declare, "Follow this decree because integration is morally *right* and because the Negro is your brother." In the midst of blatant injustices Inflicted upon the Negro I have watched white churchmen stand on the sideline and mouth pious irrelevancies and sanctimonious trivialities. In the midst of a mighty struggle to rid our nation of racial and economic injustice I have heard many ministers say, "Those are social issues with which the gospel has no real concern," and I have watched many churches commit themselves to a completely otherworldly religion which makes a strange, unbiblical distinction between body and soul, between the sacred and the secular.

We are moving toward the close of the 20th century with a religious community largely adjusted to the status quo—a taillight behind other community agencies rather than a headlight leading men to higher levels of justice.

X.

I have traveled the length and breadth of Alabama, Mississippi and all the other southern states. On sweltering summer days and crisp autumn mornings I have looked at the south's beautiful churches with their lofty spires pointing heavenward, and at her impressive religious education buildings. Over and over I have found myself asking: 'What kind of people worship here? Who is their God? Where were their voices when the lips of Governor Barnett dripped with words of interposition and nullification? Where were they when Governor Wallace gave a clarion call for defiance and hatred? Where were their voices of support when bruised and weary Negro men and women decided to rise from the dark dungeons of complacency to the bright hills of creative protest?"

Yes, these questions are still in my mind. In deep disappointment I have wept over the laxity of the church. But be assured that my tears have been tears of love. There can be no deep disappointment where there is not deep love. Yes, I love the church. How could I do otherwise? I am in the rather unique position of being the son, the grandson and the great-grandson of preachers. Yes, I see the church as the body of Christ. But, oh! How we have blemished and scarred that body through social neglect and through fear of being nonconformists.

There was a time when the church was very powerful—in the time when the early Christians rejoiced at being deemed worthy to suffer for what they believed. In those days the church was not merely a thermometer that recorded the ideas and principles of popular opinion; it was a thermostat that transformed the mores of society. Whenever the early Christians entered a town the power structure immediately sought to convict them for being "disturbers of the peace" and "outside agitators." But the Christians pressed on, in the conviction that they were "a colony of heaven," called to obey God rather than man. Small in number, they were big in commitment. By their effort and example they brought an end to such ancient evils as infanticide and gladiatorial contest.

XI.

Things are different now. So often the contemporary church is a weak, ineffectual voice with an uncertain sound. So often it is an archdefender of the status quo. Far from being disturbed by the presence of the church, the power structure of the average community is consoled by the church's silent and often even vocal—sanction of things as they are.

But the judgment of God is upon the church as never before. If today's church does not recapture the sacrificial spirit of the early church, it will lose its authenticity, forfeit the loyalty of millions, and be dismissed as an irrelevant social club with no meaning for the 20th century. Every day I meet young people whose disappointment with the church has turned into outright disgust.

Perhaps I have once again been too optimistic. Is organized religion too inextricably bound to the status quo to save our nation and the world? Perhaps I must turn my faith to the inner spiritual church, the church within the church, as the true ecclesia and the hope of the world. But again I am thankful to God that some noble souls from the ranks of organized religion have broken loose from the paralyzing chains of conformity and joined us as active partners in the struggle for freedom. They have left their secure congregations and walked the streets of Albany, Georgia, with us. They have gone down the highways of the south on torturous rides for freedom. Yes, they have gone to jail with us. Some have been kicked out of their churches, have lost the support of their bishops and fellow ministers. But they have acted in the faith that right defeated is stronger than evil triumphant. Their witness has been the spiritual salt that has preserved the true meaning of the gospel in these troubled times. They have carved a tunnel of hope through the dark mountain of disappointment.

I hope the church as a whole will meet the challenge of this decisive hour. But even if the church does not come to the aid of justice, I have no despair about the future. I have no fear about the outcome of our struggle in Birmingham, even if our motives are at present misunderstood. We will reach the goal of freedom in Birmingham and all over the nation, because the goal of America is freedom. Abused and scorned though we may be, our destiny is tied up with America's destiny. Before the pilgrims landed at Plymouth we were here. Before the pen of Jefferson etched across the pages of history the mighty words of the Declaration of Independence, we were here. For more than two centuries our forebears labored in this country without wages; they made cotton king, they built the homes of their masters while suffering gross injustice and shameful humiliation—and yet out of a bottomless vitality they continued to thrive and develop. If the inexpressible cruelties of slavery could not stop us, the opposition we now face will surely fail. We will win our freedom because the sacred heritage of our nation and the eternal will of God are embodied in our echoing demands.

XII.

Before closing I feel impelled to mention one other point in your statement that has troubled me profoundly. You warmly commend the Birmingham police force for keeping "order" and "preventing violence." I doubt that you would have so warmly commended the police force if you had seen its angry dogs sinking their teeth into six unarmed, nonviolent Negroes. I doubt that you would so quickly commend the policemen if you were to observe their ugly and inhuman treatment of Negroes here in the city jail; if you were to watch them push and curse old Negro women and young Negro girls; if you were to see them slap and kick old Negro men and young boys; if you were to observe them, as they did on two occasions, refuse to give us food because we wanted to sing our grace together. I cannot join you in your praise of the Birmingham police department.

It is true that the police have exercised discipline in handling the demonstrators. In this sense they have conducted themselves rather "nonviolently" in public. But for what purpose? To preserve the evil system of segregation. Over the past few years I have consistently preached that nonviolence demands that the means we use must be as pure as the ends we seek. I have tried to make clear that it is wrong to use immoral means to attain moral ends. But now I must affirm that it is just as wrong, or perhaps even more so, to use moral means to preserve immoral ends. Perhaps Mr. Connor and his policemen have been rather nonviolent in public, as was Chief Pritchett in Albany, Georgia, but they have used the moral means of nonviolence to maintain the immoral end of racial injustice. As T.S. Eliot has said, there is no greater treason than to do the right deed for the wrong reason.

XIII.

I wish you had commended the Negro sit-inners and demonstrators of Birmingham for their sublime courage, their willingness to suffer and their amazing discipline in the midst of great provocation. One day the south will recognize its real heroes. They will be the James Merediths, with a noble sense of purpose facing jeering and hostile mobs and the agonizing loneliness that characterizes the life of the pioneer. They will be old, oppressed, battered Negro women, symbolized in a 72-year-old woman in Montgomery, Alabama, who rose up with a sense of dignity and with her people decided not to ride segregated buses, and who responded with ungrammatical profundity to one who inquired about her: "My feet is tired, but my soul is rested." They will be the young high school and college students, the young ministers of the gospel and a host of their elders courageously and nonviolently sitting in at lunch counters and willingly going to jail for conscience' sake. One day the south will know that when these disinherited children of God sat down at lunch counters they were in reality standing up for what is best in the American dream and for the most sacred values in our Judeo-Christian heritage, thereby bringing our nation back to those great wells of democracy which were dug deep by the founding fathers in their formulation of the Constitution and the Declaration of Independence.

Never before have I written so long a letter. I can assure you that it would have been much shorter if I had been writing from a comfortable desk, but what else can one do when he is alone for days in a narrow jail cell, other than write long letters, think long thoughts and pray long prayers?

If I have said anything in this letter that overstates the truth and indicates an unreasonable impatience, I beg you to forgive me. If I have said anything that *under* states the truth and indicates my having a patience that allows me to settle for anything less than brotherhood, I beg God to forgive me.

I hope this letter finds you strong in the faith. I also hope that circumstances will soon make it possible for me to meet each of you, not as an integrationist or a civil rights leader but as a fellow clergyman and a Christian brother. Let us all hope that the dark clouds of racial prejudice will soon pass away and the deep fog of misunderstanding will be lifted from our fear-drenched communities and in some not too distant tomorrow the radiant stars of love and brotherhood will shine over our great nation with all their scintillating beauty.

QUESTIONS

1. In this great letter, the Rev. Martin Luther King, Jr. demonstrated an extensive background in ethical philosophy. In particular, his letter directly quotes some of the philosophers we have studied in this course. There are implicit references to others, such as Thoreau. How many can you spot? Note also the reference to "a degenerating sense of 'nobodiness'" as the alternative to moral action. *Materials, supra* at 6F. Ralph Ellison's book *Invisible Man* was already well known in 1963.

2. If the Rev. King were a lawyer, instead of a theologian and a minister, could he have written this letter the same way? What changes, or additions, would he have had to make? How would you have written the letter?

3. What would Locke have thought of this letter? Thoreau? Chief Justice Shaw?

RONALD DWORKIN, TAKING RIGHTS SERIOUSLY
206–217, 222 (1977)

Chapter 8
Civil Disobedience

How should the government deal with those who disobey the draft laws out of conscience? Many people think the answer is obvious: The government must prosecute the dissenters, and if they are convicted it must punish them. Some people reach this conclusion easily, because they hold the mindless view that conscientious disobedience is the same as lawlessness. They think that the dissenters are anarchists who must be punished before their corruption spreads. Many lawyers and intellectuals come to the same conclusion, however, on what looks like a more sophisticated argument. They recognize that disobedience to law may be *morally* justified, but they insist that it cannot be *legally* justified, and they think that it follows from this truism that the law must be enforced. Erwin Griswold, once Solicitor General of the United States, and before that Dean of the Harvard Law School, appears to have adopted this view. 'MI is of the essence of law,' he said, "that it is equally applied to all, that it binds all alike, irrespective of personal motive. For this reason, one who contemplates civil disobedience out of moral conviction should not be surprised and must not be bitter if a criminal conviction ensues. And he must accept the fact that organized society cannot endure on any other basis.'

The *New York Times* applauded that statement. A thousand faculty members of several universities had signed a *Times* advertisement calling on the Justice Department to quash the indictments of the Rev. William Sloane Coffin, Dr. Benjamin Spock, Marcus Raskin, Mitchell Goodman, and Michael Ferber, for conspiring to counsel various draft offenses. The *Times* said that the request to quash the indictments 'confused moral rights with legal responsibilities.'

But the argument that, because the government believes a man has committed a crime, it must prosecute him is much weaker than it seems. Society 'cannot endure' if it tolerates all disobedience; it does not follow, however, nor is there evidence, that it will collapse if it tolerates some. In the United States prosecutors have discretion whether to enforce criminal laws in particular cases. A prosecutor may properly decide not to press charges if the lawbreaker is young, or inexperienced, or the sole support of a family, or is repentant, or turns state's evidence, or if the law is unpopular or unworkable or generally disobeyed, or if the courts are clogged with more important cases, or for dozens of other reasons. This discretion is not license—we expect prosecutors to have good reason for exercising it—but there are, at least *prima facie*, some good reasons for not prosecuting those who disobey the draft laws out of conscience. One is the obvious reason that they act out of better motives than those who break the law out of greed or a desire to subvert government. If motive can count in distinguishing between thieves, then why not in distinguishing between draft offenders? Another is the practical reason that our society suffers a loss if it punishes a group that includes—as the group of draft dissenters does—some of its most loyal and law-respecting citizens. Jailing such men solidifies their alienation from society, and alienates many like them who are deterred by the threat. If practical consequences like these argued for not enforcing prohibition, why do they not argue for tolerating offenses of conscience?

Those who think that conscientious draft offenders should always be punished must show that these are not good reasons for exercising discretion, or they must find contrary reasons that outweigh them. What arguments might they produce? There are practical reasons for enforcing draft laws, and I shall consider some of these later. But Dean Griswold and those who agree with him seem to rely on a fundamental moral argument that it would be unfair, not merely impractical, to let the dissenters go unpunished. They think it would be unfair, I gather, because society could not function if everyone disobeyed laws he disapproved of or found disadvantageous. If the government tolerates those few who will not 'play the game,' it allows them to secure the benefits of everyone else's deference to law, without shouldering the burdens, such as the burden of the draft.

This argument is a serious one. It cannot be answered simply by saying that the dissenters would allow everyone else the privilege of disobeying a law he believed immoral. In fact, few draft dissenters would accept a changed society in which sincere segregationists were free to break civil rights laws they hated. The majority want no such change, in any event, because they think that society would be worse off for it; until they are shown this is wrong, they will expect their officials to punish anyone who assumes a privilege which they, for the general benefit, do not assume.

There is, however, a flaw in the argument. The reasoning contains a hidden assumption that makes it almost entirely irrelevant to the draft cases, and indeed to any serious case of civil disobedience in the United States. The argument assumes that the dissenters know that they are breaking a valid law, and that the privilege they assert is the privilege to do that. Of course, almost everyone who discusses civil disobedience recognizes that in America a law may be invalid because it is unconstitutional. But the critics handle this complexity by arguing on separate hypotheses: If the law is invalid, then no crime is committed, and society may not punish. If the law is valid, then a crime has been committed, and society must punish. This reasoning hides the crucial fact that the validity of the law may be doubtful. The officials and judges may believe that the law is valid, the dissenters may disagree, and both sides may have plausible arguments for their positions. If so, then the issues are different from what they would be if the law were clearly valid or clearly invalid, and the argument of fairness, designed for these alternatives, is irrelevant.

Doubtful law is by no means special or exotic in cases of civil disobedience. On the contrary. In the United States, at least, almost any law which a significant number of people would be tempted to disobey on moral grounds would be doubtful—if not clearly invalid—on constitutional grounds as well. The constitution makes our conventional political morality relevant to the question of validity; any statute that appears to compromise that morality raises constitutional questions, and if the compromise is serious, the constitutional doubts are serious also.

The connection between moral and legal issues was especially clear in the draft cases of the last decade. Dissent was based at the time on the following moral objections: (a) The United States is using immoral weapons and tactics in Vietnam.

(b) The war has never been endorsed by deliberate, considered, and open vote of the peoples' representatives. (c) The United States has no interest at stake in Vietnam remotely strong enough to justify forcing a segment of its citizens to risk death there. (d) If an army is to be raised to fight that war, it is immoral to raise it by a draft that defers or exempts college students, and thus discriminates against the economically underprivileged. (e) The draft exempts those who object to all wars on religious grounds, but not those who object to particular wars on moral grounds; there is no relevant difference between these positions, and so the draft, by making the distinction, implies that the second group is less worthy of the nation's respect than the first. (f) The law that makes it a crime to counsel draft resistance stifles those who oppose the war, because it is morally impossible to argue that the war is profoundly immoral, without encouraging and assisting those who refuse to fight it.

Lawyers will recognize that these moral positions, if we accept them, provide the basis for the following constitutional arguments: (a) The constitution makes treaties part of the law of the land, and the United States is a party to international conventions and covenants that make illegal the acts of war the dissenters charged the nation with committing. (b) The constitution provides that Congress must declare war, the legal issue of whether our action in Vietnam was a 'war' and whether the Tonkin Bay Resolution was a 'declaration' is the heart of the moral issue of whether the government had made a deliberate and open decision. (c) Both the due process clause of the Fifth and Fourteenth Amendments and equal protection clause of the Fourteenth Amendment condemn special burdens placed on a selected class of citizens when the burden or the classification is not reasonable; the burden is unreasonable when it patently does not serve the public interest, or when it is vastly disproportionate to the interest served. If our military action in Vietnam was frivolous or perverse, as the dissenters claimed, then the burden we placed on men of draft age was unreasonable and unconstitutional. (d) In any event, the discrimination in favor of college students denied to the poor the equal protection of the law that is guaranteed by the constitution. (e) If there is no pertinent difference between religious objection to all wars and moral objection to some wars, then the classification the draft made was arbitrary and unreasonable, and unconstitutional on that ground. The 'establishment of religion' clause of the First Amendment forbids governmental pressure in favor of organized religion; if the draft's distinction coerced men in this direction, it was invalid on that count also. (f) The First Amendment also condemns invasions of freedom of speech. If the draft law's prohibition on counseling did inhibit expression of a range of views on the war, it abridged free speech.

The principal counterargument, supporting the view that the courts ought not to have held the draft unconstitutional, also involves moral issues. Under the so-called 'political question' doctrine, the courts deny their own jurisdiction to pass on matters—such as foreign or military policy—whose resolution is best assigned to other branches of the government. The Boston court trying the Coffin, Spock case declared, on the basis of this doctrine, that it would not hear arguments about the legality of the war. But the Supreme Court has shown itself (in the reapportionment cases, for example) reluctant to refuse jurisdiction when it believed that the gravest issues of political morality were at stake and that no remedy was available through the political process. If the dissenters were right, and the war and the draft were state crimes of profound injustice to a group of citizens, then the argument that the courts should have refused jurisdiction is considerably weakened.

We cannot conclude from these arguments that the draft (or any part of it) was unconstitutional. When the Supreme Court was called upon to rule on the question, it rejected some of them, and refused to consider the others on grounds that they were political. The majority of lawyers agreed with this result. But the arguments of unconstitutionality were at least plausible, and a reasonable and competent lawyer might well think that they present a stronger case, on balance, than the counterarguments. If he does, he will consider that the draft was not constitutional, and there will be no way of proving that he is wrong.

Therefore we cannot assume, in judging what should have been done with the draft dissenters, that they were asserting a privilege to disobey valid laws. We cannot decide that fairness demanded their punishment until we try to answer further questions: What should a citizen do when the law is unclear, and when he thinks it allows what others think it does not? I do not mean to ask, of course, what it is legally proper for him to do, or what his legal rights are—that would be begging the question, because it depends upon whether he is right or they are right. I mean to ask what his proper course is as a citizen, what, in other words, we would consider to be 'playing the game.' That is a crucial question, because it cannot be unfair not to punish him if he is acting as, given his opinions, we think he should.

There is no obvious answer on which most citizens would readily agree, and that is itself significant. If we examine our legal institutions and practices, however, we shall discover some relevant underlying principles and policies. I shall set out three possible answers to the question, and then try to show which of these best fits our practices and expectations. The three possibilities I want to consider are these:

(1) If the law is doubtful, and it is therefore unclear whether it permits someone to do what he wants, he should assume the worst, and act on the assumption that it does not. He should obey the executive authorities who command him, even though he thinks they are wrong, while using the political process, if he can, to change the law.

(2) If the law is doubtful, he may follow his own judgment, that is, he may do what he wants if he believes that the case that the law permits this is stronger than the case that it does not. But he may follow his own judgment only until an authoritative institution, like a court, decides the other way in a case involving him or someone else. Once an institutional decision has been reached, he must abide by that decision, even though he thinks that it was wrong. (There are, in theory, many subdivisions of this second possibility. We may say that the individual's choice is foreclosed by the contrary decision of any court, including the lowest court in the system if the case is not appealed. Or we may require a decision of some particular court or institution. I shall discuss this second possibility in its most liberal form, namely that the individual may properly follow his own judgment until a contrary decision of the highest court competent to pass on the

issue, which, in the case of the draft, was the United States Supreme Court.)

(3) If the law is doubtful, he may follow his own judgment, even after a contrary decision by the highest competent court. Of course, he must take the contrary decision of any court into account in making his judgment of what the law requires. Otherwise the judgment would not be an honest or reasonable one, because the doctrine of precedent, which is an established part of our legal system, has the effect of allowing the decision of the courts to *change* the law. Suppose, for example, that a taxpayer believes that he is not required to pay tax on certain forms of income. If the Supreme Court decides to the contrary, he should, taking into account the practice of according great weight to the decisions of the Supreme Court on tax matters, decide that the Court's decision has itself tipped the balance, and that the law now requires him to pay the tax.

Someone might think that this qualification erases the difference between the third and the second models, but it does not. The doctrine of precedent gives different weights to the decisions of different courts, and greatest weight to the decisions of the Supreme Court decision, but it does not make the decisions of any court conclusive. Sometimes, even after a contrary Supreme Court decision, an individual may still reasonably believe that the law is on her side; such cases are rare, but they are most likely to occur in disputes over constitutional law when civil disobedience is involved. The Court has shown itself more likely to overrule its past decisions if these have limited important personal or political rights, and it is just these decisions that a dissenter might want to challenge.

We cannot assume, in other words, that the Constitution is always what the Supreme Court says it is. Oliver Wendell Holmes, for example, did not follow such a rule in his famous dissent in the *Gitlow* case. A few years before, in *Abrams*, he had lost his battle to persuade the court that the First Amendment protected an anarchist who had been urging general strikes against the government. A similar issue was presented in *Gitlow*, and Holmes once again dissented. 'It is true,' he said, 'that in my opinion this criterion was departed from [in *Abrams*] but the convictions that I expressed in that cases are too deep for it to be possible for me as yet to believe that it . . . settled the law.' Holmes voted for acquitting Gitlow, on the ground that what Gitlow had done was no crime, even though the Supreme Court had recently held that it was.

Here then are three possible models for the behavior of dissenters who disagree with the executive authorities when the law is doubtful. Which of them best fits our legal and social practices?

I think it plain that we do not follow the first of these models, that is, that we do not expect citizens to assume the worst. If no court has decided the issue, and a man thinks, on balance, that the law is on his side, most of our lawyers and critics think it perfectly proper for him to follow his own judgment. Even when many disapprove of what he does—such as peddling pornography—they do not think he must desist just because the legality of his conduct is subject to doubt.

It is worth pausing a moment to consider what society would lose if it did follow the first model or, to put the matter the other way, what society gains when people follow their own judgment in cases like this. When the law is uncertain, in the sense that lawyers can reasonably disagree on what a court ought to decide, the reason usually is that different legal principles and policies collided, and it is unclear how best to accommodate these conflicting principles and policies.

Our practice, in which different parties are encouraged to pursue their own understanding, provides a means of testing relevant hypotheses. If the question is whether a particular rule would have certain undesirable consequences, or whether these consequences would have limited or broad ramification, then, before the issue is decided, it is useful to know what does in fact take place when some people proceed on that rule. (Much anti-trust and business regulation law has developed through this kind of testing.) If the question is whether and to what degree a particular solution would offend principles of justice or fair play deeply respected by the community, it is useful, again, to experiment by testing the community's response. The extent of community indifference to anti-contraception laws, for example, would never have become established had not some organizations deliberately flouted those laws.

If the first model were followed, we would lose the advantages of these tests. The law would suffer, particularly if this model were applied to constitutional issues. When the validity of a criminal statute is in doubt, the statute will almost always strike some people as being unfair or unjust, because it will infringe some principle of liberty or justice or fairness which they take to be built into the Constitution. If our practice were that whenever a law is doubtful on these grounds, one must act as if it were valid, then the chief vehicle we have for challenging the law on moral grounds would be lost, and over time the law we obeyed would certainly become less fair and just, and the liberty of our citizens would certainly be diminished.

We would lose almost as much if we used a variation of the first model, that a citizen must assume the worst unless he can anticipate that the courts will agree with his view of the law. If everyone deferred to his guess of what the courts would do, society and its law would be poorer. Our assumption in rejecting the first model was that the record a citizen makes in following his own judgment, together with the arguments he makes supporting that judgment when he has the opportunity, are helpful in creating the best judicial decision possible. This remains true even when, at the time the citizen acts, the odds are against his success in court. We must remember, too, that the value of the citizen's example is not exhausted once the decision has been made. Our practices require that the decision be criticized, by the legal profession and the law schools, and the record of dissent may be invaluable here.

Of course a man must consider what the courts will do when he decides whether it would be *prudent* to follow his own judgment. He may have to face jail, bankruptcy, or opprobrium if he does. But it is essential that we separate the calculation of prudence from the question of what, as a good citizen, he may properly do. We are investigating how society ought to treat him when its courts believe that he judged wrong; therefore we must ask what he is justified in doing when his judgment differs from others. We beg the question if we assume that what he may properly do depends on his guess as to how society will treat him.

We must also reject the second model, that if the law is unclear a citizen may properly follow his own judgment until the highest court has ruled that he is wrong. This fails to take into account the fact that any court, including the Supreme Court, may overrule itself. In 1940 the Court decided that a West Virginia law requiring students to salute the Flag was constitutional. In 1943 it reversed itself, and decided that such a statute was unconstitutional after all. What was the duty as citizens, of those people who in 1941 and 1942 objected to saluting the Flag on grounds of conscience, and thought that the Court's 1940 decision was wrong? We can hardly say that their duty was to follow the first decision. They believed that saluting the Flag was unconscionable, and they believed, reasonably, that no valid law required them to do so. The Supreme Court later decided that in this they were right. The Court did not simply hold that after the second decision failing to salute would not be a crime; it held (as in a case like this it almost always would) that it was no crime after the first decision either.

Some will say that the flag-salute dissenters should have obeyed the Court's first decision, while they worked in the legislatures to have the law repealed, and tried in the courts to find some way to challenge the law again without actually violating it. That would be, perhaps, a plausible recommendation if conscience were not involved, because it would then be arguable that the gain in orderly procedure was worth the personal sacrifices of patience. But conscience was involved, and if the dissenters had obeyed the law while biding their time, they would have suffered the irreparable injury of having done what their conscience forbade them to do. It is one thing to say that an individual must sometimes violate his conscience when he knows that the law commands him to do it. It is quite another to say that he must violate his conscience even when he reasonably believes that the law does not require it, because it would inconvenience his fellow citizens if he took the most direct, and perhaps the only, method of attempting to show that he is right and they are wrong.

Since a court may overrule itself, the same reasons we listed for rejecting the first model count against the second as well. If we did not have the pressure of dissent, we would not have a dramatic statement of the degree to which a court decision against the dissenter is felt to be wrong, a demonstration that is surely pertinent to the question of whether it was right. We would increase the chance of being governed by rules that offend the principles we claim to serve.

These considerations force us, I think, from the second model, but some will want to substitute a variation of it. They will argue that once the Supreme Court has decided that a criminal law is valid, then citizens have a duty to abide by that decision until they have a reasonable belief, not merely that the decision is a bad law, but that the Supreme Court is likely to overrule it. Under this view the West Virginia dissenters who refused to salute the Flag in 1942 were acting properly, because they might reasonably have anticipated that the Court would change its mind. But once the Court held laws like the draft laws constitutional, it would be improper to continue to challenge these laws, because there would be no great likelihood that the Court would soon change its mind. This suggestion must also be rejected, however. For once we say that a citizen may properly follow his own judgment of the law, in spite of his judgment that the courts will probably find against him, there is no plausible reason why he should act differently because a contrary decision is already on the books.

Thus the third model, or something close to it, seems to be the fairest statement of a man's social duty in our community. A citizen's allegiance is to the law, not to any particular person's view of what the law is, and he does not behave unfairly so long as he proceeds on his own considered and reasonable view of what the law requires. Let me repeat (because it is crucial) that this is not the same as saying that an individual may disregard what the courts have said. The doctrine of precedent lies near the core of our legal system, and no one can make a reasonable effort to follow the law unless he grants the courts the general power to alter it by their decisions. But if the issue is one touching fundamental personal or political rights, and it is arguable that the Supreme Court has made a mistake, a man is within his social rights in refusing to accept that decision as conclusive.

One large question remains before we can apply these observations to the problems of draft resistance. I have been talking about the case of a man who believes that the law is not what other people think, or what the courts have held. This description may fit some of those who disobey the draft laws out of conscience, but it does not fit most of them. Most of the dissenters are not lawyers or political philosophers; they believe that the laws on the books are immoral, and inconsistent with their country's legal ideals, but they have not considered the question of whether they may be invalid as well. Of what relevance to their situation, then, is the proposition that one may properly follow one's own view of the law?

To answer this, I shall have to return to the point I made earlier. The Constitution, through the due process clause, the equal protection clause, the First Amendment, and the other provisions I mentioned, injects an extraordinary amount of our political morality into the issue of whether a law is valid. The statement that most draft dissenters are unaware that the law is invalid therefore needs qualification. They hold beliefs that, if true, strongly support the view that the law is on their side; the acts that they have not reached that further conclusion can be traced, in at least most cases, to their lack of legal sophistication. If we believe that when the law is doubtful people who follow their own judgment of the law may be acting properly, it would seem wrong not to extend that view to those dissenters whose judgment come to the same thing. No part of the case that I made for the third model would entitle us to distinguish them from their more knowledgeable colleagues.

We can draw several tentative conclusions from the argument so far: When the law is uncertain, in the sense that a plausible case can be made on both sides, then a citizen who follows his own judgment is not behaving unfairly. Our practices permit and encourage him to follow his own judgment in such cases. For that reason, our government has a special responsibility to try to protect him, and soften his predicament, whenever it can do so without great damage to other policies. It does not follow that the government can guarantee him immunity—it cannot adopt the rule that it will prosecute no one who acts out of conscience, or convict no one who reasonably disagrees with the courts. That would paralyze the government's ability to carry out its policies; it would, moreover, throw away the most important benefit of following the third model. If the state never prosecuted, then the courts could not act on the experience and the arguments the dissent has generated. But it does follow that when the practical reasons for prosecuting are relatively weak in a particular case, or can be met in other ways, the path of fairness lies in tolerance.

The popular view that the law is the law and must always be enforced refuses to distinguish the man who acts on his own judgment of a doubtful law, and thus behaves as our practices provide, from the common criminal. I know of no reason, short of moral blindness, for not drawing a distinction in principle between the two cases.

I anticipate a philosophical objection to these conclusions: that I am treating law as 'brooding omnipresence in the sky'. I have spoken of people making judgments about what the law requires, even in cases in which the law is unclear and indemonstrable. I have spoken of cases in which a man might think that the law requires one thing, even though the Supreme Court has said that it requires another, and even when it was not likely that the Supreme Court would soon change its mind. I will therefore be charged with the view that there is always a 'right answer' to a legal problem to be found in natural law or locked up in some transcendental strongbox.

The strongbox theory of law is, of course, nonsense. When I say that people hold views on the law when the law is doubtful, and that these views are not merely predictions of what the courts will hold, I intend no such metaphysics. I mean only to summarize as accurately as I can many of the practices that are part of our legal process.

Lawyers and judges make statements of legal rights and duty, even when they know there are not demonstrable, and support them with arguments even when they know that these arguments will not appeal to everyone. They make these arguments to one another, in the professional journals, in the classrooms, and in the courts. They respond to these arguments, when others make them, by judging them good or bad or mediocre. In so doing they assume that some arguments for a given doubtful position are better than others. They also assume that the case on one side of a doubtful proposition may be stronger than the case on the other, which is what I take a claim of law in a doubtful case to mean. They distinguish, without too much difficulty, these arguments from predictions of what the courts will decide.

These practices are poorly represented by the theory that judgments or laws on doubtful issues are nonsense, or are merely predictions of what the courts will do. Those who hold such theories cannot deny the fact of these practices; perhaps these theorists mean that the practices are not sensible, because they are based on suppositions that do not hold, or for some other reason. But this makes their objection mysterious, because they never specify what they take the purposes underlying these practices to be; and unless these goals are specified, one cannot decide whether the practices are sensible. I understand these underlying purposes to be those I described earlier: the development and testing of the law through experimentation by citizens and through the adversary process.

Our legal system pursues these goals by inviting citizens to decide the strengths and weaknesses of legal arguments for themselves, or through their own counsel, and to act on these judgments, although that permission is qualified by the limited threat that they may suffer if the courts do not agree. Success in this strategy depends on whether there is sufficient agreement within the community on what counts as good or bad argument, so that, although different people will reach different judgments, these differences will be neither so profound nor so frequent as to make the system unworkable, or dangerous for those who act by their own lights. I believe there is sufficient agreement on the criteria of the argument to avoid these traps, although one of the main tasks of legal philosophy is to exhibit and clarify these criteria. In any event, the practices I have described have not yet been shown to be misguided; they therefore must count in determining whether it is just and fair to be lenient to those who break what others think is the law.

* * *

Some lawyers will be shocked by my general conclusion that we have a responsibility toward those who disobey the draft laws out of conscience, and that we may be required not to prosecute them, but rather to change our laws or adjust our sentencing procedures to accommodate them. The simple Draconian propositions, that crime must be punished, and that he who misjudges the law must take the consequences, have an extraordinary hold on the professional as well as the popular imagination. But the rule of law is more complex and more intelligent than that and it is important that it survive.

QUESTIONS

1.   Do you agree with Dean Erwin Griswold that "[it] is of the essence of law that it is equally applied to all, that it binds all alike, irrespective of personal motive?" *Materials, supra* at 6F. Suppose a distraught husband or wife aids in a "mercy killing" of a suffering, terminally ill spouse, and most certainly would never kill again? *See Repouille v. U.S.*, 165 F.2d 152 (2d Cir. 1947). Or suppose the motive for a burglary is not pecuniary gain, but to steal dangerous nuclear secrets for reasons of patriotism? Suppose that an anti-abortion activist murders a doctor to "save the lives of hundreds of children?" Should the prosecutions in all these cases be equally vigorous? Should the penalties be more or less severe, and why?

2.   Do you agree with Dworkin that those who disobey laws out of conscience should sometimes get special treatment? How exactly would you define the difference between such a person and a "common criminal?" Are "common criminals" necessarily more dangerous?

3.   Should Dworkin's principles also apply to cases of professional discipline against lawyers, or is that a very different matter?

JUDITH A. McMORROW, CIVIL DISOBEDIENCE AND THE LAWYER'S OBLIGATION TO THE LAW
48 WASHINGTON AND LEE LAW REVIEW 139, 139–141, 151–155, 161–162 (1991)

Lawyers work with, under, for, and around the law as their professional livelihood. Lawyers are called "officers of the court," "officers of the law," and "ministers," and swear allegiance to support and defend the Constitution of the United States.[51] Even the title "lawyer" reinforces the relationship between the

---

[51]   C. WOLFRAM, MODERN LEGAL ETHICS § 1.6 (1986) (discussing officers of the court), § 13.2.1 (discussing officers of the law), and § 15.3 (discussing oath of office); ABA CANONS OF PROFESSIONAL ETHICS Canon 32 (1908) ("[n]o client, corporate or individual, however powerful, nor any cause, civil or political, however

person and the law. The very nature of law binds the lawyer to the content of law because, as every lawyer knows, the law is not a series of set rules plucked from universal concepts of right and good. Rather, law is an ongoing process that reflects shifting societal views.[52] This ever changing nature of the law forces lawyers to be active participants in the shaping of law.[53] Because the lawyer plays a significant role in the shaping of law and benefits materially from and has special knowledge of the law, scholars and aspirational codes assert strongly and persuasively that the lawyer has special obligations both to uphold the law and to strive to make the law just.[54]

If indeed lawyers have two special obligations—to uphold the law and to work to assure the law is just—then we understandably are confused about whether a lawyer should engage in civil disobedience or should counsel clients to engage in civil disobedience.[55] Civil disobedience is the public and nonviolent violation of law for which the actor accepts punishment willingly.[56] Civil disobedience is a commonly accepted method of attempting to make the law more just. If the

---

important, is entitled to receive nor should any lawyer render any service or advice involving disloyalty to the law whose ministers we are . . .”). States generally require an oath of office. *See, e.g.*, VA. CODE ANN. § 54.1-3903 (1988) (“[b]efore an attorney may practice in any court in the Commonwealth, he shall take the oath of fidelity to the Commonwealth, stating that he will honestly demean himself in the practice of law and execute his office of attorney-at-law to the best of his ability”). *See generally* Gaetke, *Lawyers as Officers of the Court*, 42 VAND. L. REV. 39 (1989) (arguing that phrase “officer of the court” is “vacuous and unduly self-laudatory” and that lawyers should “either stop using the officer of the court characterization or give meaning to it”).

[52] Consequently, the law is constantly at tension with itself as society attempts to find the appropriate balance between tradition (heritage) and change (heresy). *See* Brion, *An Essay of LULU, NIMBY, and the Problem of Distributive Justice*, 15 B.C. ENVTL. AFF. L. REV. 437, 439 (1988).

[53] This phrasing is the product of Claire Horisk, Oxford University exchange student at Washington & Lee University. *See also* Phelps, *No Place to Go, No Story to Tell: The Missing Narratives of the Sanctuary Movement*, 48 WASH. & LEE L. REV. 123 (1991); Wilkins, *Legal Realism for Lawyers*, 104 HARV. L. REV. 468, 477 (1990) (“lawyers have more practical power than judges to manipulate the legal terrain”).

[54] *See, e.g.*, Gibson, *Civil Disobedience and the Legal Profession*, 31 SASKATCHEWAN BAR REV. 211, 219 (1966) (“[t]hat a person is a lawyer imposes on him an obligation to uphold the authority and dignity of the law, but it also involves a duty to ensure that the law remains just and adequate”); MODEL CODE OF PROFESSIONAL RESPONSIBILITY Canon 8 (1981) [hereinafter MODEL CODE] (“[a] Lawyer Should Assist in Improving the Legal System”) and MODEL CODE EC 8-2 (“[i]f a lawyer believes that the existence or absence of a rule of law, substantive or procedural, causes or contributes to an unjust result, he should endeavor by lawful means to obtain appropriate change in the law”); MODEL RULES OF PROFESSIONAL CONDUCT 6.1 (1983) [hereinafter MODEL RULES] (“[a] lawyer is a representative of clients, an officer of the legal system and a public citizen having special responsibility for the quality of justice”).

[55] This article discusses the lawyer as counselor and does not address directly other roles that a lawyer might play, such as lawyer as judge, legislator, or law-enforcement officer. The conclusions drawn in this article, however, obviously would affect the lawyer's role in these other circumstances.

[56] Civil disobedience writers have multiple definitions of civil disobedience. Indeed, authors in this symposium reflect various shades of meaning when they discuss civil disobedience. *See e.g.*, Phelps, *supra* note 68, at 127 n. 17 and accompanying text. In this article I use civil disobedience to mean the public, nonviolent breaking of the law and the willing acceptance of the punishment. *Cf.* J. Rawls, A Theory of Justice 364 (1971) (stating civil disobedience is “a public, nonviolent, conscientious yet political act contrary to law usually done with the aim of bringing about a change in the law or policies of the government”). Philosopher John Rawls distinguishes between civil disobedience and conscientious refusal. He defines conscientious refusal as “noncompliance with a more or less direct legal injunction of administrative order.” *Id.* at 368.

lawyer's primary obligation is to uphold the law, then the lawyer's ability to engage in civil disobedience or counsel clients to do so might be reduced.[57]

The purpose of this essay is to propose and justify a theory of the proper role of the lawyer faced with issues involving civil disobedience. I begin with an initial assumption that in certain circumstances an individual, including a lawyer as an individual, may feel morally compelled to engage in acts of civil disobedience.[58] The authors in this symposium have debated the scope and extent of the use of civil disobedience, but no author has asserted that civil disobedience is *never* appropriate.[59] If one believes civil disobedience is wrong for *everyone*, then it is wrong for the lawyer, and the question of the lawyer's responsibility is easy.

*   *   *

Professional Regulation and Civil Disobedience

How should the obligation to obey the law affect how lawyers regulate themselves? Because only licensed attorneys may practice law, state bars control who may be admitted to practice and what justifies expulsion from the practice.[60] All jurisdictions have adopted a code or standard of ethics. The two dominant models, the ABA Model Code of Professional Responsibility [Model Code] and the ABA Model Rules of Professional Conduct [Model Rules], provide two ways to address the question of the lawyer's relationship to the law.[61] Both models contain broad ambiguities. Those ambiguities, however, are both tolerable and appropriate.[62]

---

[57] Throughout this introduction the word "law" is used in its "generic sense" to refer to the "rules of action or conduct duly prescribed by controlling authority, and having binding legal force." United States Fidelity & Guar. Co. v. Guenther, 281 U.S. 34 (1930).

[58] The assumption that civil disobedience is sometimes at least morally correct necessarily includes the recognition that law and morality do not overlap completely. This is hardly a startling conclusion. *See* Hart, *Positivism and the Separation of Law and Morals*, 71 Harv. L. Rev. 593 (1958).

[59] Nazi Germany provided us with a recent horrifying example of why positive law should not be blindly followed in all circumstances. I find it personally troubling that the Nazi regime assumed control of the German legal system with relative ease. Exploring whether this takeover was made easier by the nature of lawyers is, unfortunately, a topic too far afield to discuss here.

[60] *See generally* C. Wolfram, *supra* note 66, at § 2.1-.7.

[61] The Model Code and Model Rules were drafted by the American Bar Association. Like a uniform law, they have no force until adopted, with whatever amendments might be made, by the individual jurisdiction. *See generally* C. Wolfram, *supra*, note 66, at § 2.6.

[62] Every jurisdiction requires that a lawyer meet some criteria of "character." Rhode, *Moral Character* as a Professional Credential, 94 Yale L. J. 491, 493 (1985). Most jurisdictions generally list some relevant characteristics, usually focusing on "qualities that demonstrate a lack of good moral character." Brennan, *Defining Moral Character and Fitness*, 58 The Bar Examiner 24 (1989). The list of qualities, both positive and negative, varies with the jurisdiction. "Criminal conviction is by far the most commonly reported reason for denying admission, but very few, if any, offenses are so disabling that a person will be excluded from the bar in every state because of the offense." C. Wolfram, *supra* note 66, at § 15.3.2. The few opinions to deal with the issue have concluded that not every intentional violation of law shows lack of fitness to practice law. *See* Hallinan v. Committee of Bar Examiners of State Bar, 55 Cal. Rptr. 228, 237, 421 P.2d 76, 85 (1966). Although bar admission information often is confidential, one study indicated that only about 50 bar applicants a year are denied admission to practice on character grounds. Rhode, *supra*, at 516. Denying admission requires a prediction, which we tend to be hesitant

The Model Code prohibits a lawyer from engaging in "illegal conduct involving moral turpitude" or engaging in "conduct prejudicial to the administration of justice."[63] The ABA formal pronouncements under the Model Code reject any distinction between professional and personal conduct, stating that a lawyer must comply with applicable rules at all times whether or not the lawyer is acting in a professional capacity.[64] In contrast, the Model Rules state that it is professional misconduct for a lawyer to "commit a criminal act that reflects adversely on the lawyer's honesty, trustworthiness or fitness as a lawyer in other respects" or to "engage in conduct that is prejudicial to the administration of justice."[65] This language reflects a conscious policy in the Model Rules to cover only offenses that "indicate lack of those characteristics relevant to law practice."[66] Although both statements are sufficiently vague to allow for a variety of interpretations, the Model Rules seem to narrow the range of possible illegal conduct that would affect a lawyer's professional status.

Which vision, the full or part-time lawyer, is correct? Is an individual a lawyer, and therefore charged with upholding the integrity of the rule of law, only when doing lawyer-like things? Or, like a priest or a parent, do lawyers hold their role all the time?

As a practical matter one cannot draw sharp lines between the lawyer and personal self.[67] Lawyers struggle constantly with the question of how to reconcile personal beliefs with their role in the legal system.[68] One cannot humanly shed all personal perspectives when acting as a lawyer, even when one might have a responsibility to minimize them.[69] Certainly some acts performed in the privacy of one's home and late in the evening might spill over to one's role as a lawyer. For example, most would question the fitness of a lawyer to practice law if that lawyer

---

to make, so that the concept of good moral character in practice "quickly becomes meaningless, conceptual, and highly individualized." C. WOLFRAM, *supra* note at 66, at § 15.3.2; *see also* Rhode, *supra*; *cf.* Sciortino, *A Rite of Passage*, 68 THE BAR EXAMINER 14, 15 (1989) (stating that it is "difficult to validate theory of the lineage" between past behavior and future conduct; but that "it may be prudent for bar examiners to act as if the hypothesis has not been disprove[d]"). Admission to the bar, then, gives us few insights into what role breaking the law should play in professional discipline. Decisions whether to discipline a practicing lawyer provide a better vehicle for discussion.

[63] MODEL CODE DR 1 102(A)(3) & (A)(5).

[64] ABA Comm. On Ethics and Professional Responsibility, Formal Op. 336 (1974) (stating that lawyer should not engage in conduct that tends to lessen public confidence in legal profession).

[65] MODEL RULES Rule 8.4 (b), (d). The preamble to the MODEL RULES, which is aspirational rather than directive, states that "[a] lawyer's conduct should conform to the requirements of the law, both in professional service to the clients and in the lawyer's business and personal affairs." MODEL RULES, preamble.

[66] MODEL RULES Rule 8.4 comment 1 (stating that "[al]though a lawyer is personally answerable to the entire criminal law, a lawyer should be professionally answerable only for offenses that indicate lack of those characteristics relevant to law practice").

[67] Trying to sharply distinguish between the lawyer and person is like trying to make sharp, clear distinctions between public and private law. *See generally A Symposium: The Public/Private Distinction*, 130 U. PA. L. REV. 1289 (1982).

[68] *See, e.g.*, Calhoun, *Conviction Without Imposition: A Response to Professor Greenawalt*, 9 J.L. & RELIGION (1991) (forthcoming); Levinson, *supra* note 12.

[69] *See infra* notes 74–88 and accompanying text.

had sought to embezzle funds, even if the embezzlement concerned strictly personal business dealings. That act shows a defiance of the basic rules of how to allocate rights and responsibilities in our society.

We can envision other contexts in which there is no clearly identifiable person whose rights have been violated, but rather the amorphous concept of the public interest. When Washington, D.C. Mayor Marion Barry was sentenced to six months in prison for a first-time misdemeanor drug offense, some found the sentence, as "compared to other sentences of people equally situated, to be surprisingly harsh."[70] The judge candidly stated that "[o]f greatest significance to me in sentencing this defendant is the high public office he has at all relevant times occupied . . . [B]ecause of the defendant's unique position, he's not an ordinary misdemeanant."[71] As Mayor, Marion Barry had a special duty to obey the law and that duty extended even into "private" time.

Consequently, a lawyer does not avoid the problem of special responsibility simply by asserting publicly that the act of civil disobedience is being done as a citizen, not a lawyer. Nonetheless, this does not mean that the formal bar mechanism should sanction all attorneys who engage in civil disobedience. The bar as a regulator of conduct suffers from serious limitations. The lawyer's system of self-regulation struggles under mixed motives—or at least a strong perception of mixed motives. One reason lawyers work to develop codes is altruistic: they seek to develop standards to educate both lawyers and the public, to reinforce notions of right and wrong, and to provide a method of deterring misconduct.[72] Those with a more jaundiced view see the system of self-regulation as motivated by economic and class self-interest.[73]

Even assuming that the altruistic goals dominate, the codes evidence the struggle to identify which altruistic goal should dominate. Should the codes serve primarily to educate lawyers, reinforce their notions of right and wrong, or deter the most harmful conduct? The codes have evolved from the 1908 "Canons of Professional Ethics," which were largely aspirational, to the 1969 "Model Code of Professional Responsibility," which contained a blend of aspirational and directive statements, to the 1983 "Model Rules of Professional Conduct," which contain only a limited number of aspirations' statements. This evolution from "ethics" to "responsibility" to "rules of conduct" indicates that the bars have functionally—and

---

[70] Gellman, *Barry's 'High Public Office' Led Judge to Stronger Sentence*, WASH. POST, Oct. 27, 1990, at A14, col. 1.

[71] *Id.*

[72] See C. WOLFRAM, *supra* note 66, at § 2.6.1 (explaining possible reasons why group might agree on code of member conduct); Schwartz, *The Professionalism and Accountability of Lawyers*, 66 CALIF. L. REV. 669, 682 (1978) (stating three limitations on enforcing professional standards that restrict lawyers from counseling civil disobedients).

[73] See C. WOLFRAM, *supra* note 66, at § 2.6.1 (explaining possible motivation of professional code drafters); Abel, *Why Does the ABA Promulgate Ethical Rules?*, 59 TEX. L. REV. 639 (1981); DiSalvo, *The Fracture of Good Order: An Argument for Allowing Lawyers To Counsel the Civilly Disobedient*, 17 GA. L. REV 109, 135 (1982) (stating that elite of bar often undertake actions to punish lawyers who exercise their rights to challenge authority); Rhode, *Why the ABA Bothers: A Functional Perspective on Professional Codes*, 59 TEX. L. REV. 689 (1981) (discussing concerns of codification and wisdom of placing codification under bar control).

perhaps properly—recognized the inherent limits of trying to use aspirational goals rather than concrete standards. These self-developed standards, which require group approval and, consequently, a certain measure of consensus, inevitably focus on the lowest common denominator.[74]

Even assuming that lawyers would all agree that they should exercise special caution before engaging in civil disobedience, lawyers inevitably will disagree about what constitutes special caution. The resolution of that issue is grounded in how much one believes our legal system deviates from the norm of perfect justice, how much one weighs the harm caused by the injustice, and other variables not subject to even quasi-objective proof. As a system based on consensus, lawyer regulation is particularly ill-suited to be a directive basis for setting standards of caution.[75]

Lawyer self-regulation can pick up the most egregious cases of repeated defiant acts, and the current standards are sufficient to capture those instances. For example, one state bar committee suggested that a single act of civil disobedience did not call into question an attorney's fitness to practice law, but concluded "that frequent and/or continual misdemeanor convictions of this nature may result in more serious professional consequences."[76]

The standard of special caution, then, is one that each lawyer should assume individually. The law is not well suited to command all aspects of moral behavior.[77] Given that law and morality do not always dictate the same behavior and given the possible existence of unjust laws within a valid legal system, individual lawyers must define some standards for themselves.

Counseling the Client: A Working
Concept of Lawyer

Even when lawyers are not breaking the law themselves, they are likely to- have some relationship with nonlawyers who engage in civil disobedience. Many acts of civil disobedience are part of a broad-based attack on an unjust law or situation. The "war" against the injustice will have many fronts, both legal and illegal. For example, the civil rights movement proceeded not only through lawsuits and political action, but also through acts of civil disobedience used to highlight and reinforce the judicial and legislative fronts.[78] Lawyers obviously will be integrally

---

[74] C. WOLFRAM, *supra* note 66, at § 2.6.1 (stating that professional code by necessity can regulate only a narrow range between marginally enforceable rules and insubstantial rules).

[75] *Id.* (stating that once a number of lawyers defy a code rule, other lawyers will ignore the rule based on competitive pressures and sense of unfairness); Luban, *Calming the Hearse Horse: A Philosophical Research Program for Legal Ethics*, 40 MD. L. REV. 451, 460–61 (1981) (ethics and regulation do not coincide). Any issues in which deeply felt views of what is right or wrong arise are inevitably inappropriate for self-regulation. C. WOLFRAM, *supra* note 1 at § 2.6.1. If a critical mass of lawyers disagree with whether the lawyer is disqualified from practicing law because of engaging in civil disobedience, then they will act to keep the bars from either expressly or impliedly developing that standard. *Id.* If a critical mass of lawyers disagree with a standard, the rule will probably be ignored. *Id.*

[76] *Virginia Legal Ethics Opinion No. 1185*, Virginia Lawyer Register, October 1989, at 14, col. 1.

[77] *See St. T. Aquinas*, *supra* note 38, at 95 (stating that human law does not bind man in conscience).

[78] *See* Whitehead, *Civil Disobedience and Operation Rescue: A Historical and Theoretical Analysis* 48 WASH. & LEE L. REV. 77 (1991) (stating that civil disobedience activities provided unity and focus to

involved in judicial and legislative battles. (As argued above, that is also where the lawyer's energies ought to be directed.) Many individuals contemplating civil disobedience may turn for legal advice to the same lawyers who are pursuing the social goal through traditional means. Even when a person anticipating civil disobedience is not part of a larger social movement, the individual contemplating a known violation of the law likely will seek the advice and counsel of an attorney, if only to arrange to have counsel available after arrest.

*　　*　　*

The reality of counseling and the duty to respect the client's autonomy shape the nature of any counseling. Civil disobedience is a serious, personal choice because the client will suffer negative legal consequences from engaging in civil disobedience. The lawyer cannot tell the client how to make that serious personal choice. Consequently, the lawyer can never "advise" the client to engage in civil disobedience. The lawyer can, however, affirm the client's decision by stating that in light of the client's goals, civil disobedience indeed may be the only way to achieve those goals. Because of the complex conversation that lawyer and client will have, persuading a client to engage in civil disobedience against the client's inclinations is unlikely to happen.

The more troublesome counseling question is whether the lawyer may or must raise the possibility of civil disobedience. Perhaps the client's goals would justify civil disobedience as one possible alternative. Political reality confirms that in some situations civil disobedience has been extremely effective.[79] If one goal of counseling is to allow the client to come to morally correct decisions, then it is not wrong to give the client information about the possibility of civil disobedience.[80]

Despite the lawyer's duty to provide information to the client, it is troubling to consider that information provided by the lawyer may instill the idea of civil disobedience in the client's mind.[81] This question is similar to the question whether juries should be told that they have the power to ignore the law.[82] Only a handful of jurisdictions inform the jury that it has the power to disregard the law. The rest balance the precarious tension between the rule of the law and positive law by not expressly telling the jury of its potential power. Presumably if the law is sufficiently unjust, then the jury's innate desire to do the right thing will give rise to the recognition that perhaps they should decline to apply the law.

Whatever the parallels between jury nullification and civil disobedience, civil disobedience has an additional significant factor. With jury nullification the jury is the representative of the state. The jury is meting out the punishment. With civil disobedience the individual actor is breaking the law of the state and will be the

---

civil rights movement and educated those not witnessing movement first hand).

[79] *See supra* note 78 [Editor's note: Citation is to original text] and accompanying text.

[80] *See* MODEL RULES Rule 1.2(d) comment (implying that what client does with raw information is not lawyer's responsibility).

[81] Drinan, *Changing Role of the Lawyer in an Era of Non-Violent Action*, 1 LAW IN TRANSITION Q. 123, 125–26 (1964) (stating that lawyer may not only be justified, but also morally compelled to advise clients to disobey laws they regard as offensive).

[82] *See supra* note 91 and accompanying text (discussing jury nullification).

recipient of any punishment. This personalizes the question to an even greater extent. It involves the individual's most fundamental beliefs about the relationship between the individual and the state. The lawyer has a delicate role to play because the lawyer's superior position of power may unduly influence the client. Even telling the client about the option of civil disobedience implies that engaging in disobedience is a co-equal option with all others. That it is generated from the lawyer might give civil disobedience an additional imprimatur, despite disclaimers.

Affirmatively telling the client about the option of civil disobedience also reaches to the heart of the lawyer's relationship to the law. *Requiring* a lawyer to raise the possibility of civil disobedience would be like compelling a doctor who personally is opposed to abortion to tell a patient about the possibility of an illegal late-term abortion. It may be an option. It may be the right thing to do in the eyes of many. But it nonetheless reaches very deeply into the personal belief structure of the doctor (that late-term abortion is wrong) which has been affirmed by the state (that late-term abortion is illegal). Once the state has affirmed a well-considered value judgment (e.g., one should obey the law), than I see no moral basis to compel the lawyer to raise the question of civil disobedience.

At the same time, the complex conversation that occurs between lawyer and client makes me hesitate to say that a lawyer should *never* raise the possibility of civil disobedience. Recognizing the potential for unduly influencing the client, recognizing the inherently personal nature of the decision, and recognizing the importance of the idea of the rule of law, the lawyer certainly should reflect very carefully before ever independently raising the topic with the client. But if the client appears to be strongly committed to seeking all available means to remedy the injustice, the lawyer may properly raise civil disobedience as one social response to the injustice. (These instances in which civil disobedience has not already occurred to the client will obviously be rare.) Although this solution will not satisfy those who wish clear lines and firm guidance, we have all lived long enough to know that sometimes nice, tidy lines are not available.

Conclusion

As essential agents of our legal system, lawyers have a special obligation to exercise special caution before engaging in civil disobedience. Because of the limitation of the concept of self-regulation, this standard appropriately is not incorporated in to narrow "rules" of conduct, but should be part of the individual lawyer's consideration when evaluating an unjust law.

When counseling a client the primary focus is no longer on the lawyer and his or her special relationship with the law. Rather, the primary focus is on assisting the client to make a fully informed decision. The lawyer cannot "tell" a client to engage in civil disobedience because that is a uniquely personal decision and because to do so would violate the lawyer's duty to respect the decision-making authority of the client. To evaluate the legal consequences of engaging in civil disobedience, however, the lawyer will likely have to engage in a wide-ranging discussion about the necessity defense and jury nullification—both of which are "legal" ways of curing "illegality." Because of the reality of the complex conversation, placing any practical limitations on the lawyer as counselor is inherently problematic. We can only urge the lawyer to respect the idea of the rule of law, to respect the inherently personal nature of the decision for the client, and to respect the client's autonomy.

QUESTIONS

1.   Professor McMorrow found it, "personally troubling that the Nazi regime assumed control of the German legal system with relative ease." *Materials, supra* at 6F. Assuming that this was the case, would the problem be, as Professor McMorrow suggests, "the nature of lawyers?" Or would it be the prevailing jurisprudence? As to the actual record, there is much controversy. *See* MAX WEINREICH, HITLER'S PROFESSORS (2d ed. 1999); KONRAD JARAUSCH, THE UNFREE PROFESSIONS (1990).

2.   McMorrow observes that "[a]s essential agents of our legal system, lawyers have a special obligation to exercise special caution before engaging in civil disobedience?" Do you agree? In the end, why should a lawyer's loyalty to the positive law be greater than any other citizen? She continues: "Because of the limitations of the concept of self-regulation, this standard appropriately is not incorporated in to narrow 'rules' of conduct, but should be part of the individual lawyer's consideration when evaluating an unjust law." *Materials, supra* at 6F. If a lawyer's obligation not to participate in civil disobedience is greater than an "ordinary" citizen's, why should the standard be left up to "the individual lawyer's consideration," rather than enforced by professional rule?

3.   McMorrow argues that "[r] *equiring* a lawyer to raise the possibility of civil disobedience would be like compelling a doctor who personally is opposed to abortion to tell a patient about the possibility of an illegal late-term abortion." *Materials, supra* at 6F. What do you think of this analogy?

4.   Why should a lawyer *ever* counsel clients to engage in civil disobedience?

5.   McMorrow observes: "One cannot humanly shed all personal perspectives while acting as a lawyer, even when one might have a responsibility to minimize them." *Materials, supra* at 6F. *See also* ABA Model Rule 2.1. Is it *ever* appropriate to "minimize" your "personal perspectives while acting as a lawyer?" Why or why not?

Chapter VII

THE VALUE OF ALLEGIANCE AND DUTY FOR DUTY'S SAKE

A. THE LESSONS OF THE CRITO

Socrates' trial had been carefully timed by his accusers. On the prior day, the annual Athenian Mission to Delos had been launched, and the State Galley had "been crowned" for the trip.[1] While this ceremonial ship was absent, by custom, no death penalty could be inflicted. The trip usually took a month.

It is obvious that Socrates' enemies knew that his execution would be delayed for weeks after conviction. Why did they choose this time? Because they knew that Socrates' influential and, in certain cases, wealthy friends could arrange for his escape. It is doubtful that the likes of Anytus, Meletus, or Lycon wanted to create a martyr. Suppose Socrates were convicted, and then conveniently "disappeared," only to appear later abroad living in comfort with his wife and family. If he were "roistering in Thessaly" as Socrates put it, his accusers would be vindicated in principle, without any backlash of resentment for cruelty or injustice. Indeed, it is quite possible that Socrates' accusers, when they asked for the death penalty, had no real intention that Socrates suffer such a fate. First, they doubtless hoped he would offer a "reasonable" penalty upon conviction, and that the jury would accept it. Socrates' wealthy friends could have offered a large fine. Instead, Socrates initially offered "free maintenance [for himself] at the State's expense," doubtless a surprise. Finally, Socrates' friends clearly had the political and financial power to arrange his escape, and his accusers carefully gave them the opportunity. In fact, it turns out that Socrates' old, loyal friend Crito had made all the arrangements, including a warm welcome in Thessaly with complete protection.

We know from the *Apology* that Socrates believed he was wrongly convicted. Why, then, did he deliberately choose to be executed, loyal to the "Laws and Constitution of Athens"? The message of the *Crito*, that personal allegiance to the laws must supersede all individual provocation and necessity, remains one of the most powerful assertions of loyalty ever made. Remember, Socrates was married to Xanthippe, and had young children. She had attended him on his last day, "with the little boy on her knee," but Crito's servants took her home, at Socrates' request. She was "crying hysterically."[2] There was nothing automatic or easy about Socrates' choice. In the end, he obeyed the law to the last degree, not because of fear of a "sanction" (his escape was easy), nor because he believed the outcome was just or

---

[1] See the explanation by Phaedo to Echecrates at the beginning of Plato's dialogue the *Phaedo*, Plato, Last Days of Socrates 99–100 (H. Tredennick trans., 1969).

[2] *Materials, infra* at 7F; *see also* the *Phaedo*, Plato, Last Days of Socrates, *supra* note 1, at 102.

advantageous to himself. He also knew other innocent people, including his own loved ones, would suffer. His submission to the "Laws and Constitution of Athens" was an article of moral conviction, unto death.

In the end, it is pointless to paraphrase the reasoning and eloquence of this great essay. Read it with care. It is not a typical "Socratic" analysis, but a powerful expression of faith.[3] As Socrates said in the final line of the *Crito*, "Then let me follow the intimation of the will of God." God's will was, to Socrates, obedience to the Laws and Constitutions. It was part of the good person's duty, and, as Socrates had asserted earlier in the Apology, "nothing can harm a good man either in life or after death, and his fortunes are not a matter of indifference to the gods."[4]

Fyodor Dostoevsky (1821-1881) was familiar with Socrates' death and the *Crito*. He must have reflected on it at the moment of his own death sentence. On December 22, 1849, Dostoevsky was brought under guard to Semyonovsky Square in St. Petersburg before dawn. With him were 14 other prisoners. When they arrived at the square, they were told that they were to be executed upon direct order of the Tzar. The death sentence was read and three of the group were set against the execution post. Only then did the reprieve arrive, with the actual sentence imposed.[5]

The "actual" sentence was bad enough—prison in Siberia. Dostoevsky spent four years in a concentration camp at Omsk. There he became very ill with epilepsy. He was released at the beginning of the fifth year, on the condition that he serve six more years in the Russian army. When Dostoevsky finally returned home, after nearly 10 years, he was dreadfully ill, and had frequent violent seizures. He lived in continuous fear of the next epileptic seizure for the rest of his life.

What was Dostoevsky's offense? Only 28 years old at conviction, Dostoevsky had already established himself as a great Russian author and a philosopher. With other young intellectuals, he had been meeting secretly to discuss political affairs. They had socialist leanings, and were called the "Petrashevsky Circle." That was all.

In his great book, *Crime and Punishment*, first printed in installments in 1866, Dostoevsky examined closely issues of legal order, human freedom, and moral obedience to the law. Surprisingly, he—an established genius—expressed great distrust of placing any individual morally "above the law." One of his most powerful statements on this subject revolved around the character Raskolnikov and a dialogue between Raskolnikov and the skeptical Razumihin. Raskolnikov argued that the truly great, the moral and political leaders of a generation, were inherently

---

[3] The typical "Socratic Method" involved a series of questions directed by Socrates at his "students" or interlocutors. Their replies usually contained contradictions or inconsistencies compared to their earlier statements. The *Ion, Euthyphro, Protagoras*, and *Gorgias* were typical examples of this mode of "instruction" by demonstrating to the student internal inconsistencies in the student's own thought. Similar teaching techniques in American law schools became known as the "Socratic Method." Notice how far the *Apology* and the *Phaedo* really are from this relatively simplistic approach. Plato's later writings, including the *Philebus* and the *Sophistes* are even more subtle.

[4] *Materials, infra* at 7F.

[5] *See Publisher's Preface, in* FYODOR DOSTOEVSKY, CRIME & PUNISHMENT (Constance Garnett trans., 1966).

free from an obligation to obey the law—and this was all in the public good.[6] This, in turn, was reflected in the philosophy of Dostoevsky's contemporary, the German Friedrich Nietzsche (1844-1900). Nietzsche, especially in his early works, believed that the highest moral good was achieved in the greatest "outreach" of the human creative genius, including music, art, and politics. This moral energy was, by its nature, highly individualistic and subjective. Napoleon, for example, reflected Nietzsche's human ideal, and later Nietzsche described this ideal as "the Roman Caesar with Christ's soul."[7] Nietzsche's superior, creative human was called the "übermensch" or the man "who transcends."[8]

Such a view of the human ideal could not have been further from that of the figure of Socrates, humbly awaiting his execution. For Dostoevsky's Raskolnikov, the rule of law was a prison for the truly creative, powerful, and innovative leader, a chain to be broken.[9] As Raskolnikov argued: "[a]ll . . . legislators and leaders of men, such as Lycurgus, Solon, Mahomet, Napoleon, and so on, were all without exception criminals, from the very fact that, making a new law, they transgressed the ancient one, handed down from their ancestors and held sacred by the people, and they did not stop at bloodshed either, if that bloodshed—often of innocent persons fighting bravely in defense of ancient law—were of use to their cause." He continued:

> It's remarkable, in fact, that the majority, indeed, of these benefactors and leaders of humanity were guilty of terrible carnage. In short, I maintain that all great men or even men a little out of the common, that is to say capable of giving some new word, must from their very nature be criminals—more or less, of course.[10]

By the end of Dostoevsky's dialogue between the skeptical Razumihin and the earnest Raskolnikov, it becomes clear that Raskolnikov regards himself as such an Übermensch, and free "to rob and murder."[11] Given Dostoevsky's cruel treatment by his own legal order, his portrayal of moral superiority to law, as symbolized by Raskolnikov, is striking. Raskolnikov emerges, not as the ultimate realization of the power of the human condition, but as an ominous danger.

---

[6] *Materials, infra* at 7F.

[7] *See* ALASDAIR MACINTYRE, A SHORT HISTORY OF ETHICS 225 (1998).

[8] *Id.* at 225. How fair it is to blame Nietzsche for the exploitation of his philosophy by Hitler and Nazism is open to debate. For one plainly prejudiced view, see BERTRAND RUSSELL, A HISTORY OF WESTERN PHILOSOPHY 760–773 (2007). Russell observed of Nietzsche in 1945, immediately following the defeat of Hitler, "I dislike Nietzsche because he likes the contemplation of pain, because he erects conceit into a duty, because the men whom he most admires are conquerors, whose glory is cleverness in causing men to die. . . . Nietzsche despises universal love; I feel it the motive power to all that I desire as regards the world. His followers have had their innings, but we may hope that it is rapidly coming to an end." *Id.* at 772–773.

[9] *See* ALASDAIR MACINTYRE, AFTER VIRTUE 109–120 (2d ed., 1984). Though Nietzsche clearly despised systematizers such as Aristotle, his views on Socrates are much more complex. *See* WALTER KAUFMAN, NIETZSCHE: PHILOSOPHER, PSYCHOLOGIST, ANTICHRIST ch. 13 (1974).

[10] *Materials, infra* at 7F.

[11] *Materials, infra* at 7F.

Although separated by nearly 2300 years, Socrates and Dostoevsky shared a strong conviction. Moral superiority does not bring with it immunity from the rule of law and, even more important, immunity from a personal allegiance to the legal order. They maintain this view despite grievous wrongs suffered by any individual. The Übermensch, representing Nietzsche's repudiation of such an allegiance, was anathema to Socrates and Dostoevsky alike. Theirs was a faith passionately articulated, and articulated by men of genius whose faith in law was no idle speculation, but honed in the face of their own execution orders.

Is there a potential inconsistency in Socrates' position? Socrates "broke" one law, according to the vote of the jurors in his trial, yet refused to break a second law by escaping punishment. The ideas in Chapter V on natural law may help you reconcile these acts. Other philosophical principles, including duty for duty's sake and right's theory, might also help us better understand the value of allegiance presented by both Socrates and Dostoevsky.

B. "DEEP THEORIES": KANT AND RAWLS

These Materials have set out some of the classic dilemmas of modern legal and ethical thought. The solutions, so far, have been limited. One option, thoroughly explored by Lon Fuller's puzzles like the "Grudge Informer" and the "Case of the Speluncean Explorers," is straight positivism, backed by a system of coercive rewards and punishments.[12] The legitimacy of such a system, at least in a democracy, is the legitimacy of the political process, no more and no less.

A second solution, represented by the writings of Saint Thomas Aquinas, is a "God-centered" natural law theory.[13] Represented today by the writings of John Finnis and others, this approach sees law and the legal order as a subset of God's will for us.[14] Nearly 770 years after Saint Thomas' birth, the "Neo-Thomism" explored in Chapter IV, remains widely influential, particularly in the Catholic Church.

But are there solutions for those who do not believe in God, or wish to convince others who do not, or wish to convince others who believe in other conceptions of God? Here we must begin to explore what Dworkin terms "deep theories"—theories that expose and define the fundamental assumptions of juristic systems.[15] Dworkin divides these into three rough categories: "goal-based" theories, "right-based" theories, and "duty-based" theories.[16]

"Goal-based" theories are easy to understand. Let us take a fundamental goal like "improving the general welfare," "preserving a democracy," or establishing a "classless society." All laws which, in net effect, promote these ends are legitimate. This beneficial effect can be tested empirically, and the laws can be enforced by positivist rewards and benefits. People subjected to such a system do not need to

---

[12] *Materials, supra* at 5E.

[13] *Materials, supra* at 4E.

[14] *See* selected writings suggested at *Materials, supra* at 4E.

[15] *Materials, infra* at 7F.

[16] *Materials, infra* at 7F.

agree about the nature of God, or the nature of virtue. The only issue for the individual is whether the nature of the goal, or the system that sets the goal, commands allegiance. And, as the *Crito* illustrates, allegiance can be seen as an independent virtue even by those who profoundly disagree with a system's philosophy, procedures, and outcomes.

But "goal-based" theories are inherently unsatisfactory for those who are concerned about both the legitimacy of goals and the means employed in pursuit of goals, and seek independent criteria to assess both these ends and the means. Here "duty-based" and "right-based" deep theories become useful. These theories share one characteristic: at some level, they cannot be tested empirically, but assume *a priori* some fundamental values.

The leading proponent of a "duty-based" *a priori* system remains Immanuel Kant (1724-1804). Kant lived his entire life near Konigsberg in Prussia. He was a quiet, academic bachelor without children, a point likely to be raised by spouses if one endlessly cites his postulates of duty and virtue. Despite his quiet life, Kant's writing was, and is, of the utmost importance.

Although personally religious, Kant believed that the fundamental tests of virtue could be demonstrated without resort to divine revelation. He also believed that such fundamental principles could be demonstrated, like mathematics, by *a priori* deductive reasoning, and not inferred inductively from experience.[17] This kind of principle he called a "categorical imperative." "The categorical is synthetic and *a priori*. Its character is deduced by Kant from the concept of law."[18] Once a categorical imperative is discovered, and Kant defined three versions, they can be used to test all laws and actions.

Kant is hard to read, even in a good translation.[19] For the purpose of these materials, we have selected a short excerpt, translated well by E. B. Ashton, and then a more extensive description of Kant's philosophy by A. C. Ewing.[20] In reading these challenging selections, note one very important point. Just as the fundamental categorical imperatives cannot be discovered by empirical means—but only by *a priori* deduction—so they cannot be tested empirically for beneficial results or outcomes. For example, being successful and happy is not a test of whether your professional career stands scrutiny under Kant's principles of duty. Kant would say that a person of great virtue who followed his categorical imperative could end up poor and disgraced. True, it is good when a virtuous person is successful and happy, and Kant makes this point, but achieving success and happiness is certainly not implicit in a duty-based system.[21] Doing your duty, as defined by Kant's principles, is an end unto itself, not a means to any other empirically verifiable good.

---

[17] *See* BERTRAND RUSSELL, A HISTORY OF WESTERN PHILOSOPHY, *supra* note 8, at 706.

[18] *Id.* at 710. The term "synthetic" means, in philosophy, linking two concepts not necessarily linked. For example, "mammal" is necessarily implied by "dog," but "stop" is not necessarily implied by "red light." The sentence "red light means stop" is a "synthetic" sentence. Our thanks to Eric Bjorgum for this definition.

[19] For suggestions of original sources, see *Materials, infra* at 7F.

[20] *Materials, infra* at 7F.

[21] *Materials, infra* at 7F.

As harsh as it may seem, such a duty-based system can be a great solace in law practice. Experienced lawyers know that adherence to professional duty, whether defined by Kantian ethics or a similar system, often is not rewarded. But, as Kant points out, there is no need for guilt if you have done your duty. Likewise, truly evil conduct is frequently rewarded in law practice, and is often safe from detection or punishment. But as Kant observed: "The violation of one's duty, even without taking into consideration the disadvantages that follow, directly affects the mind of the agent and makes him reprehensible and punishable in his own eyes."[22] There is a very real comfort in duty-based systems in times of personal failure, and a corresponding wise restraint in times of success, that has been recognized by veteran professionals.

Also included is a selection by F. H. Bradley, "My Station and Its Duties" that reveals a different approach. Bradley argues that people are "real only because [they] are social" and that "[t]he mere individual is a delusion of theory; and the attempt to realize it in practice is the starvation and mutilation of human nature, with total sterility or the production of monstrosities."[23] "Duty" derives from the role given to each of us by the society which alone makes us real. "[A] man's life with its moral duties is in the main filled up by his station in that system of wholes which the state is, and that this, partly by its laws and institutions, and still more by its spirit, gives him the life which he does live and ought to live."[24]

Bradley's ideas are quite different from Kant's. They derive from George Wilhelm Friedrich Hegel (1770-1831), who, like Kant, was a Prussian. Hegel believed that individuals are inherently less perfect than a collective of individuals in a state. He even argued that "[t]he State is the Divine Idea as it exists on earth."[25] The selection from Bradley is to illustrate this "collectivist" approach to duty, in contrast to Kant's definition by individual imperatives. Indeed, Hegel's ideas have lent themselves to misuse by goal-based systems,[26] although Hegel actually looked to deduction from universal truths as the source of his philosophy. Despite his idealization of the state, much of Hegel's jurisprudence is highly useful, particularly his analysis of property, contract, and tort law.[27]

---

[22] *Materials, infra* at 7F.

[23] *Materials, infra* at 7F.

[24] *Materials, infra* at 7F.

[25] *See* BERTRAND RUSSELL, A HISTORY OF WESTERN PHILOSOPHY, *supra* note 8, at 740, for a good, if somewhat prejudiced, summary.

[26] For Hegel, the individual "only has objectivity, truth, and morality in so far as he is a member of the State." *Id.* at 740. The State itself is "its own highest law." *Id.* at 742. Russell observes "such is Hegel's doctrine of the State—a doctrine which, if accepted, justifies every internal tyranny and every external aggression that can possibly be imagined." *Id.* at 742. This is unfair to Hegel. *See* HUNTINGTON CAIRNS, LEGAL PHILOSOPHY FROM PLATO TO HEGEL 503–550 (1949). "[Hegel's] conclusion is not quite so entirely absurd and despicable as it is sometimes represented to be. . . . Hegel can rightly be called a conservative; but insofar as he praises the state, it is because the state incarnates in fact—so he believes—certain social and moral values." ALASDAIR MACINTYRE, A SHORT HISTORY OF ETHICS, *supra* note 7, at 209. Hegel had a major influence on Marx's early philosophy. *Id.* at 210–211. *See also* LOUIS DUPRE, THE PHILOSOPHICAL FOUNDATIONS OF MARXISM (1966).

[27] *See* HUNTINGTON CAIRNS, LEGAL PHILOSOPHY FROM PLATO TO HEGEL, *supra* note 26, at 524–531.

We now move to a very different approach, "right-based" deep theories. Here the leading exponent is John Rawls, whose great book, *A Theory of Justice* (1972), is one of the most important of our time. Rawls, like Kant, can be hard to read in the original.[28] Fortunately, he has a remarkable interpreter and critic in Ronald Dworkin, another leading modern jurist. Included in these Materials is Dworkin's lucid exposition of Rawl's "right-based deep theory," plus Dworkin's own analysis, taken from his own remarkable book, *Taking Rights Seriously* (1977).[29]

In one way, "right-based" and "duty-based" deep theories are alike. Unlike "goal-based" theories, both "right-based" and "duty-based" theories "place the individual at the center, and take his decision or conduct as of fundamental importance."[30] But, as Dworkin points out, here the similarity stops.

> [T]he two types put the individual in a different light. Duty-based theories are concerned with the moral quality of his acts, because they suppose that it is wrong, without more, for an individual to fail to meet certain standards of behavior. Kant thought that it was wrong to tell a lie no matter how beneficial the consequences, not because having this practice promoted some goal, but just because it was wrong. Right-based theories are, in contrast, concerned with the independence rather than the conformity of individual action. They presuppose and protect the value of individual thought and choice. Both types of theory make use of the idea of moral rules, codes of conduct to be followed, on individual occasions, without consulting self-interest. Duty-based theories treat such codes of conduct as of the essence, whether set by society to the individual or by the individual to himself. The man at their center is the man who must conform to such a code, or be punished or corrupted if he does not. Right-based theories, however, treat codes of conduct as instrumental, perhaps necessary to protect the rights of others, but having no essential value in themselves. The man at their center is the man who benefits from others' compliance, not the man who leads the life of virtue by complying himself.[31]

As we will see, because "the man at the center" of a right-based theory is "the man who benefits from others' compliance, not the man who leads the life of virtue by complying himself," a "right-based" theory is very helpful in testing conduct toward others, and less helpful in setting affirmative individual goals for yourself.

Dworkin also explains one of the most famous features of Rawls work, the idea of the "original position."

> It imagines a group of men and women who come together to form a social contract. Thus far it resembles the imaginary congresses of the classical social contract theories. The original position differs, however, from these theories in its description of the parties. They are men and women with ordinary tastes, talents, ambitions, and convictions, but each is temporarily

---

[28] Indeed, there is even an excellent book by Robert Paul Wolff entitled UNDERSTANDING RAWLS (1977).

[29] *Materials, infra* at 7F.

[30] *Materials, infra* at 7F.

[31] *Materials, infra* at 7F.

ignorant of these features of his own personality, and must agree upon a contract before his self-awareness returns.[32]

In the popular jargon of law students, Rawls' original position is visualized as a meeting before the participants are born—the "room before the womb." The participants are thus totally ignorant of their own health, physical nature, wealth, intelligence, family, ethnic group, sex, race, skills, etc., including disadvantages and advantages of every kind.

Rawls postulates that, if these people are rational and "act only in their own self-interest," they will select two "principles of justice," put "roughly" by Dworkin:

> 1. "[T]hat every person must have the largest political liberty compatible with a like liberty for all," and;

> 2. "[T]hat inequalities in power, wealth, income, and other resources must not exist except in so far as they work to the absolute benefit of the worst off members of society."[33]

It is a source of great amusement to test these principles in class, although this group can only pretend to be disinterested. As Dworkin notes, some will always argue that Rawls two principles are too conservative; even human beings utterly ignorant of their place in life might be willing to gamble more.[34] But Dworkin's analysis of Rawls contains far more profound insights, and is worth careful study as an excellent evaluation of a leading "right-based deep theory." Consider also the questions following the sections on both Kant and Rawls. Which "deep theory" most comfortably supports the system of professional regulation represented by the ABA Code and Model Rules we have discussed so much? Which provides the most guidance for professional conduct? What difference does it make?

C. THE ETERNAL PROBLEMS OF "DIRTY HANDS" AND "BILLY BUDD"

Now that we have at least a couple of well-known secular "deep theories" to assist us, we can return to our old friend of Chapter I, Niccolò Machiavelli, and two more classic problems: the problem of "Dirty Hands" and that of "Billy Budd." Of all ethical problems in law practice, these are the most commonly encountered.

The problem of "Dirty Hands" was articulated clearly by Machiavelli (1469-1527) in *The Prince* (1513), nearly five centuries ago.

> It remains now to be seen what are the methods and rules for a prince as regards his subjects and friends. And as I know that many have written of this, I fear that my writing about it may be deemed presumptuous, differing as I do, especially in this matter, from the opinions of others. But my intention being to write something of use to those who understand it, it appears to me more proper to go to the real truth of the matter than to its

---

[32] *Materials, infra* at 7F.

[33] *Materials, infra* at 7F.

[34] Dworkin does not "think this criticism is well-taken." *Materials, infra* at 7F.

imagination; and many have imagined republics and principalities which have never been seen or known to exist in reality; for how we live is so far removed from how we ought to live, that he who abandons what is done for what ought to be done, will rather learn to bring about his own ruin than his preservation. A man who wishes to make a profession of goodness in everything must necessarily come to grief among so many who are not good. Therefore it is necessary for a prince, who wishes to maintain himself, to learn how not to be good, and to use it and not use it according to the necessity of the case.

*   *   *

I know that every one will admit that it would be highly praiseworthy in a prince to possess all the above-named qualities that are reputed good, but as they cannot all be possessed or observed, human conditions not permitting of it, it is necessary that he should be prudent enough to avoid the disgrace of those vices which would lose him the state, and guard himself against those which will not lose it him, if possible, but if not able to, he can indulge them with less scruple. And yet he must not mind incurring the disgrace of those vices, without which it would be difficult to save the state, for if one considers well, it will be found that some things which seem virtues would, if followed, lead to one's ruin, and some others which appear vices result, if followed, in one's greater security and well being.[35]

In short, if the good are going to survive and be effective, they are going to have to get "dirty hands" when necessary. Otherwise they may lose what they hold most dear to those who are genuinely without any principle.

The two selections excerpted to illustrate this problem are Bernard Williams' "Politics and Moral Character" and Michael Walzer's "Political Action: The Problem of Dirty Hands."[36] These essays, like Machiavelli's *The Prince*, both focus primarily on the "profession" of the politician. But their arguments also apply directly to lawyers. Like politicians, lawyers are not just responsible for their own well-being, but also the well-being of others for whom they are officially accountable. It is one thing, out of scruple, to lose a key advantage for yourself—but what if the effect is to lose something vitally important to others who have chosen or elected you to represent them and to safeguard them and their families? Both politicians and lawyers face this frequently in the "real world."

There is another similarity. As Walzer points out, politicians have available to them special power over others, the coercive power—the "official violence" of the State. So do lawyers, through the legal process, whether they act as judges, prosecutors, or in private practice. This power represents both the means to do good, and the opportunity to do evil in an official capacity.

---

[35] *Materials, infra* at 7F.

[36] *Materials, infra* at 7F.

Examine the two examples given by Walzer, the "deal" with the ward boss and the decision of how to deal with a terrorist.[37] Do you agree with how Walzer presents the issues? How does Walzer answer Machiavelli? How would Kant resolve these issues? Rawls?

It is easy to imagine very similar, although perhaps less dramatic, issues in ordinary law practice. Bernard Williams presents these issues by the following argument:

> (1) In any complex society (at least) the enforcement of some legal rights involves morally disagreeable acts.
>
> (2) It is bad that legal rights which exist should not be enforceable.
>
> (3) Enforcement of many rights of the kind mentioned in (1) requires lawyers.
>
> (4) Any lawyer really effective in enforcing those rights must be fairly horrible.
>
> Ergo (5) It is good that some lawyers are fairly horrible.[38]

Which of these propositions would you attempt to negate, if any? How would Kant approach this challenge? Rawls? Williams adds a second set of propositions, this time in terms of politicians, although you can easily substitute "lawyer" for "politician" and "getting a court order" for "ordering."

> I shall set out a list of four propositions which some would regard as all true, and which, if they were all true, would make the hope of finding politicians of honourable character, except in minor roles and in favourable circumstances, very slim.

(i)   There are violent acts which the state is justified in doing which no private citizen as such would be justified in doing.

(ii) Anything the state is justified in doing some official such as, often, a politician is justified in ordering to be done.

(iii) You are not morally justified in ordering to be done anything which you would not be prepared to do yourself.

(iv) Official violence is enough like unofficial violence for the preparedness referred to in (iii) to amount to a criminal tendency.[39]

Again, how do you counter Williams' assertions? The hope of finding lawyers "of honourable character" depends on being able to answer these challenges. Which helps more, "duty" or "right" based theories?

Herman Melville (1819-1891) has been mentioned before in our discussion of Holmes' views on natural law[40] and because he was Chief Justice Shaw's son-in-

---

[37] *Materials, infra* at 7F.

[38] *Materials, infra* at 7F.

[39] *Materials, infra* at 7F.

[40] *Materials, infra* at 7F.

law.[41] Certainly Melville's book, *Moby Dick* (1851), is one of the greatest of all American books. *Moby Dick* is a symbolic treatment of the nature of God and good and evil in the human soul. Without digressing into the finer points, Melville believed in an awesome natural God, but one apparently indifferent to our fate. If one chooses to follow a course of individual or collective self-destruction, a constant danger of our human nature, God will not intercede, and may not care.[42] Just as the whale ship Pequod was destroyed by the Great White Whale, so may we all be destroyed, out of human folly or evil.

Such religious views were not acceptable in Melville's America. Thus *Moby Dick* was written in a kind of symbolic code. But the message was clear that good and kind men could be led to their destruction, without salvation, by the forces of evil.

Melville wrote another great book, a much shorter book on the nature of crime, punishment, and legal authority. It was called *Billy Budd*, and was only published in 1924, long after Melville's death.

Billy Budd focuses on a central issue of this course: how does a person acting solely in an official capacity under law justify disregarding that law for moral reasons? Billy Budd was a virtuous young seaman, whose life was practically a caricature of the "romantic" 19th century British tar. He was forcibly impressed, from the private merchant vessel called Rights-of-Man, to a British warship. (No "tacit consent" from Lockean theory here!) He is hated for his beauty and innocence by the twisted and malevolent Claggart, the petty officer. Billy cannot understand Claggart's hatred, or even how such pure evil can exist. In his innocence, Billy also cannot defend himself from Claggart's plot to accuse Billy, falsely, of planning a mutiny. When Claggart makes the accusation before the Captain, Billy cannot speak, frustrated by a vocal impediment. Instead, in desperation, he strikes wildly at Claggart. It is a fatal blow.

The excerpt in the Materials is the account of Billy's court martial, and the analysis of the situation by Captain Vere. He is convinced of Billy's innocence of the charge of mutiny, but the King's military code will not excuse the killing of Claggart.

---

[41] *Materials, infra* at 7F.

[42] The classic critical account is D. H. Lawrence, HERMAN MELVILLE'S MOBY-DICK, Studies in Classic American Literature (1964), excerpted in HERMAN MELVILLE, MOBY DICK 581–587 (Charles Child Walcutt ed., 1967). D. H. Lawrence was no ordinary literary critic. Here is a sample:

Doom! Doom! Doom!
Something seems to whisper
It is the very dark
Trees of America! Doom!
Doom of what?
Doom of our white day. We are doomed,
Doomed. And the doom is in America.
Doom!

*   *   *

The *Pequod* went down. And
the *Pequod* was the ship of
the white American soul.

Id. at 586–587. For a more conventional analysis, see the suggestions under "Further Reading," *Materials, infra* at 7F.

"Struck dead by an angel of God. Yet the angel must hang." But what of the scruples of fundamental fairness and natural law? The Captain exclaims:

> But your scruples: do they move as in a dusk? Challenge them. Make them advance and declare themselves. Come now: do they import something like this: If, mindless of palliating circumstances, we are bound to regard the death of the master-at-arms as the prisoner's deed, then does that deed constitute a capital crime whereof the penalty is a mortal one? But in natural justice is nothing but the prisoner's overt act to be considered? How can we adjudge to summary and shameful death a fellow creature innocent before God, and whom we feel to be so?—Does that state it aright? You sign sad assent. Well, I too feel that, the full force of that. It is Nature. But do these buttons that we wear attest that our allegiance is to Nature? No, to the King.[43]

The Captain then turns to the collective, Hegelian purpose of the ship. It is to fight at command, and they are soldiers, submerged in the apparatus of the State. So, too, is the nature of their obedience to law.

> Though the ocean, which is inviolate Nature primeval, though this be the element where we move and have our being as sailors, yet as the King's officers lies our duty in a sphere correspondingly natural? So little is that true that, in receiving out commissions, we in the most important regards ceased to be natural free agents. When war is declared are we, the commissioned fighters, previously consulted? We fight at command. If our judgments approve the war, that is but coincidence. So in other particulars. So now. For suppose condemnation to follow these present proceedings. Would it be so much we ourselves that would condemn as it would be martial law operating through us? For that law and the rigor of it, we are not responsible. Our vowed responsibility is in this: That however pitilessly that law may operate, we nevertheless adhere to it and administer it.[44]

The Captain's reference to the "inviolate Nature primeval" of the ocean brings to mind Melville's indifferent God. Here again, as in *Moby Dick*, evil triumphs. An innocent man will be executed. But this time, the evil triumphs through the operation, not of nature, but of the law.

This, then, is the "Billy Budd" problem. In the absence of God, how do we, as officers of the laws, provide a framework that tests the operation of the positive law and legitimately subject it to a higher moral standard? Simplistic appeals to "private conscience" will not do. As Captain Vere challenged:

> But something in your aspect seems to urge that it is not solely the heart that moves in you, but also the conscience, the private conscience. But tell me whether or not, occupying the position we do, private conscience should not yield to that imperial one formulated in the code under which alone we officially proceed?[45]

---

[43] *Materials, infra* at 7F.

[44] *Materials, infra* at 7F.

[45] *Materials, infra* at 7F.

Only a "deep theory" with principles that can be universally defended and uniformly applied, will suffice. This, in the end, is the problem that Kant, Rawls, and Dworkin have set out to solve.

One particularly striking passage by Melville anticipates modern feminist jurisprudence. The Captain describes compassion as "the feminine in man," as opposed to, here, the cruel operation of the positive law, which is masculine.

> But the exceptional in the matter moves the hearts within you. Even so too is mine moved. But let not warm hearts betray heads that should be cool. Ashore in a criminal case will an upright judge allow himself off the bench to be waylaid by some tender kinswoman of the accused seeking to touch him with her tearful plea? Well the heart here denotes the feminine in man, is as that piteous woman and, hard though it be, she must here be ruled out.[46]

Is it wise to have "the feminine . . . ruled out"? What happens to the fabric of law when this perspective is pushed aside? We will explore insights from feminist jurisprudence in greater detail in Chapter IX.

Melville's story of *Billy Budd* was written long after his father-in-law, Chief Justice Shaw, felt bound by his official station to return black Americans, in chains, to slavery. Yet *Billy Budd* cries out against the evil of this jurisprudence. New schools of juristic thought, evolving from the experience of racism and sexual oppression, may help provide new answers to the "Billy Budd" problem. As Robin West noted, in reference to the Fugitive Slave Act cases, "[w]hatever may have been the claims of the historical positivists, or even the apparent logic of positivism, if it facilitated judicial acquiescence in the most abominable, ignoble moment in American legal history, there is something deeply wrong with it."[47]

D. FURTHER READING

The best readily available text of the *Crito* is in PLATO, THE LAST DAYS OF SOCRATES (trans. with intro., Hugh Tredennick, new ed., 1959), a "Penguin Books" paperback. There is an extensive listing of references for the study of Plato under Chapter ID.

A good paperback, unabridged edition of FYODOR DOSTOEVSKY'S CRIME AND PUNISHMENT is the translation by Sidney Monas (1968), available as Signet Classic paperback. This includes an excellent analytical "Afterword" by Monas and a good bibliography of selected criticism. *Id.* at 529–544. For a good discussion of Friedrich Nietzsche (1844-1900) and the *Übermensch,* see ALASDAIR MACINTYRE, A SHORT HISTORY OF ETHICS 222–226 (1966); and ALASDAIR MACINTYRE, AFTER VIRTUE 109–120 (2d ed., 1984). Walter Kaufman, a great scholar and popularizer of Nietzsche,

---

[46] *Materials, infra* at 7F.

[47] Robin West, *Natural Law Ambiguities,* 25 CONN. L. REV. 831, 832 (1993). West, however, argues that "It may well be that the nineteenth-century abolitionist judges were seduced by positivism toward acquiescence in the evil legal system of their time. But it is not clear they would have done any differently had they been natural lawyers." *Id.* at 837. She goes on to argue that positivism is a "necessary," but not a "sufficient" condition of constitutional criticism. *Id.* at 839.

devotes a full chapter of his treatise on Nietzsche to meticulously tracing Nietzsche's views on Socrates. *See* Walter Kaufman, *Nietzsche's Attitude Toward Socrates, in* NIETZSCHE: PHILOSOPHER, PSYCHOLOGIST, ANTICHRIST (4th ed., 1974). There is also a highly amusing account in BERTRAND RUSSELL, A HISTORY OF WESTERN PHILOSOPHY 770–773 (1945). ("His [Nietzsche's] general outlook . . . remaining very similar to that of Wagner in the Ring: Nietzsche's superman is very like Siegfried, except that he knows Greek. This may seem odd, but that is not my fault.")

Our reliable philosophy manuals are good on both Kant (1724-1804) and Hegel (1770-1831). *See* ALASDAIR MACINTYRE, A SHORT HISTORY OF ETHICS, 190–198 ("Kant"), 199–214 ("Hegel and Marx"); BERTRAND RUSSELL, A HISTORY OF WESTERN PHILOSOPHY, 701–718 ("Kant"); 730–746 ("Hegel"). *See also* HUNTINGTON CAIRNS, LEGAL PHILOSOPHY FROM PLATO TO HEGEL 391–463 ("Kant"), 503–550 ("Hegel") (1949). For well-translated collections of Kant's writing, see THE PHILOSOPHY OF KANT (Carl J. Friedrich ed., 1949), which includes a good biography, and IMMANUEL KANT, LECTURES ON ETHICS (trans. L. Insfield, 1963). The classic scholarly exposition of Kant on ethics is H. J. PATON, THE CATEGORICAL IMPERATIVE (1971, orig. printed 1947).

For an excellent introduction to Rawls, read in its entirety Ronald Dworkin, *Justice and Rights, in* TAKING RIGHTS SERIOUSLY 150–183 (1977), and, better still, read the entire book. Also most helpful is ROBERT PAUL WOLFF'S UNDERSTANDING RAWLS (1977). ROBERT NOZICK'S ANARCHY, STATE AND UTOPIA (1974), is the most influential analysis of Rawls and, of course, there is the great book itself, JOHN RAWLS, A THEORY OF JUSTICE (1971).

Good resources on the problem of "Dirty Hands" are the two anthologies in which the Williams and Walzer articles originally appeared: PUBLIC AND PRIVATE MORALITY (S. Hampshire ed., 1968) and PRIVATE AND PUBLIC ETHICS: TENSION BETWEEN CONSCIENCE AND INSTITUTIONAL RESPONSIBILITY (D. G. Jones ed., 1978), respectively. *See also* Robin West's excellent *Natural Law Ambiguities*, 25 CONN. L. REV. 831 (1993).

For an "in print" edition of Billy Budd, see SHORTER NOVELS OF HERMAN MELVILLE (1978), a "Liveright Paperback" and HERMAN MELVILLE, BILLY BUDD AND OTHER TALES (rev. Willard Thorp, 1979), a "Signet Classic" paperback. There is also an excellent article by Christopher James Serritt, as Commissioner to the Chief Judge of the United States Court of Military Appeals, *Ode to "Billy Budd": Judicial Professionalism in Modern American Military*, 38 FED. BAR NEWS & J. 208 (1991). For a fine edition of *Moby Dick*, complete with a good introduction, biographical note, contemporary letters of Melville, a selection of contemporary and recent criticism, and bibliography, see HERMAN MELVILLE, MOBY DICK (intro. Charles C. Walcutt ed., 1984), a "Bantam Classic" paperback.

Excellent introductions to feminist jurisprudence include the entirety of Phyllis Goldfarb, *A Theory-Practice Spiral: The Ethics of Feminism and Clinical Education*, 75 MINN. L. REV. 1599 (1991), the article excerpted at *Materials, infra* at IXE; Robin West, *Jurisprudence and Gender*, 55 U. CHI. L. REV. 1 (1988); Katherine T. Bartlett, *Feminist Legal Methods*, 103 HARV. L. REV. 829 (1990); and Leslie G. Espinoza, *Constructing a Professional Ethic*, 4 BERKELEY WOMEN'S L.J. 215 (1989). A particularly helpful comparative study is Katharine Bartlett's review of Catharine

Mackinnon's well-known book FEMINISM UNMODIFIED: DISCOURSES ON LIFE AND LAW (1987). *See* Katharine T. Bartlett, *Mackinnon's Feminism: Power on Whose Terms?*, 75 CAL. L. REV. 1559 (1987).[48]

For more discussion of what is often called "role differentiated behavior" of lawyers, see Richard Wasserstrom, *Lawyers as Professionals: Some Moral Issues*, 5 HUM. RTS. 1 (1975). Wasserstrom's ideas have been extensively discussed in legal ethics literature. For additional discussion of the idea that lawyers should not be morally accountable for what they do in their representative capacity, as long as it is within the bounds of the law, see D. LUBAN, LAWYERS AND JUSTICE: AN ETHICAL STUDY 12 (1988); Charles Fried, *The Lawyer as Friend: The Moral Foundation of the Lawyer-Client Relationship*, 85 YALE L.J. 1060 (1976); Robert W. Gordon, *Why Lawyers Can't Just Be Hired Guns*, in ENRON CORPORATE FIASCOS AND THEIR IMPLICATIONS 797 (Nancy B. Rapoport & Bala G. Dharan eds., 2004); Stephen L. Pepper, *The Lawyer's Amoral Ethical Role: A Defense, a Problem, and Some Possibilities*, 1986 AM. B. FOUND. RES. J. 613; David Luban, *The Lysistratian Prerogative: A Response to Stephen Pepper*, 1986 AM. B. FOUND. RES. J. 637; Andrew L. Kaufman, *A Commentary on Pepper's The Lawyer's Amoral Ethical Role*, 1986 A.B.F. RES. J. 651, 651–652.

E. DISCUSSION PROBLEMS

PROBLEM XVII

If your response to the problems in Chapter VI on Justified Disobedience was to break the law, would you turn yourself in for punishment?

Consider:

ABA Model Rules of Professional Conduct.

Rules 1.2, 2.1, 3.1, 3.2, 3.3, 8.3, and 8.4

PROBLEM XVIII

You have been asked to assist in revisions (if any) of the Preamble, paragraph [1], of the Model Rules of Professional Conduct. Your first step is to present a position paper on the question of to whom do you owe your "duty" as a citizen and/or as a lawyer? Will your professional role as a lawyer change the content of that "duty"? Do you owe allegiance to the courts and the bar if you are censured unfairly? What is your professional duty to the public?[49] Can you articulate a 1–2 paragraph position that addresses these questions.

As you prepare your position paper, consider Robert E. Lee, who said that "Duty is the sublimest word in the English language." In 1852, Lee was Superintendent at West Point, charged with the training of the future elite officer

---

[48] We are grateful to Phyllis Goldfarb for help in compiling these suggestions.

[49] Our thanks to Dan Coquillette's former research assistant, Tom Peele, for this problem and some of the assigned reading.

corps of the United States. In 1860, following brilliant duty in Mexico and Texas, he was offered the command of the United States Army. Instead, he resigned his commission and accepted command of the rebel Virginia forces. To whom did Lee owe his "duty"? Did he deserve greater moral censure than Lemuel Shaw? Analyze the concept of duty in light of Lee's decision. Do you agree with Kant's formulation? Dworkin's? Rawls'?

PROBLEM XIX

F. H. Bradley states: "There is nothing better than my station and its duties, nor anything higher or more truly beautiful. It holds and will hold its own against the worship of the 'individual,' whatever form that may take." Do you agree? For the same Model Rules study group, prepare a one paragraph analysis about your "station" as a lawyer?

PROBLEM XX

Bernard Williams argues that "it is good that some lawyers are fairly horrible." He notes that "[i]t is a personal fact about somebody that [being a lawyer] is his [her] profession." It is a short logical step to note that there may be times that a good lawyer must do something "fairly horrible." Is Williams' description accurate? If true, is it possible to be both a good lawyer and a good person? Does Michael Walzer's analysis of the politician's professional role provide any assistance? Is it a comparable "profession"?

Return to Problem I. Are your views about this classical debate any different now? Should it effect your decision to join the American legal profession?

PROBLEM XXI

You have been asked to give a Graduation Speech at your Law School. Beyond the podium are row after row of shining, expectant faces. Beyond them are the proud families who sacrificed for this day. You have been asked to speak on "Professional Duty." This allows you to speak more broadly than a position paper for the Model Rules of Professional Conduct. What do you say? To help you prepare your talk, consider what the story of Billy Budd suggests about Melville's view of duty and the legal order. As mentioned before, Chief Justice Lemuel Shaw was Melville's father-in-law, and we know they had long walks and discussions together. Do you think they agreed about the nature of professional duty? What do you think of Captain Vere and the fate of Billy Budd? Do you agree with Captain Vere that "the heart here denotes the Feminine in man . . . and, hard though it be, she must be ruled out?"

As you prepare your speech, consider your answer, as a lawyer, to Captain Vere's final question, "But tell me whether or not, occupying the position we do, private conscience should not yield to the imperial one formulated in the Code under which alone we officially proceed?" What would Shaw's answer be? Thoreau's? Melville's? Martin Luther King's? A feminist perspective?

F. MATERIALS

PLATO'S DIALOGUES, CRITO
Translation from Benjamin Jowett (1871)

Persons of the Dialogue
Socrates
Crito

Scene: The Prison of Socrates

Socrates. Why have you come this hour, Crito? it must be quite early.

Crito. Yes, certainly.

Soc. What is the exact time?

Cr. The dawn is breaking.

Soc. I wonder the keeper of the prison would let you in.

Cr. He knows me because I often come, Socrates; moreover, I have done him a kindness.

Soc. And are you only just come?

Cr. No, I came some time ago.

Soc. Then why did you sit and say nothing, instead of awakening me at once?

Cr. Why, indeed, Socrates, I myself would rather not have all this sleeplessness and sorrow. But I have been wondering at your peaceful slumbers, and that was the reason why I did not awaken you, because I wanted you to be out of pain. I have always thought you happy in the calmness of your temperament; but never did I see the like of the easy, cheerful way in which you bear this calamity.

Soc. Why, Crito, when a man has reached my age he ought not to be repining at the prospect of death.

Cr. And yet other old men find themselves in similar misfortunes, and age does not prevent them from repining.

Soc. That may be. But you have not told me why you come at this early hour.

Cr. I come to bring you a message which is sad and painful; not, as I believe, to yourself, but to all of us who are your friends, and saddest of all to me.

Soc. What! I suppose that the ship has come from Delos, on the arrival of which I am to die?

Cr. No, the ship has not actually arrived, but she will probably be here to-day, as persons who have come from Sunium tell me that they have left her there; and therefore to-morrow, Socrates, will be the last day of your life.

Soc. Very well, Crito; if such is the will of God, I am willing; but my belief is that there will be a delay of a day.

Cr. Why do you say this?

Soc. I will tell you. I am to die on the day after the arrival of the ship?

Cr. Yes; that is what the authorities say.

Soc. But I do not think that the ship will be here until to-morrow; this I gather from a vision which I had last night, or rather only just now, when you fortunately allowed me to sleep.

Cr. And what was the nature of the vision?

Soc. There came to me the likeness of a woman, fair and comely, clothed in white raiment, who called to me and said:

O Socrates

"The third day hence, to Phthia shalt thou go."

Cr. What a singular dream, Socrates!

Soc. There can be no doubt about the meaning, Crito, I think.

Cr. Yes: the meaning is only too clear. But, O! my beloved Socrates, let me entreat you once more to take my advice and escape. For if you die I shall not only lose a friend who can never be replaced, but there is another evil: people who do not know you and me will believe that I might have saved you if I had been willing to give money, but that I did not care. Now, can there be worse disgrace than this—that I should be thought to value money more than the life of a friend? For the many will not be persuaded that I wanted you to escape, and that you refused.

Soc. But why, my dear Crito, should we care about the opinion of the many? Good men, and they are the only persons who are worth considering, will think of these things truly as they happened.

Cr. But do you see, Socrates, that the opinion of the many must be regarded, as is evident in your own case, because they can do the very greatest evil to anyone who has lost their good opinion?

Soc. I only wish, Crito, that they could; for then they could also do the greatest good, and that would be well. But the truth is, that they can do neither good nor evil: they cannot make a man wise or make him foolish; and whatever they do is the result of chance.

Cr. Well, I will not dispute about that; but please to tell me, Socrates, whether you are not acting out of regard to me and your other friends: are you not afraid that if you escape hence we may get into trouble with the informers for having stolen you away, and lose either the whole or a great part of our property; or that even a worse evil may happen to us? Now, if this is your fear, be at ease; for in order to save you, we ought surely to run this or even a greater risk; be persuaded, then, and do as I say.

Soc. Yes, Crito, that is one fear which you mention, but by no means the only one.

Cr. Fear not. There are persons who at no great cost are willing to save you and bring you out of prison; and as for the informers, you may observe that they are far from exorbitant in their demands; a little money will satisfy them. My means, which, as I am sure, are ample, are at your service, and if you have a scruple about spending all mine, here are strangers who will give you the use of theirs; and one of them, Simmias the Theban, has brought a sum of money for this very purpose; and Cebes and many others are willing to spend their money too. I say, therefore, do not on that account hesitate about making your escape, and do not say, as you did in the court, that you will have a difficulty in knowing what to do with yourself if you escape. For men will love you in other places to which you may go, and not in Athens only; there are family and friends of mine in Thessaly, if you like to go to them, who will value and protect you, and no Thessalian will give you any trouble. Nor can I think that you are justified, Socrates, in betraying your own life when you might be saved; this is playing into the hands of your enemies and destroyers; and moreover I should say that you were betraying your children; for you might bring them up and educate them; instead of which you go away and leave them, and they will have to take their chance; and if they do not meet with the usual fate of orphans, there will be small thanks to you. No man should bring children into the world who is unwilling to persevere to the end of their nurture and education. But you are choosing the easier part, as I think, not the better and manlier, which would rather have become one who professes virtue in all his actions, like yourself. And, indeed, I am ashamed not only of you, but of us who are your friends, when I reflect that this entire business of yours will be attributed to our want of courage. The trial need never have come on, or might have been brought to another issue; and the end of all, which is the crowning absurdity, will seem to have been permitted by us, through cowardice and baseness, who might have saved you, as you might have saved yourself, if we had been good for anything (for there was no difficulty in escaping); and we did not see how disgraceful, Socrates, and also miserable all this will be to us as well as to you. Make your mind up then, or rather have your mind already made up, for the time of deliberation is over, and there is only one thing to be done, which must be done, if at all, this very night, and which any delay will render all but impossible; I beseech you therefore, Socrates, to be persuaded by me, and to do as I say.

Soc. Dear Crito, your zeal is invaluable, if a right one; but if wrong, the greater the zeal the greater the evil; and therefore we ought to consider whether these things shall be done or not. For I am and always have been one of those natures who must be guided by reason, whatever the reason may be which upon reflection appears to me to be the best; and now that this fortune has come upon me, I cannot put away the reasons which I have before given: the principles which I have hitherto honored and revered I still honor, and unless we can find other and better principles on the instant, I am certain not to agree with you, no, not even if the power of the multitude could inflict many more imprisonments, confiscations, deaths, frightening us like children with hobgoblin terrors. But what will be the fairest way of considering the question? Shall I return to your old argument about the opinions of men, some of which are to be regarded, and others, as we were saying, are not to be regarded? Now were we right in maintaining this before I was condemned? And has the argument which was once good now proved to be talk for the sake of talking; in fact an amusement only, and altogether vanity? That is what I want to consider with your help, Crito: whether, under my present circumstances, the argument appears to be in any way different or not; and is to be allowed by me or disallowed. That argument, which, as I believe, is maintained by many who assume to be authorities, was to the effect, as I was saying, that the opinions of some men are to be regarded, and of other men not to be regarded. Now you, Crito, are a disinterested person who are not going to die to-morrow—at least, there is no human probability of this, and you are therefore not liable to be deceived by the circumstances in which you are placed. Tell me, then, whether I am right in saying the some opinions, and the opinions of some men only, are to be valued, and other opinions, and the opinions of other men, are not to be valued. I ask you whether I was right in maintaining this?

Cr. Certainly.

Soc. The good are to be regarded, and not the bad?

Cr. Yes.

Soc. And the opinions of the wise are good, and the opinions of the unwise are evil?

Cr. Certainly.

Soc. And what was said about another matter? Was the disciple in gymnastics supposed to attend to the praise and blame and opinion of every man, or of one man only—his physician or trainer, whoever that was?

Cr. Of one man only.

Soc. And he ought to fear the censure and welcome the praise of that one only, and not of the many?

Cr. That is clear.

Soc. And he ought to live and train, and eat and drink in the way which seems good to his single master who has understanding, rather than according to the opinion of all other men put together?

Cr. True.

Soc. And if he disobeys and disregards the opinion and approval of the one, and regards the opinion of the many who have no understanding, will he not suffer evil?

Cr. Certainly he will.

Soc. And what will the evil be, whither tending and what affecting, in the disobedient person?

Cr. Clearly, affecting the body; that is what is destroyed by the evil.

Soc. Very good; and is not this true, Crito, of other things which we need not separately enumerate? In the matter of just and unjust, fair and foul, good and evil, which are the subjects of our present consultation, ought we to follow the opinion of the many and to fear them; or the opinion of the one man who has understanding, and whom we ought to fear and reverence more than all the rest of the world: and whom deserting we shall destroy and injure that principle in us which may be assumed to be improved by justice and deteriorated by injustice; is there not such a principle?

Cr. Certainly there is, Socrates.

Soc. Take a parallel instance; if, acting under the advice of men who have no understanding, we destroy that which is improvable by health and deteriorated by disease—when that has been destroyed, I say, would life be worth having? And that is—the body?

Cr. Yes.

Soc. Could we live, having an evil and corrupted body?

Cr. Certainly not.

Soc. And will life be worth having, if that higher part of man be depraved, which is improved by justice and deteriorated by injustice? Do we suppose that principle, whatever it may be in man, which has to do with justice and injustice, to be inferior to the body?

Cr. Certainly not.

Soc. More honored, then?

Cr. Far more honored.

Soc. Then, my friend, we must not regard what the many say of us: but what he, the one man who has understanding of just and unjust, will say, and what the truth will say. And therefore you begin in error when you suggest that we should regard the opinion of the many about just and unjust, good and evil, honorable and dishonorable. Well, someone will say, "But the many can kill us."

Cr. Yes, Socrates; that will clearly be the answer.

Soc. That is true; but still I find with surprise that the old argument is, as I conceive, unshaken as ever. And I should like to know whether I may say the same of another proposition—that not life, but a good life, is to be chiefly valued?

Cr. Yes, that also remains.

Soc. And a good life is equivalent to a just and honorable one—that holds also?

Cr. Yes, that holds.

Soc. From these premises I proceed to argue the question whether I ought or ought not to try to escape without the consent of the Athenians: and if I am clearly right in escaping, then I will make the attempt; but if not, I will abstain. The other considerations which you mention, of money and loss of character, and the duty of educating children, are as I hear, only the doctrines of the multitude, who would be as ready to call people to life, if they were able, as they are to put them to death—and with as little reason. But now, since the argument has thus far prevailed, the only question which remains to be considered is, whether we shall do rightly either in escaping or in suffering others to aid in our escape and paying them in money and thanks, or whether we shall not do rightly; and if the latter, then the death or any other calamity which may ensue on my remaining here must not be allowed to enter into the calculation.

Cr. I think that you are right, Socrates; how then shall we proceed?

Soc. Let us consider the matter together, and do you either refute me if you can, and I will be convinced; or else cease, my dear friend, from repeating to me that I ought to escape against the wishes of the Athenians: for I am extremely desirous to be persuaded by you, but not against my own better judgment. And now please to consider my first position, and do your best to answer me.

Cr. I will do my best.

Soc. Are we to say that we are never intentionally to do wrong, or that in one way we ought and in another way we ought not to do wrong, or is doing wrong always evil and dishonorable, as I was just now saying, and as has been already acknowledged by us? Are all our former admissions which were made within a few days to be thrown away? And have we, at our age, been earnestly discoursing with one another all our life long only to discover that we are no better than children? Or are we to rest assured, in spite of the opinion of the many, and in spite of consequences whether better or worse, of the truth of what was then said, that injustice is always an evil and dishonor to him who acts unjustly? Shall we affirm that?

Cr. Yes.

Soc. Then we must do no wrong?

Cr. Certainly not.

Soc. Nor when injured injure in return, as the many imagine; for we must injure no one at all?

Cr. Clearly not.

Soc. Again, Crito, may we do evil?

Cr. Surely not, Socrates.

Soc. And what of doing evil in return for evil, which is the morality of the many—is that just or not?

Cr. Not just.

Soc. For doing evil to another is the same as injuring him?

Cr. Very true.

Soc. Then we ought not to retaliate or render evil for evil to anyone, whatever evil we may have suffered from him. But I would have you consider, Crito, whether you really mean what you are saying. For this opinion has never been held, and never will be held, by any considerable number of persons; and those who are agree and those who are not agreed upon this point have no common ground, and can only despise one another, when they see how widely they differ. Tell me, then, whether you agreed with and assent to my first principle, that neither injury nor retaliation nor warding off evil by evil is ever right. And shall that be the premise of our argument? Or do you decline and dissent from this? For this has been of old and is still my opinion; but, if you are of another opinion, let me hear what you have to say. If, however, you remain of the same mind as formerly, I will proceed to the next step.

Cr. You may proceed, for I have not changed my mind.

Soc. Then I will proceed to the next step, which may be put in the form of a question: Ought a man to do what he admits to be right, or ought he to betray the right?

Cr. He ought to do what he thinks right.

Soc. But if this is true, what is the application? In leaving the prison against the will of the Athenians, do I wrong any? or rather do I not wrong those whom I ought least to wrong? Do I not desert the principles which were acknowledged by us to be just? What do you say?

Cr. I cannot tell, Socrates, for I do not know.

Soc. Then consider the matter in this way: Imagine that I am about to play truant (you may call the proceeding by any name which you like), and the laws and the government come and interrogate me: "Tell us, Socrates," they say; "what are you about? are you going by an act of yours to overturn us—the laws and the whole State, as far as in you lies? Do you imagine that a State can subsist and not be overthrown, in which the decisions of law have no power, but are set aside and overthrown by individuals?" What will be our answer, Crito, to these and the like words? Anyone, and especially a clever rhetorician, will have a good deal to urge about the evil of setting aside the law which requires a sentence to be carried out; and we might reply, "Yes; but the State has injured us and given an unjust sentence." Suppose I say that?

Cr. Very good, Socrates.

Soc. "And was that our agreement with you?" the law would say; "or were you to abide by the sentence of the State?" And if I were to express astonishment at their saying this, the law would probably add: "Answer, Socrates, instead of opening your eyes: you are in the habit of asking and answering questions. Tell us what complaint you have to make against us which justifies you in attempting to destroy us and the State? In the first place did we not bring you into existence? Your father married your mother by our aid and begat you. Say whether you have any objection to urge against those of us who regulate marriage?" None, I should reply. "Or against those of us who regulate the system of nurture and education of children in which you were trained? Were not the laws, who have the charge of this, right in commanding your father to train you in music and gymnastic?" Right, I should reply. "Well, then, since you were brought into the world and nurtured and educated by us, can you deny in the first place that you are our child and slave, as your fathers were before you? And if this is true you are not on equal terms with us; nor can you think that you have a right to do to us what we are doing to you. Would you have any right to strike or revile or do any other evil to a father or to your master, if you had one, when you have been struck or reviled by him, or received some other evil at his hand?—you would not say this? And because we think right to destroy you, do you think that you have any right to destroy us in return, and your country as far as in your lies? And will you, O professor of true virtue, say that you are justified in this? Has a philosopher like you failed to discover that our country is more to be valued and higher and holier far than mother or father or any ancestor, and more to be regarded in the eyes of the gods and of men of understanding? also to be soothed, and gently and reverently entreated when angry, even more than a father, and if not persuaded, obeyed? And when we are punished by her, whether with imprisonment or stripes, the punishment is to be endured in silence; and if she leads us to wounds or death in battle, thither we follow as is right; neither may anyone yield or retreat or leave his rank, but whether in battle or in court of law, or in any other place, he must do what his city and his country order him; or he must change their view of what is just: and if he may do no violence to his father or mother, much less may he do violence to his country." What answer shall we make to this, Crito? Do the laws speak truly, or do they not?

Cr. I think that they do.

Soc. Then the laws will say: "Consider, Socrates, if this is true, that in your present attempt you are going to do us wrong. For, after having brought you into the world, and nurtured and educated you, and given you and every other citizen a share in every good that we had to give, we further proclaim and give the right to every Athenian, that if he does not like us when he has come of age and has seen the ways of the city, and made our acquaintance, he may go where he pleases and take his goods with him; and none of us laws will forbid him or interfere with him. Any of you who does not like us and the city, and who wants to go to a colony or to any other city, may go where he likes, and take his goods with him. But he who has experience of the manner in which we order justice and administer the State, and still remains, has entered into an implied contract that he will do as we command him. And he who disobeys us is, as we maintain, thrice wrong: first, because in disobeying us he is disobeying his parents; secondly, because we are the authors of his education; thirdly, because he has made an agreement with us that he will duly obey our commands; and he neither obeys them nor convinces us that our commands are wrong; and we do not rudely impose them, but give him the alternative of obeying or convincing us; that is what we offer, and he does neither. These are the sort of accusations to which, as we were saying, you, Socrates, will be exposed if you accomplish your intentions; you, above all other Athenians." Suppose I ask, why is this? They will justly retort upon me that I above all other men have acknowledged the agreement. "There is clear proof," they will say, "Socrates, that we and the city were not displeasing to you. Of all Athenians you have been the most constant resident in the city, which, as you never leave, you may be supposed to love. For you never went out of the city either to see the games, except once when you went to the Isthmus, or to any other place unless when you were on military service; nor did you travel as other men do. Nor had you any curiosity to know other States or their laws: your affections did not go beyond us and our State; we were your special favorites, and you acquiesced in our government of you; and this is the State in which you begat your children, which is a proof of your satisfaction. Moreover, you might, if you had liked, have fixed the penalty at banishment in the course of the trial—the State which refuses to let you go now would have let you go then. But you pretended that you preferred death to exile, and that you were not grieved at death. And now you have forgotten these fine sentiments, and pay no respect to us, the laws, of whom you are the destroyer; and are doing what only a miserable slave would do, running away and turning your back upon the compacts and agreements which you made as a citizen. And first of all answer this very question: Are we right in saying that you agreed to be governed according to us in deed, and not in word only? Is that true or not?" How shall we answer that, Crito? Must we not agree?

Cr. There is no help, Socrates.

Soc. Then will they not say: "You, Socrates, are breaking the covenants and agreements which you made with us at your leisure, not in any haste or under any compulsion or deception, but having had seventy years to think of them, during which time you were at liberty to leave the city, if we were not to your mind, or if our covenants appeared to you to be unfair. You had your choice, and might have gone either to Lacedæmon or Crete, which you often praise for their good government, or to some other Hellenic or foreign State. Whereas you, above all other Athenians, seemed to be so fond of the State, or, in other words, of us her laws (for who would like a State that has no laws?), that you never stirred out of her: the halt, the blind, the maimed, were not more stationary in her than you were. And now you run away and forsake your agreements. Not so, Socrates, if you will take our advice; do not make yourself ridiculous by escaping out of the city.

"For just consider, if you transgress and err in this sort of way, what good will you do, either to yourself or to your friends? That your friends will be driven into exile and deprived of citizenship, or will lose their property, is tolerably certain; and you yourself, if you fly to one of the neighboring cities, as, for example, Thebes or Megara, both of which are well-governed cities, will come to them as an enemy, Socrates, and their government will be against you, and all patriotic citizens will cast an evil eye upon you as a subverter of the laws, and you will confirm in the minds of the judges the justice of their own condemnation of you. For he who is a corrupter of the laws is more than likely to be corrupter of the young and foolish portion of mankind. Will you then flee from well-ordered cities and virtuous men? And is existence worth having on these terms? Or will you go to them without shame, and talk to them, Socrates? And what will you say to them? What you say here about virtue and justice and institutions and laws being the best things among men? Would that be decent of you? Surely not. But if you go away from well-governed States to Crito's friends in Thessaly, where there is great disorder and license, they will be charmed to have the tale of your escape from prison, set off with ludicrous particulars of the manner in which you were wrapped in a goatskin or some other disguise, and metamorphosed as the fashion of runaways is—that is very likely; but will there be no one to remind you that in your old age you violated the most sacred laws from a miserable desire of a little more life? Perhaps not, if you keep them in a good temper; but if they are out of temper you will hear many degrading things; you will live, but how?—as the flatterer of all men, and the servant of all men; and doing what?—eating and drinking in Thessaly, having gone abroad in order that you may get a dinner. And where will be your fine sentiments about justice and virtue then? Say that you wish to live for the sake of your children, that you may bring them up and educate them—will you take them into Thessaly and deprive them of Athenian citizenship? Is that the benefit which you would confer upon them? Or are you under the impression that they will be better cared for and educated here if you are still alive, although absent from them; for that your friends will take care of them? Do you fancy that if you are an inhabitant of Thessaly they will take care of them, and if you are an inhabitant of the other world they will not take care of them? Nay; but if they who call themselves friends are truly friends, they surely will.

"Listen, then, Socrates, to us who have brought you up. Think not of life and children first, and of justice afterwards, but of justice first, that you may be justified before the princes of the world below. For neither will you nor any that belong to you be happier or holier or juster in this life, or happier in another, if you do as Crito bids. Now you depart in innocence, a sufferer and not a doer of evil; a victim, not of the laws, but of men. But if you go forth, returning evil for evil, and injury for injury, breaking the covenants and agreements which you have made with us, and wronging those whom you ought least to wrong, that is to say, yourself, your friends, your country, and us, we shall be angry with you while you live, and our brethren, the laws in the world below, will receive you as an enemy; for they will know that you have done your best to destroy us. Listen, then, to us and not to Crito."

This is the voice which I seem to hear murmuring in my ears, like the sound of the flute in the ears of the mystic; that voice, I say, is humming in my ears, and prevents me from hearing any other. And I know that anything more which you will say will be in vain. Yet speak, if you have anything to say.

Cr. I have nothing to say, Socrates.

Soc. Then let me follow the intimations of the will of God.

QUESTIONS

1.   Poor Crito was certainly one of the classic "foils" or "straight men" in the history of thought. Accurately described by Hugh Tredennick as "old . . . kindly, practical, simple-minded,"[50] he loved Socrates and was generous to a fault. He was worried about Socrates' family, particularly his children, and saw Socrates' death to be the needless waste of a great teacher. Socrates' death was completely unnecessary, because Crito and others had bribed the jailers and arranged for a safe rescue. Besides, the trial was entirely political and the conviction unjust. Crito, ever a practical and loyal friend, blamed himself. He pleaded with Socrates to be reasonable, arguing "The trial need never have come on, or might have been brought to another issue; and the end of all, which is the crowning absurdity, will seem to have been permitted by us, through cowardice and baseness, who might have saved you, as you might have saved yourself, if we had been good for anything (for there was no difficulty in escaping)." Put yourself in Crito's shoes, as one of Socrates' most devoted friends. What would you have done?

2.   Assume, as a lawyer, you have a client like Socrates. What could and would you do in such a situation? How much can a lawyer be like the generous, loyal and practical Crito when the solution is illegal? Or should the lawyer always be an embodiment of the "Laws of Athens," who came in to Socrates' mind to interrogate him and demand obedience? What do your professional rules say about this? *See* ABA Model Rules 1.2, 2.1, 3.1, 3.2, 3.3, 8.3, and 8.4. Note, many immigration lawyers

---

[50]   PLATO, THE LAST DAYS OF SOCRATES 79 (trans. and Intro. Hugh Tredennick, new ed., 1959).

know that their clients can easily avoid detection in America as "illegal" immigrants. Should that influence their "legal" advice?

FYODOR DOSTOEVSKY, CRIME AND PUNISHMENT (1866)
(Constance Garnett trans., 1914)

*   *   *

"Only fancy, Rodya, what we got on to yesterday. Whether there is such a thing as crime. I told you that we talked our heads off."

"What is there strange? It's an everyday social question," Raskolnikov answered casually.

"The question wasn't put quite like that," observed Porfiry.

"Not quite, that's true," Razumihin agreed at once, getting warm and hurried as usual. "Listen, Rodion, and tell us your opinion, I want to hear it. I was fighting tooth and nail with them and wanted you to help me. I told them you were coming. . . . It began with the socialist doctrine. You know their doctrine; crime is a protest against the abnormality of the social organisation and nothing more, and nothing more; no other causes admitted! . . ."

"You are wrong there," cried Porfiry Petrovitch; he was noticeably animated and kept laughing as he looked at Razumihin, which made him more excited than ever.

"Nothing is admitted," Razumihin interrupted with heat. "I am not wrong. I'll show you their pamphlets. Everything with them is 'the influence of environment,' and nothing else. Their favourite phrase! From which it follows that, *if society is normally organised, all crime will cease at once*, since there will be nothing to protest against and all men will become righteous in one instant. Human nature is not taken into account, it is excluded, it's not supposed to exist! They don't recognise that humanity, developing by a historical living process, will become at last a normal society, but they believe that a social system that has come out of some mathematical brain is going to organise all humanity at once and make it just and sinless in an instant, quicker than any living process! That's why they instinctively dislike history, 'nothing but ugliness and stupidity in it,' and they explain it all as stupidity! That's why they so dislike the *living* process of life; they don't want a *living soul*! The living soul demands life, the soul won't obey the rules of mechanics, the soul is an object of suspicion, the soul is retrograde! But what they want, though it smells of death and can be made of india rubber, at least is not alive, has no will, is servile and won't revolt! And it comes in the end to their reducing everything to the building of walls and the planning of rooms and passages in a phalanstery! The phalanstery is ready, indeed, but your human nature is not ready for the phalanstery—it wants life, it hasn't completed its vital process, it's too soon for the graveyard! You can't skip over nature by logic. Logic presupposes three possibilities, but there are millions! Cut away a million, and reduce it all to the question of comfort! That's the easiest solution of the problem! It's seductively clear and you mustn't think about it. That's the great thing, you mustn't think! The whole secret of life in two pages of print!"

"Now he is off, beating the drum! Catch hold of him, do!" laughed Porfiry. "Can you imagine," he turned to Raskolnikov, "six people holding forth like that last night, in one room, with punch as a preliminary! No, brother, you are wrong, environment accounts for a great deal in crime; I can assure you of that."

"Oh, I know it does, but just tell me: a man of forty violates a child of ten; was it environment drove him to it?"

"Well, strictly speaking, it did," Porfiry observed with noteworthy gravity; "a crime of that nature may be very well ascribed to the influence of environment."

Razumihin was almost in a frenzy. "Oh, if you like," he roared, "I'll prove to you that your white eyelashes may very well be ascribed to the Church of Ivan the Great's being two hundred and fifty feet high, and I will prove it clearly, exactly, progressively, and even with a Liberal tendency! I undertake to! Will you bet on it?"

"Done! Let's hear, please, how he will prove it!"

"He is always humbugging, confound him," cried Razumihin, jumping up and gesticulating. "What's the use of talking to you! He does all that on purpose; you don't know him, Rodion! He took their side yesterday, simply to make fools of them. And the things he said yesterday! And they were delighted! He can keep it up for a fortnight together. Last year he persuaded us that he was going into a monastery: he stuck to it for two months. Not long ago he took it into his head to declare he was going to get married, that he had everything ready for the wedding. He ordered new clothes indeed. We all began to congratulate him. There was no bride, nothing, all pure fantasy!"

"Ah, you are wrong! I got the clothes before. It was the new clothes in fact that made me think of taking you in."

"Are you such a good dissembler?" Raskolnikov asked carelessly.

"You wouldn't have supposed it, eh? Wait a bit, I shall take you in, too. Ha-ha-ha! No, I'll tell you the truth. All these questions about crime, environment, children, recall to my mind an article of yours which interested me at the time. 'On Crime'. . . . or something of the sort, I forget the title, I read it with pleasure two months ago in the *Periodical Review*."

"My article? In the *Periodical Review*?" Raskolnikov asked in astonishment. "I certainly did write an article upon a book six months ago when I left the university, but I sent it to the *Weekly Review*."

"But it came out in the *Periodical*."

"And the *Weekly Review* ceased to exist, so that's why it wasn't printed at the time."

"That's true; but when it ceased to exist, the *Weekly Review* was amalgamated with the *Periodical*, and so your article appeared two months ago in the latter. Didn't you know?"

Raskolnikov had not known.

"Why, you might get some money out of them for the article! What a strange person you are! You lead such a solitary life that you know nothing of matters that concern you directly. It's a fact, I assure you."

"Bravo, Rodya! I knew nothing about it either!" cried Razumihin. "I'll run to-day to the reading-room and ask for the number. Two months ago? What was the date? It doesn't matter though, I will find it. Think of not telling us!"

"How did you find out that the article was mine? It's only signed with an initial."

"I only learnt it by chance, the other day. Through the editor; I know him. . . . I was very much interested."

"I analysed, if I remember, the psychology of a criminal before and after the crime."

"Yes, and you maintained that the perpetration of a crime is always accompanied by illness. Very, very original, but . . . it was not that part of your article that interested me so much, but an idea at the end of the article which I regret to say you merely suggested without working it out clearly. There is, if you recollect, a suggestion that there are certain persons who can. . . . that is, not precisely are able to, but have a perfect right to commit breaches of morality and crimes, and that the law is not for them."

Raskolnikov smiled at the exaggerated and intentional distortion of his idea.

"What? What do you mean? A right to crime? But not because of the influence of environment?" Razumihin inquired with some alarm even.

"No, not exactly because of it," answered Porfiry. "In his article all men are divided into 'ordinary' and 'extraordinary.' Ordinary men have to live in submission, have no right to transgress the law, because—don't you see?—they are ordinary. But extraordinary men have a right to commit any crime and to transgress the law in any way, just because they are extraordinary. That was your idea, if I am not mistaken?"

"What do you mean? That can't be right?" Razumihin muttered in bewilderment.

Raskolnikov smiled again. He saw the point at once, and knew where they wanted to drive him. He decided to take up the challenge.

"That wasn't quite my contention," he began simply and modestly. "Yet I admit that you have stated it almost correctly; perhaps, if you like, perfectly so." (It almost gave him pleasure to admit this.) "The only difference is that I don't contend that extraordinary people are always bound to commit breaches of morals, as you call it. In fact, I doubt whether such an argument could be published. I simply hinted that an 'extraordinary' man has the right . . . that is not an official right, but an inner right to decide in his own conscience to overstep . . . certain obstacles, and only in case it is essential for the practical fulfilment of his idea (sometimes, perhaps, of benefit to the whole of humanity). You say that my article isn't definite; I am ready to make it as clear as I can. Perhaps I am right in thinking you want me to; very well. I maintain that if the discoveries of Kepler and Newton could not have been made known except by sacrificing the lives of one, a dozen, a hundred, or more men, Newton would have had the right, would indeed have been in duty bound . . . to *eliminate* the dozen or the hundred men for the sake of making his discoveries known to the whole of humanity. But it does not follow from that that Newton had a right to murder people right and left and to steal every day in the market. Then, I remember, I maintain in my article that all . . . well, legislators and leaders of men, such as Lycurgus, Solon, Mahomet, Napoleon, and so on, were all without exception criminals, from the very fact that, making a new law, they transgressed the ancient one, handed down from their ancestors and held sacred by the people, and they did not stop short at bloodshed either, if that bloodshed—often of innocent persons fighting bravely in defense of ancient law—were of use to their cause. It's remarkable, in fact, that the majority, indeed, of these benefactors and leaders of humanity were guilty of terrible carnage. In short, I maintain that all great men or even men a little out of the common, that is to say capable of giving some new word, must from their very nature be criminals—more or less, of course. Otherwise it's hard for them to get out of the common rut; and to remain in the common rut is what they can't submit to, from their very nature again, and to my mind they ought not, indeed, to submit to it. You see that there is nothing particularly new in all that. The same thing has been printed and read a thousand times before. As for my division of people into ordinary and extraordinary, I acknowledge that it's somewhat arbitrary, but I don't insist upon exact numbers. I only believe in my leading idea that men are *in general* divided by a law of nature into two categories, inferior (ordinary), that is, so to say, material that serves only to reproduce its kind, and men who have the gift or the talent to utter *a new word*. There are, of course, innumerable subdivisions, but the distinguishing features of both categories are fairly well marked. The first category, generally speaking, are men conservative in temperament and law abiding; they live under control and love to be controlled. To my thinking it is their duty to be controlled, because that's their vocation, and there is nothing humiliating in it for them. The second category all transgress the law; they are destroyers or disposed to destruction according to their capacities. The crimes of these men are of course relative and varied; for the most part they seek in very varied ways the destruction of the present for the sake of the better. But if such a one is forced for the sake of his idea to step over a corpse or wade through blood, he can, I maintain, find within himself, in his conscience, sanction for wading through blood—that depends on the idea and its dimensions, note that. It's only in that sense I speak of their right to crime in my article (you remember it began with the legal question). There's no need for much anxiety, however; the masses will scarcely ever admit this right, they punish them or hang them (more or less), and in doing so fulfil quite justly their conservative vocation. But the same masses set these criminals on a pedestal in the next generation and worship them (more or less). The first category is always the man of the present, the second the man of the future. The first preserve the world and people it, the second move the world and lead it to its goal. Each class has an equal right to exist. In fact, all have equal rights with me—and *vive la guerre éternelle*—till the New Jerusalem, of course!"

"Then you believe in the New Jerusalem, to you?"

"I do," Raskolnikov answered firmly; as he said these words and during the whole preceding tirade he kept his eyes on one spot on the carpet.

"And . . . and do you believe in God? Excuse my curiosity."

"I do," repeated Raskolnikov, raising his eyes to Porfiry.

"And . . . do you believe in Lazarus' rising from the dead?"

"I . . . I do. Why do you ask all this?"

"You believe it literally?"

"Literally."

"You don't say so . . . I asked from curiosity. Excuse me. But let us go back to the question; they are not always executed. Some, on the contrary. . . ."

"Triumph in their lifetime? Oh, yes, some attain their ends in this life, and then. . . ."

"They begin executing other people?"

"If it's necessary; indeed, for the most part they do. Your remark is very witty."

"Thank you. But tell me this: how do you distinguish those extraordinary people from the ordinary ones? Are there signs at their birth? I feel there ought to be more exactitude, more external definition. Excuse the natural anxiety of a practical law-abiding citizen, but couldn't they adopt a special uniform, for instance, couldn't they wear something, be branded in some way? For you know if confusion arises and a member of one category imagines that he belongs to the other, begins to 'eliminate obstacles,' as you so happily expressed it, then. . . ."

"Oh, that very often happens! That remark is wittier than the other."

"Thank you."

"No reason to; but take note that the mistake can only arise in the first category, that is among the ordinary people (as I perhaps unfortunately called them). In spite of their predisposition to obedience very many of them, through a playfulness of nature, sometimes vouchsafed even to the cow, like to imagine themselves advanced people, "destroyers," and to push themselves into the "new movement," and this quite sincerely. Meanwhile the really *new* people are very often unobserved by them, or even despised as reactionaries of groveling tendencies. But I don't think there is any considerable danger here, and you really need not be uneasy for they never go very far. Of course, they might have a thrashing sometimes for letting their fancy run away with them and to teach them their place, but no more; in fact, even this isn't necessary as they castigate themselves, for they are very conscientious: some perform this service for one another and others chastise themselves with their own hands. . . . They will impose various public acts of penitence upon themselves with a beautiful and edifying effect; in fact you've nothing to be uneasy about. . . . It's a law of nature."

"Well, you have certainly set my mind more at rest on that score; but there's another thing worries me. Tell me, please, are there many people who have the right to kill others, these extraordinary people? I am ready to bow down to them, of course, but you must admit it's alarming if there are a great many of them, eh?"

"Oh, you needn't worry about that either," Raskolnikov went on in the same tone. "People with new ideas, people with the faintest capacity for saying something *new*, are extremely few in number, extraordinarily so in fact. One thing only is clear, that the appearance of all these grades and subdivisions of men must follow with unfailing regularity some law of nature. That law, of course, is unknown at present, but I am convinced that it exists, and one day may become known. The vast mass of mankind is mere material, and only exists in order by some great effort, by some mysterious process, by means of some crossing of races and stocks, to bring into the world at last perhaps one man out of a thousand with a spark of independence. One in ten thousand perhaps—I speak roughly, approximately—is born with some independence, and with still greater independence one in a hundred thousand. The man of genius is one of millions, and the great geniuses, the crown of humanity, appear on earth perhaps one in many thousand millions. In fact I have not peeped into the retort in which all this takes place. But there certainly is and must be a definite law, it cannot be a matter of chance."

"Why, are you both joking?" Razumihin cried at last. "There you sit, making fun of one another. Are you serious, Rodya?"

Raskolnikov raised his pale and almost mournful face and made no reply. And the unconcealed, persistent, nervous, and *discourteous* sarcasm of Porfiry seemed strange to Razumihin beside that quiet and mournful face.

"Well, brother, if you are really serious. . . . You are right, of course, in saying that it's not new, that it's like what we've read and heard a thousand times already; but what is really *original* in all this, and is exclusively your own, to my horror, is that you sanction bloodshed *in the name of conscience*, and, excuse my saying so, with such fanaticism. . . . That, I take it, is the point of your article. But that sanction of bloodshed by conscience is to my mind . . . more terrible than the official, legal sanction of bloodshed. . . ."

"You are quite right, it is more terrible," Porfiry agreed.

"Yes, you must have exaggerated! There is some mistake, I shall read it. You can't think that! I shall read it."

"All that is not in the article, there's only a hint of it," said Raskolnikov.

"Yes, yes." Porfiry couldn't sit still. "Your attitude to crime is pretty clear to me now, but . . . excuse me for my impertinence (I am really ashamed to be worrying you like this), you see, you've removed my anxiety as to the two grades' getting mixed, but . . . there are various practical possibilities that make me uneasy! What if some man or youth imagines that he is a Lycurgus or Mahomet—a future one, of course—and suppose he begins to remove all obstacles. . . . He has some great enterprise before him and needs money for it . . . and tries to get it . . . do you see?"

Zametov gave a sudden guffaw in his corner. Raskolnikov did not even raise his eyes to him.

"I must admit," he went on calmly, "that such cases certainly must arise. The vain and foolish are particularly apt to fall into that snare; young people especially."

"Yes, you see. Well then?"

"What then?" Raskolnikov smiled in reply; "that's not my fault. So it is and so it always will be. He said just now (he nodded at Razumihin) that I sanction bloodshed. Society is too well protected by prisons, banishment, criminal investigators, penal servitude. There's no need to be uneasy. You have but to catch the thief."

"And what if we do catch him?"

"Then he gets what he deserves."

"You are certainly logical. But what of his conscience?"

"Why do you care about that?"

"Simply from humanity."

"If he has a conscience he will suffer for his mistake. That will be his punishment—as well as the prison."

"But the real geniuses," asked Razumihin frowning, "those who have the right to murder? Oughtn't they to suffer at all even for the blood they've shed?"

"Why the word *ought*? It's not a matter of permission or prohibition. He will suffer if he is sorry for his victim. Pain and suffering are always inevitable for a large intelligence and a deep heart. The really great men must, I think, have great sadness on earth," he added dreamily, not in the tone of the conversation.

He raised his eyes, looked earnestly at them all, smiled, and took his cap. He was too quiet by comparison with his manner at his entrance, and he felt this. Every one got up.

"Well, you may abuse me, be angry with me if you like," Porfiry Petrovitch began again, "but I can't resist. Allow me one little question (I know I am troubling you). There is just one little notion I want to express, simply that I may not forget it."

"Very good, tell me your little notion," Raskolnikov stood waiting, pale and grave before him.

"Well, you see. . . . I really don't know how to express it properly. . . . It's a playful, psychological idea. . . . When you were writing your article, surely you couldn't have helped, he-he, fancying yourself . . . just a little, an 'extraordinary' man, uttering a new word in your sense. . . . That's so, isn't it?"

"Quite possibly," Raskolnikov answered contemptuously.

Razumihin made a movement.

"And, if so, could you bring yourself in case of worldly difficulties and hardship or for some service to humanity—to overstep obstacles? For instance, to rob and murder?"

And again he winked with his left eye, and laughed noiselessly just as before.

"If I did I certainly should not tell you," Raskolnikov answered with defiant and haughty contempt.

*   *   *

QUESTIONS

1.   Razumihin is deeply hostile to the idea that crime is "the influence of environment, and nothing else." ("From which it follows that, if society is normally organized all crime will cease at once. . . . Human nature is not taken into account, it is excluded. . . ."). *Materials, supra* at 7F. To what extent do you believe that crime is "caused" by society? Socrates, in defending his allegiance to Athenian law, did recall all Athens had done for him, but remained true even when Athens turned on him most cruelly. Dostoevsky, too, was cruelly treated by his beloved Russia, imprisoned, and nearly executed. Both, however, were deeply reluctant to permit cruel treatment by their society to be an excuse from allegiance to the legal order. Why is that? Do you agree?

2.   Raskolnikov saw himself in the role of a morally superior person, the kind Nietzsche would describe as an "*Übermensch.*" As with Nietzsche's "superior man," Raskolnikov saw himself exempt from normal legal obedience, for the good of all. Dostoevsky, despite his own harsh treatment by the legal order of his home land, developed Raskolnikov as an ominous figure. How does one define the difference between Nietzsche's moral "*Übermensch*" and the criminal mentality? Do the Crito and Dostoevsky change your views as to the problems in Chapter VI on *Justified Disobedience*?

3.   Razumihin observed to Raskolnikov: "[W]hat is really *original* in all this . . . to my horror, is that you sanction bloodshed *in the name of conscience*. But that sanction of bloodshed by *conscience* is to my mind more terrible than the official, legal sanction of bloodshed. . . ." *Materials, supra* at 7F. We have discussed before whether a person who commits a crime out of moral conviction should be punished more or less severely than an ordinary criminal. Do these excerpts from *Crime and Punishment* change your views? Why is bloodshed sanctioned by conscience "more terrible" than a "legal" execution?

IMMANUEL KANT, ON THE OLD SAW: THAT MAY BE RIGHT IN THEORY BUT IT WON'T WORK IN PRACTICE
(Approx. 1785) (E. B. Ashton trans., 1974)

* * *

The concept of duty in its total purity is not only incomparably simpler, clearer, and more comprehensible and natural for everyone's practical use than any motive drawn from happiness, or mixed with happiness and with considerations of happiness (which always require a great deal of skill and thought). In the view of even the most common human reason, the concept of duty is far stronger, more penetrating, and more promising than any motives borrowed from the self-interested principle of happiness—provided only it is presented to our will in detachment from, or even in opposition to, those considerations of happiness.

Suppose, for instance, that someone is holding another's property in trust (a deposit) whose owner is dead, and that the owner's heirs do not know and can never hear about it. Present this case even to a child of eight or nine, and add that, through no fault of his, the trustee's fortunes are at lowest ebb, that he sees a sad family around him, a wife and children disheartened by want. From all of this he would be instantly delivered by appropriating the deposit. And further that the man is kind and charitable, while those heirs are rich, loveless, extremely extravagant spendthrifts, so that this addition to their wealth might as well be thrown into the sea. And then ask whether under these circumstances it might be deemed permissible to convert the deposit to one's own use. Without doubt, anyone asked will answer "No!"—and in lieu of grounds he can merely say: "It is wrong", i.e., it conflicts with duty. Nothing is clearer than that. And assuredly it is not his own *happiness* that the man promotes by surrendering the deposit. For if happiness were the end that he expected to determine his decision, he might, for example, think along these lines: "If you give up, unasked, what does not belong to you, you will gain a widespread good reputation that may become quite lucrative for you." But all this is very uncertain. On the other hand, many misgivings arise as well: "To end your straitened condition at one stroke, you might embezzle what has been entrusted to you; but if you made prompt use of it, you would evoke suspicions concerning how and by what means your circumstances had so quickly improved; however, if you were slow about it, your distress would increase in the meantime to a point beyond help."

The will thus pursuant to the maxim of happiness vacillates between motivations, wondering what it should resolve upon. For it considers the outcome, and that is most uncertain: one must have a good head on his shoulders to disentangle himself from the jumble of arguments and counterarguments and not to deceive himself in the tally. But if he asks himself where his duty lies, he is not in the least embarrassed for what answer to give himself; he is instantly certain what he must do. In fact, if the concept of duty carries any weight with him, he will actually shudder to think of benefits he might derive from its violation, just as if he still had a choice.

It is clear, that these distinctions are not the niceties they seem to be to Herr G. They are graven into the human soul in the crudest, most legible script, and Herr G.'s argument that *they evaporate altogether when it comes to action* contradicts our experience. Not, of course, the experience embodied in the history of maxims derived from one principle or the other, for this unfortunately shows that most of these maxims flow from the principle of self-interest. But it contradicts the experience, which can only be an inner experience, that no idea does more to lift the human spirit and to fan its enthusiasm than the very idea of a pure moral character. Due to this idea, man will revere his duty above all else, will wrestle with the countless ills of life as well as with its most seductive temptations, and yet (as we correctly assume that he can) will overcome them. That he knows he can do this because he ought to—this is the revelation of divine tendencies within himself deep enough to fill him with sacred awe, as it were, at the magnitude and sublimity of his true destiny. And if it were more frequently brought to the attention of men, if they became accustomed to divesting virtue of the rich loot of advantages to be gained by the performance of duty, and to envisioning virtue in all its purity; if constant use of this view were made a principle of private and public education (a method of inculcating virtue that has been neglected in almost every age)—if these things were done, the state of human morality would improve in short order. The fact that historical experience until now has not yet proved the doctrines of virtue successful may well be due to the wrong premise. The motivating force derived from the idea of duty itself has been considered far too refined for the vulgar understanding; while the cruder idea of duty, based upon certain benefits expected in this world (and indeed in a future world) from following the law (without regard to its motivating force) was credited with a more vigorous effect upon the mind. And it may be due to the adoption of the educational and homiletic principle of preferring the pursuit of happiness over the supreme requirement of reason: being worthy of happiness. The *prescriptions* how to gain happiness, or at least to keep from harm, are not *commandments*. They are not downright obligatory on anyone. Having been warned, man may choose what seems good to him if he is willing to suffer the consequences. Ill effects are apt to result from his failure to take the advice received, but he has no reason to regard them as punishment. Punishment is reserved for a will that is free but unlawful; nature and inclination cannot legislate for freedom. With regard to the idea of duty the situation is entirely different. The violation of one's duty, even without taking into consideration the disadvantages that follow, directly affects the mind of the agent and makes him reprehensible and punishable in his own eyes.

Here we have clear proof that in ethics what is right in theory must work in practice.

*   *   *

QUESTIONS

1. Do you agree with Kant's "practical" example of the needy trustee and the spendthrift heirs?

2. A famous contracts professor of the "Old School," who later became a distinguished judge, found the idea of teaching "ethics" in law school deeply ridiculous. He was finally *required* to teach ethics as part of a new rule mandating 20 minutes of ethical instruction in every class weekly, a rule he described as "absurd." His first 20 minutes consisted of telling the following story: "A new lawyer was eager but destitute. He stood to lose his house if he didn't pay his mortgage soon, but the next money due him was months away. He had a rich client, a kindly widow who had entrusted some of her accounts to his care. Without telling her, the lawyer "borrowed" enough from her accounts to save his home. When his money finally came, he replaced the sum with full interest. *She was none the wiser*, and both lived happily ever after." The professor then said, "You've had your ethics lesson!" and stalked from the room. What was the lesson?

A. C. EWING, ETHICS
(1953)

Chapter 4
Duty for Duty's Sake

Having examined theories which based ethics on happiness, it is well to turn to the other extreme and take the theory of the great German philosopher Kant (1724-1803). His ethics was to a large extent motivated by a reaction against hedonism, especially the egoistic variety of it, and his theory took the form that the primary thing to *consider* is not the happiness or unhappiness produced by an action, or indeed any of its consequences, but the nature of the action itself. Central to his ethics is the concept of the good will. By this he means not good will in the sense of kindly feeling, but the doing one's duty because it is one's duty, or as he put it, "out of respect for the moral law." He begins his ethics by declaring that this good will is the only thing which can be held to be unconditionally good, and he insists again and again on its supreme and incomparable worth, which it retains even if unable to achieve any of the external results valued and desired by us. There is something splendid about a self-sacrificing and disinterested act, even if through no fault of the agent it fails entirely. Kant does not indeed deny all value to happiness, but he maintains that happiness (which he like the utilitarians equates with pleasure) is only conditionally good. By this he means that, if we have the good will, it is good that we should also be happy, but not otherwise. This is not to say happiness is only good as a means: for if a person has the good will, it is better that he should also be happy, even apart from any future consequences of his happiness. But it is to say that happiness, unlike the good will, is not good under all circumstances but only under some, namely, in the presence of the good will. Kant never suggests that anything else besides the good will and happiness can be intrinsically good and, strange to say, it seems that he valued knowledge, love, and all qualities of the mind other than the good will merely as means. Nor does he like Mill draw any distinction in quality between pleasures, but treats all pleasures and all desires as on the same level, as being neither good nor bad but ethically indifferent. His main contribution to ethics was to develop the idea of duty for duty's sake which previous moralists had usually neglected. Of the other things generally accounted as values he says little.

In developing his concept of dutiful action Kant insists on a very important distinction he draws between hypothetical and categorical imperatives. A hypothetical imperative tells us to act in a certain way because it will tend to produce a certain result, and the need for the action is thus conditional on our desiring the result in question; but a categorical imperative commands us unconditionally. For example, "take such and such a road if you want to go to London" (which you may not do) is a hypothetical imperative; "do not tell lies" a categorical. Categorical imperatives alone, he holds, are ethical. Obedience to them is a duty, while obedience to hypothetical imperatives is at the best prudential. But what is the motive for obeying categorical imperatives? It is not a desire for some future result of the action, whether for ourselves or even others, otherwise they would be hypothetical; it is the motive to do the right as such, *respect for the moral law*, which Kant regards as essentially different from desire, though it can like desire serve as a motive for action. Kant further draws a very sharp distinction between actions which are outwardly in accordance with the moral law but really are motivated by self-interest and actions which are done from a sense of duty. The first kind of action may be externally the same as the second, but this does not give it any inner worth whatever. We cannot praise a tradesman for his honesty if he is honest merely because he thinks it good business policy.

A difficulty that strikes most readers of Kant is that men seem often to perform the most noble and self-sacrificing actions under the influence of love rather than out of a conscious sense of duty, and it seems unfair to deny all intrinsic value to such actions. We should actually think better of a father who did his duty to his children from love without thinking of it as a duty than we should of one who felt no love for his children but without desiring to benefit them did his duty to them just because it was his duty. Commentators are not agreed exactly how far Kant lays himself open to this criticism, but according to the interpretation which I am on the whole inclined to favour he did not commit himself to the view that a person's action had no moral value if it was motived both by some desire and by respect for the moral law in such a way that either motive by itself would have been sufficient to bring about the act, but only to the view that it had no moral value if it was motived entirely by desire. In that case at any rate he has a reasonable defence. He might urge that any desire, however fine in itself, may lead us to act wrongly, and therefore, if we let ourselves be guided solely by it we are risking doing wrong, and cannot lay claim to any merit even if by good luck we are right. It is obvious that the love of any one individual or group of individuals may lead us to further their interests at the expense of others or in ways which are normally wicked. We may disagree with Kant and ascribe intrinsic value to some forms of love and some desires other than respect for the moral law, but at any rate we cannot ascribe to them or to action motived solely by them the particular kind of value known as moral value which Kant has so effectively brought to our notice. On the other hand we must recognize that the supreme ethical motive which Kant felt as respect for an abstract law is felt by others as an urge to pursue the supreme good for humanity, and by others still as the love of God. We must not of course condemn as unethical anyone who does not envisage it in just Kant's way.

Now let us consider the application of Kant's theory to the chief question of Ethics, namely, what acts are right and why are they right. He was debarred by his principles from answering this question simply by a straightforward reference to their consequences. For to make consequences decisive is to base the rightness or wrongness of an action on the good or evil it produces. Now the only goods Kant recognized were, as we have seen, the good will and happiness. The former is a matter of the action and its motives and not of the consequences at all, and the latter could not be made the supreme criterion of what is right without adopting utilitarianism, a view with which Kant had no sympathy. He was therefore constrained to look for a means of explaining why some actions are right and some wrong otherwise than by reference to consequences.

He had another reason for this attitude. In philosophy one of the most fundamental distinctions is that between empirical knowledge, or knowledge based on observation, and *a priori* knowledge, or knowledge based on pure thought and reasoning, as in mathematics. Now Kant was convinced that ethical knowledge is *a priori* and not empirical. Observation can only tell us what is, and you cannot derive what ought to be from what is, he argued, and he also thought that ethical principles have a necessity which cannot find a place in the merely empirical world. He concluded that the general principles of Ethics like those of mathematics were discoverable *a priori* by thinking and not by generalization from experience, though of course they have to be applied to empirical facts, as indeed are the principles of mathematics. For instance, he held we could know *a priori* that we ought not to tell lies, though we obviously need empirical knowledge to decide what is the true thing to say and how best to say it so as to make ourselves understood by others.

How are the principles of Ethics then to be established? *A priori* conclusions are commonly proved in other fields of thought by showing that there would be a contradiction in denying them, and Kant tried to apply this method to Ethics. Thus he argued that it is wrong to tell lies because, if everybody lied whenever he thought it suited him, the lies would not be believed and would therefore lose all point and be self-defeating. Kant regards this as showing universal lying to be logically impossible, but he does not think it can be shown of all wrong ethical principles that their universal application would be impossible, but merely that it would contradict our nature to will it. Thus in discussing why we ought to help other men who are in need he says that society could still subsist if the principle of not helping others in need were universalized, but we could not consistently will it universalized because there are many possible circumstances in which we should wish to be helped ourselves. This sounds as if Kant were after all falling back on an egoistic motive, but I do not think it is really so. Kant's point is not—Give to others so that they may give to you in return, but—It is not consistent, we might put it "not fair," to benefit by the kindness of others, as you must, and yet refuse to do others a kindness when they need it. While the former motive is prudential, the latter is certainly moral. Kant's general principle is—"Act as if the maxim of your action were to become by your will law universal." When we act according to a principle which we could not wish to be generally applied, Kant thinks we are acting immorally.

Kant here has clearly hold of something very important, though the detailed applications he makes of his principle are harder to defend. Let us see what plain ethical truths we can learn from him. In the first place, it is significant that what the man who does wrong believing it to be wrong usually wishes is by no means that everybody should act in the way he proposes to do. The thief is the last person who would wish others to steal from him. What the bad man wishes in general is not that the rule he breaks should cease to hold, but that an exception should be made to it in his own favour. It is this arbitrary making of exceptions in one's own interest which is essentially immoral, Kant is saying. Secondly, it does seem that in some cases the use of a criterion like Kant's is more in accord with our ordinary ethical thinking than is straightforward utilitarianism. There are cases where the harm a particular action does is insignificant but we condemn it because it is one of a class of actions. Thus, if I tried to evade taxation and argued that I was under no obligation to pay my taxes because the loss of that amount of money would make no appreciable difference to the functioning of the State but made a considerable difference to me, the usual answer would be to ask in return—What would happen if everybody acted like that? But it should be noted that, while it is a common test of the rightness or wrongness of an action to ask what would happen if everybody acted in that way, what the person who asks has in mind is usually the good or bad consequences that would accrue if everyone so acted, while Kant claimed to base the obligatoriness of his laws not on the harm their general breach would do but on the supposition that there would be some kind of contradiction in a general defiance of them, since universal breach of a law would take away the point in breaking it. Thirdly, it is true that there is really something inconsistent about wickedness in the sense that it aims at an end the attainment of which is at the same time by its inherent nature self-defeating. For the man who is guilty of it seeks satisfaction for himself, yet real satisfaction cannot be attained by evil but only by good. This was perhaps the main point made by both Plato and Hegel in Ethics.

Finally, we must admit that all our answers to the question what is right are of universal application in the sense that, granted an act is right for me, it must be right under the same conditions for everybody. In this sense any moral decision claims universality. Only we should in some cases have to include among the conditions to be taken into account not only external circumstances but differences of individual psychology. It does not follow that, because it was right for Kant to engage on a philosophical career, it would be right for everybody, and a man cannot decide whether it is right for himself or not without considering his own psychology. It may be objected that this makes the principle of universality of no importance, since the circumstances will never be exactly the same for two different agents, if only because the agents are different men, and indeed even for the same agent on two different occasions. But only a small proportion of the circumstances will be ethically relevant, and these might well be similar. Of all the multitudinous circumstances of past history and psychological make-up which differentiate me from another man, only a relatively few will be relevant to the question whether either of us should take up philosophy and probably none at all to the obligation to pay our ordinary debts. One might just as well argue that the "uniformity of nature," or the principle that the same event may be expected under the same conditions, has no relevance to physical science because the conditions are never quite the same on two different occasions. The main point is that I am never entitled to advance on behalf of my own action an excuse which I should not be prepared to accept from anybody else. If I am to maintain that some act is obligatory for A and not for B, I must be able to point to some difference between the circumstances or dispositions of A and B which will account for the difference in obligation, just as the point of the uniformity of nature for the scientist lies in the rule that, if different things happen, the difference must be explained by a difference in the conditions.

Kant, however, held not merely that the same act was always right or wrong for everybody under the same conditions, physical and psychological, but that there are a number of classes of acts which are always wrong under all conditions. Thus he maintained that it was never right to tell lies even in order to save human life from a murderer. This conclusion is very difficult to accept, but if we do not accept it we must admit that Ethics is not *a priori* in the way in which Kant held it was, since we may then occasionally set a general rule aside on account of empirical consequences.

This point has sometimes been expressed by saying that Kant's ethics ignores consequences. This is unfair, and if true would make his ethics a complete absurdity not worth serious study. The truth is that Kant allows us to take account of consequences in order to apply an ethical law but not in order to establish the validity of the law or to make an exception to the law. In order to apply the law that we must not lie we are obviously bound to take account of consequences up to a point. We must take account of the likely effects of our words on the person to whom they are addressed if we are to be understood. But we must not, Kant thinks, justify the general law against lying by arguing that lying usually does more evil than good. This he would say was true, but did not constitute the reason why lying was wrong. Still less, Kant insists, must we argue that we are entitled to lie in a particular case because in this case lying will do more good than evil. It is in this sense that Kant objected to taking account of consequences in deciding what we ought to do. We may note that the law that we ought to help others still more obviously requires a consideration of consequences for its application, but Kant still seems to say that the ultimate justification of it is to be found not in its good consequences but in the fact that we should be in some way acting inconsistently if we broke it, i.e. making an arbitrary exception in our own favour to a rule which we cannot help wishing should be generally observed.

Further, we should note a sense in which Kant is quite obviously right in saying that consequences do not matter, namely, when he insists that the morality of an action and the worth of the agent are not affected by the actual as opposed to the intended or at least foreseeable consequences. In many novels the most dastardly act of the villain turns out to be just the unintended means of bringing about the triumph of the hero and his marriage to the heroine, but if this really happened the beneficial effects of the villain's action could not in the least be accounted to his credit since he intended the reverse, nor could a well-intentioned man be blamed for any unforeseeable consequences of his acts, however deplorable.

But very few writers on ethics since Kant have been prepared to attach so little importance to consequences as he did in deciding how we ought to act. Kant conceived ethics as a set of *a priori* laws which each possessed strict universality, but this view is hard to maintain. The question is of great practical importance especially, though not only, in connection with war. In all wars some, and in the last war almost all, generally accepted ethical rules of action were violated, and their violation was justified as a necessary means to averting still greater evils. So it seems that anybody who refuses to admit that consequences can ever justify the breach of a general ethical law ought to be a conscientious objector to military service?[51] But, even apart from war, there are liable to be cases where conflict if I am asked by a murderer about the whereabouts of his intended victim, or by an invalid on the verge of heart failure for news of a son who I know has died when he still thinks him alive and well. When this happens we must admit an exception to at least one of the laws, for since I must either lie or not, it must be right either to lie or to sacrifice a life which I could have saved. We cannot escape the difficulty by

---

[51] Kant, however, did not take this view, arguably inconsistent with his underlying principle.

saying we ought to keep silent, because there are circumstances in which refusal to answer a question would be equivalent to letting the questioner know the truth. Kant apparently intended to meet such situations by always giving preference to the negative over the positive law, but this seems arbitrary. And in cases where two laws conflict it is hard to see how we can rationally decide between them except by considering the goodness or badness of the consequences. However important it is to tell the truth and however evil to lie, there are surely cases where much greater evils still can only be averted by a lie, and is lying wrong then? Would it not be justifiable for a diplomat to lie, and indeed break most general moral laws, if it were practically certain that this and this alone would avert a third world-war? Some people would answer—No, but they could only defend their position not by argument but by appeal to self-evidence—which Kant does not make—and while it may be self-evident that lying is always evil, it is surely not self-evident that it is always wrong. To incur a lesser evil in order to avert a much greater might well be right, and if that is the case as regards a lie, the lie is evil but not wrong. Without committing myself to the view that absolute pacifism is right, I must however add that I feel considerable sympathy with those who say that it must be wrong to pursue even a good end by evil means because the bad means will taint and poison the results they produce, and because once we adopt this line we are on a slippery slope and do not know where to stop. (Almost all the great political crimes of history have been justified by their perpetrators as means to the greatest good, but of course the fact that a line of justification is often grossly abused does not prove that it is never to be adopted at all, though as I have suggested it is exceedingly difficult to draw the line.) But I do not see how this argument can possibly be carried so far as to exclude all deceit or injustice even, e.g., to save life, and it is at any rate one which appeals to consequences, so as against Kant it must be admitted that it is hard to avoid giving the latter a decisive role where two laws conflict.

Kant introduces two other supreme principles besides the one which tells us to act as if the principle of our action were to be law universal. He indeed for obscure reasons (with which the general reader need not bother) claims that the three are only different formulations of the same truth, but I do not think this can be defended. In any case they are to all appearance different. The second principle reads, "Act so as to treat humanity both in your own person and in that of every other man always as an end and never only as a means." (Note the word "only": we treat a man as a means whenever we allow him to do us a service, and that of course is not wrong, provided we treat him also as an end-in-himself.) Now these words of Kant have had as much influence as perhaps any sentence written by a philosopher, they serve indeed as a slogan of the whole liberal and democratic movement of recent times. They rule out slavery, exploitation, lack of respect for another's dignity and personality, the making of the individual a mere tool of the State, violations of rights. They formulate the greatest moral idea of the day, perhaps one might add the greatest moral (as distinct from "religious") idea of Christianity. But without casting any aspersions on their value, we must point out that they can only serve as a guide to tell us which particular actions to perform if we have some positive idea of the ends of man, so the second principle like the first seems to need supplementation by reference to the positive goods which are to be brought about by its adoption.

The third principle is defined as "the idea of the will of every rational being as a universally legislating will," but this, beyond saying that we are bound by the laws of morality because we realize that we are so bound, adds little to the first law and does not itself give further help in determining what we ought to do in particular cases.

The main upshot of the argument of this chapter is to suggest that Kant's ethics, in so far as it is regarded as a means to determining what is right, needs at any rate to be supplemented and possibly altogether replaced by a point of view which will be more utilitarian, not in the sense of admitting that happiness is the only good, but in the sense of deriving the rightness or wrongness of acts from the good or harm they do. We might disagree with the hedonistic utilitarian as to what is good and yet agree with him in holding that the only thing which makes an act right or wrong is the good or evil it produces or is liable to produce. We have seen how Kant's principles require utilitarian supplementation, the first in order to enable us to decide which ethical precept to obey when there is a conflict between two, the second in order to provide that concrete idea of end without which the principle of treating humanity as an end-in-itself cannot be practically applied. Kant may possibly have been right in holding that the essence of morality and the supreme good for man lies in the nature of the will and yet mistaken in holding that the criterion needed to tell us which acts are right and wrong is to be found in anything but the consequences which can reasonably be anticipated from action. The strength of such a position was not apparent to Kant because he kept thinking of some form of hedonism as the only alternative to his view, and ignored the possibility of a theory which, without taking the hedonist view of good and evil, still derived the obligatoriness or wrongness of an action from its good or bad effects. It remains to consider, in the next chapter, whether this type of utilitarianism is itself capable of defence. In the mean-time we must note with gratitude Kant's description of the specifically moral element in our nature, which may be able to stand in the main independently of his theory of the criteria for determining what is right, as it does stand independently of the general philosophy which he connects with it.

QUESTIONS

1. Kant believed that lying was always wrong. The evil of lying was, for him, an *a priori* truth, that is, like the "truths" of mathematics. It was, therefore, independent of any empirical "test" of good and bad consequences. Do you agree? Would you lie to prevent an evil result? If the evil of lying is not an *a priori* moral truth, what is?

2. Ewing notes that all wars involve evil means justified by compelling ends. He further observes that "[w]ithout committing myself to the view that absolute pacificism is right, I must however add that I feel considerable sympathy with those who say that it must be wrong to pursue even a good end by evil means because the bad means will taint and poison the results they produce, and because once we adopt this line we are on a slippery slope and do not know where to stop." Do you agree? This philosophy is reflected in the "exclusionary" doctrine used by the Supreme Court to enforce constitutional rights by barring the "fruits of the

poisonous tree." *See* Mapp v. Ohio, 367 U.S. 643 (1961). Does this doctrine make any sense?

3.   Many Quakers believe that it is always wrong to lie and to fight in wars. Was Kant's view different? If so, why?

F. H. BRADLEY, ETHICAL STUDIES
(1927)

My Station and Its Duties

* * *

Let us take a man, an Englishman as he is now, and try to point out that, apart from what he has in common with others, apart from his sameness with others, he is not an Englishman—nor a man at all; that if you take him as something by himself, he is not what he is. Of course we do not mean to say that he can not go out of England without disappearing, nor, even if all the rest of the nation perished that he would not survive. What we mean to say is, that he is what he is because he is a born and educated social being, and a member of an individual social organism; that if you make abstraction of all this, which is the same in him and in others, what you have left is not an Englishman, nor a man, but some I know not what residuum, which never has existed by itself, and does not so exist. If we suppose the world of relations, in which he was born and bred, never to have been, then we suppose the very essence of him not to be; if we take that away, we have taken him away; and hence he now is not an individual, in the sense of owing nothing to the sphere of relations in which he finds himself, but does contain those relations within himself as belonging to his very being; he is what he is, in brief, so far as he is what others also are.

The "individual" man, the man into whose essence his community with others does not enter, who does not include relations to others in his very being, is, we say, a fiction.

* * *

We have seen that I am myself by sharing with others, by including in my essence relations to them, the relations of the social state. If I wish to realize my true being, I must therefore realize something beyond my being as a mere this or that; for my true being has in it a life which is not the life of any mere particular, and so must be called a universal life.

What is it then that I am to realize? We have said it in "my station and its duties". To know what a man is (as we have seen) you must not take him in isolation. He is one of a people, he was born in a family, he lives in a certain society, in a certain state. What he has to do depends on what his place is, what his function is, and that all comes from his station in the organism.[52] Are there then such organisms in which

---

[52] We pass here from negation of individualism, and assertion of social life as essential to the 'organism' and the individual's place in it; (i) The family, (ii) social position, and particular profession, (iii) the state, (iv) and a still wider society are all mentioned.

he lives, and if so, what is their nature? Here we come to questions which must be answered in full by any complete system of Ethics, but which we can not enter on. We must content ourselves by pointing out that there are such facts as the family, then in a middle position a man's own profession and society, and, over all, the larger community of the state. Leaving out of sight the question of a society wider than the state, we must say that a man's life with its moral duties is in the main filled up by his station in that system of wholes which the state is, and that this, partly by its laws and institutions, and still more by its spirits, gives him the life which he does live and ought to live. That objective institutions exist is of course an obvious fact; and it is a fact which every day is becoming plainer that these institutions are organic, and further, that they are moral. The assertion that communities have been manufactured by the addition of exclusive units is, as we have seen, a mere fable; and if, within the state, we take that which seems wholly to depend on individual caprice, e.g. marriage, yet even here we find that man does give up his self so far as it excludes others; he does bring himself under a unity which is superior to the particular person and the impulses that belong to his single existence, and which makes him fully as much as he makes it. In short, man is a social being; he is real only because he is social, and can realize himself only because it is as social that he realizes himself. The mere individual is a delusion of theory; and the attempt to realize it in practice is the starvation and mutilation of human nature, with total sterility or the production of monstrosities.

QUESTIONS

1. Bradley argues that "[m]an is a social being; he is real only because he is social." He goes on to state that "[l]eaving out of sight a society wider than the state, we must say that a man's life is filled up by his station in that system of wholes which the state is, and that this, partly by its laws and institutions and still more by its spirit, gives him the life which he does live and ought to live." Do you agree? How does this perspective, deeply indebted to Hegel, differ from Kant's views?

2. What consequences follow if you adopt Bradley's views about individualism? How would it affect your life as a lawyer?

RONALD DWORKIN, TAKING RIGHTS SERIOUSLY
150–151, 133–155, 159–161, 164–166, 168–183 (1977)

Justice and Rights

I trust that it is not necessary to describe John Rawls's famous idea of the original position in any great detail.[53] It imagines a group of men and women who come together to form a social contract. Thus far it resembles the imaginary congresses of the classical social contract theories. The original position differs, however, from these theories in its description of the parties. They are men and women with ordinary tastes, talents, ambitions, and convictions, but each is temporarily ignorant of these features of his own personality, and must agree upon

---

[53] JOHN RAWLS, A THEORY OF JUSTICE (1972).

a contract before his self-awareness returns.

Rawls tries to show that if these men and women are rational, and act only in their own self-interest, they will choose his two principles of justice. These provide, roughly, that every person must have the largest political liberty compatible with a like liberty for all, and that inequalities in power, wealth, income, and other resources must not exist except in so far as they work to the absolute benefit of the worst-off members of society. Many of Rawls's critics disagree that men and women in the original position would inevitably choose these two principles. The principles are conservative, and the critics believe they would be chosen only by men who were conservative by temperament, and not by men who were natural gamblers. I do not think this criticism is well-taken, but in this essay, at least, I mean to ignore the point. I am interested in a different issue.

Suppose that the critics are wrong, and that men and women in the original position would in fact choose Rawls's two principles as being in their own best interest. Rawls seems to think that that fact would provide an argument in favor of these two principles as a standard of justice against which to test actual political institutions. But it is not immediately plain why this should be so.

If a group contracted in advance that disputes amongst them would be settled in a particular way, the fact of that contract would be a powerful argument that such disputes should be settled in that way when they do arise. The contract would be an argument in itself, independent of the force of the reasons that might have led different people to enter the contract. Ordinarily, for example, each of the parties supposes that a contract he signs is in his own interests but if someone has made a mistake in calculating his self-interest, the fact that he did contract is a strong reason for the fairness of holding him nevertheless to the bargain.

Rawls does not suppose that any group ever entered into a social contract of the sort he describes. He argues only that if a group of rational men did find themselves in the predicament of the original position, they would contract for the two principles. His contract is hypothetical, and hypothetical contracts do not supply an independent argument for the fairness of enforcing their terms. A hypothetical contract is not simply a pale form of an actual contract; it is no contract at all.

*   *   *

The technique of equilibrium does play an important role in Rawls's argument, and it is worth describing that technique briefly here. The technique assumes that Rawls's readers have a sense, which we draw upon in our daily life, that certain particular political arrangements or decisions, like conventional trials, are just and others, like slavery, are unjust. It assumes, moreover, that we are each able to arrange these immediate intuitions or convictions in an order that designates some of them as more certain than others. Most people, for example, think that it is more plainly unjust for the state to execute innocent citizens of its own than to kill innocent foreign civilians in war. They might be prepared to abandon their position on foreign civilians in war, on the basis of some argument, but would be much more reluctant to abandon their view on executing innocent countrymen.

It is the task of moral philosophy, according to the technique of equilibrium, to provide a structure of principles that supports these immediate convictions about which we are more or less secure, with two goals in mind. First, this structure of principles must explain the convictions by showing the underlying assumptions they reflect; second it must provide guidance in those cases about which we have either no convictions or weak or contradictory convictions. If we are unsure, for example, whether economic institutions that allow great disparity of wealth are unjust, we may turn to the principles that explain our confident conviction, and then apply these principles to that difficult issue.

*   *   *

2.

A. Equilibrium

I shall start by considering the philosophical basis of the technique of equilibrium I just described. I must spend several pages in this way, but it is important to understand what substantive features of Rawls's deep theory are required by his method. This technique presupposes, as I said, a familiar fact about our moral lives. We all entertain beliefs about justice that we hold because they seem right, not because we have deduced or inferred them from other beliefs. We may believe in this way, for example, that slavery is unjust, and that the standard sort of trial is fair.

These different sorts of beliefs are, according to some philosophers, direct perceptions of some independent and objective moral facts. In the view of other philosophers they are simply subjective preferences, not unlike ordinary tastes, but dressed up in the language of justice to indicate how important they seem to us. In any event, when we argue with ourselves or each other about justice we use these accustomed beliefs—which we call "institutions" or "convictions"—in roughly the way Rawls's equilibrium technique suggests. We test general theories about justice against our own institutions, and we try to confound those who disagree with us by showing how their institutions embarrass their own theories.

Suppose we try to justify this process by setting out a philosophical position about the connection between moral theory and moral intuition. The technique of equilibrium supposes what might be called a "coherence" theory of morality.[54] But we have a choice between two general models that define coherence and explain why it is required, and the choice between these is significant and consequential for our moral philosophy. I shall describe these two models, and then argue that the equilibrium technique makes sense on one but not the other.

I call the first a "natural" model. It presupposes a philosophical position that can be summarized in this way. Theories of justice, like Rawls's two principles, describe an objective moral reality; they are not, that is, created by men or societies but are rather discovered by them, as they discover laws of physics. The main instrument of this discovery is a moral faculty possessed by at least some men, which produces

---

[54] *See* Feinberg, *Justice, Fairness and Rationality*, 91 Yale L.J. 1004, 1018–21 (1972).

concrete intuitions of political morality in particular situations, like the intuition that slavery is wrong. These intuitions are clues to the nature and existence of more abstract and fundamental moral principles, as physical observations are clues to the existence and nature of fundamental physical laws. Moral reasoning or philosophy is a process of reconstructing the fundamental principles by assembling concrete judgments in the right order, as a natural historian reconstructs the shape of the whole animal from the fragments of its bones that he has found.

The second model is quite different. It treats intuitions of justice not as clues to the existence of independent principles, but rather as stipulated features of a general theory to be constructed, as if a sculptor set himself to carve the animal that best fits a pile of bones he happened to find together. This "constructive" model does not assume, as the natural model does, that principles of justice have some fixed, objective existence, so that descriptions of these principles must be true or false in some standard way. It does not assume that the animal it matches to the bones actually exits. It makes the different, and in some ways more complex, assumption that men and women have a responsibility to fit the particular judgments on which they act into a coherent program of action, or, at least, that officials who exercise power over other men have that sort of responsibility.

This second, constructive, model is not unfamiliar to lawyers. It is analogous to one model of common law adjudication. Suppose a judge is faced with a novel claim—for example, a claim for damages based on a legal right to privacy that courts have not heretofore recognized.[55] He must examine such precedents as seem in any way relevant to see whether any principles that are, as we might say, "instinct" in these precedents bear upon the claimed right to privacy. We might treat this judge as being in the position of a man arguing from moral intuitions to a general moral theory. The particular precedents are analogous to intuitions; the judge tries to reach an accommodation between these precedents and a set of principles that might justify them and also justify further decisions that go beyond them. He does not suppose, however, that the precedents are glimpses into a moral reality, and therefore clues to objective principles he ends by declaring. He does not believe that the principles are 'instinct' in the precedents in that sense. Instead, in the spirit of the constructive model, he accepts these precedents as specifications for a principle that he must construct, out of a sense of responsibility for consistency with what has gone before.

*   *   *

B. The Contract

I come, then, to the second of the three features of Rawls's methodology that I want to discuss, which is the use he makes of the old idea of a social contract. I distinguish, as does Rawls, the general idea that an imaginary contract is an appropriate device for reasoning about justice, from the more specific features of the original position, which count as a particular application of that general idea.

---

[55] I have here in mind the famous argument of Brandeis and Warren. *See* Brandeis & Warren, *The Right to Privacy*, 4 HARV. L. REV. 193 (1890), which is a paradigm of argument in the constructive model.

Rawls thinks that all theories that can be seen to rest on a hypothetical social contract of some sort are related and are distinguished as a class from theories that cannot; he supposes, for example, that average utilitarianism, which can be seen as the product of a social contract on a particular interpretation, is more closely related to his own theory than either is to classical utilitarianism, which cannot be seen as the product of a contract on any interpretation. In the next section I shall consider the theoretical basis of the original position. In this section I want to consider the basis of the more general idea of the contract itself.

*   *   *

Right-based and duty-based theories . . . place the individual at the center, and take his decision or conduct as a fundamental importance. But the two types put the individual in a different light. Duty-based theories are concerned with the moral quality of his acts, because they suppose that it is wrong, without more, for an individual to fail to meet certain standards of behavior. Kant thought that it was wrong to tell a lie no matter how beneficial the consequences, not because having this practice promoted some goal, but just because it was wrong. Right-based theories are, in contrast, concerned with the independence rather than the conformity of individual action. They presuppose and protect the value of individual thought and choice. Both types of theory make use of the idea of moral rules, codes of conduct to be followed, on individual occasions, without consulting self-interest. Duty-based theories treat such codes of conduct as of the essence, whether set by society to the individual or by the individual to himself. The man at their center is the man who must conform to such a code, or be punished or corrupted if he does not. Right-based theories, however, treat codes of conduct as instrumental, perhaps necessary to protect the rights of others, but having no essential value in themselves. The man at their center is the man who benefits from others' compliance, not the man who leads the life of virtue by complying himself.

We should therefore, expect that the different types of theories would be associated with different metaphysical or political temperaments, and that one or another would be dominant in certain sorts of political economy. Goal-based theories, for example, seem especially compatible with homogeneous societies, or those at least temporarily united by an urgent, overriding goal, like self-defense or economic expansion. We should also expect that these differences between types of theory would find echoes in the legal systems of the communities they dominate. We should expect, for example, that a lawyer would approach the question of punishing moral offenses through the criminal law in a different way if his inchoate theory of justice were goal-, right- or duty-based. If his theory were goal-based he would consider the full effect of enforcing morality upon his overriding goal. If this goal were utilitarian, for example, he would entertain, though he might in the end reject, Lord Devlin's arguments that the secondary effects of punishing immorality may be beneficial. If his theory were duty-based, on the other hand, he would see the point of the argument, commonly called retributive, that since immorality is wrong the state must punish it even if it harms no one. If his theory were right-based, however, he would reject the retributive argument, and judge the utilitarian argument against the background of his own assumption that individual rights must be served even at some cost to the general welfare.

All this is, of course, superficial and trivial as ideological sociology. My point is only to suggest that these differences in the character of a political theory are important quite apart from the details of position that might distinguish one theory from another of the same character. It is for this reason that the social contract is so important a feature of Rawls's methodology. It signals that his deep theory is a right-based theory, rather than a theory of either of the other two types.

QUESTIONS

1.   What is the fundamental difference between a "right-based deep theory" and a "duty-based deep theory," at least according to Dworkin? Are they both fundamentally incompatible with "goal-based theory"? With each other?

2.   How would your choice of "deep theory" affect your attitude toward the problems discussed in this book? Does the choice of a "right-based deep theory" or a "duty-based deep theory" make a practical difference in how you would conduct yourself as an attorney?

BERNARD WILLIAMS, POLITICS AND MORAL CHARACTER
in PUBLIC AND PRIVATE MORALITY 66–71 (S. Hampshire ed., 1978)

* * *

One has to ask how the desired product of legal activity, justice, is related to an adversarial system, and to what extent the sorts of behavior that concerned Fried are encouraged or required by such a system. That is, in fact, only the start of the problem, for if the adversarial system succeeds in producing justice, one factor in that must be the presence of a judge—and judges are lawyers, and usually former advocates. The judicial disposition is not the same as the adversarial disposition, but as our system of recruitment for judges works, the one has somehow to issue from the other.

Let us, however, stick to the adversarial case. Concentrating on the morally disagreeable activities which may be involved in the enforcement of some legal rights (e.g. some legal rights of the strong against the weak), we might be tempted by the following argument:

(1) In any complex society (at least) the enforcement of some legal rights involves morally disagreeable acts.

(2) It is bad that legal rights which exist should not be enforceable.

(3) Enforcement of many rights of the kind mentioned in (1) requires lawyers.

(4) Any lawyer really effective in enforcing those rights must be fairly horrible.

Ergo (5) It is good that some lawyers are fairly horrible.

How might this argument be met, if at all? The conventional answer presumably lies in denying (1) but in our context of discussion, we will not accept as sufficient the conventional reason for denying it, namely that there is a sufficient moral justification for the system that requires those acts (which is in effect equivalent to (2)). Another line would be to deny (2). This is perhaps the approach of Waserstrom,[56] who inclines to view that if (1) carries much weight with regard to some rights, then it may just be better that those rights be not enforced. If this goes beyond the position of refusing to act when one knows that someone else will (not necessarily an objectionable position), it runs into difficulties about the operation of the law as a roughly predictable system. Fried denies (4), by putting the acts required in (1) into the framework of loyalty and friendship. Others might combat (4) by using notions of professionalism, insisting that since those acts are done in a professional role, in the name of a desirable system, it cannot follow that they express a horrible disposition—they are not, in that sense, personal acts at all.

The phenomenology of the states of mind invoked by that answer is very complex. The limitations of the answer are, however, fairly obvious and indeed notorious. One limitation, for instance, must lie in the consideration that it is a personal fact about somebody that that is his profession. However, whatever we think in general about those ideas of professionalism, there is at least one thing that can be allowed to the lawyer's situations which it is hard to allow to the politician's. Even if we accepted the disagreeable conclusion of the argument, we could at least agree that the professional activities of lawyers are delimited enough to make the fact that some are fairly horrible of limited account to the public: the ways in which the argument, if sound, shows them to be horrible are ways which their clients, at any rate, have no reason to regret. But there is much less reason for such comfort in the politician's case, and if a comparable argument can be mounted with them, then the public has reason to be alarmed. The professional sphere of activity is very much less delimited, and there are important asymmetries, for example in the matter of concealment. The line between the client and the other side is one which in an adversarial system governs a great deal of the lawyer's behaviour, and certainly the sorts of reasons he has for concealing things from the opposition are not characteristically reasons for concealment from his client. But the reasons there are for concealing things in politics are always reasons for concealing them from the electorate.

Another reason for concern in the political case lies in the professional (and in itself perfectly proper) commitment to staying in power. I have already suggested that it involves an essential ambivalence: it is impossible to tell, at the limit, where it merges into simple ambition, and into that particular deformation of political life, under all systems, which consists in the inability to consider a question on its merits because one's attention is directed to the consequences of giving (to one's colleagues, in the first instance) a particular answer. Where that has widely taken over, the citizens have reason to fear their politician's judgment.

The dispositions of politicians are differently related to their tasks and to their public than are those of a profession such as the legal profession for which partly analogous questions arise. Those differences all give greater reason for concern,

---

[56] *Lawyers as Professionals: Some Moral Issues*, 5 HUMAN RIGHTS 2–24 (1975). I am grateful for discussion of these issues to Dick Wasserstrom, Andy Kaufman, and other participants in the Council for Philosophical Studies Institute on Law and Ethics, Williams College Mass., 1977.

and make more pressing the question: what features of the political system are likely to select for those dispositions in politicians which are at once morally welcome and compatible with their being effective politicians? What features of the system can help to bring it about that fairly decent people can dispose of a fair degree of power? How does one ensure a reasonable succession of colonists of the space between cynicism and political idiocy?

It is a vast, old, and in good part empirical question. If one adapts Plato's question, *how can the good rule?*, to Machiavelli's, *how to rule the world as it is?*, the simplest conflation—*how can the good rule the world as it is?*—is merely discouraging. It is also, however, excessively pious: the conception of the good that it inherits from Plato invites the question of how the good could do anything at all, while the Machiavellian conception of the world as it is raises the question of how anyone could do anything with it. (A popular sense of 'realism' gets its strength from the fact that the second of those questions has some answers, while the first has none.) But if one modifies from both ends, allowing both that the good need not be as pure as all that, so long as they retain some active sense of moral costs and moral limits: and that the society has some genuinely settled politics and some expectations of civic respectability: then there is some place for discussing what properties we should like the system, in these respects, to have. There are many: I will mention, only in barest outline, four dimensions of a political system which seem to bear closely on this issue.

(a) There is the question, already touched on, of the balance of publicity, and the relations of politician and public, particularly of course in a democracy. The assumption is widespread, particularly in the USA, that public government and a great deal of public scrutiny must encourage honest government, and apply controls to the cynicism of politicians. There is, however, no reason to suppose that the influence of such practices and institutions will be uniformly in one direction. The requirements of instant publicity in a context which is, as we are supposing, to some mild degree moralized, has an evident potential for hypocrisy, while, even apart from that, the instant identification of particular political acts, as they are represented at the degree of resolution achievable in the media, is a recipe for competition in pre-emptive press releases.

(b) A similar question is that of the relations of politicians to one another; and there is another approved belief, that it is in the interest of good government that politicians should basically be related to one another only functionally, that they should not share a set of understandings which too markedly differentiate them from people who are not politicians. Yet it is not clear how far this is true, either. For it is an important function of the relations of politicians to one another, what courses of action are even discussible, and that is a basic dimension of a moral culture. Very obviously, a ruthless clique is worse than a clique checked by less ruthless outsiders, but that is not the only option. Another is that of a less ruthless clique resisting more ruthless outsiders.

(c) A very well-known point is that of the relation of potential politicians to actual ones, the question of political recruitment. Notoriously, systems where succession is problematic or discontinuous have the property of selecting for the ruthless. No sensible critic will suggest that if that is so, it is all easy to change, but it is nevertheless an important dimension of assessment of a political system.

(d) A slightly less obvious variant of the same sort of issue concerns the promotion-pattern within a political organization: in particular, the position of the bottleneck between very top jobs and rather less top jobs. Except in very favoured circumstances, it is likely to be the case that getting to the top of a political system will require properties which, while they need not at all necessarily be spectacularly undesirable or even regrettable, may nevertheless perhaps lean in the direction of the kind of ambition and professionalism which does not always make for the best judgment, moral or practical. It is desirable that the system should not put too heavy stress on those properties too soon in the business; there can then be an honourable and successful role, below the final bottleneck, for persons without the elbow-power to get into or through the bottleneck. Government concentrated on a few personalities of course tends to weaken this possibility. Related is the question of the prestige of jobs below the top one. It was a notable fact, remarked by some commentators that when the English politician R.A. (now Lord) Butler retired from politics, it was suggested that his career had been a failure because—and although—he had held almost every major office of state except the Premiership itself.

These are, of course, only hints at certain dimensions of discussion. The aim is just to suggest that it is such ways that one should think about the disagreeable acts involved in (everyday) politics—that fruitful thought should be directed to the aspects of a political system which may make it less likely that the only persons attracted to a profession which undoubtedly involves some such acts will be persons who are insufficiently disposed to find them disagreeable.

Last, I should like to make just one point about the further dimension of the subject, in which one is concerned not just with the disagreeable or distasteful but with crimes, or what otherwise would be crimes. This is a different level from the last: here we are concerned not just with business but, so to speak, with the Mafia. My question, rather as before, is not directly whether actions of a certain kind—in this case such things as murders, torture, etc.—are ever justified, but rather, if they are justified, how we should think of those who politically bring them about. I shall call the actions in question, for short, *violence*. It might be worth distinguishing, among official acts of violence, what could be called *structured* and *unstructured* violence: the former related to such processes as executions under law, application of legal force by the police, etc., while the latter include acts (it may be, more abroad than at home) pursued in what is regarded as the national interest.

I shall set out a list of four propositions which some would regard as all true, and which, if they were all true, would make the hope of finding politicians of honourable character, except in minor roles and in favourable circumstances, very slim.

(i) There are violent acts which the state is justified in doing which no private citizen as such would be justified in doing.

(ii) Anything the state is justified in doing, some official such as, often, a politician is justified in ordering to be done.

(iii) You are not morally justified in ordering to be done anything which you would not be prepared to do yourself.

(iv) Official violence is enough like unofficial violence for the preparedness referred to in (iii) to amount to a criminal tendency.

QUESTIONS

1.   Our thanks to former BC law student Tom Peele for spotting this article. He suggests that in considering Williams' "four propositions," above, one simply replace the word "politicians" with "lawyers" and the phrase "ordering to be done" with "seeking a court order that it be done." The result would be "a list of four propositions which some would regard as all true, and which, if they were all true, would make the hope of finding [lawyers] of honourable character, except in minor roles and in favourable circumstances, very slim." Do you think the "four propositions" are true for lawyers?

2.   Williams argues that "[o]fficial violence is enough like unofficial violence for the preparedness referred to in (iii) to amount to a criminal tendency." What do you think of the death penalty? Should it be regarded as "official violence"?

MICHAEL WALZER, POLITICAL ACTION: THE PROBLEM OF DIRTY HANDS,
in PRIVATE AND PUBLIC ETHICS[57] 97–123 (Donald G. Jones ed., 1978)

The preceding essay first appeared in *Philosophy & Public Affairs* as a symposium on the rules of war which was actually (or at least more importantly) a symposium on another topic.[58] The actual topic was whether or not a man can ever face, or even has to face, a moral dilemma, a situation where he must choose between two courses of action both of which it would be wrong for him to undertake. Thomas Nagel worriedly suggested that this could happen and that it did happen whenever someone was forced to choose between upholding an important moral principle and avoiding some looming disaster.[59]

The argument relates not only to the coherence and harmony of the moral universe, but also to the relative ease or difficulty—or impossibility—of living a moral life. It is not, therefore, merely a philosopher's question. If such a dilemma can arise, whether frequently or very rarely, any of us might one day face it. Indeed, many men have faced it, or think they have, especially men involved in political activity or war. The dilemma, exactly as Nagel describes it, is frequently discussed in the literature of political action—in novels and plays dealing with politics and in the work of theorists too.

In modern times the dilemma appears most often as the problem of "dirty

---

[57] An earlier version of this paper was read at the annual meeting of the Conference for the Study of Political Thought in New York, April 1972. We are indebted to Charles Taylor, who served as commentator at that time and provided encouragement to think that its arguments might be right.

[58] PHILOSOPHY & PUBLIC AFFAIRS 1, no. 2 (Winter 1972).

[59] ***Bernard Williams has made a similar suggestion, though without quite acknowledging it as his own: "many people can recognize the thought that a certain course of action is, indeed, the best thing to do on the whole in the circumstances, but that doing it involves something wrong" (MORALITY: AN INTRODUCTION TO ETHICS 93 [1972]).

hands," and it is typically stated by the Communist leader Hoerderer in Sartre's play of that name: "I have dirty hands right up the elbows. I've plunged them in filth and blood. Do you think you can govern innocently?"[60] My own answer is no, I don't think I could govern innocently; nor do most of us believe that those who govern us are innocent—as I shall argue below—even the best of them. But this does not mean that it isn't possible to do the right thing while governing. It means that a particular act of government (in a political party or in the state) may be exactly the right thing to do in utilitarian terms and yet leave the man who does it guilty of moral wrong. The innocent man, afterwards, is no longer innocent. If on the other hand he remains innocent, chooses, that is, the "absolutist" side of Nagel's dilemma, he not only fails to do the right thing (in utilitarian terms), he may also fail to measure up to the duties of his office (which imposes on him a considerable responsibility for consequences and outcomes). Most often, of course, political leaders accept the utilitarian calculation; they try to measure up. One might offer a number of sardonic comments on this fact, the most obvious being that by the calculations they usually make they demonstrate the great virtues of the "absolutist" position. Nevertheless, we would not want to be governed by men who consistently adopted that position.

The notion of dirty hands derives from an effort to refuse "absolutism" without denying the reality of the moral dilemma. Though this may appear to utilitarian philosophers to pile confusion upon confusion, I propose to take it very seriously. For the literature I shall examine, is the work of serious and often wise men, and it reflects, though it may also have helped to shape, popular thinking about politics. It is important to pay attention to that too. I shall do so without assuming, as Hare suggests one might, that everyday moral and political discourse constitutes a distinct level of argument, where content is largely a matter of pedagogic expediency.[61] If popular views are resistant (as they are) to utilitarianism, there may be something to learn from that and not merely something to explain about it.

i

Let me begin, then, with a piece of conventional wisdom to the effect that politicians are a good deal worse, morally worse, than the rest of us (it is the wisdom of the rest of us). Without either endorsing it or pretending to disbelieve it, I am going to expound this convention. For it suggests that the dilemma of dirty hands is a central feature of political life, that it arises not merely as an occasional crisis in the career of this or that unlucky politician but systematically and frequently.

Why is the politician singled out? Isn't he like the other entrepreneurs in an open society, who hustle, lie, intrigue, wear masks, smile and are villains? He is not, no doubt for many reasons, three of which I need to consider. First of all, the politician claims to play a different part than other entrepreneurs. He does not

---

[60] Jean-Paul Sartre, *Dirty Hands* in NO EXIT AND THREE OTHER PLAYS, trans. Lionel Abel (New York, n. d.), page 224.

[61] *** "[T]he simple principles of the deontologist . . . have their place at the level of character formation" (moral education and self-education)."

merely cater to our interests; he acts on our behalf, even in our name. He has purposes in mind, causes and projects that require the support and redound to the benefit, not of each of us individually, but of all of us together. He hustles, lies, and intrigues for us—or so he claims. Perhaps he is right, or at least sincere, but we suspect that he acts for himself also. Indeed, he cannot serve us without serving himself, for success brings him power and glory, the greatest rewards that men can win from their fellows. The competition for these two is fierce; the risks are often great, but the temptations are greater. We imagine ourselves succumbing. Why should our representatives act differently? Even if they would like to act differently, they probably cannot: for other men are all too ready to hustle and lie for power and glory, and it is the others who set the terms of the competition. Hustling and lying are necessary because power and glory are so desirable—that is, so widely desired. And so men who act for us and in our name are necessarily hustlers and liars.

Politicians are also thought to be worse than the rest of us because they rule over us, and the pleasures of ruling are much greater than the pleasure of being ruled. The successful politician becomes the visible architect of our restraint. He taxes us, licenses us, forbids and permits us, directs us to this or that distant goal—all for our greater good. Moreover, he takes chances for our greater good that put us, or some of us, in danger. Sometimes he puts himself in danger too, but politics, after all, is his adventure. It is not always ours. There are undoubtedly times when it is good or necessary to direct the affairs of other people and to put them in danger. But we are a little frightened of the man who seeks, ordinarily and every day, the power to do so. And the fear is reasonable enough. The politician has, or pretends to have, a kind of confidence in his own judgment that the rest of us know to be presumptuous in any man.

The presumption is especially great because the victorious politician uses violence and the threat of violence—not only against foreign nations in our defense but also against us, and again ostensibly for our greater good. This is a point emphasized and perhaps overemphasized by Max Weber in his essay "Politics as a Vocation".[62] It has not, so far as I can tell, played an overt or obvious part in the development of the convention I am examining. The stock figure is the lying, not the murderous, politician—though the murderer lurks in the background, appearing most often in the form of the revolutionary or terrorist, very rarely as an ordinary magistrate or official. Nevertheless, the sheer weight of official violence in human history does suggest the kind of power to which politicians aspire, the kind of power they want to wield, and it may point to the roots of our half-conscious dislike and unease. The men who act for us and in our name are often killers, or seem to become killers too quickly and too easily.

Knowing all this or most of it, good and decent people still enter political life, aiming at some specific reform or seeking a general reformation. They are then required to learn the lesson Machiavelli first set out to teach: "how not to be good."[63] Some of them are incapable of learning; many more profess to be

---

[62] In FROM MAX WEBER: ESSAYS IN SOCIOLOGY, trans. and ed. Hans H. Gerth and C. Wright Mills (New York, 1946), pages 77–128.

[63] See THE PRINCE, chap. XV; cf. THE DISCOURSES, bk. I, chaps. IX and XVIII. I quote from the Modern

incapable. But they will not succeed unless they learn, for they have joined the terrible competition for power and glory; they have chosen to work and struggle as Machiavelli says, among "so many who are not good." They can do no good themselves unless they win the struggle, which they are unlikely to do unless they are willing and able to use the necessary means. So we are suspicious even of the best of winners. It is not a sign of our perversity if we think them only more clever than the rest. They have not won, after all, because they were good, or not only because of that, but also because they were not good. No one succeeds in politics without getting his hands dirty. This is conventional wisdom again, and again I don't mean to insist that it is true without qualification. I repeat it only to disclose the moral dilemma inherent in the convention. For sometimes it is right to try to succeed, and then it must also be right to get one's hands dirty. But one's hands get dirty from doing what it is wrong to do. And how can it be wrong to do what is right? Or, how can we get our hands dirty by doing what we ought to do?

ii

*   *   *

All this may become clearer if we look at a more dramatic example, for we are, perhaps, a little blasé about political deals and disinclined to worry much about the man who makes one. So consider a politician who has seized upon a national crisis—a prolonged colonial war—to reach for power. He and his friends win office pledged to decolonization and peace, they are honestly committed to both, though not without some sense of the advantages of the commitment. In any case, they have no responsibility for the war; they have steadfastly opposed it. Immediately, the politician goes off to the colonial capital to open negotiations with the rebels. But the capital is in the grip of a terrorist campaign, and the first decision the new leader faces is this: he is asked to authorize the torture of a captured rebel leader who knows or probably knows the location of a number of bombs hidden in apartment buildings around the city, set to go off within the next twenty-four hours. He orders the man tortured, convinced that he must do so for the sake of the people who might otherwise die in the explosions—even though he believes that torture is wrong, indeed abominable, not just sometimes, but always.[64] He had expressed this belief often and angrily during his own campaign; the rest of us took it as a sign of his goodness. How should we regard him now? (How should he regard himself?)

Once again, it does not seem enough to say that he should feel very badly. But why not? Why shouldn't he have feelings like those of St. Augustine's melancholy soldier, who understood both that his war was just and that killing, even in a just war, is a terrible thing to do?[65] The difference is that Augustine did not believe that it was wrong to kill in a just war; it was just sad, or the sort of thing a good man

---

Library edition of the two works (New York, 1950), page 57.

[64] I leave aside the question of whether the prisoner is himself responsible for the terrorist campaign. Perhaps he opposed it in meetings of the rebel organization. In any case, whether he deserves to be punished or not, he does not deserve to be tortured.

[65] Other writers argued that Christians must never kill, even in a just war; and there was also an intermediate position which suggests the origins of the idea of dirty hands. Thus Basil the Great (Bishop of Caesarea in the fourth century A.D.): "Killing in war was differentiated by our fathers from murder

would be saddened by. But he might have thought it wrong to torture in a just war, and later Catholic theorists have certainly thought it wrong. Moreover, the politician I am imagining thinks it wrong, as do many of us who supported him. Surely we have a right to expect more than melancholy from him now. When he ordered the prisoner tortured, he committed a moral crime and he accepted a moral burden. Now he is a guilty man. His willingness to acknowledge and bear (and perhaps to repent and do penance for) his guilt is evidence, and it is the only evidence he can offer us, both that he is not too good for politics and that he is good enough. Here is the moral politician: it is by his dirty hands that we know him. If he were a moral man and nothing else, his hands would not be dirty; if he were a politician and nothing else, he would pretend that they were clean.

iii

Machiavelli's argument about the need to learn how not to be good clearly implies that there are acts known to be bad quite apart from the immediate circumstances in which they are performed or not performed. He points to a distinct set of political methods and stratagems which good men must study (by reading his books), not only because their use does not come naturally, but also because they are explicitly condemned by the moral teachings good men accept—and whose acceptance serves in turn to mark men as good. These methods may be condemned because they are thought contrary to divine law or to the order of nature or to our moral sense, or because in prescribing the law to ourselves we have individually or collectively prohibited them. Machiavelli does not commit himself on such issues, and I shall not do so either if I can avoid it. The effects of these different views are, at least in one crucial sense, the same. They take out of our hands the constant business of attaching moral labels to such Machiavellian methods as deceit and betrayal. Such methods are simply bad. They are the sort of thing that good men avoid, at least until they have learned how not to be good.

Now, if there is no such class of actions, there is no dilemma of dirty hands, and the Machiavellian teaching loses what Machiavelli surely intended it to have, its disturbing and paradoxical character. He can then be understood to be saying that political actors must sometimes overcome their moral inhibitions, but not that they must sometimes commit crimes. I take it that utilitarian philosophers also want to make the first of these statements and to deny the second. From their point of view, the candidate who makes a corrupt deal and the official who authorizes the torture of a prisoner must be described as good men (given the cases as I have specified them), who ought, perhaps, to be honored for making the right decision when it was a hard decision to make. There are three ways of developing this argument. First, it might be said that every political choice ought to be made solely in terms of its particular and immediate circumstances—in terms, that is, of the reasonable alternatives, available knowledge, likely consequences, and so on. Then the good man will face difficult choices (when his knowledge of options and outcomes is

---

. . . nevertheless, perhaps it would be well that those whose hands are unclean abstain from communion for three years." Here dirty hands are a kind of impurity or unworthiness, which is not the same as guilt, though closely related to it. For a general survey of these and other Christian views, see Roland H. Bainton, CHRISTIAN ATTITUDES TOWARD WAR AND PEACE (New York, 1960), esp. chaps. 5–7.

radically uncertain), but it cannot happen that he will face a moral dilemma. Indeed, if he always makes decisions in this way, and has been taught from childhood to do so, he will never have to overcome his inhibitions, whatever he does for how could he have acquired inhibitions? Assuming further that he weighs the alternatives and calculates the consequences seriously and in good faith, he cannot commit a crime, though he can certainly make a mistake, even a very serious mistake. Even when he lies and tortures, his hands will be clean, for he has done what he should do as best he can, standing alone in a moment of time, forced to choose.

This is in some ways an attractive description of moral decision-making, but it is also a very improbable one. For while any one of us may stand alone, and so on, when we make this or that decision, we are not isolated or solitary in our moral lives. Moral life is a social phenomenon, and it is constituted at least in part by rules, the knowing of which (and perhaps the making of which) we share with our fellows. The experience of coming up against these rules, challenging their prohibitions, and explaining ourselves to other men and women is so common and so obviously important that no account or moral decision-making can possibly fail to come to grips with it. Hence the second utilitarian argument: such rules do indeed exist, but they are not really prohibitions of wrongful actions (though they do, perhaps for pedagogic reasons, have that form). They are moral guidelines, summaries of previous calculations. They ease our choices in ordinary cases, for we can simply follow their injunctions and do what has been found useful in the past; in exceptional cases they serve as signals warning us against doing too quickly or without the most careful calculations what has not been found useful in the past. But they do no more than that; they have no other purpose, and so it cannot be the case that it is or even might be a crime to override them.[66] Nor is it necessary to feel guilty when one does so. Once again, if it is right to break the rule in some hard case, after conscientiously worrying about it, the man who acts (especially if he knows that many of his fellows would simply worry rather than act) may properly feel pride in his achievement.

But this view, it seems to me, captures the reality of our moral life no better than the last. It may well be right to say that moral rules ought to have the character of guidelines, but it seems that in fact they do not. Or at least, we defend ourselves when we break the rules as if they had some status entirely independent of their previous utility (and we rarely feel proud of ourselves). The defenses we normally offer are not simply justifications; they are also excuses. Now, as Austin says, these two can seem to come very close together—indeed, I shall suggest that they can appear side by side in the same sentence—but they are conceptually distinct, differentiated in this crucial respect an excuse is typically an admission of innocence.[67] Consider a well-known defense from Shakespeare's Hamlet that has often reappeared in political literature: "I must be cruel only to be kind."[68] The words are spoken on an occasion when Hamlet is actually being cruel to his mother.

---

[66] Brandt's rules do not appear to be of the sort that can be overridden—except perhaps by a soldier who decides that he just won't kill any more civilians, no matter what cause is served—since all they require is careful calculation. But I take it that rules of a different sort, which have the form of ordinary injunctions and prohibitions, can and often do figure in what is called "rule-utilitarianism."

[67] J. L. Austin, "A Plea for Excuses," in PHILOSOPHICAL PAPERS, ed. J. O. Urmson and G. J. Warnock (Oxford, 1961), pages 123–152.

[68] HAMLET 3-4-178.

I will leave aside the possibility that she deserves to hear (to be forced to listen to) every harsh word he utters, for Hamlet himself makes no such claim—and if she did indeed deserve that, his words might not be cruel or he might not be cruel for speaking them. "I must be cruel" contains the excuse, since it both admits a fault and suggests that Hamlet has no choice but to commit it. He is doing what he has to do; he can't help himself (given the ghost's command, the rotten state of Denmark, and so on). The rest of the sentence is a justification, for it suggests that Hamlet intends and expects kindness to be the outcome of his actions—we must assume that he means greater kindness, kindness to the right person, or some such. It is not, however, so complete a justification that Hamlet is able to say that he is not really being cruel. "Cruel" and "kind" have exactly the same status; they both follow the verb "to be," and so they perfectly reveal the moral dilemma.[69]

When rules are overridden, we do not talk or act as if they had been set aside, canceled, or annulled. They still stand and have this much effect at least: that we know we have done something wrong even if what we have done was also the best thing to do on the whole in the circumstances.[70] Or at least we feel that way, and this feeling is itself a crucial feature of our moral life. Hence the third utilitarian argument, which recognizes the usefulness of guilt and seeks to explain it. There are, it appears, good reasons for "overvaluing" as well as for overriding rules. For the consequences might be very bad indeed if the rules were overridden every time the moral calculation seemed to go against them. It is probably best if most do not calculate too nicely, but simply follow the rules; they are less likely to make mistakes that way, all in all. And so a good man (or at least an ordinary good man) will respect the rules rather more than he would if he thought them merely guidelines, and he will feel guilty when he overrides them. Indeed, if he did not feel guilty, "he would not be such a good man."[71] It is by his feelings that we know him. Because of those feelings he will never be in a hurry to override the rules, but will wait until there is no choice, acting only to avoid consequences that are both imminent and almost certainly disastrous.

The obvious difficulty with this argument is that the feeling whose usefulness is being explained is most unlikely to be felt by someone who is convinced only of its usefulness. He breaks a utilitarian rule (guideline), let us say, for good utilitarian reasons: but can he then feel guilty, also for good utilitarian reasons, when he has no reason for believing that he is guilty? Imagine a moral philosopher expounding the third argument to a man who is likely to feel guilty. Either the man won't accept the utilitarian explanation as an account of his feeling about the rules (probably the best outcome from a utilitarian point of view) or he will accept it and then cease to feel that (useful) feeling. But I do not want to exclude the possibility of a kind of superstitious anxiety, the possibility, that is, that some men will continue to feel

[69] Compare the following lines from Bertold Brecht's poem "To Posterity." "Alas, we/Who wished to lay the foundations of kindness/Could not ourselves be kind. . . ." (*Selected Poems*, trans. H. R. Hays [New York, 1969], page 177). This is more of an excuse, less of a justification (the poem is an *apologia*).

[70] Robert Nozick discusses some of the possible effects of overriding a rule in his "Moral Complications and Moral Structures," NATURAL LAW FORUM 13 (1968): 34–35 and notes. Nozick suggests that what may remain after one has broken a rule (for good reasons) is a "duty to make reparations." He does not call this "guilt," though the two notions are closely connected.

[71] Hare, page 59.

guilty even after they have been taught, and have agreed, that they cannot possibly be guilty. It is best to say only that the more fully they accept the utilitarian account, the less likely they are to feel that (useful) feeling. The utilitarian account is not at all useful, then if political actors accept it, and that may help us to understand why it plays, as Hare has pointed out, so small a part in our moral education.[72]

iv

One further comment on the third argument: it is worth stressing that to feel guilty is to suffer, and that the men whose guilt feelings are here called useful are themselves innocent according to the utilitarian account. So we seem to have come upon another case where the suffering of the innocent is permitted and even encouraged by utilitarian calculation.[73] But surely an innocent man who has done something painful or hard (but justified) should be helped to avoid or escape the sense of guilt; he might reasonably expect the assistance of his fellow men, even of moral philosophers, at such a time. On the other hand, if we intuitively think it true of some other man that he should feel guilty, then we ought to be able to specify the nature of his guilt (and if he is a good man, win his agreement). I think I can construct a case which, with only small variation, highlights what is different in these two situations.

Consider the common practice of distributing rifles loaded with blanks to some of the members of a firing squad. The individual men are not told whether their own weapons are lethal, and so though all of them look like executioners to the victim in front of them, none of them know whether they are really executioners or not. The purpose of this stratagem is to relieve each man of the sense that he is a killer. It can hardly relieve him of whatever moral responsibility he incurs by serving on a firing squad, and that is not its purpose, for the execution is not thought to be (and

---

[72] There is another possible utilitarian position, suggested in Maurice Merleau-Ponty's HUMANISM AND TERROR, trans. John O'Neill (Boston, 1970). According to this view, the agony and the guilt feelings experienced by the man who makes a "dirty hands" decision derive from his radical uncertainty about the actual outcome. Perhaps the awful thing he is doing will be done in vain; the results he hope for won't occur; the only outcome will be the pain he has caused or the deceit he has fostered. Then (and only then) he will indeed have committed a crime. On the other hand, if the expected good does come, then (and only then) he can abandon his guilt feelings; he can say, and the rest of us must agree, that he is justified. This is a kind of delayed utilitarianism, where justification is a matter of actual and not at all of predicted outcomes. It is not implausible to imagine a political actor anxiously awaiting the "verdict of history." But suppose the verdict is in his favor (assuming that there is a *final* verdict or a statute of limitations on possible verdicts): he will surely feel relieved—more so, no doubt, than the rest of us. I can see no reason, however, why he should think himself justified, if he is a good man and knows that what he did was wrong. Perhaps the victims of his crime, seeing the happy result, will absolve him, but history has no powers of absolution. Indeed, history is more likely to play tricks on our moral judgment. Predicted outcomes are at least thought to follow from our own acts (this is the prediction), but actual outcomes almost certainly have a multitude of causes, the combination of which may well be fortuitous. Merleau-Panty stresses the risks of political decision-making so heavily that he turns politics into a gamble with time and circumstances. But the anxiety of the gambler is of no great moral interest. Nor is it much of a barrier, as Merleau-Ponty's book makes all too clear, to the commission of the most terrible crimes.

[73] *Cf.* the cases suggested by David Ross, THE RIGHT AND THE GOOD (Oxford, 2002), pages 56–57, and E. F. Carritt, ETHICAL AND POLITICAL THINKING (Oxford, 1947) page 65.

let us grant this to be the case) an immoral or wrongful act. But the inhibition against killing another human being is so strong that even if the men believe that what they are doing is right, they will still feel guilty. Uncertainty as to their actual role apparently reduces the intensity of these feelings. If this is so, the stratagem is perfectly justifiable, and one can only rejoice in every case where it succeeds—for every success subtracts from the number of innocent men who suffer.

But we would feel differently, I think, if we imagine a man who believes (and let us assume here that we believe also) either that capital punishment is wrong or that this particular victim is innocent, but who nevertheless agrees to participate in the firing squad for some overriding political or moral reason—I won't try to suggest what that reason might be. If he is comforted by the trick with the rifles, then we can be reasonably certain that his opposition to capital punishment or his belief in the victim's innocence is not morally serious. And if it is serious, he will not merely feel guilty, he will know that he is guilty (and we will know it too), though he may also believe (and we may agree) that he has good reasons for incurring the guilt. Our guilt feelings can be tricked away when they are isolated from our moral beliefs, as in the first case, but not when they are allied with them, as in the second. The beliefs themselves and the rules which are believed in can only be *overridden*, a painful process which forces a man to weigh the wrong he is willing to do in order to do right, and which leaves pain behind, and should do so, even after the decision has been made.

v

That is the dilemma of dirty hands as it has been experienced by political actors and written about in the literature of political action. I don't want to argue that it is only a political dilemma. No doubt we can get out hands dirty in private life also, and sometimes, no doubt we should. But the issue is posed most dramatically in politics for the three reasons that make political life the kind of life it is, because we claim to act for others but also serve ourselves, rule over others, and use violence against them. It is easy to get one's hands dirty in politics and it is often right to do so. But it is not easy to teach a good man how not to be good, nor is it easy to explain such a man to himself once he has committed whatever crimes are required of him. At least, it is not easy once we have agreed to use the word "crimes" and to live with (because we have no choice) the dilemma of dirty hands. Still the agreement is common enough, and on its basis there have developed three broad traditions of explanation, three ways of thinking about dirty hands, which derive in some very general fashion from neoclassical, Protestant, and Catholic perspectives on politics and morality. I want to try to say something very briefly about each of them, or rather about a representative example of each of them, for each seems to me partly right. But I don't think I can put together the compound view that might be wholly right.

The first tradition is best represented by Machiavelli, the first man, so far as I know, to state the paradox that I am examining. The good man who aims to found or reform a republic must, Machiavelli tells us, do terrible things to reach his goal. Like Romulus, he must murder his brother; like Numa, he must lie to the people.

Sometimes, however, "when the act accuses, the result excuses."[74] This sentence from THE DISCOURSES is often taken to mean that the politician's deceit and cruelty are justified by the good results he brings about. But if they were justified, it wouldn't be necessary to learn what Machiavelli claims to teach: how not to be good. It would only be necessary to learn how to be good in a new more difficult, perhaps roundabout way. That is not Machiavelli's argument. His political judgments are indeed consequentialist in character, but not his moral judgments. We know whether cruelty is used well or badly by its effects over time. But that it is bad to use cruelty we know in some other way. The deceitful and cruel politician is excused (if he succeeds) only in the sense that the rest of us come to agree that the results were "worth it" or, more likely, that we simply forget his crimes when we praise his success.

It is important to stress Machiavelli's own commitments to the existence of moral standards. His paradox depends upon that commitment as it depends upon the general stability of the standards—which he upholds in his consistent use of words like good and bad.[75] If he wants the standards to be disregarded by good men more often than they are, he has nothing with which to replace them and no other way of recognizing the good men except by their allegiance to those same standards. It is exceedingly rare, he writes, that a good man is willing to employ bad means to become prince.[76] Machiavelli's purpose is to persuade such a person to make the attempt, and he holds out the supreme political rewards, power and glory, to the man who does so and succeeds. The good man is not rewarded (or excused), however, merely for his willingness to get his hands dirty. He must do bad things well. There is no reward for doing bad things badly, though they are done with the best of intentions. And so political action necessarily involves taking a risk. But it should be clear that what is risked is not personal goodness—*that is thrown away*—but power and glory. If the politician succeeds, he is a hero; eternal praise is the supreme reward for not being good.

What the penalties are for not being good, Machiavelli doesn't say, and it is probably for this reason above all that his moral sensitivity has so often been questioned. He is suspect not because he tells political actors they must get their hands dirty, but because he does specify the state of mind appropriately to a man with dirty hands. A Machiavellian hero has no inwardness. What he thinks of himself we don't know. I would guess, along with most other readers of Machiavelli, that he basks in his glory. But then it is difficult to account for the strength of his original reluctance to learn how not to be good. In any case, he is the sort of man who is unlikely to keep a diary and so we cannot find out what he thinks. Yet we do want to know; above all, we want a record of his anguish. That is a sign of our own conscientiousness and of the impact on us of the second tradition of thought that I want to examine, in which personal anguish sometimes seems the only acceptable excuse for political crimes.

The second tradition is best represented, I think, by Max Weber, who outlines its

---

[74] THE DISCOURSE, bk. I, chap. IX (page 139).

[75] For a very different view of Machiavelli, see Isaiah Berlin, "The Question of Machiavelli," THE NEW YORK REVIEW OF BOOKS, 4 November 1971.

[76] THE DISCOURSES, bk. I, chap. XVIII (page 171).

essential features with great power at the very end of his essay "Politics as a Vocation." For Weber, the good man with dirty hands is a hero still, but he is a tragic hero. In part, his tragedy is that though politics is his vocation, he has not been called by God and so cannot be justified by Him. Weber's hero is alone in a world that seems to belong to Satan, and his vocation is entirely his own choice. He still wants what Christian magistrates have always wanted, both to do good in the world and to save his soul, but now these two ends have come into sharp contradiction. They are contradictory because of the necessity for violence in a world where God has not instituted the sword. The politician takes the sword himself, and only by doing so does he measure up to his vocation. With full consciousness of what he is doing, he does bad in order to do good, and surrenders his soul. He "lets himself in," Weber says, "for the diabolic forces lurking in all violence." Perhaps Machiavelli also meant to suggest that his hero surrenders salvation in exchange for glory, but he does not explicitly say so. Weber is absolutely clear: "the genius or demon of politics lives in an inner tension with the god of love. . . . [which] can at any time lead to an irreconcilable conflict."[77] His politician views this conflict when it comes with a tough realism, never pretends that it might be solved by compromise, chooses politics once again, and turns decisively away from love. Weber writes about this choice with a passionate high-mindedness that makes a concern for one's flesh. Yet the reader never doubts that his mature, superbly trained, relentless, objective, responsible, and disciplined political leader is also a suffering servant. His choices are hard and painful, and he pays the price not only while making them but forever after. A man doesn't lose his soul one day and find it the next.

The difficulties with this view will be clear to anyone who has ever met a suffering servant. Here is a man who lies, intrigues, sends other men to their death—and suffers. He does what he must do with a heavy heart. None of us can know, he tells us, how much it costs him to do his duty. Indeed, we cannot, for he himself fixes the price he pays. And that is the trouble with this view of political crime. We suspect the suffering servant of either masochism or hypocrisy or both, and while we are often wrong, we are not always wrong. Weber attempts to resolve the problem of dirty hands entirely within the confines of the individual conscience, but I am inclined to think that this is neither possible nor desirable. The self-awareness of the tragic hero is obviously of great value. We want the politician to shave an inner life at least something like that which Weber describes. But sometimes the hero's suffering needs to be socially expressed (for like punishment, it confirms and reinforces our sense that certain acts are wrong). And equally important, it sometimes needs to be socially limited. We don't want to be rifled by men who have lost their souls. A politician with dirty hands needs a soul, and it is best for us all if he has some hope of personal salvation, however that is conceived. It is not the case that when he does bad in order to do good he surrenders himself forever to the demon of politics. He commits a determinate crime, and he must pay a determinate penalty. When he has done so, his hands will be clean again, or as clean as human

---

[77] "Politics as a Vocation," pages 125–128. But sometimes a political leader does choose the "absolutist" side of the conflict, and Weber writes (page 127) that is "immensely moving when a mature man. . . . Aware of a responsibility for the consequences of his conduct . . . reaches a point where he says: 'Here I stand; I can do no other:'" Unfortunately, he does not suggest just where that point is or even where it might be.

hands can ever be. So the Catholic Church has always taught, and this teaching is central to the third tradition that I want to examine.

Once again I will take a latter-day and a lapsed representative of the tradition and consider Albert Camus's *The Just Assassins*. The heroes of this play are terrorists at work in nineteenth-century Russia. The dirt on their hands is human blood. And yet Camus's admiration for them, he tells us, is complete. We consent to being criminals, one of them says, but there is nothing with which anyone can reproach us. Here is the dilemma of dirty hands in a new form. The heroes are innocent criminals, just assassins, because, having killed, they are prepared to die—*and will die*. Only their execution, by the same despotic authorities they are attacking, will complete the action in which they are engaged: dying, they need make no excuses. That is the end of their guilt and pain. The execution is not so much punishment as self-punishment and expiation. On the scaffold they wash their hands clean and, unlike the suffering servant, they die happy.

Now the argument of the play when presented in so radically simplified a form may seem a little bizarre, and perhaps it is marred by the moral extremism of Camus' politics. "Political action has limits," he says in a preface to the volume containing *The Just Assassins*, "and there is no good and just action but what recognizes those limits and if it must go beyond them, at least accepts death."[78] I am less interested here in the violence of that "at least"—what else does he have in mind?—than in the sensible doctrine that it exaggerates. That doctrine might best be described by an analogy: just assassination, I want to suggest, is like civil disobedience. In both men violate a set of rules, go beyond a moral or legal limit, in order to do what they believe they should do. At the same time, they acknowledge their responsibility for the violation by accepting punishment or doing penance. But there is also a difference between the two, which has to do with the difference between law and morality. In most cases of civil disobedience the laws of the state are broken for moral reasons, and the state provides the punishment. In most cases of dirty hands moral rules are broken for reasons of state, and no one provides the punishment. There is rarely a Czarist executioner waiting in the wings for politicians with dirty hands, even the most deserving among them. Moral rules are not usually enforced against the sort of actor I am considering, largely because he acts in an official capacity. If they were enforced, dirty hands would be no problem. We would simply honor the man who did bad in order to do good, and at the same time we would punish him. We would honor him for the good he has done, and we would punish him for the bad he has done. We would punish him, that is, for the same reasons we punish anyone else; it is not my purpose here to defend any particular view of punishment. Short of the priest and the confessional, there are no authorities to whom we might entrust the task.

I am nevertheless inclined to think Camus's view the most attractive of the three, if only because it requires us at least to imagine a punishment or a penance that fits the crime and so to examine closely the nature of the crime. The others do not require that. Once he has launched his career, the crimes of Machiavelli's prince, seem subject only to prudential control. And their crimes of Weber's tragic hero are

---

[78] CALIGULA AND THREE OTHER PLAYS (New York, 1958), p. x. (The preface is translated by Justin O'Brian, the plays by Stuart Gilbert).

limited only by his capacity for suffering. In neither case is there any explicit reference back to the moral code, once it has, at great personal cost to be sure, been set aside. The question posed by Sartre's Hoerderer (whom I suspect of being a suffering servant) is rhetorical, and the answer is obvious (I have already given it), but the characteristic sweep of both is disturbing. Since it is concerned only with those crimes that ought to be committed, the dilemma of dirty hands seems to exclude questions of degree. Wanton or excessive cruelty is not at issue, any more than is cruelty directed at bad ends. But political action is so uncertain that politicians necessarily take moral as well as political risks, committing crimes that they only think ought to be committed. They override the rules without ever being certain that they have found the best way to the results they hope to achieve, and we don't want them to do that too quickly or too often. So it is important that the moral stakes be very high—which is to say, that the rules be rightly valued. That, I suppose, is the reason for Camus's extremism. Without the executioner, however, there is no one to set the stakes or maintain the values except ourselves, and probably no way to do either except through philosophic reiteration and political activity.

"We shall not abolish lying by refusing to tell lies," says Hoerderer, "but by using every means at hand to abolish social classes." I suspect we shall not abolish lying at all, but we might see to it that fewer lies were told if we contrived to deny power and glory to the greatest liars—except, of course, in the case of those lucky few whose extraordinary achievements make us forget the lies they told. If Hoerderer succeeds in abolishing social classes, perhaps he will join the lucky few. Meanwhile, he lies, manipulates, and kills, and we must make sure he pays the price. We won't be able to do that however, without getting our own hands dirty, and then we must find some way of paying the price ourselves.

QUESTIONS

1. Walzer claims that the "dilemma of dirty hands" is "a central feature of political life." He goes on to say that a politician is distinct from "other entrepreneurs in an open society" in three ways: (1) "[h]e does not merely cater to our interests; he acts on our behalf, even in our name," (2) he "rule[s] over us," and (3) he has access to the power of "official violence." For this purpose, is there any difference between a lawyer and a politician?

2. Walzer observes that "just assassination . . . is like civil disobedience," referring to Camus's *The Just Assassins*. Walzer adds, "In both ['just' assassination and civil disobedience] men violate a set of rules, go beyond a moral or legal limit, in order to do what they believe they should do. At the same time, they acknowledge their responsibility for the violation by accepting punishment or doing penance." Is this comparison between civil disobedience and assassination fair?

3. Walzer concludes section ii as follows: "Here is the moral politician [lawyer]: it is by his dirty hands that we know him. If he were a moral man and nothing else, his hands would not be dirty; if he were a politician [lawyer] and nothing else, he would pretend that they were clean" ("lawyer" inserted). Do you agree? What is Walzer's primary point in writing this article?

HERMAN MELVILLE, EXCERPTS FROM BILLY BUDD, FORETOPMAN

(1928)

* * *

All being quickly in readiness, Billy Budd was arraigned, Captain Vere necessarily appearing as the sole witness in the case, and as such temporarily sinking his rank, though singularly maintaining it in a matter apparently trivial, namely, that he testified from the ship's weather-side, with that object having caused the court to sit on the lee-side. Concisely he narrated all that had led up to the catastrophe, omitting nothing in Claggart's accusation and deposing as to the manner in which the prisoner had received it. At this testimony the three officers glanced with no little surprise at Billy Budd, the last man they would have suspected, either of mutinous design alleged by Claggart, or of the undeniable deed he himself had done. The First Lieutenant, taking judicial primacy and turning towards the prisoner, said, "Captain Vere has spoken. Is it or is it not as Captain Vere says?" In response came syllables not so much impeded in the utterance as might have been anticipated. They were these:

"Captain Vere tells the truth. It is just as Captain Vere says, but it is not as the Master-at-arms said. I have eaten the King's bread and I am true to the King."

"I believe you, my man," said the witness, his voice indicating a suppressed emotion not otherwise betrayed.

"God will bless you for that, your honour!" not without stammering said Billy, and all but broke down. But immediately was recalled to self-control by another question, with which the same emotional difficulty of utterance came: "No, there was no malice between us. I never bore malice against the Master-at-arms. I am sorry that he is dead. I did not mean to kill him. Could I have used my tongue I would not have struck him. But he foully lied to my face, and in the presence of my Captain, and I had to say something, and I could only say it with a blow. God help me!"

In the impulsive above-board manner of the frank one the court saw confirmed all that was implied in words which just previously had perplexed them, coming as they did from the testifier to the tragedy, and promptly following Billy's impassioned disclaimer of mutinous intent—Captain Vere's words, "I believe you, my man."

Next it was asked of him whether he knew of or suspected aught savoring of incipient trouble (meaning a mutiny, though the explicit term was avoided) going on in any section of the ship's company.

The reply lingered. This was naturally imputed by the court to the same vocal embarrassment which had retarded or obstructed previous answers. But in main it was otherwise here; the question immediately recalling to Billy's mind the interview with the after guardsman in the fore-chains. But an innate repugnance to playing a part at all approaching that of an informer against one's own shipmates—the same erring sense of uninstructed honour which had stood in the way of his reporting the matter at the time; though as a loyal man-of-war man it was incumbent on him and failure so to do charged against him and, proven, would have subjected him to the heaviest of penalties. This, with the blind feeling now his, that nothing really was being hatched, prevailing with him. When the answer came it was a negative.

"One question more," said the officer of marines now first speaking and with a troubled earnestness. "You tell us that what the Master-at-arms said against you was a lie. Now why should he have so lied, so maliciously lied, since you declare there was no malice between you?"

At that question unintentionally touching on a spiritual sphere wholly obscure to Billy's thoughts, he was nonplussed, evincing a confusion indeed that some observers, such as can be imagined, would have construed into involuntary evidence of hidden quilt. Nevertheless he strove some way to answer, but all at once relinquished the vain endeavor, at the same time turning an appealing glance towards Captain Vere as deeming him his best helper and friend. Captain Vere, who had been seated for a time, rose to his feet, addressing the interrogator. "The question you put to him comes naturally enough. But can he rightly answer it?—or anybody else? unless indeed it be he who lies within there," designating the compartment where lay the corpse. "But the prone one there will not rise to our summons. In effect though, as it seems to me, the point you make is hardly material. Quite aside from any conceivable motive actuating the Master-at-arms, and irrespective of the provocation of the blow, a martial court must needs in the present case confine its attention to the blow's consequence, which consequence is to be deemed not otherwise than as the striker's deed!"

This utterance, the full significance of which it was not at all likely that Billy took in, nevertheless caused him to turn a wistful, interrogative look towards the speaker, a look in its dumb expressiveness not unlike that which a dog of generous breed might turn upon his master, seeking in his face some elucidation of a previous gesture ambiguous to the canine intelligence. Nor was the same utterance without marked effect upon the three officers, more especially the soldier. Couched in it seemed to them a meaning unanticipated, involving a prejudgment on the speaker's part. It served to augment a mental disturbance previously evident enough.

The soldier once more spoke, in a tone of suggestive dubiety addressing at once his associates and Captain Vere: "Nobody is present—none of the ship's company, I mean, who might shed lateral light, if any is to be had, upon what remains mysterious in this matter."

"That is thoughtfully put," said Captain Vere; "I see your drift. Ay, there is a mystery; but to use a Scriptural phrase; it is a mystery of iniquity, a matter for only psychologic theologians to discuss. But what has a military court to do with it? Not to add that for us any possible investigation of it is cut off by the lasting tongue-tie of him in yonder," again designating the, mortuary state-room. "The prisoner's deed. With that alone we have to do."

To this, and particularly the closing reiteration, the marine soldier, knowing not how aptly to reply, sadly abstained from saying aught. The First Lieutenant, who at the outset had not unnaturally assumed primacy in the court, now over-rulingly instructed by a glance from Captain Vere (a glance more effective than words), resumed that primacy. Turning to the prisoner: "Budd," he said, and scarce in equable tones, "Budd, if you have aught further to say for yourself, say it now."

Upon this the young sailor turned another quick glance towards Captain Vere; then, as taking a hint from that aspect, a hint confirming his own instinct that silence was now best, replied to the Lieutenant, "I have said all, Sir."

The marine—the same who had been the sentinel without the cabin-door at the time that the foretopman, followed by the Masters-at-arms, entered it—he, standing by the sailor throughout their judicial proceedings, was now directed to take him back to the after compartment originally assigned to the prisoner and his custodian. As the twain disappeared from view, the three officers, as partially liberated from some inward constraint associated with Billy's mere presence—simultaneously stirred in their seats. They exchanged looks of trouble indecision, yet feeling that decide they must, and without long delay; for Captain Vere was for the time sitting unconsciously with his back towards them, apparently in one of his absent fits, gazing out from a sashed port-hole to windward upon the monotonous blank of the twilight sea. But the court's silence continuing, broken only at moments by brief consultations in low earnest tones, this seemed to assure him and encourage him. Turning, he to-and-fro paced the cabin athwart; in the returning ascent to windward, climbing the slant deck in the ship's lee roll; without knowing it symbolizing thus in his action a mind resolute to surmount difficulties even if against primitive instincts strong as the wind and the sea. Presently he came to a stand before the three. After scanning their faces he stood less as mustering his thoughts for expression, than as one in deliberating how best to put them to well-meaning men not intellectually mature—men with whom it was necessary to demonstrate certain principles that were axioms to himself. Similar impatience as to talking is perhaps one reason that deters some minds from addressing any popular assemblies; under which head is to be classed most legislatures in a Democracy.

When speak he did, something both in the substance of what he said and his manner of saying it, showed the influence of unshared studies, modifying and tempering the practical training of an active career. This, along with his phraseology now and then, was suggestive of the grounds whereon rested that imputation of a certain pedantry socially alleged against him by certain naval men of wholly practical cast, captains who nevertheless would frankly concede that His Majesty's Navy mustered no more efficient officers of their grade than "Starry Vere."

What he said was to this effect: "Hitherto I have been but the witness, little more; and I should hardly think now to take another tone, that of your coadjutor, for the time, did I not perceive in you—at the crisis too—a troubled hesitancy, proceeding, I doubt not, from the clashing of military duty with moral scruple—scruple vitalized by compassion. For the compassion, how can I otherwise but share it. But, mindful of paramount obligation, I strive against scruples that may tend to enervate decision. Not, gentlemen, that I hide from myself that the case is an exceptional one. Speculatively regarded, it well might be referred to a jury of casuists. But for us here, acting not as casuists or moralists, it is a case practical and under martial law practically to be dealt with.

"But your scruples! Do they move as in a dusk? Challenge them. Make them advance and declare themselves. Come now—do they import something like this: If, mindless of palliating circumstance, we are bound to regard the death of the Master-at-arms as the prisoner's deed, then does that deed constitute a capital crime whereof the penalty is a mortal one? But in natural justice is nothing but the prisoner's overt act to be considered? Now can we adjudge to summary and shameful death a fellow-creature innocent before God, and whom we feel to be so?—Does that state it aright? You sign sad assent. Well, I, too, feel that, the full force of that. It is Nature. But do these buttons that we wear attest that our allegiance is to Nature? No, to the King. Though the ocean, which is inviolate Nature primeval, though this be the element where we move and have our being as sailors, yet as the King's officers lies our duty in a sphere correspondingly natural? So little is that true, that in receiving our commissions we in the most important regards ceased to be natural free-agents. When war is declared, are we the commissioned fighters previously consulted? We fight at command. If our judgments approve the war, that is but coincidence. So in other particulars. So now, would it be so much we ourselves that would condemn as it would be martial law operating through us? For that law and the rigour of it, we are not responsible. Our vowed responsibility is in this: That however pitilessly that law may operate, we nevertheless adhere to it and administer it."

"But the exceptional in the matter moves the heart within you. Even so, too, is mine moved. But let not warm hearts betray heads that should be cool. Ashore in a criminal case will an upright judge allow himself when off the bench to be waylaid by some tender kinswoman of the accused seeking to touch him with her tearful plea? Well, the heart here is as that piteous woman. The heart is the feminine in man, and hard though it be, she must here be ruled out."

He paused, earnestly studying them for a moment; then resumed.

"But something in your aspect seems to urge that it is not solely that heart that moves in you, but also the conscience, the private conscience. Then, tell me whether or not, occupying the position we do, private conscience should not yield to that imperial one formulated in the code under which alone we officially proceed?"

*   *   *

QUESTIONS

1.   What does Billy Budd suggest about Melville's view of duty and the legal order?

2.   We know that Herman Melville took long walks and had lengthy conversations with his father-in-law, Chief Justice Lemuel Shaw, who had ordered the return of escaped slave Thomas Sims even though Shaw personally opposed slavery. Do you think they agreed about the nature of professional duty?

3.   What do you think of Captain Vere and the fate of Billy Budd? Do you agree with Captain Vere that "the heart here denotes the Feminine in man . . .? and, hard though it be, she must be ruled out?" What would Phyllis Goldfarb think of this characterization of positivist legal obligation?

4.   What is your answer, as a lawyer, to Captain Vere's final question, "But tell me whether or not, occupying the position we do, private conscience should not yield to the imperial one formulated in the Code under which alone we officially proceed?" What would Shaw's answer be? Thoreau's? Melville's? Martin Luther King's?

Chapter VIII

VIRTUE ETHICS

A. YOU ARE CONVINCED BUT . . . AN INTRODUCTION TO THE NEXT THREE CHAPTERS

You may be fully convinced that you are responsible for the choices in your lives (Chapter I), and that there is some notion of the right or the good even if you cannot define it with precision (Chapter II). As a lawyer, you understand "the legal mentality," with both the strength that this construct offers and the danger that it may sometimes serve to define away moral concerns (Chapter III). You understand that the value of your role as a lawyer turns on the moral foundation of the underlying system in which you function and that there are moral constraints to rule making (Chapter IV). You even accept that there are some fundamental limits on behavior (Chapter V) so that you may, in times of dire necessary, consider breaking the very law you have been sworn to uphold (Chapter VI). Yet there is the value of allegiance, which means you may also place value on duty even if that means adhering to an unjust law or application of law (Chapter VII).

In the end, you have to live in this world and make daily decisions, large and small, that often have ethical dimensions. Many of us strive to grow as a person of practical wisdom as we do so. The problems in this book have demonstrated that the devil is always in the details. The challenge is not just to *be* ethical but to *do* ethics. The next three chapters provide some additional guidance on how you "do" ethics. These ideas are part of your toolbox, or arsenal if you prefer the imagery of war, as you live in this world. Virtue ethics (Chapter VIII) and pragmatism and casuistry (Chapter IX) are not merely broad philosophical concepts, but very practical ideas for how to improve your decision-making. And we know from many case studies of flawed decisions that errors often occur because individuals simply do not see the ethical dimensions of their decisions, get blinded by their role, or become paralyzed by factual, legal, or moral uncertainty. We strive in Chapter X to address some of these concerns as well as some organizational and political constraints on ethical decision-making.

B. BEYOND ARISTOTLE

Recall our discussion of Aristotle's *Nicomachean Ethics* in Chapter II. Aristotle was an ancient Greek philosopher and student of Plato whose work influenced modern theorists such as Alasdair MacIntyre, Bernard Williams, Phillipa Foote, and Stanley Hauerwas. Aristotle believed that human beings are fundamentally different from other animals because they have the capacity to use reason to seek for and contemplate the truth, and because they can subordinate their more basic sensualities and appetites to advance desired ends. For Aristotle and virtue ethicists who followed him, a discussion of moral responsibility must begin with the question "What does it mean to be fully human"?

As Professor Michael Cassidy's article suggests, the primary concern of virtue ethics is with personal integrity; that is, the coherence of one's actions with one's values and character. It is thus an inward-looking moral theory that focuses on what it means to lead a good life. Recall Ronald Dworkin's comparison of goal-based, duty-based, and rights-based moral philosophies, *infra* at 7F. Like utilitarianism, virtue ethics is a teleological, or "goal-based" philosophy. The course that a moral agent takes is directed toward a "telos," or goal. But unlike utilitarianism, where the ultimate goal of human action is maximizing happiness, the "telos" for a virtue ethicist is promoting human flourishing. For a virtue ethicist, the concept of the good is determined by intrinsic human excellence rather than by external outcomes. This philosophical tradition understands moral virtue as a *rightly ordered way of being*; that is, an integration of head and heart, of intellect and behavior. For a virtue ethicist, moral judgment is about nurturing good *character* so that individuals can form appropriate responses to external situations or problems that arise.

A virtue ethicist believes not only that our character influences our actions, but also that our actions influence our character. That is, the accumulation of prior actions habituates us toward certain forms of future behavior. Virtues, like vices, dispose us to act in a certain way, and to perceive the world in a certain way. When confronted with a moral dilemma, a person who ascribes to virtue theory would thus ask herself at least two questions: (1) what direction do the virtues of justice, courage, honesty, prudence, etc. point me in making this decision; and (2) what type of person will I become if I behave in a certain way, and do I want to become that sort of person?

Virtue ethics may cause you, once again, to question what value there is to embracing "values." Professor Martha Nussbaum's article urges us to confront such skepticism head on. This challenge is particularly acute for lawyers, for whom it is so easy to disengage from values. There were probably several times in your discussion of problems where you were tempted to (or did) throw up your hands and say that the right answer is contested, and therefore that we should not make any claim to right behavior. Each individual should decide for himself or herself. This turns conversation about values into simply a way to make a personal choice, with little or no values to others, and a way to distance ourselves from any deep commitment to care about these questions. Nussbaum urges that there is in fact value in values talk. And she challenges the common logical slip to shrug our shoulders and believe that all values are equal. We certainly don't believe all facts are equal. Just because there are Holocaust deniers does not mean that their position is equal to those who have meticulously documented the existence of the Holocaust. And even when we have the tragic clash of two important values, it does not make the losing value worthless.

So what does this mean for your life as a lawyer? There is a crisis in the legal profession, and there is strong evidence that this is a crisis in values. As Professor Daniel Markovits points out, American lawyers and theorists spend an inordinate amount of time justifying the lawyer's conduct through the adversary system. This is often called the "adversary system excuse," which uses the adversary system as a third-person impartial moral justification for the lawyer's conduct. But Markovits sets out an alternative, first-person, point of view. "Even if the modern lawyer can justify her morally troubling actions to third parties in impartial terms, she cannot cast them as components of a life she can happily endorse and therefore cannot construct an acceptable self-image as their author; even where the modern lawyer can justify her morally troubling actions, the justification she offers leaves her alienated from her own moral life." If Markovits' analysis rings true to you, does virtue ethics offer some hope to reconcile the crisis in values? Ursula LeGuin raises a similar question of personal integrity in her provocative short story, *The Ones Who Walk Away from Omelas*. LeGuin imagines a world where it simply may not be possible to reconcile a life of virtue with the choice offered. Has our legal system reached that crisis point?

C. FURTHER READING

For a comprehensive but concise treatment of Aristotle's Ethics, see ALASDAIR MACINTYRE, A SHORT HISTORY OF ETHICS 57–83 (1998). For a discussion of virtue ethics generally, see James F. Keenan, *Virtue Ethics: Making a Case as It Comes of Age*, 67 THOUGHT 115, 115 (1992). For an excellent discussion of virtue ethics and how moral reasoning might be brought to bear on issues surrounding professional responsibility of lawyers, see Robert Araujo, S.J., *The Virtuous Lawyer, Paradigm and Possibility*, 50 SMU L. REV. 433, 446 (1997).

D. DISCUSSION PROBLEMS

PROBLEM XXII

Consider the following ethical conundrum first posed by Bernard Williams in *A Critique of Utilitarianism*, discussed in Daniel Markovits' article *infra* at 8E.

Jim is captured along with 19 other political prisoners. A mad dictator offers Jim a choice: select one of his fellow prisoners and shoot him, or the dictator will have all 20 prisoners (including Jim) shot. Should Jim kill one innocent person in order to save 19 others? Choose the role of the Utilitarian, the Deontologist, and the Virtue Ethicist, and build an analysis of what you should do.

Consider:

ABA Model Rules of Professional Conduct, Rule 8.4

E. MATERIALS

R. MICHAEL CASSIDY, CHARACTER AND CONTEXT: WHAT VIRTUE ETHICS CAN TEACH US ABOUT A PROSECUTOR'S ETHICAL DUTY TO "SEEK JUSTICE"
82 NOTRE DAME L. REV. 635 (2006) (footnotes omitted)

Part II.

Legal theorists typically distinguish between two types of moral theories—deontological and consequentialist. Deontologists such as Immanuel Kant posit that we must look to prior principles in order to decide upon a moral course of action. One can deduce these prior principles (or moral truths) by asking whether one would be happy living in a world where everyone behaved as proposed. If the answer is no, then one has a duty not to behave that way. The categorical imperative—"the moral law according to which one should act only on principles that one can accept everyone's acting upon" provides the source of the duty to determine right action. In a deontological ethical system, the right is prior to the good; good outcomes will be achieved if everyone behaves according to their rights and responsibilities.

A consequentialist moral theory looks at the outcome of human decisions. A course of action is morally proper if it increases human happiness (pleasure) and improper if it increases human suffering (pain). Determining a proper course of action requires an actor to weigh the social utility and disutility of his conduct to determine whether it produces, on balance, beneficial consequences. Although a so-called "rights-utilitarian" would concede that respect for individual rights and human autonomy is a value that contributes to aggregate social welfare, even this more finely calibrated form of consequentialism would allow an actor to violate the rights of certain individuals in order to protect the rights of many others.

Approaching professional ethics from either a purely deontological perspective or a purely consequentialist perspective presents several problems. To paraphrase Bernard Williams, if someone needs to rationalize saving his wife from a burning building on background principles [either deontological (duty) or consequentialist (maximizing happiness and minimizing pain)] he is "having one thought too many." Values and principles alone cannot determine proper outcomes, because moral judgment is not just about arriving at appropriate answers—or what Gerald Postema facetiously termed "getting our moral sums right." Moral judgment is also about nurturing the appropriate attitudes and reactions to the situations in which individuals find themselves. For these reasons, it is critical to approach problems of professional ethics from a perspective that recognizes the importance of character.

A focus on character may help to bridge the gap where both deontological and utilitarian reasoning fail. For example, there is an important difference between "being a truthful person," which is a good character trait, and "telling the truth," which is a rule. One might violate the proscription on lying in certain compelling circumstances without being an untruthful person (e.g., lying about whether Anne

Frank and her family are hiding in your attic in order to protect them from arrest by the Nazi forces). Deontological reasoning simply fails to provide meaningful guidance in that situation. Moreover, to be an authentically truthful person one must at times speak honestly, even if it might cause great pain to others. Cheating on your tax return is wrong, even where it is necessary to finance a life-saving medical procedure for a family member. In this situation, purely utilitarian forms of moral reasoning also fail us. These examples illustrate that if lawyers are expected to be honest throughout their professional activities, they must be taught to prize the truth, and not simply admonished "not to lie."

Virtue ethics is a teleological philosophy rooted in the classical humanism of Aristotle. The course which a moral agent takes is directed toward a "telos," or goal. But unlike consequentialist theories such as utilitarianism, where the ultimate goal of human action is maximizing happiness, the "telos" for a virtue ethicist is individual human flourishing. The concept of the good is prior to the concept of the right, but what is good is determined by intrinsic human excellence rather than external outcomes.

Aristotle emphasized the sort of person we must become if we want to live a good life. Virtue is acquired through practice. Repetition of virtuous actions will lead to virtuous character (habit), which in turn will lead to more virtuous action. Just as men "become builders by building houses," they become just persons by practicing just actions and self controlled persons by practicing self control. Only by putting the virtues into practice does the good becomes "integrated" in our character, in the words of Germain Grisez. An action is right if it is in conformity with the virtues, and improper or unethical if it is contrary to the virtues.

The proper threshold question for virtue ethicists is thus not "what should one do?" but "what kind of person should one be?" Only when we answer that question can we possibly hope to discern what to do. Whereas deontological theories are concerned with universal principles or rules (what is "right"), virtue ethics is concerned with the goal of becoming a good person. Goodness conveys the agent as "striving out of love to realize the right." For a virtue ethicist, "how it is best or right to conduct oneself is explained in terms of how it is best for a human being to be." Virtue ethics makes the characteristics of a good person the focus of analysis, "on the assumption that one who is good is likely to do the right thing in most situations."

It is important to distinguish virtue from two related but distinct concepts: value and honor. Values are about personal preference (I might prefer fame to money, leisure time to material goods, or friendship to autonomy). Virtues, on the other hand, are internal dispositions of character or mind that lead to human excellence. The virtues exert control on our external preferences, but they are both prior and superior to our value systems.

Virtue is also distinct from honor. Honor is often equated with status—the social prestige, accolades, and privilege that come from having a good reputation. Honor is not a virtue because it depends on the approval of others—"the gossip of the town and the judgment of circumstantial elites." We honor others only because they have done something to merit the honor. Character, by contrast, comes from within, and is directed at helping us to become our best selves rather than attaining the approval of others. For Aristotle, honor was at best only a goal secondary to virtue.

Individuals are not born with virtue, but they are born with the capacity to learn the virtues through nurturing and training. Aristotle believed that we are not by nature either good or evil, although we may have tendencies toward one pole or another. During childhood and adolescence we acquire good or bad dispositions through the process of rewards and discouragement. A student of virtue performs virtuous acts, makes them a habit (integration), and then approaches particular situations by combining intellect and character through the process of practical wisdom, which will be discussed later in this section. Once moral virtues become habitual dispositions and are coupled with reason, they allow the individual "to choose freely the just and beautiful action."

Aristotle classified the virtues into two distinct categories: the moral virtues and the intellectual virtues. The moral virtues are those virtues that perfect the part of the soul which can be controlled or influenced by rationality. Aristotle emphasized eleven moral virtues: temperance, courage, industriousness, generosity ("magnanimity"), pride, good temper ("mildness"), truthfulness, friendliness, modesty, justice, and pleasantness (being "ready witted"). The intellectual virtues, for Aristotle, are those virtues that perfect the part of the soul which itself reasons, that is, the virtues that shape the capacity to reason. The five intellectual virtues are understanding (intuition), science, theoretical wisdom (philosophy), craft (the art of production), and practical wisdom.

In the thirteenth century, St. Thomas Aquinas synthesized Aristotelian philosophy and Christian tradition in his treatise Summa Theologica. For Aquinas, virtue is one of the necessary means by which a person is led to his perfection; that is, achieving the beatific vision and coming to know God. Aquinas agreed with Aristotle on what he termed the "natural" virtues (both intellectual and moral) but added to Aristotle's framework the "theological" virtues of faith, hope and charity. Moreover, Aquinas grouped Aristotle's natural virtues into what he termed the four "cardinal" virtues—prudence, justice, temperance, and courage. Aquinas saw all of Aristotle's other moral virtues as subsumed or grouped within one of these four cardinal virtues.

In a grouping reminiscent of Aquinas, modern virtue ethicist Alasdair MacIntyre has seized upon justice, courage, and honesty as the most important virtues for individuals striving to be responsible moral agents. For the purposes of this paper, I intend to analyze these three key virtues identified by MacIntyre, in addition to the "cornerstone" Aristotelian and Thomistic virtue of practical wisdom (or "prudence").

*   *   *

Justice. Aristotle identified justice as the "complete virtue," and spent all of Book V of Nichomachean Ethics discussing what it means to be a just person. Aristotle distinguished between universal justice—which is the complete or perfect virtue ("kratiste")—from particular justice, which is a moral virtue on par with courage, temperance, etc. Universal justice is concerned with law abidingness and compliance with rules. Particular justice—the context in which I will use the term throughout this article—is concerned with right relations towards others.

For Aristotle, particular justice is the virtue by which a person "lives in right relation with his neighbor." Individuals must recognize each other's existence and their right to co-exist. Justice occurs where there is reciprocity, that is, where "every person renders to one another those concerns which each has for the self." Aristotle believed that justice was closely related to friendship. One can have friendship for pleasure, for advantage, or for good. The best and highest form of friendship is a friendship of the third variety. Where individual "A" is concerned for individual "B" for B's own sake, rather than for the result accruing to A, A essentially recognizes B as another self. Justice is the virtue that prompts me to act for the sake of another's well being, rather than just my own.

Bernard Williams equated the Aristotelian notion of justice (justice "in the particular") to "fairness." According to Williams, an unjust person is one who is "not . . . affected or moved by considerations of fairness." The vice of injustice is seen as "settled indifference" to others.

*   *   *

Courage. Courage is the virtue that enables an individual to do what is good notwithstanding harm, danger or risk to themselves. For Aristotle it was the mean between cowardice and false confidence, or "boldness." Alasdair MacIntyre saw courage as related to care and concern for others: "If someone says that he cares for some individual, community, or cause, but is unwilling to risk harm or danger on his, her or its own behalf, he puts in question the genuineness of his care and concern." Similarly, Reed Loder has captured the virtue of courage as the ability to "withstand[ ] pressure, even at some personal sacrifice." With respect to the conduct of public officials, the virtue of courage is also implicated in the willingness to sacrifice short term benefits for longer range goals; that is, courage may enable a prosecutor, legislator or judge to "strike a balance between the immediate demands and concerns of the public and the long range public good."

Honesty. Aristotle recognized the importance of being truthful in speech and action. For Aristotle, the excess of truthfulness was boastfulness and the deficiency of truthfulness was "self deprecation," with the virtue of honesty being the mean between these two vices. In giving these examples, Aristotle clearly was focusing on truthfulness as important to an individual's self assessment. But this virtue also has important implications for an individual's assessment of external facts. Thomas Shaffer characterized the virtue of honesty as "tolerance for ambiguity." A person is honest if he is comfortable with incongruity, and is willing to accept circumstances and other people for the way they are, rather than feeling the need to make them consistent with his own predispositions. An honest person is thus open to evidence that discredits his own ideas or world view.

Prudence. Prudence, or "practical wisdom," is the one intellectual virtue which Aristotle also considered to be a moral virtue. In fact, Aristotle treats practical wisdom as the "keystone of all virtues." Ethical judgment ends in action for Aristotle through the process of practical wisdom, or "phronesis." For Aristotle, the moral virtues are those characteristics of the soul that allow us to desire and to select good ends. But practical wisdom is the virtue that allows us to take aim and decide on a course of action to achieve these good ends. Practical wisdom enables one to act at the time "when one should," "in the way one should," and "for the reasons one should."

In Aristotle's view, the gap between priority rules and action is bridged by the virtue of practical wisdom. Arriving at the ability to know and recognize what is good cannot be accomplished without this intellectual virtue. All choice involves consideration and deliberation of the alternatives. Practical wisdom is the ability to deliberate well—to recognize and perceive proper ends, and then to select those means that are likely to achieve such ends. Deliberation toward *any* end is cleverness; deliberation toward a *good* end is practical wisdom.

Aristotle recognized that in certain situations the moral virtues may be in conflict (for example, courage may point in one direction and temperance in another). However, Aristotle believed that practical wisdom was the key to discerning a proper course of action in those instances where the virtues might conflict. What might be cowardice in one situation might be courage in another. For Aristotle "the virtues of character are unified through practical wisdom." "Virtuous action cannot be specified without reference to the judgment of a prudent man." This emphasis on context is distinctly Aristotelian. To be a virtuous person requires "sensitivity to the salient features of [particular] situations," and not merely the capacity to apply or follow explicit rules.

Practical wisdom involves a three step process—deliberation, judgment, and decision. It is a dialectic rather than a purely deductive approach. Individuals who possess the virtue of practical wisdom are reflective; they are willing and able to deliberate well about what it means to pursue the good in a particular circumstance. A person who is good at deliberation combines both compassion (the power of generating feelings for potential outcomes, even those that affect others rather than ourselves) and then detachment (the power to moderate or confine those feeling in balancing interests and making decisions between alternatives). The prudent lawyer is able both to identify the salient features of particular situations, and then to synthesize the multiplicity of concerns at stake.

How does an emphasis on practical wisdom differ from the so-called "new casuistry" approach to legal ethics? Casuistry has been defined as a "particularized, context driven method" of ethical decisionmaking, whereby one extrapolates from the principles underlying an ethical rule, and then determines the right course of action in gray areas by giving full considerations to the details of the situation and the motives and circumstances of the various actors involved. But as proponents of new casuistry recognize, the proper exercise of casuistry requires not only attention to and reflection on the particulars of a concrete ethical dilemma, but also a form of expertise. Casuistry is not just going with your best "hunch" or intuition. Those who are successful at casuistry as a form of moral reasoning are those that have developed the wisdom necessary to develop considered moral judgments. Casuistry and virtue theory thus share an emphasis on the importance of practical wisdom and experience. Where casuistry and virtue theory diverge, however, is on the issue of what personal attributes of the decisionmaker apart from wisdom (and perhaps the other intellectual virtues such as the ability to listen attentively and to reason) are necessary to considered moral judgment. Unlike casuistry, virtue ethics looks inward and emphasizes the importance of the good *character* of the decisionmaker. For Aristotle and other virtue ethicists, a person's character is akin to the muscles of an athlete; successful performance in any particular endeavor depends not only on attention to the external circumstances of the contest, but also on conditioning and development of the inner self.

QUESTIONS

1.   If an attorney embraces virtue ethics, is the attorney putting his or her own desire for human flourishing above the interests of his or her client?

2.   Cassidy acknowledges that sometimes different virtues will point us in different directions. What then? Is this a flaw in virtue theory, or does it just make all deliberation come down to a matter of prudence?

MARTHA C. NUSSBAUM,[1] VALUING VALUES: A CASE FOR REASONED COMMITMENT
6 YALE JOURNAL OF LAW & HUMANITIES 197 (1994) (footnotes renumbered)

I begin with two stories about values in a "postmodern world"—that is, a world in which the norms and standards by which people habitually guide their actions have come under attack, and the norms are suddenly seen to be nonnecessary, historical, and "all-too-human." The first story is from Ancient Greece, where this assault on the normative began; it concerns the skeptical philosopher Pyrrho, the legendary author of the assault.

*   *   *

Pyrrho is on the deck of a ship at sea.[2] A storm comes up suddenly. The other passengers begin to rush around, filled with anxiety. Because they have not followed the advice of philosophy to suspend their normative commitments—because, we might say, they do not think that they live in a postmodern world—they have definite beliefs about what is good and what is bad, and attach considerable importance to those beliefs, as giving them good reasons for, as opposed to simply causing, action. So they try to protect themselves, their loved ones, their possessions—and they wonder anxiously what is best to do. Meanwhile, on the deck of the ship, a pig goes on eating contentedly at its trough. Pyrrho points to the pig and says, "The wise person should live in just such freedom from disturbance."

---

[1] I am very grateful to Steven Winter and Pierre Schlag for arranging the panel, and to Cass Sunstein for comments on a previous draft.

[2] The story is told in Diogenes Laertius's Life of Pyrrho, IX.66. All translations from the Greek are my own. I discuss the ancient Greek skeptics in detail in chapter 8 of The Therapy of Desire: Theory and Practice in Hellenistic Ethics (Princeton: Princeton University Press, 1994). I discuss some of the modern parallels in more detail in "Skepticism about Practical Reason in Literature and the Law," Harvard Law Review 107 (January 1994): 714–44, hereinafter "Skepticism."

II

*   *   *

Let me illustrate the problem with an example that was central to Marty Chen's articulate study of the question.[3] Metha Bai, a young widow in Rajasthan, needs to take a job outside the home if she and her children are to have enough to eat. Since she belongs to a social caste that forbids women to work outside the home, her in-laws strenuously oppose her plan; they beat her if she tries to go out. They prefer the ill-health and possible death of Metha Bai and her children to the shame they would incur through her working. Interviewed by Chen, she summarized her predicament as follows: "I may die, but I cannot go out." It would appear that this is a case that calls urgently for moral standtaking.

Let me now illustrate the procedure of the ancient skeptics; in a moment I shall show that they have numerous descendants on the contemporary scene. First, they produce a belief, and for these purposes I shall stick to evaluative beliefs, although in fact they do this across the board with all beliefs.[4] Let us say, sticking with an example actually used in the ancient texts, that it is the belief that incest is a bad thing. The skeptics then produce from somewhere or other the opposite of this belief, showing that it is held by somebody or other. Thus, the first belief is not uncontested. In this case, they produce the practice of incest in the Egyptian royal family, in order to show that someone thinks incest is a good thing.[5] Faced with the conflict of opposing beliefs, the follower of Pyrrho feels their "equal weight." There seems to be nothing to do, then, but to suspend commitment to both of them because we have available to us no criterion for sorting things out that itself commands universal agreement. And this suspension, the ancient Greek skeptics note, produces a delightful state of freedom from disturbance, like the calm after the storm.[6] They add that it is this security and freedom from disturbance that ethical people wanted from their ethical commitments and values anyhow; however, since no values are ever uncontested, no values really bring this calm.[7]

Faced with the case of Metha Bai, how would the skeptic proceed? Let me imagine that Marty Chen, the fieldworker who interviewed her and described her case, is such a skeptic. The skeptical Chen would take note of Metha Bai's predicament and her beliefs, registering the fact that some women think that

---

[3] See Marty Chen, "A Matter of Survival: Women's Right to Work in Rural India and Bangladesh," in Women, Culture.

[4] The relevant ancient texts are in Diogenes Laertius, Life of Pyrrho. See the Loeb Classical Library edition, Lives of the Philosophers (Cambridge: Harvard University Press, 1936), and Sextus Empiricus, Outlines of Pyrrhonism and Against the Professors, gathered in the Loeb Classical Library edition of Sextus (Cambridge: Harvard University Press, 1933). The translation given in the Loeb of Sextus is highly defective, so the reader should consult the extracts available in Julia Annas and Jonathan Barnes, eds., The Modes of Skepticism (Cambridge: Cambridge University Press, 1985), and Anthony A. Long and David Sedley, eds., The Hellenistic Philosophers, vol. 1 (Cambridge: Cambridge University Press, 1987), 1–24, 468–88.

[5] See Sextus, Outlines, III.234

[6] Sextus, Outlines, I.8.

[7] Sextus, Outlines, I.25. For detailed analysis and further references, see chap. 8 of Therapy and "Skepticism."

women need the right to work outside the home. She would also take note of the prevalent and deeply entrenched beliefs of upper-caste Indians, to the effect that it is terrible and shameful for women to work outside the home. Faced with this evident conflict of opposing beliefs, Chen would suspend judgment, because it would appear that there is something like equal weight on both sides. This suspension of judgment leads to a state of freedom from disturbance. Chen, who was initially inclined to be upset about Metha Bai, no longer feels the disturbing temptation to get involved in her predicament, since she understands that there is no resolving the matter. She can go her way unaffected.[8]

The detached skeptic will continue to act, but she will realize that motives for action are just behavioral causes that derive from her feelings and habits and from the customs and conventions and practices of her society, as well as—Sextus Empiricus adds—the habits of the profession in which she was trained. She will realize that there is no justifiable ground for commitment to any of them, though she may continue to feel bound by them as causes. What this means is that Marty Chen can continue on with her professional activity of doing fieldwork and writing up its results; she can even follow her own entrenched habits, helping others to the extent to which it is habitual to do so, though she will cease to feel that this help is demanded by a moral principle to which she is committed. This is likely to have consequences in action: without a sense of urgency about the moral commitment, one will be less likely to undertake ambitious, costly, or risky action for the sake of doing something about Metha Bai's predicament. It may be questioned whether, if a skeptic, Marty Chen would ever have found herself in a rural village in India in the first place, given that her profession can be exercised in other, more comfortable surroundings. The moral commitment that drives her to undertake hardship cannot be removed, it seems, without affecting the pattern of her choices. I can add that skepticism would alter her writing as well, for in the writing of the real-life Marty Chen one feels a powerful compassion and anger at the injustices faced by women such as Metha Bai. If informed by skepticism, this disturbed style of writing would be replaced by a style more detached, distant, or even playful.

*   *   *

The ancient skeptics have their modern followers. They do not characteristically call themselves skeptics, but this is on the whole because they associate the term with modern epistemological skepticism, and not with the very different strategy of the ancient skeptics, which is really quite close to their own. The modern skeptic simply attempts to drive a wedge between knowledge and belief; the ancient skeptic wants people to suspend all their commitments, especially normative commitments. What is especially strange is that people who think of themselves as occupying very different political commitments join hands in following the general skeptical path. On the left, we find versions of this argument, for example, in both Jacques Derrida[9] and Stanley Fish. To focus on the example that is most pertinent to the law, Fish's

---

[8] This example is very close to some produced by Sextus, who mentions the pain people have when they look at the suffering of others, and holds that this pain would be removed if we understood that the belief that the person's condition is bad can, like other beliefs, be countered by an opposing belief.

[9] See "Skepticism" for a treatment of the complexities of this case.

article "Anti-Professionalism"[10] announces that we would have good reasons for an evaluative judgment only if we had both universal agreement and criteria that transcended human history. Lacking this, we must simply follow the practices of the professions in which we are trained, viewing these as causes of action rather than as giving sound reasons for action. This manifestation of power takes the place of our old notions of fitness and rightness.

*　　*　　*

What is wrong with these arguments? Returning to Metha Bai and Marty Chen, I shall point to three serious difficulties: an unrealistic goal, loaded dice, and the fact that freedom from disturbance is presupposed as the goal.[11] First, the skeptics, both ancient and modern, demand nothing less than universal agreement as the criterion of acceptability for a normative principle. If we come up with anyone at all who believes the contradictory of a given proposition, this is sufficient to get us started on the road that ends up in suspension of commitment. But why should we think this? There are many different reasons why people have the beliefs they have; many of these are bad reasons. It is only because the skeptic has already given up on the distinction between reasons and causes that all values look equal. The skeptic is not supposed to be assuming this distinction, but showing it. Until the skeptic has shown it, we should not be troubled by the fact that Egyptians like incest (if they do) or that some people love cannibalism. Such facts have no weight, independently of the reasons and arguments that are given for holding the belief.

If we consider the case of Metha Bai, we see this rather clearly. Hardly ever, when social injustice and hierarchy are present, will we find universal agreement about a project of reform. It is no surprise that Metha Bai's in-laws do not agree with her; it was no surprise when whites in the South opposed the Civil Rights movement. In these cases, a claim of justice and human need conflicts with a claim based on prejudice and entrenched power. In real life, we do not hesitate to make these distinctions, nor do we hesitate to say that the reasons Metha Bai gives for working are weightier, more deserving of respect, than the reasons the in-laws give for forbidding her to work. The absence of unanimity in no way prevents moral argument from reaching a conclusion.

We now can notice the second serious difficulty with the fused left and right characterization of the postmodern predicament: the skeptic really does not bring forward arguments that are equal in force on both sides of all questions. The movement from assertion and counter-assertion to suspension is rigged by ignoring arguments with good, strong human credentials that really do help people decide in life for one view as against another, even in the absence of universal agreement. It is because the skeptic has set the goal so unreasonably high that these humble human arguments are of no interest to him or her. The skeptic assumes, in the act of constructing his arguments, a stance of detachment from commitment that is supposed to be the outcome of the arguments, not their prerequisite. It is only

---

[10] In Stanley Fish, Doing What Comes Naturally: Change, Rhetoric, and the Practice of Theory in Literary and Legal Studies (Durham: Duke University Press, 1989); see also the related account in Fish, There's No Such Thing as Free Speech.

[11] For more detail, see "Skepticism."

because the skeptic stands back so far, refusing to be swayed by reasons in the usual human way, that each claim seems exactly as strong as its contradictory.

Again, think of the skeptical Marty Chen. Why has she concluded that the arguments of Metha Bai and her in-laws have equal weight? (To the real-life Chen, this is not at all how things seem.) It is because she has antecedently refused involvement, refused to assess these arguments against any moral beliefs or commitments of her own. Standing back from them, she has seen them simply as one argument clashing against another argument, and, seen in this way, they really do appear to have equal weight. That suspension of commitment was supposed to be the outcome of the argument, not its prerequisite.

What explains this departure from our usual human immersion in the strength of reasons? The ancient skeptics are very forthright about this: it is the allure of freedom from disturbance, the goal to which detachment from normative commitment allegedly leads. They announce that they deliver reliably a goal that everyone wants, but committed people all too rarely get, and they allow their commitment to this goal to order the whole enterprise, carefully devising antithetical arguments so as to bring themselves into detachment about any proposition whatsoever. Modern skeptics and their relatives are less forthright about this—but in Derrida's allusions to the pleasure of "free play"; in Fish's evident pleasure in the way the power of the profession takes its course, revealing some as high-salaried, others as poor; in the economist's preference for low decision costs; in Bork's preference for turning things over to the majority—we see clear analogues to the ancient commitments. The skeptical Marty Chen I have imagined seems to be eager not to get too close to the people she studies, eager to avoid the disturbance of being involved in their predicament. She assumes the detached posture of an onlooker watching the play of forces because the cost of immersion and concern would be too great a disturbance.

*   *   *

It seems, furthermore, that we might not want to live in the world these skeptics would give us. In that world there may be no fear of shipwreck and no terror of barking dogs, but as Sextus Empiricus makes clear, there would also be no commitment to fight for justice against a tyrant's pressure, no commitment to engage in any sort of unpopular or radical reform, no commitment to help a friend in trouble when help would impose difficulty, and no commitment to help Metha Bai in her struggle for survival. The story goes that one day Pyrrho's colleague Anaxarchus fell into a swamp. Pyrrho sees him floundering, but walks on by without helping. When others start criticizing him, Anaxarchus (by this time, let us hope, out of the mud) praises Pyrrho's lack of normative commitment.[12] Even so, we can imagine the fictional Marty Chen, who walks away from Metha Bai, winning the praise of Stanley Fish. Fish, by way of characterizing his theoretical position, describes himself as the sort of character who cannot remember a commitment for more than a few hours.

---

[12] Ibid., IX.6.

III

Nevertheless, I want to take on the difficult task of saying something on behalf of abstract values. In the process, I shall use examples from Plato, where the push to the abstraction Schlag describes got going in the Western tradition, and I shall also, as before, use the example of Metha Bai and Marty Chen.

What, then, is abstraction good for in value-talk? Or, to put things Nietzsche's way,[13] what is the value of these values? I suggest four roles that the creation of detached and to some extent acontextual norms might play in ethical life.

A

First, and most obviously, there is the point developed by Pierre Schlag: sometimes, indeed, the appeal to abstraction is a way of stopping debate by saying that there is something unchanging out there, and we are bound by it. To his son, who proposes to beat him, Aristophanes's character Strepsiades points to the laws of the external (as he thinks) value-order. The son points out that this is a human order, and, since he is a human being, he can make a new order. It might have been better for this son to have gone on believing in the external.[14]

This order-giving role for abstract values is defended not only by old metaphysical types, but by some of the postmodernists themselves. Many philosophers who actually think values are historical and contextual also think that it is dangerous to let people recognize this, because if they do they will not feel as bound and will have a tendency to behave badly. This argument has been made in different ways by Nietzsche[15] and by Charles Taylor,[16] both of whom are inclined to believe that people will not prove capable of reliably binding themselves to a moral way of life without the belief (even if false) that there is an order "out there" commanding their actions.

---

[13] See, for example, Friedrich Nietzsche, On the Genealogy of Morals, trans. W. Kaufmann (New York: Vintage, 1967), preface section 3:

> [U]nder what conditions did man devise these value judgments good and evil? and what value do they themselves possess? Have they hitherto hindered or furthered human prosperity? Are they a sign of distress, of impoverishment, of the degeneration of life? Or is there revealed in them, on the contrary, the plenitude, force, and will of life, its courage, certainty, future?

[14] Aristophanes, Clouds, ed. Kenneth J. Dover (Oxford: Clarendon Press, 1972).

[15] Consider especially the essay "On Truth and Lying in the Extra-Moral Sense," in which Nietzsche argues that coherent discourse would not be possible if we were at all times aware of the human origins of our distinctions and categories. Gay Science, sec. 111 argues in a related way that lack of awareness of the noncorrespondence of our categories to any immutable and ahistorical reality is highly functional: "At bottom every high degree of caution . . . and every skeptical tendency constitute a great danger for life." See also Gay Science, sec. 121 ("We have arranged for ourselves a world in which we can live—by positing bodies, lines, planes, causes and effects, motion and rest, form and content; without these articles of faith nobody now could endure life."). On the special danger posed by awareness of the "death of God," see ibid., sec. 125, in which the speaker doubts that human beings will be capable of ordering their own ethical lives without the illusion of an externally given order. This is the worry developed in the final section of Charles Taylor's Sources of the Self: The Making of the Modern Identity (Cambridge: Harvard University Press, 1989).

[16] See Taylor, Sources of the Self, chap. 25.

*   *   *

Let me return here to Metha Bai. We find in her case that much of the trouble comes from a certain sort of abstraction, which for far too long has bound people's behavior as if from without. Far from ordering beliefs in a fruitful way, the Hindu caste system, thought of as "out there," simply fortifies people's resistance to legitimate human claims. If we were to remove from these caste norms their sense of externality, we would not, I believe, have a standoff. We would be able to present a very powerful moral argument in support of Metha Bai's claim to work. This argument would make use of nontranscendent abstractions such as the right to food, personhood, and autonomy. Even if we could not persuade the actual in-laws of Metha Bai—for they are probably using her for their own selfish ends and are not really interested in engaging in argument—we could convince the local government, or the local development authority, that Metha Bai's autonomous choice to work should be respected. Getting rid of the alleged authority of the transcendent will permit the good human abstractions to have their full argumentative weight.

B

To appeal to an abstraction such as Justice or Personhood is a way of saying that we are appealing to standards that are above and beyond our momentary whims and preferences. We are expressing a commitment not to be ruled by whim and preference. We are saying that there is something very important that binds us, whether we feel like it or not. In effect, we are expressing a mistrust of the preference or desire of the moment, whether our own or that of others. We are recognizing that these preferences may have been deformed by lack of information, by greed, by appetite, by many things that do not represent the best of which we, and our reflection, are capable. This clearly need not mean that the abstract standard is extra-historical. It can be a way of talking about the gap between a deep layer of reflection and a superficial impulse. When Plato's Cephalus says that Justice is telling the truth and paying back what you owe,[17] he means that you do it, even when you do not feel like it, because you have endorsed this norm at a level of your personality deeper than the way you happen to feel.

*   *   *

Moreover, when a value so respected clashes with another one that is equally deserving of our respect—let us say, Justice with Liberty—we cannot dispose of its claim lightly, nor reduce it to merely a quantity of something else. We will in that case think of the conflict as tragic, in a way that other conflicts are not. In that sense, the recognition of these binding abstractions, each distinct from every other, each continuing to exert its claim, generates an attitude to the conflict of values that is opposed in spirit to the attitude of economic utilitarianism, and, I think, opposed in a deep and a good way.[18] Some moral views—notably those associated with cost-benefit analysis—reduce tragic conflicts of values to choices in which an agent

---

[17] Plato, Republic, 331AB. Cephalus in fact believes that the values have an external religious origin, but that is not a necessary concomitant of this sort of value-talk.

[18] Oddly, Kant himself does not take up this attitude toward tragedy, because, I think, he is reluctant to admit that worldly circumstances can have such power over one's capability for goodness. On this, see

weighs up the costs and benefits. The view I recommend, by contrast, recognizes that in a case in which two major values collide, even when we can decide which option for action is preferable on balance, the losing option may continue to exert a moral claim if it is a value to which we have given our commitment. The fact that events have produced a situation in which we cannot do justice to all the claims to which we are committed does not mean that we are no longer committed to all of them. Thus in ancient Greek ethics, the recognition that there are many gods, that one must honor all the gods, and that the gods do not always agree generates a sense of the binding force of each separate ethical obligation, even in circumstances of tragedy.[19] This sense of tragedy remains alive even for those for whom the divinities in question are seen as human in origin; indeed it is important to point out that many ancient Greek divinities are difficult to distinguish from ethical abstractions that do not have transcendent status. Antigone, announcing her commitment to the binding claim of family love, even in tragic circumstances, points to the existence of "unwritten laws" that transcend human life.[20] But other characters similarly placed simply speak of the obligations imposed by virtue and loyalty, taking these to have a merely human origin.[21] The point of alluding to abstractions remains much the same, and it is thought to be possible so to allude to them, whether or not one believes in their transcendence.[22]

This recognition of tragedy has several serious consequences for the ethical life. First, it means that we will seek ways to make good on our commitment to a value that has lost out, for example, by making reparations, or by devoting particular care to that area of our lives at other times. Second, it means that we will seek to remake the world in such a way that such conflicts more rarely arise. The recognition, for example, that many parents face painful conflicts between their commitment to and love of their children and the demands of their work can be the beginning of a creative rethinking of the structure of work, until a structure is found that can do justice to all of the claims, or at least do far better by them. If the conflict is never seen as a conflict, the rethinking is less likely to take place.

*   *   *

---

my The Fragility of Goodness: Luck and Ethics in Greek Tragedy and Philosophy (Cambridge: Cambridge University Press, 1986), chap. 2.

[19] See ibid.

[20] Sophocles, Antigone, lines 454–55; see Nussbaum, Fragility of Goodness, chap. 3.

[21] See Nussbaum, Fragility of Goodness, chaps. 2 and 11 for discussion of examples in tragedy and Aristotle. An excellent recent treatment of the whole issue, and of Aristotle's position, is in Michael Stocker, Plural and Conflicting Values (Oxford: Clarendon Press, 1989). For contemporary legal consequences of this way of viewing conflict, see Cass Sunstein, "Incommensurability and Valuation in Law," Michigan Law Review 92 (February 1994): 779. An excellent treatment of the whole issue in connection with the criticism of utilitarian models of deliberation is in Henry Richardson, Practical Reasoning about Final Ends (forthcoming 1995).

[22] Of course, it would not be possible to admit tragic conflict if one believed that the world were governed entirely by divine justice; hence, Christian ethical views often have difficulty with the topic. Aquinas famously holds that if two values appear to conflict there must be some error, for otherwise the agent's scheme of imperatives would be logically inconsistent. For an effective discussion of the difference between the ancient Greek and the Christian views, see Alasdair MacIntyre, After Virtue (Notre Dame: Notre Dame University Press, 1981).

IV

Now of course all of this is subject to abuse. . . . Abstract value-talk may conceal manipulative intentions; it may obscure the issue, rather than clarifying it. It may short-circuit the work of reflection and argument, by suggesting that what is right to do is given in heaven, and we need not work to find it. It may abnegate responsibility by representing the choices as dictated from outside, rather than chosen by us. All these are indeed serious dangers, and the recent criticism of metaphysical realism and abstraction in philosophy has done a great service by alerting us to these dangers. But let us also not forget the positive role that the moral abstractions of the Enlightenment can play, in a world increasingly riven by all sorts of particularism and contextualism and religious communitarianism, many of them quite horrifying, most of them dangerous to the well-being of women and of ethnic and sexual minorities.

QUESTIONS

1.   What does Nussbaum mean when she states that a "detached skeptic" would operate "in a state of freedom from disturbance" when there are reasonable arguments on both sides of a moral or ethical dilemma?

2.   Is there any difference between an "abstract value," as Nussbaum uses that term, and a "virtue" in the Aristotelian tradition?

3.   Nussbaum argues that moral claims will sometimes conflict, but that when they do an appeal to "abstract values" can help us to order our priorities and to decide on a proper course of action. Do you agree? Does this appeal to "abstract values" help solve the conundrum faced by Marty Chen? How?

DANIEL MARKOVITS, LEGAL ETHICS FROM THE LAWYER'S POINT OF VIEW

15 YALE JOURNAL OF LAW & HUMANITIES 209 (2003) (footnotes renumbered)

Lawyers, I suppose, were children once.
—Charles Lamb

Introduction
(The Form of the Argument)

These pages present a philosophical argument about legal ethics. Although this general approach to legal ethics is a common one, the specific form of the argument that follows is unusual and warrants some comment. In particular, the argument does not attempt (at least not as its primary goal) to say whether the present regime of legal ethics—the law governing lawyers as it stands—is justified or wrongheaded, nor does it attempt to say what ethical principles should ideally govern the professional conduct of lawyers. Instead, the argument takes the present regime (or some recognizable variation of this regime) as given and employs philosophical analysis to explain the moral condition of lawyers who practice under this regime. My aim is to develop an account of what it is like—of what it is like not psychologically but ethically—to practice law under the present regime, with a special emphasis on the moral tensions that practicing lawyers face.

In this sense, my argument proceeds not from the point of view of the philosopher (or policy-maker) who stands outside the system of legal ethics as it is, but instead develops the point of view of the lawyer practicing within this system. Hence my title.

*　　*　　*

[M]uch contemporary scholarship in legal ethics . . . passes over the important question what it is like—what it is like ethically—to be a lawyer practicing under the system of ethical rules that we now have.

An effort at answering this question will, I think, readily justify itself. There is a widely remarked upon crisis in the modern legal profession, but the character of the crisis and indeed its very existence are hotly debated.[23] If my philosophical analysis of the lawyer's point of view is right, then the lawyer's ethical position is deeply troubled and is growing ever more intractable as time passes and the legal profession evolves. Accordingly, the commonly observed crisis in the legal profession is justified. (Whether or not this is why the crisis is felt, or indeed how widely the crisis is felt at all, I am in no position to say.) Finally, the crisis in the legal profession is in this case also profound, which is to say that it reflects, and indeed is intricately involved in, other crises of moral justification that are present in the modern world.

Part of my aim, then, is to recast familiar arguments in legal ethics in unfamiliar ways in order to reveal both the depth of the lawyer's ethical crisis and the connections between this crisis and other problems of contemporary ethics.[24] In particular, I shall show that the principal argument of contemporary legal ethics, the adversary system excuse in its several variations, is inadequate to the moral

---

[23] See, e.g., American Bar Ass'n, Young Lawyers Division Survey: Career Satisfaction 13 (1995) (reporting that more than a quarter of young lawyers are dissatisfied with the practice of law); Mary Ann Glendon, A Nation Under Lawyers 85 (1994) (revealing that a majority of lawyers would not choose the law as a career again, and over three quarters do not want their children to become lawyers); Anthony Kronman, The Lost Lawyer: Failing Ideals of the Legal Profession 2 (1993) (arguing that the legal profession suffers "a crisis of morale"); G. Andrew et. al., Comprehensive Lawyer Assistance Programs: Justification and Model, 16 L. & Psychol. Rev. 113, 114 nn.6–7 (1992) (citing empirical evidence of elevated levels of depression among lawyers in Wisconsin and Florida); G. Andrew et. al., The Prevalence of Depression, Alcohol Abuse, and Cocaine Abuse Among United States Lawyers, 13 Int'l J. L. & Psychiatry 233, 240–41 (1990) (reporting that lawyers in Washington and Arizona displayed statistically significantly higher levels of depression than the general population, specifically 20% as compared to 3–9%); William W. Eaton et. al., Occupations and the Prevalence of Major Depressive Disorder, 32 J. Occupational Med. 1079, 1081 (1990) (reporting that lawyers experience decidedly higher rates of depression that the 3–5% found among the general population); Chris Klein, Big Firm Partners: Profession Sinking, Nat'l L.J., May 26, 1997 at A1 (noting that over 80% of surveyed partners at large law firms believe that the profession has changed for the worse); Deborah Rhode, The Professionalism Problem, 39 Wm. & Mary L. Rev. 283, 284 (1998) ("Discontent with legal practice is increasingly pervasive . . ."). But see John Heinz et. al., Lawyers and Their Discontents: Findings from a Survey of the Chicago Bar, 74 Ind. L.J. 735, 735 & n.3 (1999) (reporting that 84% of Chicago lawyers surveyed were either satisfied or very satisfied with their jobs, characterizing the research presented in support of discontent among lawyers as mostly "dreadful," and attributing assertions of an ongoing crisis in the legal profession to the phenomenon that "[every] generation of lawyers appears to think that the golden era of the bar occurred just before they entered it").

[24] The richness and vividness of the lawyer's ethical position will also enable me to illuminate these more general ethical problems in a new way.

problems that face practicing lawyers—inadequate in the strict sense that some of
the most important and pressing of these problems survive even the correctness of
the adversary system excuse. If I succeed in this aim, then approaching the
problems of legal ethics from the lawyer's point of view will have enabled me to
present these problems more clearly to the philosopher's point of view (and also to
the policy-maker's) than has so far been possible. And quite apart from its intrinsic
interest, this is an important first step towards the more traditional aim of solving
them.

I. The Wellsprings of Legal Ethics
   (Two Charges of Immorality)

Lawyers in an adversary legal system inhabit an extraordinarily subtle and
complex ethical position. They represent particular clients rather than justice writ
large, and they represent these clients by means of "zealous advocacy," that is, with
"warm zeal."[25] Unlike legislators, adversary lawyers are not charged fairly to
balance the interests and claims of all persons. Instead, they care disproportion-
ately and at times almost exclusively about their clients' interests. And unlike juries
and judges, adversary lawyers are not charged to discern a true account of the facts
of a case and to apply the law dispassionately to these facts. Instead, they try
aggressively to manipulate both the facts and the law into a shape that benefits their
clients. In each of these ways, adversary lawyers commonly do, and indeed are often
required to do, things in their professional capacities, which, if done by ordinary
people in ordinary circumstances, would be straightforwardly immoral . . . This
effort reveals that the charge that adversary lawyers commit ordinarily immoral
acts should in fact be separated into two distinct charges. The relationship between
these two charges and the effects of their distinctness on the power and relevance
of several of the best-known and most important arguments in contemporary legal
ethics will form the centerpiece of my investigation. It will turn out that, at least
when approached from the lawyer's own point of view, legal ethics is substantially
more difficult (and perhaps bleaker) than has heretofore been supposed. I will
elaborate upon and defend these claims in the sections to come. In the remainder
of this section, I separate out the two charges of immorality that lawyers face.

First, lawyers are partial; they prefer their clients' interests over the interests of
others in ways that would ordinarily be immoral. The most famous statement of this

[25] Canons of Professional Responsibility Canon 15 (1908) (requiring a lawyer to represent a client
with "warm zeal"); Model Code of Prof'l Responsibility Canon 7 (1969) (requiring a lawyer to "represent
a client zealously within the bounds of law"); Model Rules of Prof'l Conduct R. 1.3 cmt. (1983) (requiring
a lawyer to "act with zeal in advocacy upon the client's behalf").

This characterization focuses on lawyers acting as litigators, that is, prosecuting or defending lawsuits.
Lawyers who act as negotiators or as legal compliance advisers will generally be less one-sided or
aggressive than the characterization implies (although even here lawyers will be influenced by what they
think they can achieve by resorting to litigation or the threat of litigation).

One should not therefore overstate lawyers' one-sidedness or zeal. Indeed, even litigators remain officers
of the court, subject to certain limitations on zealous advocacy (limitations that could undoubtedly be
made more substantial than they are at present without abandoning the core of the lawyer's adversary
position). But the ethical attacks on lawyers I consider in the main text remain robust even on the most
cautious account of these matters. Even the most mildly adversary lawyer remains a fundamentally
different figure from the judge. And that difference, it will become clear, is enough to get my argument
off the ground.

preference, and also one of the most extreme, was of course made by Lord Brougham, who said that a lawyer ". . . by the sacred duty which he owes his client, knows, in the discharge of that office but one person in the world—THAT CLIENT AND NONE OTHER . . ." and added that a lawyer must continue pressing his client's interests "by all expedient means" and "reckless of the consequences," and even though (as in the case of Lord Brougham's own defense of Queen Caroline's divorce case) he should "involve his country in confusion for his client's protection."[26] Perhaps few today (or few among Lord Brougham's contemporaries[27]) would accept so extreme a view, but the essential idea—that the lawyer should be partial—remains firmly entrenched in our legal practice. At the very least, lawyers must, as Charles Fried has pointed out, dedicate greater energies to promoting their clients' interests than is consistent with the efficient, let alone fair, distribution of their professional talents.[28] Furthermore, and much more immediately, lawyers are called on to engage their talents in support of outcomes their clients favor even when these outcomes are themselves unfair[29]—they must provide legal services and offer legal arguments in support of clients who are morally in the wrong. A tort lawyer, for example, might help a client avoid liability by pleading a technical defense involving a statute of limitations even though she knows the client committed the tort in question and has a moral duty to compensate the victim.

---

[26] 1 Speeches of Henry Lord Brougham 105 (1838), quoted in Lord MacMillan, Law and Other Things 195 (1937). MacMillan, it should be noted, did not himself approve of this extreme position.

[27] Brougham's statement probably did not represent the mainstream view among his English contemporaries, and it is not clear that even Lord Brougham himself believed what he said: he later characterized his statement, made in the course of an extraordinary trial, as "anything rather than a deliberate and well-considered opinion." See William Forsyth, Hortensius: An Historical Essay on the Office and Duties of an Advocate 389 n. (2d. ed. 1875); see also David J.A. Cairns, Advocacy and the Making of the Criminal Trial, 1800–1865, at 139 (1998). In the United States, David Hoffman and George Sharswood, the two most prominent legal ethicists of the nineteenth century, both accepted what today seem surprisingly strong limits on the lawyer's partisan commitment to his clients' interests. Hoffman thought that the lawyer should "ever claim the privilege of solely judging" whether and how far to pursue his clients' cases, and that he should not pursue cases if he concluded that the client ought to lose. David Hoffman, 2 A Course of Legal Study Resolution xiv, at 755 (2d ed. 1836). Indeed, Hoffman even thought it was wrong for a lawyer to offer purely technical defenses, for example involving statutes of limitations, against honest claims. Id. Resolution xiii at 754–55. Sharswood may have held similar views, for example that a lawyer "should throw up his brief sooner than do what revolts against his own sense of honor and propriety," although in this case the interpretive question is more complicated. George Sharswood, An Essay on Professional Ethics, 74–75 (5th ed. 1907). Sharswood, after all, originated the language of "Entire devotion of the interests of the client [and] warm zeal in the maintenance and defense of his rights . . ." that survives in the codes of ethics even today. Id. at 78–80.

[28] Fried, supra note 4, at 1061–62.

[29] Lawyers act unfairly in another way also. Lawyers commonly choose clients based not on the righteousness of their claims or on their need for legal services but rather based on their ability to pay fees. Thus lawyers don't just act unfairly to benefit the clients they have, they also choose clients in an unfair fashion (that is, in a fashion that creates an unfair distribution of legal services). I do not include this feature of legal practice in my main argument because lawyers' roles cannot plausibly be said to obligate them to distribute their services on the basis of people's ability to pay their fees. In civil cases, at least, probably no one has a right to a lawyer, and certainly no one has a right to whatever lawyer he can afford. Lawyers act immorally in choosing their clients, but they do so because of their greed and not because of their roles. Accordingly, this immorality is not distinctive to lawyers (doctors behave in similar ways) and is less interesting from the point of view of legal ethics, even if it is no less important in practice.

Similarly, a contract lawyer might help his client escape liability by arguing that the parol evidence rule supports enforcing the terms of a writing even though he knows that the parties orally agreed to different terms, terms his client has a moral duty to honor.[30]

A lawyer must raise these and other legally available arguments on behalf of his morally undeserving clients. As one court has observed, a lawyer has a duty to "set[] forth all arguable issues, and the further duty not to argue the case against his client."[31] Certainly a lawyer may not undermine a client's case on the ground simply that his own beliefs—and especially his moral beliefs—instruct him that his client should lose.[32] Thus it is hornbook law that under the ABA Model Rules of Professional Conduct, "[a] lawyer may not sabotage a client's lawful case because . . . the lawyer considers the cause repugnant."[33] Indeed, the principle that a lawyer may not damage a client's case on the ground that his conscience dictates that the client should lose is so deeply ingrained in lawyers' professional consciousness that it is rarely tested in practice or remarked upon by courts or disciplinary tribunals. . . .

*   *   *

The second charge of immorality leveled at lawyers accuses them not of generic unfairness but rather of particular vices with familiar names. (This charge focuses less on whose or what interests lawyers promote and more on what lawyers do for clients, whoever they are and whatever positions they take.) Thus lawyers, in the course of practicing their profession, attempt to convince others of characterizations of the facts and the law that they themselves believe to be false. They engage in sharp practices—papering cases, filing implausible claims and counterclaims, and delaying or extending discovery—in order to force advantageous settlements. And they badger and callously attack truthful but vulnerable opposition witnesses in order to discredit them. Furthermore, in many cases lawyers are permitted and indeed even required to act in these ways. Although lawyers may not aid in their clients' perjury by eliciting testimony they know to be straightforwardly false,[34] and although lawyers may not simply misreport precedent,[35] they are required by their duty of zealous advocacy to present colorable versions of the facts that they do not

---

[30] Charles Fried has thus observed, "[w]ould it not be intolerable if it were known that lawyers would not plead the defense of the Statute of Frauds or of the statute of limitations." Fried, supra note 4, at 1085.

[31] People v. Lang, 11 Cal. 3d 134, 139 (Cal. 1974).

[32] See Model Code of Prof'l Responsibility DR 7-101(A) (1969) (a lawyer "shall not intentionally fail to seek the lawful objectives of the client").

[33] Geoffrey C. Hazard & W. William Hodes, The Law of Lawyering § 6.2 at 6–5 (3d ed. 2001). Hazard and Hodes add, as an example of this principle, that where a client seeks to interpose a statute of limitations defense against a morally valid debt, "a lawyer who remains on the case may not refuse to assert the defense on the ground of his own conscience." Id.

[34] See Model Rules of Prof'l Conduct R. 3.3(a)(2) (1983) ("A lawyer shall not knowingly offer evidence the lawyer knows to be false.").

[35] See Model Rules of Prof'l Conduct R. 3.3(a)(1) (1983) ("A lawyer shall not knowingly fail to disclose to the tribunal legal authority in the controlling jurisdiction known to the lawyer to be directly adverse to the position of the client . . .").

themselves believe and to make colorable legal arguments that they reject. They are "required to be disingenuous," that is, "to make statements as well as arguments which [they do] not believe in."[36] Similarly, although lawyers may not file frivolous lawsuits or obstruct discovery,[37] they are allowed, and might in some circumstances even be required, to pursue claims for their clients which, while facially valid, are in fact pressed to gain a strategic advantage or even to distract or delay the course of a lawsuit.[38] And finally, even though the rules of ethics limit the extent to which lawyers may directly attack opposition witnesses,[39] they are required to confuse these witnesses in order to undermine even testimony they believe to be truthful—certainly they may not refuse to cross-examine a vulnerable witness solely as a matter of conscience, on the ground that they believe the witness is telling the truth. . . . [40]

A question now arises whose answer will form the foundation of the argument to come, namely what does the second charge add to the first—what do accusations that lawyers commit particular, lawyerly vices add to the accusation that lawyers unjustifiably prefer their clients over others? One answer is that these particular charges add nothing to the general charge that lawyers are unjustifiably partial, or at least that they add nothing substantial. According to this view, which I shall call the dependence thesis, the lawyerly vices are simply further elaborations or further specifications of the general charge of partiality. Lawyers prefer their clients' interests over the interests of others in ways that are unfair. How so? They will injure others by lying, cheating, and abusing if this best serves their clients' interests. These are vices, to be sure. But they are wrong only as species of unjustified partiality. They carry no independent moral weight because they involve no additional moral ideals.

I shall argue that the dependence thesis is wrong—that when lawyers are accused of lying, cheating, or abusing these accusations carry moral weight that does not depend on, and cannot be explained by, the idea that lawyers unjustifiably prefer their clients' interests over the interests of others. Furthermore, this feature of legal ethics—that the vices lawyers are accused of exhibiting cannot be reduced

---

[36] Charles Curtis, The Ethics of Advocacy, 4 Stan. L. Rev. 3, 9 (1951).

[37] See Model Rules of Prof'l Conduct R. 3.1 (1983) (declaring that a lawyer may not press frivolous claims); see also Fed. R. Civ. P. 11(b)(1) (requiring that those who present a submission to a court certify that "it is not being presented for any improper purpose, such as to harass or to cause unnecessary delay or needless increase in the cost of litigation").

[38] See Model Rules of Prof'l Conduct R. 3.1 cmt. 1 (1983) (declaring that while the advocate may not abuse procedure, she also "has a duty to use legal procedure to the fullest benefit of the client's cause").

[39] See Model Rules of Prof'l Conduct R. 4.4 (1983) ("In representing a client, a lawyer shall not use means that have no substantial purpose other than to embarrass, delay, or burden a third person, or use methods of obtaining evidence that violate the legal rights of such a person.").

[40] As Justice White has observed, if a defense counsel "can confuse a witness, even a truthful one, or make him appear at a disadvantage, unsure, or indecisive, that will be his normal course." United States v. Wade, 388 U.S. 218, 256–58 (1967) (White, J., dissenting in part and concurring in part). See also ABA Defense Function Standards 4-7.6(b) [KF 9640.A93 1993] ("Defense counsel's belief or knowledge that the witness is telling the truth does not preclude cross-examination."). But note the exceptional rule that a criminal prosecutor may not use cross-examination to discredit or undermine a witness whom the prosecutor knows to be telling the truth. See American Bar Ass'n, The Prosecution Function, Standards for Criminal Justice 3-5.7(b) (3d. ed. 1993).

to forms of impermissible partiality—is not merely a surface phenomenon, and no archaeology of these vices (no matter how thorough or how deep) will ever reveal them to be merely special cases or forms of partiality. The reason for this, I shall argue, is that the two charges leveled at lawyers in the end play themselves out on two distinct moral registers, tuned to two distinct moral points of view. Accusations of viciousness are independent of the accusation of partiality because the two points of view these accusations address are themselves independent of each other.

The charge that lawyers are impermissibly partial appeals to what I shall call third-personal moral ideals, according to which morality is about a person's duty to others, always construed in light of the fact that everyone's life is as important and valuable as everyone else's, including, for that matter, her own. To answer this charge, lawyers must demonstrate that their preference for their clients' interests in fact respects or promotes everyone's interests (even those whose interests they appear to disprefer) by being a part of the proper protection of everyone's legal rights. The charges involving lawyerly vices, by contrast, all play in a very different, first-personal moral register, according to which morality aims to direct a person's efforts at formulating and then living up to appropriate ideals and ambitions for herself, at constructing a life that is a success from the inside and that she can (and should want to) endorse as her own, a life that displays a kind of authenticity or narrative integrity in her own mind. To answer these charges, lawyers must recast their professional activities so as to show that, rather than involving vices of the sort ordinary good people seek to disavow and avoid, these activities instead involve virtues that belong to a form of life that a person might reasonably aspire to make her own.

*   *   *

II. Two Ethical Points of View
   (The Idea of Integrity)

Although my main focus is on legal ethics, my argument will depend on and develop certain ideas about ethics that have a more general application and whose origins lie in the broader traditions of moral philosophy. Accordingly, I devote this section of my argument to introducing a set of quite general philosophical ideas about ethics. More specifically, I shall investigate and develop certain philosophical ideas about the independent, and possibly divergent, demands of third-personal and first-personal ethical justification. This divergence, applied to legal ethics, reveals the falsehood of the dependence thesis and introduces into legal ethics the pathologies that are responsible, I shall argue, for the extraordinary complexity and intractability of the modern lawyer's ethical position.

The dominant theme in modern ethical thought is the idea of what I shall call third-personal impartial moral justification. This idea begins from the proposition that everyone's life is as important as everyone else's and, in particular, that each person is equally the source of independent, authoritative moral claims on all others. Accordingly, modern moral thought insists that an agent must justify her actions in terms that take into account—and indeed give equal consideration to—all persons whom they affect. Someone who does not grant equal concern and respect to all whom her actions affect denies those whom she fails to consider their equal status as sources of authoritative moral claims, and to this extent she acts immorally.[41]

Modern moral philosophy has focused on this dominant theme, but ethics itself continues to contain a second set of ideas about ethical justification, ideas that the theme of third-personal impartial justification has not, in spite of its dominance, quite obscured or erased. These ideas approach ethical justification in what I shall call the first-person, from the agent's own point of view. They involve the thought that ethically justified acts are those that promote the actor's success writ large (as opposed to his narrow self-interest)—his success at living according to his own suitable life plan and at achieving his own admirable ends.[42]

---

[41] Both the utilitarian and the Kantian moral traditions make this focus on third-personal impartial justification central to their philosophical ambitions. Utilitarianism's express focus on maximizing total utility is built upon an ideal of impartiality, namely that each person's utility should count equally, as under Bentham's famous dictum "everybody to count for one, nobody for more than one." See John Stuart Mill, Utilitarianism 60 (George Sher ed., 1979). (The citation to Mill here reflects something of a curiosity. Although the quoted words are attributed to Bentham by Mill, I know of no place at which Bentham actually committed his dictum to print, and Mill provides no citation. Bentham would, of course, have approved of the dictum, and he did say, in a passage that Mill's immediately prior remarks suggest Mill had in mind when making the reference to Bentham, that "[t]he happiness and unhappiness of any one member of the community—high or low, rich or poor—what greater or less part is it of the universal happiness and unhappiness, than that of any other?" Jeremy Bentham, Plan of Parliamentary Reform in the Form of a Catechism, with Reasons for Each Article: With an Introduction Showing the Necessity of Radical, and the Inadequacy of Moderate, Reform, in 3 The Works of Jeremy Bentham, supra note 29, at 433, 459.) In the Kantian tradition, this emphasis on impartiality may be seen beginning in Kant's own work, especially in the formulation of the Categorical Imperative that commands one always to treat all others as ends in themselves and never merely as means. Immanuel Kant, Groundwork of the Metaphysic of Morals 95–96 (The Formula of the End in Itself) (HJ Paton trans., 1958) (1785). It may be seen equally clearly in the efforts of modern Kantians, beginning with John Rawls, to develop Kantian moral ideas through the several mechanisms of social contract theory—mechanisms expressly designed to construct moral principles that would be generally acceptable to equally situated people. See, e.g., Bruce Ackerman, Social Justice and the Liberal State (1980); John Rawls, Political Liberalism (1993); John Rawls, A Theory of Justice (1971) [hereinafter Rawls, A Theory of Justice]; T.M. Scanlon, What We Owe to Each Other (1998) [hereinafter Scanlon, What We Owe to Each Other]; T.M. Scanlon, Contractualism and Utilitarianism, in Utilitarianism and Beyond (Amartya Sen & Bernard Williams eds., 1982) [hereinafter Scanlon, Contractualism and Utilitarianism]. The dispute between utilitarians and Kantians is properly understood as being not about the importance of impartiality to moral thought but rather about which conception of impartiality is the correct one. I will have more to say about this dispute later in this section. For an extended treatment of the idea that modern moral and political philosophy quite generally is best understood as a debate among competing conceptions of equality and impartiality, see Will Kymlica, Contemporary Political Philosophy (1990).

[42] In speaking, as I am doing, of first-personal ethical justification, I shall be using language in a somewhat (although not entirely) unconventional way. The most common usage, in the philosophical tradition that I am considering, is not to limit the enquiry to ethical justifications but instead to consider the broader class of all practical reasons—that is, reasons about what to do. (Practical reason is distinguished, in the philosophical tradition, from theoretical reason—reason about what to believe.) Under the common usage, the class of practical reasons is then divided into third-personal (or "agent-neutral") reasons and first-personal (or "agent-relative") reasons, with the paradigmatic case of the former being moral reasons involving impartiality and the paradigmatic case of the latter being prudential reasons involving self-interest.

This broader approach has the advantage over mine of making it possible to consider how other-regarding reasons and self-regarding reasons—for example reasons of impartiality and self-interest—should be balanced against each other in reaching all-things-considered decisions about what to do. But the paradigmatic association between first-personal reasons and self-interest makes it easy to

This theme recalls the venerable Aristotelian tradition that constructed an entire ethical theory around the idea that virtue promotes the general well-being or flourishing (eudaimonea) of the virtuous.[43] This idea—that a person's ethics and her first-personal success are intertwined and that ethics is about forming and satisfying appropriate ambitions and desires, so that a person does well by doing good—has been thought natural (even self-evident) in many periods of human history; and the modern idea that a person's ethical duties are measured in the third-personal currency of self-sacrifice may even, viewed historically, be the more unusual position. Indeed, although this claim is not necessary for my larger argument, the modern association between ethics and self-sacrifice may find its historical origins in certain forms of perversity—including most notably in early Christian asceticism (most extremely, in the asceticism of St. Benedict and St. Simon the Stylite, but also, and more moderately, in the thought of St. Augustine), which sought to soften the pains of wordly impotence by teaching that self-sacrifice in this world clears the path to heaven in the next.[44]

. . . On the one hand, modern ideas of equality and impartiality rightly

---

forget that first-personal reasons—reasons based not on the impartial value of others but rather on the reasoning agents' own distinctive ambitions and plans—can also be other-regarding and in this sense ethical. And, relatedly, the paradigmatic association between first-personal reasons and self-interest makes it difficult to credit that first-personal reasons may sometimes outweigh conflicting third-personal reasons in all-things-considered practical judgments.

My slightly unusual usage is designed to counteract both of these tendencies, and my substantive argument will expressly reject the two conclusions that they encourage. Thus, the problem of legal ethics that I am concerned to understand involves precisely the form of conflict between third-personal and first-personal ethical reasons that the conventional usage obscures. And my argument concerning this problem will insist on precisely the possibility that first-personal reasons can outweigh third-personal reasons that the conventional usage renders implausible.

[43] See Aristotle, The Nichomachean Ethics, bk. I chs. 4–12 (W.D. Ross, trans.), in The Basic Works of Aristotle (Richard McKean ed., 1941). Plato, incidentally, also believed the just man to be happier than the unjust one. Specifically, Plato argued that "[t]he just soul and the just man then will live well and the unjust ill" and that "he who lives well is blessed and happy, and he who does not the contrary." Plato, The Republic 353e—354a (Paul Shorey trans., 1930) in The Collected Dialogues of Plato (Edith Hamilton & Huntington Cairns eds., 1961). Plato's position, however, is in fact the polar opposite of Aristotle's. Thus, Aristotle took well-being to be the fundamental idea and derived an ethical theory from the conditions for promoting well-being. Plato, by contrast, took ethical obligation to be the fundamental idea and sought to explain why a person who violates the principles of ethics will always and inevitably suffer diminished well-being. (This is the source of Plato's well-known concern to show that even a person possessing the power to violate ethical principles with impunity—even, to use Plato's own example, the wearer of the Ring of Gyges—will be happiest if he nevertheless resists temptation and acts justly. See id. at 359c ff.).

[44] This view of Christianity owes much to Isaiah Berlin. See Isaiah Berlin, Two Concepts of Liberty § III The Retreat to the Inner Citadel, in Four Essays on Liberty (1969). Of course, the reference to Christianity in this context proceeds only by way of presenting a historically familiar example. There is no reason to think that the form of perverse asceticism that I am discussing is peculiarly Christian, and certainly none to think that Christianity possesses a monopoly on this form of self-abnegation. One can see, for example, a non-Christian version of such asceticism in Arthur Koestler's old communist Rubashov and his view that "honor is to be useful without fuss." See Arthur Koestler, Darkness at Noon (1941).

Finally, as Pascal's wager makes plain, it is a dubious proposition whether asceticism adopted with this motive involves any genuine self-sacrifice at all. Indeed, even an ascetic who did not take heaven seriously might (as Berlin observed) adopt asceticism as simply a self-interested effort to limit her desires in the face of the prospect that whatever desires she has will be frustrated.

emphasize the third-personal aspect of moral argument—the idea that each person must justify her actions to others in light of the fact that her own life is no more important than theirs. On the other hand, this emphasis leads modern ethical thought to underplay certain first-personal elements of morality that remain important. In particular, modern ethical thought underplays the idea that even with equality and impartiality in place, each person continues to need to identify specifically with his own actions, to see them as contributing to his peculiar ethical ambitions in light of the fact that he occupies a special position of intimacy and concern—of authorship—with respect to his own actions and life plan.

*   *   *

Modern ethical thought has opened up a gap between the demands of third- and first-personal moral justification, and the modern lawyer has fallen in. Even if the modern lawyer can justify her morally troubling actions to third parties in impartial terms, she cannot cast them as components of a life she can happily endorse and therefore cannot construct an acceptable self-image as their author; even where the modern lawyer can justify her morally troubling actions, the justification she offers leaves her alienated from her own moral life. She suffers, as Hegel might say, the diremption of modernity. . . .

*   *   *

The originator of the movement of thought I shall expand upon is Bernard Williams, and I begin from the same thought experiment from which he began.[45] Imagine that Jim is confronted by a dictator who has captured twenty political prisoners and offers Jim the following choice: either Jim must kill one of the prisoners or the dictator will kill all twenty. What should Jim do?

Now Jim is certainly in a difficult position, which, were it real, would cry out for an effort of practical and moral creativity directed at finding a way to avoid both horns of the dilemma at once. This obvious observation makes it somewhat silly to use thought experiments like the one at hand to say what a real Jim should, all-things-considered, do: a real Jim should undoubtedly consider many alternatives that the stylized rigidity of the thought experiment disallows. Instead, I shall employ the thought experiment for a more limited purpose, namely to elaborate one set of considerations that Jim should not ignore in deciding what ultimately to do, considerations that involve the independent demands of first-personal ethical justification and suggest that Jim should refuse to kill the one.

Jim, we may suppose, accepts the moral principle that one should not kill innocents. Indeed, this is probably something of an understatement—the idea that one should not kill innocents is likely foundational, or at least comes very early, among Jim's ethical ideals. But he notes that he is presently faced with a case in which his violating this principle himself, by killing one innocent, will minimize the total number of innocents killed, by causing the dictator to refrain from killing not only that innocent but also nineteen others. Moreover, Jim's refusing to kill the one is better for nobody, so that there is likely no third person who has any grounds for

---

[45] See Bernard Williams, A Critique of Utilitarianism, in J.J.C. Smart & Bernard Williams, Utilitarianism: For and Against 98 ff. (1973) [hereinafter Williams, A Critique of Utilitarianism].

objecting to Jim's killing. Even the one Jim kills will be killed in any case, and (barring special circumstances, such as being Jim's lover) she has no grounds for specially objecting to being killed by Jim. We might even imagine that the innocents ask Jim to join them in adopting a (fair) procedure for choosing which innocent he will kill and that the chosen innocent accepts being killed by Jim's hand. Jim's (admittedly artificial) situation has been constructed so that it appears, on almost any accounting, to be impartially preferred for him to kill the one. Accordingly, third-personal impartial morality appears to recommend that Jim kill.

Nevertheless, Jim may have a good first-personal ethical reason for refusing to kill the one. The root of this reason is that if Jim refuses to kill, then, as Williams has observed, the result will not be simply that twenty innocents are dead or even that Jim has caused twenty innocents to die, but rather that the dictator (and not Jim) has killed twenty innocents.[46] This much, Williams points out, is made plain by the observation that if the dictator responds to Jim's refusal to kill by telling Jim, "You leave me no alternative but to kill twenty," then he is, straightforwardly, lying.[47] If Jim declines the dictator's offer and refuses to kill, then he is, in some measure at least, enforcing the distinction between his agency and the dictator's and insisting upon the moral significance of this distinction, in particular with respect to the intimacy of each of their connections to whatever killings are committed. But if Jim accepts the dictator's offer and kills the one, then he allows himself to become a partner in the dictator's active malevolence. If Jim kills, then he must abandon his own benevolent projects, which include (indeed begin from) the project to avoid killing innocents. Instead, Jim must allow his projects to be determined by the dictator's evil ends. . . .

Now because of the numbers involved in this case, Jim may reasonably decide that he should in the end kill the one. He may conclude that when nineteen additional killings (or twenty times as many killings) are at stake, it is self-indulgent to refuse to kill; he may conclude that the badness of becoming the dictator's malevolent instrument is simply outweighed by the nineteen lives that his doing so will save. But even if it is right, when the numbers are large enough, for Jim to think in this way, the numbers may not always be large enough, and the moral relevance of his having killed the one will certainly not be erased by these ideas and will continue to be felt by Jim. Once again, nothing in Jim's situation forces him to kill; if Jim refuses, then the dictator, acting alone, will be the only one who kills. But if he accepts the dictator's offer, Jim must recognize that the dictator's malevolence has induced him to violate the principle—which he had adopted as his own—that one should not kill innocents and to join in the dictator's project and to make a killing his own. Indeed, it would be grotesque for Jim to ignore this fact, to deny that he has cooperated with the dictator or killed at all, and instead to congratulate himself on cooperating with the innocents or on saving nineteen lives. Jim will help the innocents and save lives by accepting the dictator's offer, but that's not all he'll do.[48]

---

[46] Id. at 108.

[47] Id. at 109.

[48] Changing the terms of the example slightly makes this side of the question stronger still. Imagine that the dictator tells Jim that to save the remaining prisoners, he must kill not one but ten (or even

Williams uses Jim's case to emphasize and develop broader ideas about the moral importance of the special relation, which I am calling the relation of authorship, that a person has to his own actions, a relation the person does not have to other people's actions, not even to those that he could have prevented. Someone who denies the moral importance of authorship and insists that there is never a morally relevant distinction between doing something himself and failing to prevent someone else from doing the same thing—a person who thinks it straightforward that Jim should kill the one—places his own decisions at the mercy of other people's projects and thereby attacks his own moral personality. . . . But it is not clear how someone who understands himself in this way retains a well-defined moral self—a sense of his own distinctive moral agency—to understand. Such a person rejects the idea that certain actions are peculiarly his, that he is their author and that these actions should bear an especially close relationship to his own ideals and ambitions. . . .

*   *   *

Perhaps Jim can, in the shadow of the dictator's threat and offer, justify his killing either in utilitarian terms, as optimizing, or in Kantian terms, including to the one whom he would kill. But while it may be that, in the shadow of the dictator's evil, Jim is impartially justified in killing the one, Jim is not simply subsumed in the dictator's shadow. Moreover, third-personal justifications of the killing cannot resolve, and must make room for, the separate question how far and how fully Jim should enter into the dictator's shadow. And this is necessarily a first-personal question, because it involves Jim's considering whether to retreat (for the moment) from his own benevolent ideals and instead to implicate himself in the dictator's evil projects, at least in the sense of making one of these projects—the killing of the one—into his own. Jim's dilemma is not dissolved by third-personal impartial moral analysis because the problem of the intimacy of Jim's connection to the killings—of Jim's authorship—is not dissolved, or indeed even addressed, by third-personal moral analysis in either its utilitarian or Kantian forms. Nor, on reflection, could it be. Third-personal impartial moral analysis necessarily proceeds from the points of view of others, and the Kantian innovation was to focus this moral inquiry not on the single maximizing point of view of total well-being, but rather on the several, independent points of view of the innocents who might be killed. The problems of authorship and integrity that lie at the core of Jim's dilemma, on the other hand, must be addressed not from the innocents' points of view, but from Jim's.

III. The Weight of the First-Personal
    (Integrity Re-examined)

I have argued that the problem of integrity endures across conceptions of third-personal impartial morality. Throughout this argument, I have presented

---

nineteen), and that he must kill using some involved method, say a slow and deliberate torture, whose execution will command Jim's protracted effort and attention and further distract him from his own benevolent ideals and ends. (In order to continue comparing likes, we may suppose that the dictator will employ the same method on all twenty prisoners in case Jim refuses.) Although it remains impartially best for Jim to accept the dictator's offer even in these modified circumstances, the first-personal arguments for Jim's refusing the dictator's offer become even stronger. Indeed, looking ahead somewhat, one might say that if it is self-indulgent for Jim to refuse to kill, his accepting the dictator's offer involves self-indulgence of another kind—the self-indulgence of believing he can so signally betray his own ideals and yet somehow remain true to them.

integrity as a substantial value—as connected to the idea that first-personal moral ideals might sometimes outweigh third-personal moral ideals in an agent's all-things-considered practical deliberations, and certainly as underwriting deep worries when it is placed under threat. This presentation was supported by the powerful intuition that Jim's integrity, in connection with his first-personal ambition not to kill innocents, might in some circumstances give him all-things-considered most reason not to kill the one even though third-personal impartial morality, in both its utilitarian and Kantian forms, counsels that he do so.

*   *   *

My own effort to answer the hegemonic claims of third-personal morality and to sustain the independent weight of the first-personal tries, therefore, to retain Williams' focus on integrity while avoiding William's psychological turn. I set forth from the ethical (and not merely psychological) observation that persons act, at bottom, for themselves (and self-responsibly) and not just as delegates on behalf of some superior (and ultimately responsible) over-arching practical presence. (Indeed, the problem of integrity is a problem at all only because people act, in this way, on their own behalves—one does not worry about the integrity of mere representatives.) I then try to give the conditions for the continued integrity of persons—first for the continued engagement, and then for the continued coherence, of persons' independently responsible wills—an ethical (and not merely a psychological) development. My aim is to sketch (although I shall do no more than sketch) an account of the necessary architecture of the first person—to demonstrate that it is as a matter of ethics a necessary condition for maintaining the integrity of persons as engaged and separate agents that their first-personal ideals be able to resist the hegemony of the third-personal and sometimes even to outweigh third-personal ideals in all-things-considered practical deliberation.

*   *   *

My argument concerning integrity and the independence of first-personal morality simply repeats this movement of thought with respect to persons understood not as patients, but as agents—not as bearers of interests and sources of claims against others, but as doers of acts and bearers of responsibility. The separateness of persons as agents is inconsistent with understanding persons as mere locally interchangeable delegates or representatives of a single overarching scheme of third-personal impartial ethical ideals. Someone who viewed himself in this way only, and who accepted that he should sacrifice his distinctive first-personal ideals whenever it is third-person impartially best that he do so, would be unable to understand some ideals as peculiarly his, or to conceive of himself as a free-standing, self-originating, and responsible source of ideals and values for himself. He would, in this way, sacrifice his integrity as an agent. The integrity of persons as agents and the capacity of first-personal ideals sometimes to outweigh third-personal impartial morality are thus no more mysterious than the integrity of persons as patients and the capacity of their individual interests sometimes to outweigh the common interest. One might say, finally, that persons are examples only and not representatives of the moral point of view.[49]

---

[49] Samuel Scheffler has also sought to develop Williams' initial insight about integrity into a sustained

* * *

IV. Legal Ethics in the Third-Person
  (The Charge of Partiality and the Adversary System Defense)

The argument of sections two and three revealed that the dependence thesis is, as a general philosophical matter, false: claims that a person's conduct violates first-personal ethical ideals do carry content that is independent of the claim that this conduct violates the third-personal ideal of impartiality. Nevertheless, the academic tradition in legal ethics—in particular, the academic tradition that treats legal ethics as a distinctively philosophical problem (rather than, for example, a sociological problem)—has generally proceeded on the assumption that the dependence thesis is true. (Although academic legal ethicists have not expressly formulated the dependence thesis, that is only because they have not attended to the distinction between third- and first-personal morality in light of which the dependence thesis arises.) Academic legal ethicists have by and large proceeded as if the

---

argument against the hegemony of third-personal morality, at least in its consequentialist form, and in favor of what he calls an "agent-centered prerogative" which permits persons sometimes to act in ways that do not produce the third-person impartially best overall state of affairs. See Samuel Scheffler, The Rejection of Consequentialism 5 (rev. ed. 1994). Three differences between my views and Scheffler's are worth mentioning and explain why my own argument has proceeded directly from Williams' ideas. Although I recite these differences together, it is worth noting that they stand in very different positions with respect to the overall movement of thought.

First, Scheffler restricts his efforts to resisting the hegemony of the consequentialist version of third-personal morality. He does not consider the possibility that even non-consequentialist third-personal morality may threaten the integrity of persons and, indeed, takes his arguments to support not resistance to the third-personal tout court but rather incorporation of some elements of deontological (or, as I have been saying, Kantian) views into third-personal morality. See id. at 4–5. Second, although Scheffler observes that consequentialism's insistence that persons should maximize third-personal value fits poorly with "the way in which concerns and commitments are naturally generated from a person's point of view quite independently of the weight of those concerns in an impersonal [third-personal] ranking of overall states of affairs," id. at 9 (emphasis in original), and although he seeks to develop a moral theory that takes adequate account of the "independence of the personal point of view," id. at 62, "as a fact about human agency," id. at 64, Scheffler makes no sustained effort to elaborate upon this idea. Although Scheffler recognizes that moral theory must be sensitive to what it is "reasonable" to demand of human agents given how their concerns and commitments arise," id. at 125, and although he recognizes that the idea of reasonableness must in this connection refer to "the structure of a unified personality," id. at 18, he presents no substantive standard of what is, in this sense, reasonable. He presents no substantive account of what I have called the "architecture of the first person." Finally, and perhaps most importantly, Scheffler's resistance to the hegemony of third-personal morality is limited to claiming that persons may sometimes act in ways that are not impartially best; he expressly rejects the view that persons are sometimes required to act in such ways. (Scheffler expresses this position by saying that he accepts an agent-centered prerogative but rejects agent-centered restrictions. See id. at 5–6.) Scheffler takes this view because he believes that discretion to act in ways that are not impartially best is sufficient to protect a person's integrity, that "if someone wants to bring about the best state of affairs, either out of a supererogatory willingness to sacrifice his own projects or because bringing about the best is his project, there is no reason from the standpoint of integrity to forbid that." Id. at 22 (emphasis in original). Scheffler insists, therefore, that "[t]he promotion of the general good . . . can be undertaken from within one's personal standpoint." Id. at 97 (emphasis in original), and expressly rejects the view that "to have a [first-] personal point of view is to have a source for the generation and pursuit of personal commitments and concerns that is independent of the impersonal [third-personal] perspective." Id. at 57. This is precisely the position that I adopt. The account of the architecture of the first-person that I develop in the main text is designed to defend this position, and the discussion of legal ethics that follows aims to apply it to the professional circumstance of modern lawyers.

real problem of legal ethics were the third-personal problem of the lawyer's partiality and the lawyerly vices were nothing more than special (perhaps particularly egregious) cases of this partiality.

* * *

But although these movements to moderate the adversary system and tame the adversary lawyer involve substantial reforms, they do not amount to a call to eliminate the adversary system altogether. Nearly all the critics agree (at least their positions entail) that some version of the adversary system should remain in place. They continue to believe that lawyers should represent particular clients—that is, that lawyers should argue one side of a legal dispute. And they continue to believe that lawyers should, or at any rate in the end must, choose which clients to represent on some basis other than their own personal sense of who ought to win, which means that lawyers will sometimes represent clients, and argue sides, that they believe ought to lose. To reject these positions is to claim in effect that lawyers should sit in judgment over their clients or, in more practical terms, that there should be no lawyers save for judges (or judges' assistants), no lawyers whose role is something other than determining how legal disputes should be resolved. This view, as section one illustrated, precisely negates the adversary system (in any form), and it is not prominent in the contemporary academic debate about legal ethics. Instead, the academic debate remains firmly concentrated on the adversary system and firmly centered within the adversary system defense, focusing not on eliminating adversariness altogether, but rather on important questions concerning the form of adversary procedure that in fact impartially protects everyone's rights.

* * *

Participating in the adversary system assaults the good adversary lawyer's integrity. Indeed, this assault is particularly damaging, much more damaging, in fact, than the more dramatic assault the dictator commenced against Jim's integrity. Jim's saving lives requires only a single act of killing, isolated from the rest of his life by the outlandishness of the circumstance that the dictator contrived to put him in. Killing the one requires Jim to abandon his own peculiar ends and become a participant in the scheme in which the dictator plays so large a part. But the circumstances that might persuade Jim that he should abandon his first-personal ends in the service of third-personal morality, and that might cause Jim to lose his integrity, are so far removed from the circumstances of Jim's day-to-day life that Jim might conclude that in more ordinary circumstances it will (almost) always be best for him to remain true to his own ends. Jim's loss of integrity, although real, might remain isolated and contained.[50] The adversary lawyer, by contrast, can serve impartial morality only by habitually abandoning her own ends and performing

---

[50] Notice, however, that even this argument can do only limited service on Jim's behalf. Once Jim has accepted the principle that he should sacrifice his integrity when the actions of others make it impartially best for him to do so, then the most he can say for maintaining his integrity in his day-to-day life is that, as it happens, the circumstances do not then require the sacrifice. But this is a shaky foundation indeed. It remains uncertain how often the world will be so arranged that it is impartially best for Jim to abandon his own ends even in ordinary life. And it is uncertain whether a person whose attachment to his own ends hangs by only the thin thread of circumstance can properly be said to have adopted or even articulated any ends as his own at all. He seems, instead, merely to be following rules of thumb, which treat him as

what would ordinarily be wrongs, so that wrongdoing becomes a familiar part of her life, an element of her (professional) character. Her condition is, in this way, analogous not to Jim's, but rather to another case I imagined only in passing, in which the dictator tells someone he must make a career of killing and torture in order to prevent even more killing and torture. And the adversary lawyer's sacrifice of her integrity, although less dramatic than Jim's, is commensurately more complete.

When, in the course of performing her professional duties, the adversary lawyer lies, cheats, and abuses, she alienates herself from her own actions and ethical ideals and views herself as merely a component part of the scheme of adversary justice; and, in this way, she sacrifices her integrity to the requirements of the adversary system. Furthermore, the adversary system defense does nothing to alleviate the adversary lawyer's loss of integrity; indeed, it does not even address the problem of this loss. The adversary system defense proceeds in the third-person, arguing that in spite of appearances lawyers can in the end justify their professional activities to the world at large. But the adversary lawyer's loss of integrity is a first-personal problem, which arises because even if she can justify her professional activities to the rest of the world, the adversary lawyer must still explain her professional activities to herself so as to make them fit (or at least not clash) with her more general first-personal ethical aims and ideals, her first-personal account of the life of which she wishes to claim authorship. The adversary system defense cannot do this, and cannot protect the adversary lawyer's integrity, because it does not even address the lawyer's point of view.

* * *

VII. Legal Ethics from the Lawyer's Point of View
(Cosmopolitanism and the Modern Lawyer)

These observations make it possible to return to my initial question and to ask (now that all the components of the problem have been explained and put into place) what it is like (what it is like ethically) to be a modern, cosmopolitan adversary lawyer. Our adversary legal system requires lawyers not only to display ordinarily impermissible partiality in favor of their clients, but also to subordinate their ordinary first-personal ethical ideals of honesty, fair play, and kindness to a professional role in which they must, in some measure or other, lie, cheat, and abuse. Furthermore, although third-personal impartial justifications of the lawyer's professional activities—for example, the division of labor argument embodied in the adversary system defense—may resolve the ethical problem raised by the lawyer's partiality, they do not resolve the ethical problems raised by the accusations that lawyers display certain familiar vices, especially when these problems are considered from the lawyers' own points of view. This is because arguments like the adversary system defense ask lawyers to abandon, in the name of third-personal impartial morality, the first-personal ideals that they admire and the forms of life that they aspire to achieve and instead to become, themselves, liars, cheats, and abusers. In this way, third-personal justifications of the adversary system, even

an undifferentiated component of the larger world and do not, properly speaking, support his integrity at all.

when they succeed on their own terms, place the integrity of lawyers under threat by asking lawyers to pursue courses of action and adopt forms of life that separate lawyers from their first-personal ambitions and ideals.

Furthermore, although role morality might in principle salvage the lawyer's integrity even in the face of this threat, and although an attractive, distinctively lawyerly role-ethic can be articulated, the increasing cosmopolitanism that modernity has imposed on the lawyer's role renders such a role-ethic culturally unavailable to modern lawyers and in this way secures the assault on their integrity. Put succinctly, modern adversary lawyers are required to subordinate their ordinary ethical ideals to the imperatives of their professional role, but this role has been rendered too insubstantial (too cosmopolitan) to provide lawyers with alternative, role-based ethical ideals that might help them to carry this burden. Modernity has opened up a gap between the demands of third-personal and first-personal ethical justification, and modern lawyers have fallen in.[51]

*   *   *

But although some modern lawyers no doubt feel professionally dissatisfied for banal reasons only, and others manage to avoid feeling dissatisfied at all, these commonplace facts do not reduce the significance of my philosophical argument. Although the connection between philosophical ethics and lived experience is without doubt complicated and perhaps even attenuated, there can be similarly little doubt that it is also pervasive and profound. Quite simply, one cannot imagine Jim's escaping from the dictator's offer unconcerned and unscathed. And once the isomorphism between Jim's circumstance and the circumstances of modern adversary lawyers has been laid bare, an easy and uncomplicated escape for these lawyers becomes similarly incredible. Certainly the indifference of which the New Testament accused the lawyers of an earlier era—"Ye lade men with burdens grievous to be borne, and ye yourselves touch not the burdens with one of your fingers"[52]—is no longer possible. Instead, modern lawyers' literal integrity is at stake and under threat in their professional lives, and the threat endures whether lawyers notice it or not. Finally, and in light of this, the New Testament's view of lawyers is perhaps best replaced by Anthony Kronman's warning: the practice of law is at risk of "los[ing] its status as a calling and degenerat[ing] into a tool with

---

[51] The modern adversary lawyer's position is far from unprecedented in this regard. Modernity, acting in the service of egalitarianism, has quite generally dismantled forms of social organization and control that involved insular social roles and replaced these with cosmopolitan social structures (most notably bureaucracies). This process has dramatically expanded the range of application of third-personal impartial morality and has consequently also expanded the class of people who might fall subject to an integrity-threatening conflict between third- and first-personal ethical ideals. (This observation is just one way of giving structure to one of the commonplaces of the communitarian critique of modernity, namely the claim that modern social organization engenders widespread alienation). Nevertheless, although the threat to modern adversary lawyers' integrity is certainly neither unprecedented nor exceptional, lawyers plausibly do suffer an unusually stark, unusually powerful version of the threat. This is because the third-personal impartial justification of lawyers' professional conduct takes the form (in the adversary system defense) of a division of labor argument. And the division necessarily involved in this argument will inevitably separate lawyers from first-personal ideals that they hold dear.

[52] Luke 11:46.

no more inherent moral dignity than a hammer or a gun."[53]

QUESTIONS

1. Does Markovits offer a realistic alternative to the "adversary system excuse," or just a critique of that very common justification of attorney conduct?

2. What does Markovits mean by living an "integrated" life, where one's first-person ethical ideals are consistent with the third-person demands of clients? How, if at all, is such a life consistent with the Aristotelian notion of "integrity"? Is such an integrated life possible for most legal professionals?

URSULA K. LEGUIN, THE ONES WHO WALK AWAY FROM OMELAS
in THE WIND'S TWELVE QUARTERS (2000)

With a clamor of bells that set the swallows soaring, the Festival of Summer came to the city Omelas, bright-towered by the sea. The ringing of the boats in harbor sparkled with flags. In the streets between houses with red roofs and painted walls, between old moss-grown gardens and under avenues of trees, past great parks and public buildings, processions moved. Some were decorous: old people in long stiff robes of mauve and gray, grave master workmen, quiet, merry women carrying their babies and chatting as they walked. In other streets the music beat faster, a shimmering of gong and tambourine, and the people went dancing, the procession was a dance. Children dodged in and out, their high calls rising like the swallows' crossing flights over the music and the singing. All the processions wound towards the north side of the city, where on the great water-meadow called the Green Fields boys and girls, naked in the bright air, with mud-stained feet and ankles and long, lithe arms, exercised their restive horses before the race. The horses wore no gear at all but a halter without bit. Their manes were braided with streamers of silver, gold, and green. They flared their nostrils and pranced and boasted to one another; they were vastly excited, the horse being the only animal who has adopted our ceremonies as his own. Far off to the north and west the mountains stood up half encircling Omelas on her bay. The air of morning was so clear that the snow still crowning the Eighteen Peaks burned with white-gold fire across the miles of sunlit air, under the dark blue of the sky. There was just enough wind to make the banners that marked the racecourse snap and flutter now and then. In the silence of the broad green meadows one could hear the music winding throughout the city streets, farther and nearer and ever approaching, a cheerful faint sweetness of the air from time to time trembled and gathered together and broke out into the great joyous clanging of the bells.

Joyous! How is one to tell about joy? How describe the citizens of Omelas?

They were not simple folk, you see, though they were happy. But we do not say the words of cheer much any more. All smiles have become archaic. Given a description such as this one tends to make certain assumptions. Given a description

---

[53] Kronman, supra note 1, at 364.

such as this one tends to look next for the King, mounted on a splendid stallion and surrounded by his noble knights, or perhaps in a golden litter borne by great-muscled slaves. But there was no king. They did not use swords, or keep slaves. They were not barbarians. I do not know the rules and laws of their society, but I suspect that they were singularly few. As they did without monarchy and slavery, so they also got on without the stock exchange, the advertisement, the secret police, and the bomb. Yet I repeat that these were not simple folk, not dulcet shepherds, noble savages, bland utopians. There were not less complex than us.

The trouble is that we have a bad habit, encouraged by pedants and sophisticates, of considering happiness as something rather stupid. Only pain is intellectual, only evil interesting. This is the treason of the artist: a refusal to admit the banality of evil and the terrible boredom of pain. If you can't lick 'em, join 'em. If it hurts, repeat it. But to praise despair is to condemn delight, to embrace violence is to lose hold of everything else. We have almost lost hold; we can no longer describe happy man, nor make any celebration of joy. How can I tell you about the people of Omelas? They were not naive and happy children—though their children were, in fact, happy. They were mature, intelligent, passionate adults whose lives were not wretched. O miracle! But I wish I could describe it better. I wish I could convince you. Omelas sounds in my words like a city in a fairy tale, long ago and far away, once upon a time. Perhaps it would be best if you imagined it as your own fancy bids, assuming it will rise to the occasion, for certainly I cannot suit you all. For instance, how about technology? I think that there would be no cars or helicopters in and above the streets; this follows from the fact that the people of Omelas are happy people. Happiness is based on a just discrimination of what is necessary, what is neither necessary nor destructive, and what is destructive. In the middle category, however—that of the unnecessary but undestructive, that of comfort, luxury, exuberance, etc.—they could perfectly well have central heating, subway trains, washing machines, and all kinds of marvelous devices not yet invented here, floating light-sources, fuelless power, a cure for the common cold. Or they could have none of that: it doesn't matter. As you like it. I incline to think that people from towns up and down the coast have been coming to Omelas during the last days before the Festival on very fast little trains and double-decked trams, and that the trains station of Omelas is actually the handsomest building in town, though plainer than the magnificent Farmers' Market. But even granted trains, I fear that Omelas so far strikes some of you as goody-goody. Smiles, bells, parades, horses, bleh. If so, please add an orgy. If an orgy would help, don't hesitate. Let us not, however, have temples from which issue beautiful nude priests and priestesses already half in ecstasy and ready to copulate with any man or woman, lover or stranger, who desires union with the deep godhead of the blood, although that was my first idea. But really it would be better not to have any temples in Omelas—at least, not manned temples. Religion yes, clergy no. Surely the beautiful nudes can just wander about, offering themselves like divine soufflés to the hunger of the needy and the rapture of the flesh. Let them join the processions. Let tambourines be struck above the copulations, and the gory of desire be proclaimed upon the gongs, and (a not unimportant point) let the offspring of these delightful rituals be beloved and looked after by all. One thing I know there is none of in Omelas is guilt. But what else should there be? I thought at first there were no drugs, but that is puritanical. For those who like it, the faint insistent sweetness of drooz may perfume the ways of the city, drooz which first brings a great lightness and brilliance to the mind and limbs, and then after some hours a dreamy languor, and wonderful visions at last of the very arcane and inmost secrets of the Universe, as well as exciting the pleasure of sex beyond all belief; and it is not habit-forming. For more modest tastes I think there ought to be beer. What else, what else belongs in the joyous city? The sense of victory, surely, the celebration of courage. But as we did without clergy, let us do without soldiers. The joy built upon successful slaughter is not the right kind of joy; it will not do; it is fearful and it is trivial. A boundless and generous contentment, a magnanimous triumph felt not against some outer enemy but in communion with the finest and fairest in the souls of all men everywhere and the splendor of the world's summer: This is what swells the hears of the people of Omelas, and the victory they celebrate is that of life. I don't think many of them need to take drooz.

Most of the processions have reached the Green Fields by now. A marvelous smell of cooking goes forth from the red and blue tents of the provisioners. The faces of small children are amiably sticky; in the benign gray beard of a man a couple of crumbs of rich pastry are entangled. The youths and girls have mounted their horses and are beginning to group around the starting line of the course. An old woman, small, fat, and laughing, is passing out flowers from a basket, and tall young men wear her flowers in their shining hair. A child of nine or ten sits at the edge of the crowd alone, playing on a wooden flute. People pause to listen, and they smile, but they do not speak to him, for he never ceases playing and never sees them, his dark eyes wholly rapt in the sweet, thing magic of the tune.

He finishes, and slowly lowers his hands holding the wooden flute.

As if that little private silence were the signal, all at once a trumpet sounds from the pavilion near the starting line: imperious, melancholy, piercing. The horses rear on their slender legs, and some of them neigh in answer. Sober-faced, the young riders stroke the horses' necks and soothe them, whispering. "Quiet, quiet, there my beauty, my hope. . . ." They begin to form in rank along the starting line. The crowds along the racecourse are like a field of grass and flowers in the wind. The Festival of Summer has begun.

Do you believe? Do you accept the festival, the city, the joy? No? Then let me describe one more thing.

In a basement under one of the beautiful public buildings of Omelas, or perhaps in the cellar of one of its spacious private homes, there is a room. It has one locked door, and no window. A little light seeps in dustily between cracks in the boards, secondhand from a cobwebbed window somewhere across the cellar. In one corner of the little room a couple of mops, with stiff, clotted, foul-smelling heads, stand near a rusty bucket. The floor is dirt, a little damp to the touch, as cellar dirt usually is.

The room is about three paces long and two wide: a mere broom closet or disused tool room. In the room, a child is sitting. It could be a boy or a girl. It looks about six, but actually is nearly ten. It is feeble-minded. Perhaps it was born defective, or perhaps it has become imbecile through fear, malnutrition, and neglect. It picks its nose and occasionally fumbles vaguely with its toes or genitals, as it sits hunched in the corner farthest from the bucket and the two mops. It is afraid of the mops. It finds them horrible. It shuts its eyes, but it knows the mops are still standing there; and the door is locked; and nobody will come. The door is always locked; and nobody ever comes, except that sometimes—the child has no understanding of time or interval—sometimes the door rattles terribly and opens, and a person, or several people, are there. One of them may come in and kick the child to make it stand up. The others never come close, but peer in at it with frightened, disgusted eyes. The food bowl and the water jug are hastily filled, the door is locked; the eyes disappear. The people at the door never say anything, but the child, who has not always lived in the tool room, and can remember sunlight and its mother's voice, sometimes speaks. "I will be good," it says. "Please let me out. I will be good!" They never answer. The child used to scream for help at night, and cry a good deal, but now it only makes a kind of whining, "eh-haa, eh-haa," and it speaks less and less often. It is so thin there are no calves to its legs; its belly protrudes; it lives on a half-bowl of corn meal and grease a day. It is naked. Its buttocks and thighs are a mass of festered sores, as it sits in its own excrement continually.

They all know it is there, all the people of Omelas. Some of them have come to see it, others are content merely to know it is there. They all know that it has to be there. Some of them understand why, and some do not, but they all understand that their happiness, the beauty of their city, the tenderness of their friendships, the health of their children, the wisdom of their scholars, the skill of their makers, even the abundance of their harvest and the kindly weathers of their skies, depend wholly on this child's abominable misery.

This is usually explained to children when they are between eight and twelve, whenever they seem capable of understanding; and most of those who come to see the child are young people, though often enough an adult comes, or comes back, to see the child. No matter how well the matter has been explained to them, these young spectators are always shocked and sickened at the sight. They feel disgust, which they had thought themselves superior to. They feel anger, outrage, impotence, despite all the explanations. They would like to do something for the child. But there is nothing they can do. If the child were brought up into the sunlight out of that vile place, if it were cleaned and fed and comforted, that would be a good thing, indeed; but if it were done, in that day and hour all the prosperity and beauty and delight of Omelas would wither and be destroyed. Those are the terms. To exchange all the goodness and grace of every life in Omelas for that single, small improvement: to throw away the happiness of thousands for the chance of happiness of one: that would be to let guilt within the walls indeed.

The terms are strict and absolute; there may not even be a kind word spoken to the child.

Often the young people go home in tears, or in a tearless rage, when they have seen the child and faced this terrible paradox. They may brood over it for weeks or years. But as time goes on they begin to realize that even if the child could be released, it would not get much good of its freedom: a little vague pleasure of warmth and food, no real doubt, but little more. It is too degraded and imbecile to know any real joy. It has been afraid too long ever to be free of fear. Its habits are too uncouth for it to respond to humane treatment. Indeed, after so long it would probably be wretched without walls about it to protect it, and darkness for its eyes, and its own excrement to sit in. Their tears at the bitter injustice dry when they begin to perceive the terrible justice of reality, and to accept it. Yet it is their tears and anger, the trying of their generosity and the acceptance of their helplessness, which are perhaps the true source of the splendor of their lives. Theirs is no vapid, irresponsible happiness. They know that they, like the child, are not free. They know compassion. It is the existence of the child, and their knowledge of its existence, that makes possible the nobility of their architecture, the poignancy of their music, the profundity of their science. It is because of the child that they are so gentle with children. They know that if the wretched one were not there sniveling in the dark, the other one, the flute-player, could make no joyful music as the young riders line up in their beauty for the race in the sunlight of the first morning of summer.

Now do you believe them? Are they not more credible? But there is one more thing to tell, and this is quite incredible.

At times one of the adolescent girls or boys who go see the child does not go home to weep or rage, does not, in fact, go home at all. Sometimes also a man or a woman much older falls silent for a day or two, then leaves home. These people go out into the street, and walk down the street alone. They keep walking, and walk straight out of the city of Omelas, through the beautiful gates. They keep walking across the farmlands of Omelas. Each one goes alone, youth or girl, man or woman.

Night falls; the traveler must pass down village streets, between the houses with yellow-lit windows, and on out into the darkness of the fields. Each alone, they go west or north, towards the mountains. They go on. They leave Omelas, they walk ahead into the darkness, and they do not come back. The place they go towards is a place even less imaginable to most of us than the city of happiness. I cannot describe it at all. It is possible that it does not exist. But they seem to know where they are going, the ones who walk away from Omelas.

QUESTIONS

1.   Are the residents of Omelas who "walk away" after discerning the bargain the town has made acting in a morally responsible manner? Or do they have some responsibility to take affirmative action to save the child in the cellar?

2.   What about the conduct of the citizens of Omelas who do not "walk away"? Is their conduct justifiable under any theory of moral responsibility we have studied in this course? Does it matter how the child was selected for its life of misery? What if they drew lots?

3.   What does the emphasis on virtue tell us about the "ones who walk away" that other moral theories might not explain?

Chapter IX

CASUISTRY, PRAGMATISM, AND MORAL REALISM

A. CASUISTRY: WORKING FROM CASES

Most lawyers are comfortable analogizing from cases. We have, after all, been using that process of legal analysis since the first year of law school. For example, broad theories such as "due process" and "equal protection" hold powerful sway over our legal values, yet we only bring these ideas to life on a case-by-case basis using this methodology. Can the same process of analogy from prior cases also help us think through difficult ethical problems?

As Professor Paul Tremblay notes, casuistry's "most critical premise is that moral knowledge develops incrementally through the analysis of concrete cases."

> Once she identifies one or more paradigm cases, a casuist proceeds in a fashion quite familiar to lawyers: she employs a common law reasoning style, comparing the case at hand with a collection of available easy cases. Through "moral triangulation," she reasons by analogy from the exemplars, identifying the morally relevant features of the paradigm cases, the features of the cases which account for their ready acceptance, and comparing the newer, less certain case with each paradigm case to discern which comes closest to the case under consideration.

A well-developed analysis using casuistry will delve deeply into facts in context and avoid simplistic labels and hasty conclusions.

Casuistry urges that you analogize from easy cases as you strive for the best answer in the more complex case before you. Casuistry requires a commitment to understanding the facts and context of the question at hand. Your discussions of the problems in this book inevitably have resulted in a yearning for more information and facts than a simple hypothetical can provide. Chapter X explores the problem of uncertainty in greater detail. We can say at a minimum, however, that casuistry requires that you obtain as many facts as possible as you undertake the analysis of paradigm cases.

Notice that casuistry is a method of analysis, but does not provide answers for actual cases. Chances are you have used this method in ascertaining right behavior in a variety of contexts. When analyzing the Speluncean explorers, you may have considered that killing one person in the cave to steal their food would have been improper (immoral). You may have considered that we allow people to be "heroes" by giving up their lives to save another. You may have compared or contrasted suicide, which some consider to be an improper abandonment of life. By setting out these paradigms (or others you might imagine) and making comparisons, your analysis of the Speluncean Explorers problem inevitably was made richer and more nuanced.

B. PRAGMATISM: DE-EMPHASIZING THE SEARCH FOR ABSOLUTES

Professor Amy Mashburn introduces us to the work of Reinhold Niebuhr and what has become known as pragmatism. Niebuhr's "primary methodological focus was figuring out what would work . . . given the limitations of individuals and collectives."

Like casuistry, pragmatism does not spend much time articulating universal theories, instead focusing on ethical decision-making in a complex world. Niebuhr urges that we adopt a realistic perspective and understand that there is a dualism between the morality of groups and morality of individuals. As Professor Mashburn explains:

> Niebuhr taught that moral absolutes and norms do not exist and we should not exhaust or deceive ourselves looking for them. The best we can hope to achieve is an approximation of justice that is temporarily tolerable to most. In order to do this, we must use many different ethical strategies and avoid rigidity and devotion to absolutes which threaten flexibility. We should be cognizant of the dangerous propensity of contingent moral principles to transmute themselves into "inalienable rights" and "self-evident truths." The virtues we identify today have an ironic tendency to become the vices of tomorrow. Because moral standards and values are contingent, indeter- minate, and temporal, they must be constantly re-examined to bring them into conformance with the preferences of society.

Niebuhr's insights suggest that if we truly want to increase moral decision-making, we should consider the systems in which moral decisions are made. In particular, we should assure that many voices are heard to correct the natural self-interest that emerges in decision-making.

Some interpret Niebuhr as simply endorsing pure relativism: there is no moral truth, just your truth and my truth. Niebuhr would resist that argument. As Professor Mashburn notes, "Niebuhr, the pragmatist, identified unattainable moral ideals as a primary source of desirable goals and ends." The challenge is not that we cannot identify larger goals, but that in our complex world, we cannot always attain them. That does not excuse us from searching for the closest approximation by assuring a vigorous conversation that openly and honestly considers a wide range of views, particularly of the powerless.

Casuistry and pragmatism, and we would urge good moral reasoning of all stripes, requires a commitment to understanding the context of the case in front of you. If both legal and moral reasoning requires a deeper understanding of context, you might question some aspects of your legal education, which can be strikingly acontextual. Professor Phyllis Goldfarb urges greater use of clinical and feminist methodologies in law school training. These methodologies focus on narratives, which "contain painstaking renderings of competing viewpoints that check our natural tendencies to oversimplify and overlook details and perspectives that unsettle the neat conclusions that we desire." After considering Professor Goldfarb's article, do you think that your law school training has equipped you with the skills necessary for thoughtful moral analysis?

C. FURTHER READING

For an exploration of casuistry and a discussion of its modern revival as an ethical model, see ALBERT JONSEN & STEPHEN TOULMIN, THE ABUSE OF CASUISTRY: A HISTORY OF MORAL REASONING (1988). For an early work by Reinhold Niebuhr discussing the realities of collective power and how such power may influence individual moral decision-making, see MORAL MAN AND IMMORAL SOCIETY: A STUDY OF ETHICS AND POLITICS (1932).

In addition to Paul Tremblay's excellent article in the *Materials*, take a look at his further thoughts on this subject in *Teaching Values in Law School: Shared Norms, Bad Lawyers, and the Virtues of Casuistry*, 36 U.S.F. L. REV. 659 (2002). For an interesting discussion of forms of moral discourse and casuistry within a community of shared beliefs, see M. Cathleen Kaveny, *Prophecy and Casuistry: Abortion, Torture and Moral Discourse*, 51 VILL. L. REV. 499 (2006) (includes an extensive analysis of the flawed casuistry in the torture memos).

D. DISCUSSION PROBLEMS

PROBLEM XXIII

Return to the Speluncean Explorers, [Problem X Chapter V]. Prepare an outline of the opinion you would write as a judge using casuistry as a form of moral reasoning. Has your analysis changed from the prior discussion? Your conclusion?

PROBLEM XXIV

The following facts are summarized from the opinion of *In re Pautler*, contained in your materials below. (Quotation marks are omitted.) For additional details, please read the opinion.

> On June 8th, 1998, Chief Deputy District Attorney Mark Pautler arrived at a gruesome crime scene where three women lay murdered. All died from blows to the head with a wood splitting maul. After interviewing witnesses he learned that the killer was William Neal. Neal had apparently abducted the three murder victims one at a time, killing the first two at the apartment over a three-day period. After abducting and tying a third woman, J.D.Y, on a bed, Neal brought a fourth woman to the apartment. He taped her mouth shut and tied her to a chair within J.D.Y.'s view. Then, as J.D.Y. watched in horror, Neal split the fourth victim's skull with the maul. That night he raped J.D.Y. at gunpoint.
>
> The following morning, Neal returned with J.D.Y. to the apartment. Two other people arrived at the apartment and Neal held J.D.Y. and her two friends in the apartment over thirty hours. He dictated the details of his

crimes into a recorder. Finally, he abandoned the apartment, leaving instructions with J.D.Y. and her friends to contact police, and to page him when the police arrived.

When Pautler reached the apartment, Deputy Sheriff Cheryl Moore had already paged Neal according to the instructions Neal had left. Neal answered the page by phoning the apartment on a cell phone. The ensuing conversation lasted three-and-a-half hours, during which Moore listened to Neal describe his crimes in detail. She took notes of the conversation and occasionally passed messages to Deputy D.A. Pautler and police officers at the scene. Sheriff Moore developed a rapport with Neal and continuously encouraged his peaceful surrender. Meanwhile, other law enforcement officers taped the conversation with a handheld recorder set next to a second phone in the apartment. Efforts to ascertain the location of Neal's cell phone were unsuccessful.

At one point, Neal made it clear he would not surrender without legal representation; Moore passed a message to that effect to Deputy D.A. Pautler. Neal first requested an attorney who had represented him previously, Daniel Plattner, but then also requested a public defender ("PD"). Pautler managed to find Plattner's office number in the apartment telephone book. When he called the number, however, Pautler received a recorded message indicating the telephone was no longer in service. Pautler believed that Plattner had left the practice of law, and he therefore made no additional attempt to contact Plattner. Upon learning that Plattner was unavailable, Sheriff Moore agreed with Neal to secure a public defender. However, no one in the apartment made any attempt to contact a PD or the PD's office.

Pautler was concerned that Neal was at large and capable of killing again if not apprehended. Pautler believed that any defense lawyer would advise Neal not to talk with law enforcement. Pautler also did not trust lawyers at the PD's office, although he later acknowledged that there was at least one PD he did trust. (Law enforcement officials present at the Belleview apartment later stated they would not have allowed a defense attorney to speak with Neal because they needed the conversation to continue until they could apprehend Neal). Instead of contacting the PD's office, or otherwise contacting defense counsel, Pautler offered to impersonate a PD using a fictitious name of "Mark Palmer." Law enforcement agents at the scene agreed. Posing as a public defender, Pautler talked with Neal and Neal later surrendered. About two weeks later the newly assigned public defender learned about the deception by listening to the taped conversations. Neal's public defender stated that he had difficulty establishing a trusting relationship with Neal after telling Neal that there was no lawyer named Mark Palmer at the PD's office. Neal would later dismiss his PD lawyer and defend himself in court.

Pautler was charged by the Colorado Attorney Regulatory Counsel with engaging in "dishonesty, fraud, deceit or misrepresentation" in violation of Colorado Rule of Professional Conduct (RPC) 8.4 and falsely claiming to be

disinterested in speaking to an unrepresented person, in violation of
Colorado RPC 4.3.

Please select one perspective and be prepared to present the analysis of (i)
Pautler and his defense counsel, (ii) bar counsel concerned about Pautler's
impersonation of a public defender, (iii) a victim's defense group concerned about
protecting victims of crime, or (iv) the Public Defender's Association. In developing
your analysis, be sure to consider the questions at the end of the opinion.

Consider:

ABA Model Rules of Professional Conduct:

   Rules 4.3, 8.4

E. MATERIALS

PAUL R. TREMBLAY, THE NEW CASUISTRY

12 GEORGETOWN JOURNAL OF LEGAL ETHICS 489 (1999) (footnotes omitted)

I. PRACTICING PHILOSOPHY

Let us suppose, just for the moment, that "plain people" care about ethics, that
they would prefer, everything else being equal, to do the right thing, or to lead the
good life. And let us imagine that lawyers share that sentiment—they too would
prefer to practice law in an ethical manner, by and large. We could also assume,
further, that "ethics" for lawyers means something different from, and more than,
simply following a set of rules established by the legal profession, rules with
obligatory qualities implying penalties for their violation. Many within the
profession seem to think of "legal ethics" as such rule-obligations, but it is fair for
us to assume that ethics can and does mean a lot more.

We can readily accept these premises, but doing so implies some benchmark, or
standard, or similar criterion to differentiate "better" decisions from "worse" ones.
Without some identifiable method by which to evaluate ethical choice, "caring"
about ethics is meaningless. Unless we defend the proposition that any choice is
acceptable so long as it violates no outstanding rule (a proposition with few
defenders), we implicitly accept the reality of normative standards. This, of course,
comes as no surprise, but the nature and source of those standards remain
remarkably elusive, especially in the discourse of legal ethics. This Article
represents an effort to identify sources of moral agreement without descending
into the meta-discussions of the philosophers.

                              *   *   *

In the pages below, this Article argues that these dominant approaches fail to
inform   practicing   lawyers—plain   persons   usually   lacking   philosophical
training—about how best to resolve their tensions. This Article introduces here and
seeks to defend an alternative insight about ethical choice, one grounded in the
wisdom of the Jesuits of the Middle Ages, the clinical experiences of modern

bioethicists, and the practical judgments of plain persons. This alternative is casuistry. Casuistry accepts the central truths of such grand theories as consequentialism and Kantianism. It acknowledges the importance of virtue and character, with special emphasis on practical wisdom and judgment. It melds these insights, though, with a recognition of the importance of cases and context in moral thinking, in a process that offers better concrete guidance to those who must "practice philosophy."

Casuistry represents a case-based, particularized, context-driven method of normative decision making. Casuistry starts with paradigm cases, examples upon which most observers will readily agree, and reasons analogically from those agreed-upon cases to more complex cases representing ethical conflict. By understanding and emphasizing sources of agreement, casuistry elides the all-too-common stalemate in ethics talk, where "the only alternatives [are] dogmatism and relativism." The lawyer as casuist need not decide, nor know, whether she is a Kantian, a utilitarian, or a Rawlsian. Indeed, in one case a lawyer might act "deontologically," and in a different circumstance act "consequentially," and be right in both instances. Casuistry leaves the deep and difficult philosophy debates to the philosophers, and aims its insights to the clinician, the practitioner, and the plain person. In its rejection of positivism and categorical thinking, and its emphasis on context, particularity, and phronesis, casuistry claims as intellectual forebears such influences as ancient rhetoric, Aristotelian ethics, American pragmatism, and some important strains of postmodernism.

*   *   *

III. A PRAGMATIC ALTERNATIVE: CASUISTRY, CLINICAL ETHICS, AND CASE-BASED REASONING

*   *   *

Albert Jonsen and Stephen Toulmin, the scholars most responsible for its revival, describe casuistry as follows:

> [Casuistry is] the analysis of moral issues, using procedures of reasoning based on paradigms and analogies, leading to the formulation of expert opinions about the existence and stringency of particular moral obligations, framed in terms of rules or maxims that are general but not universal or invariable, since they hold good with certainty only in the typical conditions of the agent and circumstances of action. Casuistry does not pursue universal truths and it does not rely on foundations of moral belief derived from some developed intellectual scheme. It instead looks more modestly, if not intensely, at the circumstances of the particular case that demand moral inquiry, resisting abstract or formal theories in favor of identifying paradigm cases from which one can reason analogously and contextually. Casuistry then arrives at "probable certitude" through the exercise of reflective, practical judgment. Like principlism, it builds upon shared moral sentiment; like virtue ethics, it discerns that sentiment in the particulars of cases.

B. CASUISTRY'S COMPONENT UNDERSTANDINGS

1. The "Wellsprings question": cases as the source of moral knowledge

Casuistry's most critical premise is that moral knowledge develops incrementally through the analysis of concrete cases. We have already discussed the weaknesses of moral theory and mid-level principles in practice settings. Casuists credit theories and principles as developed insights formed from considered reactions to individual cases. A lawyer understanding that insight can more readily accept conflict between theories or among principles by looking more particularly at the cases that account for the competing sentiments. In the end, the cases drive the sentiment.

Casuistry, thus, is prescriptive. It advises moral actors to think through questions differently from the manner which a theorist would suggest, by beginning with cases in context. It is also ontological and metaphysical, in that its prescription arises from a particular conception of how we know what is right. That claim, best left to the philosophers for its full defense, warrants some brief development here.

Let us call this question about the source of moral truth the "wellsprings question." The casuists observe that moral theory seldom has contributed meaningful insights to the resolution of practical problems; instead, the "locus of moral certitude" remains with the particular cases. What moral theory can do well, at times, is summarize what we know about moral truth from our encounters with concrete cases. This insight is not new, and represents an important part of feminist and pragmatist thought.

*   *   *

It is therefore not at all implausible for lawyers to accept the critical premise of casuistry—that moral insight stems from the particularities of concrete cases. This is not meant to deny theory an important place in moral deliberation, nor to ignore the insights of theoretical moral philosophy. Each competing moral theory represents sentiments derived from paradigm cases, and can summarize those sentiments in effective ways. A welcome benefit of casuistry, in fact, is that one can accept the arguments of competing theories selectively, without concluding that the theory is defective when a counter-example appears for which the theory cannot account.

2. The Role of Paradigm Cases and Analogical Reasoning

Theories and principles, despite their faults, offer a semblance of comfort. The worry is that their absence leaves only relativism, or perhaps nihilism. The casuists avoid despair by recognizing the centrality of paradigm cases, "in which the actions to be taken are clear and agreed on by virtually anyone familiar with the case and its particulars." The force of paradigm cases is largely intuitive. Once she identifies one or more paradigm cases, a casuist proceeds in a fashion quite familiar to lawyers: she employs a common law reasoning style, comparing the case at hand with a collection of available easy cases. Through "moral triangulation," she reasons by analogy from the exemplars, identifying the morally relevant features of the paradigm cases, the features of the cases which account for their ready acceptance, and comparing the newer, less certain case with each paradigm case to discern which comes closest to the case under consideration.

*   *   *

4. The Role of *Phronesis* and the Importance of Context

Casuistry is impatient with "thin" descriptions of moral dilemmas and with simple hypothetical examples. It resists abstraction, claiming that appropriate judgments are only found when all of the relevant circumstances are understood. Like feminist thought, casuistry understands knowledge to be contextually acquired. Lawyers acting in good faith will understand and learn not by carefully deducing propositions through chains of reasoning, but instead by the faculty of judgment, prudence, or Aristotle's *phronesis*. Here the casuists and the virtuists meet. Good ethical judgment takes into consideration relevant relationships, roles, power imbalances, emotional needs, community expectations, vulnerabilities, and so forth, just as the virtue ethics adherents profess.

This characteristic of casuistry has implications for the teaching of ethics, if not for the teaching of law practice generally. It demands "thick" descriptions of context. Sophisticated hypothetical problems may work, but even they will usually lack sufficient texture. It is the clinic that offers the most promising environment for students to experience the levels of tension and ambiguity necessary to develop practical judgment.

Casuistry not only demands context, but it also insists upon a form of *expertise*. All practitioners are not equally "wise." Those who are better at casuistry, and therefore at moral reasoning itself, are those who have developed the wisdom, or the *phronesis*, necessary to develop considered moral judgments. These experts need not be moral philosophers; indeed, there is good reason to doubt whether philosophers have any special insight into the proper resolution of practical moral problems. At the same time, though, the wisdom so admired by casuists and Aristotelians is not unrelated to philosophical study. As Martha Nussbaum notes, immersion in the humanities and in fiction is an important and perhaps necessary means to achieving the practical wisdom that persons of great character exemplify. The idea of "moral expertise" integrates learning and practice. In this way, casuistry acknowledges the contributions of philosophical study while rejecting much of the methodology of modern applied ethics.

5. Casuistry's Rekindling of the Art of Rhetoric

*   *   *

Maxims are exemplified by paradigm cases. In law, some maxims might include, "you always follow your client's instructions"; "lawyers do not turn away clients without good reason"; "it is wrong to reveal a client's information"; "it is wrong to lie to another lawyer"; and "a lawyer should first advance her client's case." Each of these would be arguments relied upon by any good lawyer in debating an important issue. Each may, and indeed will, have exceptions arising from certain combinations of circumstances, and that is understood. The role for the case analyst is to embrace the maxims in such a way as to make the most sense of the case before her. Her arguments will not necessarily be long, complex chains of reasoning, but instead will be more abbreviated evocation of the maxims, in what classical rhetoricians called "enthymemes."

The next rhetorical device employed by casuists is that of *"taxonomies."* Any morally complex case will invoke one or more of the field's special topics. Those topics will help frame the issue at stake in the case, and that issue should suggest several maxims. If a maxim applies, then the line of inquiry ends. In most interesting cases, a maxim will not easily apply without dissonance. That being so, the next rhetorical step, according to the casuists, is to identify a *taxonomy* of cases, starting with paradigm cases on either side of the issue and continuing with cases of lesser certainty. The case at issue is then fit within the array or continuum of cases, and the case comparison process ensues.

Classical rhetoric was always intended to persuade audiences on questions of importance to the polity or the community. While that understanding of rhetoric may be diminished today, it need not be lost. The affinity between law and rhetoric, and that between casuistry and rhetoric, combined with the frequent analogies within casuistry to the common law method, only emphasizes the importance of connecting the practice of casuistry and the practice of legal ethics in an explicit way.

AMY R. MASHBURN, PRAGMATISM AND PARADOX: REINHOLD NIEBUHR'S CRITICAL SOCIAL ETHIC AND THE REGULATION OF LAWYERS

6 GEORGETOWN JOURNAL OF LEGAL ETHICS 737 (1993) (footnotes omitted)

INTRODUCTION

When called upon to prescribe the ethical conduct of others, rule drafters, unlike moral philosophers, do not rationally apply abstract principles or implement consistent ethical theories. More often, they invoke generalized, amorphous beliefs about how people are likely to behave and how they can, and should, be made to behave. Even if they do not consciously draw upon such beliefs, they nonetheless indirectly and unconsciously implicate them by drafting rules that are premised on tacit assumptions about human behavior. When the Model Rules are viewed as the collective product of numerous choices and generalizations about how people can and should behave, they reveal a curious and troubling portrait of human nature.

This article asserts that the conception of human nature consciously and unconsciously embodied in the Model Rules is false and incongruous and demonstrates the manner in which the disciplinary system founded on the Model Rules is crippled by this inherent defect. Specifically, the Model Rules embody two seemingly contradictory, but paradoxically related, false postulates: (1) that people are basically good and can be trusted with wide discretion and virtually unlimited power to affect the lives of others and (2) that lawyers, members of a privileged class legislating to protect their power and privilege, are capable of drafting rules that adequately protect their clients and the public.

*   *   *

II. THE LEGITIMACY OF USING REINHOLD NIEBUHR'S THEORETI-CAL CONCEPTION OF HUMAN NATURE

Reinhold Niebuhr was an immensely influential theologian, moral philosopher, and political theorist who wrote prolifically during the middle third of the twentieth century. His thought, which is currently enjoying a renaissance of sorts, shaped the thinking of a generation of theologians, politicians, historians, ethicists, and political theorists. Throughout his life, Niebuhr was preoccupied with achieving a proper understanding of the individual and collective capabilities, illusions, self-deceptions, limitations, and potential of human beings. Consequently, unlike most ethical theories, Niebuhr's moral philosophy is founded on an explicit, systematic, and comprehensive view of human nature.

Although Niebuhr is commonly regarded as a theologian, he was, in reality, primarily a political analyst and moral philosopher. He considered himself a teacher of "Christian Social Ethics" rather than a theologian. His theology existed pragmatically to serve his ethic, and not vice versa. Niebuhr's epistemology reflects a corresponding disregard for the metaphysical foundations of his conception of human nature. Theologian Paul Tillich observed:

> The difficulty of writing about Niebuhr's epistemology lies in the fact that there is no such epistemology. Niebuhr does not ask, "How can I know?"; he starts knowing. And he does not ask afterward, "How could I know?", but leaves the convincing power of his thought without epistemological support.

In his defense to Tillich's accusation, Niebuhr conceded that he could "find no way of proving [his revelations] by any epistemological method" and that he knew of "no way of inducing [his] faith by purely rational arguments." To Niebuhr, an epistemological foundation, adequate or otherwise, is properly viewed as religious truth that lies beyond reason and attempts to state the inconceivable.

*   *   *

Niebuhr's ethic is not a prepackaged set of opinions on every conceivable subject. Rather, it is a dialectic methodological for thinking about human beings and a system for analyzing moral problems and making ethical choices in light of a theoretical doctrine of human capabilities and limitations. The endurance and appeal of his thought across political, social, historical, and religious lines demonstrate its widespread acceptance and continuing relevancy. Thus, applying Niebuhr's prophetic insights and dialectic mode of analysis to contemporary ethical issues is a useful and legitimate exercise.

III. REINHOLD NIEBUHR'S SOCIAL ETHIC

*   *   *

E. *The Lesser Morality of Collectives*

Niebuhr deduced that the "vision prompted by the conscience and insight of individual man . . . [is] incapable of fulfillment by collective man and that no force could make the brutal character of collectives conform to individual ideals or moral standards. Because the moral differences between individuals and groups result in actions and policies embarrassing to a "purely individualistic ethic," moral tension and conflict between individuals and groups are inevitable. Justifications are then offered to obscure the straight facts of collective life which "easily rob the average individual of confidence in the human enterprise." Thus, Niebuhr identifies hypocrisy as the "most salient moral characteristic" of a collective. He explained:

> The inevitable hypocrisy, which is associated with all of the collective activities of the human race, springs chiefly from this source: that individuals have a moral code which makes the actions of collective man an outrage to their conscience. They therefore invent romantic and moral interpretations of the real facts, preferring to obscure rather than reveal the true character of their collective behavior.

*   *   *

Niebuhr assumed that ethical action does not exist in the absence of self-criticism and that self-criticism is impossible without the rational capacity for self-transcendence. In collectives, self-critical tendencies are thwarted by the need for unity and the selfishness of the controlling or dominant class within the collective. Self-criticism is an inner disunity that the "feeble mind" of the collective cannot distinguish from the other forms of conflict it finds threatening. For this reason, according to Niebuhr, collectives regard criticism from within as disloyalty and crucify moral rebels. Thus, groups do not achieve self-consciousness because of the dynamics between internally conflicting forces but rather through the unifying effect of conflict with others. Consequently, external conflict is an unavoidable prerequisite for group solidarity and, unlike internal conflict, it is not suppressed. The externally projected "will-to-live" in groups is transformed into a collective "will-to-power." Collectives develop imperial ambitions which are aggravated, but not caused solely, by the lusts and desires of their leaders and privileged classes.

*   *   *

IV. NIEBUHR'S METHODOLOGY

However compelling Niebuhr's insights into human nature may be, they do not comprise a complete ethical theory. The missing element is a coherent methodology for applying Niebuhr's themes to contemporary problems. Absent that, Niebuhr's perceptions are too broad, open-ended, and ephemeral to suggest particular resolutions of actual, moral dilemmas. Unfortunately, discerning Niebuhr's methodology is quite difficult. A search of his voluminous works exposes no clear explication of process. But Niebuhr's lack of methodological self-consciousness does not mean that he had no method. We have trouble finding Niebuhr's method because it does not look like what we expect, nor does it reveal itself in a familiar manner. Niebuhr's problem-solving approach is not formulaic, systematic, or analytical as are most other ethical theories. Instead, it is more of a "sensibility," a "constellation of perspectives, Biblically derived and validated by experience, an offer to "experience the world in a Niebuhrian way," and a mode of encountering ethical issues as a "concerned, searching, believing, understanding and acting person." From the lengthy written record of Niebuhr's encounters with moral problems, a very distinctive, if somewhat shadowy, methodology emerges.

A. *Cognitive Mode*

The first discernibly distinct aspect of Niebuhr's methodology is a radically different way of thinking about ethics and communicating those thoughts. Niebuhr consistently employed an engaging and powerful mix of cognitive strategies: analytic, pragmatic, substructuralist, and intuitive. The analytic approach adheres to the dictates of reason and relies upon the weapons of "classical logic and argumentation." Pragmatic thinkers, on the other hand, are skeptical of universal explanations. They acknowledge the "flux and pluralism of social life" and use fallibility to defeat rigidity and polarization. The substructuralist mode is characterized by "nonrational (often total) explanations for social practices, ideologies, and the core of common sense that constitutes reason. It is aimed at the "presumed objectivity of many analytic strategists" who, according to the substructuralists, undervalue experience and practice. Finally, the intuitive mode, common in normative discourse, does not analyze its foundational assumptions and relies upon the " 'given's' of institutional practices, established methodologies, and privileged texts."

* * *

C. *A Niebuhrian Approach to Ethical Problem-Solving*

After peeling away the many substantive and methodological layers of Niebuhr's thought, one confronts what is for our purposes the core inquiry: How would Niebuhr actually go about making the choices necessary to frame ethical rules and resolve moral dilemmas? His pragmatic approach is best explained through consideration of Niebuhr's answers to three hypothetical questions: (1) What standard determines the rightness of moral actions?; (2) How do we ascertain appropriate ethical objectives?; and (3) How does society achieve those objectives?

1. Consequentialism

Niebuhr's ethic is fundamentally teleological in orientation in that he believed that the rightness of an action should be determined with reference to its consequences and whether it accomplishes or furthers a desired goal or end. For Niebuhr, morality was not substantive but rather was a principle of action. Niebuhr rejected deontological ethics because he did not believe that absolute rights, norms, or rules exist and condemned our efforts to create them as contrary to history and experience. From a Niebuhrian perspective, virtue-based ethics are problematic because people are not inherently virtuous and detecting their true motives is impossible. Niebuhr simply had no use for ethical theories that could not be translated into action.

Niebuhr's rejection of absolute moral values and recognition of the contingency and indeterminacy of all values, laws, and "self-evident truths," led him to embrace a type of relativism or nominalism. Niebuhr maintained that no moral philosopher is capable of stating a final truth, and rule-makers are similarly incapable of divining immutably correct ethical norms. Niebuhr's relativist perspective not only suggests that any search for objectively correct answers to ethical questions is futile, but it also warns us of the limited ability of any laws or ethical rules to constrain bad behavior. Niebuhr cautions that

(a) No law can do justice to the freedom of man in history. It cannot state the final good for him, since in his transcendence and self-transcendence no order of nature and no rule of history can finally determine the norm of his life. . . .

(b) No law can do justice to the complexities of motive which express themselves in the labyrinthine depths of man's interior life . . . [and]

(c) Law cannot restrain evil; for the freedom of man is such that he can make the keeping of the law the instrument of evil.

Clearly, in a Niebuhrian world, ethical rule-making would be like all law-making: a series of compromises between "rational-moral ideals of what ought to be" and the "explicit formulations" that represent the collective desires of those with power who participate in the legislative process. For that reason, Niebuhr was deeply committed to pluralism and believed that advocates of all perspectives—including those of the powerless—must participate to produce a consensus that promotes societal harmony. Niebuhr's pluralistic approach consists of including a multitude of perspectives, allowing each "to contribute their treasures to [the] common fund," resisting dogma, tolerating diversity, and remaining receptive to correction.

In sum, Niebuhr's answer to the first question is that we determine the rightness of actions by examining their consequences and the legitimacy of moral norms and ethical rules with reference to the inclusiveness and balance of the consensus that produces them.

2. Realism

The second question—how do we ascertain appropriate ethical objectives—is more substantive in its focus than the first. It asks how society should go about determining the content of the goals and ends against which particular moral actions will be judged. Ironically, Niebuhr, the pragmatist, identified unattainable moral ideals as a primary source of desirable goals and ends. Niebuhr maintained: "Every truly moral act seeks to establish what ought to be, because the agent feels obligated to the ideal, though historically unrealized, as being the order of life in its more essential reality." Although unattainable, moral ideals should not be relegated exclusively to the world of transcendence because they offer "immediate possibilities of a higher good in every given situation" for which we should strive. Even though we cannot achieve ethical perfection or destroy evil simply by avowing ideals, movement in the direction of an ideal will produce substantial improvement.

*   *   *

Niebuhr was, for whatever reason, unwilling to devote much time to advancing foundational reassurances or defending the nihilistic implications of his thought. In that respect, Niebuhr was a thoroughgoing Jamesian pragmatist whose primary methodological focus was figuring out what would work. According to Niebuhr, "even the most uncompromising ethical system must base its moral imperative in an order of reality and not merely in a possibility." Moral ideals may provide directional guidance, but the primary source of societal goals and ends should be a determination of what will work given the limitations of individuals and collectives. Niebuhr called that awareness "moral realism" and defined it as "the disposition to take all factors in a social and political situation, which offer resistance to established norms, into account, particularly the factors of self-interest and power.

Stated more broadly, Niebuhr's moral realism is simply a directive to take action with the substance of his doctrine of human nature in mind. As we have seen, that doctrine teaches that society will always be a "jungle" and conflict is inevitable. We are fundamentally self-interested and will never protect others' rights adequately. All moral actions are tainted with hypocrisy. A clash of opposing interests may be the only way to limit the power of inordinate self-interest. Creating social harmony and arbitrating conflicting interests is a difficult and costly process. " 'Some coercion, however, is justified because ethical selflessness is rarely voluntary or sincere. Surprisingly, Niebuhr's realism does not lead to or advocate an ethic of cynicism; it generates hope and tolerance. Although simply recognizing our flaws will not destroy them,' " true self-knowledge—which Niebuhr defined as self-accusation coupled with examination of the "dark labyrinths of the human heart"—obliterates the illusions and hypocrisies that perpetuate evil. Additionally, we see others more charitably when we become acquainted with the evil in ourselves.

*   *   *

3. Strategies

In response to the final inquiry—how does a Niebuhrian ethic suggest that society go about achieving its objectives—Niebuhr's works suggest five strategies.

(1) Adopt a realistic perspective.—Ethical rules should be drafted with the limitations of human nature in mind, with particular attention to the shortcomings of collective behavior. We should avoid the pitfall of inculcating conveniently superficial—and most often, optimistic—generalizations about behavior into our moral systems. The pervasiveness of evil should not deter us from making moral distinctions, judging others, and holding them responsible for the consequences of their acts. Niebuhr stated: "In spite of all the moral relativism we know fairly well what good and evil are. . . . We know that . . . [t]ruth is a virtue and the lie is evil." We should not refuse to act upon our intuitive insights simply because they are nonrational or subjective. We also know that it is good to restrain self-interest and to encourage the innate tendency to consider others. Finally, Niebuhr cautioned that our realism should not be so relentless that we ignore " 'the residual capacity for justice and devotion to the larger good' even in collective life."

(2) Accept ethical dualism.—A system of ethics cannot be crafted solely or directly from the moral ideals of individuals, nor can individual morality be transferred or applied *in toto* to group ethics. Niebuhr maintained that we have to accept a "frank dualism" in ethics between the moralities of groups and individuals

in order to avoid seriously compromising the efficacy of both by attempting to bring them into congruence. Notwithstanding that limitation, however, a workable ethic must do more than unquestioningly accept the differences between the moralities of individuals and groups. It should introduce measures to curb the coercive tendencies of collectives to impose their lower morality on individuals. As Niebuhr stated, society must try to exploit and capitalize on the "latent moral capacity" in individuals. For that reason, ethical systems should be designed to allow individuals the greatest possible freedom and otherwise encourage radical moral action. On the other hand, granting individuals great freedom is very dangerous because society cannot adequately restrain their behavior and must, to some extent, always rely upon the honesty and self-restraint of those who are free to choose evil. Therefore, we should not "make individual liberty as unqualifiedly the end of life as our ideology asserts."

(3) Seek proximate justice and apply principles of relative morality.—Niebuhr taught that moral absolutes and norms do not exist and we should not exhaust or deceive ourselves looking for them. The best we can hope to achieve is an approximation of justice that is temporarily tolerable to most. In order to do this, we must use many different ethical strategies and avoid rigidity and devotion to absolutes which threaten flexibility. We should be cognizant of the dangerous propensity of contingent moral principles to transmute themselves into "inalienable rights" and "self-evident truths." The virtues we identify today have an ironic tendency to become the vices of tomorrow. Because moral standards and values are contingent, indeterminate, and temporal, they must be constantly re-examined to bring them into conformance with the preferences of society. In particular, Niebuhr directed us to "[c]hallenge [ourselves] to re-examine superficial moral judgments, particularly those which self-righteously give the moral advantage to the one who makes the judgment." A workable ethical system, therefore, accommodates relative moral judgments and facilitates change. Moral relativism, according to Niebuhr, promotes a healthy sense of moral restlessness, guilt, and responsibility.

(4) Create power equilibriums.—Conflict is inevitable and omnipresent. Discord, however, can be directed to further positive societal goals. Justice, according to Niebuhr, "is actually maintained by a tension of competitive forces" and can be achieved only if power is properly distributed among the clashing interests. We should not shirk from harnessing conflict and coercing redistribution of power because injustice will not be diminished voluntarily or without force. The legitimacy of relative moral norms depends upon the inclusiveness of the consensus which produces them. For that reason, all interests must be empowered to participate in the debate over the form and content of ethical rules and society must ensure input from critical outsiders.

(5) Maintain institutional control.—Although groups have lesser morality than individuals, and individuals are the source of self-transcendent radical moral action, reliance upon individual morality, according to Niebuhr, cannot create justice and is no substitute for institutional control with sufficient protections and constraints. Society's moral goals and directives must be adequately institutionalized or they will invariably be compromised and defeated. Niebuhr believed that legislation and other forms of political and social governance can, and ultimately must, provide

adequate safeguards against the dangers of both collective and individual self-interest.

* * *

VI. CONCLUSION

An application of Niebuhr's theories to the regulation of lawyers provides a number of intriguing and useful insights. First, Niebuhr's analysis accurately predicts and persuasively explains the current state of lawyer regulation. Second, Niebuhrian perspectives suggest a number of fundamental structural changes to the disciplinary rules and propose strategies for accomplishing them. These include, among other things, the following reforms:

- The public should participate on an equal footing with the organized bar and the judiciary in the drafting and enforcement of the rules that govern lawyers.
- The *Model Rules* should not contain aspirational standards or provisions that are not enforceable by disciplinary action.
- The *Rules* should give lawyers less discretion in the situations that they govern.
- The drafters should make, and frequently evaluate, the hard choices necessary to determine the appropriate balance between inherently conflicting duties in recurrent situations and should communicate those resolutions in a straightforward and unequivocal manner.
- Truisms, like the sanctity of client confidences, should be frequently reevaluated and brought into conformance with the moral preferences of a legitimate societal consensus.
- Rule enforcement should emphasize punishment and exclusion from the practice of law rather than rehabilitation or education.

Finally, and perhaps most importantly, Niebuhr's socio-political ethic highlights problematic aspects of lawyer regulation that moral philosophy and legal analysis overlook or obscure. Given the limitations of collective egoism, the legal profession's disregard of public discontent, inattention to consumer protection, and refusal to relinquish power are hardly surprising. External societal pressure, however, may force the legal profession to change, even if it does so only in an effort to retain control.

* * *

Perhaps it is utopian to expect the profession to achieve the level of collective self-transcendence necessary for such a radical re-orientation, but the cumulative effect of individual lawyers re-thinking their relationship to society might move the profession in that direction. At a minimum, Niebuhr's ethic urges lawyers to base their disciplinary rules on an unflinching appraisal of human limitations and potential and to acknowledge openly the roles self-interest and inordinate power play in self-governance. To inspire the self-accusation that is an essential precursor to movement in the direction of an ideal, Niebuhr often quoted Blaise Pascal who said, "There are only two kinds of men, the righteous who believe themselves sinners; the rest, sinners, who believe themselves righteous." To this, Niebuhr modified Pascal's categories to include the "infinite . . . shades of awareness of guilt from the complacency of those who are spiritually blind to the sensitivity of the saint who knows that he is not a saint."

QUESTIONS

1. What are the major differences between casuistry and pragmatism as forms of moral reasoning?

2. What would a moral realist say about the ability of a casuist to identify "universal maxims" in the law, and then to apply these maxims properly to new and unforeseen circumstances? Why are pragmatists like Reinhold Niebuhr "skeptical of universal explanations"?

3. Why would a moral realist like Niebuhr find certain norms of attorney conduct "conveniently superficial?" Which ones? And for whom are they convenient? On the contrary, why might a casuist argue that ethical norms *should* be constructed at a fairly high level of generality?

4. Neibuhr felt that moral relativism created a "healthy sense of moral restlessness, guilt, and responsibility." In what sense is such moral unease "healthy"?

PHYLLIS GOLDFARB, A THEORY-PRACTICE SPIRAL: THE ETHICS OF FEMINISM AND CLINICAL EDUCATION
75 Minnesota Law Review 1599, 1691–1698 (1991) (footnotes renumbered)
[Cross-citations are to original text.]

*   *   *

Those who malign lawyers' character and competence turn to law schools to help solve both problems.[1] By exposing students to law as it operates through people, processes, and institutions, and by promoting practices of critical reflection, law schools can do something about lawyers' competence and perhaps even more about lawyers' character. By supporting and taking seriously both clinical and feminist methods, as this Article describes them, law schools would cultivate habits of attention to matters of ethical consequence and improve the moral training of lawyers.

Taking clinical and feminist methods seriously might cause the proliferation of a few, or a few more, courses in clinical education and feminist jurisprudence in the law school curriculum. To my mind, this would be an eminently desirable result. Another way for legal education to take these movements seriously is to import the

---

[1] *See, e.g.*, Burger, *The Special Skills of Advocacy: Are Specialized Training and Certification of Advocates Essential to Our System of Justice?*, 42 Fordham L. Rev. 227, 240–241 (1973) (competence); Thomforde, *Public Opinion of the Legal Profession: A Necessary Response by the Bar and the Law School*, 41 Tenn. L. Rev. 503, 503–05 (1974) (character); Wasserstrom, *supra* note 254, at 15–24 (same).

lessons of both methodologies into the traditional classroom.[2]

If teaching doctrine is the aim of traditional education, then teaching "doctrine in a vacuum" frustrates that aim.[3] Legal rules and principles grow out of historical, social, cultural, and ethical contexts. For students to understand fundamentally and work creatively with rules and principles, they must appreciate the contexts from which these rules and principles emerged.[4] Adopting the clinical and feminist emphasis on the development of context as a prelude to understanding would enrich the traditional classroom environment.

One way to develop more context for legal rules and principles is to diversify the learning materials of the law school classroom. Feminists and clinicians would urge classroom elaboration of the stories of the persons who become the textbooks' cases, whether through visits to the class of persons involved in litigation,[5] examination of story-illuminating materials such as case histories, transcripts, and pleadings,[6] or imaginative role-playing by students based on historical materials.[7] Students could then probe these materials to ascertain whether they included the positions of all interested persons and communities and, if not, seek to remedy the exclusions.

Use of interdisciplinary tools, as advocated by feminists and clinical educators, would inform students thinking beyond the concrete history of the case itself. With interdisciplinary assistance, a student could consider a number of important questions: What were the structural forces—historical, social, and cultural—alive in the era and region in which the case was born? What were the patterns of social conflict and conditions of social distress that may have affected its birth? How did the conduct and outcome of the case affect these conditions? How can professionals

---

[2] Karl Klare's enumeration of the absences in the traditional law school curriculum reads as a prescription for the clinical and feminist methods described here:

> What is left out of the law-school curriculum? Omitted is systematic training in how to learn from others; in how to criticize one's own work and the work of others; in how to learn about lawyering from practice, that is, in how to acquire the capacity for continuing self-development over the span of a career; and in how one might act in the central relationships that constitute the lawyering process: adversary, client, coworker relationships, and so on. Omitted also is systematic training in how to work closely and cooperatively with others in situations of high vulnerability and high risk and, finally, in how to think critically about morals and politics based on the best learning available from the social sciences and from ethical discourse.

Klare, *supra* note 379, at 341 (emphasis in original).

[3] *See* White, *supra* note 14.

[4] *See* Klare, *supra* note 379, at 343.

[5] *See* Menkel-Meadow, *supra* note 233, at 297 (describing the lessons learned about a case from a plaintiff's classroom visit).

[6] *See, e.g.*, Munger, *Clinical Legal Education: The Case Against Separatism*, 29 Clev. St. L. Rev. 715, 729 (1980) (urging the use of supplementary documents in a "standard casebook course"); *see also* J. Noonan, Persons and Masks of the Law (1976) (providing case histories of the persons and problems underlying well-known cases); In the Interest of Children: Advocacy, Law Reform, and Public Policy (R. Mnookin ed. 1985) (offering case studies of five landmark Supreme Court cases affecting children's interests).

[7] Kohlberg has described the value of "reciprocal role playing," taking the roles of persons with a variety of perspectives, in facilitating moral development. *See* Richards, *supra* note 263, at 372 ("To the extent clinics and simulation techniques promote reciprocal role playing, they have, in addition to their pedagogical rationale in improving skills training, a further justification in facilitating moral development through stimulating the capacity of students to take different points of view.").

and institutions respond to the individual and social problems that they encounter?

With this broad and deep contextual background, feminists and clinicians would require students to reason from the concrete reality of the cases to principled conclusions. Feminists, in particular, would have students consider the reasoning advanced and the conclusions desired by the full array of interested persons before making any decisions, encouraging students to rethink doctrine from a variety of vantage points. Students then would compare their decisions and decision making processes to the actual reasoning and judgment in the case. In doing so, they would have to reflect on questions of fairness and justice. Was the decision and the process of decision in this case just? From whose perspectives? Can I defend my decision and my process of decision? Can I critique them? What is my defense or critique of the court's reasoning and holding?

Cross-disciplinary attention to the tools of the humanities, particularly literature and philosophy, would help students think critically about these questions of justice, fairness, and truth. Wrestling with their internal conflicts concerning ethical processes and outcomes, an active experience on which students must reflect intensively, can help students develop the cognitive and affective capacities of moral judgment needed to resolve their conflicts. In this way, students, guided by whatever tools are available, confront and articulate the inchoate philosophies by which they live and make choices. By doing so, they come to understand themselves and others and can begin to develop a conscious process of moral reasoning.

*   *   *

The feminist and clinical movements view the nature of justice and community as the stakes of education, a sensibility that the classroom can actively tap. To stimulate this sensibility, feminists and clinicians would reduce the traditional hierarchy of the classroom. A teacher wedded to this aim would not be the omniscient fount of knowledge, but would facilitate the students' active responsibility for making sense of their experience of the legal and interdisciplinary materials. Authoritarianism conflicts with the values of this project and impedes its possibilities of success. An atmosphere of open exploration, where students and teachers exchange their views and insights on matters of deep and abiding interest, encourages students to assume responsibility for developing the understanding of self and others that this classroom approach requires.[8]

If legal education followed this methodological course, it would come to resemble feminist and clinical methodologies in yet another manner. The classroom would employ particular intellectual practices, and insight would flow from participation in these practices.[9] These practices involve relating to diverse texts and materials in a way that brings one's own and others' perspectives into view, and critically reflecting on these perspectives in light of such materials. The experience of the classroom method would constitute the source of insight, and the experience of further classes

---

[8] Kohlberg's emphasis on "educational democracy" as an important pre-condition for moral education supports this insight. *See* Richards, *supra* note 263, at 372.

[9] *See* White, *supra* note 14, at 161 ("[C]an we come to see that the law we teach . . . is not a set of rules to be learned but a set of ways of thinking and talking and acting together about questions of justice, a method and a community which it should be our task to exemplify and constitute?").

and materials would test and develop these insights.[10] This classroom methodology links theory and practice in the spiral that inspires feminism and clinical education. Plainly, the lessons of these movements can enlighten legal education generally.

D. REEXAMINING ETHICS

The methodologies of the feminist and clinical education movements suggest that the story of Antigone, a case in a law school clinic, or other richly specified narratives represent promising springboards for inquiry into broad questions about law and morality. The considerable and sundry details of such narratives express the subtleties and complexities of the morally charged situations in which humans find themselves. Unlike many children's tales, a single lesson does not surface readily from these narratives. Rarely do these real-life or life-like contexts provide easily grasped answers to obvious questions. Rather, they suggest multiple interpretations and analyses. The narratives contain painstaking renderings of competing viewpoints that check our natural tendencies to oversimplify and overlook details and perspectives that unsettle the neat conclusions that we desire. We must actively engage the full breadth and depth of these narratives to honestly and effectively further our analysis. What we will come to know as a result of this inquiry will be altered by the contextualized process through which we have come to know it.

I have sought to demonstrate that such a theory-building practice is a distinctly ethical project.[11] Clinical and feminist methods represent possibilities for rescuing the morally significant details that are systematically excluded from the culture's storehouse of standard stories. Acute empirical sensitivity—foregrounding the stories of those whom cultural structures have generally relegated to the background, and supporting the voices often rendered barely audible—can help to accomplish this goal. Working through the cognitive dissonance created by the infusion of these previously neglected perspectives expands our understanding and promotes both a critique of the societal structures that obscured such knowledge and an interest in dismantling these knowledge-distorting structures.[12] This is why

---

[10] James Boyd White's vision of legal education supports the vision developed in this Article:

The heart of this education is learning to be responsible in a new way for what one thinks and says. The student has to make sense of it all herself, for no one can do it for her. She has to think for herself in circumstances forever new, to reach conclusions for which she is responsible, to decide for herself what is worth saying and what is not. This constitutes an active education, a learning-to-do, not a passive acquisition of knowledge; when it works well, it tests the limits of one's mind and the imagination . . . What one learns in law school is not law in the sense of repeatable propositions, but how to learn law—that is, how to do it and how to make it. In an important sense "the law" one studies is thus the law that is actually made in the classroom, made out of the materials of case and statute as the class thinks and talks about particular questions. A good law school is thus a school of law-making. This means that the proper focus of attention is not on what the student is learning to repeat or to describe but what she is learning to see and to do; on the doctrine or language of the law not abstracted from experience, but embodied in it, as the object and medium of thought, expression and intellectual action.

Id. at 157, 162.

[11] *See supra* notes 188–89, 263–84, 317–21 and accompanying text.

[12] *See* Minow & Spelman, *supra* note 318, stating that:

Abrham Herschel would have prophets take philosophers to the slums.[13] From the feminist-clinician-prophet-philosopher's vantage point, the distinction between epistemology and ethics collapses.

From feminists' and clinicians' relentless demand for elaborate concrete detail and for special attention to the data provided by those whom society frequently disempowers comes a reconceived notion of what qualifies as ethical inquiry. This notion of ethical inquiry is a process grounded in our experiences of social and institutional interactions and concerned with the way people actually respond to the moral choices presented by everyday life and work. The focus of ethical theory is no longer the justification of actions affecting the "generalized others" of traditional philosophy, but the justification of actions affecting the "concrete others" with whom we are enmeshed.[14] Ethical systems emerge from this network of relationships when we seek to resolve and explain our resolutions of the quotidian dilemmas that we encounter in the complex, nuanced, temporal context in which they arise. This ethical theory, then, responds to the experiences central to daily personal situations and requires reflection on such situations to develop moral consciousness.[15]

In the hands of feminists and clinicians, ethics becomes a sustained practice of empirical attention and reflection on the actions of people in actual situations. Ordinary life expresses and creates ethical theory, which is understood as having an inescapably social character.[16] The better our context-sensitive empiricism, the better our moral deliberations, and the more precise the articulation of our ethical principles will be.[17]

> Because persistent patterns of power, based on lines of gender, racial, class and age differences, have remained resilient and at the same time elusive under traditional political and legal ideas, arguments for looking to context carry critical power. In this context, arguments for context highlight these patterns as worthy of attention and, at times, condemnation.

Id. at 1651.

[13] *See* Heschel, *supra* note 199 and accompanying text. This is also why Cornel West advocates a philosophy of "prophetic pragmatism," which through the examination of actual human lives and the acknowledgment of the constraints on, and possibilities for, moral improvement, calls for cultural challenges to oppressive structures of power. West, *supra* note 325, at 228–34; *see also* Minow & Spelman, *supra* note 318, at 1612–15 (discussing this piece of West's work).

[14] *See* Benhabib, *The Generalized and The Concrete Other: The Kohlberg-Gilligan Controversy and Moral Theory*, in MORAL THEORY, *supra* note 91, at 154.

[15] *See* Held, *supra* note 319, at 112 ("I suggest that we ought to try to develop moral inquiries that will be as satisfactory as possible for the actual contexts in which we live and in which our experience is located. . . . We [should] do our best to 'test' various moral theories in actual contexts and in light of our actual moral experience.").

[16] *See* Addelson, *Moral Passages*, in MORAL THEORY, *supra* note 91, at 87–88 ("[M]oral explanation. . . . [is] constructed in social interactions, and . . . systematic social and political relations are created and maintained in the process of construction.").

[17] *See* A. MacIntyre, AFTER VIRTUE (1981) (arguing that context is necessary for understanding the significance of moral claims and decrying the loss of context for many of our important moral principles); Kittay & Meyers, Introduction, in MORAL THEORY, *supra* note 91, at 3, 12 ("[G]eneral moral principles cannot be applied without a subtle understanding of context.").

QUESTIONS

1. Goldfarb argues that "[i]n the hands of feminists and clinicians, ethics becomes a sustained practice of empirical attention and reflection on the actions of people in actual situations." *Materials, supra.* Does this mean she rejects the *a priori* assumption of Kant and/or Rawls? Or does this mean that she subscribes to a "dirty hands" theory of moral relativism, that is, morality is simply a convenient construct of society that can change depending on individual preferences and attitudes? If not, exactly what is Goldfarb's point?

2. Might the influx of women into the legal profession and the influence of the feminist perspective described by Goldfarb have the potential to result in a fundamentally new and beneficial jurisprudence of ethics? If so, what form do you think this jurisprudence might take? *See* Katharine T. Bartlett, *Feminist Legal Methods*, 103 HARV. L. REV. 829 (1990) and Robin West, *Jurisprudence and Gender*, 55 CHI. L. REV. 1 (1988).

*   *   *

IN THE MATTER OF MARK C. PAUTLER, ATTORNEY-RESPONDENT
47 P.3d 1175 (Colo. 2002) (en banc) (footnotes omitted)

In this proceeding we reaffirm that members of our profession must adhere to the highest moral and ethical standards. Those standards apply regardless of motive. Purposeful deception by an attorney licensed in our state is intolerable, even when it is undertaken as a part of attempting to secure the surrender of a murder suspect. A prosecutor may not deceive an unrepresented person by impersonating a public defender. We affirm the hearing board's finding that the district attorney in this case violated the Colorado Rules of Professional Conduct, and on somewhat different grounds, including the attorney's failure to disclose his deception immediately after the event, we also affirm the discipline imposed by the hearing board.

I.

The hearing board found the following facts by clear and convincing evidence: On June 8th, 1998, Chief Deputy District Attorney Mark Pautler arrived at a gruesome crime scene where three women lay murdered. All died from blows to the head with a wood splitting maul. While at the scene ("Chenango apartment"), Pautler learned that three other individuals had contacted the sheriff's department with information about the murders. Pautler drove to the location where those witnesses waited ("Belleview apartment"). Upon arrival, he learned that the killer was William Neal. Neal had apparently abducted the three murder victims one at a time, killing the first two at the Chenango apartment over a three-day period. One of the witnesses at the Belleview apartment, J.D.Y., was the third woman abducted. Neal also took her to the Chenango apartment where he tied her to a bed using eyebolts he had screwed into the floor specifically for that purpose. While J.D.Y. lay spread-eagled on the bed, Neal brought a fourth woman to the Chenango apartment. He taped her mouth shut and tied her to a chair within J.D.Y.'s view. Then, as J.D.Y. watched in horror, Neal split the fourth victim's skull with the maul. That night he raped J.D.Y. at gunpoint.

The following morning, Neal returned with J.D.Y. to the Belleview apartment. First one friend, a female, and then a second friend, a male, arrived at the apartment. Neal held J.D.Y. and her two friends in the Belleview apartment over thirty hours. He dictated the details of his crimes into a recorder. Finally, he abandoned the apartment, leaving instructions with J.D.Y. and her friends to contact police, and to page him when the police arrived.

When Pautler reached the Belleview apartment, Deputy Sheriff Cheryl Moore had already paged Neal according to the instructions Neal had left. Neal answered the page by phoning the apartment on a cell-phone. The ensuing conversation lasted three-and-a-half hours, during which Moore listened to Neal describe his crimes in detail. She took notes of the conversation and occasionally passed messages to Pautler and other officers at the scene. Sheriff Moore developed a rapport with Neal and continuously encouraged his peaceful surrender. Meanwhile, other law enforcement officers taped the conversation with a hand-held recorder set next to a second phone in the apartment. Efforts to ascertain the location of Neal's cell-phone were unsuccessful.

At one point, Neal made it clear he would not surrender without legal representation; Moore passed a message to that effect to Pautler. Neal first requested an attorney who had represented him previously, Daniel Plattner, but then also requested a public defender (PD). Pautler managed to find Plattner's office number in the apartment telephone book. When he called the number, however, Pautler received a recorded message indicating the telephone was no longer in service. Pautler believed that Plattner had left the practice of law, and he therefore made no additional attempt to contact Plattner. Upon learning that Plattner was unavailable, Sheriff Moore agreed with Neal to secure a public defender. However, no one in the apartment made any attempt to contact a PD or the PD's office.

Pautler later testified that he believed any defense lawyer would advise Neal not to talk with law enforcement. Pautler also testified that he did not trust anyone at the PD's office, although on cross-examination he admitted there was at least one PD he did trust. Law enforcement officials present at the Belleview apartment, testifying in Pautler's defense, said they would not have allowed a defense attorney to speak with Neal because they needed the conversation to continue until they could apprehend Neal. Instead of contacting the PD's office, or otherwise contacting defense counsel, Pautler offered to impersonate a PD, and those law enforcement agents at the scene agreed.

When Neal again requested to speak to an attorney, Sheriff Moore told him that "the PD has just walked in," and that the PD's name was "Mark Palmer," a pseudonym Pautler had chosen for himself. Moore proceeded to brief "Palmer" on the events thus far, with Neal listening over the telephone. Moore then introduced Pautler to Neal as a PD. Pautler took the telephone and engaged Neal in conversation. Neal communicated to Pautler that he sought three guarantees from the sheriff's office before he would surrender: 1) that he would be isolated from other detainees, 2) that he could smoke cigarettes, and 3) that "his lawyer" would be present. To the latter request, Pautler answered, "Right, I'll be present."

*   *   *

Pautler made no effort to correct his misrepresentations to Neal that evening, nor in the days following. James Aber, head of the Jefferson County Public Defender's office, eventually undertook Neal's defense. Aber only learned of the deception two weeks later when listening to the tapes of the conversation whereupon he recognized Pautler's voice. Aber testified at Pautler's trial that he was confused when Neal initially said that a Mark Palmer already represented him. Aber told the board that he had difficulty establishing a trusting relationship with the defendant after he told Neal that no Mark Palmer existed within the PD's office. Several months later Neal dismissed the PD's office and continued his case pro se, with advisory counsel appointed by the court. Ultimately, Neal was convicted of the murders and received the death penalty. The parties dispute whether Neal dismissed Aber out of the mistrust precipitated by Pautler's earlier deception.

Attorney Regulation Counsel charged Pautler with violating both Colo. RPC 8.4(c) and 4.3 of the Colorado Rules of Professional Conduct ("Rules"). The presiding disciplinary judge granted summary judgment against Pautler on Rule 8.4(c); the 4.3 charge went to a hearing board because the judge ruled that (1) whether Neal was represented, and (2) whether Pautler gave advice, were disputed questions of fact. The board subsequently found that Pautler violated Rule 4.3. With one dissent, the board set the sanction for both violations at three months suspension, with a stay granted during twelve months of probation. During that period, Pautler was to retake the MPRE, take twenty hours of CLE credits in ethics, have a supervisor present whenever he engaged in any activity implicating Colo. RPC 4.3, and pay the costs of the proceedings.

*   *   *

II.

Lawyers, as guardians of the law, play a vital role in the preservation of society. The fulfillment of this role requires an understanding by lawyers of their relationship with and function in our legal system. A consequent obligation of lawyers is to maintain the highest standards of ethical conduct. Colo. R.P.C. pmbl.

The jokes, cynicism, and falling public confidence related to lawyers and the legal system may signal that we are not living up to our obligation; but, they certainly do not signal that the obligation itself has eroded. For example, the profession itself is engaging in a nation-wide project designed to emphasize that "truthfulness, honesty and candor are the core of the core values of the legal profession." [Footnotes omitted]. Lawyers themselves are recognizing that the public perception that lawyers twist words to meet their own goals and pay little attention to the truth, strikes at the very heart of the profession—as well as at the heart of the system of justice. Lawyers serve our system of justice, and if lawyers are dishonest, then there is a perception that the system, too, must be dishonest. Certainly, the reality of such behavior must be abjured so that the perception of it may diminish.

With due regard, then, for the gravity of the issues we confront, we turn to the facts of this case.

III.

*   *   *

The complaint charged Pautler with violating Colo. RPC 8.4: "It is professional misconduct for a lawyer to: . . . (c) engage in conduct involving dishonesty, fraud, deceit or misrepresentation." This rule and its commentary are devoid of any exception. Nor do the Rules distinguish lawyers working in law enforcement from other lawyers, apart from additional responsibilities imposed upon prosecutors. *See* Colo. RPC 3.8; *see also Berger v. United States*, 295 U.S. 78, 88, 55 S. Ct. 629, 79 L. Ed. 1314 (1935). The two jurisdictions that have created exceptions to this blanket prohibition limited them to circumstances inapposite here.

A. *Pautler's Defense*

We are unpersuaded by Pautler's assertion that his deception of Neal was "justified" under the circumstances, and we underscore the rationale set forth in *People v. Reichman*, 819 P.2d 1035 (Colo.1991). There, a district attorney sought to bolster a police agent's undercover identity by faking the agent's arrest and then filing false charges against him. *Id.* at 1036. The DA failed to notify the court of the scheme. *Id.* We upheld a hearing board's imposition of public censure for the DA's participation in the ploy. *Id.* at 1039.

*   *   *

Thus, in *Reichman*, we rejected the same defense to Rule 8.4(c) that Pautler asserts here. We ruled that even a noble motive does not warrant departure from the Rules of Professional Conduct. Moreover, we applied the prohibition against deception a fortiori to prosecutors:

> District attorneys in Colorado owe a very high duty to the public because they are governmental officials holding constitutionally created offices. This court has spoken out strongly against misconduct by public officials who are lawyers. The respondent's responsibility to enforce the laws in his judicial district grants him no license to ignore those laws or the Code of Professional Responsibility.

Reichman, 819 P.2d at 1038–39 (citations omitted).

We stress, however, that the reasons behind Pautler's conduct are not inconsequential. In *Reichman*, we also stated, "While the respondent's motives and the erroneous belief of other public prosecutors that the respondent's conduct was ethical do not excuse these violations of the Code of Professional Responsibility, they are mitigating factors to be taken into account in assessing the appropriate discipline." *Id.* at 1039. Hence, *Reichman* unambiguously directs that prosecutors cannot involve themselves in deception, even with selfless motives, lest they run afoul of Rule 8.4(c).

B. *Imminent Public Harm Exception*

Pautler requests this court to craft an exception to the Rules for situations constituting a threat of "imminent public harm." In his defense, Pautler elicited the testimony of an elected district attorney from a metropolitan jurisdiction. The attorney testified that during one particularly difficult circumstance, a kidnapper had a gun to the head of a hostage. The DA allowed the kidnapper to hear over the telephone that the DA would not prosecute if the kidnapper released the hostage. The DA, along with everyone else involved, knew the DA's representation was false and that the DA fully intended to prosecute the kidnapper. Pautler analogizes his deceptive conduct to that of the DA in the hostage case and suggests that both cases give cause for an exception to Rule 8.4(c).

We first note that no complaint reached this court alleging that the DA in the kidnapper scenario violated Rule 8.4(c), and therefore, this court made no decision condoning that DA's behavior. But assuming arguendo that the DA acted in conformity with the Rules, one essential fact distinguishes the hostage scenario from Pautler's case: the DA there had no immediately feasible alternative. If the DA did not immediately state that he would not prosecute, the hostage might die. In contrast, here Neal was in the midst of negotiating his surrender to authorities. Neal did make references to his continued ability to kill, which Pautler described as threats, but nothing indicated that any specific person's safety was in imminent danger. More importantly, without second guessing crime scene tactics, we do not believe Pautler's choices were so limited. Pautler had several choices. He had telephone numbers and a telephone and could have called a PD. Indeed, he attempted to contact attorney Plattner, an indication that communicating with a defense attorney was not precluded by the circumstances. Pautler also had the option of exploring with Neal the possibility that no attorney would be called until after he surrendered. While we do not opine, in hindsight, as to which option was best, we are adamant that when presented with choices, at least one of which conforms to the Rules, an attorney must not select an option that involves deceit or misrepresentation. The level of ethical standards to which our profession holds all attorneys, especially prosecutors, leaves no room for deceiving Neal in this manner. Pautler cannot compromise his integrity, and that of our profession, irrespective of the cause.

C. [Omitted]

D. *Role of Peace Officer*

Finally, Pautler contends that this court has never addressed whether district attorneys, "while functioning as peace officers," may employ deception to apprehend suspects. He suggests that because peace officers may employ lethal force when pursuing a fleeing, dangerous felon, it would be absurd to sanction an officer who instead uses artifice, simply because that officer is also a licensed attorney. We disagree.

The Rules of Professional Conduct apply to anyone licensed to practice law in Colorado. *See In re C de Baca*, 11 P.3d 426, 429–30 (Colo.2000) (ruling that lawyers must adhere to the Rules of Professional Conduct even when suspended from the practice of law). The Rules speak to the "role" of attorneys in society; however, we do not understand such language as permitting attorneys to move in and out of ethical obligations according to their daily activities. Pautler cites *Higgs v. District Court*, 713 P.2d 840 (Colo.1985), for the proposition that this court has provided a test for distinguishing when prosecutors act as "advocates" and when they act as "investigators," for purposes of governmental immunity. *Id.* at 853. Such test exists, but we hold here that in either role, the Rules of Professional Conduct apply. The obligations concomitant with a license to practice law trump obligations concomitant with a lawyer's other duties, even apprehending criminals. Moreover, this case does not confront us with the propriety of an attorney using deceit instead of lethal force to halt a fleeing felon. We limit our holding to the facts before us. Until a sufficiently compelling scenario presents itself and convinces us our interpretation of Colo. RPC 8.4(c) is too rigid, we stand resolute against any suggestion that licensed attorneys in our state may deceive or lie or misrepresent, regardless of their reasons for doing so.

IV.

The complaint also charges Pautler with violating Rule 4.3:

> In dealing on behalf of a client with a person who is not represented by counsel, a lawyer shall state that the lawyer is representing a client and shall not state or imply that the lawyer is disinterested. When the lawyer knows or reasonably should know that the unrepresented person misunderstands the lawyer's role in the matter, the lawyer shall make reasonable efforts to correct the misunderstanding. The lawyer shall not give advice to the unrepresented person other than to secure counsel.

Colo. RPC 4.3. This rule targets precisely the conduct in which Pautler engaged. At all times relevant, Pautler represented the People of the State of Colorado. The parties stipulated that Neal was an unrepresented person. Pautler deceived Neal and then took no steps to correct the misunderstanding either at the time of arrest or in the days following. Pautler's failure in this respect was an opportunity lost. Where he could have tempered the negative consequences resulting from the deception, he instead allowed them to linger.

While it is unclear whether Pautler actually gave advice to Neal, he certainly did not inform Neal to retain counsel. In addition, Pautler went further than implying he was disinterested; he purported to represent Neal. Without doubt, Pautler's conduct violated the letter of Colo. RPC 4.3.

For reasons substantially similar to those above, we refuse to graft an exception to this rule that would justify or excuse Pautler's actions. Instead, we affirm the ruling of the hearing board finding a violation of Colo. RPC 4.3 and turn now to consider the sanction imposed.

*   *   *

V.

In sum, we agree with the hearing board that deceitful conduct done knowingly or intentionally typically warrants suspension, or even disbarment. *See* ABA *Standards* 7.2 ("Suspension is generally appropriate when a lawyer knowingly engages in conduct that is a violation of a duty owed to the profession. . . ."); *id.* at 5.11(b) ("Disbarment is generally appropriate when . . . a lawyer engages in any other intentional conduct involving dishonesty, fraud, deceit, or misrepresentation. . . . "). We further agree that the mitigating factors present in Pautler's case outweigh the aggravating factors, and affirm the imposition of a three-month suspension, which shall be stayed during twelve months of probation. This sanction reaffirms for all attorneys, as well as the public, that purposeful deception by lawyers is unethical and will not go unpunished. At the same time, it acknowledges Pautler's character and motive.

VI.

Therefore, we affirm the hearing board's ruling that Pautler violated Rules 8.4(c) and 4.3 of the Colorado Rules of Professional Conduct. We also affirm the hearing board's probationary period, with a three-month suspension to be imposed only if Pautler violates the terms of that probation. Finally, Pautler is to pay the costs of this proceeding as ordered by the hearing board.

QUESTIONS

1. From a casuist perspective, what rhetorical exercise would Pautler have had to go through to discern whether his action in impersonating a defense lawyer was proper? What "maxims" of attorney conduct would Pautler have identified if he had in fact engaged in casuistry? Are these "maxims" in tension with each other? If so, do they point to one course of conduct with "probable certitude," as casuists like Tremblay suggest is possible?

2. For a pragmatist, "rigidity and devotion to absolutes . . . threaten flexibility." Was the Colorado Supreme Court overly rigid in its interpretation of Rule 8.4? Should prosecutors have more "flexibility" in acting to protect public safety than other lawyers?

3. What might a moral realist like Neibuhr say about the decision to suspend Pautler from the practice of law? (Recall Blaise Pascal's suspicion of "sinners . . . who believe themselves righteous"). Will Pautler's sanction likely deter other prosecutors from engaging in deceptive conduct should they ever face similar extreme circumstances? If not, does disciplinary action in Pautler's case breed respect for—or cynicism towards—professional norms?

4. The Paulter problem above took place in a criminal context. For a civil example, consider the following problem. A family dispute over ownership of a large supermarket chain resulted in acrimonious litigation. The trial judge ordered that control of the chain be given to the plaintiffs. The defendant, the uncle in a large extended family, was firmly convinced that the trial court judge was biased and had acted improperly. In an effort to develop evidence of judicial bias, the defense

lawyers set up an undercover operation, inspired by the undercover operations frequently used in criminal matters to identify relevant evidence. The lawyers had a fake head hunter contact the former law clerk of the trial judge. Thinking that he was interviewing for a job, the law clerk took part in two interviews in which the judge and the supermarket litigation were discussed. The lawyers eventually confronted the law clerk, revealed that the job opportunity was a sham, and sought an affidavit from the law clerk that would arguably support a claim of judicial bias. Using the approaches of casuistry and pragmatism, consider the following perspectives: (1) the defense counsel, who believes there was judicial bias but is having difficulty developing facts, (2) the law clerk, and (3) the trial court. Do casuistry and pragmatism assist you in determining which perspective has the greatest weight in your ethical analysis?

For a fuller discussion of these facts and the subsequent disciplinary action, see *In re Crossen*, 450 Mass. 533 (2008).

Chapter X

IMPLEMENTATION CHALLENGES

A. CACOPHONY OF INFORMATION

Information that forms the basis of ethical and moral decision-making comes to you from many sources: clients, partners, subordinates, press, formal discovery, independent investigation, and even anonymously. The information also comes with varying degrees of reliability and specificity: the smoking gun document, rumor and innuendo (which may be true, partially true, or false), the "too good to be true" beneficial moments, or the confidential aside. In addition, the majority of lawyers function as part of organizations, whether as associates or partners in a large or small law firm, government or public interest lawyers, politicians, or the like. Both uncertainty over "facts" and the complications of group functioning make real life moral decision-making much more complicated than tidy hypotheticals often project.

B. FACTUAL, LEGAL, AND MORAL UNCERTAINTY

1. Factual Uncertainty

As Professor Paul Tremblay describes, lawyers more often differ on *facts* than values. But of greater concern to all of us are the well-documented cognitive biases that distort our ability to see and assess facts that give rise to moral problems. We are all prone to these distortion effects:

- the self-serving bias in assessing information;

- the endowment effect of giving greater weight to what we already possess;

- the belief perseverance phenomenon in which we cling to beliefs despite contrary evidence;

- the availability heuristic in which we are more likely to believe things if a similar event has recently occurred; and

- the hindsight bias, which is the distortion of historic fact as we look back and seek confirming evidence.

All of these cognitive processes may obscure our ability to even see and process whether a particular action has moral significance. It can blunt moral awareness.

These cognitive processes, coupled with a desire to avoid difficult ethical issues, may cause a lawyer to engage in what some courts have described as "deliberate ignorance." As a legal concept, deliberate ignorance occurs when there is "(1) subjective awareness of a high probability of the existence of illegal conduct, and (2) purposeful contrivance to avoid learning of the illegal conduct." *United States v. Cavin*, 39 F.3d 1299, 1310 (5th Cir. 1994). It is quite easy to see how deliberate ignorance also occurs in factual questions that have moral dimensions.

2. Legal Uncertainty

Any first-year law student confronts the reality that law is much less firm and "determinate" than they might have expected. The legal realism movement in the 1930s brought this concept into the mainstream of legal thought. Professor David Wilkins explores legal indeterminacy in the context of the lawyer's role. Legal uncertainty intersects with moral reasoning on many levels. The Rules of Professional Conduct carry the challenge of indeterminacy that is inherent in so many rules. And our habits of advocacy can cause us to read the Rules of Professional Conduct as simply one more tool in the arsenal to advance a client's interests. In other words, there is a strong tendency for lawyers to probe for legal uncertainty within the Rules of Professional Conduct so that we can exploit that uncertainty for the client's end. This legal uncertainty can muddy the waters as lawyers explore the moral and ethical dimensions of their conduct.

3. Moral Uncertainty

Much of this book focuses on the *process* of moral decision making for lawyers. We hope that a good process will yield correct decisions in most cases. Sometimes we are confronted with a circumstance that leaves us uncertain how to proceed. Too often, we freeze like the old cliché of the deer in the headlights. Examples abound of inaction that is later roundly criticized: failing to come to the aid of a child being molested in a public bathroom, doing nothing when it appears that fraudulent activity is occurring around you in a corporation like Enron, etc. While action and inaction may not be morally equivalent in all cases, failing to act is itself a moral *choice*.

Moral uncertainty, the concern that we may not know what is morally right, can be intertwined with factual uncertainty. So often we cognitively hide behind some perceived uncertainty, especially when intervening may risk harm. ("Well, I'm not absolutely certain so I'll do nothing.") Philosopher Ted Lockhart challenges us to think more rigorously about these areas of moral uncertainty. He argues that:

> In situations of moral uncertainty, I (the decision-maker) should (rationally) choose some action that has the maximum probability of being morally right.[1]

This is simple to say, but of course hard to do. Yet if we step back from the facts and think carefully about where we are uncertain (factually, legally, and morally) and consider the probability of being correct, we can hopefully compensate for at least some of the cognitive biases that are part of human decision-making.

---

[1] Ted Lockhart, Moral Uncertainty and its Consequences 26 (2000).

C. PSYCHOLOGY OF DECISION-MAKING AND WORKING IN GROUPS

1.   Ethical Awareness

If you are not already depressed about the frail nature of our human decision-making, consider as well the complexity of decision-making in groups. Recall the description of Reinhold Niebuhr's philosophy in Chapter IX. He emphasizes that moral tension between individuals and groups is inevitable. Collectives create solidarity from conflict with external sources. Conflict from within is seen as disloyal and often suppressed. There is a great danger that we confine our "role" so that we define away the moral dimensions of our work.

The most chilling example of this phenomenon of defining away the moral dimensions of conduct is the story of Adolf Eichmann, the architect of Hitler's "final solution" to exterminate the Jews of Europe. The reading from Richard Nielsen's *Politics of Ethics* draws on the work of Hannah Arendt and others to describe Eichmann as an "archetype" actor. Eichmann perceived that he was just "doing his job," and indeed advancing the virtue of obedience. He did not appear to have an evil motive himself. Hannah Arendt would later ask readers to consider:

> *Could the activity of thinking* as such, the habit of examining and reflecting upon whatever happens to come to pass, regardless of specific content and quite independent of results, *could this activity be of such a nature that it "conditions" men against evil-doing?*[2]

Arendt would disavow an interpretation that there is an Eichmann in each of us. Nevertheless, the Eichmann archetype reminds us that evil-doing can come packaged in ordinary wrapping.

Virtue Ethics once again might offer one option of how to proceed. A commitment of *honesty*, coupled with self-awareness of the distortions in our own decision-making, can hopefully offer some check on our biases. Humility to be open to assessing information that comes to us might also help check these distortionary effects.

Richard Nielsen also describes several other archetypes of people who initiate or cooperate in unethical behavior. The reading describes another common archetype, Socrates's Jailer, who complies with unethical behavior because he will be punished if he refuses to obey. Nielson's book includes a description of other archetypes:

- *Richard III* embraced "calculated wickedness," by killing his nephews to gain the throne.[3]

- *Phaedo* "was an intelligent, good person who cared about the ethical, but he

---

[2] Hannah Arendt, *Thinking and Moral Considerations: A Lecture*, 33 SOCIAL RESEARCH 417 (1970). Our thanks to Bethany Assy, *Eichmann, the Banality of Evil, and Thinking in Arendt's Thought, Contemporary Philosophy*, available at http://www.bu.edu/wcp/MainCont.htm (accessed March 11, 2009).

[3] RICHARD P. NIELSEN, THE POLITICS OF ETHICS, *Materials, infra* at 10G.

was unable to "get it right" without Socrates's help."[4]

- *Faust*, the protagonist of Goethe's play, exchanges his soul (one good) for what he believes are superior goods (knowledge and love).[5]

- *Dr. Suguro* participated in medical experiments on American prisoners of war, to determine scientifically how much blood people can lose before dying, because it was "impractical" to not go along.[6]

Staying in role, fear of punishment, calculated wickedness, ethical confusion, means-justify-the-ends analysis, or simply finding non-compliance impractical a startling list of ways in which one can easily be blown off course by organizational dynamics. Understanding more about group functioning will help us better understand how we might fall into one of these archetypes. As lawyers, we engage in "role differentiated behavior," giving priority to client interests, maintaining confidences in ways we might not do so in ordinary life, avoiding conflicts, and serving as an officer of the court. This role behavior may put us at particular risk of ethical confusion.

2.   Conformity, Deference, and Other Concerns

Most lawyers function in groups: large, medium, and small firms; prosecutor, public defender, or legal aid offices; corporate counsel, and the like.[7] Not only are we prone to the pressures from our environment (role obligations, fear of punishment, etc.), but most young lawyers will be subordinate or reporting to a superior. Again, the psychological literature on conformity indicates that we are highly prone as individuals to conform to the expectations and perceptions of the world around us. Experiments have also documented the psychological phenomenon of deference to the orders or judgment of superiors. Professor Andrew Perlman describes the literature on conformity and deference. How do you protect yourself from these group pressures?

D.   THE POLITICS OF ETHICS: THE ART OF "GOOD CONVERSATION"

Assume that as a lawyer you have considered the factual, legal, and moral uncertainty and conclude that there is an ethical issue that must be addressed. You have likely come to this conclusion by discussing the issue with individuals around you whom you trust. If you have been convinced by this book, then you have probably concluded that dispensing with moral judgment altogether is not the proper response.

At some point you may wonder how you act in a morally responsible way without losing your job. (After all, in 2009, the average U.S. law student graduated with approximately $90,000 in educational debt). Thankfully, not every moral decision

---

[4] *Id.* at 17–18.

[5] *Id.* at 18–22.

[6] *Id.* at 22–24.

[7] *See* RICHARD L ABEL, AMERICAN LAWYERS (1989).

involves falling on your sword. Indeed, many lawyers find their careers ultimately enhanced by running through the gauntlet.

Most lawyers hope that ethical issues are resolved in a positive fashion long before the lawyer faces the challenge of being a whistle-blower. Dialogue and persuasion of the important decision-makers is a common part of the process. Fortunately, advocacy and negotiation are part of our professional skills. But we rarely explore the "politics of ethics," and how to effectively discuss issues of the right behavior. Advocacy in this context requires a continued openness to explore the full dimensions of the problem we confront, while being aware of the cognitive and group pressures that can blunt our own moral awareness.

In the art of persuasion, it is worth noting two important points. First, lawyers have a tendency to assume that clients and other attorneys are indifferent to moral concerns. That is quite a dismissive attitude. This is not to suggest that the client or other attorneys will always agree with your analysis of the morally right conduct, but it is quite another thing to assume that your client has *no* moral perspective or is actively hostile to moral questions. Indeed, the authors know of several instances in which clients refused to go to lawyers because they were concerned that the lawyers would discount or ignore the moral dimensions of their legal problems!

Second, you rarely win friends by rushing in and accusing an actor of unethical conduct. It is much better to start with a more creative eye, identifying practical reasons why good ethics also makes for good strategy. For example, many experienced and successful litigators report that it is better to disclose a harmful, but discoverable, document early in discovery than attempt to hide it. In a world filled with multiple electronic copies, the chance of successfully hiding a bad document is increasingly remote. If discovery later uncovers it under a cloud of bad faith suppression of evidence, the document can take on exponentially greater importance and could subject both the client and lawyers to sanctions. Voila—a strategic reason for good ethics.

Alas, not everyone is convinced by strategic reasons. And not all good ethics can be supported by good strategy. Suppose you go to your supervising attorney and introduce the ethical issue, avoiding accusatory language and raising the issue in a non-judgmental fashion (where possible), but your supervisor brushes you off and refuses to engage in additional conversation. Model Rule 5.2 allows a subordinate attorney to comply with "a supervisory lawyer's reasonable resolution of an arguable question of professional duty." Note that the rule simply allows, but does not require, you to comply. In addition, the superior attorney's interpretation must be reasonable.

Many larger firms have an Ethics Partner or Ethics Committee that you can go to with ethical issues. The focus of these systems is to ensure compliance with the Rules of Professional Conduct and avoid malpractice. An ethics counsel or committee can sometimes serve as a useful resource.[8] With more luck, you will find a strategic advisor to help raise the issue and balance out the power dynamics as you discuss the matter with your superior. If the issue involves interpretation of a

---

[8] *See generally* Elizabeth Chambliss & David B. Wilkins, *The Emerging Role of Ethics Advisors, General Counsel, and Other Compliance Specialists in Large Law Firms*, 44 ARIZ. L. REV. 559 (2002).

Rule of Professional Conduct, most state bars have an ethics hotline. Many bars also have ethics advisory committees and members may be available to help you think through issues. One challenge you face in any external consultation is your ongoing obligation of confidentiality you owe to the client.

In the end, you as an individual must decide how to proceed. But most of the time you are not alone. There are resources to help you think carefully and thoughtfully about the issues and help protect against the cognitive and group dynamics that could distort your analysis.

E.   FURTHER READINGS

For more on the psychology of decision-making as it applies to lawyers, see Richard W. Painter, *Lawyer's Rules, Auditor's Rules and the Psychology of Concealment*, 84 MINN. L. REV. 1399 (2000); Chris Guthrie, *Framing Frivolous Litigation: A Psychological Theory*, 67 U. CHI. L. REV. 163 (2000).

Hannah Arendt's brilliant and controversial book on EICHMANN IN JERUSALEM: A REPORT ON THE BANALITY OF EVIL (1963) continues to provide a chilling account of why we cannot explain away atrocities by simply assuming that the actors are intrinsically evil.

The role-differentiated behavior of lawyers has been explored by many scholars. An excellent starting point is Richard Wasserstrom's seminal essay, *Lawyers as Professionals: Some Moral Issues*, 5 HUM. RTS. 1, 1–2 (1975). David Luban explores this idea in DAVID LUBAN, LAWYERS AND JUSTICE (1989) and in his more recent and expanded discussion in LEGAL ETHICS AND HUMAN DIGNITY (2007).

For a fascinating case study of the internal and external factors that might result in unethical conduct, we recommend MILTON C. REGAN JR., EAT WHAT YOU KILL: THE FALL OF A WALL STREET LAWYER (2004). For additional reading on group functioning in law, see Kimberly Kirkland, *Ethics in Large Law Firms: The Principle of Pragmatism*, 35 U. MEM. L. REV. 631 (2005); David Luban, *Integrity: Its Causes and Cures*, 72 FORDHAM L. REV. 279 (2003). There is increasing literature on the ethical infrastructure of law firms. *See* Alex B. Long, *Whistleblowing Attorneys and Ethical Infrastructures*, 68 MD. L. REV. 786 (2009); Elizabeth Chambliss & David B. Wilkins, *The Emerging Role of Ethics Advisors, General Counsel, and Other Compliance Specialists in Large Law Firms*, 44 ARIZ. L. REV. 559 (2002).

There has been more recent interest in the responsibilities of supervising subordinate lawyers. *See* Douglas Richmond, *Subordinate Lawyers and Insubordinate Duties*, 105 W. VA. L. REV. 449 (2003), and *Law Firm Partners as Their Brothers' Keepers*, 96 KY. L.J. 231 (2007).

F. DISCUSSION PROBLEMS

PROBLEM XXV

You are the young lawyer in Andrew Perlman's hypothetical. You are "fresh out of law school with crushing loan debt and few job offers." You accept a position at a medium-sized firm. The partner with whom you work with closely asks you to review a client's documents to determine what needs to be produced in discovery. In the stack, you find "a 'smoking gun' that is clearly within the scope of discovery and spells disaster for the client's case." You give the document to the partner, who without explanation tells you not to produce it. You ask the partner a few questions and drop the subject when the partner is obviously busy on other matters and tells you to get back to work. You return to your office. Identify the legal, factual, and moral uncertainties that you confront. Strategize how you will proceed next. What arguments will you make as you engage in conversation on this issue? To whom?

Consider:

ABA Model Rule of Professional Conduct 5.1: Responsibilities of Partners, Managers, and Supervisory Lawyers

ABA Model Rule of Professional Conduct 5.2: Responsibilities of a Subordinate Lawyer

PROBLEM XXVI

We return again to the Torture Memo (Chapter V). The Office of Legal Counsel policy group is meeting in two hours to discuss the problem. There are five members of the group, all deeply committed to protecting the country from harm. All are extremely bright, thoughtful, and share a political vision of the role of government which envisions expansive executive power, especially in times of war. Assume that you have serious reservations about the moral dimensions of torture. What new insights are available to you as present your concerns to the group?

PROBLEM XXVII

ABA Model Rule 8.3(a) requires a lawyer who has information "that another lawyer has committed a violation of the Rules of Professional Conduct that raises a substantial question as to that lawyer's honesty, trustworthiness or fitness as a lawyer in other respects to inform the appropriate professional licensing authority of the misconduct," unless the information is confidential. This so-called "snitch rule" has been widely adopted; almost all states other than California and Kentucky have similar provisions in their disciplinary rules. Nonetheless, the snitch rule is considered one of the most under-enforced of all attorney disciplinary standards.[9]

You are a prosecutor representing the state in a straightforward armed robbery case. Your evidence is strong—the alleged theft at knifepoint occurred in broad

---

[9] Nikki A. Ott & Heather F. Newton, *Current Development: A Current Look at Model Rule 8.3: How Is It Used and What Are Courts Doing About It?*, 16 GEO. J. LEGAL ETHICS 747 (2003).

daylight, and there were three eyewitnesses to the event who subsequently picked the defendant out of both a photo array and a lineup. After impaneling the jury and immediately following the lunch recess, you have a discussion with the defense attorney about a possible guilty plea. Defense counsel indicates that his client may be willing to plead guilty if the prosecutor recommends a sentence of not more than five years in state prison. During your conversation, you notice that the defense attorney has glassy eyes, is slurring his speech slightly, and appears unsteady on his feet. You also notice the smell of alcohol on his breath. You suspect that the lawyer had been drinking over the lunch recess.

If the defense attorney is willing to accept a "deal," do you go forward with the change of plea that afternoon? Do you report his conduct to the state professional licensing authority for lawyers? Do you take steps in court to protect the defendant's right to competent counsel?

What additional facts would you want to know before making a report to the bar? Would your calculus change if the defense bar has been complaining (inaccurately, you believe) that the prosecutor's office has been "going after" defense counsel? What if defense attorney was an elected state representative and chair of the powerful Criminal Justice Committee in the state legislature? The former law partner of your boss, the District Attorney?

Would your analysis change if you were the lead attorney in a large civil case involving a dispute between two corporations, and opposing counsel were visibly intoxicated? What if you were the lead attorney representing a large corporation and opposing counsel was representing an injured worker?

G. MATERIALS

PAUL TREMBLAY, MORAL ACTIVISM MANQUE[10]
44 SOUTHERN TEXAS LAW REVIEW 127 (2002) (footnotes omitted)

I. Introduction

Since the mid-1980s, legal ethics scholarship has trumpeted a commitment to lawyering for the good, and not just for instrumental gain—what David Luban has called "moral activism" or "morally ambitious lawyering." Since the mid-1980s, the moral quality of lawyering practice has, by most accounts, degenerated, perhaps significantly. In this article I explore some reasons for this apparent disconnect. The sophisticated philosophical lessons from the moral activism project may, sadly, have less influence in the actual world of high pressure and factually complicated practice settings than its adherents have hoped.

My hypothesis is that lawyers, working within the messy world of competing factual claims and arguments, rarely can be sufficiently confident about empirical facts to justify blunt betrayal of their clients. Moral activism, if it is to change the way that the professional behaviors manifest in public, means, at its core, betrayal

---

[10] Ed. Note: "manque" is defined as failing to fulfill one's aspirations or talents.

of client trust. The moral activism project encourages betrayal of client trust only when the client's demands forfeit that trust. However, before betraying or abandoning a client, a lawyer must be certain that her qualms are soundly justified. Earlier objections to moral activism argued that such justification is difficult because of competing visions of what is good. That argument, as we have seen, is unpersuasive. However, replacing it is a newer version, one that locates the uncertainty, not in the realm of value, but in the realm of fact.

The world of a lawyer is a messy, ambiguous, and complicated place. In the stories that populate moral activism project literature, the good guys and the bad guys are rather clearly defined, and the arguments proceed from those premises (consider the two examples that I used to introduce the moral activism primer, with the racist landlord and the abusive husband). In the untidy law offices where real lawyers work, bad guys do not often present themselves as unadulterated scoundrels. Indeed, the epistemological challenge confronting lawyers within ethics contexts is, almost by definition, more daunting than that facing lawyers regarding questions of substantive law. Recall that the moral activism project operates as a second-tier function. A good-faith lawyer, confronted with an unseemly undertaking, must first determine whether the questionable action requested by her client is lawful. If not, she most likely will refuse to proceed. If the undertaking is not forbidden, then, and only then, the activism equation kicks in. If the undertaking is lawful, but still unseemly, the lawyer must decide whether the unseemliness is so repugnant that she will refuse to participate in the client's cause.

My arguments here rely on the complexity and the contested quality of factual assertions underlying legal claims. But there is something else that we need to acknowledge about how lawyers function in practice. Not only is the world of the lawyer and the client complicated in the way just described, but also at the same time powerful cognitive psychological forces operate to undercut the certainty that a moral activist stance requires. Decision theorists and cognitive scientists have demonstrated the significant influence on perceptions, beliefs, and attitudes of several biases or psychological short-cuts. Researchers report how the self-serving bias, the endowment effect, the belief perseverance phenomenon, the availability heuristic, and the hindsight bias collectively affect in critical ways what a person knows, believes, and values. Each of those forces functions to support and encourage beliefs which a person wants to possess, or which are in her interest to possess.

Consider how these "cognitive illusions" might work with a lawyer encountering a scheme proposed by a client who wants to persuade the lawyer that the scheme is a sound and attractive one, and not merely legal. Let us also assume that the scheme would appear to an objective, neutral, outside observer as morally very troublesome. The lawyer, however, does not "see" the information from that neutral, outsider perspective. First, the lawyer's understanding of the scheme will be influenced by the "self-serving bias"—the tendency of individuals "to conflate what is fair with what benefits oneself." In one study, experimenters assigned groups of undergraduates randomly to one of two groups, and gave each group identical folders containing information about a personal injury lawsuit pending before a judge. Each group's task was to estimate the amount of damages the judge would award to the plaintiff (liability was conceded, so the only contested issue was the amount of recovery). The testers randomly assigned one group to pretend to be the plaintiff; they randomly assigned the other to identify with the defendant. Based on this purely-by-chance assignment, and with no other investment in the case, the plaintiff group estimated the worth of the case substantially higher than did the defendant group. In a control variation, the experimenters did not tell the two groups that they were to identify with a party until just before the end of the evaluation process. In that control variation, the differences between the groups were not significant.

This experiment, the results of which have been replicated often in related studies, demonstrates not posturing by the respective sides about how best to package a case, but instead honest, sincere beliefs about a predictive, factual judgment. The self-interest of the principal dramatically influenced the belief structures of the agents representing that principal. Put another way, those agents could not (absent some separate intervention) "know" what an objective observer would know upon looking at the same data.

As the lawyer hears the more-rosy-than-a-neutral-observer's version of the client's scheme, other cognitive processes operate at the same time. Psychologists report a phenomenon known as "belief perseverance," by which "people cling to their initial beliefs to a degree that is normatively inappropriate." The perseverance effect is connected, some think, to the "endowment effect," which leads clients to value what they already have over what they aspire to have. Beliefs are like possessions and seem to be influenced by the endowment effect. The research shows that the persistence of beliefs, even in the face of contrary evidence, is aided by the vividness of the presentation of the initial data (vivid but weak data is more powerful than abstract but logically more cogent information) and by the opportunity to generate explanations for those beliefs. All of these factors apply to our lawyer's experience. The self-interested client defending his scheme provides a vivid, personalized description of its benefits and massages any uncertainties or doubts. The influence of the vividness is an example of the "availability heuristic," a cognitive illusion by which people are more apt to believe something will happen if a similar event has occurred recently.

Now consider the effect of one further bias that wields some influence in this setting. The "hindsight bias" causes "people [to] overestimate the predictability of past events." An event occurs, and afterwards people assume that what happened could have been foreseen. . . .

The "hindsight bias" is persistent in its distortion of historical fact. This is cause for some serious concern in legal doctrine because so very much depends on the accuracy of historical accounts. For our purposes, in assessing the viability of a moral activism stance, the "hindsight bias" plays two distinct roles.

First, "hindsight bias" accompanies the self-serving bias in reinforcing the gripes of the client telling the story to the lawyer. The bias affects both lawyer and client, so claims by the client that someone is responsible for knowingly hurting the client can possess greater credence than an objective view would warrant. While it seems to be true that moral activism has a significant role in settings involving defendants, this bias still plays a part in the explanations offered by the accused for why their actions were justified, given the behaviors of the accusing plaintiffs.

There is a second way in which the hindsight bias plays an important role in the moral activism project and the critique of lawyers who engage in troublesome practices. The first hindsight bias role spoke to the review of what the client, or the client's adversary, had done. This second role speaks to what the lawyer has done, as understood at the time when the critics direct their complaints. The critics, simply put, always observe lawyer behavior with the influences of hindsight. Consider this: David Luban uses the example of prominent attorney Joseph Flom and his threats to incite international, anti-Semitic unrest if he did not succeed in obtaining his client's takeover of the corporate giant Conoco. Luban, a historian at this point, looks at the tactics and results from the perspective of hindsight—how else could he?—and finds the lawyering behavior morally unacceptable. Perhaps his view of the facts is right, but he is reviewing those facts subject to the hindsight bias. What looks to the critic as unadulterated sleaze might have looked more complicated and nuanced at the time of the actions. (Of course, that behavior might well have been simple sleaze. The hindsight bias does not mean that the behavior was not just awful to begin with.)

QUESTIONS

1. Can you identify examples in public discourse that exemplify these cognitive biases?

2. If Professor Tremblay is correct, does this mean that lawyers are incapable of "knowing" facts when they serve in a representative capacity?

DAVID B. WILKINS, LEGAL REALISM FOR LAWYERS
104 HARVARD LAW REVIEW 468 (1990) (footnotes omitted)

I. LEGAL REALISM'S CHALLENGE TO LEGAL ETHICS

A. The Traditional Model

The traditional model of legal ethics assumes that lawyers have two distinct, though complimentary, sets of responsibilities. On one hand, the lawyer is an advocate for the private interests of particular clients. On the other, she serves as an "officer of the court" with a separate duty of loyalty to the fair and efficient administration of justice. Both these responsibilities are essential to the traditional model's assertion that "[l]awyers play a vital role in the preservation of society." In their private capacity, lawyers enable members of the public to vindicate and protect their legal rights. By tempering this facilitative role with a concomitant duty to preserve the system's integrity, the traditional model promises that the pursuit of private ends will not unduly frustrate public purposes. The command that lawyers should zealously represent their clients' interests "within the bounds of the law" sets the terms under which this tempering is to take place. I call this mediating device the boundary claim.

The argument is familiar. Lawyers should help clients obtain "lawful" objectives only by "legally permissible means," with "lawful" referring both to the limitations generally applicable to all citizens and to the special obligations imposed on lawyers by the rules of professional responsibility. So long as the lawyer honors this obligation, she is privileged not to consider how achieving the client's goals might damage the legal framework. The law, in short, defines the limits of the lawyer's responsibility to clients.

Using legal boundaries as the mechanism for setting the limits on client service implies three normative claims. First, by limiting zealous advocacy to "the bounds of the law," the traditional model gives the impression that there are identifiable external constraints on lawyer conduct. These constraints are allegedly "objective" in that their content can be established by reference to some authoritative set of textual materials—statutes, court decisions, administrative regulations, or professional codes of conduct—that do not depend on the lawyer's personal moral or political judgment.

Second, the boundary claim implies that these objective constraints can be consistently applied to all lawyers in all contexts. Thus, the rules of professional conduct are both "general," in that each rule regulates a broad range of conduct, and "universal," in that they are intended to apply to all lawyers. As a result, clients should not have to worry that their lawyer operates under some idiosyncratic understanding of how to balance potentially competing obligations to clients and to the system. Similarly, each lawyer knows what to expect from other members of the bar: zealous advocacy within the objective, identifiable bounds of the law.

Finally, the constraints on lawyer conduct represented by the boundary claim are "legitimate" in that they flow directly from democratically accountable sources of power. The boundary claim invokes the traditional liberal understanding that individual freedom should be constrained only by sources of authority subject to democratic control. In modern American society, law is the quintessential form of such accountable constraint.

This last claim has always fit somewhat uncomfortably with the fact that rules of professional conduct are not the product of democratic decisionmaking. As a result, these rules place few restrictions on lawyer conduct that might interfere with the client's ability to act within generally applicable legal limits. Moreover, the traditional model strongly implies that doubts about the exact contours of the law should be resolved in the client's favor. Together, these two tendencies place client loyalty, or "partisanship," at the center of the lawyer's role. Thus, the traditional model instructs lawyers both to respect legal boundaries and to determine the practical meaning of this command by adopting the perspective of maximizing client interests. Partisan loyalty to clients, therefore, is the starting point for interpreting the bounds of the law.

By invoking these standard rule-of-law values, the traditional model promises a role for lawyers that appropriately balances the rights of individuals against the legitimate demands of civil society. This claim is persuasive only if the substance of the boundary—"the law" (including the law of professional ethics)—can fulfill the normative promises implicitly made on its behalf. The idea that legal rules are objective, consistent, and legitimate, however, is precisely what the legal realists denied. To determine whether the traditional model of legal ethics can fulfill its promise to confine partisan zeal within reasonable bounds, therefore, we must investigate the relevance of the realist critique of formal rules for the practicing lawyer.

B. The Realist Critique

The broad outlines of the realist movement are familiar and need only be restated briefly. In the 1920s and 1930s, the realists challenged prevailing understandings about the nature of law and the process of legal reasoning. A central theme of this broad attack on classical legal thought was the claim that law is indeterminate. Given the limitations of deductive logic and analogic reasoning and the existence of vague, internally contradictory premises and rules, the realists argued that it was almost always possible to derive multiple and often inconsistent "legal" answers to particular problems. I call this claim the indeterminacy thesis.

Recently, the validity, importance, and continuing relevance of the indeterminacy thesis has become a hot topic in American legal scholarship. Adopting the position of several original realists, some commentators argue that legal rules rarely, if ever, provide determinate answers. Others claim that the law is only moderately indeterminate. Virtually all this discussion, however, has taken place at the level of abstract legal theory or has centered on the judge's role. Until recently, lawyers and legal ethics were essentially ignored.

This omission has two unfortunate consequences. First, it enables advocates of the traditional model to avoid confronting the potentially troubling implications of the indeterminacy thesis for the boundary claim. Specifically, how can an indeterminate boundary provide the objectivity, consistency, and legitimacy promised by the traditional model of legal ethics? If, as some have argued, it is possible to provide a "legal" justification for virtually any action, it is hard to see how the requirement that zealous advocacy must occur within the bounds of the law meaningfully restrains a lawyer's decisionmaking. Put somewhat differently, indeterminacy threatens to collapse the distinction between the lawyer's public responsibility to obey the law and her private responsibility to represent her client effectively.

Second, the focus on judges obscures consideration of the effect institutional roles might have on the practical meaning of indeterminacy. Despite all the attention to the potential for contradictory premises within the law itself, most scholars discussing this topic assume the universality of the legal reasoning process. If it is possible for a law professor to provide "legal" justifications for multiple and contradictory outcomes, judges and lawyers can accomplish the same result. Or, to take the opposite example, if a proper understanding of interpretive method renders the law substantially determinate, any actor in the system can successfully employ the method.

Given the substantial differences among lawyers, judges, and legal academics, however, this universalist assumption seems doubtful. Lawyers and judges do inhabit a common universe. They work with many of the same materials—statutes, opinions, and regulations—and attempt to understand many of the same institutions—courts, legislatures, and regulatory tribunals. Moreover, each sector of the profession tries to influence the other. Nevertheless, the many differences between lawyers and other actors in the system highlight the danger of uncritically applying arguments relevant to the indeterminacy debate in academic theory or judicial decisionmaking to the realm of professional ethics.

Two such differences seem particularly important. First, unlike lawyers, judges do not have "clients" in any traditional sense. When the lawyer seeks to determine "the bounds of the law," she does so at the request of a specific client. Moreover, what she has agreed to do for that client is to argue a particular interpretation of disputed legal terms. These differences plausibly affect how the legal boundary will be perceived.

Second, lawyers and judges occupy quite different positions in the hierarchy of adjudication. On the formal level, judges have more official power to change the legal terrain. They can overrule precedent, declare statutes unconstitutional, and substantially influence the development of the official record upon which the merits of the decision will ultimately be reviewed. Lawyers, of course, are denied these formal powers.

Conversely, lawyers have more practical power than judges to manipulate the legal terrain. Lawyers operate in a broader sphere than judges—they resolve many legal matters that will never go before a judge. Even in contested cases, there are whole areas of conduct outside the judge's attention. As a result, as Sanford Levinson accurately notes, "[t]he advice lawyers feel free to give their clients has far more to do with structuring our legal system than does the legal opining of judges in specific cases."

Given these differences in position, authority, and motivation, one might suspect that "lawyer's law" will be different from "judge's law." Assessing the challenge that legal realism presents to legal ethics, therefore, requires that we specifically address how lawyers experience indeterminacy in the law and how that experience either affirms or undermines the boundary claim. To address these issues, we need not resolve the larger jurisprudential debate about whether the law is radically or only marginally indeterminate. Instead, we must examine how lawyers actually discover and interpret legal rules. With this knowledge, we can then evaluate the traditional model's claim that the bounds of the law meaningfully constrain zealous advocacy.

II. LEGAL REALISM AND THE BOUNDARY CLAIM

A. *The Argument for Indeterminacy*

The legal realists and their followers marshal three arguments to support the claim that law is largely indeterminate. First, they argue, there are in most cases a number of sources from which a "legal" answer might be derived. Second, legal doctrines contain vague or ambiguous language susceptible to multiple, inconsistent interpretations. Finally, they argue that by shifting the focus of analysis between the general and the particular, it is often possible to alter the perception of the proper application of the law to the facts. Each of these potential sources of ambiguity is relevant to the practicing lawyer.

1. Multiple Theories and Sources.—Specific legal questions often present lawyers with many potential avenues of investigation. Consider from a lawyer's point of view the simple case of a fired black employee. Several fields of law seem potentially relevant. Can the employee bring a contract action? What about a tort action, perhaps for slander or for wrongful interference with prospective business advantage? Can a claim be made under federal or state antidiscrimination law? What about arguing for a constitutional right to employment? Which of these potentially applicable legal fields the lawyer actually chooses to investigate depends on several factors, including how the client has described the circumstances surrounding the termination and the lawyer's knowledge and intuitive judgment about the "state of the law" in each of these fields. Even after this narrowing process, however, several ways of characterizing the problem are likely to remain available. More important, the "answers" yielded by these potentially applicable legal fields may conflict.

Moreover, many areas of the law contain competing, and sometimes conflicting, rules that might be applied to the facts of any case. A similar argument can be made about that aspect of the legal boundary that focuses directly on the lawyer: the rules of professional conduct. In his seminal statement of realist philosophy, Karl Llewellyn argued that the law of ethics simultaneously claims that a lawyer should believe in the justice of his client's cause and that no lawyer should be the judge of his client's case. Because these two norms conflict, Llewellyn asserted, a lawyer may always select the one that best fits his preexisting interests.

Finally, within any particular field, a vast array of legal materials may be relevant to any given problem. Statutes, legislative history, judicial decisions from various jurisdictions, constitutional provisions, and scholarly commentary all contain potentially relevant insights. These materials are likely to generate a range of arguments that a thoughtful lawyer might raise in a particular case.

2. Vague and Ambiguous Terms.—The frequent use of vague, open-ended language adds to the potential for conflict created by the multiplicity of legal authority. Many statutes and other legal rules contain terms like "good faith," "reasonableness," "duress," and "proximate cause." Such general terms are always open to multiple and conflicting interpretation.

Again, the rules of professional responsibility provide a potent example. The ABA's Model Code of Professional Responsibility is rife with vague and ambiguous terms. For example, the rules prohibiting conflicts of interest instruct the lawyer not to engage in multiple representation if "the exercise of his independent professional judgment . . . will be or is likely to be adversely affected," without further defining what constitutes such an "adverse effect." Similarly, in litigation, a lawyer may not advance a claim or defense "unwarranted" under existing law or unsupported by a "good faith argument for an extension, modification, or reversal of existing law." Finally, Canon 9 instructs the lawyer to avoid "even the appearance of impropriety."

Indeed, the widespread perception that the Code was too vague to give meaningful guidance to lawyers was one of the primary forces motivating the ABA's decision to promulgate new standards of professional conduct. Thus, the resulting Model Rules of Professional Conduct self-consciously attempt to bring more determinacy to the field of professional responsibility by adopting a rule-like structure. Though this shift in structure and tone has eliminated some of the more pervasive ambiguities, vagueness and open-endedness remain. For example, Model Rule 1.1 defines competent representation as that amount of "legal knowledge, skill, thoroughness and preparation reasonably necessary for the representation." Similarly, the Rules provide that in litigation, a lawyer shall not "make a frivolous discovery request or fail to make reasonably diligent effort to comply with a legally proper discovery request by an opposing party." As under the Model Code, the meaning of "reasonable" or "diligent" performance continues to be susceptible to multiple and conflicting interpretations.

3. Framing and Application.—Finally, indeterminacy may result from a dispute over the level of generality at which a legal issue should be framed or the manner in which a chosen rule should be applied to a particular case. No rule can determine the scope of its own application. Thus, in determining the bounds of the law, we must always choose whether a given rule should be construed broadly, so as to govern a wide range of conduct, or narrowly, so as to apply only to the facts of a particular case. This choice may in turn rest on the perceived relevance of the rule's underlying legislative purpose.

Consider the effect of *Nix v. Whiteside* on a lawyer's decision to reveal her client's intention to commit perjury. In *Nix*, the Supreme Court rejected the claim that a lawyer who successfully dissuaded a client from testifying falsely by threatening to disclose the perjury violated the defendant's sixth amendment right to effective assistance of counsel. The Court broadly intimated that disclosure is the universally proper response to client perjury. As a result, the case can be cited for the proposition that the underlying purposes of the adversary system require that client perjury be revealed, even when the prevailing view before *Nix* would have considered disclosure inappropriate. However, *Nix* can also be read narrowly to authorize only the *threat* of disclosure and to be silent as to the permissibility of *actual* disclosure. That the issue of disclosing client perjury can either be framed broadly, in terms of its effect on the adversary system's underlying purposes, or narrowly, in terms of the specific textual provisions of the codes of professional conduct, undoubtedly contributes to the "great uncertainty" that lawyers face after *Nix*.

Uncertainty is not limited to the purely legal elements of adjudication, for every interpretation of a legal rule depends on some underlying conception of the relevant facts. But like the law, the facts are also open to a variety of interpretations. Confronted with the same factual material, various legal actors may easily reach different conclusions about the significance of a series of events. * * * * For the practicing lawyer, therefore, frequent ambiguity as to the proper characterization of the facts contributes to the problem of indeterminacy.

4. Indeterminacy and the Lawyer's Role.—Each of the three standard arguments in favor of the indeterminacy thesis is important to lawyers. Their impact, however, is greatly magnified by the traditional model's allegiance to partisanship, which strongly suggests that it is the lawyer"s job to uncover and exploit the multiple meanings of legal rules.

The entire reason that the lawyer is engaged in the process of legal interpretation is to facilitate her client's ability to achieve some concrete objective. She has, in other words, a particular purpose for engaging in legal analysis. This purpose will invariably lead her to attempt to discover the subset of plausible legal interpretations that best supports her client"s goals, a tendency expressly sanctioned by the rules of professional conduct. When the weight of the relevant legal rules supports her client's objectives, this task will seem sufficiently distant from "the bounds of the law." When the client's aim is novel or controversial, however, the goal of achieving the client's objectives is destined to push the lawyer toward discovering gaps, conflicts, and ambiguities in the relevant legal materials. Partisanship, therefore, encourages lawyers to exploit indeterminacy.

This interaction between legal materials and the lawyer's role creates serious difficulties for the boundary claim. By highlighting the open-textured nature of many legal questions, the indeterminacy thesis has the potential for generating an argumentative nihilism in which any construction of the law is as good as any other and in which there are no restrictions on zealous advocacy. In such a regime, the lawyer's "public" responsibilities as an officer of the court would either collapse into the duty to advance the client's private interests or be relegated to the personal moral and political discretion of individual lawyers. In either case, the objectivity, consistency, and legitimacy promised by the boundary claim would, at the very least, be substantially compromised.

QUESTIONS

1.   If representing a client "within the bounds of the law" does not give a sufficiently clear boundary to limit lawyers behavior, is there a better alternative available?

2.   Wilkins notes that the Model Rules of Professional Conduct were intended to bring more determinacy to the field of legal ethics than their predecessor, the Model Code of Professional Responsibility. Are the attorney conduct rules still too vague?

RICHARD NIELSEN, THE POLITICS OF ETHICS: METHODS FOR ACTING, LEARNING, AND SOMETIMES FIGHTING WITH OTHERS IN ADDRESSING ETHICS PROBLEMS IN ORGANIZATIONAL LIFE
(Ruffin Series 1996)

THE EICHMANN

Hannah Arendt was a philosopher and political theorist who died in 1975. One of her most noted works was *Eichmann in Jerusalem: A Report On The Banality of Evil* (1964), originally commissioned and published by *The New Yorker* and later expanded into a book. Her analysis of Eichmann and his organizational situation, while an extreme case, is a valuable example of a certain type of cooperation with unethical behavior in organizations.

From Arendt (1964, 1978) we learn that Eichmann was an upper-middle-level manager in a Nazi institution engaged in, as Arendt phrases it, the "administrative massacre" of millions of people. Eichmann never belonged to the higher Nazi Party circles and did not participate in policy decisions. He was a manager in an organization where obeying authority was valued, expected, and required.

According to Arendt, Eichmann believed that he was practicing the virtue of obedience when he did his work. He obeyed orders without thinking about ethical implications. Hitler ordered Goering, Goering ordered Himmler, Himmler ordered Heydrich, Heydrich ordered Eichmann, and Eichmann obeyed. Arendt explains what she thinks Eichmann thought: "His guilt came from his obedience, and obedience is praised as a virtue. His virtue had been abused by the Nazi leaders. But he was not one of the ruling clique, he was a victim, and only the leaders deserved punishment" (1964, p. 247).

Arendt concludes with the judgment that Eichmann was guilty, but that instead of being insane or monstrously evil, Eichmann was, perhaps more horribly, well within the range of sanity and normality. He was a "thoughtless" and "banal" man who did not think about distinguishing right from wrong in his role as a manager in an organization that harmed people. His job was not, as he saw it, to think about the ethics of policies or decisions made by higher authority. His thinking was narrowly directed toward efficient implementation.

Arendt explains: "Despite all the efforts of the prosecution, everybody could see that this man was not a monster . . . he certainly would never have murdered his superior in order to inherit his post. He merely, to put the matter colloquially, never realized what he was doing. . . . He was not stupid. It was sheer thoughtlessness—something by no means identical with stupidity. . . ." (1964, p. 287).

Eichmann was a good technical manager, but was very narrow, "ignorant of everything that was not directly, technically and bureaucratically connected with his job" (p. 287).

The key characteristic of the Eichmann archetype is a narrow, routinized, "in the box" mentality that does not recognize ethical dimensions—as Arendt phrased it, "the banality of evil." Are there such unthinking managers and employees in modern business, government, and nonprofit organizations? Many examples could be cited; a few will suffice.

Ford Pinto (Gioia, 1992) The Ford automobile company had a field recall coordinator at the time Ford Pinto gas tanks were exploding and passengers were burning and dying from rear-end collisions at speeds as low as twenty-five miles per hour. The recall coordinator later asked himself the question, "Why didn't I see the gravity of the problem and its ethical overtones?" (Gioia, 1992, p. 383). He answered his own question as follows: "Before I went to Ford I would have argued strongly that Ford had an ethical obligation to recall. After I left Ford I now argue and teach that Ford had an ethical obligation to recall. But while I was there, I perceived no strong obligation to recall and I remember no strong ethical overtones to the case whatsoever" (Gioia, 1992, p. 388).

On a different scale from Eichmann, but in a similar way, the recall coordinator did not think about the ethical dimensions of the decision. Sometimes people use schemata that are too narrow (Bartunek and Moch, 1987; Bartunek, 1993a). In the case of the recall coordinator, he explained:

> Most models of ethical decision making in organizations implicitly assume that people recognize and think about a moral or ethical dilemma when they are confronted with one. I call this seemingly fundamental assumption into question. The unexplored ethical issue for me is the arguably prevalent case where organizational representatives are not aware that they are dealing with a problem that might have ethical overtones. If the case involves a familiar class of problems or issues, it is likely to be handled via existing cognitive structures or scripts—scripts that typically include no ethical component in their cognitive content. . . . Scripts are built out of situations that are normal, not those that are abnormal, ill-structured, or unusual (which often can characterize ethical domains). The ambiguities associated with most ethical dilemmas imply that such situations demand a "custom" decision, which means that the inclusion of an ethical dimension as a component of an evolving script is not easy to accomplish. (Gioia, 1992, p. 388)

The Eichmann phenomenon may be more common than we would like it to be.

C. R. Bard, Inc., and faulty heart catheters (Zuckoff and Kennedy, 1993) In 1993, C. R. Bard, Inc., one of the largest medical equipment manufacturers in the world, pleaded guilty to 391 counts of conspiracy, mail fraud, lying to government regulators, and selling "adulterated products" for human experimentation. Individuals within the company knew that the heart catheters it was selling for use in balloon angioplasty surgery were faulty. Sometimes the tips of catheters inserted into heart arteries broke off inside the artery. Sometimes the balloon did not deflate, causing heart attacks, emergency bypass surgery, and deaths.

Perhaps as many as fifty Bard managers and technicians, at the upper-middle, middle, and lower levels, knew for about three years that the products being sold were faulty. Apparently, none thought that they had any personal ethical responsibilities. They didn't make the decisions, they were just obeying orders and implementing policy decisions. The ethics issues were not part of their narrowly defined in-the-box thinking.

United Fruit Company (McCann, 1976, 1984) The United Fruit Company in the early 1950s decided to improve local business conditions by helping to overthrow the government of Guatemala. According to an assistant vice president of United Fruit, who later became a vice-president, "At the time, I identified so closely with the company and my job that I didn't think about it as a moral or ethical issue" (McCann, 1984).

This manager was narrowly focused on improving the market share and profitability positions of United Fruit. It did not occur to him to think about the people who would be disenfranchised or killed in the government overthrow that United Fruit was financing and that he as communications assistant vice president was covering up.

*   *   *

SOCRATES'S JAILER

> Soon the jailer, who was the servant of the Eleven, entered and stood by him, saying: To you, Socrates, whom I know to be the noblest and gentlest and best of all who ever came to this place, I will not impute the angry feelings of other men, who rage and swear at me, when, in obedience to the authorities, I bid them drink the poison—indeed, I am sure that you will not be angry with me; for others, as you are aware, and not I, are to blame. And so fare you well, and try to bear lightly what must needs be—you know my errand. Then bursting into tears he turned away and went out. (Plato, *Phaedo: The Death of Socrates;* quoted in Jowett, 1903, p. 271)

This may be the most common archetype of all. Socrates's Jailer was under the power and orders of "the Eleven." If he did not obey, he knew he would be punished. He may have had a family, responsibilities, obligations. Plato gives him no name in the dialog. None may be needed, since we have so many already. Many of us have experienced similar pressures. The following cases illustrate this archetype.

Raymond Smith and General Electric. Almost all employees who knew about the price fixing and market allocations at General Electric went along with them. Raymond Smith, a G.E. vice president and general manager of the transformer division, told the U.S. Department of Justice and the Kefauver Senate Subcommittee on Antitrust and Monopoly that throughout his career he and all the other managers in the relevant areas went along with the unethical and illegal behavior because it was condoned by higher authority.

And at G.E. one obeyed orders or suffered the consequences. He "readily acknowledged that he had met with competitors," in violation of the antitrust laws and internal organization ethics codes, because, as Smith explained,

> to my knowledge . . . during the entire period from 1940 through 1956, it was common practice . . . to discuss prices and other competitive matters with competitors. . . . I was also aware that similar practices were being followed not only in other areas of the company, but also in other companies in the electrical manufacturing industry . . . although the General Electric Policy . . . regarding antitrust practices had been issued in 1946, it had been constantly disregarded in major areas of the company with . . . the *tacit* approval and agreement of the managers and the officers of the company at the time responsible for those areas. (Herling, 1962, pp. 30–31)

John Geary and U.S. Steel. John Geary was a salesman for U.S. Steel when the company decided to enter a new market with a new product, deep oil well casings. Geary protested to several groups of managers that the casings the company was producing and asking him to sell had what the engineers indicated was too high a failure rate and were therefore unsafe.

> According to Geary, even though the managers, engineers, and salesmen believed him and the test results, "the only desire of everyone associated with the project was to satisfy the instructions of Henry Wallace [then sales vice president]. No one was about to buck this man for fear of his job" (Ewing, 1983b, p. 86). Geary was fired, and other employees did the work.

Radiation experiments. During the late 1940s and early 1950s the United States department of Defense conducted radiation experiments on people, both civilians and soldiers. Several hundred experiments were undertaken. According to the *New York Times* "Most experiments involved exposing troops to varying amounts of radiation, usually without informing them of the risks or seeking their consent" (Hilts, 1994, p. A14). A lot of debate and opposition to the practice took place among many of the scientists conducting the experiments. For example, Dr. Shields Warren, the chief medical officer of the Atomic Energy Commission, stated in July 1949 that he was "taking an increasingly dim view of human experimentation" (Hilts, 1994, p. A14).

In a 1947 document the Atomic Energy Commission stated, "It is desired that no document be released which refers to experiments with humans and might have an adverse effect on public opinion or result in legal suits. Documents covering such work in this field should be classified 'secret' " (Hilts, 1994, p. A14). Both the ethical debates about the experiments and the experiments were classified secret by the Department of Defense.

Despite their ethical opposition, several of the scientists and doctors obeyed orders, cooperated, and did not blow the whistle. They did so largely because of fear of the penalties for violating the military "secret" classification, which in the late 1940s and early 1950s were quite severe. The experiments continued until at least 1953.

QUESTIONS

1.   Eichmann embraced the virtue of obedience. Does this suggest that Virtue Ethics offers little guidance in ethical decision-making, if we end up selecting the "wrong" virtue to follow? Recall the material in Chapter VIII on Virtue Ethics. Where did Eichmann go wrong in his ethical analysis?

2.   Socrates' jailer, and the business examples that follow, demonstrate a clear problem for young lawyers as well: "Will I lose my job if I don't cooperate?" The pressure on the other side is "Will I lose my license to practice if I do cooperate?" But as discussed in Chapter III, acting merely from fear of sanction is a fairly superficial form of moral analysis. While concern about losing one's job is very real and important, what else should lawyers be considering as they think through ethical issues?

ANDREW M. PERLMAN, UNETHICAL OBEDIENCE BY SUBORDINATE ATTORNEYS: LESSONS FROM SOCIAL PSYCHOLOGY
36 Hofstra Law Review 451–459 (2007) (footnotes omitted)

I. Introduction

Consider the plight of a lawyer—fresh out of law school with crushing loan debt and few job offers—who accepts a position at a medium-sized firm. A partner asks the young lawyer to review a client's documents to determine what needs to be produced in discovery. In the stack, the associate finds a "smoking gun" that is clearly within the scope of discovery and spells disaster for the client's case. The associate reports the document to the partner, who without explanation tells the associate not to produce it. The associate asks the partner a few questions and quickly drops the subject when the partner tells the associate to get back to work.

We would like to believe that the young lawyer has the courage to ensure that the partner ultimately produces the document. We might hope, or expect, that the lawyer will report the issue to the firm's ethics counsel, if the firm is big enough to have one, or consult with other lawyers in the firm, assuming that she has developed the necessary relationships with her colleagues despite her junior status.

In fact, research in the area of social psychology suggests that, in some contexts, a subordinate lawyer will often comply with unethical instructions of this sort. This basic, but crucial, insight into human behavior suggests that there is often a significant gap between what the legal ethics rules require and how lawyers will typically behave. Indeed, lawyers will too often obey obviously unethical or illegal instructions or fail to report the wrongdoing of other lawyers.

II. Basic Lessons from Social Psychology About Conformity and Obedience

Studies on conformity and obedience suggest that professionals, whom we would ordinarily describe as "honest," will often suppress their independent judgment in favor of a group's opinion or offer little resistance in the face of illegal or unethical demands. These studies demonstrate that we ascribe too much weight to personality traits like honesty, and that contextual factors have far more to do with human behavior than most people recognize. Indeed, a number of experiments have amply demonstrated that situational forces are often more powerful predictors of human behavior than dispositional traits like honesty.

A. Foundational Studies on Conformity

The importance of context is apparent from a number of experiments related to conformity, the most celebrated of which is a 1955 study by Solomon Asch. Asch wanted to determine how often a group member would express independent judgment despite the unanimous, but obviously mistaken, contrary opinions of the rest of the group.

In one version of the study, the experimenter told the subject that he was about to participate in a vision test and asked the subject to sit at a table with four other individuals who were secretly working with the experimenter.

All five people were shown the two cards and asked to identify which line in the card on the right (A, B, or C) was the same length as the line shown in the card on the left. Each person was asked his opinion individually and answered out loud, with the subject of the experiment going near the end. After each person had answered, a new set of cards was produced, and the participants were once again asked their opinions.

During the initial rounds, all of the confederates chose the obviously right answer. Not surprisingly, under this condition, the subject also chose the right answer.

In some subsequent rounds, however, Asch tested the subject's willingness to conform by prearranging for the confederates to choose the same wrong answer. Even though the four confederates were obviously mistaken, subjects of the experiment nevertheless provided the same wrong answer as the confederates 35.1% of the time, with 70% of subjects providing the wrong answer at least once during the experiment.

Most importantly, Asch found that the introduction of certain variables dramatically affected conformity levels. For example, Asch found that conformity fell quickly as the confederate group size dropped from three (31.8% of the answers were wrong) to two (13.6% were wrong) to one (3.6% were wrong), but did not increase much in groups larger than seven (maxing out at about 37%). Moreover, conformity fell by more than 50% in most variations of the experiment when one of the confederates dissented from the group opinion.

Not surprisingly, other studies have shown that conformity levels increase when (as is true in the law) the answer is more ambiguous. For example, in studies predating Asch's, Muzafer Sherif placed a subject in a dark room and asked the person to look at a projected spot of light and guess how far it moved. Notably, the light did not move at all, but only appeared to move due to an optical illusion called the autokinetic effect. The precise extent of the perceived movement was thus impossible for subjects to determine objectively.

In one variation of the experiment, a subject gave individual assessments and was subsequently put in a room with a confederate, whose opinion intentionally varied from the subject's. As expected, the subject's assessments quickly came into line with the confederate's or (when the subject was placed in a group) with the group's. Thus, Sherif found that questions with ambiguous answers tended to produce more conformity, because people were understandably less certain of their original assessments.

The Asch and Sherif studies offer compelling evidence—also supported by more recent experiments—that a group member's opinion is easily affected by the group's overall judgment. Critically, the studies also reveal that this effect varies considerably, depending on situational variables, such as the level of ambiguity in the assigned task, the number of people in the group, the status of the person in the group (e.g., high status people feel more comfortable offering a contrasting view), and the existence of dissenters. The situation, in short, has a powerful effect on human behavior.

B. Foundational Studies on Obedience

Not long after Asch's provocative study, Stanley Milgram focused on a different but related question: When will people follow the unethical or immoral orders of an authority figure?

The answer turned out to be both surprising and alarming. Milgram found that, under the right conditions, an experimenter could successfully order more than sixty percent of people to administer painful and dangerous electric shocks to an innocent, bound older man with a heart condition, despite the man's repeated pleas to be let go.

Critically, Milgram, like Asch and Sherif before him, found that context was essential. Obedience varied a great deal depending on a number of situational factors, such as whether the learner was in the same room as the teacher, whether the person issuing the orders was in the same room as the teacher, whether subjects assisted a confederate with the shocks instead of administering the shocks themselves, and whether someone dissented (such as when the experiment occurred in a group setting).

Milgram's findings have been replicated throughout the world, with similar results in both genders, different socioeconomic groups, and different countries. Moreover, because of new ethics guidelines that make Milgram's work difficult to reproduce today, his work still stands as one of the most significant contributions to our understanding of human obedience to authority. We know from his work that, given the right situation, most people will follow orders that they would ordinarily consider blatantly immoral.

C. The Power of the Situation

The basic point of these studies is not that people are social conformists, mindless followers of authority, or latent sadists. Indeed, the studies do not suggest that "people are disposed to obey authority figures unquestioningly." Rather, the point is that "manipulations of the immediate social situation can overwhelm in importance the type of individual differences in personal traits or dispositions that people normally think of as being determinative of social behavior." As a result, "subtle features of . . . [the] situation . . . prompt[] ordinary members of our society to behave . . . extraordinarily."

The importance of context is clear. Asch's studies showed that a single variable, such as reducing the number of people in the group or introducing a dissenting group member, could dramatically reduce conformity levels. Milgram also found that the existence of a dissenter could reduce obedience and that other factors, such as placing the experimenter outside of the room or moving the "learner" into the same room as the subject, produced a similar effect. Social psychologists, in short, have found that conformity and obedience are heavily context-dependent and that social forces play a much greater role—and dispositional traits a much weaker role—in determining human behavior than most people assume.

III. Situational Conformity and Obedience: Implications for Lawyer Behavior

Conformity and obedience are different in subtle but important ways. According to Milgram, "obedience to authority occurs within a hierarchical structure in which the actor feels that the person above has the right to prescribe behavior. Conformity regulates the behavior among those of equal status. . . ." So, for example, the discovery hypothetical primarily implicates issues of obedience, because a superior is issuing an order to a subordinate. The hypothetical would implicate conformity if the young lawyer saw her colleagues at the firm concealing "smoking guns" and consequently followed their lead without being instructed to do so. Despite the differences in the two concepts, both of them can exist in many law practice settings.

A. Situational Factors that Produce Conformity in Law Practice

Recall that numerous factors contribute to conformity, including the size of the group, the level of unanimity, the ambiguity of the issues involved, group cohesiveness, the strength of an individual's commitment to the group, the person's status in the group, and basic individual tendencies, such as the desire to be right and to be liked.

Many of these factors frequently exist in law practice. For instance, lawyers often have to tackle problems that contain many ambiguities of law and fact. Even questions that, at first, seem to have well-settled answers are often susceptible to an analysis that can make the answers seem unclear. Indeed, law students are trained to perform this particular art of legal jiu jitsu.

Given the uncertainty of many legal answers and lawyers' expertise in identifying (or manufacturing) those uncertainties, lawyers are especially susceptible to the forces of conformity. The hierarchical structure of lawyering also makes conformity more likely. Studies suggest that strong conformity forces exist even in "arbitrarily constructed groups . . . that hold no long-term power to reward conformity or punish dissent." Lawyers, however, work in groups that are not arbitrarily constructed and actually do hold long-term power to reward conformity or punish dissent. Attorneys typically work in settings where other group members, such as senior partners or corporate executives (e.g., in-house counsel jobs), control the professional fates of subordinates, a condition that increases the likelihood of conformity. So, for example, the young lawyer in the initial hypothetical would feel a powerful, though perhaps unconscious, urge to conform, especially given that she had trouble finding a job and faced significant financial burdens.

Social status also affects conformity. There is evidence that people with more social prestige feel more comfortable deviating from the prevailing opinion. By contrast, a person with a lower status, such as the junior law firm associate in the hypothetical, will be more likely to conform to protect her more vulnerable position.

Unanimity also encourages conformity, and unanimity is common among lawyers who are working together on the same legal matter. Studies have shown that zealous advocacy tends to make lawyers believe that the objectively "correct" answer to a legal problem is the one that just so happens to benefit the client. This tendency causes teams of lawyers to agree on many issues, making it even more difficult for dissenting voices to be heard. So in the discovery example, the absence of a dissenting voice would make the subordinate more likely to assume that her initial position was incorrect or, at the very least, not worth pursuing.

The point here is not that lawyers will always conform to the views of superiors or colleagues. Plenty of lawyers express their own beliefs, even under very difficult circumstances. The claim is that powerful social forces exist in many law practice settings that make conformity more likely than most people would expect.

B. Situational Factors that Produce Obedience in Law Practice

Law practice also tends to produce excessive obedience. First, lawyers can usually frame unethical or illegal requests in ways that fit the first and second factors. For example, the partner who requested the withholding of the smoking gun document could articulate a legitimate reason for the request, such as "it's not within the scope of discovery" or "it's arguably privileged," even though neither statement is objectively accurate. The partner could also explain that withholding the document will produce the salutary effect of promoting zealous advocacy and advancing the client's cause. In these ways, the authority figure—in this case, a partner—could give the subordinate a seemingly plausible explanation for refusing to disclose the document and argue that it promotes a positive outcome (factors one and two respectively).

The partner could also frame the instruction as part of litigation's unwritten "rules of the game" (factor three). In this way, the demand appears entirely benign. Moreover, the consequences may also appear inconsequential. Unlike Milgram's experiments, where obedience resulted in painful electric shocks to a man with a heart condition, compliance in many (but not all) lawyering contexts produces far less dire consequences. For instance, in the discovery example, the lawyer is "merely" withholding a document as part of the discovery "game" that all lawyers play, not causing somebody physical pain or risking someone's life. The seemingly benign nature of the request can enhance the subordinate's willingness to obey.

This factor is likely to have more weight if the subordinate has little litigation experience and does not have the necessary expertise to question the partner's authority. In contrast, if the subordinate has handled numerous document productions and has a strong experiential basis to know that the partner's request is impermissible, the subordinate is less likely to give the partner's demand a benign gloss. Of course, even when it is absolutely clear that the partner's behavior is unethical or illegal, the subordinate may still comply if some of the other factors favoring obedience are present.

Factors four (an agreement to help the authority figure) and five (the presence of assigned roles) also frequently exist in law practice. The lawyer-client relationship itself is essentially an agreement to help clients achieve their goals (factor four). When combined with the common perception that a lawyer's morality is distinct from individual morality (i.e., role differentiation), lawyers are more apt to view arguably legal conduct as part of their job as an advocate (factor five). Thus, subordinates, such as the associate in the discovery example, will view the authority's instructions as part of the agreement to help the client, with the mindset of role-differentiation only adding to the belief that any moral consequences are not the subordinate's primary concern.

Another factor that contributes to obedience is that attorney misbehavior will typically affect victims who are more remote in time and place than the victims in Milgram's experiments (factor six). For example, the failure to produce a smoking gun document will affect an adverse party, but in a much more indirect way than the application of an electric shock. Similarly, assisting a company's financial fraud (e.g., the Enron scandal) will primarily harm shareholders and lower level employees, people with whom lawyers have little contact. Because a lawyer will perceive these harms to be less immediate and proximate than someone suffering painful electric shocks in an adjoining room, this factor favors obedience in the lawyering context even more strongly than what Milgram found in many of his experiments.

Not only will the victims of legal misconduct be relatively remote, but the person issuing the orders will be nearby. Milgram found that obedience increased when the authority figure and the subordinate were in the same room and decreased when the experimenter issued orders using a tape recorder or from another location. For lawyers, the authority figure who issues the instruction will typically be a colleague or a client with whom the subordinate has a great deal of contact and who may exercise considerable power regarding the subordinate's future at the firm, thus further adding to the likelihood of obedience (factor seven).

Subordinates may also discount their responsibility for their conduct (factor eight) by shifting moral responsibility to the person issuing the orders. Indeed, when Milgram's subjects asked who was responsible for what happened in the laboratory, the experimenter said that he (the experimenter) was ultimately responsible for any harm to the learner. This shifting of responsibility is especially likely in the legal ethics context, where Model Rule 5.2(b) states that "[a] subordinate lawyer does not violate the Rules of Professional Conduct if that lawyer acts in accordance with a supervisory lawyer's reasonable resolution of an arguable question of professional duty." Given the ambiguity of so many legal and ethical duties, subordinates will frequently find that a supervisory lawyer's instructions reflect a "reasonable resolution of an arguable question of professional duty." Thus, subordinate lawyers are likely to believe that responsibility for their actions ultimately lies with superiors.

Another significant factor that contributed to obedience in Milgram's subjects was the incremental nature of the experiment (factor nine). Each new shock was only modestly larger than the last, making it difficult for subjects to distinguish morally what they were about to do from what they had already done. This phenomenon of justifying past actions in a way that makes conduct of a similar type in the future seem ethical is known as cognitive dissonance.

Social prestige (factor ten) is another of those forces. Many law firms, especially larger firms, are held in high esteem among lawyers. These firms are thus likely to produce the same social forces that Yale University produced in Milgram's subjects. Moreover, smaller firms can also produce the same effect, especially if the superior is an experienced and respected partner.

In addition to the factors that contributed to obedience in Milgram's experiment, there is one factor that favors obedience in the lawyer situation that did not exist for Milgram: professional and financial self-interest. [A] subordinate lawyer has a lot to lose by refusing to obey: a job. The subordinate's concern for her job, particularly a junior lawyer who may have had few other professional opportunities, is likely to be substantial. Thus, this factor also weighs heavily in favor of compliance and suggests that lawyers might be even more likely to comply than the subjects of Milgram's experiments.

There is, however, one factor that weighs against the hypothetical lawyer's compliance: obedience could lead to monetary sanctions or disbarment. If the lawyer believes that she faces a real chance of discipline, she arguably would be more likely to resist the partner's demands. The powerful concern for professional survival might trump the other social forces that favor obedience and conformity and make compliance less likely than in Milgram's experiments, where subjects had no equivalent incentive to dissent.

There are three problems with this view. First, it assumes that the subordinate will recognize that the partner's demands implicate her ethical duties. The reality is that, given the forces at work, she may easily begin to question her initial opinion and view the partner's opinion as, at the very least, justifiable. This tendency to interpret the situation so that it does not implicate one's ethical or moral responsibility is sometimes called ethical fading. Specifically, the actor reinterprets the situation in such a way that the ethical nature of the situation fades from view. If the subordinate does not even identify the ethics issue, the concern for professional survival cannot override the social forces favoring conformity and obedience.

Second, even if the subordinate recognizes the ethical dilemma, she is not likely to be terribly concerned about discipline. Rule 5.2 only imposes discipline if the superior's instructions were clearly unethical. So unless the instruction is blatantly impermissible, the subordinate is not likely to fear any disciplinary consequences.

Third, even if the instruction is blatantly unethical or illegal, a lawyer may still not fear discipline, at least in the discovery context. Bar discipline for this sort of misconduct occurs rarely, and sanctions are usually far below what would be necessary to discourage this sort of behavior.

To summarize, the hypothetical associate faces considerable pressures to conform and obey and few risks from compliance and obedience. Even if the misconduct is uncovered, a risk that may be rather small, she is unlikely to face any punishment that will adversely affect her career. The ultimate and disturbing result is that she is prone to obey the partner who has issued the unethical and illegal command.

QUESTIONS

1. You began the journey through this material by exploring the idea of the moral person (Chapter I) and moral responsibility (Chapter II). Does Perlman's description undermine the vision of responsibility set out by Aristotle in Chapter II?

2. Recall Telford Taylor's insights in Chapter II on responsibility in Nuremburg and Vietnam. What is the supervisor's responsibility when he or she pressures the young associate to engage in wrongful conduct?

TABLE OF CASES

[References are to pages]